THE EVOLUTION OF NUCLEAR STRATEGY

THE EVOLUTION OF NUCLEAR STRATEGY

Lawrence Freedman

Professor of War Studies
King's College, London

Second Edition

St. Martin's Press
New York

First published in the United States of America in 1981
Second edition 1989

Printed in the People's Republic of China

ISBN 0-312-02817-2 cloth
ISBN 0-312-02843-1 paper

Library of Congress Cataloging-in-Publication Data
Freedman, Lawrence.
The evolution of nuclear strategy.
Bibliography: p.
Includes index.
1. Nuclear warfare.   2. Military policy.   I. Title.
U263.F698   1989   355'.0217   88-35558
ISBN 0-312-02817-2
ISBN 0-312-02843-1 (pbk.)

Contents

Preface to the Second Edition

Since the first edition of this book was published in 1981 there has been an almost continuous debate underway in the Western world on questions of nuclear policy. In addition there has been a substantial amount of original scholarship on the history of the post-war world, much of which deals directly with the subject matter of this book. I had intended to draw on this new material in a complete revision of the book. I decided against doing this, partly because of time and partly because of space. In addition much of the new research has been on the policy-making process, yet my main focus was on the public and academic debates surrounding nuclear strategy. The bulk of this book is therefore as it was first published.

I have however added a new chapter outlining some of the main themes of the 1980s, which has turned out to be one of the most critical decades in the history of nuclear strategy. In a sense it might be argued that the intensity and variety of the developments of the 1980s contradict the suggestion made in the first edition that nuclear strategy had run its course – at least intellectually. However, my view is that this suggestion has if anything been reinforced by the developments of the past decade. During this period those who argued that nuclear strategy could be reinvigorated if only sensible and courageous policies were adopted have had ample opportunity to prove their point, for the Reagan Administration was receptive to their views. The main result of their efforts would appear to be that the intellectual exhaustion of nuclear strategy is now matched by its political exhaustion.

In addition to this new chapter, I have rewritten the introduction, largely to draw attention to the new scholarship in this area, and the conclusions, so as to reflect some of the more recent policy debates. The bibliography and the index have also been revised to incorporate the new material. Some of the material in the new Chapter 26 first appeared as 'The Reagan Legacy' in Joe Kruzel (ed.), *The American Defense Annual 1988/89* (Lexington, Mass.: Lexington Books, 1988).

Lawrence Freedman
June 1988

Acknowledgments

The issues discussed in the following pages have been the common fare of strategists wherever and whenever they have met during the post-war years. Since 1975, when I began writing this book, I have been fortunate enough, as a member of the staff of, first the International Institute for Strategic Studies, and then the Royal Institute of International Affairs, to have had many opportunities to discuss questions of contemporary strategy with most of the leading members of the profession. In the course of my research I have therefore benefited from discussion and often argument with large numbers of people on aspects of this study. They are too numerous to mention by name but some deserve particular thanks. Christoph Bertram not only asked me to undertake this study in the first place, but has given me constant encouragement, and not a little prodding, to complete it. In this he has been ably assisted by Jonathan Alford who suggested some valuable improvements to an early version of this manuscript. Michael Howard, who has served as my mentor from my days as a graduate student at Oxford, provided not only guidance on how to treat the subject but, in his own books, offers a model for any aspiring historian of strategic thought. In 1976 he chaired a series of seminars I gave at Oxford, which provided an early opportunity to try out my ideas on a critical audience. A number of people have either read individual chapters or have served as a sounding board for my ideas: Des Ball; Richard Burt; Richard Haas; Frank Klotz; Barry Posen; Greg Treverton; and Phil Williams. Albert Wohlstetter has shown kindness not only in discussing the development of strategic studies but in providing copies of relevant documents. James King permitted me to read a copy of his own masterly unpublished study entitled *The New Strategy.*

Debbie Van Opstall Ginsberg, who also read and commented upon many of the chapters, helped in the construction of the bibliography. Jean Pell typed many of the chapters. Jane Capper took on the main burden of typing and organizing the manuscript into a form suitable for the publishers as well as helping with the bibliography and occasionally advising on syntax. My wife Judith has shown remarkable tolerance with my continued fascination with the rather disagreeable subject of nuclear war.

My final acknowledgment is to the late Alastair Buchan. Not long before his premature death, as I was starting to organize my thoughts on how best to approach this subject, I was able to talk to him a number of times. The advice he gave which stuck most firmly in my mind was 'if you are writing a history of ideas you must be bold'. It is this advice that I have tried to follow. Whether the attempt has been successful I leave it to the reader to judge.

L.D.F.

Introduction

On 6 August 1945 the first atomic bomb was dropped on the Japanese city of Hiroshima. At least 66,000 people died almost immediately from the explosion and fire-storm that followed. Tens of thousands more died in the aftermath. Three days after the first explosion, a second bomb was dropped on the Japanese city of Nagasaki. The immediate dead numbered some 40,000 people. The smaller size of the city and the hilly terrain meant that the devastation was not as complete as with Hiroshima. About 40 per cent of the city's structures were destroyed or severely damaged, as against 80 per cent in Hiroshima.

The weapons that destroyed Hiroshima and Nagasaki produced explosions equivalent to that produced with 14,000 and 20,000 tons of TNT respectively, an explosive power described as being 14 or 20 kilotons. Many of the nuclear warheads now in the possession of the major powers are in the megaton range; that is they would result in explosions equivalent to that produced with 1 million or more tons of TNT. If a 1-megaton bomb is exploded at the height necessary to achieve maximum destruction, all brick houses would be destroyed out to $3\frac{1}{2}$ miles, with comparatively minor damage out to 13 miles. The blast would create winds sufficient to hurl objects (and even people) through the air at lethal speeds, out to $6\frac{1}{2}$ miles. Within a radius of about 6 miles most fabrics and paper will burst into flame. As far out as 11 miles the explosion could cause second-degree burns and ignite dry leaves. The explosion would take its toll in human life for the following weeks and months through radiation sickness and the spread of disease and hunger that can be expected to follow the breakdown of social organization. Any unborn children subjected to irradiation would be likely to be born deformed. It is not altogether clear whether or not a human society could recover from the aftermath of a nuclear war. The material, physical, and psychic destruction might well be too severe.

Most frightening of all, perhaps, is how quickly all or much of this could be accomplished. If the deed were to be done it could be done quickly. It is within human decision. Our collective future is hostage to continuing acts of self-restraint by the leaders of the world's major powers. It is not surprising that at times these leaders do not seem wholly suited to this responsibility, or that events appear to be propelling them to a point where caution, and eventually everything else, might be thrown to the winds. Mass movements have been mobilized on the basis of such anxieties, and have forced the question of prevention of nuclear war high on to the political agenda. The remedies proposed range from attempting to make nuclear weapons more usable by controlling their effects, to attempting to make them virtually impossible to use on the grounds that it would be impossible to control their effects should they be used. Some address the problem as essentially one of command and control; others are concerned with the size of the nuclear inventories and argue that they can and should be reduced dramatically – if possible to zero.

Ronald Reagan early in his Presidency made the case for reinforcing nuclear deterrence by reinvigorating nuclear strategy, so helping to animate the protest movements of the 1980s. But later he came to join those arguing for total abolition of nuclear weapons. He first sought to deal with the matter by exploiting what he believed to be encouraging trends in defensive technology; he later endorsed the vision of complete nuclear disarmament. What was notable about this endorsement was that it was shared by his Soviet counterpart, Mikhail Gorbachev.

Despite this common vision of a nuclear-free world its practical realization remains distant. The knowledge of how to develop and produce nuclear weapons is widely known. So long as we do not have a conflict-free world the fear that this knowledge will be exploited by the unscrupulous limits the possibilities for complete disarmament. Even if current stocks were eliminated, during the course of a conflict new stocks could be produced (especially if civilian nuclear facilities had not been eliminated). Nor do nuclear explosions exhaust the possible horrors that human beings can inflict on each other. More positively, the record suggests – even if it cannot prove – that the risk of nuclear disaster has been the source of a welcome caution in international politics over the past four decades. Given all this a nuclear-free world is likely to remain little more than a vision. It is as difficult to comprehend a future without nuclear weapons as it is to comprehend the consequences of their use. The awfulness of the weapons, and the inescapable vulnerability of all to nuclear attack, at the very least suggest the degradation of their use as instruments of policy. Despite this there remains a desire to exploit them to the full in the construction of security policies. The problem of gaining military advantage or effective deterrence from a nuclear arsenal in conditions of apparent stalemate has preoccupied some of the best minds of our time.

It is a problem for which there can be no definitive answer. The thankful lack of experience of nuclear warfare, since 1945, has rendered highly speculative all thoughts on the likely causes of nuclear war, its course and its finale. On the other hand, the weapons involved and the physical consequences of their detonation are well known. Indeed, technical details on warheads, delivery systems, and basing modes, often of the sort that would once have deserved the highest classification, are widely distributed. Because of the pace of technological change, and a series of arms control negotiations between the superpowers, there is always something new for discussion. Nevertheless, the fundamental questions of how, when, and why to use these weapons remain matters for inference and conjecture.

Because of the difficulty of keeping up to date with the detail of new weapons or the latest arms control proposals, plus the desire to influence future decisions, those engaged in contemporary strategic studies tend to be technically sophisticated, forward-looking and policy-orientated. This led, with a few notable exceptions,[1] to a neglect of the history of the subject. During the 1980s there has been a growing interest in the history of nuclear weapons, doctrines and strategies and a number of studies have catered to this interest. As post-war archives have been opened, and as American scholars have learned to exploit the Freedom of Information Act, the first post-war decades have been thoroughly studied. These studies include the attempts to use the new atomic weapons to support post-war American diplomacy,[2] the later role of nuclear weapons in East–West relations,[3] analysis of key decisions, such as that to build the hydrogen bomb,[4] and the detailed development of nuclear plans.[5] Transcripts of the meetings of senior policy-makers during the Cuban Missile Crisis have cast a completely new light on the established views of the crisis.[6] In addition to one book based on interviews with key figures in the development of nuclear thinking,[7] there have been studies of some of the key figures who have helped to shape both policy and our general understanding of nuclear issues, such as Paul Nitze,[8] while others such as Glenn Seaborg and Herbert York have written valuable memoirs.[9] In Britain and France too there has been a growing interest in both early thinking about nuclear weapons,[10] and the continuity in doctrine.[11] With the Soviet Union historical studies still have to rely on a limited amount of material in the public domain,[12] although there are hopes that the new spirit of *Glasnost* will extend to the opening up of Soviet archives.

There is still a shortage of critical studies of the development either of key figures in the strategic studies community[13] or some of the key concepts.[14] However two books have provided histories of the strategic studies community. Both take a much greater interest than have I in the personalities of the key figures in the community and how they related to each other. Inevitably this leaves less space for analysis of the substance of their ideas or consideration of just how influential these ideas were when it came to policy-making.[15] Of the two Greg Herken's *Counsels of War* is the more ambitious, but Fred Kaplan's *Wizards of Armageddon* is more reliable and less error-prone.

The use of the word 'evolution' in the title of this book is somewhat misleading for it suggests progress along a learning curve, implying a higher level of present understanding than thirty, twenty or even ten years ago. This was the assumption with which I began. Now, having completed the study, I believe it to be false. What is impressive is the cyclical character of the debates. Much of what is offered today as a profound and new insight was said yesterday; and usually in a more concise and literate manner. The past decades have encouraged a rich literature that is barely appreciated by many contemporary students of strategy, especially those close to policy-making circles. If there is an underlying trend, it is less towards the refinement of a theory strong in its inner core, but towards a steady disillusion with the idea of an operational nuclear strategy.

The richness of the literature, however, provides a powerful disincentive to anyone contemplating a comprehensive survey. It is difficult not to be overwhelmed by the sheer volume of the material that has been generated. In addition to professional writings of military men and reflections of politicians presiding over nuclear arsenals, there has been a vast outpouring of books, articles, papers, and memos from civilians representing many academic disciplines and often organized into new research institutes concerned with few things other than the problems of modern strategy. The literature is thus immense, threatening to overwhelm any would-be historian of ideas. In addition, the literary style is often atrocious. To help order and explain such a novel situation, new and arcane concepts have been developed, which sometimes serve to clarify but often only obfuscate. The uninitiated has to work his way through a forbidding miasma of acronyms and jargon.

An attempt to note each intended contribution to contemporary strategy would result in a work of great length and tedium. Inevitably a large proportion of the material is repetitive and derivative. In the same way that a military historian is not expected to record every campaign so a historian of ideas does not have to record every documented thought. This work is selective, and in consequence the discussion of some areas such as conventional strategy, and particularly naval warfare, is inadequate; also, I have concentrated on the strategic debate in the United States, the most vigorous and fertile, though without neglecting the parallel debates in the Soviet Union, Britain, France, and China. The aim is to provide a systematic and reasonably comprehensive treatment of the major themes of nuclear strategy. To this end, the most important individual contributions to the debate have been analysed in some detail, but this is not a collection of critiques of great texts and so some favourite authors may not have got the attention they deserve. Similarly, while I have been concerned to examine the interaction between theory and policy, this is not a history of decision-making.

Finally, to complete this list of what the book does not offer, it provides neither a theory of strategy nor a new strategic theory. What it does attempt to offer is a detailed and critical history of official and unofficial attempts to construct a plausible nuclear strategy. As these attempts have come from a variety of sources and appeared in a variety of forms there is no fixed pattern to this investigation and it is only loosely chronological. I believe this approach to be necessary, not only to highlight the major issues, but also to illuminate the more general expectations, understandings, and preoccupations that have characterized strategic thinking since 1945. If there is an underlying theme it is the attempt to develop a convincing strategy for extended deterrence, to make the United States' nuclear guarantee to Europe intellectually credible rather than just an act of faith. As will be seen, this is one of those areas where a policy has worked far better in practice than an assessment of the theory might lead one to expect.

A book about strategy ought to begin with a definition of the subject. A comparable book in the Soviet Union would open with elaborate distinctions between military strategy, art, science, and doctrine. But as indicated above I have avoided restrictive terms of reference. Furthermore, there has been no constant and generally accepted definition of strategy, even during the post-war years. The origins of the world 'strategy' lie in the Greek *strategos*, meaning the art of the general. There was little need to significantly alter the meaning even up to the time of General von Clausewitz (1780–1831) who defined the concept of strategy as the use of battles to forward the aim of war.

By the twentieth century such a definition was blatantly inadequate. The preoccupation with battles, always questionable, failed to allow for the great variety in the methods of employing military forces and the choice of targets. Furthermore, the link with war itself was too direct. When war-fighting was so distasteful, it might be as important to preserve the peace by reminding a potential enemy of the costs of war or even to achieve aggressive objectives by encouraging a weaker country to give in without a fight.

For this century, the definition of strategy developed by Basil Liddell Hart – 'the art of distributing and applying military means to fulfil ends of policy'[16] – seems more appropriate. It is non-committal about how the military means are to be distributed while stressing, as would Clausewitz, the role of the political sphere as the source of strategic objectives. It also maintains the connection with military means, and in this differs from other contending definitions for twentieth-century strategy. It has been argued that in an age of total war, especially when the value of military instruments has been blunted by the excessive costs attendant on their use, all the means of national power – political and economic as well as military – should be incorporated into a definition of strategy. It is probably best to resist this temptation. If we have to focus on all methods of prevailing in any given conflict, the study of strategy ceases to be distinct from the study of diplomacy or of international relations in general and the sense that we are dealing with 'functional and purposive violence' is lost.[17]

If some have sought to broaden the term, others have sought to constrict it. When fledgling air forces, after World War I, were anxious to demonstrate that they possessed a means for getting right to the heart of the enemy's power and destroying it with some well-chosen blows, they described this as a 'strategic' capability. Thus they spoke of 'strategic bombardment', using 'strategic bombers', eventually under a 'Strategic Air Command' (SAC). After 1945 nuclear weapons, best able to perform this mission, came to be known as 'strategic weapons', and a war in which they were to be used would be a 'strategic war'. This use of the adjective 'strategic' has very little to do with the noun 'strategy'. The connection has now become even more tenuous, with 'strategic' now tightly defined, in the 'strategic arms limitation talks' by reference to the ranges of certain weapons. A weapon that can be directed from the homeland of one superpower against the homeland of the other is strategic. It is difficult to avoid this sort of use, as it is now the language in which nuclear issues are discussed. However, the definition of Liddell Hart's remains the best, and unless the context indicates otherwise, it is the one adopted for this study.

The developing muddle in use of this fundamental term prepares us for the muddle of nuclear strategy itself. Initially, when atom bombs first made their dramatic entrance on to the international stage, they were discussed and understood in terms derived from the established theories of airpower. Eventually, nuclear weapons became more powerful, more numerous and, crucially, possessed by more than one nation. New concepts and approaches developed in an attempt to come to terms with a situation in which a war in which the most formidable weapons available were used would, in all probability, be catastrophic for all concerned.

The question has been whether any useful purpose could be served by employment of devices which invited discussion using words such as 'holocaust', 'doomsday' and 'armageddon', and whether any employment could be sufficiently deliberate and controlled to ensure that political objectives were met. Which means that at issue has been whether a 'nuclear strategy' is a contradiction in terms.

Section 1

First and Second Thoughts

1 The Arrival of the Bomb

The Transformation of War

It might be thought that the introduction of nuclear weapons created a wholly unprecedented situation rendering all previous strategic theories and concepts immediately obsolete. In fact such a demarcation line is hard to establish. The concepts with which nuclear weapons were first understood were derived from a prior era; many of the post-1945 debates were, in essence, continuations of those of pre-war days. The main link was provided by the doctrine of strategic bombardment, which assumed that the most effective use of aircraft was to attack the social and industrial heart of the enemy, so producing internal collapse and obviating the need for a traditional battlefield victory. Support for this doctrine grew with the quality of aircraft performance and also out of the desire to avoid a repetition of the murderous stalemate of the Great War.

The terrible slaughter from 1914 to 1918, as both sides attempted to penetrate the other's defence, had thrown into sharp relief the meaning of all the developments in technology and industrial organization of the past century. The whole society, rather than just an armed segment, had become intimately involved in the waging of war. Success was dependent upon the numerical and industrial strength of nations, and the willingness to concentrate them in a titanic struggle. This struggle was channelled onto a battlefield, which became an arena in which the two sides engaged in a process of mutual exhaustion. It was a war of attrition in which defeat came to the nation which

3

collapsed first, with the victor left in a state only marginally less sorry.

Such a war involved a severe drain on national resources and energies. It demanded patience and perseverance; a satisfaction with the enemy's lack of progress rather than tangible progress of one's own. Few military thinkers have applied themselves to the perfection of the means of fighting a war of attrition.[1] Soldiers do not like to plan for long-drawn-out and inconclusive campaigns. That is why they are often so unprepared to fight such a campaign when it is forced upon them. The generals of the Great War could think of no better way of breaking the deadlock than throwing large numbers of men at the enemy in the hope of somehow achieving a breakthrough.

After 1918 no one was prepared to contemplate a repeat performance. The more innovative sought ways to achieve a quick and decisive victory. It was recognized that this would have to be based on the new means of mobility demonstrated but not fully exploited in the war: tanks and aircraft. There were two approaches: one (explored in Britain by Basil Liddell Hart and Major-General Fuller, and applied for Germany in 1939–40 by General Guderian) was to use both tanks and aircraft to extend the traditional range of instruments available to a military commander, providing him with added scope for manoeuvre; the other was to use the aircraft's range for direct attacks on the enemy homeland and so avoid the need for any surface conflict at all.

Strategic Bombardment

The possibility of using aircraft to attack cities had been noted almost with their invention. In fact, there had already been experiments with balloons in two unsuccessful attempts to drop explosives on an enemy – by the Russians on the French in 1812 and the Austrians on the Venetians in 1847. The first actual victims of air war were Arab villagers in Libya, bombed during the Italian war on Turkey of 1911–12. Books prior to World War I described vividly the horror-struck panic, the vast loss of life and the obliteration of centres of population, industry and government expected to accompany attacks from the sky. In 1908 H. G. Wells published his prophetic *The War in the Air*, which even spoke of airborne atomic warfare.

These visions gained even wider currency and credibility in the 1920s and 1930s. This was a consequence of the panic generated in

London following the small-scale Zeppelin and aircraft raids of World War I; an awareness of the growing range, speed and capacity of aircraft; and a pessimism as to the possibilities of effective defence. The growing expectations of a war dominated by vicious air attacks was summarized succinctly in a famous 1932 speech of Stanley Baldwin:

> Any town which is within reach of an aerodrome can be bombed within the first five minutes of war from the air, to an extent that was inconceivable in the last war, and the question will be whose morale will be shattered quickest by the preliminary bombing? I think it is well for the man in the street to realise that there is no power on earth that can protect him from being bombed. Whatever people may tell him, the bomber will always get through.[2]

The apparent strength of the bomber offensive in bringing matters to a swift conclusion could be contrasted with that of the defence on the ground in preventing a conclusion. A final but not insignificant factor encouraging the promotion of air operations against the heartland of the enemy was that it strengthened the claims of ambitious airmen for a separate and autonomous service commanding a major share of the military budget.

This use of airpower was described as 'strategic bombardment'. The terminology was appropriate only if the premise was accepted that bombardment of socioeconomic targets behind the enemy lines provided an independent means to the strategic end of enemy defeat. Adding the adjective 'strategic' to blockade or invasion or territorial defence would seem superfluous. Its use in the case of bombardment came from a desire to distinguish the envisaged role from that of a tactical variety, undertaken in support of surface forces in battle. This distinction between 'strategic' and 'tactical' roles made little sense for armies and navies. Here battlefield success, or the probability of such success, was an inevitable concomitant of the attainment of the strategic end. The distinction did seem to make sense for airpower. It differentiated between independent operations and those dependent upon other services, and also expressed a belief, that later turned out to be fallacious, that strategic bombardment did not involve contact with the enemy's forces. Air Marshal Trenchard explained: 'It is not necessary, for an air force, in order to defeat the enemy nation, to defeat its armed forces first. Airpower can dispense with that intermediate step...'.[3]

It was the Italian Giulo Douhet (1869–1930) who did most to organize the apparent logic of airpower into a systematic theory. Though the theory of strategic bombardment has come to be associated with his name it would be a mistake to overestimate his influence. Similar notions occurred to many airmen in many countries quite independently. The theory had a simple appeal. Here was an exciting, and still improving, new medium of warfare, capable of speedier and more distant operations than hitherto considered possible. Rather than dabble inconclusively in surface engagements on the periphery, how much more effective to aim right at the centre of the enemy's power – the industries and workforce which sustained his military effort.

Much advocacy of strategic bombardment was immoderate and simplistic, relying on intuition more than analysis. In part, this was because it was propaganda for a new branch of the armed services. But even the most detached writers on this subject were working in the realm of speculation. They could not be sure what changes new technological advances would bring; they could only guess at the impact of bombardment on modern social structures. (In Britain, for example, much of the RAF's confidence in strategic bombing derived from its apparent efficiency in controlling wild tribesmen in Somalia and Iraq.) Under the influence of these theories, military writers were straying beyond their area of competence. It might be hard to challenge military expertise on the tactics of battle; but now they were commenting on the ability of civilians, indeed whole societies, to withstand a certain sort of pressure. To illustrate the problems this created we can examine some of the precepts of strategic bombardment.

The Political Science of Airpower

Douhet had few doubts about the unassailable primacy of the offence in the air and of the defence on the ground. For an adequate military posture it would be necessary and sufficient to be in a position to gain command in the air. This would be when one was 'in a position to prevent the enemy from flying while retaining the ability to fly oneself', achieved by aggressive bombardment of the enemy's air bases rather than through aerial combat. These bases would be a key feature of the set of targets marked out for immediate attack. In these attacks the essential motto would appear to be 'hit first and hit hard'.

Whatever its aims, the side which decides to go to war will unleash all its aerial forces in mass against the enemy nation the instant the decision is taken, without waiting to declare war formally.[4]

The belief in the critical importance of the first blow was based on the premise that this could be a war-winning event, less because of the physical than the psychological consequences. The total paralysis of society would require time and favourable conditions. However, the proponents of strategic bombing believed that the desired result would come earlier because of the vulnerability of civilian morale to aerial attacks. Before bomb damage had made it impossible to produce war *materiel*, the collapse of morale would lead to offers of surrender.

The identification of morale as a critical target was borrowed from those conventional theories of warfare in which the morale of the armed forces was emphasized as being as much a critical determinant of strength as numbers and equipment. Clausewitz wrote of the importance of 'spirit', describing physical force as the 'wooden hilt' of the sword, whereas moral force was the 'shining blade'. At the time when the early theories of strategic bombardment were being formulated 'morale' was a central concept in military thought. The French Army in particular, inspired by the theories of Du Picq and Foch, saw war as the clash of opposing wills, with defeat the punishment of the force whose will broke first. There had been a tendency, which Foch mournfully acknowledged after World War I, to believe that 'morale alone counted', seeing victory as almost a triumph of mind over matter. But even those who kept the moral factor more in perspective did not deny its importance and recognized the virtue of an *esprit de corps*. Bad morale meant indiscipline and desertion; good morale meant resourcefulness and courage on the battlefield.

Focusing attention on to civilian morale as well as that of the armed forces seemed appropriate to an age when warfare was losing its separateness and becoming a test of strength between whole societies rather than simply the armed representatives of those societies. The welfare of civilians had always been at stake in warfare, but until the nineteenth century their contribution to performance in war had not been significant. Even in sieges non-combatants were more of a drag than a spur, spoken of as *bouches inutiles* – useless mouths. As warfare came to rely more upon a society's total resources of manpower and industrial capacity, the rôles of 'national will' and a smooth process of war production grew in relative importance. The ability to interfere with production and undermine the national will might be as important as battlefield successes in weakening the enemy. Civilian suffering might be a cause of defeat – not just a consequence.

Furthermore, civilian morale appeared as a more choice target than military morale. Civilians were unready to face military danger and lacked discipline when it came. So Douhet argued that there would be no need to pound at the sturdy and prepared military shield provided by the army and navy. The 'air arm ... will strike against entities less well able to resist, and helpless to act or counteract. It is fated, therefore, that the moral and material collapse will come about more quickly and easily.'[5]

But while it was true that military morale could be built and reinforced more readily than that of civilians, the consequences of its collapse were proportionately greater. A despondent and dispirited leadership was a recipe for battlefield disaster. Even for the individual soldier – normally controlled within a command structure – often, because of the physical proximity of the enemy, there was an option to desert or surrender. Direct and immediate results could flow from a collapse in military morale in a way in which they were unlikely to do with a collapse in civilian morale. Because of the lack of immediate consequences and the added difficulties facing an enemy attempting to press an advantage, recovery was more possible at home than at the front. So long as the economy was functioning sufficiently well to service the military machine, and this was itself performing adequately in combat, the strategic impact of a miserable and dejected population was limited, though it might be a source of vicarious pleasure for the raider. It could be hoped that a government that sympathized with, or indeed experienced, the suffering of the people would be so appalled that the desire for relief would cause a reconsideration of the national commitment, but there would be no compelling need for this.

There was a prevalent belief in a basic division between the mass and the élite. Mass hysteria and panic after populations had been bombed would lead to demands for merciful release through national capitulation. On the actual mechanisms through which the mass would force the élite to change its conduct of the war, the theorists and practitioners of strategic bombardment were notably vague. Their writings were replete with references rarely more specific than 'breaking morale', attacking the 'will to resist' and bringing a nation 'to its knees'. Douhet explained how:

A complete breakdown of the social structure cannot but take place in a country being subjected to ... merciless pounding from the air. The time would soon come when, to put an end to horror and suffering, the people themselves, driven by the instinct of self-preservation, would rise up and demand an end to the war.[6]

Writing in 1923 the British military theorist Major General J. F. C. Fuller wrote about how London would be transformed into a 'vast raving Bedlam' following an air attack and how the Government at Westminster would be 'swept away by an avalanche of terror'.[7]

On both sides during World War II there were assertions that the enemy élite in crucial ways was alienated from the mass, committed to the war for its own purposes but able to use the state apparatus to mobilize the mass to follow its lead. There was an obvious propaganda element in such assertions. Nevertheless the assumption can be detected that the government's hold over the population was tenuous. In this sense the mass was the élite's 'Achilles heel' – a soft target that was also the foundation of the national effort. Aerial bombardment would jolt the populace into an awareness of the risks they were running for the government's war policy. The relationship between the mass and the élite would be disrupted: either the people would cease to do the bidding of the government through a generally lacklustre approach to war projects or else, preferably, they would demand of the government that it sued for peace.

Even accepting a crude élite/mass distinction the above expectation suffered from two fallacies. The first was the belief that a change in attitudes would automatically result in a change in behaviour and that this would take the form of activism rather than apathy; and second, that the means would be available for mass activism to transform the government's conduct of the war. The objective misery of the population, whether resulting from bombardment or scarcities or battlefield losses, was not the key variable in the government–citizen relationship. Basic factors of social cohesion and political structure, as well as more specific ones relating to the extent of the understanding of and support for the war policy and its execution, were as crucial. To replace a government, or to get an existing one to change its mind, required both political means and an alternative policy. 'Peace' could suggest far greater evils if it was firmly believed that 'democracy' or 'civilization' was imperilled. Most important, for a fundamental change to take place there needed to be an environment in which some form of political opposition could develop and grow.

The Experience of World War II

At the start of World War II, rather than embark on the course of uninhibited bomber offensives as anticipated by Douhet, the major belligerents exercised restraint. This was a consequence of uncertainty as to whether strategic bombardment could bring the war to an early and satisfactory conclusion plus the knowledge that it could well lead to reprisal raids.[8] The devastation resulting from the systematic pounding of each others' cities appeared as a frightening prospect. No government wished to cope with the consequent social and economic strains.

The British and French had an exaggerated sense of German bomber strength, while Hitler was anxious to prevent major damage to German cities. The *Luftwaffe*'s role was more of a tactical one, acting in support of ground forces. In issuing his commands at the start of the war, Hitler laid down a 'guiding principle' not to provoke the initiation of aerial warfare by an action on the part of Germany.

The erosion of this mutual restraint, which did not take place until after the fall of France, stemmed from the fact that any use of airpower, whether seen as being 'tactical' or 'strategic' tended, at some point, to degenerate into an attack on civilians. Attempts to use airpower as a purely military and discriminating instrument floundered on inherent inaccuracies and the regular proximity of 'civilian' and 'military' targets, especially when 'military' was broadly defined. The 'tactical' use of airpower implied that it was to be contained within the combat zone. But a 'combat zone' was not a fixed space with rigid boundaries, though it had sometimes taken that appearance during the Great War. Aircraft had been responsible for extending the area of the combat zone and, with tanks and other armoured vehicles, for allowing much greater forward momentum in the battlefront. Compared with the static fronts of 1914–18, the battle arenas of 1939–45 were remarkable for their scale, variability, and fluidity. The success of the German offensive of the first year of the war meant that cities were frequently to be found in the combat zone. As 'tactical' obstacles, and easier to denote as such when actively defended, they suffered aerial attack.

When the Germans reached the channel the potential combat zone included southern England. The *Luftwaffe* attempted to gain command of the air by destroying the aircraft, bases, and facilities of the RAF. The purpose of this effort was not, as Douhet would have expected, to put British cities at the mercy of the Germans, but to provide clear skies for the planned invasion. It was in the course of the battle for the command of the air – the Battle of Britain – that the restraints on aerial warfare finally eroded. As a result of symbolic British raids of late August against Berlin, the blitz of London began. Rather than a catastrophe for Britain, by allowing the RAF a chance to recover from the severe damage inflicted to its facilities, the blitz was a relief, despite the suffering that Londoners had to endure.

The first year of the war demonstrated that the more extravagant claims of airpower enthusiasts had been erroneous. The sweep of the German armies through Europe upset notions of surface deadlock; there were forms of defence against bombers, such as radar-aided fighter aircraft, that could cause serious casualties in the offensive force; and the fragility of the civilian population in the face of air attack had been over-estimated.

The Germans became involved in a major effort to test civilian morale, for the blitz continued after the invasion plans had been shelved in the vague and futile hope that it might force the British to reconsider their commitment to the war. What started as a support for an invasion turned into a surrogate. By 1942 the RAF had recovered, built up its strength and was being joined by the US air force. It was now the Allies' turn to test theories of strategic bombardment. Here too, their adoption of the strategy was a surrogate. Unable to open a second front on the land, they contented themselves with battering the enemy from the sky.

An attack on the socioeconomic structure of the enemy was not a novel feature of British strategic policy. Accustomed to having weaker land armies than those found on the continent the means to victory had been seen to be the ability of the Royal Navy to enforce an economic blockade. This had contributed to victory in 1918 and was the foundation of British hopes in 1939. It demanded no great conceptual leap to suggest that bombers might achieve through direct assault what the Navy could only achieve through an indirect squeeze. If merchant shipping could be considered a legitimate military target so could industry, fuel, and communications. Here problems arose because airpower was an extremely blunt instrument. At sea there was no adjacent property to be damaged. This was not the case on the land where, even if the target was missed, something would be hit.

On top of this the RAF were sceptical as to their ability to pinpoint key industrial targets and destroy them with sufficient efficiency and on a sufficient scale to affect the course of the war. The bluntness of the air instrument stemmed from a requirement, if prohibitive losses were to be avoided, of night action which added to the already considerable inaccuracy of aerial bombardment. What was practically easier became strategically desirable. Point attacks against specifically identified vulnerabilities in the military or industrial structure were dismissed as 'panaceas' and the effort was concentrated against 'the morale of the German civil population and in particular of the industrial workers'. As Liddell Hart caustically noted: 'inaccuracy of weapon-aim fostered inhumanity of war-aim'.[9]

The American airmen were more anxious to aim for military – industrial targets and even attempted day-time raids, in which they were extremely vulnerable to enemy air defences, to improve accuracy. While obviously less costly in civilian lives than area attacks, civilian losses could not be avoided, even when the targets were in occupied territories. Nevertheless, purposeful attacks on vulnerable parts of the military–industrial structure did show results over time. Eventually, the allied bombing offensive disrupted the war economy and denied key supplies to the enemy forces. The value of attacks on civilians were less obvious though strongly asserted by those promoting the attacks. The bombing surveys conducted after the war cast doubts as to whether civilian morale was seriously strained through bombing attacks. Even accepting that there was a threshold of tolerance for a society and that it could adapt to a systematic pounding only up to a certain point, this point was not reached early in the war. The long-range bomber did not appear as an instrument of a decisive early blow, but as another instrument of attrition.

As an attempt to regulate political behaviour and decisions through inflicting pain on the populace it was not impressive. The limitations on this form of attack were widely recognized after the war. During the war they were suspected by some, but the prevailing atmosphere on both sides was one in which the capacity of the enemy to withstand pain was doubted and the desire to inflict pain, by way of retribution for past 'atrocities', was very strong. It was in this atmosphere that the early versions of the weapons that dominated post-war strategic thinking were created.

Retaliation and the 'V' Weapons

War provides a great stimulus to technological innovation. Among the many innovations of World War II, two were crucial to the future of strategic planning and thought – the 'V' weapons and the atomic bomb. The operational deployment of both was limited, though sufficient in each case to demonstrate potential. Both were seen to be of greatest value against civilian targets. Both were seen to be effective because of their capacity to cause shock and terror as much as actual destruction. Both were barely considered in terms of aiding the conventional military effort.

Hitler had often expressed the belief that retaliation in kind was the only way to get the enemy to desist from terror-bombing of German cities. But, once the Allies had air supremacy, it became harder to retaliate with equivalent effect to massive attacks on Germany. As the war progressed this problem faced Hitler with increasing intensity. One way round the problem was to use available resources to greater effect through improvements in weapon design. The V-1 flying bomb was such an advanced weapon. Though somewhat unreliable, it saved on fuel and air crew. It has been estimated that the campaign cost the British four times as much to deal with it as it cost the Germans to wage. The V-2 rocket however, though a greater technical achievement, was inefficient. For improvements in performance (greater speed and reliability in penetrating air defences) and an added sense of spectacle, it cost one hundred times as much as the V-1.

The production of V-1s and V-2s got under way too late to demonstrate their full potential. Their introduction was delayed by technical problems and hampered by allied bombing; their operation was eventually curtailed as the Germans were forced out of France. The use that was made of the weapons was very much conditioned by Hitler's belief in the need to retaliate against Britain. The very name of the new weapons – *Vergeltungswaffe* (revenge weapon) – underlined their purpose. The main arguments concerning the operational plans for their use appear to have been concerned with the most effective way of breaking British morale. David Irving quotes a conversation between Lieutenant-General von Axthelm, who favoured a 'really sadistic bombardment', and Field Marshal Milch, who argued that a sustained drizzle of pilotless aircraft was 'the most evil burden imaginable for a city' with nobody knowing where the next one would fall. 'Twenty days of that will have them all folding at the knees'.

Any alternative use for the 'V' weapons, for example against the ports which would be used for an invasion fleet, was not countenanced by Hitler. The V-1 was seen to be 'of use only as an instrument of terror, and not for attacking military objectives' though, when used against the port of Antwerp in a bid to impede the allied invasion, the attack was of some success. So the use of the weapons was conditioned by Hitler's view that the only way 'to smash terror was with counter-terror' and that these weapons were, to quote Goebbels, 'awe-inspiring murder weapons'.[10]

The Atom Bomb

The most revolutionary development of all was the atom bomb. As the war in Europe had begun in 1939 the world's scientific community had been in a state of some professional ferment over a rapid series of discoveries on the process by which uranium atoms split under bombardment from neutrons. This phenomenon was named fission by O. R. Frisch, because of its similarity to the division of a biological cell. The scientific community involved in this research was international in character, with contributions coming from all over Europe and North America. However, by 1939 the political tensions within Europe were causing the relevant scientists to congregate in Britain and the US. The story of the scientific and engineering achievement which resulted in the production of the first bombs has been well told elsewhere.[11] Because of the central importance of this achievement for everything that follows in this book, it might be useful to summarize briefly the scientific principle involved.

Our textbook image of the atom is one of a small solar system, with a heavy, positively charged nucleus, made up of protons and neutrons, orbited by light negative electrons. As each atom is electrically neutral, the number of protons in the nucleus is equal to that of the outer electrons. The atomic number of an atom, and its fundamental chemical properties, is determined by this number of protons. The number of neutrons in atoms of the same element is not necessarily constant. Variations, which can lead to differing physical and nuclear properties, are known as isotopes. They are distinguished from one another by quoting the total number, neutrons plus protons, of particles contained in the nucleus (e.g. uranium-235).

A key characteristic of neutrons, which makes them potential agents of change in a nucleus, is that they are uncharged. Only certain combinations of neutrons and protons are stable. When few in number, equal amounts of protons and neutrons result in stability, but for larger nuclei, the proportion of neutrons required is much greater. The two heavy elements relevant to the design of nuclear weapons are uranium (U) and plutonium (Pu).

By 1939, the process of fission was becoming appreciated in the scientific community. It was known that when uranium atoms were bombarded with neutrons, they could split into approximately equal parts with the release of enormous quantities of energy. Furthermore, when fission occurred some free neutrons were released which were capable of causing fission in other nuclei. It was realized that if more than one secondary neutron became available as a result of each fission, then in principle a chain-reaction was possible, spreading through a mass of fissile material and yielding enormous energy. The first man-initiated self-sustaining nuclear chain-reaction was achieved on 2 December 1942 in Chicago as part of the war-time Manhattan project organized in the US for the purpose of building atomic bombs.

An atom (or fission) bomb is one which exploits such a chain-reaction to create an explosion. The amount of fissionable uranium or plutonium isotopes (U233, U235 or Pu-239) required is known as the *critical size*. This is reached when free neutrons, sufficient to sustain a chain-reaction, cannot escape or be captured by non-fissionable material. In addition, for explosive purposes, this reaction must build up extremely rapidly, for otherwise the device will fly apart and the reaction will stop. It was the brevity of this period that caused most technical problems in the construction of the first bomb.

The impetus behind the atom bomb project in Britain and the United States came from a fear of the consequences of a unilateral German success in the military exploitation of atomic energy. The German atomic threat did not materialize. What would have happened if it had done so is by no means clear. Hitler presumably would have viewed atomic bombs in the same manner that he viewed the 'V' weapons: as an instrument of counter-terror which if produced and delivered to the enemy in sufficient quantities might well turn the tide of the war. It was this prospect which made the Allies nervous.

Originally the bomb was seen only as an insurance policy against a successful German project. However, once the US programme was well under way, the responsible officials expected a substantial return on their investment. When and if the bomb became available it would be a weapon to be employed against the enemies of the United States, whatever these enemies had available in their own arsenals. Henry Stimson, Secretary of War from 1940 to 1945, made it clear that the

common objective throughout the war was to be the first to pro-duce an atomic weapon and use it. The possible atomic weapon was considered to be a new and tremendously powerful explosive, as legitimate as any other of the deadly explosive weapons of modern war. The entire purpose was the production of a military weapon; on no other ground could the wartime expenditure of so much time and money have been justified. The exact circumstances in which that weapon might be used were unknown to us until the middle of 1945.[12]

It was not until mid-1945, with the New Mexico test of the first bomb, that the full enormity of atomic power could be properly appreciated. In August 1941, after being informed that a weapon equivalent to 1800 tons of TNT could be produced, Churchill noted his contentment with 'existing explosives' before recognizing that 'we must not stand in the path of improvement'. Compare this with his apocalyptic exclamation to Henry Stimson on hearing of the successful test at New Mexico: 'Stimson, what was gunpowder? Trivial. What was electricity? Meaningless. This Atomic Bomb is the Second Coming in Wrath!'.[13] Truman recalled that, on being told by Stimson after he became President that the US was near to completing 'the most terrible weapons ever known in human history, one bomb which could destroy a whole city', the first comparison that came into his mind was with the shells that the large German gun, Big Bertha, had sent into Paris in World War I.[14]

The atom bomb was not simply 'just another weapon'. It was still for use in war, as legitimate as any other weapon, but with implications and ramifications far beyond those which had ever accompanied the introduction of a new piece of military equipment.

The Strategy of Hiroshima[15]

The eventual strategic use of the bomb was determined by the conditions prevailing at the time at which the first bomb became available. By the middle of 1945 Japan was a spent force, unable to project her strength beyond her boundaries. Having lost command of both the sea and the air, she was being starved of resources through blockade and was being subjected to a regular and unmerciful burning and battering by waves of B-29 bombers. The problem for the Americans was how to turn this defeat into surrender. The problem for the Japanese, once they recognized that there was no path left to victory, was how to surrender under the most favourable political conditions.

The Japanese leadership's unwillingness to surrender in 1945, despite the blatant hopelessness of the position, was not so much based on a lingering sense of glory and honour as on a deep sense that the constitutional essence of Japan, embodied in the personage of the Emperor, was at stake. The Japanese continued to fight in the hope that the further costs they could impose on the Americans during the course of an invasion would encourage the United States to modify its war aims. This hope rested on sufficient resilience in the face of blockade and bombardment to force the United States into an invasion, and then an ability to make this invasion as bloody as possible. There was also a hope that the Russians, neutral in the Pacific War, might be able to act as mediators.

A successful Allied invasion which would lead to the physical occupation of the key decision-making centres in Japan would settle the matter. But the calculations of possible Allied losses, fortified by the experience of the heavy fighting over Okinawa, led to estimates of casualties approaching the million. The military alternative was to continue, through blockade and bombardment, to inflict so much punishment on the enemy that this would lead to a reconsideration of the obstinate refusal to surrender unconditionally. The use of nuclear weapons was constrained by the lack of key military targets available. In the first meeting to discuss bomb use, in May 1943, the Japanese fleet at Truk was considered a suitable target. By mid-1945 the Japanese fleet was virtually non-existent. Use of bombs in a 'tactical' mode was considered for an invasion of Japan. But an invasion was still the very thing US policy-makers wished to avoid.

The Air Force preference for precision, as against area, bombardment that had been displayed in Europe had all but vanished in the Pacific War. Japan seemed particularly suited for area raids: industry was dispersed rather than concentrated and the people, crowded into wooden structures, were consequently extremely vulnerable to incendiaries. After limited fire-bombing raids in January and February 1945, the Air Force embarked upon a remorseless campaign, beginning in March with an all-out attack on Tokyo that left nearly 300,000 buildings destroyed and over 80,000 dead. In April General Curtis LeMay, who was in charge of this campaign, wrote:

I am influenced by the conviction that the present stage of development in the air war against Japan presents the AAF for the first time with the opportunity of proving the power of the strategic air arm. I consider that for the first time strategic air bombardment faces a situation in which its strength is proportionate to the magnitude of its task. I feel that the destruction of Japan's ability to wage war is within the capability of this command.[16]

It was in this same month that General Groves set down criteria for a committee he had appointed to choose appropriate targets for the bomb. The 'governing factor' was that the targets chosen should be places the bombing of which should 'adversely affect the will of the Japanese people to continue the war'. This was similar wording to that customarily used by the Air Force to explain the purpose of terror-bombing.[17] In fact the Air Force leadership saw the bomb as a dramatic supplement to the campaign of conventional bombing currently being waged against Japan. These conventional raids did not stop as a prelude to the introduction of the bomb; they continued up to the very moment of Japan's surrender. Indeed many in the Air Force appear to have been surprised at the apparent decisiveness of atom-bombing.

The key influences on the bomb's use were those such as Stimson, Marshall, Oppenheimer, Groves, Bush, and Conant, who had been involved in atom-bomb questions from early on in the project and were *au fait* with the properties of the new weapon. To them the bomb was not seen purely as an intensive form of strategic bombardment. To get full benefit in the Manhattan project it was necessary to emphasize the unique and awesome properties of the bomb. After it had been noted in the Interim Committee that the effect of one bomb would not be that different from 'any Air Corps strike of current dimensions', Oppenheimer pointed out that 'the visual effect of an atomic bombing would be tremendous. It would be accompanied by a brilliant luminescence which would rise to a height of 10,000 to 20,000 feet.' It was on the basis of this spectacular quality that those considering the use of the bomb began to move away from the previous, implicit, strategy of cumulative pressure to one of maximum shock.

Many nuclear scientists argued that to demonstrate the bomb's power would suffice, for the knowledge of its existence would be shock enough. The humanitarian advantages of this course were discounted because of practical disadvantages: failure, after a portentous announcement, could be counterproductive while the full meaning of success could be lost if a spectacular display was unaccompanied by equally spectacular destruction.

The problem was to induce a sense of hopelessness in a people, still resisting despite immense suffering, by impressing upon them their vulnerability to an unprecedented form of horror. In discussing the value of airpower Liddell Hart noted that 'so long as the process is gradual' human beings can accommodate to degradation of their standard of life. 'Decisive results come sooner from sudden shocks than long-drawn-out pressure. Shocks throw the opponent off balance. Pressure allows him time to adjust to it.'[18] To throw the enemy off balance was precisely what was required. Stimson wrote in 1947: 'I felt that to extract a genuine surrender from the Emperor and his military advisers they must be administered a tremendous shock which would carry convincing proof of our power to destroy the Empire.' The atomic bomb 'was more than a weapon of terrible destruction; it was a psychological weapon'. He noted that Marshall was 'emphatic in his insistence on the shock value of the new weapon'.[19]

A key feature of a strategy of shock was that it required an element of surprise. Here there was a contrast with a strategy of cumulative pressure. If the aim was to convince the enemy of the horror ahead if resistance continued, then a declaration of intent to devastate the enemy's homeland was a natural part of the strategy. But, if the aim was to shock, surprise was necessary. General Marshall explained; 'It's no good warning them. If you warn them there's no surprise. And the only way to produce shock is surprise'.[20]

With the prompt surrender of the Japanese following Nagasaki the impression was left that the strategic concepts that guided the use of the bomb were valid. The accumulation of evidence since 1945 has suggested that the bomb was less important than it appeared at the time in terminating the war.

Surrender is a political decision, usually controversial, and so may require a shift in the national power structure before it can take place. It was the movement of this shift, dependent on the delicate handling of the hard-line militarists and a hope of tolerable surrender terms, that determined the date of the Japanese surrender. If the bomb did have a role it was in accelerating and intensifying the process of political change. But even here caution is due. The dropping of the bomb was not the only shock that the Japanese received in the four days beginning 6 August 1945. Combined with the atom bomb was the Soviet Union's entry into the war against Japan. This dashed any lingering hopes of Soviet support in mediating for more favourable conditions for surrender. The bomb, however, did result in the sort of dislocation that the administration of strategic shock is supposed to bring. According to Butow:

It was not that the military men had suddenly become reasonable in the hours following the Hiroshima and Nagasaki disasters; it was rather that they ... had momentarily been caught off balance. They were also at a loss for words which could make any lasting impression upon the end-the-war faction. Prior to the dropping of the two A-bombs they had been able to pledge their belief in their ability to meet effectively any action taken by the enemy, but now whatever they said made them look foolish and insincere.[21]

Even assuming that the bomb was the major source of surrender the lessons that could be drawn from the minimal operational experience were limited. It was like administering poison on the death bed. The target was a fragile one. It was a structure not only weak, but on the point of collapse. There were few operational problems. The 'command of the air' had already been won; there were no Japanese defences or threats of retaliation. Furthermore the advantage of shock was unique; thereafter there could be horror but not surprise in the bomb's use.

Nevertheless, the appearance was more compelling than the reality, and the worth of the bomb was taken to have been proven in action. Its use was symptomatic of a period in warfare which had seen the development of a number of weapons suitable only for the indiscriminate destruction of large targets, and the erosion of restraints on the employment of these weapons. The legitimacy of these targets, which tended to be cities, was found in the character of total warfare, in which victory depended on the effective utilization of the total resources of a society, and not just the armed forces.

In a remarkable book, written in the closing months of the war, Basil Liddell Hart pondered the meaning of the new V-weapons. He saw them as the culmination of a process that had been anticipated some 2000 years before by the Spartan king, Archidamus, who had exclaimed on seeing a dart fired by a machine brought from Sicily: 'O Hercules, the valour of men is at an end'. In the past century the mechanization of war had been progressing steadily. With heavy artillery and aircraft the 'gulf which had separated the fighting zone from the hinterland' had been leapt, and now, with the V-weapons, the human element was being removed altogether. In the future:

the most virile nation might not be able to withstand another, inferior to it in all natural qualities, if the latter had some decisively superior technical appliance.

The flying bomb may well tear away the veil of illusion that has so long obscured the reality of the change in warfare – from a fight to a process of destruction. Being palpably an 'inhuman' instrument, it creates the *feeling* – which counts more than a truth apprehended by reason – that war is no longer a matter of *fighting*. Thus its introduction on June 15, 1944, may come to be regarded as the start of a new era.

The book was not published till after the war. By that time Liddell Hart had had time to write an epilogue. The introduction of the atom bomb reinforced his arguments concerning the danger of conceiving warfare in terms of unlimited aims and unlimited methods. The bomb was 'merely a further stage in the evolution of "automatic warfare"', but one that by virtue of its apparent success was liable to make a more dramatic impact than either the V-1 or the V-2. These had not gone 'far enough in their *actual* effort to convince the world that the problem of security had undergone a fundamental change'. They had not succeeded in their strategic aim and public opinion did not 'probe into the underlying causes of failure, but tends to be swayed by the outcome'. The speed with which the use of the atomic bomb was followed by Japan's surrender meant that 'its decisive effect can hardly be disputed'.[22]

2 Offence and Defence

The Persistence of the Doctrine of Strategic Bombardment

The dramatic finale of World War II at Hiroshima and Nagasaki rescued the doctrine of strategic bombardment. Without the atom bomb the theorists of airpower would have been pushed on to the defensive, hard put to justify the pounding of cities for limited rewards. With the atom bomb, airpower could be said to have come of age.

The great bomber offensives of the war had failed to validate the expectations of the pre-war years. The bomber had not always 'got through', and when it had done the results had been less than decisive. Air raids took their toll, but only over time. The bomber was not a means of breaking a deadlock, but yet another instrument of attrition, another method by which industrial societies could beat each other down.

Now two spectacular advances had occurred in the destructive capacity of weapons and their means of delivery. There was no known way of stopping a V-2 type rocket, while atom bombs were absolutely devastating and, if the experience of the Japanese surrender was anything to go by, promised immediate results. The old axioms could be reformulated: the rocket would always get through; atomic bombardment offered an independent and swift route to total victory. The terms of the debate on the strategic significance of the new technology was thus set by the existing debate on the value of strategic bombardment.

Amongst airmen, an ideology had been created around a single weapon of war – the heavy bomber. They could not contemplate a truly effective defence against the bomber, nor accept that airpower had value in any rôle other than strategic bombardment. Perry Smith explains this, in the USA, by reference to the Air Force objective of institutional independence from the Army, an objective realized in 1947. But this does not explain the persistence of this ideology well after autonomy was achieved. It is unwise to isolate a single motive. Bureaucratic and operational independence, the élan of the airmen, the primacy of the strategic bombardment mission were all bound up in a general sense of the uniqueness, in its power and directness, of the heavy bomber.

The Air Force had its critics – from civilians who were repelled by the reliance on mass destruction, to sailors and soldiers who sensed an unwarranted downgrading of their own importance. The immediate impact of Hiroshima and Nagasaki was to silence such criticism, at least for a couple of years. 'Strategic bombing had won its case, and the ignored lessons of World War II could remain ignored by the public, Congress and all others except the inquiring scholar or the parochial Army or Navy man'.[1] When, in 1946, the first reports of the US Strategic Bombing Survey were released, one newspaper columnist commented: 'What might have become a good old fashioned row now becomes an academic discussion thanks to the atomic bomb. Come the next war there will be no fleets of bombers pouring down death on civilian populations. Just one little atom bomb will do the work of a thousand blockbusters'.[2] The detailed analyses contained in the reports were seen to refer to an era that had just past. The challenge they represented to Air Force articles of faith failed to make an impact.

In November 1945, in his Final Report to the Secretary of War, General Arnold, the Chief of Air Staff, stated:

> The influence of atomic energy on air power can be stated very simply. It has made air power all important . . . [The] only known effective means of delivering atomic bombs in their present state of development is the very heavy bomber . . .

> This country . . . must recognize that real security . . . in the visible future will rest on our ability to take immediate offensive action with overwhelming force. It must be apparent to a potential aggressor that an attack on the United States would be followed by an immensely devastating air attack on him.

The atom bomb was a weapon that could only be delivered by air and against large targets, which basically meant cities. As long as the supplies of the bomb were limited there would be no point in wasting them against small point targets of limited value on a battlefield or at sea. It was a palpably blunt instrument and would be used in a blunt manner. It made airpower more efficient by decreasing the 'cost of destruction'. General Arnold calculated that substituting atomic for conventional explosives would make a given amount of destruction 'at least six times more economical'. Less aircraft would be needed; the dropping of a single atom bomb by a B-29 on Hiroshima caused as 'much damage as 300 planes would have done'.[3] Not only would less planes be required but also effective range would be increased, as an atom bomb would represent a lighter load than a full complement of conventional exposives. The violence would be more concentrated in terms of both space and time.

The New Strategic Environment

The military tend to have an ambivalent attitude to technological advance. They will embrace readily those incremental developments that allow them to perform their traditional rôles even better, but view with suspicion anything new that appears to require radical departures from established methods or, worse still, suggests the progressive obsolescence of their own brand of warfare. Up till now the air force had seen itself as the most futuristic force. But it had been discriminating, preferring the technology of the long-range offence to that of the defence or tactical support. Now it was faced with a technology capable of replacing the heavy bomber with a pilotless machine, so rendering airmen redundant. The Air Force was luke-warm to the prospect of intercontinental missiles and therefore pursued their development with only the minimum of enthusiasm.[4]

Visionaries, anticipating a new era of automatic warfare, assumed that the military would naturally follow wherever the new technology took them. As the conjunction of V-2s with atom bombs seemed the obvious solution to all the practical problems of strategic bombardment it was taken for granted that this was the way of the future. Writing just after Hiroshima, Hanson Baldwin noted how in years to come 'The first line of defense . . . will be the directors of "push-button" war – the men who fling gigantic missiles across the seas'.[5] Major-General J. F. C. Fuller, whose vivid imagination was as inventive with the bomb as it had been in the 1920s and 1930s with the tank, described a future 'laboratory-inspired war of destruction'. It would be a duel between two 'tactical organizations of atom-charged and propelled rockets – the one offensive and the other defensive':

> [M]iles above the surface of the earth, noiseless battles will be fought between blast and counterblast. Now and again an invader will get through, and up will go London, Paris, or New York in a 40,000 foot high mushroom or smoke and dust; and as nobody will know what is happening above or beyond or be certain who is fighting whom—let alone what for—the war will be a kind of bellicose perpetual motion until the last laboratory blows up'.[6]

The strength of this and similar imagery dominated much of the popular debate, though regretted in more 'serious' quarters. The Compton Report noted in 1947:

> [T]he era of push-button warfare, in which inter-continental rockets with atomic warheads wipe out tens of millions over-night has not yet arrived. It is extremely unfortunate that the mistaken idea has been planted in so many minds that that era is now present.

It suggested that a weapon of the 'transpolar or trans-oceanic' ranges was some twenty-five years away.[7] This estimate was shared by many others, including the Navy: '[I]t seems a wholly reasonable and safe assumption that rockets with atomic warheads capable of thousands of miles of range are not to be expected for at least another 25 years'.[8]

The problem was not that of range; the method of travelling intercontinental distances was understood. The main difficulties were lack of accuracy, uncertain reliability and high cost. General Arnold, extrapolating from the V-2's low accuracy of 4 miles over a 200-mile range, pointed out that over 3000 miles range this would lead to an average error of 60 miles. Though he expected guidance mechanisms to improve he put this well into the future.[9] The intercontinental missile, noted Bush, 'is not so effective from the standpoint of cost or performance as the airplane with a crew aboard'.

> [A]s long as atomic bombs are scarce and highly expensive in terms of destruction accomplished per dollar disbursed, one does not trust them to a highly complex carrier of inherently low precision, for lack of precision decidely increases such costs.[10]

Because of the loss of accuracy with range, the expectation grew that no rocket with a range of over 1000 miles would be feasible. Some recognized that one might possibly compensate for this lack of range by placing rockets on ships or submarines. The Navy noted that such a deployment would provide for retaliatory attacks with the 'flexibility and surprise available only to mobile instruments'. Bush considered submarines as effective carriers because the 'scales have recently tipped in favour of attack as far as undersea warfare is concerned'; Blackett acknowledged the possibility but suggested this 'could hardly be considered an effective method of waging war'.[11]

There were also a number of fanciful methods of delivery canvassed with some seriousness in 1945 and 1946. One such method was the 'suitcase bomb', considered by many, especially scientists viewing matters in narrow, technical terms, as one of the more probable methods of delivery. For example, Leo Szilard in a May 1945 memo devoted three paragraphs to the danger of bombs being physically carried to US cities, noting America's peculiar vulnerability because of the concentration of its population in large cities along a long coastline accessible to enemy agents, before observing in one sentence that it might one day be possible to deliver atom bombs great distances by means of rockets.[12] Henry Stimson wrote to President Truman in April 1945: '[T]he future may see a time when such a weapon may be constructed in secret and used suddenly and effectively by a wilful nation or group of much greater size and material power'. After Hiroshima this warning was given emphasis:

> The beginning of a new war will surely involve not only the launching of the missiles, but the explosion of the mines that have secretly been set near key targets to provide the pinpoint accuracy that long-range weapons may possibly lack. Government buildings will fall, the great communications facilities will be destroyed, ports of rail and air and sea traffic will be disabled, the crucial industrial installations will be attacked.[13]

Few were ready to dismiss the problem completely, but gradually it came to be accepted that to introduce the component parts of a bomb and then assemble them without detection would not be as simple as had been presumed. An aggressor would worry that his plans might be exposed by untimely detection of just one bomb, or, more generally, it would be risky to depend on planted bombs whose reliability he could not readily check. After having written in 1945 that atom bombs would place 'an extraordinarily high premium' on 'national competence in sabotage on the one hand and in counter-sabotage work on the other',[14] a year later Brodie was writing: 'The new potentialities which the atomic bomb gives to sabotage must not be overrated'.[15]

The consensus that grew during the 1940s, encouraged by the Air Force's expert opinion, was that for the forseeable future, exotic methods would be unnecessary for carrying atomic bombs to their targets. The 'only vehicle for the delivery of an atomic bomb with adequate accuracy over the next ten years will be the conventionally piloted aircraft'.[16] Push-button warfare was a matter for long-term speculation, not immediate planning.

Another pertinent question concerned the number of atomic bombs that would be available for delivery. It did not become apparent until later just how limited the US nuclear stockpile was during the 1940s. There was in fact virtually no stockpile, only unassembled components, until 1947 when post-war production got under way.

The figure on the size of the US stockpile was a closely guarded secret, accepted by those 'not in the know' to be small, though how small was not realized. In 1946 Bernard Brodie guessed a figure of twenty bombs while recognizing that it might be smaller. The next year he chastised the US Navy for assuming that the weapon would be scarce for some time to come. While acknowledging that '[t]oday the atomic bomb is apparently a commodity of great scarcity and very high unit cost' he speculated that this situation 'may evaporate a good deal faster than the Navy expects'.[17] But generally the expectation was of steady rather than spectacular growth in the stockpile so that plans should still assume it to be a scarce resource.

Nor, as the decade progressed, was the danger of a Soviet stockpile considered pressing. In 1945 informed scientific opinion put the date of the first Soviet test two to five years away. This accurate estimate was gradually dismissed as being too alarmist. There was a slide into complacency. The War Department paper of 1947 estimated that: 'For a number of years, perhaps as many as 8 to 15, only the U.S. will possess atomic bombs in significant quantities'. The Compton Report, also of 1947, noted that: 'We cannot safely assume that we will have sole possession of atomic explosives beyond 1951, although most scientists and engineers familiar with the production of the atomic bomb believe it will be 1955 at the earliest before an attack in quantity can be made.' In 1949, at the time of the Soviet test it was reported that the Joint Chiefs of Staff had not been expecting the first Soviet A-bomb until 1952.[18]

These relaxed views of Soviet atomic prospects were even more marked outside of official circles. William Fox in June 1948 was assuming a 'decade or two' before the Soviet Union acquired bombs 'in significant or decisive quantities'.[19] The most surprising complacency in this matter, in view of his earlier accuracy, came from Vannevar Bush in a book that went to press as the first test was announced. 'Opinion now', he noted 'indicates a longer time than it did just after the end of the war.' The reason:

> They [the Russians] lack men of special skill, plant adapted to making special products, and possibly materials . . . [T]hey lack the resourcefulness of free men, and regimentation is ill-adapted to unconventional efforts. [Before the time when] a war would be primarily an atomic war, many things may happen. We may be living by then in a different sort of world.[20]

In time other countries as well as the Soviet Union might become atomic powers; the trend towards war-fighting becoming the sole prerogative of great and wealthy nations could be reversed. Few countries might be able to afford thousand-strong fleets of heavy bombers but, as atomic secrets spread, many could, at tolerable cost, accumulate a modest stockpile of atomic weapons. This might 'equalize' international relations. Nations both great and small would have the power to devastate each other. Jacob Viner commented:

> The small country will again be more than a cipher or a pawn in power politics, provided it is big enough to produce atom bombs. The small country will still not have a defense against an aggressor great country, but even the strongest country will no longer have any reasonable prospects of a costless victory over even the smallest country with a stock of atomic bombs.[21]

But this again was a problem for the future. In the near-term the only three conceivable nuclear powers were the 'big three' – Britain, the United States and the Soviet Union.

The strategic implications of the atom bomb could therefore be treated in two distinct ways. First, as a speculative exercise, postulating a world with a number of powers possessing significant stockpiles of atomic bombs and the means to deliver them. Second, as an immediate question of military planning based on capabilities either in existence or under development. In both cases there was some confusion over time-frames and the mix of capabilities that would be available at any moment. The latter debate was the major one. It involved the military services and influential civilians. The Air Force was lobbying for defence resources to be devoted to airpower, while the Navy and Army were anxious lest over-reliance on atom bombs resulted in the neglect of provisions for traditional forms of warfare.

The new Air Force recognized the bomb to be their strongest bargaining card and played it for all it was worth, carefully fudging the question of whether the vast destructive power concentrated in a single device ought really to allow for contraction, rather than expansion, in numbers of aircraft. The other services felt this competition keenly in the tough struggle to keep forces intact and prepare for the future in the atmosphere of post-war demobilization and budgetary stringency. The Navy was particularly anxious to secure support for its own expensive investment programme, for 'super-carriers', and felt it had little choice but to oppose the Air Force and its atomic strategy head-on. Admirals warned of the unreality of expectations of quick and easy victory, the need to prepare for a wide variety of contingencies and the affront to American values represented by strategies based on mass destruction. This did little to dampen the enthusiasm for an atomic strategy or to promote the Navy's case. The Navy was seen as parochial and backward-looking, desperate to justify its existence in a world in which the reach of airpower was being extended all the time, and in which the most likely enemy was virtually land-locked and had only a slight maritime tradition.

The budgetary battle came to a head in 1949 and the Admirals lost. A new Navy leadership accepted that if the proponents of an atomic strategy could not be beaten then they would have to be joined. The Navy's own potential for delivering nuclear weapons came to be stressed by noting how aircraft carriers could obviate the need for fixed bases close to enemy territory. This new approach was far more successful in gaining support in both the executive branch and Congress.

Two distinguished scientists, Vannevar Bush in the United States and Patrick Blackett in Britain, wrote important books, already cited, contributing to the general debate on nuclear strategy. Most of the literature written by those outside official circles was, however, of the more speculative variety. Some were little more than collections of sensational predictions. The most substantial effort to develop a new strategic theory for the atom bomb was made by Bernard Brodie and his colleagues, at the Yale Center for International Studies, with support from Professor Jacob Viner of Chicago. But this work, which now in retrospect stands out, was peripheral to the main concerns of the 1940s. The question for immediate consideration was whether atomic bombs meant that strategic bombardment was now the most profitable strategy for the West to adopt. The most challenging criticism to the prevailing view that it was came from Blackett and Bush, supported by some self-interested arguments from the Navy.

The Possibility of Defence

It was generally agreed that little could be done to spare cities if aircraft carrying atom bombs got through active defences.[22] Passive measures would involve protecting key targets through dispersion and by encasing them, as much as possible, in reinforced concrete. To survive nuclear war a society would have to be cellular, consisting of thin, independent and self-sufficient units. Few could believe that any such measures were practicable in Europe, let alone in the United States where the pattern of life was well established and had never been disrupted by air raids. In the absence of such radical measures, only Blackett argued forcefully that a city might recover from bombardment with atomic weapons with sufficient speed to restart industrial operations.

The possibility of countering an atomic attack became the main question during the 1940s. There were those who took comfort in the thought that an effective antidote to the bomb itself would eventually be discovered. On 23 October 1945 President Truman told Congress: 'Every new weapon will eventually bring some counter defence to it.' Earlier the same month Fleet Admiral Chester Nimitz commented on the 'historical truth' that 'there has never yet been a weapon against which man has been unable to devise a counter-weapon or a defense'. There was no such historical truth. As Bernard Brodie pointed out, there had been little noteworthy progress on defences against the V-2 and that 'after five centuries of the use of hand arms with fire-propelled missiles, the large number of men killed by comparable arms in the recent war indicates that no adequate answer has yet to be found for the bullet'.[23] Informed opinion came strongly round to the view that there was no direct counter – such as jamming the bomb's inner workings – to the atom bomb.

Interest centred on an attack on delivery vehicles. If the bomb could be readily delivered by rocket or secret agent then the tasks of defence might be too great. But if the offence was to be concentrated in the long-range bomber then the problem was restricted to its vulnerability to air defences. The issue was over the race between the technologies of the offence and the defence. The Strategic Bombing Survey noted that:

> The capacity to destroy, given control of the air and an adequate supply of bombs, is beyond doubt. Unless both of these conditions are met, however, any attempt to produce war decisive results through atomic bombing may encounter problems similar to those encountered in conventional bombing.[24]

There was agreement in the 1940s that for the moment the offensive was dominant. There were, however, indications that the defence was about to mount a serious challenge. 'The present technical trend', noted the Navy optimistically, 'is decidedly in favour of the defense against the offense in ordinary strategic bombing'.[25] Radar would improve methods of detection; jet fighters and, eventually, guided missiles, would improve methods of interception. The new technology of missilery would suit the defence rather than the offence because it would only be at the shorter ranges suitable for defensive action that missiles would be cost-effective. Bush, impressed by the developing defensive technology noted:

> No fleets of bombers will proceed unmolested against any enemy that can bring properly equipped jet pursuit ships against them in numbers, aided by effective ground radar, and equipped with rockets or guided air-to-air missiles armed with proximity fuses.[26]

Against this the offence offered two likely technical improvements. First, the ability to fly faster,[27] and second, the ability to fly at higher altitudes. But, came the rejoinder, if bombers flew high their accuracy would be impaired, and cunning defence tactics involving camouflage and decoys could exacerbate this problem. The bombers would be unable to engage in precision attacks but would have to rely on area bombings, unlikely – if the strategic bombing survey was to be believed – to produce significant results unless prosecuted in greater strength and numbers than possible during the war.

The atom bomb seemed to swing the scales back to the offence. Even if attrition rates were high, it would not need many bombs to get through for decisive results. If, with conventional bombing, a 10 per cent attrition rate was intolerable, with atom bombs a rate of up to 90 per cent would be manageable. The argument against this was twofold. First, it was suggested that the logic of a 90 per cent attrition rate had been accepted without an analysis of the practicalities. If enough young men would fly on virtually suicidal raids, might not the defence also find such courageous young men to engage in suicidal attacks on the incoming aircraft? What would happen to the bombs aboard the 90 per cent of the planes that were shot down? Would they explode or, perhaps, fall into enemy hands? More important, it was pointed out that the readiness to accept large losses in making the attack presumed a plentiful supply of bombs.

So long as bombs were scarce then the offence had problems in mounting attacks. A lone bomber would be extremely vulnerable to a dedicated defence. A fleet of aircraft dedicated to the carriage of atomic weapons would be wasteful, constituting the sort of attack that could only be occasional. If the need to ensure that some atom bombs got through had to be balanced with the need to use available supply in an economical fashion, then the most likely form of attack would consist of a fleet of bombers, most armed with conventional explosives and a few with atom bombs. This would increase the chances of each atom bomb reaching its target, but at the cost of mounting an attack of World War II dimensions. 'If it takes a whole fleet to carry an atomic bomb, then most of the advantage is lost, and we get right back to the question of whether mass bombing pays at all.'[28] If the defending country had put all its resources in defensive, rather than offensive, equipment, such as jet fighters, ground-to-air missiles and radar, then any attack 'would have to be launched on a huge scale to have a good chance of decisive success'.[29] And in this huge attack it would be necessary to ensure that many atom bombs reached their targets. Blackett estimated that it would take 400 atom bombs of the Hiroshima type to reproduce the damage inflicted on Germany by strategic bombardment during World War II. When allowances were made for interceptors, more than a thousand atom bombs would have to be launched. 'The principal point is that the atomic bomb is for the immediate future a very important but by no means an absolute weapon, that is, one so overpowering as to make all other methods of waging war obsolete.'[30]

The argument did not stop at analysis of the relative advantages of the offence and defence when locked in a straightforward duel. An attacker aware of a strong defence is unlikely to desire a head-on clash. Instead, he will turn to the attacker's traditional advantage of surprise, selecting the time and place to attack. The selection of targets is less of a problem in air warfare than ground warfare. There are only a limited number of strategic targets and, as important, only a limited number of routes by which they can be approached. The advantage of choice of time was more significant. The defence might not be able to mobilize quickly enough and, even if prepared, might not reach peak performance at once. Combat experience would be required. Thus, the atom bomb gained over conventional bombard-ment because of the impact of the first blow. Conventional bombs had been shown not to be decisive in the first attack and so the defence would get time to prepare itself. 'War . . . always starts with a Pearl Harbor kind of attack. In an atomic war the first attack, no matter how well prepared for it we may be, will really be a disaster.'[31] Indeed any improvement in the technology of the defence merely enhanced the importance of the surprise first strike.

3 Aggression and Retaliation

The Vital First Blow

In order to understand the development of post-war strategic thought it is necessary to recognize the deep-rooted nature of the belief in the inevitability of a massive surprise attack as the opening shot in any war. It was particularly strong in the US, because of the experience of Pearl Harbor, but was widely accepted in Europe. It was not based simply on a calculation of tactical need, to beat a strong defence, but on a presumption that this was the way of aggressors. Whether atom bombs were scare or plentiful, the defence weak or strong, was irrelevant.

Aggression, by definition, involved making the first military move. In making such a move the aggressor would aim for maximum military advantage which, it was presumed, would require the maximum possible exercise of force. With the stakes so high the benefit of surprise would not be squandered for mere 'tactical' benefit; the gain would have to be of 'strategic' dimensions and the most decisive 'strategic' act was atomic bombardment. The aggressor would aim for an immediate paralysis of the victim's socioeconomic organization rather than his military capabilities. The diplomatic niceties of 'ultimata' and formal declarations of war could be ignored. The surprise would be complete. Some even suspected that it would take guesswork to identify the aggressor.

Historical experience was less than conclusive on this matter. Both the Japanese and the Germans had used surprise attacks to weaken the conventional military position of their enemies; but then neither Britain nor France entered the war as the victim of a surprise attack. An attack on cities would only make sense if it could be decisive. Otherwise it would be more sensible to weaken the enemy's means of counter-attack. Maximum hurt to the victim is not the same as maximum gain to the attacker. Nevertheless the consensus on this score was almost overwhelming.

In the discussion amongst scientists connected with the Manhattan Project, the value of atomic bombs to a surprise attack was a major theme. Some of the earliest thoughts on the future military role of nuclear weapons were collected in a September 1944 Report entitled 'Prospectus on Nucleonics' by a committee of scientists headed by Zoy Jeffries:

> A nation, or even a political group, given the opportunity to start aggression by a sudden use of nuclear destruction devices, will be able to unleash a 'blitzkrieg' infinitely more terrifying than that of 1939–40. A sudden blow of this kind might literally wipe out even the largest nation – or at least all its production centers – and decide the issue on the first day of the war.[1]

These ideas appeared in the June 1945 Franck Report of nuclear scientists urging caution in the use of the first bomb,[2] and were endorsed by H. R. Smyth, one of the Manhattan Project scientists, who prepared the account of the development of atom bombs for official publication immediately after the first use of the bombs. In his conclusion Smyth wrote:

> A weapon has been developed that is potentially destructive beyond the wildest nightmares of the imagination; a weapon so ideally suited to sudden unannounced attack that a country's major cities might be destroyed overnight by an ostensibly friendly power.[3]

Such a view soon became the conventional wisdom; Caryl Haskins called it 'An ideal weapon for aggressors'; with 10,000 bombs costing some $10 billion there would be the means to 'eliminate a great nation'. Major George Fielding Eliot of the *New York Herald Tribune* wrote that the atom bomb sets aside 'the old theories of attack and defense. It gives to the surprise attack the power to destroy utterly, without warning.' Robert Oppenheimer described it as 'A weapon of aggression, of surprise, and of terror.' David Lilienthal, recording the conclusion of a January 1947 discussion at the Pentagon between top military and scientific leaders, said 'Value of surprise increased with every increase in potency of weapons; with atomic bomb surprise achieves supreme value.'[4]

By contrast, the United States and other peaceful nations would be effectively constrained from making a surprise attack despite the military benefits that might accrue. Edward Mead Earle observed that the new weapons (atom bombs and rockets) would 'put an enormous premium on the surprise attack, planned in secrecy and waged *a outrance*'. An open and democratic society would be incapable of such planning and, in any case, the populations of liberal democracies only became interested in military preparedness after the outbreak of war. Because of the increased value of the sudden and provoked 'knockout blow', 'the peacefully inclined and the militarily careless' were put at a disadvantage. A similar point was made in a 1947 paper expressing War Department thinking: 'We are prevented by our form of Government and our constitutional processes from launching surprise attacks against potential enemies'. The requirement for any declaration of war to be passed by Congress, the pressure of public opinion and a sense of America's moral position in the world would all militate against any behaviour that could be remotely classified as 'aggressive'.[5]

The Atom Bomb and Aggressors

It is worthwhile pausing here to consider briefly the concept of aggression. In the nineteenth century this term had been limited, technical, and neutral, referring to any 'military attack by the forces of a state against the territory or vessels of another state'. War was still a legitimate, if regrettable, last resort in pursuit of legal rights. Any attempt to interfere with the *status quo*, to harass a nation's subjects or upset its sense of honour could be used to justify a declaration of war. As the view of war changed so did the concept of aggression. By 1914 the term had become pejorative, referring to a military attack that was not justified by law. After 1918 it became hard to justify any use of military force. The Great War was such a disaster that it was considered incumbent upon all states to prevent any recurrence. The League of Nations set up mechanisms to settle disputes peacefully. Illegitimate *casus belli* came to include not only attempts at conquest but even redress of legitimate grievances. In such declarations as the Kellogg–Briand pact of 1927 war was renounced as an 'instrument of national policy'. Short of self-defence and collective actions sanctioned by the League, there could be no just recourse to war, whatever the provocation. Such a recourse would be 'aggression'. Unfortunately, this use of the term confused a military judgment with a moral stance. There was a desire (and still is) to use it to distinguish right from wrong in any dispute, but this distinction was rarely straightforward. Technically, it placed far too much emphasis on the 'first shot', the responsibility for which was rarely clear nor necessarily significant. Strategically, no allowances were made for pre-emptive action. In part because of this, but also because of the tendency of pejorative terms to be generalized to encompass all unwelcome acts, aggression eventually came to be 'applied to any instrument of state policy which affects the interests of other states in a significant way'. It is now necessary to talk of 'armed aggression'.[6]

In 1945 the common approach to international affairs was legalistic. Though subjective in practice and rarely doing justice to the complexity of disputes, the distinction between peace-loving and aggressive states was adopted as a guide to the proper assignment of blame for the outbreak of a war. 'Our position', explained the American prosecutor before the International Military Tribunal at Nuremberg, 'is that whatever grievances a nation may have, however objectionable it finds the *status quo*, aggressive warfare is an illegal means for settling those grievances or for altering those conditions'.[7] Aggression was seen to be the most deviant form of international behaviour. It was deviant not only because it violated an international code of conduct, but also because it was patently foolish. As it inevitably led to disaster, it could never be an act of men possessed of rationality and moral sensibilities, who would use peaceful means to settle disputes.

The adoption of violent means betrayed more than an aggressor's strategic calculus. It also betrayed something about the nature of his society. It was symptomatic of a particular culture, one that bred in profusion 'authoritarian' or 'aggressive' personalities, or else a 'mass society' that allowed an unsavoury and totalitarian political philosophy to prosper and gain control. Social scientists and psychologists, convinced of the essential irrationality of war, searched for its causes in the alienation of industrial man, patterns of child-rearing, the ambition of megalomaniacs, the dreams of political utopias, and the potency of unthinking nationalism, rather than such mundane things as geographical vulnerabilities, a sense of grievance, or straightforward conflicts of national interests.

War was an irrational act and thus had an irrational cause. In consequence, aggressors could not be relied upon to listen to reason. What they might listen to was their own language – that of force. If that was the only language they understood then the communication must be loud and clear. Aggression was more than a military move to be met by a counter-move. It was a crime deserving of punishment. The perpetrators could not be expected to act as international statesmen, with whom it might be possible to negotiate and compromise. They could only be communicated with by force. The experience of the pre-war years underlined the danger of 'appeasing' an insatiable aggressor through continual concessions. 'International blackmail', based on the threat of aggression, could only be dealt with by firm resistance and preparation for a trial of strength. Reliance on the conventional panoply of diplomatic instruments could be counterproductive, for aggressors must never think you 'soft'. Clark Clifford, Special Counsel to the President, wrote to Truman in 1946:

> The language of military power is the only language which disciples of power politics understand. The United States must use that language in order that Soviet leaders will realize that our government is determined to uphold the interests of its citizens and the rights of small countries. Compromise and concessions are considered, by the Soviets, to be evidences of weakness and they are encouraged by our 'retreats' to make new and greater demands.[8]

If it came to war, military power should be applied in such a way as to inhibit future aggression. It should not be applied according to narrow strategic criteria. Military defeat was not enough. Power had also to be used in a retributive and exemplary manner. In justifying the atomic bombing of Hiroshima, President Truman illustrated the belief in the retributive value of force:

> Having found the bomb, we have to use it. We have used it against those who attacked us without warning at Pearl Harbor, against those who have starved and beaten and executed American prisoners of wars, against those who have abandoned all pretense of obeying international laws of warfare.

Only then did he mention the need to 'shorten the agony of war' and 'to save the lives of thousands and thousands of young Americans'.[9]

Thus, the atom bomb could be used as a means of punishing aggressors, especially those that lacked atomic bombs of their own. But once these weapons were readily available, and if this would be to the advantage of the aggressive as opposed to the peace-loving, there was a good case for banishing them from international life. It was one thing to threaten a potential aggressor with an atomic attack when there was no danger of a counter-attack; it was another thing altogether when determined action might put America at risk from an atomic-armed adversary.

To many, especially the scientists who had brought the bomb into the world, the introduction of atomic weapons into an unreformed international society would be a disaster. The very structure of the international system, with its sovereign nation states each capable of preparing for war, meant that self-restraint in the use of atomic weapons could not be guaranteed. The only solution would be to banish the bombs themselves. A stark choice was identified: either the creation of a strong international organization with powers to enforce universal pledges of atomic abstinence or else the bad habits of international politics would be perpetuated until they inevitably led to an orgy of mutual destruction. The choice was 'One World or None'.[10]

There was a serious effort made to achieve a measure of international control over atomic energy. This failed because the question became mixed up with the general deterioration in East–West relations. Neither side could summon up enough trust in the other. It is important to note that even if the American plan, to put the most sensitive nuclear facilities under the control of an International Development Authority, had been accepted it would have delayed the use of atom bombs in war for over a year but not prevented their use completely.[11]

The choice facing the world was considered so stark that some argued for drastic measures to push recalcitrant nations towards sanity, even threatening them with atomic weapons. There were a number of calls made for a move against the Soviet Union, widely suspected of aggressive tendencies, before it had a chance to do the world any more damage. For example the redoubtable Senator Brian McMahon: 'I assert that for the first time in human history, the failure to agree to a sane, effective and righteous control of weapons of war constitutes in and of itself an act of aggression'.[12] Similar reasoning led to a curious and notorious call in October 1946 for nuclear threats against the Soviet Union from the philosopher Bertrand Russell. After noting that a war in the near future would lead to

American victory and then 'to a world government under the hegemony of the United States', a development he would 'welcome with enthusiasm', Russell called for the liberal democracies to pressure the Soviet Union into accepting an international government. 'The only possible way' to do this would be by 'a mixture of cajolery and threat, making it plain to the Soviet authorities that refusal will entail disaster, while acceptance will not'.[13]

Early Thoughts on Deterrence

In the absence of international control, nations who wished to avoid atomic bombardment would have to rely on their own devices. The most appropriate device for deterring the employment of atomic weapons by one state was the threat of counter-employment. There was nothing new in the notion that the best way to dissuade an enemy from using a particularly obnoxious weapon was a threat of a reprisal in kind. It was fear of reprisals that encouraged restraint over the use of gas during World War II. Hopes for a similar neutralizing effect had been expressed in connection with the bombing of cities and submarine attacks on merchantmen. Here there had been disappointment but the 'eye-for-an-eye' concept was strong and could be found in official rationales for air-raids and V-weapon attacks. A monopoly in a terror-weapon was considered a major advantage. It was fear of a German monopoly in atom bombs that led nuclear scientists, who might in other circumstances have thought better of helping to exploit atomic energy for military purposes, to bring such a sense of urgency to the Manhattan Project.

In each of these cases the reasoning was confined to threats of reprisals in kind against use of specified weapons. There was another argument of long standing that the more awful is war, the less likely that nations would resort to it to settle their disputes. But, especially in 1945, there could be little confidence in either this general proposition or the more modest hope that mankind might be spared certain horrors because of a fear of reprisals. Thus when Prime Minister Clement Attlee wrote to President Truman on atomic energy issues in September 1945 he made the point that 'The only deterrent is the possibility of the victim of such an attack being able to retort to the victor.' He then went on to cast doubt on the efficacy of such a deterrent: 'In many discussions on bombing in the days before the war it was demonstrated that the only answer to the bomber was the bomber. The war proved this to be correct. This obvious fact did not prevent bombing but resulted in the destruction of many great centres of civilization.'[14]

The logic of retaliation as the best deterrent to aggression was appreciated from the start but, as can be seen with Attlee, it was combined with a deep pessimism that 'sooner or later' these weapons would be used. In the September 1944 report of the Jeffries Committee of Manhattan Project scientists it was noted that:

> The most that an independent American nucleonic re-armament can achieve is the certainty that a sudden total devastation of New York or Chicago can be answered the next day by an even more extensive devastation of the cities of the aggressor, and the hope that the fear of such a retaliation will paralyze the aggressor.

But the Committee did not think 'much of this hope':

> The whole history of mankind teaches that this is a very uncertain hope, and that accumulated weapons of destruction 'go off' sooner or later, even if this means a senseless mutual destruction.[15]

Similarly, in 1946, General Arnold offered a formula that has lasted to this day: '[O]ur first line of defense is the ability to retaliate even after receiving the hardest blow the enemy can deliver'. With such an ability a stalemate might be possible, but Arnold took pains to emphasize that this was only a possibility.[16]

The professional military readily accepted the importance of the threat of retaliation to deter atomic aggression. In Britain – where, because of the country's size and vulnerability to strikes from Europe, the problem was seen as a defensive one from the start – an atomic stockpile was considered the only means of warding off aggressors.[17] The United States Air Force, which was more interested in exploiting superiority than compensating for possible inferiority, tended to see the value of its bombers as a deterrent to all forms of aggression, atomic or otherwise. The expectation that the threat of overwhelming force would make potential aggressors pause before hasty actions was deeply ingrained into its thinking.

It was this form of general deterrence that the Policy Planning Staff of the US State Department had in mind when it discussed the need to maintain armed strength. Deterrence was of 'outstanding importance', in creating such an impression of military strength as to make it quite clear to the Russians that they would have no hope of victory in war. Already in 1948 there was a tendency to assume that 'excessive military weakness here and in Western Europe might indeed create a factor which would operate to overcome the other reasons why the Soviet Government would not be inclined to use armed force, and might thus constitute a compelling invitation to aggression'.[18] The fear that weak peacetime forces would cause an aggressor to miscalculate the resolve of democracies (once stirred to action) provided an argument for signalling determination via military preparedness. This need embraced all forces; it was not tied to a specific weapon or type of military action. It was to demonstrate a capacity for war-fighting and thus could not be seen as an alternative form of military posture that might reduce the need for traditional forms of armed forces.

In providing the required image, the atomic stockpile was of obvious importance. But the professionals did not feel they could rely on the threat of atomic retaliation to deter war or even atomic bombs being used against them. If an attack did come it was assumed that the enemy would exploit the advantages of surprise to the full. The restraining influence of an imposing atomic stockpile on others was no more than a considered but guarded hope.

What had yet to develop was a full doctrine of nuclear deterrence. The early development of such a doctrine stemmed from a critical examination of the assumption of the inevitable surprise attack. There was tension in prevalent theories between an assumption of cities as the only appropriate targets and the decisive value of surprise, for unless the enemy's means of nuclear retaliation were destroyed, little could be gained by surprise. In Britain, Liddell Hart and Blackett argued against the assumption that the aggressor would aim first for cities. Liddell Hart pointed out that aggressors tended to be calculating. 'They plan to achieve their gains with the least possible damage both to themselves and to their acquisitions, whereas the victims of aggression are driven by an uncontrollable impulse to hit back regardless of the consequences.' Therefore, he suggested, an aggressor aiming at no more than 'profitable expansion . . . may hesitate to employ atomic bombs' because of the likelihood of retaliation.[19]

A similar point was made by Jacob Viner, Professor of Economics at Chicago and an important influence on the coming generation of academic strategists. He declared himself unconvinced by the assumption that the atom bomb would give an overwhelming advantage to the surprise attack. Even after the victim's cities had been destroyed 'why can it not nevertheless retaliate within a few hours with as effective an atomic-bomb counter-attack as if it had made the first move'.[20] Bernard Brodie also noted: 'The element of surprise may be less important than is generally assumed. If retaliation has to be accepted no victory is worth it'. Brodie suggested that a stable balance in atomic arsenals might be safer than asymmetries: 'A war in which atomic bombs are *not* used is more likely to occur if both sides have bombs in quantity from the beginning than if neither side has it at the outset or if only one side has it'. This same point was made by other contributors to *The Absolute Weapon*, the book Brodie edited, suggesting that the weapon was not as absolute as all that.[21]

One conclusion of this line of argument was that the only purpose of a surprise attack would be to destroy military facilities. It is remarkable how little this point was explored. One who did was William Liscum Borden who asked: 'Why squander the precious assets of surprise and the initiative in attacking cities, a mission which can so easily be carried out later, when the main obstacle to a lightning victory is air forces-in-being?'. Assuming that 'belligerents possess stockpiles of atom bombs and carriers numbered in the thousands', Borden forecast a future war taking the form, in the first instance, of a

one-dimensional aerial duel . . . between two highly decentralized military systems, each seeking to eliminate the offensive power of the other. If the war lasted long enough for industrial production to make itself felt, the belligerents most threatened could undertake the few brief raids necessary to paralyze his opponent's home front; and retaliation in kind would surely follow.[22]

The neglect of the plausibility of this sort of exchange was surprising. The desirability of eliminating the enemy's air offensive was, after all, an established tenet of the doctrine of strategic bombardment. If rockets were to play a major part in a future war then the best opportunity to destroy them would be on the ground, prior to launch. This neglect could be explained first by the natural obsession with what weapons of such ferocity could do to human beings. The most memorable use of airpower in World War II had been against cities and it was assumed that this pattern, confirmed at Hiroshima, was now established. Atom bombs were described habitually as 'terror' weapons with the term 'weapons of mass destruction' soon in use as a synonym, as if there were no other possible targets. Second, and more practically, it was doubted that either side would be so foolish as to concentrate facilities for the production or carriage of atom bombs in a few places susceptible to attack. Nevertheless, in the first tentative steps through the logic of deterrence, it did become apparent, at least to Bernard Brodie, that:

> The first and most vital step in the American security program for the age of atomic bombs is to take measures to guarantee ourselves in case of attack the possibility of retaliation in kind.

> Thus far the chief purpose of a military establishment has been to win wars. From now on its chief purpose must be to avert them. It can have no other useful purpose.

Brodie suggested two main requirements. First, it would be necessary to fight with men and equipment already mobilized. America could no longer wait for a war to start before building up her armed forces. Second, it would be necessary for the armed forces to make 'themselves independent of the urban communities and their industries for support'. The forces would be maintained in isolation, dispersed in secret sites, and 'protected by storage underground'.[23] One requirement for which there was much support, given the assumption that the supreme command could be easily wiped out, was that the local commander should have independent power to release an atomic strike once he was certain that his country had been the recipient of an atomic attack. This was one area where later thinking moved in the opposite direction.

The basic axioms of the nuclear age, therefore, were soon identified: the impossibility of defence; the hopeless vulnerability of the world's major cities; the attraction of a sudden attack; and the necessity of a capability for retaliation. There were inklings of the debates that were to dominate strategists in the coming decades: the danger of a successful first strike against nuclear forces; the impossibility of deterring madmen; and the paradox of intensive defensive preparations taking on the appearance of a provocative act.[24] But there was nothing systematic or emphatic about the presentation of these notions. Often they stand out only with the benefit of hindsight. They were no more than inklings.

Towards a Policy of Deterrence

4 Strategy for an Atomic Monopoly

Atom Bombs and the American Way of War

Americans were accustomed to viewing international politics, which up to 1940 was to all intents and purposes European politics, with a certain detachment. The European propensity to war was symptomatic of its dominance by reactionary and decadent élites and the persistence of imperialist instincts. Furthermore, there was little reason to view war as a grim struggle for survival, let alone a time for defiant resistance. The United States' industrial and economic resources were so vast that there were few doubts that, once she put her mind to the task, any enemy would be eventually overwhelmed. The United States was the weary policeman, slow to be roused and loath to get involved in the internecine quarrels of European states. Once aware of danger and into action, she was unbeatable.

Any threat to American security was to be found in the prospect of the hegemony of a strong and malevolent state in Europe or the Pacific. As there was little danger of a direct invasion there had been little interest in the development of forces mainly suitable for territorial defence. A strong Navy combined with sheer distance kept any enemy at bay. At the outbreak of war, US forces would be small. Mobilization would proceed and men and equipment would then be sent overseas where their intervention would inevitably be decisive. The fighting was remote – 'over there'.

This mobilization would involve time and effort, while the despatch of American 'boys' to fight abroad was considered the most evil of necessities. The Americans were happy to keep wars at a distance but felt that they should be prosecuted in an efficient manner. The enemy should be crushed expeditiously, exploiting America's technological strength rather than its precious manpower. The requirements for effective punishment of an aggressor also pointed to an unambiguous and certain sanction capable of disabling any offender, inflicted with ease and at minimal cost to the forces of law and order.

For both these purposes airpower, combined with the added strength of atomic weapons, seemed eminently suitable. Airpower put the political and economic centres of the enemy at risk. Rather than grapple with the tentacles, the octopus could now be hit right in the eye. Here was a means of defeating and punishing an aggressor not requiring the victim to be overcome laboriously before sanctions were applied. Other forms of military power took too long to have an effect and were too costly and labour-intensive. War should be similar to the spanking of a naughty child; not a wrestling match. America could both isolate itself from the effects of war and decide the issue.

Walter Lipmann noted, unsympathetically, how to many Americans the arrival of atom bombs and rockets appeared as:

> the perfect fulfillment of all wishful thinking on military matters: here is war that requires no national effort, no draft, no training, no discipline, but only money and engineering know-how of which we have plenty. Here is the panacea which enables us to be the greatest military power on earth without investing time, energy, sweat, blood and tears, and – as compared with the cost of a great Army, Navy, and Air Force – not even much money.[1]

The Limits of the Bomb

The preoccupation with the new *means* for inflicting death and destruction over great distances and at great speeds had meant that few had concerned themselves with the purposes for which these means might be employed. Strategy became separated from diplomacy and from the analysis of interests, values, and motives. The changes were coming too fast for their meaning to be properly understood and digested. Specific conflicts, with added complications supplied by geography and the weight of past military traditions, were not revisited with the new technology. There were some nightmarish speculations on the subject of how Hitler might have acted if he had been in possession of a nuclear arsenal, but there seemed no new conflict so immediate or so dangerous that it could provide an occasion for nuclear attacks. Meanwhile, politicians and the public could content themselves with the thought that these most decisive and punishing of weapons represented an Anglo-American monopoly. So long as this monopoly could be maintained the world was 'controllable'.

By 1947 this was changing. The development of the cold war provided a focus for analysis. The Soviet Union took on the mantle of 'potential aggressor' and provided an unambiguous set of targets. General questions on the rôle of the bomb in international relations became subordinate to the quite specific question of how it affected the contest between East and West.[2] One crucial consequence of the atom bomb was that it made a war between the Soviet Union and the United States conceivable. Until its arrival, it was hard to envisage any means of forcing an unequivocal result in a military conflict between the United States and the Soviet Union. A clash of two 'super-powers', each possessed of enormous human and industrial resources, was unlikely to lead to anything but a stalemate. Writing in 1944 William Fox had noted:

> [T]he points of direct contact are few and inaccessible but the centers are widely separated. The armed power of each can effectively be carried only part of the way to the other. American control over the seaward approaches to the New World will in any foreseeable future render a transoceanic operation by the Soviet Union impossible. The massive superiority of its land army should on the other hand discourage the Western powers from attempting a large-scale amphibious operation against hostile shores controlled by the Red Army.[3]

Prior to the development of atomic bombs, even Air Force planners had had to recognize that the Soviet Union posed an exception to the general rule of the primacy of strategic bombardment. Its sheer size and its demonstrated resilience – recovering after Hitler had captured half of its industrial and agricultural resources – posed a large question mark against claims that it could be made to surrender through any future Anglo-American application of air power.[4] Atomic bombs provided at least a partial answer to that question mark. Four years later, Fox recognized that 'the atomic energy inventions have largely destroyed the military function of the continent [Europe] as a buffer'.[5]

The interaction between the introduction of the atom bomb and the development of the cold war was complex. The bomb helped to accentuate the divisions among the major powers and make an East–West war feasible. The cold war then provided a context in which to assess the strategic relevance of the bomb.

As the Truman Administration began this assessment it became apparent that there were limits to the bomb's military and political value. There had been a tendency after Hiroshima for the Americans to act as if the bomb offered a major bargaining card in negotiations with the USSR. This approach suffered from a lack of credibility. In 1945–7 a new war was unthinkable. In addition it was not yet clear that the atom bomb could be a decisive weapon.

Enthusiasts had suggested that traditional military forces might be written off as obsolete in the presence of an atom bomb; a possibility that struck a responsive chord amongst those who preferred capital-intensive to labour-intensive wars. Informed opinion soon came to recognize, however, that the decisiveness of atom bombs could not be taken for granted and that conventional forces could not be so readily dismissed.

Until well into 1947 the limitations of the bomb governed US strategy. A couple of months after the end of the war, the Commanding General of the Army Air Force, H. A. P. Arnold, commissioned Generals Spaatz, Vandenberg, and Norstad to examine the implications of the bomb for the future of the Air Force. The conclusions of this report, known as the 'Spaatz Report', were determined by two factors. The first was the scarcity of atom bombs, because of their enormous expense 'in terms of critical material and industrial effort'. Such a precious commodity could not be wasted in misconceived operations against minor targets (nor risked in attempts to penetrate intensive air defences). The second was the limited range (4000 miles) of the only available delivery vehicle (the B-29 bomber). Because of this it would be necessary to gain access, perhaps by conventional military operations, to overseas bases.

A certain amount could be done in peace-time, for example in securing some overseas bases or establishing the sort of intelligence network that would help identify appropriate targets and expose the weak points in the enemy air defences. However, much of the preparation for the bomb's use would have to be undertaken in wartime. A number of overseas bases would still have to be captured and the most obstructive air defences would still have to be suppressed. So ground and naval operations, as well as a conventional strategic bombardment campaign, would be the preconditions for the employment of these weapons. A study undertaken by the Joint Staff Strategic Survey reached similar conclusions. It noted that even when the bomb had eventually been deployed, if the enemy had sufficient 'stamina' and residual force, the bomb still might not be decisive. Victory would then require the 'actual capture and occupation of the enemy homeland to the final point where resistance is no longer possible'. For this task the army and navy would be essential.[6]

While the military were anticipating, at least in the short term, only modest rewards from the bomb, the diplomats were already experiencing its limitations. American negotiators were finding the US demobilization in conventional forces a chronic weakness in diplomatic confrontations with the Soviet Union, given the latter's imposing military presence in Europe, for which possession of the atom bomb provided scant compensation.

For all these reasons the Administration had little regard for atomic bombs (or raw military power in general) as the sole foundation of American, and Western European, security. George Kennan, the ideologist of containment, wrote in his 'X' article in *Foreign Affairs*, in which he elaborated the need to resist the Soviet Union's expansive tendencies, that such resistance could come through 'the adroit and vigilant application of counterforce at a series of constantly shifting geographical and political points, corresponding to the shifts and manoeuvres of Soviet Policy'. Later he claimed this had been misunderstood, that he had been primarily talking about 'the political containment of a political threat'. He believed that any military force required could be found from within the current budget, providing sufficient to deal with localized incidents if not full-scale invasion – which he did not expect to materialize. The 'X' article contained no mention of atomic bombs.[7]

First or Last Resort

The final reason why the Administration was reluctant to make the bomb the centrepiece of US strategy was an unwillingness to see it as 'just another weapon', ready for use when and where the occasion demanded. Rather it was a weapon of 'last resort'. Truman told Lilienthal:

I don't think we ought to use this thing unless we absolutely have to. It is a terrible thing to order the use of something that is so terribly destructive beyond anything we have ever had. You have got to understand that this isn't a military weapon. It is used to wipe out women, children and unarmed people, and not for military use. So we have to treat this differently from rifles and cannon and ordinary things like that.[8]

As East–West tensions grew, more regard was paid to the balance of military forces and the atom bomb began to figure more prominently in American calculations. But its proper rôle could not be decided until the prior question was decided whether, in the event of hostilities, it was to be used as a weapon of first or last resort. To some, who believed that all-out war with the Russians was closer than the Administration realized during the second half of the 1940s, the evident deterioration in the international situation added force to their conviction that the main source of what Soviet restraint there had been was fear of the American atomic arsenal. In March 1949, Winston Churchill said: 'It is certain that Europe would have been communized and London under bombardment some time ago but for the deterrent of the atomic bomb in the hands of the United States'. As the strongest card lay in the American hands, there were many who felt that it should be played for all it was worth. To indicate any hesitation about playing it at all seemed the height of folly.

It was the Berlin Crisis that began in the middle of 1948 that brought the issue to a head. As British and American aircraft lifted in supplies to the beleaguered city, Secretary of Defense James Forrestal observed that it was difficult to carry out his responsibilities to prepare for a full military confrontation 'without resolution of the question whether or not we are to use the A-bomb in war.'[9]

At this point, discussion was inaugurated in the National Security Council on the advisability of formulating policies regarding the use of atomic weapons. The conclusion was that a decision on this question was not necessary. The tone of the final document approved by the NSC on 16 September 1948 was in favour of a decision to use them, displaying anxiety lest the Russians were given the 'slightest reason' to believe the Americans would desist from atomic use in war. This could 'provoke exactly that Soviet aggression which it is fundamentally US policy to avert'.[10]

Forrestal raised the same question at a dinner party this same month (September). He discovered 'unanimous agreement' that in the event of war not only would the American people have no qualms as to the propriety of the use of the atomic bomb, but would in fact expect it to be used. Over the next two months Forrestal solicited opinion on both sides of the Atlantic on this matter:

> He never recorded a dissent from the 'unanimous agreement' of this dinner meeting. Marshall was to quote to him a remark of John Foster Dulles that 'the American people would execute you if you did not use the bomb in the event of war'; Clay said that he 'would not hesitate to use the atomic bomb and would hit Moscow and Leningrad first'; Winston Churchill, going even further, told him that the United States erred in minimizing the destructive power of the weapon – to do so was to lend dangerous encouragement to the Russians.[11]

The Bomb Enters War Plans

The deteriorating international situation and the sentiment discovered by Forrestal for an explicit emphasis on atom bombs in US strategy was reinforced by a growing belief among the military that these bombs could be used to decisive effect in the early stages of a war. The formal conversion of the Air Force to this view began in early 1947. By the middle of 1948 it had come to form the basis of emergency war plans. It was not simply the result of a change of heart, but the specific focus provided by the unequivocal emergence of the Soviet Union as the 'potential enemy', and two extremely significant technical developments. The first was awareness that the problem of scarcity might soon be overcome through the more efficient use of fissionable materials. This was confirmed by tests in 1948. The second development was the impending delivery of the first long-range B-36 bombers which would reduce the dependence on overseas bases.

The Soviet Union would not be the easiest enemy to confront. While it would still be a number of years before any war could be brought to the US homeland, in a war fought in and over Europe, the Russian would enjoy superiority in ground forces. This would mean that not only would it be a task of some magnitude to 'mop up' resisting enemy forces in the terminal stages of a war but, more to the point, it would be very hard to defend Western Europe against invading enemy forces in the early stages. Furthermore, as the Soviet generals would recognize the importance of overseas bases for the American strategic bombing campaign, they would have an incentive to move as fast as possible to capture these bases before the Americans had an opportunity to launch their air offensive.[12]

The significance of Soviet conventional superiority suggested three reasons why, if the availability of bombs was improving and the dependence on bases slackening, it might be wise to begin with an 'atomic blitz' rather than wait until the path had been cleared by conventional operations. First, the vulnerability of bases suggested that if their aircraft were not used quickly they might never be used at all. Second, the best way of stopping a Soviet advance, in the absence of sufficient conventional forces, was to attack those elements in the Soviet rear, such as fuel depots, which supported the forces in the field.[13] In this way the enemy could be starved of essential supplies and cut off from his home base.

The third and final reason was a hope that, even if it would be well-nigh impossible to overrun the Soviet Union with conventional means, a large enough atomic attack might still gain victory. In early 1947, the Air Staff came to this conclusion in the first major reassessment of nuclear strategy since the Spaatz Report. Returning to the traditions of strategic bombardment, the report suggested that atomic bombs could both be employed and be decisive without dependence on preceding or simultaneous conventional operations:

In past wars much of the effort of the armed forces has been expended in the fight for bases within striking distance of the enemy's vital areas. The atomic bomb and the long-range bomber will permit the delivery of devastating blows to the heart of the enemy without the necessity for the conquest of intermediate bases or at least decrease the number of steps required.... Assuming a plentiful supply of atomic bombs and a war aim of complete subjugation of the enemy, it would be feasible to risk an all-out atomic attack at the beginning of a war in an effort to stun the enemy into submission.[14]

It did not take long for these ideas to work their way into military plans. In the middle of 1947 the services began to develop joint war plans. The emergency war plan, code-named Half-Moon, was ready by May 1948 and work continued on a longer-term plan throughout that year. These plans embodied the ideas discussed above and placed great reliance on an early atomic offensive with the twin objectives of slowing down the enemy advance and destroying sufficient valuable social and economic targets to compel surrender.

The most important feature was an Annex on the use of atomic bombs, included for the first time in emergency war plans prepared by the Joint Chiefs of Staff. 'Soviet urban industrial concentrations' constituted the 'highest priority target system' which, if destroyed, 'should so cripple the Soviet industrial and control centers as to reduce drastically the offensive and defensive power of their armed forces'.[15] The initial phase of a strategic air offensive would be a series of attacks, primarily with atomic bombs and taking some 30 days, against 70 target areas, where some 28 million people lived. About 10 per cent of these people would be killed and another 15 per cent wounded.

The defensive intent, of impeding an invasion of Western Europe, and the offensive intent, of stunning the enemy into subjugation, were not easily separated. There was a feeling among some of the military that too much reliance was being placed on an 'atomic blitz' to decide the war. The revised version of the war plans in May 1949 included, at the insistence of the Army and Navy, 'the retardation of Soviet advances in Western Europe' as a specific objective.

There were also doubts about the ultimate impact of an atomic offensive on the enemy. Not long after the first plans had been drawn up, a review committee of officers from all the services, headed by Air Force Lieutenant-General H. R. Harmon, reviewed the rôle to be played by atomic bombs. The Harmon Report was thoughtful and sceptical. It concluded by affirming the value of the bomb as 'the only means of rapidly inflicting shock and serious damage to vital elements of the Soviet war-making capacities'. Its military value would mainly come if the supply of all petroleum products to the Soviet Union armed forces could be impaired.

Where the Report differed markedly from the conventional wisdom was in suggesting that the use of the bomb could be politically counter-productive unless followed up with skilful propaganda and political measures. Rather than undermine the will of the enemy, as always implied by the rhetoric of strategic bombing, it could have the opposite effect: 'For the majority of Soviet people, atomic bombing would validate Soviet propaganda against foreign powers, stimulate resentment against the United States, unify these people and increase their will to fight'.[16]

This iconoclasm made the report one of the most interesting official discussions of the strategic value of atomic bombs. Yet its effect can be presumed to be limited. The general inclination was still to assume the bomb to be an irresistible force in contemporary warfare. The Air Force had done what it could to strengthen that assumption. Impressed by preponderant Soviet conventional strength in Europe, American policy-makers looked to the bomb as the best available means of redressing the military balance. It was a time to be grateful for an American monopoly that, at the start of 1949, was still expected to last for a number of years.

Atom Bombs and the Soviet Way of War

So by 1949, though it was widely accepted in the United States that atomic bombs were particularly suitable for aggressors and un-provoked surprise attacks, and thus at variance with American con-stitutional and military practice, it was equally widely accepted that for the time being they could be exploited effectively by the United States. They provided a valuable instrument for maintaining law and order in the post-war world, attractive because they were less expen-sive in terms of money, materials and manpower than conventional weapons, and, above all, because they were an American monopoly.

Meanwhile, the Soviet Union, readily identified as a potential aggressor and so in theory the most likely to embrace a nuclear strategy, dismissed such a strategy as wrong-headed and doomed to failure. This dismissal was not unrelated to a recognition of Soviet inferiority in this area, but it also followed naturally from the strategic perspectives developed during the war years in Russia.

Marxists prided themselves on a deep understanding of the sources and resolution of all forms of conflict. The Soviet leaders could draw upon a well-developed ideological framework which put war in its social context, explained its economic foundations in the contradic-tions of capitalism, and related it to the inexorable rise of the working classes throughout the world and so on. Conclusions derived from this framework were presented as scientific truths, capable of illumin-ating the future course of mankind. It lent itself to a rigid determin-ism though with a greater room for intellectual manoeuvre than often apparent. Marxism–Leninism created confidence in the ultimate victory, while admitting the possibility of severe setbacks which could be extremely unpleasant for those unfortunate to be representing the cause at the wrong moment of history. It also permitted, and even lauded, considerable flexibility in tactics, demanding only that they be based on a sober appreciation of objective realities.

Before 1917, the Russian experience had been one of a series of military disasters and humiliations, in which the potential of this vast country as a major force in international politics had never been realized. Similarly, after 1917, the Union of Soviet Socialist Republics had been on the defensive. An inordinate amount of time and effort had been spent removing foreigners from Russian soil, as well as in defeating a variety of internal enemies. Through the twists and turns of Soviet diplomacy of the 1920s and 1930s, including the activities of the Kremlin-directed Communist parties in Europe, the one constant theme was the prevention of attacks by anti-Communist nations. When, in 1941, the Germans invaded, once again their repulsion took a tremendous effort, with early disastrous setbacks and enormous loss of life.

In 1945, for the first time, the situation looked more promising. At the cost of major social dislocation, an industrial base sufficient to support a modern military power of the first order had been created. After the disasters of 1941, a disciplined and triumphant army swept back the German invader. Joseph Stalin, undisputed leader of the Soviet Union, sat, with Attlee of Britain and Truman of the United States, as one of the 'Big Three', enjoying reasonable if hardly warm relations with the wartime allies. More to the point, the Soviet armies controlled large sections of Eastern Europe contiguous to the borders of the USSR. The importance of Central Europe to the Russians cannot be over-emphasized. By securing these border countries, and by keeping Germany divided, traditional enemies and invasion routes would lose much of their former menace. In the post-war settlement assured domination of this 'sphere of influence' was to be the primary objective.

Unfortunately, there was a tension between this objective and that of maintaining relations with the Allies. As the wartime partners discussed arrangements for the post-war world, Soviet efforts to secure Eastern Europe alarmed and irritated the Americans and British. In Washington, in particular, a desire to avoid blatant sharing of the various regions of the world among the Great Powers became mingled with a profound distaste for communism. The ideological differences subdued in the fight against Germany reasserted themselves. Moves to consolidate Soviet power in Eastern Europe, instead of being seen just as power politics as usual, were presented as the retreat of democracy and the advance of communism; seen in these terms there could be no certainty as to where the advance would stop.

Anglo-American efforts to prevent the creation of a buffer zone were viewed by the Soviet leaders as an attempt to keep their country weak, as were the measures taken to strengthen the Western sphere of influence in Europe through injections of Marshall Aid, especially when this involved encouraging German economic recovery.

The more threatening the Anglo-American stance, the more Soviet leaders felt it necessary to strengthen their strategic position – and the more they did this the more relations with the former allies deteriorated. Once again, the Russians had to contemplate the hostility of the world's most powerful nations. And, to cap it all, these nations had an advantage for which there was no Soviet counter, in the short term at least. The promise of security was whisked away to be replaced by a threat from the United States, the world's most powerful and prosperous nation, now armed with atomic weapons which it seemed to be flaunting. It was also attempting to intimidate the Russians by reminding them of their new vulnerability.

In these circumstances, the Russians were anxious to demonstrate that they would not be intimidated, even by the atom bomb. The political requirement of strategic pronouncements was to assert that the USSR was strong enough to survive any new imperialist aggression. This political requirement was not at variance with Soviet predispositions in the area, for the strategic principles shaped by the traumatic experience of the Great Patriotic War provided grounds for denigrating the new weapons and asserting the primacy of the old.

The Permanently Operating Factors

In 1942, just after the Battle of Moscow, when it appeared that the German assault had been beaten back, Stalin propounded the official doctrine that was not to be challenged until his death. The doctrine was that of the 'Permanently Operating Factors'. War was seen as a massive clash between two societies, in which all the strengths and weaknesses of the belligerents influenced the final result. In principle, by assessing the respective strengths of the opposing forces, the eventual victor could be predicted.

These Permanently Operating Factors were: the stability of the rear; the morale of the army; the quantity and quality of divisions; the armaments of the army; and the organizational ability of the army commanders. Merely to list these factors was hardly profound without analysis of their interdependence or the relative weights of one against other, or acknowledgment of the fact that advantage in each rarely accrued solely to one side. The components of the list very much reflected the events of 1941-2. Stalin's sensitivity to the stability of the rear was due to the fact that he could not always take it for granted. Otherwise the message was that superior force ought to prevail in land warfare. Types of war other than those fought on land were not considered. It was assumed that, in the future as in the past, aggression would be launched from adjacent territory. Wars were fought at or close to home. No greater reach was required than that provided by tanks, artillery, and tactical airpower. The greater the available quantities of these forces the more likely was success in a land war. In the Great Patriotic War the Russians had been facing forces that were better trained and better equipped, but the apparently inexhaustible reserve of Soviet manpower and vast numbers of tanks, turned out to be sufficient to smother the advancing Germans, halt them, and eventually turn them back. Dinerstein has commented that the fact that 'the only strategy open to the Russians turned out to be a winning strategy only served to bolster their conservative prejudices'.[17]

These prejudices were in favour of size and quantity. The basic principle of Soviet force planning became lots of everything, especially for the army. With emphasis on the survival of the biggest, Soviet doctrine opposed any attempt to gain decisive advantage through concentration on a particular type of weapon or mode of warfare, or by relying on surprise. Such prejudices meant that Soviet thought was unlikely to acknowledge the possibility of radical innovation in strategy, even with the stimulus of nuclear weapons.

Strategic surprise was relegated to the category of a transitory factor. It could only provide an indecisive 'temporary success'. This did not mean the denigration of surprise as such. Considerable stress was put on its tactical importance – but it could not compensate for a general inferiority in forces. The mistaken belief that it could was held to be the key to the German failure. Soviet views on the proper composition of a force structure were similar. All types of weapons had their functions and values. The important thing was not to place disproportionate emphasis on one type of weapon or tactic. Major-General Isayev criticized pre-war military thinking in capitalist countries which 'displayed an erratic and extravagant predilection for one-sided development, now of the air force (Douhet), now of the tank force (Fuller), and to underestimate the importance of the artillery, infantry and other services'.[18]

The focal point for Soviet strategy was the land battle which resulted in respect for the qualities of infantry, tanks, and artillery. The natural rôle for air powers was seen as combat support of ground forces. In the 1930s there had been some interest in the theories of strategic bombardment and even a tendency in force planning to favour the bomber. However, a number of the most enthusiastic advocates of long-range bombing were purged and greater priority was given to tactical airpower. In 1942 a long-range bombing force was created, mainly for the purposes of deep strikes at enemy forces and supply lines. Stalin is said to have been impressed by the impact of Anglo-American strategic bombardment, and some effort was put into improving Soviet capabilities in this area. However, official Soviet doctrine allotted only a limited rôle to this sort of activity and treated with derision Western theories of the primacy of strategic airpower. The official view was summarized in a 1949 article:

Soviet military science considers that the outcome of war under contemporary conditions is decided on the field of battle by means of the annihilation of the armed forces of the enemy, and that one of the most important tasks of aviation is active assistance to the ground and naval forces in all forms of their combat activity. This definition of the fundamental mission of aviation is not contradicted by the need to employ part of its forces to strike the deep rear of the enemy, on his military–industrial targets, but our military science does not consider such blows an end in themselves, but only a helpful means of creating favourable conditions for the success of the combat operations of the ground and naval forces.[19]

It was arguments such as these, as much as the lack of the weapon, that conditioned the initial Soviet response to the atom bomb. The nature of the American advantage ensured that the Russians had little interest in dwelling on the capabilities of atomic bombs. Too much publicity would not be conducive to good morale and could suggest American success in intimidating the Russians. The sound political reasons for virtually ignoring the bomb were followed. Garthoff notes that after three articles in 1945 and 1946, 'not a single article on atomic energy or atomic weapons is known to have appeared in the period from 1947 through 1953 in the Soviet military daily and periodical press, open or restricted in circulation'.[20] When it was mentioned elsewhere it was to castigate the West for immorally threatening use of weapons of mass destruction, and to offer reminders that they could not, by themselves, produce victory:

The revival of Douhet's venturous ideas by the Anglo-American warlords mirrors their aspirations of conquest. Not having reliable reserves of manpower at their disposal and searching for obedient cannon fodder in the Marshallized countries, the warmongers boom and exaggerate the role of the Air Force out of all proportion. These venturous schemes are also based on the calculation that the peoples of the USSR and the People's Democracies will be intimidated by the so-called 'atomic' or 'push-button' war. These ideas emanate from the completely distorted view that the outcome of a war can be settled by one kind of weapon alone. History has proved the reverse more than once.[21]

It was always part of the Soviet critique of US atomic strategy that its impact would be reduced by the inevitable entrance of the Soviet atomic bomb. Atomic bombs and long-range bombers were given high priority in Soviet force planning. In fact the Russians initiated their programme for intercontinental ballistic missiles in 1947, well before the Americans.[22] In practical terms the Russians did not neglect the ingredients of 'atomic' or 'push-button' war. Yet even after their atom bomb and long-range aircraft programmes began to bear fruit, there was no significant shift in Soviet pronouncements.

In part this was because the intellectual climate of Stalin's declining years did not encourage innovation in thought of any kind. The 'Greatest Strategist of Modern Times' did not see fit to alter his views on the Permanently Operating Factors and the danger of one-sided development in the armed forces. In part, too, strategic and atomic bombardment were played down because the West remained significantly ahead in this area. But, accepting the influence of the dead-weight of Stalinism and the expedient desire not to acknowledge Western advantage, there was also a legitimate strategic perspective. At least in the 1940s, stockpiles of atomic bombs were too small to be decisive in war. Meanwhile the formidable Soviet land forces were of more value to the Kremlin in consolidating its position in Eastern Europe and deterring campaigns of 'liberation' from the West. There were others in the West at this time who also felt that atomic bombs would play only a limited role in future wars.[23] A revolution in

Soviet strategic thought had to wait until Stalin's death. By this time not only was the system better able to accommodate new ideas, but further dramatic development in nuclear technology, to some extent stimulated by the Russians' own atomic test, had rendered formulae based on World War II experience patently inadequate.

5 Strategy for an Atomic Stalemate

The Soviet Bomb

The Soviet Union broke the United States atomic monopoly with a test in August 1949. A number of years would have to pass before this would turn into an atomic stockpile, but the eventual Soviet accumulation of such a stockpile was virtually inevitable. This development had a paradoxical effect. While it discouraged doctrines based upon atomic weapons as a uniquely American advantage, it also locked the United States into a nuclear strategy.

The response in the US to the evidence of a developing Soviet capability for both the manufacture and delivery of atom bombs was not to back down from reliance on nuclear weapons but to raise the stakes, moving to the development of hydrogen bombs, so ushering in an age of nuclear plenty and confirming a trend towards ever-increasing levels of destruction. Any doubts about the 'uniqueness' of nuclear weapons, and the ease and import of nuclear strikes, were soon erased. Those limiting factors which critics of total reliance upon nuclear weapons had identified no longer seemed so limiting. The speed of technological advance rendering some of the most authoritative and reasoned writing of the period, especially that of Blackett and Bush, anachronistic; whilst those who enjoyed playing with the possibilities for novel forms of warfare now seemed quite prescient. The sensationalists were more accurate in their predictions and this meant, unfortunately, that the limited intellectual baggage that usually travels with sensationalism was given added credence.

Soviet nuclear capabilities now had to loom large in American calculations. Account had to be taken of an evolving strategic balance. By 1949, the procurement decisions relevant to a nuclear strategy had been made but had yet to take full effect. The mainstay of the Strategic Air Command (SAC) was the 4000-mile range B-29, and the longer-range derivative the B-50. To reach the Soviet Union it was necessary to employ either overseas bases within Europe or aerial tankers. In-flight refuelling permitted large distances to be flown without stopping; but without enough tankers to refuel every offensive bomber (and capabilities never approached this level) there was still dependence on overseas bases. In 1949, the first deliveries were made of a new medium-range bomber (the B-46) which could fly at much higher speeds than the B-29 and B-50 and so was more able to penetrate air defences. This aircraft became the mainstay of SAC for the first half of the 1950s. The first long-range (over 8000 miles) bomber was the B-36, first introduced in 1948. This was not a popular plane with the USAF because of the altitude at which it flew, and it was acquired only in small numbers. It was not until the B-52 became operational in 1955 that a satisfactory long-range bomber was available.

The Soviet position with regard to delivery vehicles was worse than that of the US. Its only long-range bomber, the TU-4, was a copy of the B-29 and entered service in 1948. A replacement, the TU-16 ('*Badger*') medium bomber became available in 1955. Large numbers of both bombers were produced and posed a severe threat to Western Europe. For attacks across the ocean, however, the USSR lacked the compensations of overseas bases on the periphery of the United States and a capacity for in-flight refuelling. It was not until 1956/7 that intercontinental bombers (the TU-20 *Bear* and MYA-4 *Bison*) entered the Soviet inventory. However, if both the aircraft and crew were considered expendable, the TU-4 and TU-16 could reach the continental United States on a one-way mission. Certainly US intelligence estimates took account of this potential.[1]

As true symmetry in capabilities, denying any notable strategic advantage to either side, was some years distant, there were still strong arguments for making the most of the superiority, in numbers and in quality of delivery vehicles, that the US still enjoyed. Indeed, with the Soviets seriously engaged in bomb production, not to do so would be folly. The point was that the visible entry of the Soviet Union into the arms race removed an element of choice from US policy. The decision to emphasize or de-emphasize nuclear weapons in any future conflict could not be one for the US alone.

The 'Super' Bomb

Following the Soviet test, a decision to expand production of all types of atomic (fission) bombs was not contentious. The decision to test and then produce hydrogen (fusion) bombs touched off a sharp though exclusive debate within the defence establishment on the wisdom of developing weapons of such enormous destructive force.

In the fission bomb, energy is released when heavy nuclei split. The principle of the fusion bomb is based on the energy released when the lightest atoms combine to form heavier atoms. To initiate this fusion process a considerable investment in energy is required; more than can normally be produced by artificial methods. However, a sufficiently high temperature to cause fusion reactions with the heavier isotopes of hydrogen (deuterium or tritium) can be created by the explosion of a uranium or plutonium fission bomb. There is no 'critical size' for the fusionable material; the amounts of the reacting elements included determine the size of the eventual explosion.

The possibility of a fusion bomb with a yield many times that of the first fission bombs had been recognized early in the Manhattan Project. Work in this area had proceeded with a low priority because of the urgent need to exploit the known technology of fission bombs. Following the Soviet explosion, those scientists who had been most enthusiastic about the prospects for a thermonuclear reaction took the opportunity to agitate for a major national effort directed towards this objective. They promoted the 'super', as it was known during the brief debate of the closing months of 1949, as the logical next step in nuclear development and one which would provide a substantial measure of superiority for that nation which mastered its principles before the other one.

The main arguments against this came from the senior veterans of the Manhattan Project, led by Robert Oppenheimer, who formed the General Advisory Committee (GAC) to the Atomic Energy Commission (AEC). In their Report of October 1949, in addition to arguing against diverting energies from the fission bomb programme, they provide strategic and moral grounds for not proceeding with the 'super'. The committee noted:

> There is no limit to the explosive power of the bomb itself except that imposed by the requirements of delivery. . . . Taking into account the probable limitations of carriers likely to be available for the delivery of such a weapon, it has generally been estimated that the weapon would have an explosive effect of some hundreds of times that of present fission bombs. . . .

It is clear that the use of this weapon would bring about the destruction of innumerable human lives; it is not a weapon which can be used exclusively for the destruction of material installations of military or semi-military purposes. Its use therefore carries much further than the atomic bomb itself the policy of exterminating civilian populations.

In more strongly worded appended opinions, the 'super' was described as being a 'weapon of genocide', 'beyond any military objectives' and into the 'range of very great natural catastrophes'.[2]

It was questioned whether any extra benefit even in the area of strategic bombardment could be provided by the 'super'. If the Russians used a 'super' against the United States, 'reprisals by our large stock of atomic bombs would be comparably effective to the use of the super'. David Lilienthal, the outgoing chairman of the AEC, argued that a decision to build the 'super' would be 'widely regarded as a confirmation in the clearest possible terms of our present chief and almost sole reliance upon this kind of armament against the Russians. . . .' It would 'tend to confuse and, unwittingly, hide' the fact that 'we are today relying on an asset that is readily depreciating for us, i.e., weapons of mass destruction'. As a consequence of this confusion it would become 'more difficult to find some other course'.[3] An alternative course was recommended by the GAC, involving the pursuit of small atom bombs for 'tactical' use rather than large hydrogen bombs for mass destruction.

There was a tendency among the opponents to view the lobbying for the 'super' in terms of a drive to exaggerate the possible rôle nuclear weapons could play in American strategy. Robert Oppenheimer complained that the superbomb 'appears to have caught the imagination, both of congressmen and of military people, as *the answer* to the problem posed by the Russian advance'. George Kennan, in a valedictory *crie de cœur* before he left the foreign service, described the 'crucial question' to the Secretary of State in a long paper of January 1950:

Are we to rely upon weapons of mass destruction as an integral and vitally important component of our military strength, which we would expect to employ deliberately, immediately, and unhesitatingly in the event that we become involved in a military conflict with the Soviet Union? Or are we to retain such weapons in our national arsenal only as a deterrent to the use of similar weapons against ourselves and as a possible means of retaliation in case they are used?[4]

However, this was not a new question. The question of first and early use of atomic weapons had been raised in 1948 and though not authoritatively decided, the inclination then had been to make the most of the American atomic asset. The objections in 1948 still impressed Kennan and were connected with the problems of fitting such a repugnant weapon into American military and foreign policy. The 'super' increased the amount of destructive power by dramatic orders of magnitude but, in the end, the moral and strategic issues it raised differed from those of two years earlier only in degree. The new strategic issue was the confirmation of Soviet capabilities in this area. This could provide a justification both for the hydrogen bomb *and* for less dependence on a nuclear strategy. This was the line eventually followed by the Administration.

These arguments of Kennan, Lilienthal, and Oppenheimer failed to convince the political leadership. The moment was not propitious for another initiative on arms control. In the aftermath of the Berlin airlift, the fall of the Nationalist Chinese, and the Soviet bomb, there was little optimism about the prospects for useful negotiations on almost any issue. Nor was it accepted that there was a moral distinction between one big explosion and a number of smaller explosions causing equal or greater damage. Lastly, and most important, because such a weapon was feasible, and because the Russians were not believed to be prone to eschewing weapons for ethical reasons, the issue was seen to be one of whether the United States could allow the Soviet Union to proceed with H-bomb development while it exercised restraint. As Lewis Strauss, the AEC Commission who was leading to the pro-H-bomb group put it, 'A group of atheists is not likely to be dissuaded from producing the weapon on "moral" grounds.' Through history, he contended, the policy of the US had been 'not to have its forces less well armed than those of any other country'.[5] Acheson, the Secretary of State, though sympathetic to Lilienthal's desire not to prejudge key defence issues by a hasty move to an H-bomb, and though he later was 'strongly persuaded toward an increased conventional capability', felt that the American people would tolerate neither restraint nor a new effort at arms control. Meanwhile 'our delaying research would not delay Soviet research'.[6] For similar reasons Truman authorized   development, and later production, of the H-bomb. The Soviet atom bomb had introduced a sense of an arms race in a way that it had not been felt before. It was now felt imperative to stay ahead.

Tactical Nuclear Weapons

The opponents of the 'super' had sought to strengthen their position by adumbrating an alternative strategy, in which the explosive power of nuclear weapons was to be harnessed to established forms of land and sea warfare, with soldiers and sailors for targets rather than civilians. To achieve this strategic shift, they had to change perceptions of atom bombs as something that were suitable for attacking cities and little else. Because of their cost and scarcity, and also because of the ability of military forces to disperse, it had been felt unlikely that atomic bombs could be used against conventional military targets. Joseph Viner in 1945 suggested that 'Under atom bomb warfare, the soldier in the army would be safer than his wife and children in their urban home.'[7]

Interest in the possibility of using nuclear weapons on the battlefield in a 'tactical' manner grew amongst those seeking an alternative strategy to reliance on terror-bombing of cities. Tactical nuclear weapons appeared as a means of combining the technological asset of atomic energy with a desire to fight wars in a traditional way – as a clash of professional armies rather than as a process of destruction. The US Army had displayed some interest in the tactical applications of atomic weapons. General Omar Bradley wrote in 1949 how the A-bomb 'in its tactical aspect, may well contribute towards a stable equilibrium of forces since it tends to strengthen a defensive army'.[8]

Following the strong plea of the General Advisory Committee for an alternative strategy based on small fission bombs, the relevant technologies and concepts were explored. Despite the loss of the particular fight against the H-bomb, scientists such as Oppenheimer continued to favour this option and urge it on the US military in preference to the growing reliance on threats of mass destruction. A 1951 study, Project Vista, argued that the combination of relatively small ground forces with tactical nuclear weapons could hold Western Europe against the Red Army. Oppenheimer expressed his hope that: 'Battle could be brought back to the battlefield'.

But so long as the atomic stockpile was small, diverting weapons to battlefield use meant taking them away from the SAC. This revived old arguments over whether airpower should be used in support of ground warfare or for direct attacks on the socioeconomic structure of the enemy. The Air Force continued to oppose the use of the bomb in anything other than a strategic mode, suggesting that those who advocated such things did not have the best interests of US security at heart.

Nevertheless, investigation continued into tactical weapons, which became seen, however, as *supplements* rather than *alternatives* to strategic bombardment. In November 1951 Gordon Dean, the Chairman of the AEC, could speak of a 'revolution' in atomic warfare:

> What we are working toward here is a situation where we will have atomic weapons in almost as complete a variety as conventional ones, and a situation where we can use them in the same way. This would include artillery shells, guided missiles, torpedoes, rockets and bombs for ground support amongst others and it would include big ones for big situations.[9]

NSC-68

There was a concession to Lilienthal's anxiety that the hydrogen bomb decision was made without reference to larger questions of foreign and military policy, and that the United States was drifting into commitments to the defence of Europe against communism without fully thinking through just what this might entail. At the end of January 1950, President Truman issued a directive to the Secretaries of State and Defense 'to undertake a re-examination of our objectives in peace and war and of the effect of these objectives on our strategic plans, in the light of the probable fission bomb capability and possible thermo-nuclear bomb capability of the Soviet Union'. The main drafting of the report was undertaken by Paul Nitze, who had taken over from George Kennan as Head of the State Department's Policy Planning Staff. The result, known as NSC-68, was presented to the National Security Council (NSC) in April 1950.[10]

NSC-68's main purpose was to impress upon its bureaucratic readership the Soviet threat to world peace, best blocked through increased military preparedness in the non-Soviet world. This rôle, of getting over the message of the seriousness of the Soviet challenge to all responsible sections of the State and Defense Departments, may account for the turgidity of the style. A rearguard action was fought by Secretary of Defense Louis Johnson who, as a fiscal conservative, did not support the plea for higher military expenditure. Others, such as the recently displaced Kennan, regretted the unsubtle analysis of Soviet intentions.

NSC-68 offered a prospect of persistent East–West hostility, with a danger of war not only from miscalculations in the midst of a crisis, but as a consequence of premeditated Soviet aggression. The Soviet Union, or more precisely 'the Kremlin', was identified as an ideal-type aggressor. Already an imposition on the Russian people, it was now attempting to impose its will on the rest of the world. The moves of the Kremlin were presumed to be based on a calculation of risks. At the time of writing, in 1950, the US retaliatory capability was 'probably adequate to deter the Kremlin from a deliberate direct attack against ourselves or other free people'.

It was presumed that if war did come 'it was hardly conceivable that . . . the Soviet leaders would refrain from the use of atomic weapons unless they felt fully confident of attaining their objectives by other means'. In addition NSC-68 accepted the propositions that the natural way to fight a nuclear war was to get in a surprise attack and that totalitarian states enjoyed a comparative advantage over open societies in the ability to 'strike swiftly and with stealth'. Little confidence was expressed in the proposition that two large atomic capabilities could co-exist, mutually deterred, in a stable relationship. Rather, they would threaten each other. This could serve as an 'incite-ment to war'.

Thus a nuclear strategy would be more appropriate to the Soviet Union than the United States because of the comparative ease with which it could organize a surprise attack. It would be in the interests of the United States if 'atomic weapons were to be effectively elim-inated from national peacetime armaments'. As this was now con-sidered unlikely, the US was locked into an arms race owing to the necessity of denying the Soviet Union a decisive superiority. 'Within the next four years' a Soviet capability to damage seriously the 'vital centers of the United States' would develop. Already intelligence esti-mates assigned to the Soviet Union 'an atomic bomber capability . . . in excess of that needed to deliver available bombs'. The extent of this capability, and in consequence the risk calculus of the Kremlin, would be determined by the US response. Greatly increased air and civilian defence, plus an increase in retaliatory power, including thermonuclear weapons, could 'put off for some time the date when the Soviet Union could calculate that a surprise blow would be advantageous'.

In the absence of effective arms control it would appear that we have no alternative but to increase our atomic armaments as rapidly as other considerations make appropriate. In either case, it appears to be imperative to increase as rapidly as possible our general air, ground and sea strength and that of our allies to a point where we are militarily not so heavily dependent on atomic weapons.

Until conventional forces had been built up, the United States had no choice but to rely on its nuclear arsenal, and extend its breathing space by maintaining, for as long as possible, a clear superiority in nuclear capabilities over the Soviet Union. The imbalance in conventional capabilities meant that the United States was not even able to hold back nuclear weapons as a last resort. NSC-68 rejected the proposal for a policy of no first use of nuclear weapons. 'In our present situation of relative unpreparedness in conventional weapons, such a declaration would be interpreted by the USSR as an admission of great weakness and by our allies as a clear indication that we intended to abandon them.'

The long-term alternative to a nuclear strategy was one based on strong and ready conventional forces-in-being around the periphery of the Soviet Union to support the established policy of containment. This alternative required a series of alliances with states close to the Soviet Union and its satellites, who would provide their own forces in the knowledge that, in the event of hostilities, the United States would move to support them speedily and decisively. It also required a far larger military expenditure than had hitherto been deemed desirable or necessary.

Korea

By the time Truman had approved NSC-68, in September 1950, international developments had strengthened the force of the Report's main conclusions. In June 1950 communist North Korea invaded the South. The United States, with token support from its allies and under the aegis of the United Nations, rushed to the South's defence. Under General MacArthur, the American forces regained the initiative, taking the war well into the North. Unfortunately they took it too far, provoking China into joining the fight to keep the enemy away from its borders. The Chinese intervention was effective and the war degenerated into stalemate.

In terms of nuclear strategy, the Korean War demonstrated that, in a period when the world's two greatest powers were nervous about getting into an all-out war with each other, any conflict would be subjected to major political constraints. The experience suggested that when it came to the crunch, atomic bombs were not perceived as ordinary weapons but as something special to be handled with care, almost as if a taboo prevented their use. President Truman's distaste for atomic weapons was shared by America's Allies, particularly the British. When Truman hinted in a press conference that atom-bomb use might be considered, Prime Minister Clement Attlee hurried over the Atlantic to urge restraint. The US State Department suspected even fiercer reactions from countries far less friendly than Britain.

The atomic stockpile was still small and many felt it had to be kept in reserve for a clash in Europe. It was widely assumed that Korea was merely a diversion from a big Soviet push being prepared for Europe. Finally, it was not clear to local commanders how atomic weapons could be profitably employed.[11] Targets of strategic value in North Korea could be dealt with readily by conventional bombardment, and those North of the Yalu were out of bounds. Targets of tactical value, such as the position of enemy troops, could rarely be reported accurately and sufficiently quickly to permit destruction with atomic weapons. Furthermore, they were often too close to friendly troops to be attacked with atomic weapons safely.

However, it cannot be taken for granted that nuclear use was unthinkable. Plans for a number of contingencies may well have involved nuclear weapons. One of the most likely was large-scale attacks on United Nations forces from communist aircraft based in China and the Soviet Far East. In the event of such attacks, the US might have retaliated by destroying the relevant bases, a task that could well have required atomic bombs.

The Conventional Strategy

Prior to NSC-68, serious thought had been given to strengthening European defences against the possibility of Soviet attack. A key element in this was the Atlantic Alliance, committing the United States to come to the aid of Western Europe if attacked. Senator Vandenburg, who sponsored the Senate resolution ratifying the North Atlantic Treaty which was passed in July 1949, explained:

[W]hen Mr Hitler was contemplating World War Two, I believe he would never have launched it if he had had any serious reasons to believe that it might bring him into armed collision with the United States. I think he was sure it would not do so because of our then existing neutrality laws. If an appropriate North Atlantic Pact is written, I think it will reverse this psychology so far as Mr Stalin is concerned if, as and when he contemplates World War Three.

This indicates the extent to which the Treaty was seen as a means of reassuring Europeans that the United States would be involved at the start of any new war, rather than, as in the previous two wars, deliberating for a couple of years over whether or not to come to the aid of embattled European democracies. What it did not involve, initially, was an actual commitment of troops to Europe to help hold back a Soviet invasion. The Berlin crisis of 1948, during which the situation had only been saved by the successful expedient of an airlift, had forced military planners in the West to recognize the local Soviet strategic advantages. Nevertheless, the position was not considered hopeless as it was presumed that the Soviet Union preferred to move forward through subversion and political opportunism rather than direct military confrontation, and because the United States still enjoyed its atomic monopoly.[12]

This relaxed view was undermined first by the Soviet atom bomb test of 1949 and then by the invasion of South Korea by the North in 1950 (even though no direct analogy could be drawn with the European situation). Once a Soviet invasion moved from being a hypothetical possibility to a serious prospect, then the military position was taken to be urgent. The problem had been faced in September 1949 when the North Atlantic Treaty had acquired the rudiments of a military organization. The plans then had gone little beyond ideas for a division of labour, in which the United States would look after the sea lanes and provide strategic bombardment (already assumed in Europe to be of critical importance) while the Europeans would provide ground forces.

When agreeing to the North Atlantic Treaty, which came into force in April 1949, American Senators believed themselves to be making an important political gesture, in itself an act of deterrence, by promising that an attack on one or more of the alliance countries 'should be considered an attack against them all'. They would, however, have been appalled at the suggestion that the result would be to station a large American force in Europe for the indefinite future.

Yet in September 1950 President Truman announced 'substantial increases in the United States forces to be stationed in Western Europe in the interests of the defence of that area'. This was assumed to be only a temporary measure, until either the Europeans sorted themselves out or some grand East–West settlement was reached. The forces are still in Europe.

Proposals to this effect had been around for some time but it was the North Korean attack of June 1950 that was taken by the Administration to demonstrate the dangers of unpreparedness. The comparatively swift American response was helped by the intellectual ground that had been prepared by the 'bludgeon' of NSC-68.

The character of the response was conditioned by alliance politics as much as military logic. Any military exertions by the Europeans themselves, when funds were scarce and there were many pressing social needs, required American participation. The Europeans needed reassurance, if the effort was to be worthwhile, that this time they were to be defended rather than 'liberated' after suffering through devastating battles and occupation. From the start, the force structure of NATO was assessed as much in terms of what it told the Europeans about the strength and extent of the US commitment to their defence and what it told the Americans about the seriousness of the Europeans in helping themselves, than of what it told the Soviet Union about the likely consequences of aggression.

The rearmament, and the American commitment of ground forces to Europe, was opposed by those who distrusted this departure from the past norms of American policy ('do not commit yourself to any fighting abroad unless it can not possibly be avoided'), by those who felt that the costs would be intolerable and that NATO Allies ought to look after themselves more, and by supporters of the Air Force, with a confidence in airpower as the sole requirement for US security.

In arguing for strong ground forces to counter Soviet aggression, the Administration relied on the rationale that had been developed in NSC-68. Dean Acheson explained that blocking all enemy moves when and where they occurred was necessary because of the importance of persuading an aggressor against grabbing a piece of Europe, of discouraging unruly Soviet satellites (such as the North Koreans) from initiating 'overt moves which could be disclaimed by the real center of aggression', and because of the diminishing value of the American lead in retaliatory atomic power.

[T]he best use we can make our our present advantage in retaliatory air power is to move ahead under this protective shield to
build the balanced collective forces in Western Europe that will
continue to deter aggression after our atomic advantage has been
diminished.[13]

The acceptance of this argument led directly to the adoption by
NATO of a Forward Strategy, aimed at holding any Soviet offensive
as close to the original lines as possible, and then to the ambitious
Lisbon force goals of NATO of February 1952 and, beyond that, to
German rearmament.

Once adopted, the strategy soon faced problems. First, it was extremely expensive; a flaw that was eventually to be its undoing.
Second, in practice it was a frustrating approach to war, offering no
easy and painless route to victory. The Korean War demonstrated
just how frustrating a conventional strategy could be. The past American insistence on a 'no-holds-barred' and often ferocious response to
aggression was replaced by the imposition of strong limitations on the
conduct of war. The Truman Administration nevertheless felt that it
had little choice. The US nuclear superiority was destined to be lost,
and so provided no basis for a long-term strategy. Increasingly,
nuclear forces would be expected to do little more than neutralize
those of the other side. The struggle for advantage would have to be
waged with conventional arms.

6 Massive Retaliation

The diminishing credibility of a nuclear strategy and the consequent advisability of a more conventional approach impressed the Truman Administration, but not its successor, the Administration of General Dwight Eisenhower. A year after taking office, in January 1954, in a speech to the Council on Foreign Relations, Eisenhower's Secretary of State, John Foster Dulles, outlined a change of direction from the strategic doctrines that had been developing under Truman. This new doctrine, known as one of 'massive retaliation', was widely assumed to be founded on an undiscriminating threat to respond to any communist-inspired aggression, however marginal the confrontation, by means of a massive nuclear strike against the centres of the Soviet Union and China. In this chapter the origins of this doctrine will be discussed.

Dulles's speech, and a later article in *Foreign Affairs*, in which he attempted to clarify some of those points where he felt he had been misunderstood, indicated that he was talking more about 'flexible retaliation', with 'massive retaliation' just one option among many. The new policy was based on giving far greater emphasis to nuclear weapons in US strategy, but it was much more complex than a simple belief in the value of all-out nuclear threats as a deterrent to virtually any unwelcome Soviet move.

It revolved around a strong feeling that the West was being forced into fighting the cold war and would have to fight any future hot war according to ground rules laid down by the communists in order to exploit their tactical advantages. The West's policy of containment meant that it had been left to the communists to initiate each successive crisis, allowing them to pick the time and place for each new challenge. The West, however much on the offensive with its broad ideological, political, and economic challenge to communism, was always on the defensive in particular military crises. The 'first move' had to be ceded to the East.

The Republicans toyed with the idea of reversing this pattern by picking fights with communism where its writ had been established in a particularly illegitimate manner. But this policy of 'roll-back' never moved beyond rhetoric. The policy of containment was maintained by the Eisenhower Administration and the first move was left to the East. What was not to be tolerated was the imposition of communist rules for fighting following the first move. In Korea they had picked the point of attack and had chosen the weapons – conventional forces. The West had accommodated them by restricting fighting to the original combat zone, accepting areas crucial to the enemy's war effort but outside North Korea's territory as sanctuaries, and obliging further by resisting the temptation to use the most modern weapons in the American arsenal – atomic weapons. The consequences of this attempt to fight on communist terms meant that no benefit was gained from the nuclear programme and an excessive strain was being placed on the US economy by the attempt to match the communists in conventional forces.

An important contributory factor to the new strategy was a change in the perception of nuclear weapons. By 1953, many of the various projects initiated during the Truman years had come to fruition. The United States now had a range of nuclear capabilities, from hydrogen bombs large enough to take out a city of any size, to small weapons for battlefield use. While 'strategic' and 'tactical' nuclear weapons each had their own proponents, and were often presented as alternatives, they could be presented as two sides to a comprehensive nuclear strategy, in which the 'strategic' weapons would threaten devastation of Soviet and Chinese cities, while 'tactical' weapons would compensate for the West's lack of manpower by increasing available firepower.

Proponents of smaller, 'tactical' nuclear weapons argued that these employed the most modern explosives for traditional purposes. The military found this idea seductive. In December 1953 the Chairman of the Joint Chiefs of Staff observed that 'Today atomic weapons have virtually achieved a conventional status within our armed forces'. In a March 1955 press conference, President Eisenhower argued that

'Where these things are used on strictly military targets and for strictly military purposes, I see no reason why they shouldn't be used just exactly as you would use a bullet or anything else'.

This dual approach was made possible by the fact that both tactical and strategic weapons were now being produced in large quantities. The age of nuclear plenty had arrived. In early 1954, Brodie noted that nuclear weapons 'can no longer be regarded as exceedingly scarce or costly'.[1]

The net effect of the move towards small tactical weapons, even though it was parallel to development of massive terror weapons for destroying cities, was to make nuclear weapons seem quite ordinary. As 'just another weapon' it could be used without any special qualms.

The other major reason for promoting nuclear weapons as the centrepiece of American strategy was economic. The rearmament in conventional forces was proving inordinately expensive, and was throwing the Government budget out of balance. To Democrats, subject to some Keynesian influences, this was regrettable but not a tragedy. To Republicans it was a tragedy. It could, they suggested, even be part of the communist plot – to force the West into high military expenditure and so cause economic turmoil. They wished to avoid choosing between 'security or solvency'. The belief of the fiscal conservative in the need to reduce the budgetary burden of military expenditures encouraged strategies based on nuclear rather than conventional weapons because the former promised 'a bigger bang for a buck'.

The British Conversion

Taken together, conservative economic theories and the availability of large numbers of nuclear weapons of all shapes and sizes, created formidable pressures in favour of a nuclear strategy. The final factor was the conversion of the British to such a strategy prior to the Eisenhower Administration taking office. This was a conversion that required further proselytization. The British could not introduce such a strategy by themselves. All they could do was point the way forward for the US.

Fiscal conservatism returned in Britain, in the shape of the Conservative Party, in 1951, a year before the Republican victory over the Democrats in the United States. Official British thoughts on nuclear weapons had been similar to those in America. Margaret Gowing has observed how the British decision to develop the bomb had been almost instinctive, based on:

a feeling that Britain must possess so climacteric a weapon in order to deter an atomically armed enemy, a feeling that Britain as a great power must acquire all major new weapons, a feeling that atomic weapons were a manifestation of the scientific and technological superiority on which Britain's strength, so deficient if measured in sheer numbers of men, must depend.[2]

After the Soviet test in 1949 the British had come to accept the disadvantages of a strategy based solely on nuclear weapons and even came to view with concern the common American belief that nuclear weapons could serve as a 'panacea' for all defence problems – 'something entirely new with which aggression could be quickly, easily and permanently eliminated'. The Labour Government saw atomic bombs very much as weapons of last resort and therefore supported the Truman Administration's drive for conventional rearmament in the West, despite the heavy burden it imposed on Britain's weak economy.

Winston Churchill, back in power in October 1951, was disquieted by the inflationary impact of the rearmament programme. In addition he was strongly of the opinion that nuclear weapons deserved more of a rôle in Western strategy. Churchill had always felt a proprietary interest in nuclear matters, and had often expressed his view that the main source of Western strength was the American nuclear arsenal: only this had held back the advance of communism. Once briefed in the United States on the recent advances in nuclear technology he became even more convinced of the bomb's vital rôle. Also, the scare that had prompted the massive conventional rearmament programme was now subsiding. It was evident that Korea was not just the decoy or a prologue for a Soviet attack on Western Europe. The communists would present a challenge for many years to come. Events were not moving inexorably to a great showdown. Preparation would have to be made for a long period of bad relations with the Soviet Union which would be punctuated by high and low points, including some moments of great danger.

In the summer of 1952 the British Chiefs of Staff went to Greenwich, unencumbered by staff support, and constructed a global strategy for Britain, which reflected the above concerns. They noted that there was no defence against atomic attack, and suggested that the primary deterrent against this or any other aggression should be the knowledge that it would invite immediate and crushing retaliation. For this reason priority ought to be given to the long-range air forces of NATO. The Allies could not afford to build up sufficient conventional strength in Europe to defeat the Soviet Union in a clash of land armies. What was needed was sufficient forces in Europe to hold the Russians until the atomic counter-offensive made its impact felt. Given the fact that Britain was only on the verge of testing its first atomic bomb, and were therefore unable to contribute much to the Great Deterrent, the Chiefs of Staff were not so much offering guidelines for the British Government as sending a message to the United States.

When Sir John Slessor, Chief of Air Staff, arrived in Washington with the British paper in July 1952, his reception was cool. The Joint Chiefs in Washington saw it as 'a rationalization of a British intent to renege on their NATO force commitment'. In six months, with a new Administration, the atmosphere changed. The British approach, in its sense of economic realities and the forward-looking perspective of a 'long haul', was now viewed with sympathy. Strategic Air Command, in particular, saw in the British enthusiasm a recognition of the importance of airpower which was lacking amongst many of their compatriots. The British document, noted Charles Murphy with gratitude, 'gives substance to abstractions and theories on air power'. It was now recognized 'as an actuality, feared by Soviet Russia, and therefore a potent instrument for military and diplomatic action.[3]

Sir John Slessor became a major propagandist for the nuclear armed long-range bomber – 'the Great Deterrent'. In a July 1953 article he recorded his frustration at the lack of regard paid to SAC – 'ready to strike a mortally decisive blow, against which there is at present no defence' – because of the preoccupation with conventional rearmament. Yet this 'Great Deterrent' was 'the counter-threat to the vast armies and tactical air forces of our potential enemy. Moreover it gives us some degree, and an increasing degree, of initiative in the cold war, instead of always dancing to the enemy's tune'. This theme of using the Western advantage in air power to regain the initiative was a major feature of Dulles's presentation of the New Look, and reappeared in a later article by Slessor:

> We cannot rely on [the enemy] solving our problems for us by using the bomb first . . . it would suit him admirably to fight a war with the weapons in which he would have a decisive advantage . . .

... The atomic weapon may well be used to do what thousands of high explosive bombs were formerly required to do; and the striking force need not necessarily again be restricted by another YALU. Both will depend upon whether they are to our tactical and strategic advantage rather than to that of the enemy.[4]

The New Look

Influenced by the British arguments, but also by the logic of a situation in which the new Administration expected existing military commitments to be met at low cost, the US Joint Chiefs of Staff moved towards a commitment to use nuclear weapons whenever it was deemed appropriate. If the uncertainty surrounding the question of the use of nuclear weapons could be resolved, the Chiefs argued, they would be able to relinquish requirements for forces that would only be necessary if nuclear weapons were unlikely to be used. Adoption of a nuclear strategy promised a rationalization of defence requirements, with a cut in the most expensive component of the military force structure – manpower.

On 30 October 1953 these conclusions were enshrined in a National Security Council Paper (NSC-162/2) on *Basic National Security Policy*.[5] It began by defining the basic problem of national security policy as 'meeting the Soviet threat' while, at the same time, avoiding 'seriously weakening the US economy or undermining our fundamental values and institutions' (Para 1b). The description of the Soviet 'threat' was grim; any diplomatic moves of apparent peaceful intent from the East were dismissed as gestures. '[T]he basic Soviet objectives continue to be consolidation and expansion of their own sphere of power and the eventual domination of the non-communist world' (Para 3a). It also warned that the capability of the Soviet Union to attack the United States with atomic weapons and soon, hydrogen bombs, using aircraft on one-way missions, was growing. Nevertheless, there was little expectation that this growing Soviet power would tempt the Kremlin into deliberately launching a general war. 'The uncertain prospects for Soviet victory in a general war, the change of leadership, satellite unrest, and the US capability to retaliate massively, make such a course improbable' (Para 6a).

For the future it was considered essential to develop and maintain:

1. a strong military posture, with emphasis on the capability for inflicting massive retaliatory damage by offensive striking power;

2. US and Allied forces in readiness to move rapidly initially to counter aggression by Soviet bloc forces and to hold vital areas and lines of communication; and
3. a mobilization base, and its protection against crippling damage, adequate to insure victory in the event of general war (Para 9a).

The paper also emphasized the importance of allies – to provide forces, to accommodate bases and to co-operate in the general conduct of the cold war. It was necessary to build up 'the strength, cohesion and common determination of the free world'. Confidence was placed in collective security systems. These would dissuade aggressors through the prospect of a united front. To create this moral strength in the free world it was necessary that allies understood the purposes and assumptions that informed US strategy.

In Europe, both allies and adversaries had to be convinced of the 'manifest determination of the United States to use its atomic capability and massive retaliatory striking power if the area is attacked'. The US military forces now based in Europe had become an index of the commitment to the allies. Though America's armed forces were 'over-extended', any major withdrawal of US forces from Europe or from the Far East 'would be interpreted as a diminution of US interest in the defense of these areas and would seriously undermine the strength and cohesion of the coalition'. However, elsewhere, in areas 'not gripped by war conditions', allies needed to accept that US forces should not be further extended but should have 'mobility and initiative'. Any blatant gaps should be filled with indigenous forces. Unwillingness to base more conventional forces overseas would be compensated for by a greater readiness to issue deterrent threats, even in areas other than Europe, and to employ 'tactical' nuclear weapons.

39a   In specific situations where a warning appears desirable and feasible as an added deterrent, the United States should make clear to the USSR and Communist China, in general terms, or with reference to specific areas as the situation requires, its intention to react with military force against any aggression by Soviet bloc armed forces.

b   . . . In the event of hostilities, the United States will consider nuclear weapons to be as available for use as other munitions.

Before moving on to the manner in which the judgments of this paper were publicly presented, a few points can be noted. First, the term 'massive retaliation' (or a derivative) was used a number of times. It was not invented by journalists and academics as a useful label to hang on to the Administration's policy. It was however, used solely in connection with the deterrence of Soviet moves towards a general war, most likely to begin with an assault on Europe. The doctrine extended deterrence through threat of punishment to areas other than Europe in place of a US contribution to local defence, but it was not stated that this punishment would take the form of massive retaliation.

Second, the paper anticipated the major arguments of the opponents of 'massive retaliation'. It was not oblivious to the fact that current US superiority in nuclear weapons would not last for ever. Indeed, the President personally added to the original paper a requirement to reconsider the 'emphasis on the capability of inflicting massive retaliatory damage' if this came to 'work to the disadvantage of national security', thus anticipating a 'New New Look' of 1956. Unlike NSC-68, it was expected that when the two major powers reached 'a stage of atomic plenty and ample means of delivery' the result could be a 'stalemate, with both sides reluctant to initiate general warfare'. Or, as Churchill put it, peace could become the 'sturdy child of terror'. Drawing on the experience of the Korean War it was suggested that if general war came it would, as likely as not, be the result of miscalculation rather than deliberate intent. 'To avoid this, it will in general be desirable for the United States to make clear to the USSR the kind of actions which will be almost certain to lead to [general war]'. But it was recognized, as the Administration's opponents later claimed had not been recognized, that 'as general war becomes more devastating for both sides the threat to resort to it becomes less available as a sanction against local aggression' (Paras 6b and c).

The third feature of the new strategy was a distinction, often only implicit, between nuclear forces for strategic and for tactical purposes. There was felt to be a major qualitative difference between area bombing resulting in enormous destruction, and improved munitions, which would allow a shrinking Army to maintain or even increase its firepower. This distinction was blurred by Dulles and emphasized by many of the Administration's critics. The main innovation was to attempt to convince allies and enemies that there were to be no abnormal inhibitions on the use of either type of weapon. As Field

Marshal Montgomery, then Deputy Supreme Allied Commander, Europe (DSACEUR), explained in late 1954:

> I want to make it absolutely clear that we at SHAPE are basing all our planning on using atomic and thermonuclear weapons in our defence. With us it is no longer: 'They may possibly be used'. It is very definitely: 'They will be used, if we are attacked'.[6]

Dulles and Massive Retaliation

The controversy over the new policy was largely a result of John Foster Dulles's interpretation and presentation. He already had great confidence in America's strategic airpower as a means of deterring the Soviet Union from any military adventures in Europe. In December 1950, reflecting views popular in Republican circles, he had spoken of 'the capacity to counter-attack . . . by action of our own choosing' as the 'ultimate deterrent' and the 'only effective defense', and in May 1952 of 'instant massive retaliation' and the need for the 'free world to develop the will and organize the means to retaliate instantly against open aggression by Red armies, so that if it occurred anywhere, we could and would strike back where it hurts, by means of our choosing'.[7]

Dulles was not greatly involved in developing the Administration's 'New Look'. He understood it in terms of his own concepts and theories concerning the importance of punishing aggression and the value of collective security. Perhaps more important, he had a diplomat's view of the utility of nuclear power which he believed to have been validated in the first year of the new Administration in ending the stalemate in Korea.

One of the Republican complaints against the Truman Administration was that it had been too feeble in prosecuting the Korean war. The hesitation over the use of atomic weapons, plus the recognition of sanctuaries beyond the Yalu River, in Chinese territory, had meant that the Western forces were severely constrained. When the Eisenhower Adminstration took over in January 1953, the Korean Armistice talks were deadlocked. Over the next year the deadlock was broken. The Administration believed that this was due to skilful employment of nuclear threats. The first break in the deadlock came in February 1953 after 'discreet' suggestions that 'in the absence of satisfactory progress, we intended to move decisively without inhibition in our use of weapons, and would no longer be responsible for confining hostilities to the Korean Peninsula'. Then, as the talks bogged down again, more hints were dropped in July 1953 to the effect that it would not be possible to observe the self-imposed restriction on US activity and that hostilities might not, in the future, be confined to Korea. In April 1954 Dulles claimed that progress had been achieved because the communists had realized that in its absence 'the battle area would be enlarged so as to endanger the sources of aggression in Manchuria'. The enemy could not rely on their sanctuaries.[8]

This must have been in Dulles's mind when, in his speech in January 1954, he emphasized the need for the free world to keep the initiative, if necessary with nuclear weapons and against any suitable targets – not only those in the immediate combat zone – even after the Soviet Union had taken it upon itself to commence hostilities.

The speech began by surveying the events of the cold war, approving the fact that responses had been taken to communist actions, but regretting that these had been hurried. 'Emergency measures are costly; they are superficial; and they imply that the enemy has the initiative. They cannot be depended on to serve our long-term interests.'[9] It would be necessary to plan for a 'long haul', to rebuff Soviet challenges but to do this 'without exhausting ourselves':

We need allies and collective security. Our purpose is to make these relations more effective, less costly. This can be done by placing more reliance on deterrent power and less dependence on local defensive power. . . .

. . . Local defense will always be important. But there is no local defense which alone will contain the mighty landpower of the Communist world. Local defenses must be reinforced by the further deterrent of massive retaliatory power. A potential aggressor must know that he cannot always prescribe battle conditions that suit him. Otherwise, for example, a potential aggressor, who is glutted with manpower, might be tempted to attack in confidence that resistance would be confined to manpower. He might be tempted to attack in places where his superiority was decisive.

The basic decision that had been made was to 'depend primarily upon a great capacity to retaliate, instantly, by means and at places of our own choosing'.

The immediate interpretation given to the doctrine was that this meant a US response, to any aggression anywhere, of massive retaliation with nuclear weapons. This was not the Administration's actual policy as set out in NSC-162/2 but was an impression easily taken from Dulles's statements on reinforcing local defences by 'the further deterrent of massive retaliatory power'. The respected columnist James Reston wrote in the *New York Times* on 16 January 1954 that Washington was saying to the Chinese and Russians 'as clearly as Governments ever say these things, that in the event of another proxy or bushfire war in Korea, Indochina, Iran or anywhere else, the United States might retaliate instantly with atomic weapons against the USSR or Red China'. The same paper, on 14 March 1954, reported Vice President Nixon as saying: 'Rather than let the Communists nibble us to death all over the world in little wars we would rely in the future primarily on our massive mobile retaliatory power which we could use in our discretion against the major source of aggression at times and places that we choose'.

Some clarification was considered to be in order. This duly appeared in *Foreign Affairs* in April 1954.[10] In this article Dulles recognized, as had done NSC-162/2, that the US 'air striking power', 'while now a dominant factor, may not have the same significance forever. Furthermore, massive atomic and thermonuclear reaction is not the kind of power which could most usefully be evoked under all circumstances'. He repudiated the notion that the US 'intended to rely wholly on large-scale strategic bombing as the sole means to deter and counter aggression'. Though such an option would always be available, it was only one of a wide variety of means available for responding to aggression. Exactly the most appropriate form of response to any given enemy action should not be disclosed publicly:

> It should not be stated in advance precisely what would be the scope of military action if new aggression occurred. . . . That is a matter as to which the aggressor had best remain ignorant. But he can know and does know, in the light of present policies, that the choice in this respect is ours and not his.

This was in contrast to NSC-162/2 where great clarity in the description of deterrent threats had been considered necessary to avoid general war through miscalculation. In opting for ambiguity, Dulles hinted at a posture later known as 'brinkmanship', whereby caution is forced on the aggressor, uncertain as to how far to the 'brink' the

United States would be willing to go. The worth of a massive retaliatory threat, declining in the face of an equivalent threat from the Soviet Union, would be upheld by bold diplomatic action.

There was an indication of a formula that might be used to measure the amount of retaliation deemed necessary as a reponse to a given amount of aggression: 'The heart of the problem is how to deter attack. This, we believe, requires that a potential aggressor be left in no doubt that he would be certain to suffer damage outweighing any possible gains from aggression'. This formula – that the costs to the aggressor must always outweigh his gains – was repeated thereafter. The important thing was to have the *capacity* to retaliate massively, because that would be the only fitting punishment to the greatest crime – an all-out attack on Western Europe. For lesser crimes a more appropriate measure of retaliation would have to be found. Dulles was thus talking about 'flexible retaliation'. This suggested a continuum of nuclear responses, and thus blurred any distinctions which may have been in the mind of the Joint Chiefs of Staff between 'strategic' and 'tactical' weapons.

As formulated the policy attempted to introduce a certainty into adversary calculations through the threat of severe sanctions that the prospective gains of any provocative military action would be outweighed by the costs. However, this did not do justice to the variety of forms a policy of deterrence could take. If the aim was to ensure that costs outweighed gains, then an alternative to the imposition of costs was the denial of gains. This was often described as 'defence' to be distinguished from 'deterrence', but if it involved local forces sufficient to beat off any attack then it could act to deter any adventures. NATO seemed to be moving towards this sort of strategy in the early 1950s.

In reversing the trend, the 'New Look' uncoupled the response from the offending action. The West would not reply in kind to an Eastern invasion but raise the stakes of war. Thereafter Western strategy would depend on convincing the Soviet leaders that it had the nerve to do this. This problem would become progressively more difficult as the Soviet capabilities to fight at the new level increased.

The obvious analogue to a policy of deterrence in international relations was deterrence in a national legal system. In order to convince anti-social elements that 'crime does not pay' costs were made explicit through punishment designed not only to stop a particular offender from making further trouble, but also to serve as warning to others. John Foster Dulles frequently employed this analogy. In the

January 1954 speech he spoke of what he was advocating for the international community as being 'accepted practice as far as local communities are concerned':

> We keep locks on our doors; but we do not have an armed guard in every home. We rely principally on a community security system so well equipped to punish any who break in and steal that, in fact, would-be-aggressors are generally deterred. That is the way of getting maximum protection at bearable cost. What the Eisenhower Administration seeks is a similar international security system.

The analogy was, however, somewhat misleading. A legal system normally involves one supreme authority capable of definitively pronouncing on matters of interpretation and of taking the responsibility for the general maintenance of law and order, because of a general monopoly of legitimate and effective violence. When challenges can be made with impunity or important constraints exist on the legitimate use of force, then there is a breakdown of law and order.

For a sanction of tough punishment to be an effective deterrent it is necessary for a would-be offender to know that there is a high chance of (a) being apprehended and (b) being punished severely. The most dire threats diminish in impact when there is little certainty that they can ever be put into effect. It is the fact that one is to be put at the mercy of the court, as much as what the court does, that constitutes the deterrent.

In strategic terms, with airpower any country could put another country at its mercy. There were no problems of making the offender available for punishment. The sanction could be applied with, in all probability, a minimum of resistance. The offender, nevertheless, would not have to be apprehended by the forces of the law (which strategically would take the form of occupation of his territory) and so would remain a free agent. Moreover, he might well have means of replying to the punishment. The fact that a transgressor maintained options other than full compliance with the dictates of international law, including the option of replying in kind to any sanction, undermined the credibility of the threat of sanctions. This represented the central problem in all deterrence theory. How credible was a threat of punishment that would literally, as the schoolmaster says as he prepares to spank a naughty schoolboy, 'hurt me as much as it hurts you'?

The Spirit of the Offence

An immediate and lasting result of the 'New Look' was that NATO strategy became oriented around a hope that nuclear weapons could be employed in such a way as to particularly favour the West. However, events in Indo-China, where there was concern that the Chinese might intervene on behalf of the Viet Minh in their war against the French, suggested that the Administration was not quite as daring with atomic weapons as it might care to think. In September 1953 Dulles warned China that any physical involvement in the dispute 'could not occur without grave consequences, which might not be confined to Indo-China'. The timing of his 'massive retaliation' speech was widely seen as being geared to Indo-China. The use of nuclear weapons was being considered at the time, to help the French out at the battle of Dien Bien Phu. It was then dismissed, but not purely because of a loss of nerve at the crunch. If the United States had decided to intervene, nuclear weapons might well have been used. The constraining factor was that this would still have involved committing large numbers of ground forces to Indo-China. Contrary to the view that the use of nuclear weapons in a tactical mode would obviate the necessity for a large number of troops, the Army insisted that such use of nuclear weapons 'would not reduce the number of ground forces required to achieve a victory in Indo-China'.[11]

How then are we to view the 'New Look'? On one level it was a revival of the spirit of the offence in military strategy. The strategic concepts of the Truman years were cautious and restrained. The communists would be only contained; the main aim was defence. In battle there should be nothing provocative, nothing that might extend the conflict into a cataclysmic war. To those reared in the tradition of total war for unconditional surrender this all seemed unnecessarily restrictive. MacArthur spoke of 'no substitute for victory', the Strategic Air Command scornfully of a 'Maginot Line mentality' as if the German circumvention of France's static defences in 1940 served as a judgment on all attempts to 'hold a line'. With a cry that the 'best defence is offence' and a conviction that the communists had far more to fear from a general war than had the free world, the opponents of Truman argued that the American advantages should be capitalized to the full. The Republican Administration endorsed these sentiments but not the policies associated with them. It too, through Dulles, spoke, at length, about the need to 'seize the initiative' and refused to accept any restrictions on targets or weapons. But, though the new

Administration's policy appeared more muscular in practice, there was still a recognition of the restraints imposed by the horrendous consequences of a slide into total war, and of the growing strength of the Soviet Union's own capacity for massive retaliation.

If anything the strategy was more retrospective than prospective. It explained how the Korean War ought to have been fought. It explained how a new war might be fought during the remaining period of grace of patent nuclear superiority. Observing the influence of US airpower on Soviet conduct, it sought to exploit this to avoid meeting the cost of conventional rearmament. A nuclear strategy was far cheaper than a conventional strategy.

Because of this strong economic point in the New Look's favour, one that has remained impressive ever since, the emphasis on nuclear weapons became a permanent feature of NATO's strategy. Apart from one moment in the Kennedy Administration when serious consideration was given to dealing with the Warsaw Pact on its own terms, the notion that the West cannot afford to match the East in conventional forces became firmly established in NATO minds. American troops in Europe served to signify a US commitment to NATO – not a means of blocking a Soviet advance. Their rôle was not as a shield but as a 'trip-wire', capable of triggering the entry into a war of America's nuclear arsenal.

The economic logic remained forceful if the military logic could be only temporary. The circumstances which made the strategy plausible would pass. Dulles, however, appeared to suggest that the new posture was a statement of basic principles appropriate for the new age, and not just the coming few years. His rigid presentation offered critics a ready target. When he attempted to qualify and elaborate, he only made it worse. A flawed strategy that arguably increased the risk of nuclear war sufficed to stimulate an interest in military matters amongst intellectuals. A strategy that was also inconsistent and contradictory was a positive incitement for intellectual criticism.

Section 3

Limited War

7 Limited Objectives

Consensus on a Nuclear Strategy

The strategic debate that developed in the US during the mid-1950s was impressive both for its vigour and, viewed in retrospect, its underlying consensus. The debate found the Administration, with qualified support from the Air Force, ranged against almost every other interested party. The immediate stake was the size and composition of the defence budget. The Army and the Navy sought to check the rise in the proportion of the budget devoted to strategic air power. There have been few greater stimuli to creative thought than competition over the allocations of men, money, and equipment to the armed services.

A stimulus to the debate more powerful to those without a direct interest in the defence budget was the meaning of the awesome properties of thermonuclear weapons which was gradually sinking into the public consciousness. As information became available on the growth of destructive capabilities and the lingering after-effects of radioactive fallout,[1] and as it became apparent that Western cities were becoming vulnerable to these weapons, awareness of the gravity of the situation was heightened. With the cold war still the defining characteristic of international relations and an arms race gathering pace, the manner in which statesmen spoke of nuclear arsenals and their readiness to brandish them in power games became a topic of abiding interest.

The prospect of nuclear annihilation had yet to become a cliché;

the 'shadow of the bomb' was still a novel sensation. Given the feeling that one false and ill-considered move could result in the 'end of civilization as we know it' the significance of the slightest nuance or element of style became amplified. A rigorous analysis of the utterances of both Dulles and his critics can reveal great similarities by way of premises, logic, and conclusions, but what mattered at the time were the variations in attitudes over the use of nuclear weapons as instruments of international politics.

The danger of nuclear war put a premium on stable, calm personalities for those with 'a finger on the button'. Equally, the danger of Soviet aggression, generally taken seriously, put a premium on being 'tough' and courageous. People wished to be neither 'dead' nor 'red'. The effort to avoid having to make the choice had become the central problem of Western strategic thought. A contribution to its resolution, especially if it came from a statesman such as Dulles, was judged by reference to actions as well as words. These factors provided the broad political and emotional context in which the debate triggered by the 'Massive Retaliation' speech of Dulles took place.

Having said that, it is as well to note just how much was agreed between the various participants in this debate. First, arguments on the efficacy of strategic bombing had been settled conclusively. Nuclear weapons were available in abundance and there was no known defence against their use. Even Blackett, once the most sceptical of all regarding the claims made on behalf of strategic bombardment, now worked on the assumption that 'there is no effective defence at present, nor is there one in sight, against a large-scale and determined atomic attack on cities and centres of population. In relation to strategic air power, offence has now definitely the ascendancy over defence'.

Second, as Blackett also noted, 'this applies to both East and West'.[2] A stalemate was perceived to be evolving. An early and dramatic warning of its imminence came from Robert Oppenheimer in mid-1953:

> We may anticipate a state of affairs in which the two Great Powers will each be in a position to put an end to the civilization and life of the other, though not without risking its own. We may be likened to two scorpions in a bottle, each capable of killing the other, but only at the risk of his own life.[3]

As the aircraft carrying atomic weapons of both sides would be able to 'get through', the net effect would be for each force to neutralize the other. Both sides would hold back out of a fear of retaliation. Recognition of the extent to which that retaliatory capability would have to be cared for and protected did not become widespread until the late 1950s. For most of the decade the imminence of a strategic stalemate was taken as a basic premise.

Third, there was little doubt that the Soviet Union was a 'potential aggressor'. In fact aggression, in various forms and guises, was considered to be the normal mode of behaviour for the Soviet Union. If the integrity of the non-communist world, often described euphemistically as the 'free world', was to be preserved there was a requirement for constant vigilance. Diplomatic means to solve the cold war were considered impractical and dangerous, in that they involved concessions to Soviet demands. The result of this, it was supposed, would be only to add to the Kremlin's appetite. To any suggestion to the contrary, attention was drawn to the sorry consequences of appeasement in the 1930s. Nor was there much disagreement with the proposition that communist aggression in the coming years, under the shield of the nuclear stalemate, would take the form of local, controlled actions, often on a small scale, using all available means, political, psychological, economic and military, short of general war. The terminology of the time admitted of 'brush-fire wars', something that would rapidly expand unless beaten down promptly, and of 'salami tactics', in which the aggressor would attain his objectives in the shape of numerous, small, thin slices – each by itself not worth a major Western response but taken together constituting substantial gains.

Fourth, there was a consensus that a nuclear strategy could work to the advantage of the West. The Soviet Bloc had a tremendous superiority in manpower which, in its designated role as aggressor, it was able to deploy at times and places of its own choosing in order to initiate a confrontation. If the West could not avoid the reactive second move, it need not feel bound by the East's definition of the character of the contest; it should respond in a manner to its own choosing. And it was accepted also, though not quite as unanimously, that in most cases the West would not choose conventional weapons, an area in which it was, numerically at least, patently inferior. The area where the West was still superior over the East, in terms of quality and quantity, was that of nuclear weapons. Where there was a debate in the West was over the types of nuclear weapons, the most suitable targets for them, and the contingencies in which their use should be considered.

The critics (a collection of Democrats, soldiers, sailors, and a growing band of academic specialists in defence) charged the Administration with being wedded to a view of war as inevitably an all-encompassing, no-holds-barred, struggle for the highest stakes. The Administration was prepared, on occasion, to acknowledge the imminence of a stalemate in general war capabilities, but it was doubted whether it had really come to terms with the strategic implications of this. As it was now in everyone's interest to avoid general war, a diplomacy based upon it would be inhibited. Both the Administration and its critics spoke of the need for a full range of nuclear capabilities (only some of the critics sought a major conventional option) but the critics saw little political or military benefit, other than neutralizing the comparable Soviet forces, in a capability for massive retaliation.

As we shall see, those critics who argued for a 'tactical' nuclear option succeeded in getting themselves in as much of an intellectual tangle as the Administration and its supporters. This was, in part, because of a lack of clarity in the concept of 'tactical' nuclear weapons, apparently a tolerable species of an unpleasant genus, and how they were to be distinguished from 'strategic' nuclear weapons. It was also because of a confusion over how tactical nuclear weapons were to be used. Was this to be in a conventional mode, to enhance traditional war-fighting capabilities and so block any Soviet agressive move, at whatever level it occurred, without having to resort to strategic attacks on cities and so total war? Or was it to be a form of deterrence, a smaller punishment for a smaller crime, though carrying with it the implied threat of the larger punishment if the aggressive activity persisted and expanded?

Tactical nuclear weapons could therefore be seen in terms of deterrence either through the denial of gains or through the imposition of excessive costs. To the critics, the Dulles version of deterrence could be faulted for its lack of 'credibility'. An intellectual search began for a method to inject this magic ingredient into strategy. The basic principle of deterrence – that the potential enemy's behaviour could be manipulated through threats – was not subjected to severe scrutiny.

One key source of credibility was the setting of limited and attainable objectives to guide the use of military means. Much of limited war theory is a plea for moderation in political rhetoric, a warning against a diplomacy based on belligerence and the rigid adherence to war-aims that permit nothing but the enemy's unconditional surrender.

The problem was underlined when **Paul Kecskemeti** of the RAND Corporation published a book with 'surrender' in the title which examined the problems of pursuing total objectives when this could lead to the destruction of one's own society. Kecskemeti pointed to the tension between the US tradition of fighting for 'unconditional surrender' so as to eradicate the evil enemy system completely and the need, resulting from the mutual fear of nuclear annihilation, of coming to terms with the enemy. War aims which required the destruction of the enemy leadership were becoming unattainable, yet the rhetoric of the cold war made compromise with the Kremlin appear quite unsatisfactory.[4]

When garbled reports of this book reached the US Congress, Senator Russell of Georgia, Chairman of the Armed Services Committee, became convinced that Kecskemeti's book was concerned with 'how, when, where or under what circumstances the Government would surrender this country and its people'. He introduced an amendment to a military appropriation bill which would ensure that taxes would not be used 'to conduct any studies concerning the circumstances under which the United States would surrender to any aggressor'. The Defense Department, in defending the study, indicated their sensitivity to the prevailing mood when it claimed, quite inaccurately, that the book discussed how the US might win a war and cause the surrender of its enemies.[5]

The task before the limited war theorists was difficult, involving basic changes in the climate of opinion. If that could be achieved, narrower strategic problems would be more soluble. The hope was that once it was recognized that any wars could only be fought for limited ends, the problem of controlling a military conflict, through the process which later came to be known as escalation, would become more manageable.

The prospect of total victory would have to be eschewed in return for reprieve from possible total defeat. This raised one of the most significant hypotheses of contemporary strategic thought – the possibility that a modern war, even a nuclear war, could be fought according to some conventions, tacit or explicit, that could contain hostilities.

The Concept of Limited War

The intellectual father of contemporary theories of limited war was Captain Basil Liddell Hart. Liddell Hart's advocacy of this approach to war stemmed from his whole philosophy. It was not, as it was with many of the 1950s adherents, a pragmatic response to the exigencies of the moment. To Liddell Hart it was axiomatic that, because of the suffering and the disruption of normal relations between nation states caused by war, wars should be limited.

Liddell Hart's achievement was to develop an alternative to the prevailing strategies of total war based on sound principles rather than simply an emotional response to the horror of it all. Since the late nineteenth century, at a series of international conferences, there had been attempts to agree on means of containing war as a social institution and to maintain a sharp distinction, through bans on indiscriminate weapons and prohibitions on attacks on commerce and cities, between the military and the civilian spheres.[6] The attempt had been to preserve the traditional forms of warfare in response to the steady progress of military technology. It had been to little or no avail.

Liddell Hart sought to remind his audience that wars were but an unpleasant episode in relations between nations, and were usually avoidable. The country that you now called an enemy might be needed as a friend in the future. War should therefore be a controlled affair, conducted with the minimum of fuss and bother and without the barbarous excesses to which the most civilized democracies seemed capable once their ire had been raised, the result of which was to inflict superfluous suffering, encourage reprisals and lower all standards.

The development of airpower had introduced a source of tension into Liddell Hart's theories. At first he saw the ability to move right to the heart, and the brain, of the enemy without the painful necessity of proceeding through battlefields as a logical development. It seemed to fit in with his own preference for an 'indirect strategy', that is one aimed at the 'dislocation of the enemy's psychological and physical balance', rather than a predictable struggle 'along the line of natural expectation'.[7] However, though a method of paralysing the enemy's will, airpower was a blunt instrument. It resulted in brutal attacks on civilians which would increase the hostility between the two sides and render the objective of a moderate, negotiated peace more distant. The bluntness of the air instrument also offended against Liddell Hart's sense of the military art. By the start of World War II he had come round to a view, that became quite prevalent after the war, namely that airpower did not constitute a means of delivering a decisive, paralysing blow but was merely another means of attrition – but one that pushed the dehumanizing trend of modern warfare a stage further.

Thus Liddell Hart's critique of total war pre-dated the atomic bomb and had indeed been articulated throughout World War II. The atomic bomb served to confirm his worst fears. Writing just after Hiroshima, he did not look to the immediate future but anticipated the age of large nuclear stockpiles and rocket carriers available to both sides in a war. In such circumstances nothing of benefit to anybody could result from a war:

> When both sides possess atomic power, 'total warfare' makes non-sense. Total warfare implies that the aim, the effort, and the degree of violence are unlimited. Victory is pursued without regard to the consequences. . . . Any unlimited war waged with atomic power would be worse than nonsense; it would be mutually suicidal.

He further argued, almost uniquely at the time and in contrast to the strong belief that atomic bombs would make *all* warfare unthinkable, that it was by no means certain that 'warfare will completely disappear. But, unless the belligerent leaders are crazy, it is likely that any future war will be less unrestrained and more subject to mutually agreed rules. Within such limits it may develop new forms.' For instance, aggressors might avoid direct confrontations but prefer subtle means of 'infiltration' that would 'check the employment of atomic bombing in retort'.[8]

Liddell Hart's views on limited war were not readily accepted in the 1940s. However preferable in principle, in practice such wars were hard to arrange. War appeared to many as an activity limited only by the quantity and quality of military capabilities. It might be best to understand the enemy in human terms, unless, as in the last war, the enemy was so genuinely barbarous that compromise was impossible. For restraints on weapons and targets to hold, a modicum of trust was needed, and this tended to be in short supply in war. When the issues were the survival of whole civilizations, a way of life or a national identity, there was little inclination to admit defeat, or to show mercy, or to miss any opportunity to bring it all to a satis-factory conclusion, even if that meant the employment of distasteful methods. Perhaps the strongest charge against Liddell Hart was that he was out of touch with his time. The distinguished American strategist Edward Mead Earle accused him of being 'nostalgic'. 'Wars are an inherent part of the societies within which they are fought', which meant that they were now 'primarily battles of production and logistics'. 'No nation possessed of sea power has ever abandoned the blockade; it is unlikely that any nation possessed of air power will abandon bombing as a means of immobilizing the enemy'.[9]

Liddell Hart found no reason to change his views. The stupendous accretions of destructive power represented by H-bombs underlined his arguments. Not long after Dulles's 'massive retaliation' speech, he repeated his earlier arguments.

> Would any responsible government, when it came to the point, dare to *use* the H-bomb as an answer to local and limited aggression? . . . To the extent that the H-bomb reduces the likelihood of full-scale war, it *increases* the possibilities of limited war pursued by widespread local aggression: . . . the value of strategic bombing forces has largely disappeared – except as the last resort.[10]

By now Liddell Hart was not alone. The approach of a thermonuclear stalemate had alerted many to the danger of assuming the inevitability of total war. Bernard Brodie wrote to Liddell Hart how 'I became in effect a follower of yours early in 1952, when I learned . . . that a thermonuclear weapon would be tested in the following autumn and would probably be successful'.[11]

In 1954 Brodie, who had always recognized the role of nuclear threats as a source of restraint, argued that 'The availability of this threat as a deterrent will be increasingly limited to only the most outrageous kind of direct aggression'. A prudent regard for the suicidal character of nuclear exchanges, when the West seemed to be relying on a threat of total war, would create a 'diplomacy straightjacketed by fear'. It was therefore necessary to 'explore ways of consciously limiting those conflicts we may be unable entirely to avoid'.[12]

This message was frequently repeated over the next two years. In 1956 a collection of essays edited by William Kaufmann, entitled *Military Policy and National Security* appeared, providing a forum for a number of critics of 'massive retaliation'. In his introductory essay, which had been distributed as a monograph in 1954, Kaufmann stressed the importance of 'credibility'. In assessing the risk of an American response to any aggression, the enemy would use three sources of information: the statements and behaviour of the US government; the attitudes of public opinion; and also the 'government's performance in comparable contingencies'. He then noted, with justice, that the up-to-date evidence of East–West confrontations would suggest that it would be 'out of character' for the US to retaliate massively. In fact, it would suggest 'rather strongly that the United States is willing – and, it should be added, able – to meet [Soviet efforts at expansion] successfully on the grounds and according to the rules set by the opponent'. If the United States was unable to respond in this way, because of the communists' own ability to retaliate on a massive scale, then any threats it cared to make with regard to less-than-total provocations would not be taken seriously.

> It the Communists should challenge our sincerity and they would have good reasons for daring to do so, we would either have to put up or shut up. If we put up, we would plunge into all the immeasurable horrors of atomic war. If we shut up, we would suffer a serious loss of prestige and damage our capacity to establish deterrents against further Communist expansion.[13]

The same message – that the choice was between having to put up or shut up – was repeated in different forms throughout the 1950s. It would be 'holocaust or humiliation'; 'suicide or surrender', 'sudden destruction or slow defeat'.

In 1957 Robert Osgood published a book which sought to establish the theoretical and historical credentials of limited war. He stressed that the 'principal justification of limited war lies in the fact that it maximises the opportunities for the effective use of military force as a rational instrument of policy', and then argued that America's experience in the twentieth century had proved to be so unsatisfactory because of a failure to establish this link between military power and national policy. Recognition had been forced upon her since 1945, but the process of adaptation had been partial and *ad hoc*. The Korean War, fought according to the right principles, especially that of the primacy of politics, had proved to be so traumatic for the American people because these principles had been inadequately explained. It was now necessary, to achieve success in the cold war, to confront this problem in an organized and systematic manner. If there was to be a strategy of deterrence it had to be credible, and 'credibility, in turn, requires that the means of deterrence be proportionate to the objectives at stake'.[14] This was the essential principle of the limited war theorists.

The most stimulating book of the mid-1950s, bringing this debate to a wider public, was Henry Kissinger's *Nuclear Weapons and Foreign Policy*, also published in 1957. Kissinger was acting as rapporteur for a Council on Foreign Relations study group which included a number of Democrats and supporters of the army. Though not original in its basic formulations, it was written in a challenging, confident, and assertive style. Kissinger too attacked the propensity of the Americans to think in total, absolute categories, in which war and peace, the military and politics, were seen as separate and opposite. The only available doctrine was one concerned with the repulsion of overt aggression. Atomic bombs had been seen as 'merely another tool in a concept of warfare which knew no goal save total victory and no mode of war except all-out war'. But now the problem of limited war had 'forced itself on American strategic thought despite itself'. With the end of the atomic monopoly 'it is no longer possible to impose unconditional surrender at an acceptable cost' nor could one 'combine a deterrent based on a threat of maximum destructiveness with a strategy of minimum risk'.

This problem of limited war could not be understood in purely military terms. To stop when ahead but not triumphant, or when behind but not defeated, was against military logic. 'The prerequisite for a policy of limited war is to reintroduce the political element into our concept of warfare and to discard the notion that policy ends when war begins or that war can have goals distinct from those of national policy'.[15]

Limited Objectives

Much of the effort of the limited war theorists was educational, attempting to explain the realities of international life, and in particular of the growth of Soviet power, to an audience that appeared to be temperamentally unsuited to a moderate approach to war. The need was to calm the spirit of the offence, potent in air force circles and influential in the Administration. The Administration might recognize the need for restraint in actual crises, but its rhetoric encouraged a view of war that was out-moded and dangerous, with an expectation of a decisive showdown between East and West.

This is why these theorists – Brodie, Kaufmann, Kissinger and Osgood – all made a special point of insisting on the need to scale down America's political and military aspirations. Brodie wrote: 'The one basic proposition which must be established in the minds of men if progress is to be made towards resolving our terrible military dilemma is this: limited war must mean also limited objectives'.[16]

This basic proposition was true as far as it went. Limited objectives would be a necessary condition for limited war. But they would not guarantee a limited war. The Great War had started amidst considerable confusion over war-aims, and those that were clear were not immoderate. In this conflict, as in others, the war-aims began to grow in scope and intensity with the steady expansion of the fighting. What was being asserted was not a fundamental truth but an observation related to the circumstances of the time. Thus, the best historical precedents could be found in the eighteenth century, before the Industrial Revolution. This point needs some further elaboration.

Osgood defined limited war as one in which 'the belligerents restrict the purposes for which they fight to concrete, well-defined objectives that do not demand the utmost military effort of which the belligerents are capable and that can be accommodated in a negotiated settlement'.[17] There is a clear suggestion of a symmetry between the two belligerents in both capabilities and intentions. One could argue that the question of *intentional* limitation of war arose only when there was a reasonable symmetry of capabilities, sufficient to ensure that the outcome of a conflict was not a foregone conclusion. Many wars are limited unavoidably, for example because of logistical problems caused by the awkward location of the territories in contention, or because large distances between the territories of the combatants makes invasion impossible. Or else a war is limited for one side, in the sense mentioned by Osgood with 'economic, social and political patterns of existence' continuing without 'serious disruption', while the experience for the other is of total war. A war between a major power and a minor power would take on this appearance.

For the United States in the 1950s, war with any potential enemy other than the Soviet Union would be 'limited' for she would have no reason to extend herself. It was only when facing a country with approximately equivalent capabilities for general war, which meant the Soviet Union, that a victory became less than a 100 per cent certainty. Then the United States would have to accept, as other countries with more limited resources had often before had to accept, that the successful conclusion of a war could not be guaranteed and would only come at substantial cost. This was a novel idea *only* to the United States.

There was little doubt that if either super-power tried to attack the other the resulting clash would be anything but limited. It was also suspected that a full-scale Soviet attack on Europe, because of the objectives inherent in the action, would also be total. The problems would come in the 'grey areas' – disputed territories between East and West. The key assumption was that any trouble, whether subversion, civil war, or claims on the territory of another, would be inspired, or at least supported by, the Soviet Union.

Not only did the Kremlin have an interest in fomenting trouble everywhere, but also it was assumed to be actually in control of the individual conflicts and thus able to negotiate settlements. Recalling the necessity for the symmetry of intentions as well as capabilities, this adversary, despite persistent efforts for new gains, must recognize the logic of limited war, of the need to accept restraints.

> The basic assumption for this kind of conflict – and it is one that appears to correspond accurately with reality under existing conditions – is the assumption of a calculating individual with a multiplicity of values, aware of cost and risk as well as advantage, and capable of drawing significant inferences from symbolic acts.[18]

With this interpretation of the likely motives and behaviour of the Soviet Union, the prospect of limited war, though more appealing than total war, was still one of permanent but indecisive hostilities between East and West. There was to be little resemblance to the limited wars of the past, which had not been limited through recognition of a capacity for mutual destruction but because the objectives were genuinely limited. Wars were not over fundamentals and, at least in the pre-Napoleonic days, had had a low ideological content. They were not expected to lead to irreparable damage between nations. Alliances and enmities were fragile. In the 1950s the argument between East and West was considered to be fundamental and the two positions irreconcilable. It was only the possibility of mutual destruction that provided the incentive for restraint.

The difficulty lay in deciding upon objectives that were moderate enough to permit eventual compromise yet worthy enough to impel the necessary mobilization and risk-taking that even a limited war required. If only a restricted amount could be achieved and the stakes were small, could the effort be justified? If the stakes were high enough, could each side be persuaded to pull punches? In practice, the limitation of objectives meant that there could be no attempt to force the unconditional surrender of the Soviet Union. In the past the elimination of the offending country, or at least its regime and armed forces, had sometimes been adopted as a war-aim. Such a demand would now be unrealistic. It had to be accepted that even if hostilities could be concluded to the West's satisfaction, the East would live to fight another day.

This was spelled out in a 1957 article by James King:

> We cannot win the cold war by military means alone. We cannot be confident of our ability to destroy International Communism as we destroyed National Socialism, because International Communism is armed with weapons that would very likely destroy us too. We cannot liquidate the cold war; we must live with it and fight it on terms that make sense.

The only victories to be expected were gains in the cold war balance of advantage. The result would always be frustrating; the basic stalemate would remain. 'Properly considered, then, limited wars are but episodes of increased tension and irritation in this ceaseless striving to retain a political position and to gain political advantage'.[19]

If the Soviet Union lacked the bomb or could not be linked with those occasional hostilities, such as colonial wars, with which Western countries were getting involved, there would have been no great enthusiasm for limited war. It was not a theory about the primacy of political objectives over military means, but of the primacy of military realities over political objectives.

8 Limited Means

Limited Nuclear War

Henry Kissinger wrote that 'The more moderate the objective, the less violent war is likely to be', as if the choice of weapons and the manner of their use would be governed by the war-aims of the contestants. Yet the choice of means had to be decided on the basis of those available, and the problem faced by the proponents of limited war was that the means most appropriate for limited objectives – strong, local conventional forces – were by far the most expensive. However strong the argument for conventional forces in terms of military logic, it would not carry the day if there were no funds available from hard-pressed and restricted national budgets (paradoxically, limited budgets did not make for limited war). In consequence many, but not all, of the proponents opted for 'tactical' nuclear weapons. This was not with great reluctance for, it should be remembered, there had long been an interest in the use of small nuclear weapons in a tactical mode amongst those who had been seeking an alternative to strategic bombardment as the centre-piece of Western defence.

Therefore, what many were writing about was limited *nuclear* war. Bernard Brodie wrote:

Whether or not we can relinquish strategic bombing as a way of war, we can hardly afford to abjure tactical use of such weapons without dooming ourselves and allies to a permanent inferiority to the Soviet and satellite armies in Europe.

106

Robert Osgood said much the same:

> With the Communist superiority in trained manpower, magnified
> by our own reductions in ground troops, these weapons may be
> virtually the only effective means the West possesses for checking
> local Communist advances, short of massive strategic retaliation.[1]

It was believed that this was likely to be an area of overwhelming
Western superiority for some time to come, at least until the end of
the 1950s. Soviet nuclear technology was still in its infancy. Not only
were the Russians some way from refining small fission bombs for
tactical use, but they were still building up their stockpile for strategic
use and could not spare any for battlefield operations.

The argument in favour of tactical nuclear weapons was not simply
that this was an area of Western superiority. It was felt that these
were weapons that favoured the defender of territory – the position
the West expected to be in when facing communist aggression. The
proposition was that offensive action required the concentration of
forces, and that once so concentrated these forces would provide an
attractive target for nuclear weapons. Furthermore, with a quantum
jump in available firepower per man, a smaller army would suffice. As
Denis Healey noted in Britain: 'An army equipped with tactical
nuclear weapons should be able to hold up an enemy many times its
own size.' Blackett, his compatriot, gave a qualified endorsement of this
view, while adding that 'it may prove false': 'Highly trained and heavily
equipped land forces might exploit tactical atomic weapons for effective
offence.'[2]

Others also noted this possibility. Could not the offence use the
extra firepower to breach a hole in the defence through which it could
then move? In these circumstances the defence would have to remain
dispersed, making it harder to concentrate its firepower and hold a
line. All that this indicated was that, in preparing to fight war in
which *both* sides would be armed with nuclear weapons, new tactical
doctrines would have to be developed.

The most celebrated effort to develop a doctrine for limited nuclear
war was that of Henry Kissinger. He insisted on the need to be rid of
the concepts of old-fashioned land warfare, taking sea warfare as a
more appropriate model, 'in which self-contained units with great
firepower gradually gain the upper hand by destroying their enemy
counterparts without physically occupying territory or establishing a
front-line'. Thus the units for tactical nuclear warfare should be small

so as not to provide a worthwhile target for the enemy. Because nuclear firepower would not depend on numbers these small units should be mobile (to avoid detection and thus easy destruction) and self-contained 'because the supply system of World War II is far too vulnerable to interdiction'. The ability of these units to carry their own supplies and maintain their own equipment was important in Kissinger's scheme of things. Forces would be much less dependent upon lines of supply. The lines of supply therefore, which usually passed through centres of population, would be less attractive as targets. In an age of nuclear plenty, forces in being at the start of hostilities would suffice. Future wars would be less 'wars of production' and there would be less interest in attacking cities as centres of production. Cities might therefore be spared completely the horror of bombardment, so keeping the war limited. 'With cities no longer serving as key elements in the communications system of the military forces, the risks of initiating city bombing may outweigh the gains which can be achieved.'[3]

It was not, as Kissinger himself eventually came to realize, quite as easy as that. Certainly the US Army had already by 1957 come to the conclusion, which it was not too unhappy to reach, that nuclear weapons could not be relied upon to reduce manpower requirements. Once involved with large ground forces, a support organization was needed. Large forces were required because the rates of attrition must be expected to be high and because, presumably, there would still be an advantage in having superior numbers of nuclear delivery systems and warheads. Furthermore, these would constitute a prize for the other side. Nuclear weapons were useful mainly against fixed targets rather than moving 'targets of opportunity'. In consequences, so as to be less vulnerable to the other side, the units were to be mobile. But could they not be attacked by mobile *conventional* forces? To guard against this eventuality conventional forces of some size would be needed, not only to beat off a conventional attack but also to protect the nuclear delivery systems – and then it would be necessary to provide a logistics organization to support them, and once any form of logistics organization is set up this too has to be protected.

Kissinger's arguments on how to do away with such an organization were the least satisfactory aspect of his case, depending on futile hopes of technological advances. As tactical nuclear weapons were considered particularly suitable for interdiction, lines of communication would soon be under attack. Once this began to happen the consequences for the society playing host to the battle would be horrific. As James King, who developed these arguments in one of the most penetrating critiques of the Kissinger strategy, observed, there could be no promise of 'immunity to society and its facilities'.

On the contrary, sizeable opposing forces nervously trying to get in the first effective nuclear blow will use far more nuclear weapons than the one-per-battle unit theoretically necessary to do the job if all hit their marks, and civilian facilities and centers will be used because using them will enable both sides to increase their forces.[4]

William Kaufmann, reviewing Kissinger's work emphasized the implausibility of civilians surviving a limited nuclear war with as much ease as in a conventional war. 'In his version of warfare, airmen do not get panicky and jettison their bombs, or hit the wrong targets, missiles do not go astray, and heavily populated areas – whether rural or urban – do not suffer thereby. Surely this is wishful thinking.'[5]

All the practical exercises with simulated tactical nuclear weapons also suggested that it was wishful thinking. This would be a war in which the 'fog of war' would be even murkier than usual. With both sides dispersed, one's own troops would be hard to identify and communication would be extremely difficult. These would be battles of great confusion; the casualties would be high; troops would be left isolated and leaderless; and morale would be hard to maintain. It would be difficult to ensure uncontaminated supplies of food and water or even of spare parts. The Army found it extremely difficult to work out how to prepare soldiers for this sort of battle and to fight it with confidence.[6]

A more alarming conclusion was that there seemed little hope of protecting civilians from the worst effects of nuclear explosions. Two exercises became notorious: Operation Sage Brush, a war game in Louisiana (the size of Greece and Portugal) in which, after some seventy bombs, each of not more than 40 kilotons yield, had been dropped on military targets, the umpires ruled that all life in the state had 'ceased to exist'. In an exercise called Carte Blanche in West Germany in the same year tactical weapons were 'used' only by the NATO Allies. The results showed that the German people would be devastated in this sort of nuclear war through the effects of blast and fallout. Over two days, 355 devices were exploded, mostly over West German territory. Even without the effects of residual radiation, this would have left up to 1.7 million West Germans dead and 3.5 million wounded – more than five times the number of German civilian casualties in World War II. West German public opinion was alarmed. This could hardly be considered to be either a 'tactical' or a 'limited' matter.

The recognition that tactical nuclear weapons could not be used in such a precise, discriminating manner as to spare civilians had two consequences. First, it meant that if they were to be used it was best that they were used early on in a conflict and before the invading forces had captured much territory. If it were true that nuclear weapons favoured the defence, then they would be of little use in regaining lost ground and a forward defence would avoid too much of Germany becoming a nuclear battleground. Some felt that the results of these exercises did no more than preclude defending Europe with tactical nuclear weapons. Elsewhere, where the population was less dense and there were large open spaces, their use might still be appropriate. This view was criticized as rendering the West vulnerable to the charge that it only considered nuclear weapons appropriate for use against Asians.

The second consequence of appreciating the local consequences of limited nuclear war was to cast grave doubts on the notion that tactical nuclear weapons could be considered virtually conventional in nature. Many nations, especially those whose allegiance to the West was wavering, would not be pleased to be defended with these weapons. There would therefore be strong grounds for holding back on their use. If not quite 'weapons of last resort' they would be of 'penultimate resort'. But any employment after defeats in conventional battles would be over friendly territory, accentuating the problem of inflicting nuclear devastation on people whose rights to self-determination justified the fighting in the first place. What was certain was that the use of nuclear weapons could never be a purely 'tactical' decision, taken by the local commander according to the state of battle. It would be a strategic decision to be taken at the highest level and with reference to the prevailing, overall political and military situation.

The Soviet View

It takes two to keep a war limited. The United States might wish to fight for limited objectives but the Soviet Union could be intending to annex a large segment of Western Europe. The United States might hope to confine its firepower to the battlefield, but it might suit the

Soviet purpose to expand the combat zone. In principle Soviet doctrine allowed for wars of virtually any type. Little interest was claimed in starting a war, so strategy was ostensibly reactive. In addition, there was a congruity between the Soviet and the Western limited war advocates when it came to a preference for directing attacks at the armed forces of the enemy rather than his civilian population. Where the Soviet Union refused to go along with many of the Western theorists was in the proposition that a war in which nuclear weapons were used could in any way be described as 'limited'.

The development of Soviet nuclear strategy will be discussed in Chapter 17. For the moment only Soviet reactions to the notion of 'tactical' nuclear weapons need be noted. It was only very rarely that Soviet commentators admitted that such a category was at all legitimate. They would still be 'weapons of mass destruction' and, however restrained in their first use, they would still result in all-out exchanges. For small tasks on the battlefield, conventional weapons were usually sufficient, and employment on a wide scale, especially against such targets as railway junctions and munition plants, would result in huge loss of life. Grave doubt was expressed over the prospects for precise use and over the possibility of separating military targets from the civilian population.

The Russians certainly expected nuclear weapons to be used on the battlefield. In early 1956 Marshal Zhukov told the 20th Party Congress that: 'In recent years considerable work on the training of troops in the art of conducting combat operations under conditions of the use of atomic weapons and other new weapons in the ground forces, aviation, and the navy has been conducted.'[7] Soviet field manuals reassured troops as to the prospects for survival when under nuclear attack. The tactical response to tactical atomic weapons was similar to that anticipated in the West: greater dispersion and mobility. More use would be made of airborne forces and of tanks, considered less vulnerable to atomic explosions. A Major-General of the Tank Troops proposed in 1957 that 'Under conditions of the employment of atomic weapons, troops will in general operate dispersed in order to save men and material, collecting into a striking concentration only at the time of attack.' Another suggestion was a 'hugging' technique, 'The best defence against an atomic strike is precipitate closing with the enemy', so that he could not use the weapons without putting his own troops at risk.

This was one example of the extent to which the threat of employment of atomic weapons on the battlefield could stimulate offensive action. Another example was in the encouragement of pre-emptive strikes. To quote Major-General Pokrovsky: 'The role of timely detection and destruction of the enemy's atomic weapons ... increases.' Finally it was argued that 'atomic weapons significantly increase the offensive potentialities of the ground troops'. This would be by means of 'a swift breakthrough of defensive lines and destruction of the tactical and close operational reserves of the enemy'.

Official Soviet writing thus gave little encouragement to the view that employment of tactical nuclear weapons was either consistent with a desire for limited war or liable to favour the defence. Once the Soviet Union had accumulated its own stockpiles then, with its offensive strategy, it could still gain the advantage. It was acknowledged that ground combat under atomic conditions would involve great loss of life. Lieutenant-General Krasilnikov of the General Staff commented in 1956 that nuclear warfare 'calls, not for the reduction in the numbers of various divisions of the combatants, but for their logical further increase, since the threat of wiping out large divisions grows, and for their replacement large reserves will be needed'. In such a grisly war of nuclear attrition, the mass armies of the East would be an advantage.

Graduated Deterrence

Though there were problems in using 'tactical' nuclear weapons purely for the purposes of local defence they might still have a rôle in strengthening the credibility of deterrence. There is an important distinction, which has already been mentioned, between deterrence through denial and deterrence through punishment. This distinction was elaborated by Glenn Snyder.[8] Denial capabilities, he suggested, worked through influencing the aggressor's estimate of his probability of gaining his objective, while punishment capabilities influenced the estimate of possible costs, and might have little effect on his chances for territorial gain.

The proponents of limited nuclear war were arguing that the use of tactical nuclear weapons would strengthen both these types of deterrence. The Russians would be deterred from aggression not only because any advance would be blocked but because the process of being blocked would be extremely painful. The invader would be punished.

This theme emerged clearly in the writings of the British 'graduated deterrence' school. Though the term originated with Basil Liddell Hart[9] the ideas associated with the term were promoted most vigorously by Rear-Admiral Sir Anthony Buzzard, a former chief of British Naval Intelligence. In addition to articles by Buzzard, the concept was elaborated in a Chatham House pamphlet which remains one of the most succinct statements of the limited war position.[10] The main proposition was that punishment should fit the crime. Economy of force was a prevalent moral theme. 'We should not cause, or threaten to cause, more destruction than is necessary', Buzzard wrote. Another principle was the need to concentrate on military rather than civilian targets. But this did not mean that the use of nuclear weapons against military targets would not hurt – they were more than 'hand-grenades'. 'Let there be no mistake, therefore. The threat of tactical atomic war is a terrible and tremendous deterrent in itself, without the additional threat of total, global war.'[11]

It was argued against this that, if the aim was to punish aggression, then ought not the threat to be made as fearsome as possible and would it not be best to abstain from doubting its worth? As the London *Economist* wrote: 'If the effectiveness of the deterrent resides precisely in its certainty and horror, then any attempt to reduce either the certainty or the horror will reduce the power to deter.'[12] The graduated deterrent theorists disagreed. They could offer punishment enough. Most importantly there would be less of a credibility problem for graduated deterrence need not be as suicidal as massive retaliation.

One of the earliest suggestions for a policy of punishing the aggressor through devastating attacks on his armed forces came from an American, Colonel Richard Leghorn, who was in correspondence with the British proponents of 'graduated deterrence'. Leghorn believed in the defensive value of tactical nuclear weapons – their use could 'render a battlefield virtually inoperable'. In order to spare local populations, he suggested attacks on reinforcements and logistics behind the enemy lines (interdiction). Leghorn's formula for deterrence was quite simple: whatever types of forces were used to support aggression, these forces would be destroyed. Ground armies would be decimated by tactical nuclear weapons, conventional airpower destroyed through hot pursuit and attacks on bases, and nuclear forces through attacks on stockpiles and delivery vehicles. In addition, nuclear attacks on hostile cities should be 'unilaterally renounced . . . unless the cities of the Free World are first attacked with weapons of mass effect'.[13]

Leghorn was aiming for a carefully graded and efficient deterrent. The response to an aggressive act would be a disabling attack that would prevent any repetition. It would be like chopping off the hand of a pickpocket or castrating a rapist rather than relying on fines, imprisonment, or corporal punishment. The retaliation would be more credible than if it were massive because it would not be suicidal and the punishment would fit the crime. It nevertheless supposed that the US would be in a sufficiently superior position to permit the USSR to raise the stakes of any conflict. At each level of combat the Russians must fear defeat. Even if it got to the stage of the use of strategic airpower, the Americans could have the confidence to absorb a first blow and then find and attack, with little trouble over access to the enemy's stockpiles and bases. This was optimistic, but if it had not been optimistic then the question would be raised as to why it was necessary to wait. If the capability for a disarming strike on Soviet airpower existed, should this not be exploited at an early rather than at a late stage in the conflict? This question will be examined in the next chapter.

The British theorists had a less elaborate approach. Their aim was to develop a form of warfare that would be 'sufficiently costly to an aggressor to make local aggression not worthwhile' but not 'automatically so terrible that any threatened country or its allies would shrink from using atomic weapons to defend itself'. In order to prevent it becoming too terrible, ideally there should be mutual understanding on restricting attacks to military targets. But even if the Soviet Union did not agree to these restrictions, it would still be preferable for the West to adopt them unilaterally. As it would be difficult to establish rules in the middle of a war, the educational process ought to begin immediately. As it would also be better if the Soviet Union had the onus of extending the conflict, Buzzard advocated saying to the 'prospective aggressor':

If you do attack, we will, if necessary, use atomic and perhaps chemical weapons against your armed forces. But we will not, on this issue, use hydrogen or bacteriological weapons at all, unless you do, and we will not use any mass destruction weapons against centres of population, unless you do deliberately.[14]

The argument was based on two premises: first, that there were two distinct types of war that could be fought using nuclear weapons – one limited, the other not – and, second, that there was a mutual interest between East and West in fighting the former rather than the latter. It was also felt that the Western interest might be greater, based on the hypothesis that 'tactical nuclear weapons favour the defence'. There seemed little reason to doubt that if matters ever came to blows, the major powers would have every incentive to contain the fighting.

The main question was whether a method of war-fighting awesome enough to deter the Soviet Union from embarking on a provocative action could still be limited. The deterrent value of tactical nuclear weapons was that they favoured the defence by impeding offensive operations in a particularly painful way. But there were good reasons for doubting whether those weapons conveyed any particular advantage to the defence and there was a great danger, if used, that the defended population would be punished as much as, if not more than, the aggressor. Both these considerations suggested *early* use of tactical nuclear weapons, at least so long as they were in effect a Western monopoly. But once the East was similarly armed it would be a time for second thoughts. If nuclear-use could not guarantee any particular advantage to the defence, then might not the result be an indecisive nuclear exchange? In this case the only result of relying on these weapons would be to introduce inconclusive but horrific nuclear devastation earlier into the conflict than might otherwise have been the case. In 1955 Bernard Brodie hinted at this possibility. After noting that 'with the unrestricted reciprocal use of nuclear weapons tactically no substantial forces will be able to live in the field at all', he commented that 'Thus we tend in the end to get the same kind of utterly nihilistic result in considering unrestricted tactical war in the future that we get in unrestricted strategic war.'

Four years later he was convinced of this. Once reciprocal use was visualized no 'overwhelming advantages' could be seen. Futhermore, 'a people saved by us through our free use of nuclear weapons over their territories would probably be the last that would ever ask us to help them'.[15]

This undermined the claim that graduated deterrence was more 'credible' than massive retaliation. For, while it did not entail as great a risk of suicide for those well away from the combat zone (though fallout could travel), it would involve sacrifice for those allies within and around the combat zone. An appreciation of this fact would inhibit rushing into nuclear use in a land battle. The inhibition would only get stronger once battle commenced, for either the enemy would be held by conventional means or else, if his invasion prospered, the local sacrifice consequent on nuclear use would become that much greater. The more tactical nuclear weapon use appeared comparable to the use of strategic nuclear weapons and the less comparable to conventional weapons, the more difficult it would be to maintain limitations.

Some considerable effort was devoted to ways of establishing convincing demarcation lines between tactical and strategic use of nuclear weapons. Factors such as size of weapon, type of target and relation to the combat zone, the enemy's military effort and centres of population were all carefully examined. Some plausible and even practical distinctions were identified, mainly with regard to targets. But there was an air of unreality about the whole effort for the most obvious way to limit a modern war was to avoid using nuclear weapons at all.

The limited nuclear war theorists insisted that there was nothing particularly reprehensible about tactical nuclear weapons as opposed to any other type of weapon. They warned how communists would do what they could to encourage faint-heartedness in the West on this matter. But it was more than communist propaganda that had led to the development of a 'nuclear taboo'. What was known of the character of nuclear explosions, including such features as radioactive fallout, was extremely disturbing. The actual behaviour of politicians and the military, aside from their brave rhetoric, demonstrated that they, too, were worried and would think more than once before authorizing nuclear attacks. Nuclear weapons were occupying a category of their own in the public mind and, though sub-categories might be acknowledged, they could not override this basic division. As Brodie noted when reviewing the Chatham House pamphlet 'the use of any kind of nuclear weapon greatly increases the difficulties in the way of making limitations'.[16] Others put it more strongly. James King insisted that the distinction between nuclear and non-nuclear weapons was 'sharp, clear and convincing'. 'General nuclear war is implicit in the employment of nuclear weapons. Their non-employment is the most obvious of all possible limitations.'[17]

Gradually many of those who had flirted with the idea of limited nuclear war came round to see it virtually as a contradiction in terms. Brodie's conversion has already been noted. Blackett came out unequivocally against it, while Liddell Hart saw it as complicating an already confused situation without solving anything. He was ready to acknowledge some possible advantages of 'small atomic weapons' but felt that their use should not be considered in isolation from the stockpiles of larger weapons for strategic use. 'Once any kind of nuclear weapon is actually used, it could all too easily spread by rapid degrees, and lead to all-out nuclear war.'[18]

In 1960 even Kissinger, acknowledging the failure of the services to develop a coherent doctrine for tactical nuclear weapons, the disagreements within NATO and the build-up of Soviet forces of this type, came out against a limited nuclear strategy:

> The more the pressures build up against *any* use of nuclear weapons, the greater will be the gap between our deterrent policy, our military capability and our psychological readiness – a gap which must tempt aggression. The years ahead must therefore see a substantial strengthening of the conventional forces of the free world.[19]

On Strategy and Tactics

Arguments over the use of tactical nuclear weapons did not stop then. The 1950s debate did not resolve anything. The development and deployment of these weapons was encouraged before an appropriate doctrine had been evolved. There was then a marked lack of success in explaining how they could solve, in anything other than the short term, the problems of the West. As with strategic nuclear weapons, once Warsaw Pact forces acquired the tactical versions, NATO could not ignore them. They always had to be available lest the East should use them first. The contingencies in which the West should initiate their use remained unclear. If the defence could hold the territorial boundaries without tactical nuclear weapons, there would be no value in gratuitous use. But, if it could not, any army so numerically and logistically weak that it could not satisfactorily wage a conventional war could not guarantee success in nuclear war. Conventional weakness might only become evident after battle had commenced, but retreat would not be the most propitious moment to adopt a nuclear strategy. A scorched-earth policy can never be popular with the local population. Furthermore, the basic problem of credibility remained. A way of punishing an aggressor without causing undue suffering to oneself had not been found.

To talk of 'tactical' nuclear weapons was a misnomer. Strategy and tactics properly refer to different aspects of warfare. Strategy is about the overall relationship between military means and the ends of policy, while tactics is concerned with the specific application of military means for direct military ends. The responsibility for the confusion that arose with this terminology lay with the airmen. They used the adjective 'strategic' to distinguish independent attacks on the heartland of the enemy, in anticipation of decisive results, from mere 'tactical' support of surface forces in battle, which they considered to be a secondary, unadventurous, and wasteful use of airpower. Eventually the adjective came to be applied not only to a rôle – 'strategic' bombardment – but to a capability – 'strategic' airpower – and then on to particular weapons – 'strategic' aircraft and missiles. It soon became common to talk of 'strategic' war, one in which these weapons were used.

But 'strategic' war is a nonsense term, for strategy is a feature not a type of war. To talk of 'strategic' war is like talking about a political election or a musical concert; the use of the word 'strategic' is redundant. Similarly, to talk of a 'tactical' weapon is nonsensical. The use of any weapons in battle involves judgments on targeting, the avoidance of counter-measures and concentration on immediate objectives, i.e. tactics. It is as difficult to imagine a non-tactical weapon as it is to imagine a non-strategic war.

There are nevertheless certain distinctions that are worth making. One is between orthodox and unorthodox types of warfare. Orthodox types are those which bear strong resemblance to the classical conflicts of the past and are distinguished by the fact that they involve clashes between professional armed forces and do not involve, except inadvertently, attacks on civilians. Unorthodox warfare, which includes both guerrilla warfare and strategic bombardment, knows no boundary between the military and civilian spheres of society. In place of the term 'strategic war', it would be preferable to use the old-fashioned 'total war', to be contrasted with 'limited war'. Finally there is the clear-cut and unambiguous distinction between conventional and nuclear explosives.

These distinctions overlap, but not completely. We might expect a total war to involve nuclear explosives and attacks on civilians, but there have been unrestricted attacks on civilians with conventional explosives, before and during the nuclear age. The question with tactical nuclear weapons was whether the orthodox/unorthodox war and the limited/total war distinctions could override the conventional/nuclear explosives distinction. By using the adjective 'tactical', it was hoped to link nuclear weapons to weapons of the past and to traditional land warfare. By the end of the 1950s it was apparent that this link was illusory. Nuclear weapons, whatever their shape, size or ostensible purpose, could not be considered 'just another weapon'. But what sort of weapons these 'tactical' nuclear weapons really were remained a mystery.

Section 4

The Fear of Surprise Attack

9 The Importance of Being First

On Winning Nuclear Wars

By the mid-1950s it was already becoming habitual to put the word 'win' in quotation marks when using it in connection with nuclear war. Traditional notions of victory and defeat dissolved in the face of the unavoidable level of destruction that even the technical winner would suffer. Every victory would be pyrrhic. Such a view lay behind the efforts of limited war theorists to encourage moderation in war-aims. There was little point in fighting for total objectives when this would require an unattainable total victory.

This did not make total war completely unthinkable, for men will often claim to be ready to fight 'to the death' in defence of values they cherish. The benefit of war, in terms of horrors prevented if not of advantages gained, might still outweigh the costs even though the costs be high. The issue was whether or not the destruction likely to be visited upon a country in the course of a nuclear war could ever be compensated for by prospective gains. The judgment turned on the anticipated levels of the costs and benefits, and the values attached to them. The resolution of a war would decide the prevailing ideology and the dominant group or nation. After a nuclear war, wrote Paul Nitze (the author of NSC-68):

> The victor will be in a position to issue orders to the loser and the loser will have to obey them or face complete chaos or extinction. The victor will then go on to organize what remains of the world as

best he can. Certainly he will try to see to it that there is never again a possibility that the loser possesses nuclear weapons.[1]

Those who could conceive of victory in nuclear war believed that its foundation would lie, to quote Nitze once more, in the West maintaining 'indefinitely a position of nuclear attack–defense superiority versus the Soviet Union and its satellites'. The value of such superiority would not be in added increments of destructive power. There was a clear law of diminishing marginal returns involved with attacks on cities. After the first few blows, additional bombs would, as Churchill put it, 'only make the rubble bounce'. The only worthwhile superiority would be in methods of depriving the adversary of his nuclear armaments and then blocking any retaliatory forces that he might still be able to muster before they reached their targets. By such means the costs of a nuclear war *might* be brought down to a tolerable level, given the issues at stake.

The ability to prevail in a nuclear exchange depended on the exploitation of new technologies that were improving both the means of offence and defence. The strategic concepts involved were derived from the traditional theory of strategic airpower. This placed great emphasis on securing command of the air so as to make it impossible for the enemy air force to operate, by destroying it either on the ground or in the air. The professional airmen were therefore ready to view the new technology as facilitating further moves in an old game.

If it was becoming possible to mount a serious attack on the enemy's nuclear stockpiles and delivery vehicles, it appeared good sense to get in this attack before the enemy forces had a chance to do any damage. And if Americans thought in that way, then there were good reasons to believe that Russians might be having similar thoughts. It was, in fact, widely assumed that many in the Kremlin would be full of such thoughts. As the 'potential aggressors', they would wish to ensure that they derived the maximum benefit from their first blow. If the Soviet leadership felt that there was a good chance of getting away with a surprise attack which deprived the US of means of retaliation, the whole strategy of deterrence would rest on shaky foundations.

The first theorists of the atomic age were impressed by how little one had to do to ensure devastating effects with atomic bombs. If only a few weapons-carriers could penetrate determined defences, the result would be an unprecedented disaster for the victim country. In the early 1950s the new thermonuclear bombs had been hailed as individual 'city-busters'. One such weapon on a major city was presumed to deter all but the most cold-blooded aggressor. Even with some uncertainty as to the victim's threshold of pain, the basic requirement was for a stockpile of bombs that could almost be counted in tens rather than hundreds. But as time went on awkward questions began to be raised on the likely character of nuclear exchanges and the opportunities available to a skilful, imaginative and well-prepared attacking force. As strategists in both East and West pondered the advantages of getting in a surprise first blow, they became impressed by just *how much* one had to do to ensure devastating effects.

Prevention or Pre-emption

The theories of limited war were premised upon an assumption of growing nuclear stalemate. Once the problem of production of nuclear weapons had been solved, there seemed no reason to believe that the problem of delivering them to targets would prove insuperable. And once that problem had been solved little could be done by a prospective victim, whatever the size of his own nuclear arsenal, to free himself from the threat of destruction. Large nuclear stockpiles, accumulated in parallel, would cancel each other out, so resulting in a stable balance of terror. It would be in everybody's interest to discourage nuclear exchanges. Those who felt this to be self-evident saw their task as being to point it out to those who seemed disposed not to notice.

It must be remembered that it had been felt originally that deterrence depended on an *imbalance* of terror in the West's favour. It was the preponderance of US nuclear forces, enhanced by the dynamism of her technology, that would keep the Soviet Union's expansive tendencies in check. The East was considered to have both the manpower and the inclination to make trouble; the West had neither. World peace would not, for this reason, benefit from a balance of terror, for the West did not need to be deterred. No community rests soundly when the forces of law and order and the criminal fraternity have an equality of strength. The emergence of a balance of terror thus threatened the utility of nuclear weapons for the West as an instrument of general deterrence. To those convinced that the West had no alternative, given its inferiority in conventional arms, to the pursuit of a nuclear strategy stalemate was best avoided. Acknowledging the growth of Soviet nuclear power, ways had to be found for the West to use its own nuclear forces in a more effective way than the East, in order to maintain a measure of superiority.

There were two distinct alternatives. One was to arrest the growth of Soviet military power through bold and timely action, exploiting America's comparative nuclear advantage while it lasted. Occasional calls to this effect – for *preventive* war – were heard during the period of US monopoly and overwhelming superiority. They intensified as it became apparent that this period was coming to an end. In 1954, the feasibility of an attack upon Soviet nuclear installations was even reported to have been discussed at the level of the National Security Council. Public advocacy of preventive war was not encouraged amongst serving officers though the sentiment could, now and again, be detected. It was a minority opinion. Though it was generally felt that the Soviet Union would have few qualms about suddenly launching an unprovoked attack if the moment was considered right, it was equally generally thought that it would be quite out of character, given the prevailing morality and constitutional provisions, for the US ever to do such a thing. This was considered to be one of the key matters of principle that set democratic apart from totalitarian societies. American leaders always reacted with considerable disbelief to the suggestion that the Soviet Union might not be as confident in America's good behaviour.[2]

The other alternative was taken more seriously. This was *pre-emptive* war. The distinction in terms of both practical requirements and outside appearances between this and preventive war could seem to be no more than a couple of letters and a hyphen. Both came down in essence to a readiness to be the first to launch a nuclear attack. Nevertheless there were differences. One was over the appropriate moment for a nuclear strike. Preventive war advocacy was based on a concern over an historical shift in the military balance. Any moment before that shift had been completed would be favourable for a strike; any moment after completion would be unfavourable. Pre-emptive war was, on the other hand, tied to a specific situation, most likely to arise after the completion of this historical shift, when there were strong grounds for believing that a Soviet strike was imminent. The second difference followed from the first. Preventive war would be based upon straightforward strategic superiority. Pre-emptive war would be launched in all probability against an enemy of equivalent strength if slower in movement. The technical requirements would be exacting: a reliable intelligence system, to ensure adequate warning of attack, and an ability, including a capacity for quick movement, to abort this attack. Captain W. D. Puleston USN (Retd) formulated the policy in a book which appeared in 1955:

> In order to make atomic retaliation effective as a deterrent to aggression, we must decide now and prepare to strike first whenever we have positive evidence that an attack is being mounted against the United States. Such a policy does not contemplate preventive war or a sneak attack. We would only strike if the prospective enemy did not cease preparing to attack us or our allies by a certain time.[3]

The reactive aspect of this strategy satisfied the moral principle of attack only in self-defence, though how certain the Americans would have to be of the imminence of a Soviet attack before launching one of their own was never made completely clear. The military principle was that of getting in the first blow. To the proponents of pre-emptive war that was the paramount consideration. Colonel Jack Nicholas wrote: 'conceding the initiative in the thermonuclear age is an enormous concession. At best it could produce a critical military situation for us. At worst it carries the seeds of a national disaster'.[4] The Air Force was not prepared to concede the initiative to the Soviet Union, especially if the first blow could be decisive. For if it could be decisive then it was still possible to imagine a clear victory in a confrontation with the Soviet Union through the effective use of nuclear weapons. This represented the last chance for a plausible alternative to nuclear stalemate.

The Virtues of Counter-Force

To its opponents one of the more deplorable features of the policy of massive retaliation was that it put the threat of unprecedented genocide at the centre of American strategy. Those who objected to targeting cities sought for ways in which the wars of the nuclear age could be fought along traditional lines, concentrating on an effort to destroy the enemy's armed forces rather than his civilian population. Limited war theorists placed great emphasis on this point. In the process they began to explore the possibility of developing capabilities for 'counter-force' as opposed to 'counter-city' strikes. Writers such as Richard Leghorn argued for the development of counter-force capabilities in the terminology of limited war. In his scheme the West would only use nuclear weapons against military bases in the Soviet Union if weapons from these bases had already been used against the West.

To the Air Force the virtue in counter-force lay not so much in its respect for non-combatants, though they were pleased to point to this humanitarian bonus. It was certainly hoped that by refraining from attacking cities the loss of life would be kept down, but there was little pretence that civilian suffering could be avoided. T. F. Walkow-icz, a former senior Air Force officer and one of the main advocates of counter-force, recognized the difficulty of making clear distinctions between military and counter-economy targets. He noted that 'major air bases are frequently located near cities; troops can be con-centrated in cities; and submarine bases are associated with major seaports. Thus, even counter-force operations will inevitably lead to some destruction of Soviet cities'.[5] The real value was in the oppor-tunity it provided for actually defeating the enemy. It was seen as a method of fighting a *total* not a *limited* war. Limited war was con-sidered an unrealistic proposition. There was no reason to believe that the Kremlin would fight with hands tied behind its back or would forsake its long-term objectives for more modest gains. If war came it would be fought for the highest stakes with no holds barred. Senior Air Force officers argued that this was the sort of war the US had to prepare to fight and should not be diverted by the hope that fighting could be confined to battlefields comparable to those of the last war.

The airmen also wished for a greater purpose in war than merely neutralizing the airpower of the other side and were eager to prove that the first blow could be decisive. The most consistent theme of USAF doctrinal pronouncements throughout its whole existence has been the insistence on a critical rôle in warfare for the manned bomber. It has influenced and coloured all beliefs as to what is right, proper, and necessary in the nuclear age. The Air Force has always had a view on how a nuclear war *ought* to be conducted. The only countermeasure to the bomber given any credence by the airmen (except for those who piloted fighter aircraft) was the bomber. The Air Force and its supporters scoffed at the very idea that a bomber offensive could be seriously impeded by air defence.[6] Air defence was seen more as a competitor for a share of the budget than a comple-ment in an overall strategy.

The US Air Force had initially been pleased with the doctrine of massive retaliation. It recognized the qualities of airpower which became the Great Deterrent. Gradually, however, it became unhappy with the thought that if the deterrent ever failed there would be little to be done but engage in an attack on Soviet cities, which was becoming increasingly suicidal. This was hardly a rational response to aggression. The most effective deterrent, Air Force officers began to argue, would be based on power that could be actually used with confidence. A threat that would, in all probability, turn out to be empty when challenged lacked credibility. A credible threat would be an American capability to *win* a nuclear war without intolerable loss. The Soviet Union's growing nuclear strength was reducing the American interest in a counter-economy war. As it would be impossible to mobilize the country's industrial base after the start of war (because of the likely disruption and destruction from nuclear attacks) the war would have to be decided with forces-in-being at the start of hostilities. A decisive result was more likely if the enemy's forces-in-being could be reduced significantly by a timely attack. The main effect of bombardment of cities, however, would be to invite retaliation against ones own cities. Striking out at all forces, not just nuclear forces, offered a way of winning a war at tolerable cost.

The 1955 policy statement of the Air Force Association pointed to the significance of the growing capabilities for surprise attack:

Given modern weapons and the advantages of initiating surprise attack, one nation can paralyze and conquer other nations without undue risk to itself.

Massive retaliation, as a deterrent to war, as a hope for survival, is steadily becoming obsolete. There can be no practical retaliation, after an all-out surprise attack with thermonuclear weapons, which destroys military bases simultaneously with centers of industry and population.

... We must have the ability and the determination to apply our airpower the instant active aggression becomes evident on the part of the Soviet Union.[7]

The requirements for actually fighting a nuclear war were exacting. It must be worth fighting and the destruction received must not be so great as to be terminal. To do this, it was necessary to explore all means of reducing the enemy's strike forces to manageable quantities as well as all his means of defence. This included any methods available for protecting the civilian population from blast and fallout, and implied that the offence-minded Air Force must reverse a past position. It involved a vigorous pursuit of superiority in all departments. The essential message was that thermonuclear war need not be suicidal; America could survive, battered but capable of recovery. It would be possible 'to live through a major nuclear war and even to re-establish a national economy and society'.[8]

The Blunting Mission

In the traditional theory of strategic airpower, critical importance was assigned to securing command of the air by making it impossible for the enemy air force to operate, either by destroying it on the ground or in the air. Leading figures in the British and American Air Forces saw no reason to change this view after the war.[9] This 'blunting mission' was considered in the first post-war operational plans for the use of air and atomic weapons against the Soviet Union. An internal Air Force document of January 1948 described the concepts of operations 'in a war which might take place in the next 4 to 15 years' (by which time it was hoped plans for a greatly expanded Air Force had been endorsed and acted upon).

[W]e will first employ our long-range strategic bombers in a retaliatory action as expeditiously as possible. Atomic bombs will be used and the system of targets to be attacked will be those which would produce the maximum 'blunting' effect. That is, the results we would hope to obtain would be those that will produce the greatest immediate damage and destruction to the enemy, thus reducing his capability to operate against vital objectives of the United States and its allies.[10]

William Liscum Borden provided a forceful presentation of the argument that the opening shots of a future war would be directed against military facilities rather than cities.[11] However, few of the major works of strategic thought of the time gave the idea much prominence. While nuclear stockpiles were small, the available weapons had to be devoted to attacks on cities. Furthermore, it was thought unlikely that any nation would permit vital military resources to be concentrated in a few vulnerable targets.

Interest in counter-force attacks revived in the 1950s. The growth in nuclear stockpiles meant that a variety of offensive missions could be considered. Furthermore, advances in reconnaissance capabilities could be contemplated to make it possible to pinpoint key enemy targets with sufficient accuracy.[12] The object was to devastate the enemy's retaliatory capability on the ground. If this could be done then all the effort that the Russians had put into catching up with the Americans would be as nought. One well-aimed blow would disarm them, prevent a response in kind, and render them vulnerable to the remaining American bombers.

But as with all attempts to discover a form of nuclear war that would work to the advantage of the West, problems arose as soon as the Soviet Union attained comparable capabilities. Once both sides enjoyed a disarming capability then the whole course of a war could be decided by the first blow. It was not a situation to appeal to those of a nervous disposition yet, if this was feasible, the thought that the Russians might acquire such a capability first was incentive enough to push ahead with an American acquisition. Developments along these lines would steer the arms race towards something almost directly opposite to a stalemate. The feasibility of the blunting mission thus had tremendous implications for the whole character of the nuclear balance.

The significance of this was recognized by Bernard Brodie in 1954, in an impressive essay in which he set out the case for limited war:

We have a number of alternative possibilities for the future oriented around a single criterion – that is, the expected degree of success of a blunting mission. Now it should be clear that a political or military strategy suitable to one condition may be most unsuitable to another. If, for example, we are living in a world where either side can make a surprise attack upon the other which destroys the latter's capability to make meaningful retaliation (which is almost a minimum definition of 'success' for the enterprise), then it makes sense to be trigger-happy with one's strategic air power. How could one afford under those circumstances to withhold one's SAC from its critical blunting mission while waiting to test other pressures and strategies? This would be the situation of the American gunfighter duel, Western frontier style. The one who leads on the draw and the aim achieves a good clean win. The other is dead. But if, on the other hand, the situation is such that neither side can hope to eliminate the retaliatory power of the other, that restraint which was suicidal in one situation now becomes prudence, and it is trigger-happiness that is suicidal![13]

Preparing for War

The agitation for counter-force capabilities might have been dismissed as Air Force self-interest were it not for the disturbing thought that it was not inconceivable that the United States would find itself engaged in a thermonuclear war. If this was the case, it was infinitely preferable that a considerable fraction of the country's population and industry should survive intact. In the late 1950s, with Soviet military strength growing (apparently) daily and a series of crises in Asia, in the Middle East and in Europe (where the uncertain status of Berlin was proving to be a persistent source of tension), it was possible to conceive of war.

In these circumstances many considered preparation for war the only responsible course of action. 'The danger of total war is real and finite', wrote Bernard Brodie. 'So long as there is a finite chance of war, we have to be interested in outcomes; and although all outcomes will be bad, some would be very much worse than others.' If war came, getting in the first blow would provide an undoubted advantage. So it was necessary to ensure that one's own retaliatory force was protected and it was necessary, to the extent possible, to prepare for an American first blow. Brodie recoiled with horror from the offence-minded wish for total solutions. He recognized that it was virtually impossible to create a first-strike capability which could, if used expeditiously, completely spare North America the full horrors of nuclear war. Even the drifting fallout resulting from an American attack would ensure a measure of reflexive retribution. He suspected that, given the choice, the US would prefer to fight a limited war, even though this would mean deliberately not using 'these existing instruments which from a strictly military point of view are far the most efficient'. However, it would be difficult to do without some first-strike capabilities and the necessary superiority in equipment to provide it. Apart from anything else, this was necessary to fulfil alliance commitments. 'We have and will probably continue to have obligations under treaties which require us to defend our partners with all the resources at our command from nuclear attack. For this and other reasons we need the capability for a first strike both in spirit and military power.[14] The other requirement was for a measure of civil defence: protecting key elements in the fabric of society; constructing fallout shelters; and planning and practising evacuation. Reading Brodie's book one senses a gap between the desirable and the practical. *Strategy in the Missile Age* is a gloomy book because of its awareness that there is no escape from the possibility of war, nor from horrific levels of destruction should worst fears be realized.

A comparable message is contained in another book by a member of the RAND Corporation's staff, Herman Kahn, though here the message is presented in a somewhat bizarre manner. In his effort to persuade people to 'think about the unthinkable' Herman Kahn employed a style designed to shock and bemuse. Kahn had worked on a major investigation of possibilities for civil defence and had come to the conclusion that thermonuclear war could be survived more easily than many people thought. There were alternative postwar states, all 'tragic' but 'distinguishable'. The distinctions were important, argued Kahn, because they were relevant to America's willingness to take on the Soviet Union. Kahn reported somewhat macabre conversations with representative Americans on the sacrifice in lives 'acceptable' to prevent a Communist take-over in Europe. Apparently the threshold of tolerance was the loss of a third of the population; a half would be too much. So if casualties could be kept down, Americans could bravely contemplate war, the deterrent threat would be strengthened and, if the threat failed to deter, war could be fought to something less than the ultimate disaster. 'Sober study shows', reported Kahn using his favourite adjective, 'that the limits on the magnitude of the catastrophe seem to be closely dependent on what kinds of preparations have been made, and on how the war is started and fought'.

Making those preparations was a form of insurance, a means of reducing the chance of war, and of seeing to it that, after the war, the survivors did not envy the dead. Not to take these precautions seemed the height of irresponsibility.

We must still be able to fight and survive wars just as long as it is possible to have such a capability. Not only is it prudent to take out insurance against a war occurring unintentionally, but we must also be able to stand up to the threat of fighting, or credibly to threaten to initiate a war ourselves – unpleasant though this sounds and is. We must at least make it risky for the enemy to force us into situations in which we must choose between fighting and appeasing.... Under current programs the United States may in a few years find itself unwilling to accept a Soviet retaliatory blow, no matter what the provocation. To get into such a situation would be equivalent to disowning our alliance obligations by signing what would amount to a nonaggression treaty with the Soviets – a nonaggression treaty with almost 200 million American hostages to guarantee performance.... These remarks will distress all who very properly view the thought of fighting a war with so much horror they feel very uneasy at having a high-quality deterrent force, much less a credible capability for initiating, fighting, and terminating all kinds of war. I can sympathize with this attitude. But I believe it borders on the irresponsible.[15]

Kahn was particularly concerned to debunk the notion that the parallel nuclear capabilities made war inconceivable. He reminded his readers, as had Brodie, that the obligations of the United States to NATO required the ability to strike against the Soviet Union even if it had not been attacked itself. 'The agonizing decision to start an all-out thermonuclear war would be ours.' He refused to accept that the threat of mutual suicide would guarantee deterrence. Moreover, it would leave the US helpless if it did 'fail'. In such circumstances the US would want a capability to prevail in the ensuing conflict. If they had such a capability then deterrence would be much stronger in the first place. Thus he argued for a 'Credible First-Strike Capability'.

A capacity for counter-force attacks was essential to such a capability. But it was not enough to rely on this alone:

Credibility depends on being willing to accept the other side's retaliatory blow. It depends on the harm *he* can do, not on the harm *we* can do. It depends as much on *air defense* and *civil defense* as *air offense*. It depends on *will* as well as *capability*. It depends on the *provocation* and on the *state of our mind* when the provocation occurs.[16]

Complementary to counter-force capabilities therefore would be adequate civil defence preparations and a suitably sacrificial frame of mind.

A Sense of Vulnerability

An occupational hazard for the military is to spend a great amount of time thinking about and preparing for what you are to do to the enemy, while neglecting the problem of what the enemy might do to you. While the US had been refining its nuclear offensive capabilities, very little attention had been given to the vulnerability of these capabilities to a Soviet surprise attack. After the first Soviet test of an atomic bomb in 1949 some thought was given to the problem.[17] Attention was focused on this problem in the 1950s through the efforts of civilian analysts with backgrounds in economics and engineering at the RAND Corporation (a non-profit research organization with close links to the Air Force). In 1951, led by Albert Wohlstetter, they began a study on the most effective acquisition, construction and use of air base facilities in foreign countries. They came to recognize that these bases were far more vulnerable to a surprise enemy attack than had previously been appreciated. By 1953 the problem had been investigated thoroughly at RAND and the Air Force leadership was being briefed on the need to protect bases.[18]

The civilians at RAND were not impressed by the Air Force response and continued to analyse the vulnerability of US facilities. By 1956 they were assessing the sort of damage that a Soviet intercontinental ballistic missile (ICBM) attack might do to US bases. Into the evolving jargon of strategic theory were introduced the concepts of first and second strikes. A *first strike* was taken to refer to a strike that was not only the opening volley of a nuclear war, but was also directed against the nuclear capability of the enemy with the intention of crippling his means of retaliation. A *second strike* force was one capable of ensuring effective retaliation even after absorbing an enemy first strike. Whereas a first strike involved counter-force, a second strike need be no more than counter-value.

In one sense, ICBMs were not as effective counter-force weapons as bombers for, in their first generation, they lacked accuracy. Against small, protected targets this could be a disadvantage, but when the targets were larger and vulnerable to nuclear explosions in the locality, such as Air Force bases, ICBMs had a crucial advantage. By the time the defending force had become aware of an incoming ICBM attack it might be too late to get the bombers safely off the ground to deliver a retaliatory blow. In Europe, American bases would be even more vulnerable, for the warning time would be minimal. If the Soviet Union was the first to achieve a significant ICBM capability, then the ease and speed with which these weapons could reach their targets could place the United States at a considerable, perhaps decisive, disadvantage.

The clearest, most sobering and most public challenge to the presumption of stability came from Albert Wohlstetter, writing with

the authority of the leader of the RAND team which had been exploring the vulnerability of US strategic forces. In a January 1959 article
he argued against the view that deterrence was an 'automatic' consequence if both sides have a nuclear delivery capability, suggesting
instead that the balance of terror was 'delicate'. The delicacy had
been missed because the 'technological race' had been construed as
being a race to develop better and more nuclear strike forces than the
other side. Deterrence required more than matching the other's ability to strike first. 'To deter an attack means being able to strike back
in spite of it. It means, in other words, a capability to strike second'.
(Here Wohlstetter introduced to the general public the distinctions
between a first and second strike outlined above). The problems of
assured retaliation had been underestimated. Wohlstetter warned: 'at
critical junctures in the 1960s, we may not have the power to deter
attack'. This warning was based on a technical assessment of the
problems of second strikes, of surviving enemy strikes, communica-
ting the decision to retaliate, reaching enemy targets through 'active'
air defences and destroying them despite 'passive' civil defence, and a
political assessment that a 'totalitarian aggressor' has considerable
advantages of flexibility and secrecy over a liberal democracy. He
concluded: 'The notion that a carefully planned surprise attack can
be checkmated almost effortlessly, that, in short, we may resume our
deep pre-Sputnik sleep, is wrong and its nearly universal acceptance
is terribly dangerous.'[19]

These concerns were echoed by others alarmed at the thought of
the US being left defenceless following a cleverly constructed Soviet
attack. For example, Bernard Brodie, who was himself at RAND,
wrote regularly of the need to provide adequate protection for essential military facilities. In his 1954 article on limited war he wrote how
'The first and most pressing item of military business before us is
therefore to reduce the vulnerability to surprise attack of our own
strategic striking forces.' Almost five years later he was still on the
same theme:

> If in this book we have frequently reiterated the importance of the
> *security* of the retaliatory force, it is because our ability to retaliate
> in great force to a direct Soviet attack is taken far too much for
> granted by almost everybody, including our highest national
> policy-makers.[20]

Few civilian strategists writing in the second half of the 1950s failed
to make the same point.[21]

Even George Kennan, long sceptical of strategic abstractions and the fantasies and phobias of cold warriors, acknowledged the need for defensive precautions:

> But now that the capacity to inflict this fearful destruction *is* mutual, and now this premium *has* been placed on the element of surprise, I am prepared to concede that the atomic deterrent has its value as a stabilizing factor until we can evolve some better means of protection. And so long as we are obliged to hold it as a deterrent, we must obviously see to it that it is in every way adequate to that purpose – in destructiveness, speed of delivery, in security against a sudden preventative blow, and in the alertness of those who control its employment. I should certainly not wish to convey the impression that I have advocated anything like a neglect or slackening of our retaliatory capacity.[22]

The Delicacy of the Balance

The question of whether or not the balance of terror was delicate was critical to the development of nuclear strategy. A delicate balance would demand hair-triggers and cool nerves, offering the possibility of overwhelming victory or an equally overwhelming defeat. An indelicate balance would calm anxieties about headlong rushes into nuclear war or sudden blows from the East, but left troubling questions as to how the United States was to meet its international responsibilities without the assistance of effective nuclear superiority.

The answer to this question would have to come largely from technical considerations, concerning the feasibility of counter-force attacks and ballistic missile defence. But complementing an evaluation of the properties of the weapons themselves was an assessment of the sort of strategies that could be sustained by the societies of the contending parties. A war-winning strategy might result from the ability to reduce the damage to one's own society to 'acceptable' levels while ensuring that the adversary could not escape 'unacceptable' damage. It could be helped by a readiness to 'act first and ask questions later' when a crisis seemed imminent and a quick move to the draw was essential to victory and survival.

In the following two chapters this question will be further explored. Chapter 10 will examine American views of Soviet advantages in the preparation and initiation of surprise first strikes, and how the Soviet theorists themselves considered these advantages in the context of the revolution in their strategic thought following the death of Stalin. Then Chapter 11 will examine the ease with which first strike aspirations could be thwarted, so stabilizing the balance of terror.

10 *Sputniks* and the Soviet Threat

The Impact of *Sputnik*

No event focused popular attention on America's vulnerabilities to attack more than the launching of the world's first artificial earth satellite, *Sputnik I*, by the Soviet Union on 4 October 1957. It brought home the fact that the United States no longer enjoyed invulnerability to the ravages of war. The peoples of Western Europe were familiar with the effects of aerial bombardment and were already growing accustomed to being well within the range of Soviet bombers and missiles. Before the capability to destroy the United States provided the Russians with a retaliatory option, the Western Europeans had served as a hostage. Now Americans also began to suffer the uncomfortable sensation of being candidates for annihilation in the event of total war.

The Russians had put only a limited effort into the development of a long-range bomber force, giving ICBMs a higher priority. As their ICBM programme had started earlier than that of the Americans, it was the first to produce results. When these results became evident there was widespread alarm and despondency in the US. Successful completion of the Soviet programme before the American would mean that there would be a couple of years during which the Russians could enjoy a decisive superiority. The US had embarked on a nuclear strategy to ensure an upper hand over the Soviet Union; now the position might be fundamentally reversed.

Sputnik pushed these dark thoughts to the fore. This achievement in space captured the popular imagination in a way that stark and subdued reports of monitored ICBM tests could not. *Sputnik* exhibited the relevant technology in an exciting and visible fashion. As important was the general shock it provided to American self-confidence. The Russians had shown that they could match – indeed exceed – the Americans in technological sophistication. Previously the cold war had been a competition between economic systems. In the West the capitalist system had been expected to triumph because of its superior performance both in developing wealth and encouraging innovation. The communist system was viewed as being so rigid that it would not be able to meet the challenges of the modern world. *Sputnik* demonstrated that the Soviet Union could operate as a modern industrial power in its ability to mobilize and exploit scientific and engineering talent. For this reason it serves as a watershed in American attitudes on technology and the strategic balance.[1] Finally, as a surprise in itself, *Sputnik* lent credibility to the notion that the Russians could, surreptitiously, steal an unexpected lead over the United States and put her at a terrible strategic disadvantage.

First Strikes for Whom?

The Air Force continued to believe that superiority could be maintained and that wars might be won in the future with nuclear weapons. Yet surprisingly, given a strategy that depended on making nuclear power an area of comparative advantage for the West, it was the Air Force who most publicized and amplified the growth of Soviet nuclear strength. Not long after the first Soviet long-range bombers had been seen flying around Moscow, the Air Force was issuing intelligence estimates warning that the Soviet Union was liable to out-produce the United States in bombers in a couple of years. In 1957, after the first Soviet ICBM tests had been monitored, the Air Force, not alone, postulated a 'missile gap' in which the Soviet Union would deploy ICBMs quicker and in greater numbers than the US.[2]

According to the Air Force, the Soviet Union was after more than a mere parity with the Union States, a matching of forces to confirm the stalemate. They sought a decisive superiority.[3] Such a stress upon the capabilities of an adversary was an odd way to support a strategy based on a preponderance of military strength. One result of the 'missile gap' clamour of the late 1950s was, in fact, to undermine the confidence of America's allies in the reliability of their super-power protection. But the Air Force was not proclaiming Soviet military power in a spirit of defeatism; rather it was in a spirit of 'act now before it is too late'.

This sense of urgency was shared by those who felt that not enough was being done to protect the retaliatory forces against a Soviet surprise attack. This was, however, primarily a defensive concern, designed to ensure a continuance of nuclear stalemate as opposed to Soviet superiority. The Air Force were not saying 'act now and then it will be all right', but that there was no alternative to continual investment in military technology and hardware to preserve the US lead. If the West did not take up the challenge, the East certainly would. Thus the ominous presentations of the 'threat'. The projections showed the Soviet Union doing those very things the Air Force believed the United States ought to do. The Soviet Union was attempting to create the conditions for winning a nuclear war; the United States should do the same.

The problem was that, according to prevailing beliefs, this task was easier for the Soviet Union. Since 1945 commentators had been stressing that nuclear weapons were particularly suitable for aggression. It was taken for granted that the Soviet Union was the most aggressive and cold-blooded of the two super-powers which suggested that, in principle, she should be best able to cope with the new situation. So long as the West enjoyed nuclear superiority this thought was not too worrisome but, once the Soviet Union had caught up in nuclear capabilities, her non-technical advantages (in manpower, secrecy and ideological determination) would start to come into play.

The West's only objective was to sustain the *status quo*. The Soviet leaders seemed to want to expand their dominion and it was therefore up to them whether or not war began. The West would have to assess the costs when deciding whether to respond, but the first judgment on costs would have to be made by the aggressor. The purpose of developing a US first-strike capability, it was insisted, would be no more than to pre-empt a Soviet attack. No such scruples were thought to inhibit the Russians. If the Americans would really only strike on receipt of unambiguous confirmation that the Soviet Union was about to attack – 'I won't strike first unless you do' – then the strategy was still reactive. For a would-be pre-empter the strain would be terrific, watching and waiting on a continual high-alert status, attempting to interpret all the incoming information and wondering whether enemy preparations were sufficiently blatant to justify a nuclear war. The aggressor, on the other hand, could choose his moment, when his victim's attention was relaxing, confident that nothing was going to happen. Apart from anything else, the openness of American society gave the Russians a clear intelligence advantage. The most important Soviet targets would be hidden from view.

A final proposition, used to challenge the presumption of nuclear stalemate, was that the Russians could tolerate a sufficiently high level of costs to contemplate launching a nuclear war. Evidence for this was found in a Russian fatalism born of a long history of disease, death and destruction, of famines and purges. The tremendous Soviet losses in World War II – some 7.5 million military and 12.5 million civilian dead – appeared to be the key. As the former Commander of SAC wrote:[4]

> With such grisly tradition and shocking record in the massacre of their own people, the Soviets cannot be expected to let the risk of even millions of Russian lives deter them from starting a nuclear war if they should consider such a war to be in the best interests of the Communist cause. Nor would they be deterred by the danger of losing some cities because widespread devastation and subsequent recovery have had numerous precedents in Russia's hectic history.[4]

On a similar theme, Albert Wohlstetter wrote:

> Russian casualties in World War II were more than 20 million. Yet Russia recovered extremely well from this catastrophe. There are several quite plausible circumstances in the future when the Russians might be quite confident of being able to limit damage to considerably less than this number – if they make sensible choices and we do not. On the other hand, the risks of not striking might at some point appear very great to the Soviets, involving, for example, disastrous defeat in a peripheral war, loss of key satellites with danger of revolt spreading – possibly to Russia itself – or fear of attack by ourselves. Then, striking first, by surprise, would be a sensible choice for them, and from their point of view the smaller risk.[5]

However, the Russians did not choose to lose 20 million people. The Soviet Union did not attack Germany; Germany attacked the Soviet Union. The question for the Russians at each point was whether to succumb to the German invasion or to fight on. The casualty lists grew at a frightening speed but the casualties were accumulated over time. A series of decisions to fight on against aggression when a level of costs had already been incurred and the future costs were indeterminate, was quite different from a single decision to launch a nuclear strike, knowing that a likely, virtually immediate and irresistible result is a catastrophic level of destruction. To know the trauma of such a catastrophe, despite recovery, was unlikely to encourage a repeat performance. The human meaning of 20 million deaths was far more comprehensible to those who had seen it than to those who knew it only as a hypothetical statistic.[6]

Patrick Blackett, who had 'no doubt' that the balance of terror was stable *against sane actions of rational governments*' and that it was ever becoming more so, argued that Wohlstetter could only have come to the opposite conclusion 'by negating the conclusions of both common sense and of formal military theory by introducing a large and arbitrary degree of moral asymmetry between the two contestants'.[7]

If one accepted this judgment of a warped Soviet psychology (once bitten, twice bold) it only confirmed that the Soviet Union was better prepared to wage a nuclear war than the United States. Thomas Power acknowledged:

> The point is that what will deter us will not necessarily deter the Soviets, and what will make them accept risks will not make us accept similar risks. Moral principles would deter us strongly from launching a pre-emptive war unless there were no other way of averting certain aggression and still greater losses. But moral considerations and the prospect of losing Russian lives and cities would not deter the Soviets from launching an aggressive war if they saw no better way of achieving their objectives.[8]

So the Soviet leaders were seen as not only acquiring the wherewithal for nuclear first strikes, enjoying the advantages of a secretive and totalitarian society in planning and executing a surprise attack, and offering a variety of plausible motives for executing such an attack, but they also appeared to gain from an insensitivity to the possible suffering for their own people. Meanwhile the Americans were respectful of human life, open in military planning, desirous only of protecting the free areas of the world, and constitutionally incapable of contemplating a first strike. It was quite clear who gained most from a nuclear strategy!

The view that an aggressive nuclear strategy would prove to be attractive to the Soviet Union followed logically from the major and minor premises that nuclear weapons were particularly suitable for aggressors and that the Soviet Union was an aggressive state. This advantage did not come into play so long as the Soviet Union lagged well behind the Union States in the development of nuclear weapons and their means of delivery. The main attraction to the West of a nuclear strategy was provided by American superiority in actual capabilities, confirmed by the stony Soviet silence on the subject of the 'bomb' except for occasional disparagement. However, once their capabilities improved, the Russians became notably less reticent and inhibited in their discussions of the bomb and more assertive in their considerations of the rôle it might play in Soviet strategy.

The changing tone was picked up by US observers of Soviet strategic affairs. In 1956 there was still a widespread presumption that the Soviet interest lay in playing down the importance of the bomb and concentrating instead on their other strengths. In one of the first serious assessments of post-war Soviet military capabilities, edited by Liddell Hart, it was argued that

> The over-publicized surprise attack with nuclear weapons against a powerful opponent, trusting to the annihilating effect of the 'first blow', is too great a gamble for cold-eyed men whose fundamental ideology tells them that time is on their side.[9]

In the post-*Sputnik* climate such an attack seemed quite plausible. In January 1958, a few months after the launch of *Sputnik I*, a leading analyst of Soviet strategy, Herbert Dinerstein, published an article in *Foreign Affairs*. He reported that 'the Soviet armed forces have greatly improved their capability both to deter and to wage war', and that they had adopted a strategy of pre-emptive war. He then speculated that this would be inherently unsatisfactory to the Soviet leaders. He concluded:

> If the Soviet Union should continue to gain technologically while the NATO alliance made little progress, the Soviet Union would be able to make war without fear of the consequences. It will be difficult to attain the ability to eliminate the opponent's nuclear striking forces in a single blow. But that is the goal which the Soviet leaders must strain to reach. If they should acquire such preponderant military strength, they would have policy alternatives

even more attractive than the initiation of nuclear war. By flaunting presumably invincible strength, the Soviet Union could compel piecemeal capitulation of the democracies. This prospect must indeed seem glittering to the Soviet leaders.[10]

The rest of this chapter will examine the shift in Soviet strategy to see whether or not fears such as these were justified.

Soviet Strategy After Stalin

Stalin's death in March 1953 had a liberating effect on Soviet strategic thought. Under Stalin, the military had been permitted little more than the incantation of official dogmas concerning Permanently Operating Factors and the selective study of their own wartime campaigns to find instances of these factors at work. All things that were difficult to explain in the past, which might undermine complacency in the present or lead to loss of confidence in the future, were ignored.

In September 1953, Major General Talensky published in the officers' journal *Military Thought*, of which he was the editor, an article entitled 'On the questions of the laws of military science'. In tentative language, Talensky argued for a military science concerned with the waging of wars and based on laws independent of those believed to be governing the socio-historical process. This was a distinct and limited discipline concerned with the conduct of wars rather than why and when and against whom they should be fought. It ought not to be full of general philosophical and sociological observations. Equally 'philosophers and sociologists ought not to intrude into the domain of military science'.

In principle the laws of war would apply equally to the armies of both capitalist and socialist societies. This view challenged the supposition that socialist societies gained imposing military strengths simply by being socialist. In another heresy, Stalin's Permanently Operating Factors were demoted. They could not be considered laws of wars, nor could it be assumed that a socialist state was inevitably superior in each of these factors. Talensky also hinted at a major departure from past dicta by suggesting that 'surprise' may not be quite so 'temporary' a factor as Stalin had insisted. 'Victory in modern war is attained by the decisive defeat of the enemy in the course of the armed conflict through the employment of successive blows accumulating in force', he wrote; then added that this 'formulation does not exclude the possibility of a decisive defeat in a limited time of one or another opponent, given the existence of certain conditions'. This was a guarded reference to nuclear weapons, still a curiously unmentionable subject. A sustained effort to educate the military in questions relating to atomic energy was about to begin. Eventually it also became possible to discuss the factor of surprise in a manner less cryptic.[11]

Talensky's article stimulated a debate in which he was criticized for paying insufficient regard to the Permanently Operating Factors. There were indications that official opinion was not prepared to endorse Talensky's views. In 1954, he was relieved of his position as editor. A more radical article by General Rotmistrov, 'On the rôle of surprise in contemporary war', was held back by the new editors. In February 1955 when Marshal Zhukov became Minister of Defence, as his reward for helping the Khruschev–Bulganin faction displace Malenkov at the top of the Soviet hierarchy, the atmosphere changed. Zhukov was well aware of the parlous and obsolescent state of Soviet military science. The month before his appointment, at a meeting of 'leading staff of the armed forces', he had advocated 'a thorough study of modern military technology and advanced military theory'.

The immediate publication of Rotmistrov's article signalled the change. Here slavish obeisance to the Permanently Operating Factors was mocked, and it was asserted that 'In the situation of the employment of atomic and hydrogen weapons, surprise is one of the decisive conditions for the attainment of success not only in battles and operations but also in the war as a whole'. He did, however, emphasize that it was not the only decisive condition. The 'operations of the ground forces' would 'also decide the outcome of war'.[12]

In March 1955, under Zhukov's guidance, the editors of *Military Thought* effectively concluded the debate that Talensky had begun. They criticized themselves for holding back Rotmistrov's article and called for more creativity in thought and less committing to memory of Stalin's writings. They endorsed Talensky's view that the 'subject of military science is, above all, the investigation of these very special laws of . . . the armed conflict'. Credence was given to the new emphasis on the importance of surprise. The official line had changed. Now the Permanently Operating Factors as an explanation for the dynamics of armed conflict was derided, though the potential significance of the individual factors was still recognized. By 1956, the term had been dropped from Soviet strategic writings.

The Logic of Pre-emption

In this reappraisal of Soviet strategy the whole question of surprise attack assumed considerable importance. There were a number of reasons for this. The refusal to attribute any significant benefits to the attainment of surprise had been the hallmark of the old strategy and was thus an inevitable target for any revisionist. In Stalinist hagiography, the sudden German invasion of 1941 had been characterized as a 'failure' because it had not resulted in an ultimate 'victory'. The Soviet Generals knew how close to victory the Germans had come, were aware that their country could have been and should have been better prepared to meet this attack, and that the price for this lack of preparedness had been extremely high in lives of Soviet soldiers and citizens.

There had never been any doubt that surprise could influence the course of a particular engagement. It had been possible to downgrade surprise as a strategic factor so long as it could be demonstrated that no single military operation could determine the outcome of a war. With the quantum jumps in destructive power brought about by atomic energy this was becoming more difficult to demonstrate. Insisting that the Soviet Union could always survive now lacked plausibility.

The gratifying growth in Soviet nuclear power promised one method of meeting this threat – deterrence. If the Imperialists could be persuaded that the Soviet Union would respond in kind they might think twice before launching aggression. This possibility had been seized upon by Stalin's successor, Malenkov. In late 1953 and early 1954 the idea was floated that the strength of the socialist camp might now bring peace to the world because it had 'sobered' the imperialists by reminding them of their own vulnerability. Malenkov and his associates put it about that the danger of war had receded, that improved relations with the West were now possible and that this was just as well for a new world war 'with the present means of warfare' would result in 'the destruction of world civilization'.

Malenkov's predictions appear to have been too optimistic for his colleagues. His views were severely criticized and in early 1955 he was replaced as leader by Khruschev and Bulganin. The criticisms were phrased in ideological terms. Claiming that the Americans could be effectively deterred forever contradicted what was claimed to be a law of history: that war was an inevitable concomitant of capitalism and that a showdown between the capitalist and socialist camps was destined to happen at some point. Stating that war could involve the destruction of world civilization suggested that instead of war being the occasion for the triumph of socialism it could be the moment of its demise; its last stage along with that of capitalism. Such a proposition involved not only the suspension of a law of history but the end of history itself.

There was, in fact, no well-established Leninist doctrine concerning the inevitability of war and, to the extent that doctrine did exist, it concerned wars between the capitalist states. Lenin and Stalin had frequently referred to a coming clash between socialism and capitalism only because this had often appeared quite likely; Stalin had found emphasis on a persistent threat useful in keeping the population mobilized.[13] It did not take Khruschev long after assuming power to denounce those who believed that war was 'fatalistically inevitable' and to proclaim the possibility of 'peaceful coexistence' between the two opposed camps. The compromise formula was to accept that a rationalist aggressor would be deterred, while acknowledging the possibility of 'madmen' failing to calculate risks. War was not inevitable, but neither was peace.

Malenkov's mistake was not so much ideological revisionism but to be too premature in his relaxed assessment of the balance of forces. The view of his group was that the Soviet Union now possessed 'everything necessary to guard the peaceful toil of our people and to bring to his senses any one who dares encroach upon our freedom and independence', and that the new conditions made possible a diversion of resources away from the military sector towards light industry. This was not favourably received by either the military or those responsible for heavy industry. The issue was less whether the imperialist aggression could be prevented and more what was the level of preparedness necessary for this task. The opposition insisted that the imperialists had not relaxed their hostility to the Soviet Union or their military build-up. Bulganin stated in March 1954: 'We would commit an irreparable error if we did not strengthen our armed forces. Very many facts indicate that the imperialist forces headed by the US are openly conducting a policy of the preparation of a new war against us'. In January 1955, as the campaign against Malenkov reached a new pitch, there was an increase in war scares[14] and calls to strengthen heavy industry. Dmitri Shepilov, the Editor of *Pravda*, attacked those who wished to downgrade this sector:

In generally understandable language this means: we surrender the advantage of forcing forward the development of heavy industry,

machine construction, energy, chemical industry, electronics, jet
technology, guidance systems, and so forth, to the imperialist
world. . . . It is hard to imagine a more anti-scientific, rotten
theory, which could disarm our people more.[15]

The call was for the Soviet Union to accept that a technological arms
race was unavoidable.

The question of the effects on a socialist society of a nuclear attack
was more difficult to deal with. Talk of the destruction of world
civilization had been attacked for encouraging fatalism and defeatism.
The impression that the destructiveness of nuclear war excluded the
possibility of its occurrence was corrected. However references to the
horrors of nuclear war increased. In 1958 Khruschev described these
horrors:

In addition to immediate destruction, the employment of nuclear
weapons will poison the atmosphere with radioactive fall-out and
this could lead to the annihilation of almost all life, especially in
countries of small territory and high population density. These all
will be literally wiped off the face of the earth.

These words were chosen with care. There was no escaping the
grievous consequences of nuclear war but they were worse for some
than for others. Particularly vulnerable were 'countries of small territory and high population density', an apt description of some of
America's allies in Europe but not of the Soviet Union (nor of the
United States). Marshal of Aviation Vershinin explained in 1957 why
'the possibility of lightning annihilation of the Soviet Union is
excluded'. The reason was that 'our country is not an island or a
point on the globe; it has enormous territory over which our vital
resources are dispersed'.[16] Thus reassurance was found in the physical character of the Soviet Union. However, with the growth of US
stockpiles there were limits to even this argument. It became increasingly difficult to demonstrate how the Soviet Union would survive nuclear exchanges and prevail over her enemies.

The only satisfactory way out of this quandary lay in finding a
means of reducing the destructiveness of the enemy attack. A recognition of the factor of surprise suggested such a way. If it was scientifically proven that the Soviet Union could thwart the imperialist's
plans for attack by a sudden blow of their own then the Soviet Union
and communist ideology might yet survive a war intact. Thus the

Soviet theorists moved, as did many in the United States, towards a theory of pre-emptive attack as a means of demonstrating how the Soviet Union could fight and win a thermonuclear war.

In the early post-Stalin period the possibility that surprise could add to the problems of a country not prepared for war was conceded. If caught unawares, tremendous damage could be suffered. The menace was one of unnecessary damage rather than defeat. Surprise was still not seen as a decisive factor until Rotmistrov's celebrated article of February 1955:

> Surprise attack, employing atomic and hydrogen weapons and other modern means of conflict, now takes on new forms and is capable of leading to significantly greater results than in the past war. . . . Surprise attack with the massive employment of new weapons can cause the rapid collapse of a government whose capacity to resist is low as a consequence of radical faults in its social and economic structure and also as a consequence of an unfavourable geographic position.

Given that neither of these latter weaknesses were admitted for the Soviet Union, Rotmistrov's argument suggested the benefit of attacks directed against the social and economic centres of a capitalist enemy rather than its armed forces. Such an attack was advocated, but only for 'pre-emptive' reasons:

> The duty of the Soviet armed forces is not to permit an enemy surprise attack on our country and, in the event of an attempt to accomplish one, not only to repel the attack successfully but also to deal the enemy counter blows, or even pre-emptive surprise blows, of terrible destructive force. For this the Soviet army and navy possess everything necessary.[17]

These statements were only true if the author was thinking of counter-value rather than counter-force nuclear attacks, or of attacks involving conventional forces.[18]

A pre-emptive attack against strategic air forces required more air power than was then available to the Soviet Union. An article published just before that of Rotmistrov spoke of nuclear weapons placed on aircraft being used to interdict airfields or to affect the course of the ground or naval battle, but not for long-range strategic missions. By 1956, with the first Soviet intercontinental bombers in service, long-range operations were considered feasible and were being openly discussed. At the 20th Party Congress in June 1956, Marshal Zhukov spoke of the increased importance of the Air Force. This then was taken up by General Krasilnikov in a contribution to a collection of essays on warfare. Krasilnikov made it clear that a war could not be won by a single blow against the armed forces of the enemy, especially if they were dispersed in a large, well-defended territory. Nor could a strategic attack against the enemy's 'deep rear' be decisive, though it would help. Victory would only come through an extended war.

This was as before. The new feature was that the initial phase could be of critical importance and could be decided itself by surprise.

The successful employment of strategic surprise in the initial phase of the war can lead to disruption of the opponent's existing plans for the strategic deployment of his main forces and to the possibility of a rapid piecemeal destruction of the troops concentrated by him. . . . An especially intense struggle to pre-empt the opponent will take place in the campaign of the initial phase of the war. . . . In as much as air forces have the greatest readiness for action and dispose of means for dealing powerful blows, campaigns will obviously be started by their active employment. In the campaign of the initial phase both sides will first seek to deal crushing destruction to the opponent's air forces, and his sources for the production of atomic weapons, and to seize mastery in the air.

Complementary to these attacks on the armed forces of the enemy would be strikes 'aimed at undermining the economic might of the opponent and weakening his will for resistance'.[19]

The ICBM completed the revolution in Soviet military affairs. During the post-Stalin thaw there had been explicit discussions on the potential of missiles. They were played down with predictions of limited range, inaccuracy and generally inefficiency as a means of delivering high-value payloads. However, from 1956 on, encouraged by an enthusiast for missiles, General Pokrovsky, it was argued that 'The future . . . belongs to long-range ballistic rockets'. By the middle of 1957 the Russians were reaping the benefits of the early start to their ICBM programme by being the first to test ICBMs. For the first time the Soviet Union appeared to be pulling ahead in the arms race. With many Americans also sharing the same belief, this was a moment for the Kremlin to savour.

With evident relish the Soviet leaders began to lecture on the primacy of the rocket over the bomber. Khruschev spoke, without the whole-hearted support of his own Air Force, of bombers being 'obsolete': 'The present period is something of a turning point. Military specialists believe that airplanes, bombers and fighters, are in their decline. Bombers have such speed and altitudes that they are vulnerable to attack by contemporary rockets'.[20] ICBMs were able to deliver thermonuclear weapons at great speed to anywhere on the globe and in any weather; air defences were incapable of stopping them. Their mobility allowed for concealed launching points and so they could be used for surprise attacks while being virtually invulnerable to attack. Major General Pokrovsky noted in 1956: 'The most effective defence against such long-range rockets is by means of their destruction in storage places, in the process of transport, and on the launching platforms where the preparation for each firing takes a rather long time'. However, these rockets would not require very complicated preliminary equipping and could be 'deployed in the most unexpected places'. Launching platforms could be 'constructed relatively quickly, quite dispersed, and well concealed'. They would be harder to detect than air-fields. 'Therefore it will be very difficult for the enemy to prevent the launching of a rocket'.[21] Once launched, the speed of the rocket would prevent 'its interception and destruction by conventional flying means, artillery fire or any other means. It is possible that some counter-weapon will be found, but without doubt for some time the probability of destruction of the rockets cannot be very great'.[22]

In March 1958, reflecting the general euphoria, General Talensky even went so far as to suggest that ICBMs were decisive – a radical departure from the consistent official line that no single weapon or mode of warfare could itself decide the outcome of wars. The movement in Soviet strategy had been dramatic. In a five-year period it had moved from assigning only minimal importance to the factors of surprise and the new technologies of nuclear weapons and long-range delivery vehicles to a strategy dominated by the concept of surprise and relying on Soviet prowess in ICBMs.

Conclusion

Khruschev attempted to gain as much political benefit as possible from his apparent lead over the Americans, capitalizing on American anxieties. In a classic case of counting chickens before hatching, he regularly boasted of his country's success in missile technology. This strategy became unstuck when it became evident in 1961 that the missile gap was in America's favour and not the other way round.[23]

It is doubtful if Soviet war-plans placed quite so much emphasis on ICBMs as did Khruschev in his rhetoric. The single-minded devotion to this particular weapon was one of the criticisms levelled at Khruschev after he was removed from office in 1964. Though it is natural to observe the similarities in the calls for pre-emptive war capabilities in each of the super-powers, there were still important differences between the two.

The Soviet assumption was that Europe would be the prize in a future war and that this prize would be gained by land forces. There was an obvious incentive not to destroy this prize by thermonuclear bombardment if it could possibly be avoided. Victory would come through the destruction of the enemy's armed forces. There was unceasing rejection of a strategy that relied solely on the bombing of the enemy's economic and population centres. Furthermore Soviet considerations of possible sources of surprise attacks did not stop with a nuclear strike. The Americans were influenced by their experience of Pearl Harbor; the Russians by their experience of land invasions. When Eastern and Western experts met in 1958 to consider ways of reducing the dangers of surprise attacks the Americans were wholly preoccupied with 'nuclear Pearl Harbors' while the Russians were concerned with a wider range of eventualities, including old-fashioned invasions over land. Their interests in the military rôle of atomic weapons was as much with their impact on land warfare as on the 'stability of the rear'. The Soviet Generals insisted that though they would have to adjust tactics to conditions of atomic bombardment they could still prevail.[24]

If it came to nuclear war the Russians did consider, as an article of faith, that their society was better suited to cope with a nuclear war than capitalist societies. They also took practical steps to improve their civil defences, though much of this took the form of reassurances to the population that atomic war could be survived if sensible precautions were taken. There was, however, an important cultural point that needs to be borne in mind when considering the pronouncements of Soviet and American commentators when assessing the strengths and weaknesses of themselves and each other. There has always been an element of reassurance in Soviet pronouncements on the state of the strategic balance, a function perhaps of the inferior position from which the Soviet Union began the nuclear age and the consequent desire to avoid defeatism (and the generally optimistic tone about all things encouraged by the prevailing ideology). The Americans, because of a sense of declining superiority, erred in the opposite direction, stressing the gains being made by the Soviet Union. Often a motive could be found in the desire to encourage a more determined national effort in the arms race. It was quite possible for the Americans to offer gloomy assessments of a decisive tilt in the balance towards the Soviet Union, have it confirmed by Soviet leaders, and yet still be wrong. As will be seen, this is precisely what happened in the late 1950s.

The Soviet Union opted for a policy of pre-emptive war as a way out of the problems posed by parallel nuclear stockpiles of vast destructive power. Given that war could not be ruled out, the Soviet military were as anxious as their Western counterparts to find means of prevailing and of limiting the damage to their own side. There is no evidence that they believed that their improving capabilities for waging nuclear war gave them the option of starting a war, or of gaining a sudden victory with only minimal harm to themselves. Whether or not even a pre-emptive strategy was viable was a question that had to be faced in both East and West.

11 The Technological Arms Race

Not everyone previously convinced of the inevitability of nuclear stalemate was ready, because of *Sputnik*, to adopt the opposite view. Many of those who had warned throughout the mid-1950s of the dangerous illusion of perpetual Western nuclear superiority saw the evident growth of Soviet nuclear capabilities as doing no more than confirming expectations. The folly of a strategy of massive retaliation was even more evident. Proponents of limited war felt their case to be strengthened. '[T]he first effect of the Sputnik on American policy has been to emphasize the thermo-nuclear stalemate and to strengthen the case for supplementing or replacing massive retaliation by limited atom war – and for giving tactical atomic weapons to America's allies', wrote British MP Denis Healey.[1]

In the United States the Army remained insistent on the need to prepare for a limited war and saw no reason to doubt the existence of a nuclear stalemate: 'It would seem that we will have a stalemate just so long as both sides retain the capacity to destroy a large segment of the other side's homeland whether or not the enemy attacks first and with surprise.' The assumption that a surprise first strike could win a war was described as 'wishful'. 'This would be a highly doubtful venture in any event and from the standpoint of the US an immensely risky one as well, because we forfeit from the outset the option of surprise under our form of government'.[2]

The Administration appeared to be moving towards a greater appreciation of limited war capabilities, sensing less value in the threat of massive retaliation. Dulles now wrote that it might well be

155

'feasible to place less reliance upon deterrence of vast retaliatory power'. This was more because of an 'alteration' in the character of nuclear weapons, which made them suitable for clean, tactical use against conventional aggression, than any changed assessment of Soviet nuclear power.[3]

The official view was that the balance would be stable for the foreseeable future. By 1956 the Administration had begun to come to terms with the balance of terror. In August of that year, Secretary of the Air Force Donald Quarles articulated a doctrine of 'sufficiency'. War had become an 'unthinkable catastrophe' from which 'neither side can hope by a mere margin of superiority in airplanes or other means of delivery to escape'. The absolute destructive power available to each side had resulted in a substantial invulnerability' to interdiction. A 'sufficiency' of force was that required to perform the essential retaliatory mission, and was already possessed by the United States. It would take 'some unforeseen technological breakthrough', perhaps in the field of air defence, to cause these requirements to change. It was not expected that technological changes would 'occur in such a revolutionary fashion'.[4] The balance of terror was tending towards a stable equilibrium. Technology was not seen as a particularly disruptive force.

When *Sputnik I* was launched, Administration spokesmen dismissed it as a 'gimmick', and attempted, unsuccessfully, to reassure the public that essential needs of national defence were being seen to and there was no need to panic. To many at the time this appeared to show extraordinary complacency; the Administration seemed unaware of the vast changes taking place in the strategic environment, unable to share the sensation and excitement of being in the midst of a technological revolution. Yet, in retrospect, the Eisenhower Administration stands out as having a more accurate assessment of the state of the strategic balance and the likely impact of technology than its critics. The programmes to which it gave high priority stabilized the balance while the more exotic programmes resulted in few changes in the military situation.[5]

This chapter will look at the developing vision of a technological arms race, particularly as it related to first-strike capabilities. Through the second half of the 1950s increasing but excessive emphasis was placed on technological change. A retrogressive tendency was introduced, resulting in an exaggerated appreciation of both the evolving technology and its impact on the strategic balance. It came to be assumed that the series of startling innovations of the past two decades set a pattern for the future; if sufficient funds and ingenuity were applied to any given problem it could be solved; the results of the growing expenditure and scientific talent being applied to military problems could be spectacular; and also (and here came the major mistake) that any improvement in technology would result in a corresponding improvement in the state of the strategic art. A tendency for strategy to lag behind technology was noted and deplored, with lectures on the need to anticipate the coming technologies so that they could be better exploited. Persistent innovation was confused with strategic revolution.

Exemplary of this sort of tendency was Herman Kahn, a devotee of science fiction since his youth and mesmerized by expectations of fantastic technical progress. He described as 'one of the most startling things that ever happened to me' his participation in 1950 on a Technical Advisory Board when he 'first came in contact with the philosophy which is willing to ask any question and tackle any philosophy'. The final one-third of his book *On Thermonuclear War* (virtually a transcript of a popular series of lectures) consisted of a set of predictions for the future. Kahn described eight wars, each one a 'technological revolution ahead of its predecessor'. The first two were the familiar World Wars I and II; the second two were hypothetical conflicts of 1951 and 1956; the final four were speculations. As the date for World War VIII was put at 1973, it can be seen that Kahn was expecting at least four technological revolutions in the means of modern warfare in the coming thirteen years. Some of the predictions were remarkably accurate, others remarkably inaccurate or at least premature. One example of the former was the prediction that there would be a landing and take-off by manned vehicles from the moon by 1969. But this illustrates the difficulty with Kahn's technological expectations. Putting a man on the moon was achieved through a well-funded crash programme which had been made a national priority. The same is true of many other of Kahn's accurate predictions. His major error was to assume that dramatic scientific breakthroughs and their immediate and rigorous exploitation was the natural state of affairs, not requiring any extraordinary effort.

Kahn recognized that certain feasible developments would be eschewed. Some would be deemed impractical because they 'cost a little too much';[6] others because of a failure to perceive the need for them, a result of the adoption of a misguided doctrine. He considered it quite likely that the US would content itself with a limited deterrent capability, one which provided no options for taking the nuclear initiative. The US might fail by neglect to do enough in boosting air defence, air offence and civil defence. By 1961, given the 'possible Soviet lead in missiles, their interest in a cheap but useful civil defense program and a sober attitude towards the risks of war and peace', the Russians could have the upper hand. Eventually Kahn suspected there would be less inhibitions about exploiting technology. He described and prescribed a frantic search for methods for improving all capabilities. It must be remembered that Kahn's basic assumption was that thermonuclear war would be an ever-present possibility and that though, if it ever came, the results would be tragic, the amount of tragedy could be reduced by the proper precautions. Thus any avenue which promised an amelioration of the effects of enemy attack was worth exploring.

The growing expectations of continual achievement in new technologies that would destabilize the strategic balance can be detected in two official reports written in 1954–5 and 1957 by panels of experts. Both were prepared under the auspices of the Science Advisory Committee of the Office of Defense Mobilization for presentation to the National Security Council. The first was the report of the Technological Capabilities Panel on 'Meeting the Threat of Surprise Attack'. The second was the report of the Security Resources Panel on 'Deterrence and Survival in the Nuclear Age'. They were known as the Killian and Gaither Reports after their respective Chairmen. Each included a forward-looking timetable, anticipating the course of the arms race in the coming decades.

The Killian Report

The Killian Report, presented to the NSC in February 1955, characterized the current period as particularly dangerous. The US had a growing offensive capability not yet quite of 'multi-megaton' dimensions, but the US lacked reliable early warning and defensive capabilities and Strategic Air Command (SAC) was not properly protected against the rapidly improving Soviet offensive capabilities. Neither side could mount an atomic strike which would 'surely be decisive', but the USSR might be tempted to attack before the US forces had achieved the ability to deliver warheads measured in 'multi-megatons'.

Soon this would be achieved. Despite improvements in defences both sides would be vulnerable to surprise attack. The difference was that 'The US can mount a surprise attack; the USSR cannot'. For a 'period of short duration', possibly up to 1960, the US military position relative to that of the USSR would be favourable so that it could hope to emerge from war a 'battered victor'. 'Our military superiority may never be so great again.' It was suggested that the possibilities for exploiting this situation for political benefit should be explored.

By the time the Russians had acquired their own 'multi-megaton' weapons, the Americans should have improved their defences and reduced the vulnerability of SAC. There was a warning that, if the US was laggard in this regard, it could be placed 'in danger of surprise attack and possibly defeat'. This situation could arise as early as 1958, especially if the Russians made faster progress than the Americans with their ICBM programme. The first to win this race would gain an important relative advantage. Not surprisingly, the report impressed upon policy-makers the urgency of speeding up the US ICBM programme and of protecting the existing SAC bases.

Eventually the two super-powers would reach a position where 'attack by either side would result in mutual destruction'. A surprise attack would produce no dividends:

> The ability to achieve surprise will not affect the outcome because each country will have the residual offensive power to break through the defenses of the other country and destroy it regardless of whether the other country strikes first.

In the 1960s, when this prediction came true, a state of mutual assured destruction came to be considered reassuringly stable. Killian's group of experts were less than pleased with the prospect. It would be 'fraught with danger', involving 'a period of instability that might easily be upset by either side'. With no defences capable of alleviating an attack 'a world catastrophe might occur'. Such a condition would be best avoided or escaped if at all possible. To this end it was necessary to 'push all promising technological developments'.

> Should we arrive at a condition where the contest is drawn and neither contestant can derive military advantage, we need not assume that this state is unchangeable or that one country or the other cannot move again into a position of relative advantage. *We see no certainty, however, that the condition of stalemate can be changed through science and technology.* This does not mean that

some new unimagined weapon or development, far afield from any present weapon system, might not provide an advantage to one side or the other.[7]

It could be argued that this statement was too dogmatic. Antiballistic missiles, multiple warheads with extraordinary accuracies, satellites and so on had yet to come. Nevertheless, a form of stalemate was created, perhaps because many developments neutralized each other. The nuances of the strategic relationship have changed enormously. Yet this picture of a stalemate impervious to technological breakthroughs captured the reality of the evolving relationship more accurately than some of the more dramatic presentations that became more popular later in the decade.

The Gaither Report

The Gaither Report, presented to the National Security Council in 1957, shared the Killian Report's anxiety over the race to deploy ICBMs, and the vulnerability of the US deterrent: 'The current vulnerability of SAC to surprise attack during a period of lessened world tension (i.e. a time when SAC is not on a SAC 'alert' status), and the threat posed to SAC by the prospects of an early Russian ICBM capability, call for prompt remedial action.' In order to maintain the US advantage and to prevent 'both the Russians and our allies', believing that the US will 'feel increasing reluctance to employ SAC in any circumstance other than when the United States is directly attacked', active and passive civil defence measures were urged, including 'a program to develop and install an area defence against ICBMs at the earliest possible date'.

In its timetable of future relative strength, the Report confirmed the accuracy of the earlier Killian prediction of the 1956–60 period as being one of comparative US advantage. 'This could be the time to negotiate from strength, since the US military position vis-à-vis Russia might never be so strong again'. The precondition would be an adequate 'alert' status for SAC. Without such, a surprise Soviet attack 'might also completely disarm' the 'air atomic strike capability' of the US. Similarly inadequate protection for the Soviet equivalent to SAC would leave them vulnerable. With neither properly protected 'a surprise attack could determine the outcome of a clash between these two major powers'.[8]

The most worrisome prediction, erroneous as it turned out, was that the USSR was leading in the race for a significant ICBM capability. If successful this would render SAC vulnerable. The period 1959–62 was thus described as 'very critical'. By the mid-1960s SAC should be protected, an early warning capability developed and a start made on anti-ICBM defences. In such circumstances, the only way in which either side could avoid total destruction would be 'a nationwide fallout shelter program'.

Neither of the two reports believed that the first strike need be critical if appropriate measures were taken in time. The latter report derived its sense of urgency from the fact these measures had yet to be taken. One of the briefings to the Gaither Committee was by Albert Wohlstetter who presented them with a similar analysis to that later published in *Foreign Affairs* on 'The delicate balance of terror'. Where they differed was on the feasibility of defence. The Killian Report saw little likelihood of defences adequate to permit survival against a full-scale attack, or that there could be much escape from a condition of stalemate. Here the Gaither Report diverged. Starting from the early 1970s it envisaged dramatic improvements in the quantity and quality of long-range ballistic missiles, but also in 'means for detecting and defending against missile attacks'. It continued:

The missiles in turn will be made more sophisticated to avoid destruction; and there will be a continuing race between the offense and the defense. Neither side can afford to lag or fail to match the other's efforts. There will be no end to the technical moves or countermoves.

The strategic balance was seen to tend not towards stability but to an 'extremely unstable equilibrium', for 'a temporary technical advance (such as a high-certainty missile defense against ballistic missiles) could give either nation the ability to come near to annihilating the other'.[9]

A situation could develop, indeed could be developing, in which groups of military technologists would be pitting their wits against each other, attempting to gain strategic advantage through technical innovation. There would be no definitive solutions to military problems. Though recent innovations had aided the offence, there was no reason in principle why future innovations should not favour the defence. Then, in solving one problem for the defence, a new one would be created for the offence. The solution to this would put new demands on the defence and so on. Thus ICBMs would render any progress in conventional air defence systems irrelevant, but it was conceivable that one day an effective anti-ballistic missile (ABM) could be developed. Putting ICBMs in concrete shelters might protect them from incoming enemy missiles, but only until the enemy missiles improved their accuracy.

There were two quite distinct views presented in the Reports concerning the likely and desirable character of the evolving strategic relationship between the two super-powers. The Killian Report pointed to the development of parallel capabilities for destruction, and viewed this with gloom because the United States would have lost its advantage and a false move by either side could result in complete catastrophe. In early 1955 to recognize that the world's two greatest powers could literally wipe out each other and much else besides, and that there was no obvious way out of this impasse, was profoundly disturbing. This was especially dangerous given the hostility between these two powers and the American responsibility for holding back Soviet expansionism.

By 1957 the desire for US superiority was still strong but there was a growing fear of Soviet superiority, in which case a balance of terror was preferable. There was concern over an offence–defence duel, fuelled by persistent technological innovations. This was viewed with gloom because of the prospect of an unending arms race driven by the prospect of moments of terrifying weakness as well as moments of transitory superiority. Henry Kissinger articulated these fears in a 1960 article:

> Technology is volatile. The advantage of surprise can be overwhelming. The forces-in-being are almost surely decisive – at least in all-out war. A major cause of instability is the very rate of technological change. Every country lives with the nightmare that even if it puts forth its best efforts its survival may be jeopardized by a technological breakthrough on the part of its opponent.[10]

George Kennan spoke of a dismal future if this weapons race was allowed to run its course:

> The technological realities of this competition are constantly changing from month to month and from year to year. Are we to flee like haunted creatures from one defensive device to another,

each more costly and humiliating than the one before, cowering underground one day, breaking up our cities the next, attempting to surround ourselves with elaborate shields on the third, concerned only to prolong the length of our lives while sacrificing all the values for which it might be worth while to live at all?[11]

Mutual Fears of Surprise Attack

Thus, by the late 1950s, prominent strategic and military figures both in the United States and the Soviet Union were advocating the development of a capacity for pre-emptive attacks. In both countries technological progress was being monitored carefully and anxiously for further indications of some imminent breakthrough that would provide one side or the other with a decisive advantage. Such a situation involved obvious dangers. To prepare for pre-emption, each side would have to build up large counter-force capabilities with an instant readiness to fire. Such an effort could suggest to the other side preparations for an unprovoked first strike, so providing an incentive to pre-empt. With both nervous about a surprise attack, even in the absence of any crisis or aggression, a climate of fear and mutual distrust could develop which could end in an unnecessary race to pre-empt. Kissinger warned in the article cited above how measures taken for self-defence could be 'indistinguishable to the other side from a desire to launch a surprise attack'. The structure of strategic forces 'may contribute to instability regardless of the intentions of the two sides'.

Fears such as these were not novel. The start of World War I was widely believed to have been accelerated because of the extra tensions generated by the rush to be the first to mobilize. There was a developing view of the cold war as a consequence of mutual fear and distrust rather than objective conflicts of interests. The precautionary measures taken by one side (based on its fears) provided cause for the fears of the other, in turn confirming the original fears. The cold war came to be seen as self-sustaining. The concern now was that a similar spiral of misperception could result in an unnecessary hot war.[12]

The possibility that war could be stimulated by purely military calculations had previously been associated with neglect. Inadequate military precautions by the peacefully inclined were seen as a temptation for aggressors. For example, failure to protect strategic forces offered an opportunity that men in the Kremlin would find hard to resist. In 1954 Brodie had spoken of how a 'vulnerable strategic air force . . . is not merely of no value as a deterrent, it positively invites an attack that might otherwise not be contemplated'. On the same theme Kahn explained how 'We do not want a potential enemy's high command contemplating for months or years a possible opportunity to eliminate most of his supposed trouble at one blow'.[13]

Now this was taken a stage further. Thomas Schelling demonstrated how the calculations of two sides normally able to resist the temptation to launch a surprise attack, could look quite different in a crisis. He called this 'the reciprocal fear of surprise attack'.

> If surprise carries an advantage, it is worth while to avert it by striking first. Fear that the other may be about to strike in the mistaken belief that we are about to strike gives us a motive for striking, and so justifies the other's motive. But, if the gains from even successful surprise are less desired than no war at all, there is no 'fundamental' basis for an attack by either side. Nevertheless, it looks as though a modest temptation on each side to sneak in a first blow – a temptation too small by itself to motivate an attack – might become compounded through a process of interacting expectations, with additional motive for attack being produced by successive cycles of 'He thinks we think he thinks we think . . . he thinks we think he'll attack; so he thinks we shall; so he will; so we must'.[14]

For such a cycle to start, two conditions would have to obtain. First strikes would have to carry a sizeable and perhaps decisive premium and both sides would require the capability to launch such a strike – otherwise the fear of pre-emption would not be mutual. This second condition added to the premium attached to the first strike, for it could now deny the enemy the benefit of his first strike. For the temptation to pre-empt to arise, there would have to be a high state of tension between the two and a reasonable chance of an outbreak of war from another cause. As Glenn Snyder noted: 'It is very hard to believe that any country would deliberately accept the *certainty* of severe retaliatory damage in preference to the *uncertain* prospect of being the recipient of a first strike.'[15]

A successful pre-emptive attack would have to reduce the potential damage of the enemy's retaliatory strike to be disarming. Counter-force capabilities required large forces. If the other side had only a moderate force, they could be saturated by a sufficiently large attack and so removed. But in such circumstances the adversary would not have a counter-force option of his own, so there would be no *mutual* fear of surprise attack and the need for pre-emption would not arise. This need would only arise if the adversary enjoyed comparable counter-force capabilities. But then the problems of a disarming first strike would be that much greater. Indeed a strike of this sort would only be conceivable if each attacking weapon could destroy more than one of the equivalent weapons. The exchange must favour the offence. The only factor that could possibly alter this calculation would be the deployment of an effective ABM system which might obstruct the enemy's retaliation. However, if ABMs were used to provide defence of the retaliatory forces, rather than cities, then the demands on the first strike would be increased further.

Technology and Stability

In terms of the model of an offence–defence duel there were therefore two profoundly destabilizing possibilities that would do grave damage to any stalemate. The first was the ability to launch a sudden disarming, counter-force attack taking out more offensive weapons than were being used to execute the attack. The second was the ability to block an incoming missile attack with active defensive measures. A possible third was civil defence measures sufficient to absorb an attack, reducing its effects to manageable levels.

The Gaither Report depicted an ABM as one of the most unsettling possibilities for the future, representing it as the logical next stage in the arms race. The early designs for air defence in the nuclear age had been concerned with bomber attacks. During the 1950s a defensive anti-aircraft system was developed in the United States. This involved a line of radars on sea and land to provide distant early warning, a variety of guided interceptors with supporting control facilities to get them to the right place at the right time, and a national command and control mechanism, intended to tie the local units together. Unfortunately, by the time the system had been developed, it had been rendered obsolete by the imminent arrival of ICBMs.

Study of ways to cope with this new threat began in 1956. The design of interceptor missiles was not the most serious problem. The real difficulty lay in detecting, identifying, tracking and predicting the trajectory of an incoming missile in sufficient time for the interceptor to be launched to meet it. To achieve this feat major improvements would be needed in a category of technological breakthroughs on a par with that of the ICBM itself. Herman Kahn noted that the statement: 'in the air and missile age the offense has an intrinsic advantage over the defense', was 'only true, if at all, because our sensors are not reliable. . . . A breakthrough in this field comparable to the invention of radar in 1935 might well make all forms of air offense incredibly costly'.[16]

Even then, as every commentator was quick to point out, the requirements for successful defence would be exacting. The opportunities for deception and confusion by the offence would be considerable, while the tolerance of failure would be minimal. Kahn approved of air defence, even given its limitations, because it would impose constraints on the offence, 'forcing the enemy to use a high-performance bomber, to put only a small number of bombs on the bomber, and to confine himself to saturation and deceptive tactics'. Its main value would be in complementing the vast civil defence effort he believed to be vital.

Whereas an effective active defence was considered a possibility, if not a probability, for the future, the specific protection of the retaliatory forces was a problem of the moment. The point was that the vulnerability of US bombers to surprise attack was not necessary and could be rectified by prompt action. The anxiety about the threat to SAC came not so much from the development of a Soviet doctrine of and capabilities for surprise attack, but because of the lack of interest in the SAC hierarchy in doing much to reduce the vulnerability of its bombers. Wohlstetter and his colleagues at RAND proposed providing each aircraft with a concrete shelter placed just below the ground as the optimum way of dealing with the problem. This was too defence-minded for the Air Force who preferred to concentrate on pre-emption to destroy Soviet offensive systems. The only precaution they would accept was continual airborne alert.[17]

The intermediate range ballistic missiles (IRBMs) – *Thor* and *Jupiter* – being deployed in Europe to provide an early missile threat to the Soviet Union were as, if not more, vulnerable because of their fixed locations, lack of protection, slow reaction time (because of liquid fuelling), and proximity to the Soviet Union.

The *Minuteman* ICBMs, then under development, would be less vulnerable. Dispersal would mean that it would not be possible for the enemy to destroy more than one with a single shot of his own. Protection in underground silos would ensure that the enemy's warhead would have to be extremely accurate to ensure destruction. Solid fuels would permit rapid launching and so a continuous high-alert status (hence the name *Minuteman*). The chances of survival could be further increased through mobility. Here the *Polaris* missiles, to be launched from submarines, also under development in the late 1950s, came into their own.

A Navy document of 1958 spoke of how the 'fortress concept' of hardened shelters and active defences merely promoted an arms race.

It challenges the enemy in an area (endless production of higher-yield, more-accurate missiles) where he is ready and able to respond impressively. Fortress-busting is always possible, since any fixed defenses, including all foreseeable anti-ICBM defenses, can be overwhelmed by numbers.

Mobility and concealment, on the other hand, would discourage an arms race:

Numbers of missiles will avail the enemy nothing, if he does not know the location of his target. We in effect take an initiative which he can overcome only by maintaining hour-to-hour fire-comb surveillance of all our land areas *and* the vast oceans.

The *Polaris* submarines, with their locations unknown and unpredictable, would be a 'comparatively cheap retaliatory system', according to Admiral Burke, the Chief of Naval Operations. 'It won't be necessary to maintain large residual forces of Polaris submarines against the possible destruction of surprise attack'. A force of invulnerable submarines carrying nuclear weapons could guarantee deterrence, releasing resources to prepare for limited war, a much more plausible eventuality than all-out nuclear exchanges.[18]

Not everyone was so convinced, including many in the Navy hierarchy who saw a strategic nuclear force as diverting funds away from the large surface ships they preferred. Another objection was the expense involved in basing missiles in submarines. Wohlstetter was concerned with the fragility of the communications links, a concern that extended to all mobile systems, whether missiles under the sea or on railroads (there was a plan to put *Minuteman* on rails) or bombers on airborne alert. The Air Force, not pleased to have another service poaching missions, argued that submarines might well be extremely vulnerable to counter-force attacks, especially given the size of the Soviet submarine fleet. Snyder noted, somewhat blandly, 'If the Soviets were to find a way to locate, identify, and trail all our Polaris submarines "on station" around the Soviet periphery, they might be able to destroy them all nearly simultaneously'.[19] Kahn suggested other means for disabling submarines including indiscriminating area attacks on the ocean, perhaps using mines on the sea-bed.

Kahn's main objection was that opting for mobility would entail the acquisition of a lower performance system. The expense would mean that fewer would be bought and those that were bought would have only small and inaccurate warheads. Fixed ICBMs would also exhibit these weaknesses to some degree. The result might well be to degrade the capacity for counter-city attacks (especially if the enemy had taken civil defence precautions) and preclude counter-force attacks altogether, so that the missiles might be inadequate for retaliation. Wohlstetter provided an example of five half-megaton weapons with an average inaccuracy of two miles. These weapons would destroy half the population of a city of 900,000 spread over 40 square miles. If the population were provided with shelters capable of resisting an over-pressure of 100 pounds per square inch, 60 weapons would be needed. If deep rock shelters were available, the requirement could be pushed up to 1000. (*Minuteman*, when it arrived, had about twice the yield and half the inaccuracy that Wohlstetter postulated.)

The short-range IRBMs, however, were suitable for counter-force attacks. Rathjens calculated that, as guidance depended on the early powered portion of the missile's flight, errors would increase with distance; a 1500-mile range IRBM should only have a quarter the delivery error of a 5500-mile ICBM. As IRBMs would be less than half the price of ICBMs, on a cost basis they might well be in the order of 35 times as effective as ICBMs against hard-point targets (i.e. bomber and missile bases). However, Rathjens added 'that it cannot be emphasized too strongly that the closeness of [IRBM] bases to the Iron Curtain would make them appallingly vulnerable'.

The effort to reduce vulnerability would require a loss of offensive capability. This is why it was felt that missiles should not completely displace bombers. Bombers could carry a greater and more differentiated payload and deliver it with higher accuracies. They could assess damage and even engage in some searches for the most appropriate victims. With men in control, a versatility was available that could not be found with a missile moving inexorably towards a single pre-planned target. Virtue could even be detected in a bomber's lack of speed; in a crisis they could be put on alert and even sent part of the way to their targets, thus signalling resolve, with the option of recall still available. Above all, they could find and attack discrete military targets, possibly including protected ICBMs.[20] Their main disadvantages in a counter-force rôle were that they could not achieve surprise and their vulnerability to air defences.

For those enamoured by counter-force and first-strike strategies the bomber was an attractive instrument of nuclear warfare. Going over completely to missiles would signal a commitment to second-strike strategies, a reduction of ambitions, a recognition that only a limited number of exceptional threats could be deterred. It would cast doubt on the extension of deterrence to other nations.

Missiles would not be very good at fighting one another. Counter-force attacks by missiles against other missiles were likely to be costly and ineffectual because of the opportunities for protection. Active defence by anti-missile missiles was also liable to be ineffectual because of the speed of the attacking weapons. The only real dual left was between the offence and passive measures for the protection of cities and economic facilities. If it were possible to afford these targets some protection comparable to that being provided for the nuclear forces themselves, then the small warheads of the missile force would have their destructive potential reduced, perhaps to levels acceptable for the defender. If, however, bombers were maintained to provide a greater range of options and more destructive power for the offence, they would also provide a greater opportunity for missile attacks. Air defence missile systems might well get sufficient warning to intercept an attacking bomber force; bombers sitting idle and in the open at air bases provided relatively easy targets for ICBMs.

As long as bombers and IRBMs existed the tasks that all strategic forces could and would be required to perform were many and various. If it were decided to concentrate solely on long-range missiles then matters would be greatly simplified. Such a decision might result from improvements in the quality and quantity of missiles, so that counter-city missions, if not counter-force missions, could be performed with greater ease and effectiveness. The replacement of bombers by ICBMs by the other side would make the counter-force mission less feasible. The situation would then become more and not less stable. With no bombers and IRBMs there would be little incentive to get forces launched at the slightest hint of an enemy strike lest they be caught on the ground. The premium on surprise attacks would be drastically reduced with both sides sure that their forces would survive a first strike and then be able to inflict a devastating retaliatory blow. As James King noted the 'dominance of the offensive', a theme that also runs right through Brodie's book *Strategy in the Missile Age*, was linked to 'the nuclear phase of the Air Age', and was likely to be replaced by the 'dominance of the deterrent' in the missile age.[21]

All this indicated the error of assigning to technology a predominantly disruptive rôle. With the move from the established bombers to the novel long-range missiles, some qualities would be gained while others would be lost. The net result would be to enhance strategies based on second strikes at the expense of those based on first strikes. One consequence of this move would be to dampen fears of a cycle of mutually reinforcing fears of surprise attacks; it would clearly take a number of missiles in a counter-force strike to be sure of destroying a single enemy missile. In such circumstances, even if one believed that war was extremely likely, rather than pre-empt it might be better to let the enemy strike first. Even if an attacker used up all his striking force, he would still not be able to obliterate the retaliatory force. The damage caused by retaliation even by a reduced force – so long as it was specifically directed at the cities of the aggressor – would probably be greater than the indirect damage to one's own cities resulting from an all-out counter-force attack.

The advantages of the resultant stability were such that some argued that the US should move to embrace it, even at the expense of renouncing counter-force as an objective, and even encouraging the development of invulnerable Soviet systems, so that they need not feel anxious about US surprise attacks. Oskar Morgenstern stated the principle: 'In order to create a nuclear stalemate under conditions of nuclear plenty it is necessary for *both* sides to possess invulnerable retaliatory forces.'[22]

Others balked at this. Snyder wrote that, given the US need to 'present the Soviets with at least some risk that we would strike first if sufficiently provoked', it could not 'be in the US interest . . . for the Soviets to make their weapons invulnerable to our counter-force fire'. In order to be able to fight all-out war more efficiently and deter less than all-out Soviet attacks on Europe, Snyder advocated keeping some IRBMs and bombers in the force, despite their vulnerability.[23]

With the US provision of credible nuclear threats providing the basis of NATO's strategy, Snyder's concern was understandable. Yet, with the declining opportunities for counter-force attacks that would result as the Russians took steps to protect their own forces, there would be a corresponding decline in the attractiveness of any strategy that could require taking the nuclear initiative. Instead of technology offering new ways out of this dilemma, it was confirming the stalemate.

The Strategy of Stable Conflict

12 The Formal Strategists

Behind the whole argument about first-strike strategies was a crisis of identity for the military, and particularly for the Air Force. Such strategies offered the last best hope of fighting a nuclear war according to established military concepts. The idea of counter-force attacks could be traced to the early doctrines of strategic air bombardment and this provided a sense of continuity with former days. Apart from the problems created for the Western Alliance, if no feasible method could be found of executing a first strike successfully, the Air Force would be left without a means of engaging in a war that could bring victory in any plausible or tolerable way.

The crisis went even deeper, for, in the construction of all conceivable strategies, the capabilities of the new weapons were far more pertinent than the qualities of the men who were to use them. With the coming of the missile age this process was accelerated. Destruction was becoming more automated and less resistible. The links with traditional military practices were tenuous. The bomber pilot, weaving through air defences, locating his target and releasing his bombs, was to be replaced by a technician, situated in some underground silo, protected by concrete and ready to launch his pre-targeted missile only on the receipt of a signal from a distant commander.

The human element was being concentrated into the decision to employ nuclear weapons and the unambiguous communication of the relevant commands. Technical skiil and ingenuity were devoted to the design and production of offensive weapons, reducing the opportunities for enemy defences, but in the process also reducing the demands on professional military talents. The implementation of an order to attack would involve the employment of modern means of communication and a strict adherence to orders. Loyalty and discipline were in fact the only traditional military virtues relevant to the missile age; heroism, leadership, quick wits and other combat virtues had little place in this sort of warfare. Soldiers were not expected to take the initiative. Every move had to wait authorization from political masters. The last vestige of a contest with the armed forces of the other side, rather than the destruction of his society, would be lost. When remote-controlled missiles dominated the force structure of both sides, the human element of war would be lost altogether.

In the United States, the military also found themselves being eclipsed by new types of experts more tuned to the perplexing demands of the nuclear age. Civilians intruded into domains once occupied solely by the professional military. The art of combat lost its relevance when the aim was to deter and when any future war would be fought in such a radically different manner from those of the past. The problems of national defence were those of the management of technical innovation, large-scale engineering projects and far-flung organizations, and of the formulation of a credible doctrine for the employment of means of unprecedented destruction. The responsible politicians turned to civilian specialists to provide guidance and assistance.

Novel forms of expertise became associated with each aspect of defence policy. This was as true for the development and manipulation of strategic concepts as it was for the design of a missile nose-cone. These specialist civilian strategists approached their subject with tools supplied by contemporary social science, particularly economics. The authors of an influential book published in 1960 by the RAND Corporation – the spiritual, and often actual, home of the new strategy – explained that 'Essentially we regard *all* military problems as, in one of their aspects, economic problems in the efficient allocation and use of resources'.[1]

The intellectual apparatus developed by the civilian strategists was designed to cope with situations characterized by complexity and uncertainty. They were masters of powerful logical reasoning based on simplifying assumptions. The essence of the strategy that emerged was that any use or threat of use of nuclear weapons should be seen as a supremely political act, reducing the potential relevance of purely military considerations. They did not devise new strategies for the military but strategies for politicians. These had the expressed intention of minimizing the influence of military considerations. For want of a better term, this might be called a strategy of stable conflict.

Military Problems and the Scientific Method

The civilian scientist's claims for his advice on military problems to be taken seriously rested upon his ability to devise solutions through disciplined reasoning and by using techniques available for handling and interpreting large quantities of conflicting data. These, he could argue, were more credible than those based on the fruits of military experience. The first attempt to use quantitative methods, by F. W. Lanchester in his book on *Aircraft in Warfare* of 1916, did little more than demonstrate mathematically certain military principles well understood in practice. During World War II opportunities arose for scientists to offer impressive guidance for actual operations, based on intensive study of the successes and failures of past operations. The practical nature of the work was captured by its description: 'Operational Research'. One of its founders, Professor Blackett, differentiated it from other areas where the scientific method was being used to study social phenomena because of 'the direct relation of the work to executive action'.[2]

Operational Research began in Britain with studies for the RAF on how to make best use of radar. Some of its early success can be seen in anti-submarine warfare. Other studies led to recommendations on the most appropriate size for convoys and on the most effective targets for air-raids on Germany. A number of features of this early work need to be emphasized in order to contrast it with post-war military applications of the scientific method. The data for operations research were taken from the accumulated experience of actual operations. The conclusions derived from the systematic analysis of these data, often with recourse to mathematical techniques, could be translated into tactical advice for future combat. It was therefore a complement to traditional forms of military planning and not a substitute for it. The operations most likely to benefit from the application of these techniques were those in which there were large numbers of comparable engagements on which to base analysis and in which sufficient factors were constant to prevent the analysis being overwhelmed by too many variables. Sir Solly Zuckerman noted that field warfare presented problems. It moved too fast for any results to be applied and because 'the situations in field warfare were infinitely more varied than in either air or sea war'.[3]

In the post-war years comparable research had to address itself to possible operations that were completely without precedent. The relevant weapons had often not been built when the studies were done and would never be tested in combat. If war came there would be no opportunity for learning through trial and error. There would be one trial in which no margin of error would be tolerable. Exchanges of nuclear firepower defied human imagination and often reason. All that was known was a considerable amount about the effect of a wide variety of types of nuclear explosions based on the aftermath of the detonations over Hiroshima and Nagasaki and subsequent nuclear tests,[4] and estimates about the properties of the alternative means of delivery and means of defence. With the improvement of methods for intelligence collection increasing amounts of information were deduced about the capabilities of the potential adversary.

There was therefore still a certain amount of material with which to continue the operational research tradition. Analysts attached to the armed forces worked on operational questions, such as the optimum altitude of bomb release or the best way to penetrate air defences. Soon the range of issues widened to provide guidance to governments on crucial policy decisions concerning the design, procurement, basing, control and operation of new weapons. In the United States there was a growth of quasi-autonomous organizations, such as RAND, funded by Government contracts for studies on these policy decisions. As the staff of these organizations also published their work in books and journals, the outside world was provided with a glimpse of the relevant analytical techniques and, on a nonclassified basis, samples of the fruits of their application. No comparable organizations emerged in Europe. The necessary information and the devices for processing this information remained scarce and monopolized by governments.

In the US the output of the operational researchers became influential. Academic strategists were exposed to it during visits to the RAND Corporation or at conferences and seminars where the two groups mixed. Nevertheless, much of their work was either classified or highly technical. Wohlstetter described analysts, such as those who worked with him on the study which discovered the SAC's vulnerability problem, as 'the largely unsung heroes of strategy in the nuclear age'.[5] The credit for developing the first-strike/second-strike distinction and recognizing the difficulties of maintaining stable deterrence, he argued, should go to those working in this empirical tradition, and not to the strategic writings of the natural and social scientists, on the whole unfamiliar to the teams working at RAND on the relevant studies in the early 1950s.

The sort of work undertaken at RAND became known as 'systems analysis'. The precise nature of this work is difficult to pin down because, in the 1950s, some sort of systems approach appeared in attempts to deal with all manner of questions from the trivial to the fundamental. The word 'system' came to be a vogue adjective, indicating a capacity to view problems as a whole, rather than in fragmented components, and to master complexity. The term was adopted in a variety of distinct occupations, each with their own literature and specialist jargon. It could be used in connection with complicated engineering projects, so that it became necessary to talk of 'weapons systems' rather than a mere weapon (to belie the notion that a single item or military equipment could perform any useful task by itself). The search for the most effective way to perform given tasks at the lowest possible cost became known as 'systems analysis'. Meanwhile, systems theory described an academic aspiration for an all-embracing conceptual framework.

A variety of systems approaches were adopted to help plan large military programmes or to aid decision-makers in some of their more difficult choices. Inevitably much of this work took for granted the underlying conflict that inspired and informed defence policy. As Albert Wohlstetter noted, for them 'conflict elements are not in the centre of analysis. They are treated by assumption or suppressed'. This is where strategists, such as Wohlstetter, came in. Their rôle was 'in the systematic study and design of the major alternatives for conflict systems'. This involved:

> [T]he *explicit* outline and study of alternative systems of interdependent parts where the comparative performance of a system is affected not only by the machines and the men who are elements in the system but also by the opposing behaviour of men and machines outside.[6]

Thus strategic studies involved the consideration of one very particular sort of system.

In this manner it was possible to make the best of the available information and even to work out how to generate some more, but it was not possible to compensate fully for the lack of hard information. The limits of this method were determined by the number and range of the variables and the extent of what could not be known. One result was to encourage a tendency, which gradually became more acute, to place an extremely sophisticated technical analysis within a crude political framework. The 'conflict systems', to use Wohlstetter's terminology, concentrated on the relationship between the capabilities of the potential belligerents and speculated on the physical consequences of their hostile interaction, varying assumptions within parameters that could be empirically determined. Where the analysis became far less effective and satisfactory was when considering the 'conflict system' as a relationship between men and political structures, rather than machines. Here most of the 'evidence' was soft – drawn from inadequate historical parallels, from limited experience of crises and from untutored intuition.

Little could be known about the likely responses of human beings to any of the situations that they were liable to find themselves in during a nuclear war – either in deciding whether to launch a nuclear attack, or in implementing this decision, or in anticipating and suffering the results. There were unavoidable uncertainties over whether it was reasonable to expect a nuclear war to have it own conventions and ground rules of the sort evident in the warfare of the past. One possibility mooted was the mutual avoidance of cities. On the other hand a nuclear exchange might be unremitting and indiscriminate. With each side able to choose from a variety of strategies there were many possible scenarios and this added further complications to military planning.

It was not only that there was a range of choice likely to face decision-makers. Many of the influences that would shape those choices lay outside the scope of any manageable 'conflict system' – in culture, economics or a series of temporary phenomena that could not be anticipated in models. The construction of 'scenarios' of East–West crises to provide a context for war-gaming could, if the scenario was presented often enough, turn doubtful hypotheses into plausible contingencies. For example, the 'Hamburg Grab' had great value in analysing how one might cope with a limited, probing action against a significant piece of territory, but it was chosen because of Hamburg's proximity to the Eastern border rather than its intrinsic value. The interests that might lead one nation to engage in provocative adventures with a high risk of disaster became less relevant in the analyses than the question of how it might succeed. It was as if police officers were being taught the art of homicide detection in terms of opportunity and murder weapon, but never motive.

The errors of adopting methodologies suited to the construction of a military force when considering its employment in complex political situations and of allowing crucial but unpredictable factors to be either excluded from the analyses for reasons of methodological rigour or else included in a wholly specious, quantified form, became exposed in the Vietnam War. However, even before this sorry experience, some of the former practitioners of operations research in Britain expressed concern over the ahistorical and apolitical bias of the American researchers, warning that more was being sought in the 'scientific method' than could ever be provided. Patrick Blackett complained of 'bizarre' recommendations based on a pseudo-science that was insensitive to the real attributes of nations and decision-makers.[7] Sir Solly Zuckerman commented that:

> [I]t is based upon assumptions about human behaviour which seem totally unreal. It neither constitutes scientific analysis nor scientific theorising, but is a non-science of untestable speculations about Western and Soviet bloc behaviour.[8]

One alternative was to rely on common sense – the sum of personal understanding of human nature and more immediate political circumstances – to develop judgments on how reasonably sensible and responsible national leaders might act under various scenarios. Such an approach could not provide definitive answers, not only because it was patently subjective, but also because by necessity it would be sensitive to changes in the prevailing conditions in international politics. It allowed for a few simple generalizations, but offered little room for systematic theorizing about nuclear strategy.

Yet another alternative was to assume the emerging situation to be wholly novel, forget the past, return to first principles and attempt to build up a new theory appropriate to the new age. The interest here was in a pure theory of strategy with premises, logic, and conclusions relevant to East–West relations but not derived from them. Those who developed their judgments and prescriptions through this sort of disciplined, formalized reasoning will be called here the 'formal strategists'. The exemplary formal strategist was Thomas Schelling, with Morton Kaplan, Glenn Snyder, Daniel Ellsberg, Malcolm Hoag and Oskar Morgenstern also having a right to inclusion. The exemplary methodology for the formal strategists was provided by game theory.

Game Theory

Game Theory provided an approach to the design and study of conflict systems. It had been invented by the distinguished mathematician John von Neumann in the 1920s and developed in a joint work with Oskar Morgenstern in 1944.[9] It was not the only type of refined theory of conflict available to formal strategists, nor was it always employed in a pure form. For a time, until the mid-1960s, the employment of matrices was the *sine qua non* of a serious strategist, though the models and mathematics were often applied in a somewhat desultory manner. Nevertheless, the appearance of quantification was taken to indicate rigorous scholarship. The conclusions and prescriptions encouraged by Game Theory could often be reached by less exotic forms of reasoning. Some leading strategists such as Kahn used it only sparingly. Others, such as Morton Kaplan, had brief flirtations with Game Theory only to abandon it later. To a large measure its notoriety resulted from the fact that one of the most original contributors to formal strategy, Thomas Schelling, and one of its most trenchant critics, Anatol Rapaport, were both leading exponents of the techniques of Game Theory.[10]

The importance of Game Theory was that it provided a means of reducing strategic problems to a manageable form in which the dilemma and the paradoxes of the age could be bared and solutions explored. It exemplified a certain type of thinking, presenting it in its purest form. It was certainly not a sufficiently powerful instrument to shape opinion itself. Nor could it be taken as some sort of scientific proof for particular policies, though it was on occasion presented as such. As a form of logical reasoning it depended on premises which were subjectively determined. It could offer valuable insights into behaviour. What it could not do was to predict how actors in the real world would respond to situations approximating to those in the theoretical models, or even to say how they ought to respond, given that the relevant decision-makers could well attribute different values to the alternative outcomes of a particular 'game'.

The aspiration of Game Theory was to suggest rules for successful participation in any conflict, be it at home, work or play, on the roads or in international relations. A game of strategy was one in which the best course of action for each player depended on what the other players did, and could be distinguished from games of skill or chance. This emphasis on the interdependence of the adversaries' decisions provided the essence of the theory.[11] The second important assumption was that of rational behaviour, based on calculations aimed at maximizing values. No particular set of values was associated with 'rational' behaviour in this sense. All that was required was that whatever the values, they were held in an explicit, transitive and internally consistent manner. The values attached to alternative outcomes of games were known as *payoffs*. The aim of a game was to maximize payoffs while being cognizant of the adversary's similar intention. The range of choices permitted to each player were decided either by rules which could be mutually agreed, or by restraints imposed by the situation. Because each player affected the moves of the other, the resources available to shape alternative outcomes influenced the other's moves through their *potential*. The actual application of resources came when the moves had been decided and were being played out.

Games could vary according to the number of participants (two-person, three-person . . . *n*-person games) and the extent of the conflict of interest. A *zero-sum game* was one in which the potential gains were fixed and so one player gained exactly what the other lost. *Non-zero sum* or *variable sum games* were those in which one's gain did not necessarily correspond to the other's loss. Both could win or both could lose, or there could be various mixes of gains and losses. For the most part, the application of Game Theory to strategic studies concentrated on two-person non-zero sum games. The two super-powers provided the players and the possibility of mutual nuclear destruction ensured that there was a shared interest in avoiding certain outcomes. If the payoffs for each player depended on decisions taken by the other player, and if there were certain outcomes which could suit the interests of both players, then what resulted was not all-out conflict but a carefully constructed bargain, which included elements of co-operation.

Some of the uses to which game theory were put by strategists were severely criticized.[12] A frequent complaint was of unreal assumptions. The concern was not so much with the assumption of interdependence of players or the possibility of co-operation. Indeed the gravamen of Rapaport's argument was that the use of theory suited to the analysis of conflict allowed far too little scope for the analysis of forms of co-operation. The basic problem was with the assumption of rationality. The prescriptions of the theory only seemed to work if the players would, in practice, be rational, calculating and 'utility-maximizing'. No regard was taken of a whole range of psychological and sociological factors – such as mental quirks, lack of awareness, domestic political pressures, value-conflicts or sheer errors of judgment. 'Purely instrumental choice unhindered either by emotional or ideological blocks on the one hand, or by ignorance on the other, exists only in the abstract world of game theory.'[13] Furthermore, the opportunities for action and thus the range of choice were determined by the structure of the game, which was the creation of the theorist. As the structure of any game was unlikely to be reproduced exactly in real life, one could not predict the course of rational decision. Finally the situations described in Game Theory were static. There was a single judgment about values, the calculation of moves, and the receipt of payoffs. Yet in international affairs policy-makers had to deal with a sequence of events in which their assumptions and circumstances were liable to rapid change. Their sense of values could also be affected as the full meaning of certain outcomes became apparent.

The tenuous relationship, between the contrived world of the theory and the real world, limited the practical validity of any conclusions. Yet, it was argued, the opposite was often believed. The excessive use of quantification and the scientific pretensions created an aura of objectivity that was quite undeserved. For example, the payoffs connected with the alternative outcomes had to be compared along some scale. One course of action that might be rational if one assigned a high value to the prevention of a Soviet take-over of Western Europe would seem less sensible if one was indifferent to the fate of Western Europe. This created a danger, through the manipulation of payoff values, of putting exceptional and awful strategic moves, that would result in mass death and destruction, in the realm of the possible and the rational.

Most strategists using Game Theory were aware of the limitations of the pure theory and provided the appropriate qualifications, though now and again extravagant claims would be made. The counter to the charge of unreal assumptions was that this was based on a misunderstanding of the role of theory. As Schelling explained, the assumption of rational behaviour was not necessarily close to the truth, but it was productive for the development of new and relevant concepts.[14] Hedley Bull commented wryly:

> A great deal of argument about military strategy . . . postulates the
> 'rational action' of a kind of 'strategic man', a man who on further
> acquaintance reveals himself as a university professor of unusual
> intellectual subtlety. In my view this kind of formal theorizing is of

great value in the discussion on strategic matters when it represents not a prediction of what will happen in the real world but a deliberate and conscious abstraction from it, which must later be related back again to the world.[15]

The model could not predict or explain actual behaviour, though it would suggest criteria for judging behaviour. The most important point, however, was that there was no valid, empirically founded theory available. Men fighting nuclear wars had not been observed in action. There were no analogous situations to draw upon. Human imagination or intuition was inadequate to cope. The abstractions of Game Theory and similar devices were useful as much because of the lack of suitable alternatives than anything else.

The success of the formal strategists was in providing a rationale for a policy of stable deterrence based on secure second-strike forces. It was a policy determined to a large extent by technology, but the strategists made the abandonment of a first-strike option a source of satisfaction rather than a disappointment. The theory was potent here because it was concerned with a basic question of strategic doctrine to be answered within reasonably well-defined parameters that were not subject to frequent and radical changes. The failure of the formal strategists came with their inability to provide a convincing answer to the problem of what to do 'if deterrence failed'. They offered a measured response as an alternative to all-out war but the arguments lacked plausibility and collapsed into paradox. To illustrate the strengths and weaknesses of the formal strategists it is necessary to examine two of the most famous 'games': 'Prisoner's Dilemma' and 'Chicken'.

Prisoner's Dilemma and Chicken

The Prisoner's Dilemma is set by a public prosecutor. He has two prisoners both under strong suspicion for committing a serious crime. Without confessions he cannot secure a conviction. He separates the two suspects and tells them that they have two alternatives; they can confess or remain silent. If both remain silent he will prosecute them on a minor charge and they will receive light sentences (1 year). If both confess they will be prosecuted but with a recommendation for a sentence below the maximum (5 years). If one confesses and the other does not then the confessor will get a lenient sentence (3 months) while the other will be prosecuted for the maximum sentence (10 years). The two players are left alone in separate cells to think things over. To predict their answers we can look at the matrix, shown in Figure 1. The answer is that they both confess. A unable to conspire with B knows that if he remains silent he risks 10 years' imprisonment; if he confesses he risks only 5 years. Furthermore, if B decides to go for the solution that would be of the greatest mutual benefit and so remains silent, by confessing A can improve his own position, though, in a sense, double-crossing B. Game Theory predicts that B will follow the same reasoning. This is known as the *minimax* strategy, in that it guarantees the best of the worst possible outcomes.

B

	1 silence	2 confess
silence$_1$	-1 $a_1 b_1$ -1	-0.25 $a_1 b_2$ -10
confess$_2$	-10 $a_2 b_1$ -0.25	-5 $a_2 b_2$ -5

A

FIGURE 1   The figures in the corners refer to expectation of sentence

The main point of this game is that the two players were forced into conflict with the result that they suffered a worse result than if they had been able to communicate and co-ordinate their answers and if they trusted each other to keep to the agreed strategy. The use of this game to illuminate an arms race is quite straightforward. If A devotes considerable resources to new weapons, at best he can gain a decisive lead over B and at worst he will deny B any advantage. However, if A and B agreed on measures to dampen down arms spending then both could enjoy equivalent security at a lower cost.

In the game of Chicken two cars are driven towards each other by delinquent teenagers anxious to prove their toughness. The first to swerve loses. If both swerve nothing is gained but if neither swerve everything is lost. If A swerves and B does not then A suffers humiliation and B gains prestige. The matrix appears as shown in Figure 2.

The minimax strategy dictates that they both swerve as the best of the worst outcomes. This is the solution that is to the greatest mutual benefit but it is not achieved by an act of co-operation or out of any sense of shared interests. Again there is no problem translating this into super-power relations. A diplomatic crisis can take on the appearance of a game of Chicken if each side is anxious to persuade the other than it is willing to go to the brink of war while both are desperately anxious to avoid an actual nuclear exchange.

$$B$$

		b_1 Swerve		b_2 Don't swerve	
		0		+20	
a_1 Swerve		a_1b_1		a_1b_2	
	0			−20	
a_2 Don't swerve		−20		−100	
		a_2b_1		a_2b_2	
	+20			−100	

A (labelled at left of the table rows)

FIGURE 2 The figures in the corners refer to values attached to alternative outcomes

Some interesting points can be drawn from a comparison of these two games.[16] The rules of Prisoner's Dilemma force two potential collaborators into conflict, while those of Chicken encourage a mutually tolerable result despite conflict.

If we analyse these games as single events between players who know nothing of each other but having the minimum information provided by the rules of the game, then the results are predictable. Working within the rules, there is no way out of the Prisoner's Dilemma. They can only be circumvented by setting up external mechanisms for establishing and confirming trust and agreeing on co-operative behaviour.

By contrast, the rules of Chicken can be manipulated. Even if both players know that they will swerve some time before collision, it is possible to win by delaying swerving to the last possible moment. If we assume that both players are equal in the quality of their cars and their driving skills, then what is at question is each player's nerve, and their assessment of the other's nerve. If A considers B weak-willed he is liable to keep on a straight course, confident that B will swerve first.

There are a number of ruses available to each player to create the impression of dedication to a collision course. He can swagger, boast, feign drunkenness, or pretend to lack the option of swerving. By throwing the steering wheel out of the window or dismantling the brakes he could convince the other that he had no choice but to go straight ahead. The point about such ruses is that a rational player, desirous of victory, has to put on a play of irrationality. The more that one could give an impression of having taken leave of one's senses, the greater the chances of prevailing in a head-on clash. The obvious difficulty when translated into nuclear confrontations was that the relevant leaders considered themselves rational and did not want a nuclear war. They might bluff, but would be unwilling to commit themselves to a patently irrational course of action without some escape. Whatever the show put on for the benefit of the other players (and spectators), in practice one foot would hover close to the brake pedal and the hands would stay firmly on the steering wheel.

The problems of playing this game become even greater if it is to be repeated. How a player performs in one game will affect perceptions of his likely performance in the future. If a player capitulates in one game he increases his problems for next time round, when the other player can expect to be more confident. If over time an impression of weakness is created then the adjustments to behaviour can create a dangerous instability, either because this player is seeking to compensate for his unfortunate image or his opponent is seeking to exploit it. Added to the particular payoffs for each individual game are the larger stakes for a larger super-game. This super-game has the characteristics of Prisoner's Dilemma. The question is whether to co-operate to call off the endless games of Chicken (with the consequent risk of a sudden challenge) or to persist in these games in the belief that each will, in the end, swerve.

There is a further problem of the tempo at which these games are played. The processes of decision-making and decision-implementation vary in time for each player. In an arms race both may decide to produce a certain type of weapon but one may get it before the other and so enjoy a significant if temporary superiority. Two powers set on a collision course may both be determined to swerve, but one may be slower to respond to the decision and so find himself an inadvertent victor. The problems of timing add to the instabilities.

Of course no discussion of this sort can do full justice to the full character of super-power relations in the nuclear age. What it does do is to illuminate, in a stark form, some of the perplexing aspects of these relations. Both games present stalemate as the predominant result. Using Prisoner's Dilemma as an analogy for an arms race, each player strives for strategic advantage because the other is likely to be doing the same, so they end up by neutralizing each other. The policy imperative that flows from this is to explore means of co-operation to secure the stalemate at a lower level. In the game of Chicken, both sides start equal and neither, if both act rationally, can 'win'. When the game is played between two nuclear powers, the rationality of swerving is increased because the consequences of collision are so horrendous. But if regular confrontations cannot be avoided, the policy imperatives that flow from this game are disturbing and ambiguous. There is a temptation to pretend to be all those things that Game Theory assumes you are not – non-calculating and 'non-utility maximizing'. These temptations are accentuated by the knowledge that the game is to be repeated.

It is possible to do more than simply to note the paradox that one game encourages a search for co-operation while the other encourages a tough and uncompromising stand. The Prisoner's Dilemma applied to the super-power arms race concerns military relationships while Chicken concerns political relationships. In the first neither side is able to gain a decisive military advantage and in the second there is no military way out of the predicament, because any clash will be mutually devastating. In both cases the answer lies in some amendment to political relations – either in the extension of areas of co-operation or in some shift in what Snyder has labelled the 'balance of resolve'.[17] These insights provided the basis for the Strategy of Stable Conflict.

13 Arms Control

The prescriptive implications of the sort of abstract theorizing discussed in the last chapter were perplexing to many. In one sense they were quite radical in that they suggested a totally new approach to strategy and dealings with a potential enemy. In another sense they were extremely conservative because they took the *status quo* as a given, and devoted their energies to its preservation. Little hope was offered that the East–West conflict might be resolved either by political or military means. Their analyses yielded neither new ideas on how to achieve a political accommodation with the Soviet Union nor military concepts that opened up the prospect of victory.

Despite an approach which encouraged strategies more political than military in nature, no answer was sought to the underlying political differences that separated East and West. One reason for this was methodology. Pure theories of strategy are preoccupied with players in opposition. Schelling explained that his theory 'degenerates at one extreme if there is not scope for mutual accommodation, no common interest at all even in avoiding mutual disaster; it degenerates at the other extreme if there is no conflict at all and no problem in identifying and reaching common goals'.[1] Morgenstern opened his book by stating some 'fundamental facts' which 'we shall not be able to get away from in our lives'. These included the impossibility of defence against nuclear weapons and the lack of any place to hide should thermonuclear war break out. Another 'fact' was of 'two hostile parties' facing each other, each claiming to be powerful enough to destroy the other and neither believing the other's protestations of his peaceful intentions. 'Rather each party recognizes the deadly and growing capabilities of the other.'[2] To the formal strategists the interesting feature of this antagonism was its incompleteness. At times interests would coincide; the challenge was to recognize and act upon this mutuality of interest. In translating theory into practice it was necessary to explain how mechanisms for facilitating co-operation could survive in an atmosphere dominated by deep antagonism.

The source of a common interest was the risk of mutual destruction if any conflict got out of hand. A major premise of the formal strategists was the existence of a nuclear stalemate – or else its possible existence, if appropriate steps were taken. The value judgment was that such a stalemate was preferable to a situation in which both sides were striving for victory, and that measures to stabilize the nuclear relationship were more promising and realistic than attempts to eliminate nuclear weapons from international affairs. Their ideas appeared timely and relevant because the late 1950s and early 1960s was a time in which a stable nuclear balance could neither be taken for granted nor ruled out.

The Strategy of Stable Conflict

If any one person can be identified as the author of the strategy of stable conflict it is Warren Amster, an operations analyst for the Convair Corporation (later part of General Dynamics). In 1954 he wrote a paper for Convair which contained the essence of the theory. This might not have been noticed but for the intervention of C. W. Sherwin, a former Chief Scientist for the Air Force, who publicized Amster's conclusions in an influential article which appeared in the *Bulletin of the Atomic Scientists* in May 1956.[3] Sherwin also employed Game Theory to help him make his points. No other article anticipates so succinctly so much of what was to become conventional wisdom by the early 1960s.

The enduring quality of the thesis lay in the relative accuracy of the technical forecasts. They compare favourably with Kahn's crystal-ball gazing discussed in Chapter 11, supporting the hypothesis that the understanding of the pace and significance of technological change was far more realistic in the mid-1950s than it became later in the decade. At the time Amster was writing, Convair was being considered (successfully) as the Air Force contractor for the ICBM programme, so it is not surprising that central to Amster's argument was a consideration of the impact of long-range missiles on the strategic balance.

Amster argued that: 'We may well expect that the conversion to intercontinental missiles will be followed shortly by the development of military strategies that are fundamentally deterrent.'[4] He identified the key features of missiles. They would not be very good at fighting each other, being too well-hidden and protected to be caught on the ground and too fast to be caught in the air. Compared with missiles, cities were extremely vulnerable – soft, immobile and sprawling.

Sherwin drew the conclusions:

If forces are very costly to attack, and cities are very cheap to attack, the optimum force will not be very large. If the forces become more vulnerable, and the economies more effectively protected, security is reduced. If this development is carried far enough ... an arms race will develop, and – considering the nature of the new weapons – great advantage will thus accrue to the initial attacker.[5]

This was precisely the fear that exercised a great many minds later in the decade and was already being seriously considered at RAND. Anticipating the introduction of missiles, Amster and Sherwin looked forward to a stable deterrent. To illustrate the consequences of this stable state, Sherwin provided a simple 'game' involving two tribes living in close proximity and armed with poison darts. They could not disarm each other, there was no defence and the poison was fatal. However, it took time to be effective, so there was a probability of retaliation. The only rational outcome was for neither tribe to start shooting.

Transposing this game to East–West relations, Sherwin reported Amster's rules for maintaining this steady state if threatened by accident, design or some expanding local conflict. The rules were only to engage in strategic bombing if attacked in this manner oneself, responding to attacks on cities with comparable attacks on the opponent's cities, and to attacks on bomb-carriers by sending off an equivalent number of carriers to those destroyed to bomb the opponent's cities. The retaliation would thus be measured, its purpose 'not to win, but to prove to the attacker that his losses are likely to be incredibly large, in the hope that by this demonstration the war will be stopped before both sides are irreparably destroyed'.[6]

Deterrence would thus work through the punitive threat of irresistible hurt to the enemy's social and economic structure, rather than through the prospect of victory in combat. Even after the outbreak of war the attempt would be made to contain it through nuclear attacks that would emphasize what might happen in the future rather than to punish past aggression. This would be possible because new technologies were liable to make stability in deterrence almost 'natural'.

Schelling's theoretical structure, reflecting his background as an economist, was much more elaborate than the one described above, yet many of its precepts were strikingly similar. He defined deterrence as being concerned with the exploitation of *potential* force, using it to persuade a possible enemy that in his own best interest he should avoid certain courses of action. Schelling realized that nuclear strategy would have to be based on the essential properties of nuclear weapons (their power to cause immense pain and destruction) rather than on properties more relevant to previous generations of weapons. In the first chapter of his later book, *Arms and Influence*, Schelling spelled out the consequences of this recognition.

He distinguished between two ways of employing military strength – as *brute force* and as the power to *hurt*. Brute force provided a means of overcoming the enemy and of acquiring his territory. The power to hurt affected the adversaries' interests and intentions rather than his capabilities, and could now be employed whatever the other's capabilities. Because it was concerned with pain, its value lay in its potential, as 'latent violence', rather than in its actual use, though it might have to be used on occasion to communicate the potency of the violence at hand. Used carefully this power could influence the adversary. By making the implementation of a threat contingent upon future behaviour, his actions could be manipulated. It was thus a form of bargaining, albeit dirty, extortionate and reluctant; a diplomacy based on coercion. Brute force could be used as an alternative to bargaining but threatening hurt involved bargaining.

Instances of emphasizing the threat of pain could be found from military history, but they had tended to come at a late stage in warfare. A military victory had been needed before the population could be put at risk. Now with nuclear weapons the threat had come to the fore while the quest for military victory was less relevant. If 'there is no room for doubt how a contest in strength will come out, it may be possible to bypass the military stage altogether and to proceed at once to coercive bargaining'. Military strategy could no longer be the science of military victory. Rather it would be the art of coercion, intimidation and deterrence.[7] If anything, he suggested, a stable balance of terror could simply be viewed as 'a massive and modern version of an ancient institution: the exchange of hostages'. The exchange provided a guarantee of good behaviour; an unpleasant device, but effective in the absence of trust, good faith and mutual respect.[8] One can note here that in his presumptions Schelling was close to the original proponents of strategic bombardment who also saw actual fighting with the enemy as an intermediate stage which could now be dispensed with. But with strategic bombardment no bargaining was envisaged – just the pounding of the enemy until he went on his knees and begged to surrender.

The notion of military victory was alien to Schelling's scheme. Bargaining strength required retaining the power to hurt and success depended on skill in exploiting it. Striving for a military victory could unsettle the whole relationship, because of the 'reciprocal fear of surprise attack' discussed in Chapter 11. In such an aggravated situation, the bargaining aspect was lost: the controlled and considered use of strength for the promotion of political interests would be displaced by the scramble to avoid military defeat. In order to ensure that military strength was used solely for the purposes of bargaining over political interests, efforts had to be made to avoid war through miscalculation. Both sides must feel confident in their second-strike capabilities. This could be assisted if each took steps to reassure the other that they were not planning a first strike.

Schelling used this criterion of stability to classify weapons. The best weapons were protected from a first strike and insufficiently accurate for counter-force attacks. Their invulnerability provided no incitement to launch on warning and would give their owner the confidence that there would always be weapons available for a second strike. Their incompetence at counter-force attacks obviously made them inadequate for first strikes. This inadequacy would demonstrate to an opponent that only a second strike was a serious option. Cities would be threatened, not weapons. A capability to kill millions of people became morally neutral because it was reactive. A first strike, killing hundreds of weapons, was the more heinous crime because that would, almost automatically, trigger a second strike. The crime was to start a nuclear war; not to prosecute it with murderous intensity.

A weapon that can hurt only people, and cannot possibly damage the other side's striking force, is profoundly defensive; it provides its possessor no incentive to strike first. It is the weapon that is designed or deployed to destroy 'military' targets – to seek out the enemy's missiles and bombers – that *can* exploit the advantage of striking first and consequently provide a temptation to do so.[9]

Such reasoning led one to conclusions that seemed quite bizarre to the military mind. The argument was to abstain from the most advanced and militarily useful weapons, while *encouraging* the enemy to improve his defences. For example Schelling discussed the 'nuclear-weapon submarine'. Because of the difficulty of detecting and destroying submarines they were considered the most invulnerable launch platforms for nuclear weapons and so admirable for second-strike purposes. Schelling noted that Americans ought not to want a monopoly of these submarines for 'if in fact we have either no intention or no political capacity for a first strike it would usually be helpful if the enemy were confidently assured of this'.[10]

If Schelling's conclusions were considered bizarre by the military, his premises were as strange to many liberals. Liberals had opposed strategic bombardment as a particularly uncivilized form of warfare. Within government they had resisted the continued effort to perfect thermonuclear means of destroying cities, attempting in the late 1940s and early 1950s to divert research on nuclear weapons to designs for tactical, battlefield use. Outside government they had deplored Western reliance on such weapons and had spoken with gloom and despondency of the future of mankind in the absence of effective international measures to promote disarmament. To turn the capacity for city destruction into a virtue and to use this as a foundation for peace and stability was quite perverse. Yet by the mid-1960s this approach had become almost the party 'line' for liberals, with few dissenters.

Disarmament to Arms Control

The approach in question can be described as 'arms control', though the meaning of this term has now been broadened to include the substance and process of all international negotiations concerned with regulating armaments. When the term was first becoming popular, it signified a shift in emphasis towards the notion of managing rather than eliminating the arms race. To be 'out of control' would be to be abandoned to fate and human destiny to be beyond human decision. Thus arms control did not offer the promise of release from the dangers and costs of war-fighting and war-preparedness; it offered no sense of a final solution to the 'curse of armaments upon mankind'. Rather there would, for an indefinite duration, be a series of mutually agreed adjustments to force structures.

Schelling had already indicated his scepticism as to the benefits of disarmament, which up to this point had described international objectives in this area. He noted how, when one started to worry about surprise attacks, one could take the opposite view from a traditional disarmer. The more weapons one had, the more difficult it was for the adversary to wipe them out in a surprise attack. An agreement involving large numbers would be also easier to maintain: '[T]he difficulty of one side's cheating, by disguising and concealing extra missiles, or breaking the engagement and racing to achieve a dominant number, is more than proportionally enhanced by any increase in the starting figures of both sides.'[11]

The second aspect of arms control as a concept was that it was not to be as alien to military thinking as disarmament. Schelling described it in a book he wrote with Morton Halperin as 'a promising, but still only dimly perceived, enlargement of our military strategy'. It rested upon the explicit recognition of the incompleteness of the antagonism between the major powers:

[W]hile a nation's military force opposes the military force of potentially hostile nations, it must also collaborate, implicitly if not explicitly, in avoiding the kinds of crises in which withdrawal is intolerable for both sides, in avoiding false alarms and mistaken intentions, and in providing – along with its deterrent threat of resistance or retaliation in the event of unacceptable challenges – reassurance that restraint on the part of potential enemies will be matched by restraint of our own.[12]

Arms control would complement deterrence by making it possible to confine nuclear weapons to this rôle, without hint of adventurism or of the sort of laxity in procedures which could result in unauthorized use.

Herman Kahn also expressed the view that arms control was beneficial. He saw advantages in mutual regulation of the conditions under which third parties might join the arms race and saw how particularly dangerous technologies might be avoided and how the risk of damage in war could be reduced. It could be confused 'with some form of premature disarmament, or at least with a general neglect of the armed services'. However, in his view, 'successful and responsible *short-run* control measures are more likely to require large military establishments on both sides than the opposite'.[13]

The final feature of the concept was the notion that it could be tacit, not always requiring institutionalized and negotiated agreements. Schelling and Halperin interpreted control to mean 'induced or reciprocated "self-control", whether the inducements include negotiated treaties or just informal understandings and reciprocated restraints'.[14] Such a concept lacked any obvious boundaries and was much the weaker for that. If all that was required was co-operation between potential enemies in the military sphere, however, ambiguous or vaguely understood, then a momentary coincidence of interests in the midst of war could be classed with a binding, negotiated agreement covering large areas of military relations. This conceptual problem indicated a more serious substantive problem. Restricting arms control to *explicit* agreements, as was to be its fate in the strategic vernacular, linked it inextricably with the processes of international negotiation. Negotiations took time, had distorting effects on nations' sense of interests and priorities, introduced special demands so as to make an agreement binding and verifiable and so on. Because of all these factors, negotiated agreements were difficult to arrange. It would be dangerous if the stability of the relationship depended on their success.

The concept might have maintained its purity at the expense of influence, if its central theme, of managing rather than eradicating the balance of terror, had not been so sympathetically received by the policy-makers. Official thinking had been moving in the same direction since the mid-1950s. The drastic surgery of disarmament was rejected as being based on over-simple theorizing and a certain innocence as to the strategic facts of life. Once the opportunity to abolish atomic bombs in the late 1940s had passed it only became a matter of time before policy-makers stopped pretending that they had any confidence in complete disarmament and began to attempt to make life with the bomb a little safer. References to nuclear disarmament in speeches were more designed to cover an exposed, humanitarian flank than to point to the way ahead. The arms controllers were following, encouraging, and developing a trend in US policy that had already commenced.

From the mid-1950s on, a shift could be discerned in the US negotiating positions at UN disarmament conferences. American negotiators accepted the bomb as a fact of international life whose influence must be controlled, rather than as an evil to be abolished. One indication of this was the change in terminology. During the drafting of the Charter of the United Nations the Americans had not been happy talking about disarmament because of its association with the futility and failure of the League of Nations. 'Regulation of armaments' had been preferred as a description of immediate objectives. After 1945 the enormity of the threat to the international system posed by the atom bomb had once again given drastic solutions greater credibility. It became more plausible to talk of disarmament. The Russians had always favoured the more radical terminology. Unfortunately the lack of movement in disarmament negotiations renewed the term's association with futility. Meanwhile, the US had allowed the useful, all-embracing term 'regulation of armaments' to become precisely defined in a 1953 General Assembly Resolution, from which it was now departing. In May 1955, Harold Stassen, President Eisenhower's new Disarmament Advisor, concluded after a major study of the arms race that the goal of total nuclear disarmament was now unobtainable and that more modest objectives were required instead. The term 'arms control' came to be adopted, indicating a move away from attempts at total elimination of nuclear weapons with balanced reduction of conventional arms to the strengthening of deterrence and the guarding against surprise attack.[15]

There has since been a minor but persistent debate over the relationship between 'disarmament' and 'arms control'. Part of the confusion lies with an earlier use of the word 'control' as 'international control', referring to the placing of armaments within some sort of international legal framework and the transfer of authority for supervising the changes in armament levels from national governments to an international organization.[16] To the Russians the notion of 'international control' had a slightly weaker meaning, implying an auditing authority. A further confusion was that strictly speaking disarmament referred to one sort of adjustment of force levels which did not preclude other forms of regulation, such as restriction on deployment or use. Schelling and Halperin said that their use of 'arms control' rather than 'disarmament' was intended 'simply to broaden the term'.[17] Alva Myrdal of Sweden, on the other hand; has seen arms control as a watered-down, bland and lesser version of disarmament:

> I wish it were not too late to start a boycott against the use of 'arms control' as an overall term. It is nothing but a euphemism, serving regrettably to lead thinking and action towards the accept-

ance as 'arms control measures' of compromises with scant or nil disarmament effect.[18]

But castigating one concept as but a mealy-mouthed version of the other, or submerging one in some larger analytical system, hid the real shift of the late 1950s which was to change the focal point of international negotiations from measures designed to remove nuclear weapons from world affairs to measures designed to make their presence more tolerable.

Arms control has thus been a deeply conservative cause. The central theme has been 'stability'. To quote Robert Osgood: '[T]he novel characteristics of contemporary military technology have placed an unprecedented burden upon the stabilizing of the military environment itself in stabilizing international relations as a whole'. The sources of instability could be found in the incredibility as much as in the incapability of constructing a deterrent system, or else dependence on 'changing and untried weapons systems', on the need for politicians with 'undeviating self-restraint and low-risk-taking propensities', and on the reliance of Western nations on nuclear weapons to deter a wide range of limited threats based on conventional weapons.[19]

Section 4 showed how this preoccupation with stability and the resultant advocacy of arms control was linked closely to the feeling that a nuclear stalemate was not going to be as automatic a development as had previously been suspected. The greatest instability would be the coincidence of an international crisis with 'the reciprocal fear of surprise attack'. The objective was therefore to reduce all temptations to pre-empt, and 'to institutionalize a less precarious balance of terror rather than to supplant it. The goal is stable mutual deterrence, which in practice amounts to playing for a stalemate rather than a win in the grimmest of games, should deterrence fail ...'.[20]

The Disarmers Disarmed

Despite the effort put into demonstrating how arms control ought to be quite congenial to the military mind as a natural complement to national military policy, it remained essentially a civilian concept. The professional military displayed little interest in making allowances for the adversary's anxieties and neuroses or in reassuring gestures designed to ease the two super-powers into a cosier and less tense relationship. To the military the most stable situation was one in which the US enjoyed overwhelming strength. Their Soviet counterparts took a similar view. There was little point in compromising the drive for superiority by schemes for mutual regulation of the balance, especially if those schemes depended on trusting communists (or imperialists). Arms control negotiations were viewed with suspicion and agreements endorsed under protest. It was not really until arms control became an entrenched feature of super-power relations in the 1970s that the military in both super-powers fully began to incorporate arms control into doctrinal thinking.

Success came earlier with another group who might have been expected to consider the institutionalization of the balance of terror to be complete anathema. This group, which might be called the *nuclear pacifists*, were not necessarily pacifists in their attitude towards the application of other types of military force, but could not sanction the use of nuclear weapons in any circumstances whatsoever. Their policy was therefore one of complete nuclear disarmament.

The nuclear pacifists could base their cause on the 'tradition of civilized warfare'[21] that had developed in the West, stemming from attempts of theologians since the days of S. Augustine to establish criteria that would make a war just. Just wars were those concerned with juridical rights rather than with adventure or plunder, they were only fought as a last resort, all peaceful means of settling the dispute having failed, and the violence employed was proportionate to the injustice suffered. Another aspect of the tradition was the concern to preserve distinctions between combatants and non-combatants, and yet another was the proper treatment of prisoners. These traditions found expression in international affairs in institutions such as the League of Nations and the United Nations, the Geneva Convention on warfare, and in a variety of disarmament conferences.

Nuclear weapons violated any attempts at proportionate violence or the preservation of distinctions between combatants and non-combatants. Even when aimed at solely military targets, the associated, unintended damage to the civilian populations would, in all probability, exceed the damage caused by pre-nuclear weapons specifically designed to attack civilians. It was difficult to justify the employment of weapons that could cause unimaginable pain and threaten the survival of whole civilizations in terms of rational, calculated acts of policy.

The moral problems were not new, having been raised by strategic bombardment during the war. Grave doubts had been voiced over the Allied bombing of Dresden, as well as that of Hiroshima and Nagasaki. These doubts could be answered by a number of arguments. There was a notion of 'just deserts'. In the justification for Dresden there had been elements of retribution for similar attacks on British cities and in that for Hiroshima remembrance of Japanese atrocities and the original act of aggression at Pearl Harbor. The other sort of justification was more instrumental. The atom bombings of Hiroshima and Nagasaki were supported out of a calculus that suggested that more human beings would have died if the bombing had not been authorized, in the heavy fighting and enormous casualties that would have accompanied an invasion. A sweetener to this argument was that the lives that were purportedly saved were mainly Anglo-Saxon. The lack of obvious results made the bombing of Dresden more difficult to support. These moral arguments thus depended on the practical context.

The use of atom bombs, as with strategic bombing, might be rationalized as a necessary evil. The necessity derived from the evil to be stopped, which had to be both stoppable by, and greater than, the evil being inflicted. But nuclear weapons were so evil in their effects that their use could only be considered a necessity in the most extreme of circumstances – when faced by a direct and potentially mortal threat to the country. A moral crusade involving nuclear weapons, no matter how good the cause, could no longer be sanctioned.

The decisive twist to the debate, as with all others that have been considered here, was the existence of two opposing nuclear arsenals. With only one nuclear capability the argument would have been over whether this evil was greater than any evil it was required to avenge or prevent. A comparable evil now existed. Each side could justify its nuclear preparedness by reference to that of the other. Each could claim that only the deterrent effect of his nuclear arsenal dissuaded the other from aggressive activity. Yet even if the *threat* of employment of nuclear weapons could in this manner be justified as a necessary evil, their actual *employment* could not. First use would be an act of gross genocide. If this invited nuclear retaliation it would worsen matters, putting the whole population at risk. On the other hand, use in retaliation would have little point, except on a retributive level. The damage would have been done and the domestic situation could not be retrieved by inflicting equivalent suffering on the enemy.

The response from those prepared to contemplate use tended to be based on a choice of values rather than strategic logic. It was considered 'better to be dead than red', to go down fighting rather than to succumb to the horrors that had come to be associated with communist rule. The nuclear pacifist might argue that the choice was not a real one. There were alternatives to suicide in order to preserve dignity and hope. He might also argue that this was a choice each individual had to make for himself. For a particular code of honour to be applied to a whole society was an imposition more absolute and authoritarian than the type of rule it was supposed to avoid. On this level not only nuclear pacifists but many others expressed concern, for example Lieutenant-General Sir John Cowley:

> The choice of death or dishonour is one which has always faced the professional fighting man, and there must be no doubt in his mind what his answer must be. He chooses death for himself so that his country may survive, or on a grander scale so that the principles for which he is fighting may survive. Now we are facing a somewhat different situation, when the reply is not to be given by individuals but by countries as a whole. Is it right for the government of a country to choose complete destruction of the population rather than some other alternative, however unpleasant that alternative may be?[22]

The arguments of nuclear pacifists centred on the act of exploding nuclear weapons in anger. It would be criminality beyond comparison, endangering the future of the whole human species. To plan to use such weapons was not only evil, it was irrational, for no gain could result. The destruction would be all-consuming. The choice appeared one of peace versus holocaust. Only the insane would choose the latter and as the leaders of the great powers had opted for nuclear arsenals, *ergo*, they must be insane. This view, that the real battle was common sense versus a mental abnormality endemic to world leaders, came through in the rhetoric of the campaigns for nuclear disarmament sponsored by the nuclear pacifists. In America there was a Committee for a SANE nuclear policy; the British campaign named its journal *Sanity*. In a book by the campaign's intellectual leader, the philosopher Bertrand Russell, the view that it was only folly and stupidity at the highest levels that prevented the abolition of nuclear weapons reverberates throughout.

Such a perspective did not leave much room for a debate with those who felt preparation for a nuclear war was the essence of a sound strategy. The nuclear pacifists could barely contain their fury at this idea. As the distinguished mathematician James Newman wrote, reviewing Herman Kahn's *On Thermonuclear War*, 'This is a moral tract on mass murder: how to plan it, how to commit it, how to get away with it, how to justify it.'[23] In a letter to the *Washington Post* in July 1956, Newman had argued that the statement 'a war of nuclear weapons is lunatic' admitted of no exceptions. 'It is an uncontingent truth, beyond niggling or casuistry.' He was reacting to a sentence in an editorial in the paper, to the effect that 'no responsible person suggests that a heavy nuclear deterrent is not necessary for employment *in extremis* despite all its awful implications'. Newman averred, pointing to the consequences of nuclear war, how in 'such a conflict the nation fighting to preserve itself cannot preserve itself, and all must perish'.

But Newman did not deal directly with the question of deterrence, of impressive nuclear forces dissuading another nuclear power from chancing an attack. The question was whether *threatening* to use nuclear weapons ought to carry the same moral stigma as actually *using* them. After all, a threat causes no death and may cause an aggressor to think twice before perpetuating a great evil. Was not this the most rational way to survive in a world of nuclear powers? The notion was unacceptable to many nuclear pacifists because holding nuclear weapons implied using them. Yet this was an implication many strategists were coming to doubt. Because of the sobering thought of retaliation in kind, neither super-power would use nuclear weapons; without the threat of use, use would be much more likely.

Two further thoughts agitated the nuclear pacifists. The first was that, despite the best efforts at restraint by leaders, nuclear war could not be avoided for perpetuity. There were a number of statements purporting to offer statistical proof that war would break out within a decade. The fear was often of miscalculation or accident. Introducing the Sherwin article mentioned earlier in this chapter, Eugene Rabinowitch, the editor of the *Bulletin of the Atomic Scientists*, expressed his doubt in the 'long-term stability of this essentially immoral deadlocked state'. A widely circulated report of 1960 concluded that 'there is a significant chance that a major accidental war may occur at some time in the 1960s'. The danger would be greatest at times of international tension. The sort of accidents discussed were 'defence system accidents', such as spurious signals from early warning systems, accidental nuclear explosions perhaps resulting from an aircraft crash, human aberrations amongst those with some responsibility over the launch of nuclear missiles and unintended expansion of limited wars and catalytic war, made possible by the spread of nuclear weapons to a large number of countries.[24] One of the best-selling novels of the early 1960s was *Fail-Safe* by Eugene Burdick and Harvey Wheeler, in which a technical malfunction unleashed a US nuclear attack. Attempts to stop all the bombers getting to Moscow failed, and the city was destroyed. Only by the reciprocal sacrifice of New York was general war avoided. So influential was this novel that the philosopher Sidney Hook felt obliged to issue a refutation, arguing that the technical dangers were exaggerated and that such writing encouraged a greater fear of the US nuclear deterrent than the Soviet desire for world domination.[25] The sort of danger highlighted by the book was more than trivial, and concern extended beyond the nuclear pacifists. Herman Kahn, despite being satirised in *Fail-Safe* as the unsavoury Groteschele, showed concern about accidents and advocated measures to limit the possibilities of their occurrence. It was his pessimism in this regard that made him doubt the ultimate stability of mutual deterrence.

The second objection of the nuclear pacifists to attempts to maintain a 'balance of terror' was that this ensured that the East–West conflict would persist. Rather than argue that only when political differences were resolved could the nuclear arsenals be dismantled, it was suggested that, on the contrary, the unease created by the arms race induced the political hostility. There was no *real* need for either side to fear the other. Such fears developed artificially with the descent into an arms race and the consequent spiral of misperception.[26] If only measures could be found to eliminate the arms race then the super-powers would find their differences to be trivial. Aaron Wildavsky described such arguments as follows:

> Tragedy replaces evil in the world drama and then turns into a comedy of errors. The final scene of *Hamlet* is played over again but a new postscript is added: the dead hero's father appears, just returned from a business trip, and discovers that everybody has died because of some trivial misunderstanding concerning his whereabouts.[27]

As Wildavsky noted, such a view could be traced to a popular interpretation of the origins of World War I as the consequence of the Anglo-German naval arms race and the thoughtless rush to mobilize at the first hint of crisis. Such a model of the sources of war could be contrasted with an alternative model, that of appeasement, in which acts of friendship are viewed as signs of weakness by a hostile power.

In this model, popular in explanations of the outbreak of World War II, the mistake was to assume reasonableness and friendship; in the former model, the mistake was to assume enmity.

Put this way the argument centred on alternative interpretations of Soviet goals and behaviour. A similar point is made by Jervis who stated that:

> [T]he explanation for differences of opinion between the Spiral theorists and proponents of deterrence lies not in differing general views of international relations, differing values and morality or differing methods of analysis, but in differing perceptions of Soviet intentions.[28]

This misrepresents the differences, in that many deterrent theorists, including Schelling, did not rest their case on the special nature of the Soviet Union. The difference was over whether or not there existed any underlying political antagonism (for which either side might be blameworthy) which made some acquisition of arms understandable and unavoidable.

If there were no real conflicts of interests and values between the super-powers then the case for doing away with nuclear weapons would be that much stronger. Unfortunately, there was nothing in the public and private behaviour and attitudes of the policy-makers of East and West to suggest that the cold war was based on anything other than genuine and mutual hostility and distrust. This both explained why these policy-makers felt unable to give up their stockpiles of nuclear weapons unilaterally and why they found it difficult to negotiate multilateral disarmament.

The nuclear pacifists faced these political realities in a variety of ways. The most prominent response was to create political pressure for disarmament. 'Ban the bomb' movements became a feature of Western countries in the late 1950s and early 1960s. As these movements failed to achieve their basic objectives they became more militant and desperate, with some coming to feel that the only hope was radical social and economic change.[29] The other response was to come to terms with the bomb's existence and to seek to keep it under tight control.

A number of campaigners for disarmament simply failed to consider the arguments for a stable deterrence. The British MP Philip Noel-Baker had been campaigning for disarmament since the days of the League of Nations. His arguments were reminiscent of the earlier period: arms races inevitably end in wars and the alternative was disarmament. He described with deep regret the loss of a 'Moment of Hope' in May 1955 when the Soviet Union at a UN Sub-Committee went a long way towards accepting a previous US disarmament position, only to discover that the US had moved away from this position, to one concerned more with a stable balance of terror. This new position Noel-Baker found indistinguishable from a pursuit of the arms race.[30]

Not everyone on Noel-Baker's 'side of the fence' found the new US position so disturbing. Leo Szilard, the formidable nuclear scientist who played such a large part in the development of the atom bomb, was continually devising elaborate schemes designed to provide for national security while phasing out nuclear weapons. In an October 1955 article he noted that current US proposals had 'little to do with disarmament' but were 'rather aimed at giving the Strategic Air Force a few days notice of surprise attack'. He saw some merit in this because, if both sides need not fear an attack, 'the Atomic Stalemate may acquire a certain degree of stability'. He then went on to discuss how disarmament could proceed from the starting point of this stalemate.[31] Others saw arms control the same way, as a gradual step on the road to disarmament, an intermediate stage, a state of limbo.[32] By 1960 Szilard had come round to the view that solving the problem of the bomb by getting rid of it was not 'a promising approach': 'I believe the time has come to face up to this situation and to ask in all seriousness whether the world could learn to live for a while with the bomb.' Szilard's answer was that it could, essentially through a balance of terror of great stability, though characteristically he designed a system of baffling complexity.[33]

Even those who could not accept the bomb as a permanent fixture began to recognize the intellectual case for a 'stable balance of terror'. Philip Green noted in the preface to his book, *Deadly Logic*:

> Although I still hold to the pro-disarmament, anti-nuclear armament bias with which I started this study, it has become obvious to me that some of the arguments for a deterrence posture are strong. Given the realities of world politics, it is perfectly understandable that many find nuclear deterrence to be the best of the practical policies available to us, although I would still demur because of moral qualms and lack of faith in the ability of national leadership on all sides to handle the complex problems of a nuclear world.[34]

Once the 'practical' case had been conceded, the political force of nuclear pacifism diminished, and the erstwhile disarmers found themselves engaged in intermediate arms control rather than ultimate disarmament. The first serious arms control measure – the Partial Test Ban Treaty of 1963 – weakened the disarmers' position further for it removed one of the most harmful side-effects of the arms race, radioactive pollution from atmospheric nuclear tests. This, plus the successful management of the Cuban Missile Crisis of October 1962 and the subsequent detente, led to the temporary removal of the nuclear issue from domestic politics in the West. Campaigners against the bomb moved on to protest against the employment of simpler weapons in Vietnam.

Nuclear pacifism persisted in contempt for 'overkill', the ability to destroy societies more than once (which somehow was seen to be morally worse than the ability to destroy them just once). This led some to advocate a minimum deterrent, i.e. the possession of sufficient nuclear weapons to inflict grievous harm on the enemy in retaliation, but no more. This was severely criticized because it took no account of the nuclear firepower that might be 'lost' or 'neutralized' in an actual exchange, nor did it concern itself with ensuring that a frightening enough retaliatory threat was retained to keep the adversary cautious. Once the case for a balance of terror was accepted, the question of at what level the balance was to be maintained became secondary. In becoming arms controllers, the nuclear pacifists had to shift their whole position: if there could be no escape from the presence of terror, then terror had to be respected.

14 Bargaining and Escalation

Bargaining

At the centre of the strategy of stable conflict was the concept of incomplete antagonism. The prospect of an all-engulfing nuclear war reminded the super-powers that they should not push their differences over ideology and geopolitical interests too far. The issue was how far was too far. Arms control was concerned with preventing any sort of war, but an armed clash could not be ruled out. Would it be possible at low levels of violence for the shared interest in avoiding the most extreme form of military collision to continue to govern the resolution of the conflict? The question aroused mixed anxieties. If a war came, something other than the uninhibited release of all nuclear arsenals would be preferable, but knowledge that war-fighting would lead to something less than a complete disaster could make it more tempting for an aggressor. Moreover, a desire to limit the use of nuclear weapons could work to the advantage of the combatant with the strongest conventional capabilities – the USSR.

The dilemma could only be solved if a way could be found of employing nuclear weapons to effect without bringing about total destruction upon oneself. The trend towards invulnerable second-strike forces, encouraged by the formal strategists, reduced the chances of fighting wars according to the principles of wars of the past. The only alternative was to develop rules suitable for this singular form of conflict, rules which would permit controlled use of nuclear weapons directed towards objectives other than military victory. This chapter is concerned with the attempts to discover such rules in known features of international activity or in postulated rational behaviour under alternative scenarios of crisis and conflict. The emphasis was on political objectives. The relationship between political ends and military means, so often forgotten in the heat of battle, now had to be more intimate and direct than ever before. There was little point in military activity for its own sake; complete victory no longer appeared as an acceptable route to a satisfactory political settlement. Without military victory there could be no unconditional surrender by the enemy. In consequence, after the military activity, there would have to be some negotiated resolution of the differences. Hostilities, however destructive they had become, could only be terminated through a process of bargaining. Consequently it was in contributing to bargaining positions that the utility, if any, of nuclear weapons could be discerned.

The theme of bargaining in Schelling's work has already been stressed. It was taken up by his contemporaries. For example, Thornton Read concluded that 'tactical nuclear war is not an alternative to a conventional ground-holding capability for NATO, but a mechanism for carrying on punitive reprisals, as part of a bargaining strategy'.[1] Herman Kahn observed that:

> Almost every analyst is now agreed that the first use of nuclear weapons – even if against military targets – is likely to be less for the purpose of destroying the other's military forces or handicapping its operations, than for redress, warning, bargaining, punitive, fining or deterrence purposes.[2]

There were a number of bargains to be struck, the most important being over the shape of the final settlement. However, understanding would also be needed on the actual conduct of the war. At the start the combatants would signal by their actions the sort of rules by which they thought the game should be played. The first nuclear salvos could signal preferences about proper targets and the scale and tempo of attacks; the riposte would signal whether these rules were acceptable.

There was in addition an interest in preventing an expansion of conflict. The process of deterrence need not stop with the first shots in anger. As 'intra-war deterrence' it could continue, in an attempt to control a deteriorating situation. Once objectives shifted from forcing an enemy to do something rather than persuading him *not* to do something, the requirement became that of compellence not deterrence. For example, if the nuclear phase did not come until well on in a war, there could well be a need to compel the adversary to withdraw from recently occupied territory.

Intra-war deterrence or compellence could not be conducted in an all-out rush to massive nuclear exchanges. To be successful, the threats had to be modulated, emphasizing what potentially *could* happen. In particular it was necessary to maintain the adversary's population as a hostage, for once one's cities were destroyed there was nothing else to lose. In this sense it was possible to speak of a limited nuclear war, growing only in stages as a result of deliberate decisions by the belligerents.

Escalation

The growth process in warfare came to be described as escalation. This word is now one of the gifts of strategic studies to everyday language, where it is used to describe the intensification of any conflict. The term was first used in the 1950s, apparently in Britain.

By the early 1960s *escalation* was in regular use, though the sort of process involved was understood well before, as shown for example by William Kaufmann in 1956: 'Because of its competitive character war places a heavy premium upon the attainment of an advantage, however fleeting and this in turn invites imitation. As the belligerents strive to gain a comparative advantage, the conflict undergoes an expansion.'[3] Theorists such as Schelling, whose ideas were essential to the elaboration of the concept, used the word only sparingly if at all.[4] The idea received prominence in the middle of the decade because of the appearance of two important books with 'escalation' appearing in the title,[5] and because of the value of the concept in describing tendencies visible in the Vietnam War.

Through all this, the concept remained somewhat vague and ambiguous. Kahn used the term broadly to describe 'an increase in the level of conflict in international crisis situations'. Elsewhere in the literature it was taken to describe both deliberate moves to raise the stakes of conflict, and an involuntary process, a phenomenon of war in which the belligerents find themselves fighting a war of ever-increasing scope and intensity. In either case the movement could be a gradual increase in the level of military force employed or the transformation into a different kind of war, for example one using only conventional, to one using nuclear, explosives. The importance of the distinction between these two types of movement was underlined by Morton Halperin. He described them as 'expansion' and 'explosion' respectively. Escalation, he felt, was inadequate as a term because it obscured this distinction.[6] To confuse matters further, Kahn suggested that he was using *escalation* as Halperin used *expansion* preferring *eruption* to Halperin's *explosion*. Both these latter terms were too dramatic to describe anything other than the most extreme form of war-transformation. Yet much of the interest and value in the concept of escalation has been found in its use to describe major transformations of a conflict, though not necessarily those occurring in an explosive or eruptive manner.

To clarify the meaning of the term it is useful to turn to a more recent investigation of the subject by Richard Smoke, who is influenced by Schelling. Smoke notes how escalation implies a step-by-step qualitative growth rather than the sort of homogeneous, quantitative growth Halperin described as expansion. Furthermore it suggests an active thrust upward rather than a mere framework with no distinct bias. (Here Smoke may be reading the metaphor a little too literally. The rhetoric surrounding nuclear war often speaks of descents downwards, warning of untold horrors at the end. Movement towards Hades rather than Heaven seems more appropriate – and one can travel downwards on escalators.) Smoke eventually defines escalation in terms of a movement across limits previously constraining both sides, or 'a step of any size that crosses a saliency'. These saliencies, which serve to contain wars, are 'objective and hence noticeable by all parties'; they are 'in some way discrete or discontinuous'.[7] This definition is quite restrictive, but this makes it analytically useful in assessing the theories of the 1960s.

Tactics in Escalation

For this bargaining between two extremely antagonistic parties, there was a need 'for some common language that permits them to hold discourse'.[8] This language was unlikely to emerge through formal negotiations or declarations; it had to be evident in the shared culture of international politics, tacit as much as explicit, with mutual understandings created and reinforced through deeds as much as words. Such a mode of communication would not allow for great subtlety or sophistication. The reference points would be prominent symbols and values in the shared culture.

The possibility of co-ordinating actions – or at least under-standings – without the benefit of formal communication was of great interest to Schelling. He explored it in some methodological detail in *Strategy of Conflict*, seeking to re-orient game theory to take account of the fact that 'people *can* often concert their intentions or expectations with others if each knows that the other is trying to do the same'. The key is some mutual focal point. It may 'depend on imagination more than on logic; it may depend on analogy, prece-dent, accidental arrangement, symmetry, aesthetic or geometric configuration, casuistic reasoning, and who the parties are and what they know about each other'. In consequence, the choices facing bel-ligerents on where to draw the lines around their conflict would not present themselves as a continuous range of possibilities. Rather, it 'is a lumpy, discrete world that is better able to recognize qualitative than quantitative differences, that is embarrassed by the multiplicity of choices, and that forces both sides to accept some dictation from the elements themselves'.[9]

In *Arms and Influence* Schelling pursued the matter further. He listed some markers and distinctions which displayed the requisite qualities of 'simplicity, recognizability, and conspicuousness':

> National boundaries and rivers, shorelines, the battle line itself, even parallels of latitude, the distinction between air and ground, the distinction between nuclear fission and chemical combustion, the distinction between combat support and economic support, the distinction between combatants and non-combatants, the distinc-tions among nationalities.[10]

He noted that tradition and precedence would be a source of guid-ance. Yet in maintaining the most important saliency – between the use of conventional and nuclear explosives – and developing new rules once that saliency had been crossed, tradition and precedence were of only marginal value.

The problem was to relate the use of nuclear weapons, an act transcendent of any immediate quarrels in its historical implications, to the course of a conflict and the interests at stake. James King, in *The New Strategy*, (as yet unpublished) placed great emphasis on 'proportionality' as a recurring theme in the writings of those strategists who were trying to come to terms with nuclear weapons; when attempting to tailor responses to aggression, sufficient military strength should be applied to counter the aggression and/or a punishment should be devised to fit the crime. This notion of proportionality provided one answer to the question of whether one could bargain with nuclear weapons. The yardstick for measuring response would be reprisal in kind, 'an eye for an eye'. This answer impressed itself on some of the first writers who attempted to come to grips with the implications for strategy of a prolonged nuclear stalemate. The assumption of Amster and Sherwin that there would be a measured response to any nuclear transgressions by the other side has already been noted.[11] In October 1955 the irrepressible Leo Szilard outlined a 'strategy of rational demolition' in which a price tag was attached to any act of aggression. For example, if a specified area was attacked, five medium-sized cities would be demolished (time would be allowed to permit evacuation). The rule of conduct would be 'Tolerate the destruction of one of your cities for each city you destroy.'[12]

Similar ideas were pursued by, amongst others, Morton Kaplan. In a 1958 article he took up Szilard's suggestion, employing a form of Game Theory. The United States could respond to a sustained attack on Europe by 'a series of installment reprisals that eventually progress to reprisals double the value of Europe'. Variations might permit the right to a return attack on a US city without further reprisal. Failure to settle matters at this level would push the schedule higher, but the assumption was that the first installment would have the requisite effect. Kaplan wondered whether public opinion would accept this plan despite its 'rational advantages'. He saw no better alternative, and advocated a peacetime announcement that nuclear war would be conducted in this manner. Because such a strategy would need Soviet compliance and understanding, 'it would be highly important to send a team of experts to the Soviet Union to explain the rationale of the strategy'.[13]

Kaplan developed his ideas in a monograph[14] and later in a contribution to a collection of essays on the subject of *Limited Strategic War*, edited by Klaus Knorr and Thornton Read.

The character of this sort of war was explained in an introduction by Knorr. It was 'strategic' because of the weapons employed, which would be nuclear and long-range (in this way the adjective 'strategic' ceased to have any relation to the original noun). Second it would be deliberately limited in the damage 'threatened, planned, and done, as well as in the types of targets attacked'. Such a war would be 'primarily a contest of resolve'.[15] The problem lay in trying to identify rational tactics for an irrational situation. Analogies could be found from lovers' tiffs to industrial strikes where two parties who needed each other entered into a mutually destructive argument before eventually reconciling their interests. Pain might be the catalyst of common sense. But once the contest of resolve had begun there was no obvious end. Furthermore, could there ever be an agreed scale, to measure damage, ensuring that it was appropriate to the situation? How did one compare in strict terms, understood on both sides, the value of Russian cities as against European cities?

On the one hand, punitive attacks could influence the opponent's will, but not control it. On the other hand attempts to use nuclear weapons to gain a decisive military advantage (and thus political control) could be the ruination of the strategy. Against military targets the effects of reprisals could not be measured. Mutual destruction of sea ports, for example, would have a more deleterious effect on the West's capabilities. Once nuclear weapons were used to affect the course of battle, the bargaining aspects would be lost and escalation could be rapid. As Kaplan explained, 'the political game must override the military one'.[16] If this was the case, political factors would be determinate, and factors such as comparative resolve would in turn be based on the issues at stake in the conflict. By itself, limited strategic war could decide nothing. It would be a means of concentrating minds.

The scheme implied something so formalized and delicate that it was difficult to conceive of it functioning properly amidst the chaos and deep passions likely to be aroused by the actual damage caused by each signal in this bizarre communication. One could not expect many subtle and complex agreements to be developed coincident with occasional volleys of nuclear weapons. There would have to be some meeting of minds, involving a recognition of basic interests. Without this there could be no other outcome but mutual destruction. However, the basic interests one might feel at the outset of hostilities would be altered quite radically once hostilities were under way. Not only would passions rise and the 'doves' run (or fly) for cover, but also the demands to be put on a country that had *actually* turned upon you were likely to be more stringent than those that would be put on a country that *might* turn on you. For these reasons it was accepted that reasonable bargaining would become more difficult as escalation progressed. Apart from anything else, unless war began with a miscalculation, it would be because of a direct conflict of interest – most probably because of a Soviet desire to expand further into Europe.

To Morton Kaplan, any settlement would need an 'aura of legitimacy'. It must have a common logic. The best possible basis would be the *status quo*. It would satisfy the Americans, even when applied against them, because in practice they were not a revolutionary power. As disaster would be unavoidable if both super-powers attempted to stir and support revolutions in the other's sphere of influence, the Soviet Union might be persuaded to accept the same criteria. But would this be essentially a cease-fire, or a return to the *status quo ante*? If war had begun because of a Soviet conventional attack, and if the West had resorted to nuclear weapons because the conventional war was going badly, then the territorial control of the contending forces would be different from that obtaining at the start of hostilities. In this sense, as both Kaplan and Read argued, local resistance was needed to limit the enemy's gains while the punitive attacks and bargaining went on. Read argued that 'a strategy of limited strategic reprisals is not a substitute for conventional ground forces. Rather its usefulness depends on having a strong conventional shield that could limit, and if possible prevent, Soviet territorial gains while the bargaining goes on'.[17]

But in such conditions there would be minimal incentive to escalate to nuclear use in the first place. If the shield was holding, why start swopping cities? Here was the flaw in the whole strategy. It was presented as a political approach, aiming at a sort of negotiated settlement without attempting to influence the course of the war on the ground. Once that was attempted, the delicate system of communication would be upset by calculations of military advantage. However, the fact remained that in the end, when the settlement was reached, it was the state of play on the ground – the territory won and lost by opposing forces – that would be decisive. Otherwise the strategy degenerated into a contest of resolve and willingness to take punishment.

Escalation Dominance

Both Kahn and Schelling contributed to the Knorr and Read volume without wholeheartedly endorsing the central message. Kahn found the situation postulated – that of two armed states playing these deadly games at regular intervals over an extended period – unrealistic. He thought matters would be resolved either by detente or by one side breaking out of the balance of terror.[18] Schelling was prepared to accept that fighting along these sort of lines might be preferable to the alternative ways of fighting a general war, but was uneasy at the ritualistic quality of the writings. In a passage that could also be directed against some of his own ideas, he spoke of how the limited nuclear war theories seemed 'to reflect a peculiar American penchant for warning rather than doing, for postponing decisions, for anaesthetizing the victim before striking the blow, for risking wealth rather than people, and for doing grand things that do not hurt rather than small things that do'.[19]

Herman Kahn's main contribution to the subject, in his own book *On Escalation*, became notorious, mainly because of his description of an 'escalation ladder' of 44 rungs, in which nuclear weapons were first used at rung 15. To many people the fact that anybody can find some 30 different ways to use nuclear weapons was quite perverse (though not every rung above number 15 does involve nuclear weapons[20]). As with his other writings, *On Escalation* defies concise exposition because of Kahn's restless writing style, full of asides, and the relish with which he discussed all manner of scenarios, however bizarre and inplausible. The situation was saved by an appendix which provided brief and lucid discussion of the 'relevant concepts and language' used by Kahn and his colleagues at the Hudson Institute (which he set up after leaving the RAND Institute where he had had disagreements with the Director).

There was a tendency to degenerate into a taxonomy of scenarios, listing all possibilities because everything was possible in a totally novel situation. Obscure aspects of deterrence and war were cited as neglected subjects, deserving of further research, as if guides might then be produced to assist policy-makers through almost any type of crisis or war. He displayed a concern for the state of both the art amongst specialists and of the general understanding of the public.

For example, in one footnote Kahn took pride in the term 'spasm war' which described the last rung on the escalation ladder. The essence of spasm war was not so much blind and overwhelming fury as the lack of control and thought. He claimed the term originated during some briefings in which he had described existing war plans as 'orgastic spasms of destruction', once even as a 'war-gasm'. He also claimed to have been innocent of any Freudian connotations though, such matters having been explained to him, he felt such connotations might not be so inappropriate. Earlier he noted that, whereas once most audiences for his briefings would have felt that spasm war was the most likely response to Soviet aggression, there was now general understanding of the possibilities for control.[20] Later he observed, in answering the objection that it was unrealistic to assume rationality, that all he required was that decision-makers were not totally irrational, adding 'coolness and rationality already have been established as part of the expectations the public has of its crisis leaders in the nuclear age'.[21]

This was the essence of Kahn's message: it was possible that controlled, discriminating patterns of behaviour would continue even in a conflict being resolved in the presence, and with the occasional use, of nuclear weapons. Where 'irrationality' was in evidence it would be for some 'rational' reason, because advantage could be gained from irrational conduct or the expectation of irrational conduct. (The more the contest represented the game of Chicken, the more useful it was if the other side thought you mad.) Nor did he believe that the various moves up the escalation ladder would be undertaken out of a narrow risk-calculus. There would be a 'competition in risk-taking' (the original term was first used by Schelling) and need for 'nerve, skill and courage'. The essential point was that even up to the very end – the spasm – the crisis leaders maintained some semblance of being the masters rather than the victims of events. The importance of many of the moves was that they were slowly implemented, allowing time to concentrate thought and bargain sensibly.

The escalation ladder was a metaphor rather than a prediction of the likely course of a conflict. Rungs could be jumped, doubled up, reversed in sequence and so on. Kahn's main aim was to illustrate options. More important than the individual rungs were six 'fire-breaks' or 'thresholds' at which very sharp changes in the character of the escalation took place. These were: (1) 'don't rock the boat; (2) nuclear war is unthinkable; (3) no nuclear use; (4) central sanctuary; (5) central war; and (6) city targeting'. The fire-breaks reflected the importance of saliencies in thoughts as well as deed. Kahn recognized the significance of the conventional weapon/nuclear weapon fire-break, but thought that as important was the one between the nation's homeland and the territory of its allies. He also believed that a distinction could be made between small, discriminating and controlled attacks on limited targets with nuclear weapons as against large attacks on cities. Whether the difference was a matter of degree or represented a recognized threshold, was the nub of the issue. If it could be maintained, then spasm war might be avoided.

Possible moves, once nuclear use had been initiated, involved, first, forms of demonstration and exemplary attacks and then hitting the

enemy's homeland, military forces, property or population in increasing amounts at an increasing tempo. Close examination of these
options was required, he argued, because they were more suitable for
the West than the East. There was no comparable dissection of the
nuances and tactics of conventional war. However, late in the book,
Kahn provided a Soviet escalation ladder in which conventional
options loomed as large as nuclear options do in the Western
ladder.[22] These options therefore were not necessarily available to
both sides (one reason for studying them was to 'guard against their
possible use by an enemy'). Different strengths made escalation easier.
Even when nuclear exchanges were at a modest level where both sides
could participate equally, the fact that one side was particularly
strong in the higher stages of escalation, i.e. had a 'credible first strike
capability', might just give him a decisive advantage. 'The stronger
may ... feel that once it has shattered its opponent's nuclear incredu-
lity, the escalation dominance available to it may be so much
strengthened that it will have its own way relatively easily'.[23]

    This concept of *escalation dominance* was thus central to Kahn's
theory. It was not defined properly until the appendix:

> This is a capacity, other things being equal, to enable the side
> possessing it to enjoy marked advantages in a given region of the
> escalation ladder. . . . It depends on the net effect of the competing
> capabilities on the rung being occupied, the estimate by each side
> of what would happen if the confrontation moved to these other
> rungs, and the means each side has to shift the confrontation to
> these other rungs.[24]

    Thus success through escalation dominance depended on a favour-
able asymmetry of capabilities. At any given level, the onus is put on
one side to escalate. Both will suffer the consequences but the problem is greater for those who have to make the decision. He acknowledged that a balance of terror might be emerging but saw ways in
which asymmetries might be created or preserved (for example,
through anti-ballistic missiles or measures to facilitate mass evacuation of cities). The suggestion was that with nerve and skill any sort
of favourable asymmetry might be turned to bargaining advantage.
However, to the extent that a stable balance of terror did come into
existence, the greater would be the similarity of the contest to the
game of Chicken, and the greater the importance of 'resolve'.

    There was a final asymmetry: 'That side which has least to lose by eruption or fears eruption the least, will automatically have an element of escalation dominance.'[25] This could refer either to advantages at a higher rung or else to a different attitude to the conflict. This latter possibility pointed, implicitly, to the key importance of the relative stakes in the conflict once all forms of strategic advantage had been neutralized.

The Threat that Leaves Something to Chance

To Schelling the value of nuclear weapons lay in the persuasive threat they posed to an adversary, even if little of value could accrue to oneself by implementing this threat. It would never be in one's interests to go the whole way, but it might always be in one's interests to threaten to do so, even in the midst of hostilities. In such circumstances the nuclear threat would be required to do much more than provide its peacetime warning against a breach of the *status quo*. The need would be to compel the aggressor to stop his aggression, or to go back to his starting point, relinquishing captured territory. Consequently, the threat would have to be particularly credible and serious, despite the fact that a deteriorating situation would indicate that a previous deterrent threat had been taken insufficiently seriously.

Nuclear threats in a situation of parity lacked credibility. With one's own well-being implicated in any threat there was a reluctance to make their execution automatic. The greatest credibility would come if implementation was linked solely to whether or not the adversary complied with the threat's provisions. However, no nation would commit itself so irrevocably. Consequently implementation would always be conditional on a decision to go ahead. An element of choice would remain, but this deprived the threat of some credibility for a conscious decision to go ahead could only be of dubious rationality. In this way the threat might well degenerate into a bluff.

This assumed that the final decision on whether or not to go ahead would remain with the deterrer. But it might be possible to arrange matters in such a way that, because of some unavoidable area of risk, no deliberate decision could be made. Schelling called it 'The Threat that Leaves Something to Chance': 'The key to these threats is that, though one may or may not carry them out, *the final decision is not altogether under the threatener's control.*'[26] The uncertain element in the decision had to come from somewhere outside the control of either the threatener or the threatened. This could be an accident, a third party, or imperfect decision-making. It was also inherent in the process of escalation.

Indeed, as a war developed and expanded it could take on a momentum of its own. This would be particularly true if the war required a nuclear dimension. The role of uncertainty in reinforcing deterrence had been widely recognized by the leading strategists of the nuclear age. Indeed the more doubtful the rationality of implementing nuclear threats, the more necessary it had become to emphasize uncertainties over rationality.[27] This was the whole point of the analysis of the game of Chicken. Schelling emphasized the ubiquity of uncertainty:

> Not everybody is always in his right mind. Not all the frontiers and thresholds are precisely defined, fully reliable, and known to be so beyond the least temptation to test them out, to explore for loopholes, or to take a chance that they might be disconnected this time. Violence, especially in war, is a confused and uncertain activity, highly unpredictable depending on decisions made by fallible human beings organized into imperfect governments depending on fallible communications and warning systems and on the untested performance of people and equipment. It is furthermore a hotheaded activity, in which commitments and reputations can develop a momentum of their own.[28]

The uncertainty created an inherent sense of risk. The risk grew as the crisis turned into a limited war and moved towards general war. 'The idea is simply that a limited war can get out of hand by degrees'.[29] Skilful tactics would exploit this fact, not shrink from it. Making a threat that left something to chance was to manipulate risk. Another word used for this process was 'brinkmanship', derived from a notorious comment of John Foster Dulles when Secretary of State – 'If you are scared to go to the brink, you are lost.' Schelling defined it as 'the deliberate creation of a recognizable risk of war, a risk that one does not completely control. It is a tactic of letting the situation get somewhat out of hand, just because its being out of hand may be intolerable to the other party and force his accommodation'. It would not only be necessary to be sufficiently rational to know the value of appearing irrational, but also to be sufficiently in control of matters to allow them to get out of control.

Any escalatory move involved pushing matters more out of control. Thus a function of limited war was to 'pose the deliberate risk of all-out war'. As such one becomes less concerned with ensuring that the war stayed limited and more with keeping the risk of escalation 'within moderate limits above zero'.[30] It would be the same with the first nuclear exchanges. The purpose of their introduction in a war that was being lost would not be 'solely or mainly, to redress a balance on the battlefield', but 'to make the war too painful or too dangerous to continue'.[31] Actually using nuclear weapons would in itself create a new situation in the opponent's mind. Using them in a small way, while the physical consequences remained quite minor, signalled that they might yet be used in a large way.

Schelling's emphasis on persuasion through risk rather than pain (initiating pain only to emphasize risk) had greater plausibility than mechanical 'tit for tat' nuclear exchanges. By the introduction and exploitation of the factor of uncertainty, the bargaining process could at least involve skill. Schelling was working with a more realistic view of the character of war than writers such as Kaplan, whose aim appeared to be one of containing its furies by devising rules which took small account of the meaning of individual moves for those suffering the consequences. However, Schelling was similar to these other writers (with the exception of Read) in his indifference to the course of the war on the ground.

Schelling acknowledged that the risk created would be a shared one, and it was not altogether clear why one side should find this risk more acceptable than the other. A 'competition in risk-taking' could develop, turning war into a contest of 'endurance, nerve, obstinacy and pain'. Like Kahn he wished to avoid such degeneration. Kahn hoped to do this through escalation dominance, based on a favourable asymmetry of capabilities at a particular stage of the escalation ladder. Because Schelling had less confidence or interest in straightforward military advantage, he saw possibilities in artful tactics. The point of these tactics would be to shift the onus of decision onto the other side. You gave him the choice of continuing with his aggression (or resistance) or complying with your demands. 'Preferably one creates the shared risk by irreversible manoeuvres or commitments, so that only the enemy's withdrawal can tranquilize the situation; otherwise it may turn out to be a contest of nerves.'[32] The emphasis was on creating a situation where only the other's compliance could relieve the shared pain and remove the shared risk. Thus, as the ideal deterrent threat made the sanction unavoidable if the adversary did what he should not, the ideal compellent threat made disaster likely if the adversary did not do what he should. In each case the element of bluff was removed. So the risk entailed in making this sort of threat was enormous. It involved placing your fate directly in the enemy's hands. It was really an abrogation of responsibility and something of an act of desperation.

Which brings us back to the question of what made one side more desperate than the other, and determined the comparative toleration of risk. In Schelling's writings, the relationship between the events that sparked off a crisis, the situation on the ground between the combatants and the 'competition in risk-taking' was uncertain. He argued that the deliberate creation of mutual risk was the strategy for the side that was losing a limited war. In a footnote, after remarking that the failure to initiate risk irreversibly would necessitate winning a 'war of nerves', he added: 'But at least this symmetrical situation replaces one in which the asymmetry favoured the opponent, who won by default if neither side acted.'[33] The suggestion was that once the conflict had moved into the nuclear realm, this was a higher plane in which the previous positions in the land battle were of only secondary importance. Elsewhere, he seemed to believe that compellent threats could in themselves reverse the advance of an invading army, and so he was barely concerned with military resistance for its own sake.

The move from the discussion of deterrence to that of compellence, from a threat made passively to persuade the other to remain passive, to one made actively to stop the other being active, removed much of the relevance of distinctions between the aggressor and the defender. After a certain point the pertinent tactics become available to either side. Schelling noted how the defender might want to contain the aggressor by the threat of escalation, while the aggressor may design his advances 'so that even local resistance seems fraught with explosive potential'. Nor was Schelling sure whether the matter which had stimulated the conflict would determine each side's interest in its resolution, for it was always necessary to consider the long-term 'supergame' between East and West. As it was anticipated that there would be a series of super-power crises – ever a series of limited wars – each contest had to be played out with the future in mind. As in the game of Chicken, reputation was crucial and once a reputation had been developed for recoiling in the face of risk then this weakness could be exploited.

In a famous passage Schelling emphasized the importance of saving 'face':

If the question is raised whether this kind of 'face' is worth fighting over, the answer is that this is one of the few things worth fighting over. Few parts of the world are intrinsically worth the risk of serious war by themselves, especially when taken slice by slice, but defending them or running risks to protect them may preserve one's commitments to action in other parts of the world and at later times. 'Face' is merely the interdependence of a country's commitments; it is a country's reputation for action, the expectation other countries have about its behaviour.[34]

In this way nuclear strategy created its own ends as well as its own means. Despite this rather definite statement, it is evident that Schelling was aware of the dangers of attacking 'face' to an unworthy enterprise and that there would be little incentive to make great sacrifice for little tangible gain.

The point was that having made a commitment to stand firm, failure to stand firm would degrade other or future commitments. It indicated the need *not* to allow one's credibility to be put to the test over matters where few interests were at stake. This qualifier was not stressed in Schelling's work. It needed the experience of Vietnam to bring it to the fore. In reminding US leaders of the interdependence of commitments, Schelling created an argument for never yielding to pressure, no matter how weak one's position in a material and moral sense.[35]

The arguments on the manipulation of risk found Schelling at his most suggestive and most confusing. He was trying to develop rational tactics for irrational situations, and in doing so attempted to turn the elements for irrationality into coercive instruments. He achieved an important shift in our understanding of the process of making threats, which would have been more valuable if he had rested with pre-war deterrent threats rather than intra-war compellence. It was easier to explain why an adversary might hesitate before setting off a chain of events that could get out of control and end in utter disaster, than why, having embarked upon this course, the same adversary should be willing not only to stop, but to turn back and give up whatever tangible had been gained. The insight was to recognize how the adversary's behaviour could be influenced not by a definite threat to do something to him but because the wrong step could provoke a situation in which terrible things *might* happen to him. It was the fear of nuclear war itself that deterred, not the specific threat of nuclear retaliation. In this way all nuclear threats became threats that leave something to chance.

From Counter-force to Assured Destruction

15 City-Avoidance

Victor Hugo's aphorism that there is no more powerful force in history than an idea whose time has come, is not as true as those many merchants of ideas who quote it so often and so hopefully would like to believe. As much as excellent and original ideas are neglected and disparaged, foolish and dangerous ones are trumpeted and celebrated. To affect history, an idea must have political strength as much as substantive content. The civilian strategists gained notice because their concepts and prescriptions were bold and imaginative. Their historical moment came in January 1961, because they succeeded in influencing an incoming Administration. To a remarkable extent their concepts were adopted as working guidelines for American defence policy. Few ideas so novel and far-reaching can have been given such a severe test so soon after their original formulation.

The strategic balance had not settled down and had yet to take on the appearance of either stability or symmetry. Instead of, as had been widely expected, the new Administration being faced by a missile gap working decidedly in favour of the Soviet Union,[1] the reverse was the case. The Eisenhower Administration had accelerated the *Minuteman* ICBM and *Polaris* SLBM programmes, and there were further boosts by the Kennedy Administration in 1961. Missiles rolled off US production lines and were put in place with impressive speed. Meanwhile the Soviet programme had been beset by a variety of technical problems. US intelligence estimates had been anticipating hundreds of Soviet missiles pointed at the US by 1961; in fact there were only a handful.

Although the situation was still ambiguous in early 1961 when the new Administration's policy was being formulated, by the Autumn of that year excellent photographs of the Soviet Union were being sent back by the new reconnaissance satellites. These made it clear that the US was in a position of considerable strength rather than weakness. In October 1961, with the Berlin crisis of that year still under way, Deputy Secretary of Defense Roswell Gilpatric, after detailing the 'tens of thousands' of nuclear delivery vehicles, tactical as well as strategic, available to the Americans, emphasized to the Russians that all was known about their relative weaknesses:

> The destructive power which the United States could bring to bear even after a Soviet surprise attack upon our forces would be as great as – perhaps greater than – the total undamaged forces which the enemy can threaten to launch against the United States in a first strike. In short, we have a second strike capability which is at least as extensive as what the Soviets can deliver by striking first.[2]

What we have called the strategy of stable conflict was thus first propounded as official doctrine at a time when the super-power relations did not seem at all stable in either political or military terms. The cold war was at its height and America was storming ahead in the quality and quantity of its nuclear arms. The new doctrines could not but be understood in the context of a build-up of military strength that spoke of a drive for superiority in all departments, which meant, inevitably, that they were misunderstood.

McNamara's Band

No single public figure has influenced the way we think about nuclear weapons quite as much as Robert S. McNamara, the US Secretary of Defense from 1961 to 1968. Under McNamara the focal point for innovation in strategic concepts shifted back to the Pentagon (though to the civilian rather than the military officers), and away from the universities and institutes. While he was in office many new concepts were introduced, of which the most important were *assured destruction, damage limitation* and *flexible response* which remain central to this day to strategic debate. Another legacy was the overall number of US ICBMs and SLBMs which were set at 1054 and 656 respectively during his term of office and stayed at that level until 1980.

Equally significant was the manner in which these concepts and policies were developed and applied. McNamara epitomized a particular style of management; so much so that he became a model for management theorists and, in his day, was taken by some sociologists to signify a new trend in the running of modern, industrial societies. He exulted in the most modern techniques of problem-solving, anxious to extend his range of choice and his devices for choosing between alternatives, attempting quantification to permit rigorous comparisons and resolutely excluding irrelevant criteria. William Kaufmann described his approach:

> He likes to see objectives concretely defined. He abhors the thought that there is only one way of doing things; he is intensely interested in alternatives. And he is a restless seeker of ways to measure the effectiveness of the alternatives.[3]

Apart from the fact that the Pentagon was the obvious position from which to lead a strategic debate, the quality of the analytical resources and the access to the vast amounts of detailed information demanded by the McNamara method could only be provided by a large, well-funded bureaucracy.

The Department of Defense had become the largest single employer in the United States, with a budget greater than that of the GNPs of many countries, bases and commitments throughout the globe, and a programme of research, development, and capital investment that made it the major source of technological innovation in the West. McNamara was taken from the top of the Ford Motor Company to apply the managerial skills he had learnt to a corporate structure of comparable size and complexity. For someone as devoted as McNamara to rational, centralized decision-making, the situation at the Pentagon was distressing. The dominant feature was inter-service rivalry, accentuated by competition for a restricted budget. Previous Secretaries of Defense had spent their time arbitrating between competing service claims, effecting compromises that moderated the disputes, often at the expense of good policy. McNamara's predecessor, Thomas Gates, had begun to take some steps to centralize decision-making, but it was left to McNamara to finish the job, a task he took on with some gusto.

The military found that the functions they were used to performing, in particular decisions on how to spend their share of the budget, were taken over by the Office of the Secretary of Defense. From this

Office, most notoriously the unit devoted to systems analysis, decisions emerged in a manner which was barely comprehensible to the military and took no account of their experience, prejudices, traditions, or sensibilities. In the first four years this bruising process was eased by sizeable increases in military expenditure. But the hostility to McNamara amongst the military was deep and bitter and, when resources flowed less freely, McNamara had to cope with formidable opposition. Having been excluded from the formation of policy, the military felt little obligation to support that policy, whatever its substantive merits, and often encouraged Congressional challenges. The revolution in decision-making sharpened the conflict between McNamara and the military.

The basic guidelines for the strategic doctrines of the Kennedy Administration were derived from the critique of the strategy of 'massive retaliation' as it had evolved during the 1950s. This critique had found considerable resonance in Democratic Party circles, and was articulated by Senator John Kennedy as he campaigned for the Presidency in 1960. The essence of the critique was that the only available response to any Soviet aggression was an all-out nuclear attack. Because this was too drastic for use except in extreme circumstances, most communist challenges could not be resisted. The Soviet advances in strategic arms had neutralized the West's major advantage. Kennedy predicted:

> Their missile power will be the shield from behind which they will slowly, but surely, advance – through Sputnik diplomacy, limited brush-fire wars, indirect non-overt aggression, intimidation and subversion, internal revolution, increased prestige or influence, and the vicious blackmail of our allies. The periphery of the Free World will slowly be nibbled away. ... Each such Soviet move will weaken the West; but none will seem sufficiently significant by itself to justify our initiating a nuclear war which might destroy us.[4]

The emphasis was thus on the danger of limited war and the availability of non-nuclear forces to fight such a war. He wanted forces capable of operating in a great variety of circumstances in a manner appropriate to the problem at hand.

McNamara had little grounding in contemporary strategic theory. The only relevant book he is reported to have read was Oskar Morgenstern's *The Question of National Defense*. Though unversed himself in the theory and methods of the new strategy, he gathered together some of the leading exponents. Many left Santa Monica in California, the home of RAND, for Washington. Charles Hitch, Alain Enthoven, Henry Rowen, Andrew Marshall, and Daniel Ellsberg all took up full-time positions in McNamara's office. William Kaufmann, though now a Professor at MIT, remained on hand as a consultant. Albert Wohlstetter, the leader of the RAND strategists, declined to join the new Administration, but his presence was still felt and the tributes paid to him by McNamara, amongst others, indicated that the old order had been overthrown and the new one installed. Thomas Schelling was a consultant, but his practical advice was less important than his notable contributions to the prevailing conceptual framework.[5]

The approach of the civilian strategists undoubtedly appealed to McNamara. It was based on disciplined reasoning rather than intuition or tradition. It presupposed a modicum of rationality at the centre and exploited this to lead to the exploration of unusual and novel strategic moves. However, whereas to the strategists 'rationality' represented a useful analytical presumption, to McNamara it was something of a creed, a goal to be aimed for. The 'homo strategicus', an abstract construct useful for theorizing, suddenly came to life. For once the real world seemed intent on approximating to a simplifying assumption.

Rational decision-making requires a position of considerable political power. The sources of 'irrationality' are not simply muddled thinking or psychological quirks, but the regular intrusion of insistent lobbyists for some cause or interests, or inadequate bureaucratic structures or the divergent pull of opposing objectives. To facilitate rational decisions, the bureaucracy has to be organized so that those at the top are aware of key decisions that have to be made and have the information with which to make them. The lobbyists have to be excluded. In fact, as few people as possible can be permitted to share in the decision. Although it was just about possible to organize the Pentagon to suit McNamara's style, it was extremely difficult to operate the American political process in a satisfactory manner, especially once key Congressmen began to appreciate the implications of McNamara's policies and refused to be blinded by his strategic 'science'. Even more difficult was operating within the Atlantic Alliance, a collection of sovereign nation states bound together by a common purpose, but each with their own particular interpretation of that purpose and how it was to be fulfilled. Finally, a measure of connivance with the Soviet Union was required. The adversary, too, needed to understand how, by co-operating with the United States, the arms race could be stabilized and wars prevented from getting completely out of hand.

McNamara's problem was how to establish Washington as not only the main but the sole decision centre in a crisis, to convince America's allies that their best interests were being looked after, and to convince the Soviet Union that her interests were appreciated, especially when they coincided with those of the United States. In fact, as McNamara eventually discovered, both allies and adversaries had their own distinctive strategic perspectives and were not inclined to follow an American lead.

Within his own domain McNamara could take steps to enhance executive control. Great stress was placed on improving and protecting the national command and control system which linked the Government to the forces in the field. Steps were taken to ensure that no moves could be made using strategic forces without the expressed authority of the President. In the design of forces, McNamara was anxious that US retaliation after the absorption of a Soviet first strike should not only be devastating, but also controlled. It would be better if it could be thoughtful and unhurried and not a reactive spasm. As McNamara explained early on, he wanted a strategic force 'to be of a character which will permit its use, in event of attack, in a cool and deliberate fashion and always under the complete control of the constituted authority'.[6]

A Strategy of Multiple Options

The greatest requirement was that the President's hand should not be forced by a lack of alternatives. He needed options to be a decision-maker. Without options there would be no decisions to be made; the President would be reduced to passivity, the victim rather than the master of events. Multiple options would mean that any American action could be tailored to the particular Soviet challenge. The choice would be greater than suicide or surrender. In an uncertain world where the contingencies were many, multiple options should mean that the Americans would not be caught unawares and unprepared. Preserving for as long as possible as wide a range of choice as possible meant that, when a choice had to be made, it could be tuned to the circumstances of the moment.

If anything, this was a non-strategy. It did not involve planning to fight a particular sort of war, but rather planning to fight a wide variety of wars. The spirit behind Dulles's espousal of a strategy of massive retaliation was that the US should not allow the adversary any benefit from taking the initiative but should force him to fight in the manner preferred by the US, insisting on one mode of warfare and refusing to be diverted. Talking of multiple options was much more reactive, preparing to accept whatever ground rules the enemy laid down for a given conflict. The reason for the shift was straightforward. Since Dulles's time there had been a declining interest in transforming any war into a nuclear contest. It was no longer as arguable that the US would enjoy any significant advantages in such a contest. The extension of options essentially meant a greater number and variety of conventional forces and indicated a US readiness to fight solely conventional wars.

It was difficult to avoid definitive choices in the earlier stages of force planning instead of at the point of confrontation with the adversary. An important consideration in persuading the Eisenhower Administration to accept a restriction in its options had been the pressures of a limited budget. The Democrats were more Keynesian, prepared to accept greater public spending for the collective good. McNamara also believed that good housekeeping could knock fat off the budget, so saving money for useful projects. Nevertheless, there could not be unlimited funding and as the decade moved on and the Vietnam War began to demand a greater share of resources allotted to defence, the purchasing of strategic options had to be restricted. It was impossible to plan for every eventuality.

Another problem was that it took two to make certain options either necessary or feasible. A war plan based on avoiding damage to both sides' civilians depended on the other side preparing to fight the same way. Also, the creation of certain options, even if for no other reason than prudent contingency planning, could be seen as an aggressive or suspicious move by potential adversaries. The association of counter-force capabilities with first strikes meant that even if such capabilities were developed and maintained for the best of motives, an adversary could be excused for assuming the worst. Their reactions might, in turn, stimulate a counter-reaction, so prompting an arms race. In this way the unintended consequences of a particular option could interfere with other objectives.

Each option could not be endowed with an equal status. Western Europeans were most concerned about the nuclear options. They were anxious at any sign that America's commitment to use nuclear weapons in the defence of Europe might be waning. The existence of plausible conventional options offered the Americans a way out, preserved a line of retreat if the time for nuclear use did not seem propitious. As time would rarely seem propitious for nuclear use, the availability of conventional options made nuclear threats less plausible. Thomas Schelling had written of the rôle of 'burning bridges' in emphasizing a commitment to stay in the fight. Creating an option could be seen as making allowance for moments of weakness.

To the chagrin of the military, McNamara did not offer a doctrine concerning how a war should be fought. According to Kaufmann he was convinced 'that the best strategy was to let the circumstances determine the choice of weapons and make sure that there was a plentiful supply in each major category'. Nevertheless, his preferences were reasonably clear: 'He wanted to have the capabilities for all the modern types of warfare and, if forced to commit himself, he wanted to place main but not sole reliance on non-nuclear weapons.' [7] The Europeans, on the other hand, still preferred to place main but not sole reliance on nuclear weapons.

It did not take McNamara long to discover the problems of interpretation caused by his simple desire for a wide choice. Section 7 will examine the difficulties caused by McNamara's ideas for relations with the Europeans. This section will discuss McNamara's forays into nuclear strategy. The first doctrine with which McNamara's name was associated was that of city-avoidance; the second was that of assured destruction. The movement from the first to the second gave the impression of a 180 degrees turn. In fact, as we shall see, the change was mainly one of emphasis, though nonetheless significant for that.

City-Avoidance

In the early studies ordered on nuclear war plans the need for flexibility, discrimination, and control in targeting were stressed. The plan inherited from the Eisenhower Administration called for the launching of all strategic forces on the initiation of nuclear war with the Soviet Union, against Soviet, Chinese, and satellite cities. No account had been taken of the growing Sino-Soviet split; millions of Chinese would be gratuitously destroyed. There was no expectation of a series of volleys; command and control facilities lacked special protection and there was no provision for strategic reserves.

The new plans involved significant changes. Reserves would be maintained and not only would US command and control facilities be protected but those of the Soviet Union would also be spared. The options created allowed for attacks ranging from those against Soviet retaliatory forces, through air defence installations distant from cities, to those near cities, to command and control systems, to an all-out 'spasm' attack. The fatalities could be varied according to the altitude of the explosions, the size of the warhead, and the amount of radio-active fallout released. If no restraints were observed and no reserves held, the US was capable of killing 360–450 million people through-out the 'Sino-Soviet bloc' in a matter of hours.[8]

By early 1962 the new strategy was ready and already affecting force planning and weapon design. McNamara began to explain publicly that the President could now spare or attack a variety of Soviet targets as the circumstances demanded. In June 1962 after explaining the new strategy privately to NATO, McNamara provided a public exposition, at the commencement address at the University of Michigan at Ann Arbor. He outlined the US approach to the 'terrible contingency of nuclear war':

> The US has come to the conclusion that to the extent feasible basic military strategy in a possible general nuclear war should be ap-proached in much the same way that more conventional military operations have been regarded in the past. That is to say, principal military objectives, in the event of a nuclear war stemming from a major attack on the Alliance, should be the destruction of the enemy's military forces, not of his civilian population.

> The very strength and nature of the Alliance forces makes it pos-sible for us to retain, even in the face of a massive surprise attack, sufficient reserve striking power to destroy an enemy society if driven to it. In other words we are giving a possible opponent the strongest possible incentive to refrain from striking our own cities.[9]

This could be seen as being derived from the theories of limited strategic war. In February 1962 McNamara had mentioned approaching nuclear exchanges in terms of bargaining: 'We may seek to terminate a war on favourable terms by using our forces as a bargain-ing weapon – by threatening further attack'.[10] The idea of attacking restricted military targets rather than restricted civilian targets as a bargaining tactic had a respectable pedigree.[11] It was consistent with the concept of populations as hostages; they would be spared great harm while the means by which they could be destroyed were demonstrated. However describing the strategy as consistent with 'more conventional military operations' did not fit in with limited nuclear war strategies. Schelling pronounced the Ann Arbor speech a 'sensible way to think about war', but complained that the attempt to create links with previous military operations was quite misleading. To him, the new approach involved concentrating on the capacity to hurt; it was 'utterly different' to the military operations of the past.[12]

McNamara was not following Schelling completely. He recognized that any war would have to be terminated somehow, and that this would be a political process, involving bargaining. He also shared the desire to keep such nuclear exchanges that did take place as limited and controlled as possible. Where he differed was in not viewing limited nuclear war in isolation from conventional war, as something totally distinct with its own unique rules of combat. Unfortunately mixing the two types of warfare could create difficulties. It could mean a rush into nuclear use, because these sort of weapons were the only ones available to meet certain contingencies. In addition, stressing the targeting of nuclear weapons against other nuclear weapons as in traditional operations involving conventional weapons, could raise fears of a disarming first strike and encourage the temptation to pre-empt.

Though counter-force was often taken to connote first-strike capabilities, this was not the major option being considered by McNamara and his aides. The relevant concepts were those developed at RAND during the 1950s. The concern of those such as Andrew Marshall and Albert Wohlstetter, who played important rôles in formulating the relevant concepts, was the conflict under way on the ground. Rather than engage in either hyper-destructive but militarily pointless attacks on cities, or formalized exchanges for bargaining purposes, the preference was for nuclear strikes that had some utility for the hard-pressed military commanders attempting to hold back the Soviet advance. Nuclear strikes would gain their effect through a combination of the impression of determination created by their actual use, and the military value of the targets attacked, which, by holding up the enemy advance, would facilitate a satisfactory settlement.

These concepts were linked to the notion of flexible options, the desire for a choice of actions according to operational circumstances. In a scenario in which a localized conflict was expanding in scope and intensity, the preferred targets might be enemy military forces being employed, or about to be employed, in and around the original combat zone, or forces threatening key ports or airfields as well as those threatening civilians. The presumption was that a future war could well be a complicated affair, in which one particular engagement would not necessarily be decisive. In fact, because it was expected that both sides would make every effort to protect their strategic forces, they would not necessarily appear as attractive targets at all. Thus the objective was not a disarming first strike but objectives geared to a type of conflict which excluded the mutual destruction of cities. Morton Halperin explained:

> In short, if both sides have well-protected forces, nuclear war, if it comes, may be much slower than we now envisage. It may involve attacks on strategic forces which are vulnerable or whose vulnerability is discovered or develops during the war; or attacks on military targets or on economic targets (such as oil fields) which are not close to major population centers.[13]

This aspect of the new strategy was not effectively explained to the public. One reason may have been the close link in the public (and the Soviet) mind between counter-force attacks and first strikes. More modest counter-force objectives had to impress an audience that associated this sort of attack with some decisive surprise blow, designed to disarm the enemy and put him at one's mercy. Many at RAND blamed some of the sensational writing of Kahn for encouraging this association. Disagreement over this may be one reason why Kahn left RAND to set up his own Hudson Institute. A second problem was indicated by the quote from Halperin given above. There could be targets well behind the front line, described as 'rear echelon' targets. They could include Soviet forces relevant both to the immediate battle and strategic attacks (such as Soviet missiles aimed at Western Europe) and their location could well mean that an attack upon them would be interpreted as a serious escalation.

A third reason was the incentive to target strategic forces for purposes of damage limitation, again more modest than a first-strike capability, but not so easily distinguished from it. This concern pulled the issue away from a land war in Europe to strategic nuclear exchanges. The influence behind damage limitation was a fear that, despite all the options – nuclear and conventional – a general nuclear war was not inconceivable. If it came, one key objective would be to keep the damage down to the minimum. The modest notion of 'damage limitation' as opposed to more ambitious 'damage prevention', captured the minimax concept of Game Theory (the best of the worst outcomes). As such it became a useful means of denoting an approach to any problem that was more preoccupied with minimizing costs than maximizing gains.

In 1961–2 it was by no means fanciful to consider nuclear war a very real danger. When Kennedy entered office, relations with the Russians were tense and the President felt himself tested continually by the Russians for signs of weakness. The Berlin crisis of 1961 intensified these feelings to the extent that it was felt that nuclear war could not be ruled out in the coming months and years. This concentrated attention on the danger of deterrence failing. The investigation of all possible means of reducing damage seemed to be only prudent insurance.

Opening up the possibility of avoiding cities in nuclear exchanges offered some hope of sparing lives. Pentagon estimates suggested that casualties might be reduced by a factor of ten, from 100 million to 10 million in the United States, if the Russians could be persuaded to avoid cities in the event of a nuclear exchange.[14] It was argued that the development of a capacity for counter-force with this objective in mind was not inconsistent with the abjuration of first-strike capabilities. Aircraft which have returned to an airfield for a second sortie or have yet to take off at all, missile launchers yet to be used or those with a reload capacity, would all provide legitimate second-strike targets. McNamara insisted during Congressional hearings that even after a Soviet first strike there would still remain 'many installations which we would wish to strike'.[15]

An effort was made to communicate to the Soviet Union an offer of city-avoidance as a rule for any future nuclear contest, rather than a threat of a first strike. McNamara who had noted the dangers of a 'reciprocal fear of surprise attack' went to great pains to try to reassure the Soviet Union on this score. His argument was that there was no incentive for the US even to contemplate a first strike. To emphasize this, that the US would neither need nor be able to pre-empt, US strategic forces were to be protected to an extent sufficient to allow them to ride out a Soviet attack and still be available for retaliation. The highly vulnerable IRBMs in Europe were phased out. The inadequacy of long-range bombers when assessed against these criteria was one reason why McNamara would not authorize procurement of a new one. Furthermore, it was assumed that the Russians would take steps to protect their own strategic forces so that it would not be in the US power to disarm the Soviet Union effectively. McNamara explained to Congress in January 1963 that:

> [I]n planning our second strike force, we have provided, throughout the period under consideration, a capability to destroy virtually all the 'soft' and 'semihard' military targets in the Soviet Union and a large number of their fully hardened missile sites, with an additional capability in the form of a protected force to be employed or held in reserve for use against urban and industrial areas.
>
> We have not found it feasible at this time, to provide a capability for insuring the destruction of any very large portion of the fully hard ICBM sites or missile-launching submarines.
>
> Fully hard ICBM sites can be destroyed but only at great cost in terms of the numbers of offensive weapons required to dig them out.
>
> Furthermore, in a second strike situation we would be attacking, for the most part, empty sites from which the missiles had already been fired.
>
> The value of trying to provide a capability to destroy a very high proportion of Soviet hard ICBM sites becomes even more questionable in view of the expected increase in the Soviet missile-launching submarine force.[16]

Retreat From City-Avoidance

Despite all the disclaimers, the logic of the strategy appeared as first strike rather than second strike. If it was at all possible to target Soviet missile forces accurately it made more sense to attack these forces in their totality, rather than destroy the residue only after the bulk were speeding towards various parts of NATO. As one Soviet strategist wrote: 'A strategy which contemplates attaining victory through the destruction of the armed forces cannot stem from the idea of a "retaliatory" blow; it stems from preventive action and the achievement of surprise'.[17]

The sort of counter-force targeting against Soviet strategic forces that McNamara claimed to have in mind could make sense only in the most limited and unlikely of circumstances. If the US was sincere in its solely second-strike intentions then it had to rely on persuasion to get the Soviet Union to follow a policy of city-avoidance. American cities were not to be spared by direct American intervention, through a strike eliminating the means of their possible destruction. Nor was the US intending to set the ground rules because she would not initiate the nuclear exchanges. She had to rely on a prior, mutual understanding that it would be best for all if a nuclear war were fought in a particular way. In addition, though the Soviet Union was to be encouraged, if she insisted on starting a nuclear war, to aim for only military targets, the sort of military targets available for attack were to be restricted through efforts to protect retaliatory forces. The Soviet Union was not going to be offered an opportunity to disarm the US. Moreover, it was expected that the attack from the Soviet Union would be less than total; some military forces and facilities would remain, serving the purpose of allowing the US to respond exactly in kind to the limited Soviet first blow. Finally, not only should the Soviet Union attempt to attack in this particular way, if she should attack at all, but her strike must be interpreted in the US as a counter-force action. Admiral Burke was not convinced. He told the Senate Armed Services Committee:

> Many of these missile bases are right close to our cities, right close, so are many of our other bases. So an attack on our major bases would necessarily destroy a great many cities and a great many of our people. When those missiles start coming over you do not know whether the intent of the enemy was to hit or not to hit a city if he hits it. The same thing is true with the Russian military installations.[18]

The doctrine as McNamara attempted to present it, therefore depended on the Soviet Union initiating a nuclear war by a limited and accurate attack against some of the less decisive US forces, situated if possible well away from cities, while holding some of her own forces in reserve, preferably vulnerable so that they would be available for the US retaliation.

McNamara did not pretend that a counter-force attack of this nature was the most likely of all Soviet nuclear attacks; on the contrary he admitted that an attack on US cities was as likely if not more so. All he argued was that it was a sufficiently plausible contingency to make it a worthy object of planning, and that if nuclear war could be fought this way, it would be less of a disaster than an all-out war.

But at the time the doctrine was being enunciated, the Soviet Union had no capability at all for mounting any sort of serious counter-force attack on the United States; it was having trouble with its ICBM and SLBM programmes while the US programme was forging ahead. Soviet missiles were few and inaccurate. As a number would have to be used to destroy with certainty each military target it would be impossible to destroy a significant segment of US forces without using up its entire stock of intercontinental strategic missiles and bombers (capabilities for use against Western Europe were much more impressive). Not only could the Soviet Union not improve its position by launching such an attack, but also its position would worsen because the US would remain strong while it would have exhausted itself. Of course the Soviet Union would not gain any positive benefits by attacking US cities, but some rewards in influencing US behaviour could be expected from threatening to do so. It was not surprising that the Kremlin rejected McNamara's ideas, preferring to concentrate propaganda on the terrible consequences of any war. The notion of 'Marquis of Queensbury rules for the conduct of nuclear war' was treated with derision, with emphasis on the inevitability of mass destruction if nuclear war should break out.

Nor was it clear to what purpose the Soviet Union might launch a counter-force attack of the type implied by McNamara's doctrine. In terms of the conventional military operations of the past, which the Russians could readily accept as a frame of reference, the only serious purpose would be a disarming pre-emptive strike. Otherwise one had to delve into concepts of signalling and bargaining, which might make for interesting diplomacy but was not the stuff of traditional military doctrine.

To get any real value out of a counter-force attack it was either necessary to destroy more weapons than were used up in making the attack (and this was not possible at the current stage of missile technology), or else accept the expenditure of extra missiles because of the possession of a much larger stock than the other side. In other words, to make military sense out of counter-force capabilities it was necessary to have superiority in the quantity and quality of weapons. This made it a much more plausible aspiration for the US than the USSR. McNamara explained to a Congressional committee the need for an invulnerable US force and also one 'larger than would otherwise be the case. Because since no force can be completely invulnerable, we will lose a portion of it under those circumstances [Soviet first strike] and we must buy more than we otherwise would buy.'[19] What were

wise precautions to McNamara could well appear as a drive to superiority by the Russians.

Apart from anything else, NATO nuclear strategy, to which the US
was the main contributor, was not rigidly oriented towards the use of
nuclear weapons solely for the purposes of retaliation. On the
contrary, despite considerable pressure in international fora, NATO
had refused to make a pledge of 'no first use' of nuclear weapons on
the grounds that deterrence rested on that very possibility. When
Kennedy came to office there were hints that he might be willing to
make such a pledge, believing that a build-up of conventional weapons might release NATO from dependence on nuclear weapons. He
hesitated for two reasons. First, America's allies were distinctly unhappy with any restrictions on what they still believed to be the
West's most efficient military asset. Second, whereas there might be
much to say on the virtues of conventional defence in the case of a
general Soviet attack across the Iron Curtain, these virtues were less
in evidence in the specific case of Berlin. Berlin was an isolated out-
post with points of access controlled by the Warsaw Pact. The
Western position could not be maintained with conventional weapons in a straightforward fight. The nuclear card was the only card to
play in this case. As Berlin was the most pressing crisis of 1961,
Kennedy felt he had no alternative but to preserve the 'first use'
option as well as search for a credible way of limiting damage in a
nuclear war should it occur. In an article in the *Saturday Evening
Post* in March 1962, Stewart Alsop spoke of Kennedy's belief that
'Khruschev must not be certain that, where its vital interests are
threatened, the United States will never strike first'.

Kennedy later clarified the remark, making it clear that he was
thinking of first use in the context of an ongoing war provoked by the
Soviet Union over the fate of Western Europe rather than some
nuclear bolt from the blue. But strategic discourse had concentrated
on massive nuclear exchanges, causing unacceptable damage to an
aggressor by way of punishment or relieving an enemy of his strategic
power in a first strike. Despite his disclaimers, and because of the
stress on damage limitation, many of the statements of McNamara
could be, and were, interpreted in these terms. Nevertheless, if McNamara's doctrine could make any sense at all it was not in the context
of a war initiated by an unprovoked nuclear attack, but as an out-
growth of a war being fought in and over Western Europe, in which
there was a degree of escalation as each side sought to improve its
position. The sensitivity of both sides to the possibilities of disarming

first strikes and the references to limiting damage to US cities in the event of general nuclear war ensured that the sort of exchanges McNamara was discussing would be viewed in isolation. The most germaine scenario of the time – a crisis beginning in Berlin – happened to be one in which early nuclear use would be especially likely.

The hostile Soviet interpretation of the 'no-cities' option concerned McNamara. However, even more disturbing than evidence that the Soviet Union was convinced that he was planning a first-strike capability was evidence that the US Air Force also believed this to be the case. The Air Force had come to associate counter-force with the capacity to fight and win a nuclear war. A USAF document of February 1963 explained how counter-city strategies lacked credibility. They relied on terror to deter, but once the 'potential aggressor' also had the means of nuclear devastation available to him, then the threat became implausible; retaliation would not be a 'rational' choice. This 'lack of credibility' increased the probability that 'deterrence will break down under stress'. However

while a potential aggressor might have cause to question the credibility of a strategy that depends on a 'city-busting' retaliatory response, he should have no doubts about the credibility of a strategy based on the ability to destroy his remaining military forces and eventually prevail. The loss of these forces is one risk he cannot afford to take, for once deprived of his military strength he is compelled to accept peace on our terms.[20]

The Air Force embraced the new doctrine with enthusiasm, to an extent that dismayed McNamara and his aides. Expensive new programmes were forwarded with a 'counter-force' label attached. The accuracy and discrimination of bombers as against missiles was underlined to justify the new B-70 bomber. As alarming was the ease with which Air Force officers spoke and wrote about nuclear war, as a normal military operation rather than as a hideous eventuality, involving deep horror and tragedy. While defending the new doctrine publicly through 1963 for the sake of consistency, by the start of that year McNamara had told the Air Force that it was not to take it 'as a criterion for strategic force proposals'.[21] In February Claude Witze was writing bitterly in *Air Force Magazine* of a 'deliberate intention to replace the necessary strategic superiority with strategic stalemate'.[22] Another fact encouraging McNamara to play down the counter-force was that, to the extent it was believed by Europeans to add credibility to the nuclear deterrent, it provided them with an excuse for not exerting themselves in the development of conventional options.

There was also a change in the political climate. The turning point was the Cuban Missile Crisis of October 1962. The first consequence of this episode for a counter-force strategy was that, in this textbook crisis of the nuclear age, the strategy had proved to be irrelevant. In presenting his warning to the Russians, Kennedy threatened a 'full retaliatory stroke'; meanwhile, by deploying US B-47 aircraft in civilian airfields, the US could be seen to be denying the Soviet Union a counter-force option.[23] Secondly, because the world had been brought so perilously close to the brink of disaster, the two super-powers were stimulated to explore ways of thawing the cold war. During 1963 a number of specific measures were taken to relax tensions, the most notable of which was the partial test ban treaty. In the changed international context, and with the President feeling more politically secure after the successful handling of the Cuban crisis, it became possible to think of ways of controlling the arms race. In one of the most impressive speeches of his Presidency, Kennedy spoke at the American University in June 1963 of the need to stabilize strategic relations. He spoke of the super-powers 'caught up in a vicious and dangerous cycle in which suspicion on one side breeds suspicion on the other, and new weapons beget counter-weapons'.[24] In a period of detente there was less of a need for 'credibility' in nuclear threats. It had become more important to emphasize that nuclear war would be the ultimate disaster.

16 Assured Destruction

The formula chosen to emphasize the disastrous nature of a general nuclear war was that of 'assured destruction'. This term is now taken to refer to a nuclear strategy based purely and simply on a threat to destroy centres of population with no alternative nuclear options contemplated at all. It is also often taken as a creation of the mid-1960s, articulated by McNamara on the rebound from an unsuccessful attempt to promote a counter-force strategy. Having first expressed a desire to avoid city destruction, he now decided to concentrate American nuclear power on little else but cities.

This is something of a caricature of the origins and character of assured destruction. Essentially what McNamara was doing was making a feature of an aspect of US deterrent doctrine which had been present from the 1940s. It had always been accepted that the most reliable deterrent force was that which would permit retaliation even after the US had been the victim of a surprise attack. This requirement gained in importance as the Soviet capacity for mounting a surprise attack grew and as the concepts of first and second strikes became widely understood.

From the beginning McNamara had insisted that the US should prepare to attack a wide range of targets, should any nuclear strike be deemed necessary. Options were to be developed to target either cities or military targets or both. Even after the counter-force strategy fell out of favour, counter-force options remained in the Single Integrated Operational Plan for Nuclear War (SIOP). McNamara did not retreat so far from his earlier statements to demand that the US be denied a city-avoidance option, though in practice such an option did prove difficult to arrange and it was pursued with an increasing lack of conviction as the decade wore on. The shift was in stressing the avoidance of war rather than the avoidance of cities within war. Emphasizing counter-city capabilities in preference to the counter-force was a declaratory policy. It was adopted to warn of the dangers of nuclear war rather than to describe how a nuclear war should be fought if it had to be fought. A secondary aspect, which eventually became more important, was to serve as a criterion for evaluating force levels. It was in this context that the concept became quite precise.

Assured Destruction

An assured destruction capability was defined as the ability to:

> Deter a deliberate nuclear attack upon the United States or its allies by maintaining at all times a clear and unmistakable ability to inflict an unacceptable degree of damage upon any agressor, or combination of aggressors – even after absorbing a surprise first strike.[1]

The levels of destruction it was thought necessary to be able to inflict would destroy 33–20 per cent of the Soviet population and 75–50 per cent of industrial capacity.

The term was first used in 1964. The concept was originally to be known as 'assured retaliation', but this was felt to be too bland. The harshness of the term and the inescapable tragedy described in its definition were intentional. McNamara was concerned that, through euphemistic language, the circumlocutions endemic to military briefings and ill-disciplined logic, the Air Force and its Congressional supporters were deluding themselves into believing that there was a tolerable way of fighting a nuclear war. Talking, for example, about 'urban-industrial fatalities' rather than 'people killed' cushioned the senses against any attempt to comprehend the extent of the human catastrophe inherent in any nuclear war. Blunt talk about assuring destruction made the nature of the exercise clear. It also, incidentally, made McNamara sound suitably tough to the right-wing who had few qualms about the nature of the exercise.

As a planning device the assured destruction criterion had the advantage of demonstrating that the burst of missile production that marked the start of the Kennedy Administration had created a sufficiency of forces. Consequently, there was no need for further crash programmes or major build-ups of any kind. McNamara and his aides used extremely conservative assumptions, including the worst possible projections of future Soviet forces, in deciding whether existing forces were sufficient. These 'worst-case scenarios' were not used, as many have assumed, to rationalize excessive military production, but rather to disarm critics opposed to ceilings on US forces. If in the worst possible case destruction could still be assured, then new investment was unnecessary. Given the size of US forces by the mid-1960s, McNamara was well aware that the horrific levels of devastation suggested by the concept were well within US capabilities. Throughout the decade the US capability was consistently higher than this level. An all-out US attack in 1968 could have destroyed nearly 50 per cent of the Soviet population and nearly 80 per cent of Soviet industrial capacity, as against the 20 per cent and 50 per cent respectively judged to be adequate by McNamara.[2]

These lower levels were described as an 'unacceptable level of destruction'. This concept was misleading. It suggested an 'acceptable' level just below the formal level, which was obviously absurd. There was no precise method of measuring levels of destruction; even in the calculations used by the Pentagon only prompt fatalities, not the effects of fallout, and general social dislocation were included.[3] Nor was there any definite view on Soviet thresholds of tolerance; the levels chosen by McNamara were more influenced by an awareness of diminishing marginal returns than any notion of what was acceptable to the Russians. After a certain point extra weapons produce few additional effects, because of the concentration of Soviet society into a finite number of large targets. Doubling the number of 1-megaton warheads from 400 to 800 would increase the destruction of Soviet population and industry by only 9 per cent and 1 per cent respectively.[4] All that was therefore necessary was for US forces sufficient to ride the 'flat of the curve'; anything beyond that would be superfluous.

Mutual Assured Destruction

The most controversial aspect of McNamara's approach was that he refused to be dismayed, in fact refused to hinder, the Soviet attainment of an assured destruction capability. The arguments for encouraging mutual assured destruction pre-date McNamara, though it was known in the late 1950s as a 'stable balance of terror'. The disadvantage of the new term was that it had an acronym – 'MAD'. In the early 1970s this acronym was seized upon by McNamara's critics as if they were making some profound strategic comment on the substance of the concept.[5] In fact MAD was no more insane and a lot more sensible than many other strategic formulations.[6]

The desirability of reassuring the other side that there was no intention of preparing for a first strike had been accepted by the Kennedy Administration from the beginning. What was underestimated was the extent to which honourable intentions could be communicated to a nervous and suspicious adversary. Arthur Schlesinger gives away some of the patronizing attitude of that Administration to its intellectual inferiors when he recalls a meeting between Walt Rostow and V. Z. Kuznetsov of the Soviet Foreign Office in the month after Kennedy's election. Kuznetsov expressed his concern over the 'missile gap' furore and warned that the Soviet Union would respond to any US build-up. Rostow replied, according to Schlesinger, that:

> any Kennedy rearmament would be designed to improve the stability of the deterrent, and the Soviet Union should recognize this as in the interests of peace; but Kuznetsov, innocent of the higher calculus of deterrence as recently developed in the United States, brusquely dismissed this explanation.[7]

There was something of the lecturer in McNamara. The presentation of doctrine in a clear and unambiguous manner was extremely important to him. The annual posture statements were written with great care and meant to be read with equal care by both allies and adversaries. He was said to be delighted at the number of copies of this statement purchased by the Soviet Embassy in Washington. The greater the convergence of doctrine and mutual understanding, the better the chances of managing US–Soviet relations.

The evidence that Moscow was putting the worst possible construction on the cities-avoidance doctrine concerned McNamara, and he sought to remedy the situation. As the retreat from counter-force began, the concern with stability became more evident. In 1962 a journal reported 'leaders in the Administration feeling that past US weapons systems developments have actually aggravated the arms race and contributed to the instability of the deterrent concept', and that US restraint in not deploying 'potentially unstabilizing weapons' was expected to lead to comparable restraint by the Soviet Union.[8]

That same month there was more authoritative evidence of such ideas at work. John McNaughton, an Assistant Secretary of Defense, introduced the concept of 'non-zero sum games'. In challenging the assumption that 'any US gain in security necessarily implies a concomitant Soviet loss', he discussed the 'possibility of mutual improvement of security through use of non-negotiated techniques' and explicitly used Schelling's phrase 'reciprocal fear of surprise attacks', with the fear 'reflected back and forth like images in a room of mirrors'. McNaughton insisted that 'We must, in every decision we make, concern ourselves with the factors of stability and of the dynamic effect on the arms race.'[9] Meanwhile, McNamara was explaining to an interviewer the virtues of a secure second-strike capability, in removing incentives to pre-empt, suggesting that it might be advantageous for the sake of a 'stable balance of terror' if both sides had such a capability.[10]

The steps that McNamara took to demonstrate a lack of interest in first strikes, phasing out weapons, such as the European IRBMs, which would only be of use in a first strike have already been noted. Though the city-avoidance doctrine suggested improvements in the quality and quantity of US missile forces so as to threaten Soviet missiles, McNamara was in little doubt that the number of these missiles would grow and that they would be protected against attack. There was no reason to believe that offensive forces by themselves could knock out the offensive forces of the adversary. The more contentious question was whether or not there was any means by which the defence could block the offence.

Disillusion with Defence

There was little hint in the early 1960s of the controversy that would surround attempts to restrict defensive systems later in the decade. The most public arguments between the Administration and Congress were over offensive systems, such as the B-70 bomber. The decision to emphasize the peaceful exploration of outer space in preference to its military exploitation also resulted in criticism of the Administration. The presumption that space would be the next great challenge for military technology was widely held, though it was hard to identify tangible strategic advantages without recourse to either psychology or romance.

Space presented fascinating opportunities for unsurpassed technological speculation and fabulous new machines, almost science
fictional in nature. The Air Force coined the word *aerospace* to indicate the limitless area of future military operations. Unfortunately the
fascination with technology, with doing more of, and better, what had
been done before, led to a neglect of considerations of objectives.
There was much fatuous talk about the moon being the classic high-
ground beloved of strategists since antiquity or of the 'psychological'
value of an orbiting nuclear bomb, but little explanation of the value
of spending vast sums of money to send weapons out to space in
order to bring them back one day, slowly, probably to the wrong
place, and in uncertain condition.[11]

Just as the Air Force was enamoured with the offence, the Administration appeared to have a proper interest in the defence. The objective of 'damage limitation' had been with the Administration from the
start and survived the collapse of the overall 'no-cities' doctrine. It
was not until later in the decade that an aversion to defensive measures became evident. Defensive measures could be divided into two
categories – active and passive. Active measures involved detecting,
tracking, and shooting down an incoming offensive force. Passive
measures involved protecting targets from the effects of an enemy
attack. In 1961 there was an elaborate system of active defences
against bomber attack in being in the United States. A system of
ballistic missile defence was under development but had not yet
reached a stage where hard decisions had to be made. Decisions were
also pending with passive defence. Apart from the protection of the
missile forces – in submarines and concrete silos dug deep into the
ground – a policy was required on defence of the civil population.

There was no doubt that unless US society was to be utterly transformed, little could be done to protect most of the effects of nuclear
weapons. For those at the centre of a nuclear detonation there was no
escape, but there were precautionary or emergency measures that, if
taken at the periphery, could save some lives. Of these the most
practical were fallout shelters. Nuclear fallout, the radioactive debris
released from an explosion, could travel great distances and linger
some time – depending, amongst other things, on the prevailing
weather conditions. A community apparently well out of harm's way
might become the victim of a radioactive cloud. By waiting a number
of days (and perhaps weeks) in a well-stocked shelter people might
escape this danger.

The Gaither Committee had advocated a fallout shelter programme, only to have it rejected by the Eisenhower Administration. Interest was revived in 1961. In terms of a desire to limit damage in the event of a nuclear war, a civil defence programme was an obvious step to take. Furthermore, fallout shelters seemed a logical component of a city-avoidance doctrine. If the enemy was good enough to attack only military targets well away from cities, then the main danger to the civilian population would be from fallout.

In July 1961 President Kennedy submitted a programme to Congress. The objective was to identify, mark, and stock the available shelter space in existing buildings. Some 50 million shelters were expected to be identified. The vulnerability of the population would depend on the pattern of the enemy attack. In an attack up to 75 per cent of the deaths might be caused by blast and thermal effects. This suggested that the 50 million shelters might save 10 to 15 million lives.[12] The programme ran into difficulties. Many critics considered it to be a dangerous delusion, lulling people into a false sense of security in the face of nuclear war. It was also thought to be provocative, suggesting the mobilization of the population and bringing them to a state of war-readiness. In addition, shelters became an emotive social issue. The rich could afford their own shelters and did not always seem disposed to share their space with less well-off neighbours.

The move away from a cities-avoidance doctrine weakened the case for a shelter programme. With a greater expectation that cities would be targets in a nuclear war, the value of the shelters diminished. Nevertheless McNamara persisted with his advocacy of such a programme, linking it to the general objective of damage limitation, which was explored in an internal study of 1962–3. For a brief period afterwards it was elevated to a central strategic concept. The advocacy became more lukewarm as it became apparent that most defensive measures could be neutralized by the adversary without a great deal of trouble. Calculations suggested that at each level of damage the defence had to spend three times as much as the offence. By 1965 the programme had been abandoned.[13]

This sense that, whatever one did to improve the defence, the offence would soon regain its position with a much more modest effort, began to colour the Administration's attitude to all defensive systems. If both sides could be persuaded to accept the inevitability of the primacy of the offence, they could save themselves a lot of money by forgoing the purchase of futile defensive systems and the consequent offensive counter-measures. It took time for this proposition to reach the centre of political debate. Available systems suffered from technical disabilities, particularly with regard to radar, which allowed McNamara to avoid meeting the issue head on.

The first serious presentation of the 'defence is a dangerous thing' argument was made in 1964 by two distinguished scientists who had recently been advising the Government on defence issues. Jerome Wiesner had been President Kennedy's science advisor and Herbert York had been Director of Defense Research and Engineering under both Eisenhower and Kennedy. They spoke for a scientific constituency that had already proved to be a significant factor in defence politics and was to be extremely influential in the late 1960s. The constituency contained many who had been working on nuclear weapons since the Manhattan project. Though a number of the leading nuclear scientists had become lobbyists for bigger and better bombs, the majority followed the lead of Robert Oppenheimer and considered it their responsibility to explain the dangers of an arms race and explore the means, both technical and political, for bringing it under control.[14] In private the scientists had access to key decisions through membership of advisory panels. Their public vehicle was the *Bulletin of the Atomic Scientists*, published since the 1940s. A second forum, which was to be of considerable importance during the 1960s and 1970s, was the journal *Scientific American*. It was in this journal that York and Wiesner published their article.

The occasion was the Partial Test Ban Treaty of 1963 and the ensuing argument over whether underground tests could now safely be banned along with the atmospheric tests covered by the Treaty. York and Wiesner demonstrated that no important weapons developments would be at risk, and in doing so provided a valuable summation for a non-specialist audience of the current state of the art in a variety of areas of defence technology. Their argument went beyond advocacy of a Comprehensive Test Ban to a warning that there was no technical solution to the problems of the vulnerability of the US (or the USSR) to nuclear attack and that attempts by either side to find a solution might only worsen the situation. They identified a search for an effective ABM system as an example of the dangers of this approach:

Paradoxically, one of the potential destabilizing elements in the present nuclear standoff is the possibility that one of the rival powers might develop a successful antimissile defense. Such a system, truly airtight and in the exclusive possession of one of the powers, would effectively nullify the deterrent force of the other, exposing the latter to a first attack against which it could not retaliate.[15]

They then explained why they believed such an effective defence was unlikely to materialize: with the potency of each offensive missile no defensive failures could be tolerated; the missile defence itself would be vulnerable to attack; and the attacker would have all the tactical advantage of surprise, knowing when, what, and how to attack, while the defender would have to be on continual alert for all eventualities. Finally there was a problem of lead times, the time taken from conception of a new system to its ultimate deployment. As the defence had to be planned against the known qualities of the offence it started the race 'a lap behind'.

The argument against ballistic missile defence thus reduced to two propositions: (a) it would not work; and (b) if one side was so misguided as to try to build one, this effort would stimulate an arms race. For most of the 1960s McNamara was content to base his opposition to ABMs on proposition (a). By 1966 this had become subject to qualification. Advances in the relevant technology made the system look more feasible. Meanwhile the Soviet Union was building its own ABM, suggesting that her leaders were unconvinced by the technical objections.

The promotion of the ABM gained even more force by the feeling amongst the military that the time had come to challenge McNamara on his whole strategic philosophy. They were distressed that few new weapons systems were being authorized and that MacNamara was unwilling to prosecute the arms race with any energy. The issue became symbolic of other complaints and frustrations connected with McNamara's disregard of military advice and sensibilities. The politics of the matter is not a subject for this book and has been dealt with elsewhere. Briefly, McNamara was faced with a recommendation from a united Joint Chiefs of Staff for a full-scale ABM system. He was forced to accede partially to this request, managing to present this as designed to protect US cities against an incipient Chinese missile threat (that in fact never materialized) rather than to protect them against a Soviet missile threat.[16] In announcing this decision in September 1967, McNamara provided an eloquent statement of his views on the dynamics of the arms race, in a manner which was to influence the defence debate for some years to come.

The Action–Reaction Phenomenon

The September 1967 speech was a remarkable statement from an American Secretary of Defense. McNamara was not content simply to say that 'none of the systems at the present or foreseeable state of the art would provide an impenetrable shield over the United States', or to add that 'were we to deploy a heavy ABM system throughout the United States, the Soviets would clearly be strongly motivated to so increase their offensive capability as to cancel out our defensive advantage'. He felt it necessary to place all this in the context of an overall view of the arms race. The situation described was one in which the arms race gained momentum unnaturally and irrationally (the adjective used was 'mad'). Both sides sought nothing else but to preserve their assured destruction capability, and were so anxious in this objective that they planned for the future on the basis of conservative assumptions concerning the adversary's future intentions and capabilities:

> What is essential to understand here is that the Soviet Union and the United States mutually influence one another's strategic plans. Whatever their intentions or our intentions, actions – or even realistically potential actions – on either side relating to the build-up of nuclear forces necessarily trigger reactions on the other side. It is precisely this action–reaction phenomenon that fuels an arms race.

He then explained the recent history of Soviet and American force development in these terms, admitting that the Soviet build-up then under way was a result of the Kremlin's misunderstanding of the objectives of the US build-up of the early 1960s which could have been seen as directed towards 'a credible first-strike capability'.

> That was not, in fact, our intention. Our goal was to ensure that they, with their theoretical capacity to reach such a first-strike capability, would not outdistance us. But they could not read our intentions with any greater accuracy than we could read theirs. The result has been that we have both built up our forces to a point that far exceeds a credible second-strike capability against the forces we each started with. In doing so neither of us has reached a first-strike capability.[17]

Such a detached analysis from a Secretary of Defense gave the proposition a credence that it did not deserve. The *action–reaction phenomenon* was soon being cited as a virtual iron law of strategic relations by liberals in an effort to encourage restraint in US policies. In this way liberals found themselves committed to the preservation of the balance of terror, rather than its elimination as had been the hope of many less than a decade before. Unfortunately there was little evidence to substantiate either McNamara's analysis of the dynamics of the arms race or his reading of history. Had he made a more modest and general observation on the extent to which the two super-powers influence each other's plans, or focused more narrowly on ABMs, where the argument that any deployment would trigger a counter-deployment in the Soviet offence was quite compelling, then he would have left himself less vulnerable to charges of over-simplification.

There were two main problems with McNamara's statement. First, the assessment of adversary intentions and capabilities were only one of a number of factors which influence weapons procurement decisions. In addition there were a number of technological, military, budgetary, and political factors at work. Second, it could not be demonstrated that there was and always had been one single, overriding strategic objective – maintenance of an assured destruction capability – guiding all actions. There remained strong pressures for a drive for outright superiority or the aggressive acquisition of damage-limiting capabilities. Indeed, these pressures had influenced McNamara during the 1960s build-up of US forces. There were powerful arguments in favour of evaluating forces according to assured destruction criteria – but that did not mean that that was how it was always done. It was the fact that the Russians did not see things this way that caused McNamara so much difficulty.

The bad history and wishful thinking detracts from, but ought not to obscure, the significance of McNamara's heartfelt plea for moderation in the pursuit of strategic objectives. He did not create the 'stimulus-misperception–response' model of the arms race. It could be found in the academic literature of the 1950s and 1960s. The rôle of ABMs in a duel with the offense had been identified in the Gaither Report ten years previously. Nor is it fair to take the logical conclusion of McNamara's message – to concentrate fire on cities in the event of nuclear war – as an expression of some perverse scale of values. The formula for stabilizing the arms race could be summed up as: 'Offence good, defence bad; killing cities good, killing missiles bad.' This was not based on timeless and universal values but the circumstances of the moment. To McNamara the super-powers could break out of the grip of the action–reaction phenomenon by refusing to react. If certain temptations could be resisted, then neither side would find its deterrent threatened and no counter-measures would be necessary. In the 1960s the ball was in the defence's court. The offence had been on the ascendant for a number of years. A sort of stability had been achieved in that both sides now enjoyed a second-strike capability to which ABMs were the only apparent source of threat. However, because, according to the Pentagon analyses, even ABMs could not create a first-strike capability, the act of restraint proposed by McNamara was somewhat easier than it would have been if a genuine advantage was available through the considerable expenditure demanded by a full-scale ABM system.

Throughout the 1960s McNamara had relied upon his powers of persuasion to convince his counterparts in the Kremlin to join him in eschewing certain weapons in order to introduce a measure of calm and stability into strategic relations. Unfortunately the actions of the US Administration did not always appear as moderate as his words. Nor was the Soviet Union willing to change its own distinctive perceptions to conform with the doctrines developed in the Pentagon. By the end of 1966 McNamara had realized that any mutual restraint would have to be negotiated. Out of this recognition came the first offer, by President Johnson in February 1967, for talks on the limitation of strategic arms.

17 The Soviet Approach to Deterrence

The Strategic Learning Curve

The dogged refusal of the Russians to endorse any of McNamara's prescriptions for intra-war deterrence or a stable arms race, undermined both confidence in McNamara's prognoses for the future and the quality of his original diagnoses. The potential convergence of Soviet and American destinies was never as great as assumed by McNamara, but nor was the actual divergence as fundamental or as damaging as his detractors suggested. In his prime, McNamara's faith in conclusions reached by a process of rigorous analysis, pushing to one side the deadweight of tradition, was contagious. It was not difficult to presume that he and his staff represented the furthest point on some strategic learning curve, to which internal opponents, allies and potential enemies were to be brought by a process of patient education in the realities of the age.

For example, Roman Kolkowicz wrote, with a number of his colleagues, of how 'Soviet strategic doctrine and capabilities appear to have lagged behind those of the United States by about five years'. His argument was that 'technology seems to have a levelling effect which subsumes political, ideological, and social differences in various political systems', and also that Western doctrine could have an 'educative' effect on Soviet leaders, persuading them to replace their own ideas and programmes by alternatives derived from 'bourgeois' societies.[1] McNamara himself explained how Soviet approaches were distinct from his own by reference to the distracting effects of tradi-

257

tion. For example, he found the Kremlin's continued expenditure of enormous sums on 'porous' defensive systems virtually incomprehensible. It was 'fanaticism', best explained, he supposed, by 'their strong emotional reaction to the need to defend Mother Russia'.[2]

It was realized that Soviet writings on nuclear strategy often diverged markedly in their formulations and conclusions from the American literature. However, three points could be noted, at least in the first half of the 1960s, to encourage the view that the American learning curve would be followed. First, Soviet doctrine had changed in the 1950s in response to the limitations and opportunities provided by thermonuclear weapons and missiles, or the 'Military–Technical Revolution', as it was known in the USSR. Presumably, therefore, it could change again. Second, Soviet military literature indicated that notice was taken of American doctrine as well as capabilities. The American strategic teachers knew that their Soviet pupils were paying attention, even if they could not count on their receptivity. Third, while it was true that a careful reading of Soviet military writings left a clear impression of an expectation of the ultimate triumph of socialism, even through a victory in nuclear war, this was so far removed from actual capabilities that it was difficult to believe the Russians themselves took it seriously. In fact, despite the proud bellicosity and ideological certainty of official pronouncements, attitudes and behaviour displayed in the context of actual international affairs were exceedingly cautious.

As the development of Soviet doctrine was kept firmly in the hands of the Kremlin, without the benefit of the independent advice from the sort of civilian specialists that flourished at RAND, it was possible to guess the reason for this lack of congruence between intentions and capabilities: the Soviet generals were anxious to secure their budgets and assert their undiminished importance to the survival of the socialist state. In the early 1960s Khrushev was obviously having trouble with his generals (as, for different reasons, was McNamara). In these circumstances it became tempting to dismiss official doctrine as largely obsolete, attempting to square a circle out of obeisance to the canons of Marxism–Leninism, and in support of requests for a higher military budget.

The growth of Soviet military capabilities during the late 1960s and 1970s encouraged people in the West to look once again, with a less critical eye, at Soviet doctrine. Some saw it as a set of statements providing notice of a clear intention to gain superiority so as to wage and win a nuclear war whenever desired.[3] As the indictment against

McNamara was being drawn up by conservatives in the 1970s, the most serious item on the charge sheet was that of a failure to appreciate the distinctiveness of the Soviet approach to strategic issues. This approach, it was argued, in contrast to that of McNamara, stressed the possibility of victory in nuclear war, an outcome other than mutual assured destruction. The Russians did not deviate from the traditional view that the role of strategy was to devise means of winning future wars, and that the role of military planners was to prepare the necessary forces. Not only did McNamara fail to convince his Soviet counterparts of the error of their ways but, by emphasizing the possibility of a coincidence of interests between the super-powers in controlling the arms race and avoiding nuclear war, he also neglected the underlying conflict of interests.[4]

Guidelines for Stability

The underlying assumptions of the Theory of Mutual Assured Destruction were that, for the foreseeable future, the offence would be able to maintain the advantage over the defence. Because of this, all one could do to prevent the other from inflicting crippling devastation was to threaten retaliation. The lesson drawn from this assumption for the purposes of force planning was that one need only ensure a sufficiency of offensive forces to assure destruction after allowing for all feasible improvements in the first-strike capabilities of the other side. The lesson drawn for arms control was that, as every improvement in one side's defence provided no extra security but merely a spurt to the offence of the other, once both sides ceased making defensive moves forces could stabilize at current levels. The lesson for crisis management was the growing uselessness of nuclear weapons for purposes other than deterring the nuclear weapons of the other side.

McNamara presented mutual assured destruction as a fact of life that everyone would do well to recognize rather than as an optimum strategy. That neither side could embark on a nuclear war, however tentatively, without a finite and probably quite large risk of complete destruction was a fact of life. But there was also a finite chance that the outcome of a nuclear war could be something other than mutual assured destruction. McNamara was therefore criticized for failing (after his early promise) to expand the opportunities for avoiding total devastation if a nuclear war did break out.

Emphasizing assured destruction might sober a potential aggressor. But once this threat had failed, and hostilities had commenced, matters would not be retrieved by exercising this threat. This was the weakest point in McNamara's whole approach. Benjamin Lambeth has provided one of the best critiques:

> Although commonly called a 'strategy', 'assured destruction' was by itself an antithesis of strategy. Unlike any strategy that ever preceded it throughout the history of armed conflict, it ceased to be useful precisely where military strategy is supposed to come into effect: at the edge of war.[5]

There were other options – restricting attacks to targets relevant to the ensuing land battle or taking care to avoid cities. These options were, of course, the ones that McNamara had been anxious to explore at the start of his term as Secretary of Defense. He never completely abandoned this exploration. So it was not quite fair to suggest, as did Lambeth, that with nuclear operations under way, all the US military could do was 'to shut its eyes, grit its teeth, and reflexively unleash an indiscriminate and simultaneous reprisal against all Soviet aim points on a pre-established target list'. The target lists drawn up in the Pentagon during the 1960s still included a number of alternative options. However, the design of these options did prove difficult and the attacks envisaged were all large. Furthermore, there was an evident decline in the interest shown in these alternatives in the Office of the Secretary of Defense. Interest was sustained slightly longer in the more modest objective of damage limitation.

Apart from the difficulty in getting a civil defence programme through Congress, McNamara became wary of damage limitation objectives. The pursuit of these objectives, he came to believe, was not only futile but might well stimulate an arms race. What was merely 'damage limitation' to one side, threatened the 'assured destruction' capability of the other.

Thus the choice McNamara made was to take every possible step to underline the danger of mutual assured destruction, *even* if this meant turning it into a self-fulfilling prophecy through undermining comprehension of, and capabilities for, alternative courses of action should war break out.

To what extent did a divergence in strategic thinking frustrate McNamara's attempt to stabilize military relations between the two super-powers? McNamara was blatantly rebuffed by the Russians twice during his term as Secretary of Defense. The Russians never accepted the notion of escalation as a set of deliberate, controlled moves. Soviet writings responded to the doctrines being propounded by McNamara in the early 1960s with great hostility, inferring rather sinister motives from his attempt to establish rules for nuclear warfare. By contrast, they argued that it was not possible to rely on 'fire-breaks' between nuclear and conventional war, or to hope that nuclear war could be contained within rigid limits.

However, McNamara's own confidence on these matters waned and rules for war-fighting played a negligible rôle in his doctrinal pronouncements of the later 1960s as he came to be preoccupied with the problems of stable deterrence. Here again there was a rebuff as the Russians persisted with their anti-ballistic missile system after McNamara had spoken long and eloquently on the destabilizing consequences of such an endeavour.

Yet McNamara did succeed here in persuading the Russians to change their views. In 1968, after he had unveiled the improvements to US offensive systems to be undertaken to penetrate the Soviet ABM defences, the Russian deployment programme faltered then stopped. Negotiations were entered into with the US to limit ABMs and these achieved their objective in 1972. So while on doctrinal grounds the Russians may have regretted the ABM Treaty, in practical terms they appeared to accept the contention that in the long run the offence could degrade any novelties which the defence might offer. This may not have been an intellectual conversion, but the result was to narrow the area in which the consequences of other disagreements might be played out.

The most difficult question is whether the Russians could ever accept that McNamara was speaking for them when he claimed:

> No meaningful victory is even conceivable in a third unlimited world war, for no nation can possibly win a full-scale thermonuclear exchange. The two world powers that have now achieved a mutual assured-destruction capability fully realize that.[6]

A 'Second-Best Deterrent'

In our earlier discussions on Soviet policy, mounting enthusiasm over the opportunities provided by the new technology of long-range missiles was noted, as was the apparent Soviet lead in their development and production. In the event, not only was this enthusiasm premature, it was also counter-productive. Khruschev's reliance on ICBMs brought him into conflict with his own military, who felt that insufficient regard was being paid to the employment of other types of forces. His regular assertions of Soviet pre-eminence impressed the Americans who took steps to strengthen their position, and impressed also the Chinese who believed that the time was now ripe to advance world revolution and then became distressed at Soviet timidity.

An anecdote from Khruschev's memoirs illustrates his fascination with rocketry and his personal involvement in the relevant decision-making – in contrast with the management of strategic innovation in the US. Khruschev recalled how he noted that one of Russia's first rockets was 'fired from a launching pad which looked like a huge tabletop and could easily be detected by reconnaissance planes or satellites in orbit around the earth'. At this point Khruschev claimed to have drawn on his experience as a coal miner and as a supervisor during the building of the Moscow Metro and suggested the idea of sinking the missile into 'sunken covered shafts'. After being told by his engineers that this 'wouldn't work' he let the matter drop. Some years later his son, Sergei, who was involved in the missile programme, informed Khruschev that 'he'd read in some American journal that the US had begun to replace launching pads with silos'. He then felt able to give some orders. A programme to dig sunken silos was initiated and completed after his 'retirement' in 1964.[7]

Khruschev's belief in the quality of his own insight into these matters inevitably led him into conflict with the military. In 1959 he remarked that he did 'not trust appraisals of generals on questions of strategic importance'. The lack of respect was mutual. Once Khruschev had been displaced in October 1964 by a leadership the generals found more congenial, they made clear their view that strategic matters demanded a competence and understanding only possessed by the professional military. General Zakharov warned in February 1965 that 'With the emergence of rocket-nuclear arms, cybernetics, electronics and computers, any subjective approach to military problems, harebrained plans, and superficiality can cause irreparable damage.'[8]

Thomas Wolfe has observed that Khruschev's policies in effect amounted to settling for a second-best strategic posture.[9] He opted for a 'minimum deterrent'. The enemy would be deterred by the devastation threatened by the nuclear power becoming available to the Soviet forces. Long-range rockets would ensure that the US land-based rockets could not escape; short-range rockets could be used to permit the reduction in army manpower without any loss in firepower.

In January 1960 Khruschev explained his position to the Supreme Soviet:

> Our state has a powerful rocket technology. Given the present development of military technology, military aviation and the navy have lost their former importance. This type of armament is not being reduced but replaced. Military aviation is now being almost entirely replaced by missiles. We have now sharply reduced and probably will further reduce and even halt production of bombers and other obsolete equipment. In the navy, the submarine fleet is assuming greater importance and surface ships can no longer play the rôle they played in the past.

He justified a cut in manpower by reference to the increase in firepower made possible by nuclear weapons. 'Firepower', Khruschev explained, was 'the main thing after all. In essence the reason why states maintain armies is precisely to have power that can withstand a possible enemy and either restrain him from attacking or repulse him if he tries to attack.'[10]

The newly formed Strategic Rocket and Air Defence (PVO-Strany) forces came out of this policy quite well, but elsewhere it was less than popular. The airmen were upset at the proposed replacement of the bomber by the missile, while the army and navy were distressed by Khruschev's determination to cut back their manpower. Their opposition resulted in some leading Soviet commanders being relieved of their posts. On the whole, however, the military response to Khruschev was not to contradict directly his theses, but to qualify them gradually. This was exemplified by the statements of Marshal R. Ya. Malinovsky, the Defence Minister, who kept his post while avoiding endorsing the Khruschevian radicalism. On the very day that Khruschev spoke to the Supreme Soviet, Malinovsky also spoke on how 'all arms' of the Soviet Armed Forces would be retained in 'relevant and sound proportions'. The emphasis on 'combined arms' soon became the hallmark of the military traditionalists. Each branch of the services provided patient accounts of its growing importance. The ground forces argued that, because of the possibilities for attrition with increased firepower, mass armies would be more necessary than ever before. Spokesmen for long-range aviation pointed to the virtues of bombers as a launch platform for air-to-surface missiles and as a means of attacking mobile targets.[11]

In 1962 the military worked out a shared position which was presented in a volume edited by Marshal Sokolovsky, entitled *Military Strategy*. This was the first major work on strategy since the 1930s and defined the new consensus that had emerged through the post-Stalin debate on nuclear strategy and the more recent arguments with Khruschev.[12] The work avoided controversy and read like a compromise document. It offered no clear priorities for the design of Soviet forces while providing support for claims for every type of force. Nor was there even an unambiguous view on the likely character of a future war. Some passages suggest that it would be long; others that it would be short. At times the hypothesis of the inevitability of the expansion of limited war into a global nuclear war was given vigorous support; elsewhere there were indications that some limits might hold. Most difficult of all was the uneasy relationship between the 'decisive' first phase involving nuclear missiles, and the final phase where the ultimate outcome depended on the strength of the surviving conventional forces. This particular problem was exacerbated by movements in US forces and doctrine (to which Sokolovsky and his team paid great attention).

The American Challenge

It was not only the suspicion of the military that caused Khruschev's strategy to be qualified, but also the continuing teething troubles of the Soviet missile programme which created an awkward lacuna in Soviet capabilities at the very time when a tangible superiority over the US had been expected. More important, this was a time of significant new directions in American policy. Many of Khruschev's formulations were reminiscent of those that had been popular in the Eisenhower Administration. They had little in common with those brought to the fore by the Kennedy Administration.

Apart from a shared belief in the obsolescence of long-range bombers, the Americans and Russians appeared in 1961 to be diverging in their strategies. While Khruschev contented himself with a minimum deterrent, McNamara worried about the problems of securing a second-strike capability. While Khruschev spoke of the obsolescence of conventional armaments, McNamara argued for extending conventional options. In addition, as once Khruschev had gloated over his imminent missile superiority, the US Administration could now

provide facts and figures on American superiority. This was diplomatically irritating and militarily alarming, for the combination of
American missile superiority, the ability using satellites to find – and
so target – Soviet missile sites with accuracy, and a new doctrine
which emphasized counter-force attacks aroused Soviet fears of an
American first strike.

Khruschev had to take steps to retrieve the situation. Having
bragged in 1960 that 'the Soviet Union is now the world's strongest
military power', he found it necessary to argue only that the two
powers were 'equal' and warn the Americans against the presumption
that they were operating from a 'position of strength'.

It was no longer asserted that Soviet casualties would be less than
those of the United States in the aftermath of a nuclear war. The need
now was to stress that *both* powers would suffer enormously. Khruschev reported that President Kennedy had told him in their meeting
in Vienna in early 1961 that the two sides were 'equal'. With his
comrades he sought to remind the Americans of this 'admission' as
reports came out of the Pentagon of a growing American superiority.
Rather defensively, Marshal Malinovsky argued in January 1962
that:

I hold that today the socialist camp is stronger than these countries
[NATO], but let us presume that the forces are equal. We are
ready to agree to this so as not to take part in stirring up a war
psychosis. But since the forces are equal the American leaders
should come to correct conclusions and pursue a reasonable
policy.[13]

In the middle of 1961, during the Berlin crisis, the cuts in conventional forces were halted. While long-range bombers remained the
largest single component of a small Soviet retaliatory force, it was felt
necessary to play down the theme of their obsolescence. To provide
for the future, major new research and development programmes
were initiated. It was hoped that by building an anti-ballistic missile
system comparable to the air defence system much of the sting could
eventually be taken out of any American attack. Development of
space weapons was also encouraged, this still being considered an
area where the USSR enjoyed a technological lead over the US.

None of this solved Khruschev's immediate problem. To compensate for his relative lack of long-range delivery vehicles he was forced
to a number of expedients. The first was to emphasize the threat to

those members of NATO which could more easily be reached and destroyed than North America. The Russians had taken the precaution of constructing a large force of medium-range aircraft and missiles. The Western Europeans could be 'hostages' to American good behaviour.[14] During the Berlin crisis pointed references were made to the vulnerability of US bases in Europe to nuclear attack and the disaster this could mean for the host countries.

A second feature of Khruschev's response was to emphasize the ferocity of the explosion of each nuclear warhead rather than the number of individual explosions that could be achieved. The 'terror quotient' was exaggerated with talks of bombs of immense megatonnage, even up to 100 million tons of TNT. A test series began in September 1961 that included, among other high-yield tests, one of 60 megatons. This was all despite the fact that the damage achieved by such weapons would not be substantially greater than that achieved with weapons of 5–10 megatons, and that there were no existing means of delivering such payloads.[15] The Americans were reminded that the mode of war-fighting they apparently preferred – using small nuclear weapons against discrete military targets as part of a controlled process of escalation – was not the sort that they would probably be engaged in. Instead an image was offered of an all-out conflict opening with massive nuclear exchanges in which few cities would escape unscathed. The notion of limitations and agreed conventions in this sort of total war was mocked and undermined by assertions of the unavoidable escalation of any war between the super-powers. In Soviet plans, nuclear and conventional forces and civilian and military targets appeared intermingled.

The first-strike menace implied by the American build-up in strategic forces, given a suspicious reading of the associated doctrine, created a major problem when the total Soviet forces were so scarce. In October 1961, speaking to the 22nd Party Congress, Marshal Malinovsky stated that:

The Presidium of the Central Committee of the Party and the Soviet Government have demanded and continue to demand of us that we devote special attention to the initial period of a possible war. The importance of this period lies in the fact that the first massive nuclear blows can to an enormous extent determine the entire subsequent course of the war and result in losses in the homeland and among the troops which could place the people and the country in a difficult situation.

The first edition of Sokolovsky's *Military Strategy* wrote of how 'primary attention' was directed 'to the study of how a future war may break out', which included 'detailed study' of, among other things, 'methods of delivering the first blow'. Elsewhere it is stated 'the main task of Soviet military strategy is working out means for reliably repelling a surprise nuclear attack by an aggressor'. The initial phase was described as 'fierce and destructive'. It would 'predetermine the development and outcome of the entire war'. The targets attacked would be the most important which, it was made clear from another part of the book, would be 'strategic nuclear weapons' located well away from theatres of military operations. 'Unless these weapons are destroyed or neutralized, it is impossible to protect the country's vital centres from destruction, and one cannot count on successfully achieving the aim of the war even if the [enemy] troop formation deployed in the military theatres are destroyed.'[16]

The logic of this line of argument led to some sort of pre-emptive attack policy. It was not one explicitly reached in this book, despite the hints. Nevertheless, there is evidence that this logic was at least partly followed.

The policy that appears to have been adopted by the Soviet military planners was that of 'launch-on-warning'. With timely warning of an incoming attack the retaliatory force could be launched in time to avoid its own destruction. In November 1967, Marshal Krylov, Commander-in-Chief of the Strategic Rocket Forces, wrote:

It must be stressed that under present conditions, when the Soviet Armed Forces are in constant combat readiness, any aggressor who begins a nuclear war will not remain unpunished, a severe and inevitable retribution awaits him. With the presence in the armament of troops of launchers and missiles which are completely ready for operation, as well as systems for detecting enemy missile launchers and other types of reconnaissance, an aggressor is no longer able suddenly to destroy the missiles before their launch on the territory of the country against which the aggression is committed. They will have time during the flight of the missiles of the aggressor to leave their launchers and inflict a retaliatory strike against the enemy. Even in the most unfavourable circumstance, if a portion of missiles is unable to be launched before the strike of missiles of the aggressor, as a result of the high degree of protection of the launchers from nuclear explosions, these missiles will be preserved and will carry out the combat missions assigned to them.[17]

While official US doctrine had not eschewed such a policy (on the grounds that ambiguity complicates the Soviet risk calculus) there were few enthusiastic proponents, and the general line was that it increased the danger of accidental war through over-reliance on the means of detecting an attack. However, the intention behind such a policy was defensive and reactive; more explicit emphasis on pre-emption would encourage an even more disturbing interpretation. Furthermore, awareness of the feasibility of launch-on-warning for Soviet forces would be an extra source of caution if a first strike was being contemplated against US forces with a similar capability. One important distinction was that a pre-emptive first strike, to make any sense, would need to destroy an extremely large proportion of the enemy's offensive forces, while with launch-on-warning it was speed that counted far more than the specific character of the targets.

The third rapid solution attempted by Khruschev, and one that back-fired dramatically, was, in October 1962, to place medium- and intermediate-range missiles on Cuba, so turning them into 'ersatz' ICBMs and, incidentally, complicating any first-strike plans the Americans may have had. Unfortunately for Khruschev the Americans detected the missiles prior to their installation and demanded their immediate withdrawal. The general sense of Soviet inferiority may have been an important factor in Khruschev's decision not to carry on with his plans, although American confidence in their position was mainly determined by local conventional superiority. The outcome of this crisis was to confirm publicly rather than redress the comparative weakness of the Soviet Union.

Sobered by this experience, Khruschev embarked on a policy of detente, seeking to hold down American military strength through arms control, obviating the need for large-scale procurement programmes in the USSR. After all that the military had been through with Khruschev – the boasting and the bluster combined with a deteriorating military position and the humiliating climb-down over Cuba – they became notably more hostile to his prescriptions for either force levels or the conduct of relations with the United States. In military newspapers and periodicals, the prospects for peaceful coexistence with the United States (and all that would entail by way of reduced military expenditure) was treated with great circumspection. The main issue was over the extent of the American threat. To pave the way for a policy of peaceful coexistence, Khruschev had begun in the 1950s to identify 'sober', 'realistic', and 'reasonable' factions in US ruling circles, with whom deals could be done, providing the other 'belligerent' and 'aggressive' faction was contained.[18] This sort of interpretation was resisted by the military, who spoke more of a 'predatory nature' inherent in imperialism itself.[19]

The Brezhnev Years

When Khruschev fell in October 1964, the military took the opportunity to reassert their position. In 1965, General Nikolai Talensky, who had retired from military service in 1958 and had become a leading supporter of Khruschev's revisionism, wrote an article warning of the 'dangerous illusion that the idea that thermonuclear war can still serve as an instrument of politics, that it is possible to achieve political aims by using nuclear weapons and still survive'. A number of military figures then attacked this notion, not so much because of its theoretical weakness but because of the bad effects on morale. Lieutenant-Colonel Rybkin wrote that: 'Any *a priori* rejection of the possibility of victory is harmful because it leads to moral disarmament, to a disbelief in victory and to fatalism and passivity. It is necessary to wage a struggle against such views and attitudes.' In addition, there was the ever-present danger of the imperialists unleashing a war.

Debate on this matter was eventually terminated in January 1967, by an unsigned and authoritative editorial in the *Krasnaia Zvezda* (Red Star) which supported the Talensky arguments. 'All peace-loving and anti-imperialist forces oppose a world nuclear war as a means of the continuation of politics.' The more exclusive journal *Military Thought* in 1968 had a more sophisticated debate, attempting to reconcile the general undesirability of nuclear war with the difficulty of admitting that such a war would mean the end of socialism as well as imperialism. General Bocharev wrote 'Recognition of the possibility of the victory of the socialist states in a global nuclear war, as is perfectly clear, by no means signifies justification for its kindling or unleashing.'[20]

The military were successful in encouraging the new leadership to initiate a major military build-up to catch up with the United States in missile power. During the second half of the 1960s Soviet military strength grew extremely fast and by the end of the decade had caught up, at least in raw numbers, with the Americans. This improvement in capabilities, which continued in the 1970s, made a number of Western observers nervous that the possibility of victory in a nuclear war was being taken more seriously, and that 'pre-emption' was becoming a serious option for Soviet planners. The frequent discussion of the importance of the factor of surprise and the stress on the need to take the tactical offensive (which pervades all Soviet military writing) gave the references, regular since the 1960s, of the possibility of 'frustrating', 'disrupting', 'forestalling' an enemy strike, a more sinister connotation.[21]

This line of reasoning pointed to a general Soviet predilection for 'war-fighting' as opposed to deterrent capabilities. Semantic confusion could set in here, for the two are not necessarily exclusive: the point has often been made in the West that the most credible form of deterrent would be a capability to fight and even win a war if necessary. This would appear to have become the Soviet view; fortified by nagging doubts over whether deterrence would hold indefinitely.[22]

Here the Soviet divergence from the views expressed by McNamara was significant. The idea of relying solely on 'assured destruction' did not provide a satisfactory answer to the question of what to do if deterrence failed. Moreover, talking of *mutual* deterrence suggested that the USSR needed to be deterred, a proposition it could not accept. Finally Soviet commentators have found it difficult to accept the idea that long-term peace could be brought about by the fear of nuclear weapons, or that some scientific breakthrough in the future would not upset the balance of terror.[23]

That said, there are two important qualifications. While Soviet leaders may not have been at ease with McNamara's approach to deterrence, it was an objective they shared. Satisfaction was gained by being able to point to the reluctance of the United States to initiate aggression because of the overall military strength of the USSR. It has been stated in the strongest possible terms that the military situation has not developed to the stage where the USSR could contemplate a war with equanimity. When the two SALT delegations met in Helsinki in November 1969, the Soviet side made the following officially cleared statement:

Even in the event that one of the sides were the first to be subjected to attack, it would undoubtedly retain the ability to inflict a retaliatory strike of crushing power. Thus evidently we all agree that war between our two countries would be disastrous for both sides. And it would be tantamount to suicide for the ones who decided to start such a war.[24]

The second point refers to the problem of capabilities. The essentials of Soviet doctrine have remained unchanged from the early 1960s until the present day, despite a wide variety in the capacity to fulfil many of the military tasks the doctrine said *ought* to be fulfilled. A problem of talking of a 'war-fighting capability' is that no self-evident limits, save the availability of resources and the requisite technology, are imposed on the procurement of new weapons. While Soviet doctrine deserved to be taken more seriously with the growth of capabilities, there remained important gaps. For example, if the civil defence forces of the Soviet Union were successful in achieving objectives set out for it – 'to rapidly liquidate the consequences of enemy nuclear strikes, promptly render extensive and diverse aid to casualties, and secure the conditions for the more normal functioning of the facilities of the national economy'[25] – then there would be serious consequences for mutual deterrence. While the USSR has made a greater effort in this area than the US, mainly to ensure a functioning government and preserve key industrial facilities, war has yet to be made more tolerable.[26]

Another example where the desiderata implied by the strategy were not matched by capability, also in the defensive area, was ABMs, in which there was a major Soviet investment through the 1960s. In 1967, a year when McNamara was making his most strenuous efforts to convince his Soviet opposite numbers of the unwisdom of ABM deployment, there was a vigorous debate in the USSR on the matter, not so much on the arms race effects of deployment, but on whether it would actually be possible to block a serious missile attack. The answer was in the negative, as limited ABM deployment around Moscow was halted in the next year.[27] When the two powers agreed in 1972 to limit ABMs in SALT I, Marshal Grechko, the Minister of Defence, wrote about how this Treaty prevented 'the emergence of a chain reaction of competition between offensive and defensive arms'.[28]

There was a real divergence between Soviet and American doctrine, but also important similarities largely imposed by the exigencies of a situation in which mutual destruction was possible. Soviet planners, like American planners, had to face the facts that offensive arms always seemed to have the edge on defensive arms and that, while war was a contingency for which preparations could be made, its initiation could not be considered as a sensible political option. The main difference was that in the USSR, unlike the US, there were not only few institutional checks on the military, as they accumulated weapons in preparation for war, but also a strong predisposition to encourage the accumulation of weapons out of the ideological need to demonstrate that the outcome of any war would be more favourable to socialism than imperialism, and a belief that the more military power possessed, the stronger its deterrent effect.

18 The Chinese Connection

Any Soviet arguments over strategic doctrine with the United States could be carried on at an arm's length. The two adversaries were not obliged to agree – each was only interested in assessing the implications of the other's deployment and declarations for its over-all position. An argument with an ally was different – divergent policies could cause problems in the planning and the conduct of war. The dependence on an ally and the possibility of exerting influence gave the argument more point. So it was that the sharpest strategic debates of the 1960s were between the Americans and French within NATO and between the Russians and the Chinese. In each case, the debate was never resolved satisfactorily and led to a loss in Alliance cohesion. With the Russians and Chinese, the link which made it still (just) possible to talk of the 'Sino-Soviet bloc' in 1960 was broken completely so that by the end of the decade the two had become enemies and, in 1969, engaged in sizeable armed clashes on the border.

Whereas American strategic precepts could be dismissed by the Russians for their lack of the correct social and historical perspective that comes with Marxism–Leninism, the Chinese claimed to be working within the same philosophical framework. Moreover their leader, Mao Tse-tung, was presented as a major Marxist theorist in his own right and a strategist with successful campaigns to his credit. The Chinese did not hesitate to make their distinctive views known, even if this undermined the leading rôle of the Soviet Union. They made claims on Soviet resources and, most sensitive of all, some Soviet territory adjacent to China which Peking insisted had been taken illegally in Tsarist days. Finally, to make the Chinese challenge even more awkward, it was mounted from the left, contrasting a revolutionary fervour and purity with the timidity of a Moscow suffering from excessive bureaucracy.

Differences over nuclear weapons – the extent of the practical help Moscow ought to extend to Peking in the construction of its own nuclear arsenal, or the cover the Soviet nuclear force could provide to the Chinese attempt to complete the civil war and gain control of Taiwan, or whether nuclear weapons could be considered decisive in modern warfare – were prominent themes in Sino-Soviet polemics. They dominated the bitter exchanges in 1963 which made it quite clear, even to doubters in the West, that there was no semblance of alliance now between the two Communist giants.[1]

The People's War

The Chinese have been most consistent of all in their views on nuclear strategy. Little has changed since Mao explained the Communist Party's stance to the American journalist Anne Louise Strong in 1946:

> The atom bomb is a paper tiger with which the American reactionaries try to terrify the people. It looks terrible, but in fact is not. Of course, the atom bomb is a weapon of mass annihilation: the outcome of a war is decided by the people, not by one or two new weapons.[2]

The emphasis on the people as the ultimate determinant of victory or defeat has been the foundation of Maoist doctrine. It was not a surprising theme to emerge out of a series of successful wars against armies that enjoyed better equipment but lacked mass support, and from a leadership imbued with a revolutionary ideology that identified the aroused masses as the source of social change.

People's War, as the Maoist strategy was described, involved galvanizing the revolutionary spirit of the masses and using this to military and political effect. In this the military sphere was at all times subordinate to the political. The main military task was not to hold territory but to gain time for the masses to be mobilized and to bring their weight to bear. At the same time enemy forces were to be depressed and demoralized, never allowed to exploit their advantages in equipment in a pitched battle, but to be drawn into the country, with lines of communication extended. There they could be bogged down in endless skirmishes and eventually drowned in a human sea. Guerrilla tactics were to be employed. Fighting at night, with local superiority in manpower, and at as close quarters as possible, would minimize the value to the enemy of his material superiority. Mao provided the formula: 'The enemy advances; we retreat. The enemy halts; we harass. The enemy retreats; we pursue.'[3]

There was much that any aspiring guerrilla leader could learn from Mao's experiences in fighting the Japanese invaders and the Kuomintang in the civil war. But the lessons were not universally applicable. They were most relevant to campaigns against unwelcome intruders into well-populated agrarian societies where the terrain afforded maximum cover for guerrillas and maximum difficulty for a conventional army. In sparsely populated and open areas, or where there were fixed strategic and industrial assets that required attention, different tactics were required. The Maoist strategy was most relevant to a campaign against an invasion of China from the south, and only partially relevant to campaigning elsewhere in different circumstances.

The professional military were aware of the limitations of People's War, though they rarely found it possible to give voice to their apprehensions. They preferred to lay less stress on political consciousness and more on equipment, wishing far more freedom of manoeuvre than being confined to either 'human wave' tactics or harassment of the enemy by the lack of modern means of warfare. The frustration was summed up by Marshal P'eng Te-Huai – 'What's the use of relying entirely on political and ideological work? It can't fly.' But then he was disgraced in 1959 for such retrograde thoughts.

The generals were not permitted to develop their forces along conventional lines, nor lay down, as did their colleagues in the Soviet Union, the essentials of strategic doctrine. These matters were at the centre of political argument and, as the Maoist faction asserted itself against internal opponents and then against the 'Khruschev Revisionists' in the Soviet Union, People's War became a dogma. Adherence to it became the touchstone of political reliability while it was presented in an ever more exaggerated form. By the time of the Cultural Revolution in the mid-1960s it had been simplified into a blanket assertion that the masses, relying on their own devices but inspired by the Thoughts of Mao Tse-tung, could achieve virtually anything against almost any odds. When Mao's Defence Minister, Lin Piao, outlined the most uncompromising and all-embracing version of this doctrine in September 1965, the opposing view was described in equally extreme terms. The 'bourgeois line', it was claimed 'ignores the human factor and sees only the material factor and ... regards technology as everything and politics as nothing'. It was hard to find any room for technology or the material factor at all: human will was dominant – a conclusion Marx would have found surprising when presented as derivative of his theories. Even nuclear technology could not overturn the basic law. 'The spiritual atomic bomb which the revolutionary people possess is a far more powerful and useful weapon than the physical atomic bomb.'[4]

In both the moderate and extreme versions of People's War the response to the atom bomb was the same: it had to be assessed in terms of the effect on morale of the guerrilla army and those masses in the process of being mobilized. In Soviet propaganda, Mao's response to the atom bomb was a desperate attempt to preserve an obsolescent doctrine by contemplating the deaths of millions of his countrymen. It was true that on occasion Mao and his followers did suggest that little would be gained by the enemy destroying hundreds of millions of Chinese because equivalent numbers would still be around to carry on the fight, but it was never suggested that these deaths would be a matter of no consequence. Nor was the disparagement of the bomb an attempt to maintain some abstract doctrinal purity. No country had been closer to nuclear attack than the Chinese since Hiroshima and Nagasaki were destroyed. Direct military confrontation came with the Americans in Korea and was close many other times in the 1950s – over Indochina and Taiwan. Later on it was feared that the Vietnam War would spill over into China. Then the hostility with the Soviet Union approached full-scale war in the late 1960s and early 1970s. There is evidence, certainly from the American side, that nuclear use was actively considered during a number of these crises. The Chinese displayed a remarkable talent for picking arguments with the super-powers.

Atom Bombs as Paper Tigers

The Maoist view was that the destructiveness of nuclear weapons ought not to be exaggerated lest the masses be demoralized. The view was best expressed through the metaphor of the 'paper tiger' – 'outwardly strong, but inwardly feeble'. The aim of the concept was to break down the superstition that left people intimidated by nuclear threats, by pointing out how unlikely it was, because of the fear of retaliation or the pressures of world opinion, that nuclear weapons would be used; how inappropriate these weapons would be in guerrilla warfare; how even after nuclear attacks the country still need not succumb to a conqueror because the basic method of People's War would still be applicable; and how, even if a nuclear weapon exploded in the vicinity, no harm would come to those that had taken the proper precautions. The essence of the concept was that the paper tiger could not, in the end, triumph. This did not mean, however, that its real qualities should be ignored, for in combat it was a 'real' or 'iron' tiger. The law was to despise the enemy strategically, but respect him tactically.[5]

During the Korean War efforts were made to demonstrate that with proper precautions the atom bomb could be survived. In November 1950 the following was published, ostensibly written by an eye-witness of Hiroshima:

> When you can get into a well-constructed air-raid shelter before the release of the bomb and put on a suit of white clothing and make sure to get to a place ten kilometres away immediately after the explosion, nothing shall happen to you. Look at myself. ... I have gone through the explosion of an atomic bomb and I am still growing strong as before. The atom bomb is in fact not as dreadful as American imperialism points it out to be.

In addition to this doubtful reassurance to the population, strategic arguments were also deployed. In the same month as the above, the following appeared in the *Current Affairs Journal* in Peking:

> The atomic bomb is no longer monopolized by the US. The Soviet Union has it too. If the US dares to use the atomic bomb she naturally will get the retaliation deserved. ...

> The atomic bomb itself cannot be the decisive factor in a war. ... It cannot be employed on the battlefield to destroy directly the fighting power of the opposing army in order not to annihilate the users themselves. It can only be used against a big and concentrated object like a big armament industry centre or huge concentration of troops. Therefore, the more extensive the opponents' territory is and the more scattered the opponent's population is, the less effective will the atomic bomb be.[6]

These arguments were not only unrealistic, and rapidly becoming more so, but somewhat premature when related to the deterrent effect of the Soviet bomb. Nevertheless, refined gradually, these practical arguments on the lack of utility of nuclear weapons were repeated over the following years. For example, during its argument with the Soviet Union, the Central Committee of the Chinese Communist Party explained in September 1963 that:

Politically recourse to this kind of weapon would place US imperialism in a position of extreme isolation, and militarily, the massive destructiveness of nuclear weapons limits their use, for in civil wars and wars of national independence where the lines zig-zag and the fighting is at close range, the use of nuclear weapons of mass destruction would inflict damage on both belligerents.[7]

It is difficult to disentangle the wishful thinking from the considered military judgment. Again one comes back to the belief that the morale of the people was the most critical factor to which all statements and actions must be geared.

This mixture of insight and credulity was illustrated by the evolution of views on the Soviet nuclear force. At the start, the first Soviet detonation of 1949 was welcomed for its deterrent effect, but the Chinese leaders took time to appreciate the full meaning of the nuclear age. By the mid-1950s the importance of the American nuclear force as an explanation for the caution in Soviet foreign policy was beginning to be recognized, as were some of the trends in Soviet strategic thinking, particularly with regard to the possible rôle of surprise attacks. In October 1957, with the launching of *Sputnik I*, the Chinese shared the Soviet pride in the spectacular achievement, but drew somewhat more optimistic conclusions than their comrades in Moscow. Mao proclaimed the ascendance of the Socialist Camp over the Imperialist Camp in a lyrical manner: 'At present, it is not the west wind which is prevailing over the east wind, but the east wind prevailing over the west wind.'

The conclusion that the Chinese drew from this happy turn of events was that the United States was no longer in a position to use its nuclear arsenal to blackmail or intimidate socialism. An argument was developed which matched the fears of the Western critics of massive retaliation – the neutralizing of American nuclear superiority created opportunities for communist advance through wars of limited

violence but large political effect, such as those of 'national liberation'. More specifically, it was felt that the moment might be ripe to
finish the business of the civil war and remove the Chinese Nationalists from their stronghold on Taiwan.

On 23 August 1958, Chinese batteries began a bombardment of
Quemoy, one of the smaller islands close to the mainland held by the
Nationalists. A month and a half later the shelling was effectively
halted. Other than that there was no military action. The Chinese
intention was to probe the extent of American support for the Nationalists. If this was found to be less than complete, the offshore
islands would probably have been seized as a prelude to the liberation of Taiwan. The Americans made it quite clear that they would
not accede to any change in the *status quo* and so the Chinese let
matters drop. They found the firm American stance unsurprising.
Less satisfactory was the extent of the limits on Soviet support for
their aspirations which became clear during the crisis. The Russians
had a largely defensive view of matters: they were pleased that the
Americans kept Chiang Kai-shek on a tight leash and that they
refused to countenance any ideas of 'rolling-back' communist power
on the mainland. What they wished to avoid was actions that might
provoke US military intervention, particularly of the sort that might
involve nuclear weapons and draw the Soviet Union into a major
confrontation. During the crisis, while Chinese propaganda spoke of
imminent landings on Quemoy and a 'joint assault of our modern
army and air force', the Russian press pointedly ignored such utterances and emphasized the improbability of war. It was only after the
shelling had stopped and the crisis had subsided that serious Soviet
warnings were issued to the United States, and even then they were
soon qualified. On 7 September Khruschev wrote to President Eisenhower 'An attack on the Chinese People's Republic, which is a great
ally, friend and neighbour of our country, is an attack on the Soviet
Union.' This suggested an automatic Soviet response to any attack on
China, but then comments appeared suggesting something more
conditional. Aid would be 'considered' and 'offered as necessary', with
reminders that the Chinese had grown sufficiently strong to have
'everything necessary to give a suitable rebuff' to an aggressor. It was
only on 19 September, when the danger of a serious confrontation
had clearly passed, that a nuclear threat was invoked, with a warning
that any use of nuclear weapons against the mainland would 'receive
a fitting rebuff by the same means'.[8]

This left the Chinese smarting under the humiliation of being forced to give up their action without tangible gains and unimpressed by the caution of their Soviet allies. The experience reinforced their view that it was necessary to become less dependent on the Soviet Union. In arguments similar to those being developed in France at the same time to justify an independent nuclear force,[9] the Chinese began to make the case that extra nuclear forces in the possession of individual members of the socialist camp would strengthen bloc security, because this would decrease the imperialists' opportunities for 'atomic blackmail'.

However, in order to attain a nuclear capability Soviet help was required. A number of Soviet concessions were made to requests for nuclear assistance but in practice little was done to satisfy Chinese aspirations. The result was to exacerbate Sino-Soviet differences as the Russians became suspicious of Chinese recklessness, while the Chinese reacted against Russian attempts to keep them dependent. Moscow observed that the Chinese Communist Party had 'developed some kind of special aims and interests which the socialist camp cannot support with its military force'. Peking took the hint: 'in fighting imperialist aggression and defending its security, each socialist country has to rely in the first place on its own defence capability and then – and only then – on assistance from fraternal countries and the people of the world'.[10]

The strategic arguments turned on the probability of any armed clash between the socialist and imperialist camps being kept localized, without all-out nuclear exchanges, and on the possibility of a meaningful victory even if the war did become nuclear. The Russians charged the Chinese with a lack of realism about the effects of nuclear war, pointing out that 'the atom bomb does not adhere to the class principle'. Peking's unfailing optimism on the inevitable triumph of the politically righteous was mocked: 'It is absurd to suppose that a war of attrition will, as it were, favour the weak and harm the strong. In such a war, the weak will be exhausted before the strong.'[11]

A bizarre anecdote from Khruschev's memoirs sums up the Soviet leader's view on the relevance of People's War in the nuclear age. After observing that he found it 'incredible that Mao could dismiss American imperialism as a paper tiger when it is a dangerous predator', he recalled an occasion when he and Mao were sitting, clad only in bathing trunks, by a swimming pool in Peking. Mao remarked on the military might of the Socialist world by reference to the number of potential divisions all the member countries could raise. Khruschev responded:

Comrade Mao Tse-tung, nowadays that sort of thinking is out of date. You can no longer calculate the alignment of forces on the basis of who has the most men. Back in the days when a dispute was settled with fists or bayonets, it made a difference who had the most men and the most bayonets on each side. Then when the machine gun appeared, the side with more troops no longer necessarily had the advantage. And now with the atomic bomb, the number of troops on each side makes practically no difference to the alignment of real power and the outcome of a war. The more troops on a side, the more bomb fodder.[12]

Chinese pronouncements became more dogmatic. This, combined with the strange events of the Cultural Revolution, helped to support the Soviet warnings that the Chinese were of doubtful rationality and of dubious purpose. Yet China's approach was less extreme than it appeared superficially. She always calculated military risks with great care and was not inclined to underestimate the strength of the enemy. Chinese arguments denying the inevitable escalation of any armed clashes into a nuclear war were also cogent. Their understanding of the political limitations of nuclear use was acute, though their views on the tactical limitations were less impressive.

In October 1964, as Khruschev was falling from power in Moscow, the Chinese detonated an atomic bomb and, two and a half years later, a hydrogen bomb. This resulted in no evident change in general attitudes on nuclear weapons. The paper tiger theme was played down, with the claim that the positive effect of the Chinese bomb on the morale of the revolutionary people made it a 'real tiger'. There was no deviation from the previous beliefs in the limited utility of nuclear weapons. In the later 1970s, warnings were still heard against 'blind belief' in nuclear weapons.[13]

China did not move beyond the most modest objectives for its nuclear force, offering no nuclear guarantees to others. It developed suitably modest capabilities, oriented towards the Soviet Union, but it was not, at the end of the 1970s, a force which met the full requirements of a second-strike capability. This demonstrated that a country burdened by enormous resource constraints could not allow itself the luxury of meeting the exacting standards for deterrence applied by the US, even though her relations with the USSR were much more precarious. Despite hostility to the USSR, and insistence on the aggressive nature of the Soviet Union, China was less than paranoid as to Soviet intentions towards China herself, conveniently discovering

Soviet motives that pointed her towards expansion on her Western and not Eastern front.

The Chinese thus managed to be the most consistent of all nuclear powers on matters of doctrine, preferring all the time to organize warfare in a way that suited the type of fighting they knew best and for which they were best (or least poorly) equipped. With the defeat of the leftist 'Gang of Four' in the mid-1970s after Mao's death, the more mystical elements of 'People's War' theory were dropped. Military leaders, allowed to spend more time on professional responsibilities, and less on raising political consciousness or administering the country, began to consider the serious difficulties connected with waging a conventional war on an around China's borders. This sort of limited campaign was a more likely contingency than that of an invader attempting to conquer the country. It required not so much a vast patriotic militia, but a more traditional sort of force, capable of a modicum of forward defence. After a short but bloody fight with former Vietnamese allies in 1979, the term 'People's War' was heard less, recognized to be referring to a form of combat more appropriate to an earlier period.

For long periods in the 1960s the Chinese managed to be wholly at odds with both super-powers. The United States was as alarmed by the Chinese as the Soviet Union. When, in September 1967, McNamara authorized the construction of a light ABM system to be in place for when the first few Chinese ICBMs were expected to be operational, there were suggestions that taking on the Chinese was politically more expedient domestically than taking on the Russians. But in itself the idea of countering a Chinese 'threat' did not seem outrageous. Unlike the USSR, the US managed to get over her sinophobia. China, for her part, grew weary of calling for a plague on both super-power houses and opted for a rapprochement with the more distant enemy, the US. Ironically, a process that began with the Chinese urging the Russians to be more militant in their dealings with America ended with a Sino-American accommodation – and the Chinese urging the Americans to be more militant with the Russians.

The European Dimension

19 A Conventional Defence for Europe

The arguments over nuclear policy between the United States and her allies were often as acrimonious as those between the Soviet Union and China, but they did not result in such a stark deterioration in political relations. France disentangled herself from NATO but the break did not turn out to be as complete as at first seemed likely. Furthermore, one result of the French withdrawal was to make possible a compromise position within NATO in which Europeans endorsed the formal US position while making it clear that they would not devote great resources to implementing it. The strategy of flexible response was adopted by NATO in 1967:

> This concept . . . is based upon a flexible and balanced range of appropriate responses, conventional and nuclear, to all levels of aggression or threats of aggression. These responses, subject to appropriate political control, are designed, first to deter aggression and thus preserve peace; but, should aggression unhappily occur, to maintain the security of the North Atlantic Treaty area within the concept of forward defence.[1]

The new strategy did not result in the major increases in the defence expenditure of America's European allies that it implied. Defence expenditure as a percentage of GNP continued its steady decline. The only time that it had risen during the 1960s was in 1961–2, and this was due as much to the crisis over Berlin as to the appeals of the US Administration. Apart from anything else, by 1967

285

the Americans had become almost completely preoccupied with Vietnam and had little extra military capacity spare for Europe.

In many ways the vehemence of the debate up to this final compromise was surprising. The concept of 'flexible response' was descended from the ideas of 'graduated deterrence' that had originated in Britain in the mid-1950s. The doctrine of 'massive retaliation' had been severely criticized in Europe for its incredibility, and the need to introduce greater flexibility into the West's military capabilities had become part of the conventional wisdom amongst centrist and social democratic parties on both sides of the Atlantic by the end of the 1950s. Two rising politicians who were later to become Ministers for Defence in their respective countries, Denis Healey in Britain and Helmut Schmidt in Germany, made their reputations by arguing against massive retaliation. Some of the acrimony of the 1960s debate can be explained by the Democrat proponents of this view coming to power in the US before their Social Democratic counterparts in Europe, so finding themselves facing an entrenched old guard. It may be that the Americans would have treated the French President, General de Gaulle, with greater sensitivity had they anticipated that he would survive the Algerian crisis which had brought him to power.

Without de Gaulle the debate might have been calmer for he introduced a challenge to the very concept of the Alliance. Equally, if the US Administration had not been so rigid in its strategic logic, cocky and arrogant in its presentation, and generally lacking in care or appreciation for European sensibilities, then it might have found its audience more receptive. That astute European observer of intellectual trends, Raymond Aron noted: 'The American theory of atomic monopoly which the experts in Washington are tireless in justifying on technical grounds, raises political difficulties which these same experts stubbornly disregard.'[2] So keen were the Americans to follow their strategic principles to logical conclusions that they neglected to weave into their theories the complications caused by European concerns. These intrusions, based on the strategic realities as seen from Europe, appeared quite non-scientific to the Americans and so were rejected through the means of rigorous argument, rather than accommodated by the political compromise that life in an Alliance necessitates.

Gaining strength through the quality of their analysis, and with a responsibility for leadership within the Alliance, McNamara and his aides managed to touch upon the most sensitive nerve-endings of the Europeans – the fear of Europe serving as a battleground; the fear of

Europe being deserted by the Americans; and the loss of dignity felt by world powers of long standing at being directed in affairs of security by such an upstart newcomer as the United States. They suspected that they needed the Americans more than the Americans needed them but resented American attempts to order them about. In this context, the final straw, particularly for the French, was for McNamara to insist that not only must the Europeans move with the United States in augmenting the conventional option, but they should deny themselves a nuclear option. All decisions on nuclear warfare should be concentrated in one centre – Washington DC.

To the French this was outrageous; it was an insult to national dignity and their sense of independence. A formidable critique of McNamara's doctrines developed in France. De Gaulle used these arguments over nuclear strategy to elaborate his own theories of European security and the need for completely new arrangements on the Continent. Few other Europeans were anxious to follow de Gaulle's example. Their irritation was with the Americans for being so infatuated with their strategic concepts that they failed to appreciate the political currents at work in the Alliance.

Factors of personality and diplomatic skill gave the debate much of its flavour and intensity, yet its source was rooted in factors of history and geography and the evolving state of the strategic environment and strategic theory.

Theories of Conventional War

The Kennedy Administration came to power in 1961 at a time when there was a groundswell amongst US strategists in favour of a strengthening of NATO's conventional defences. Former proponents of schemes for limited nuclear warfare, such as Henry Kissinger,[3] were defecting to the camp of those who believed that tactical nuclear weapons could not solve the problem of credibility that lay at the core of NATO's deterrent posture.[4] The aim was to correct NATO's over-reliance on nuclear weapons, but the desired role of conventional forces was unclear – except that it should be greater than it had been in the 1950s.

There were two distinct options: a force capable of holding back a limited Soviet conventional attack; and a force capable of repulsing a full-blooded invasion. At issue was whether NATO could develop capabilities to fight a war that was total in its intensity and objectives yet limited in its methods. When war seemed close in the early 1950s, the NATO Governments had agreed, over-optimistically as it turned out, to match Soviet conventional capabilities. The 1952 Lisbon force goals were to bring up NATO strength from 25 to 96 divisions in two years. Soviet strength was calculated, as it was through the decade, at anything from 140 to 175 divisions, with reserves able to more than double these numbers. As the war-scare subsided and the build-up turned out to be inflationary in its economic consequences, the New Look of the Eisenhower Administration was embraced because it offered a robust deterrence at a manageable cost. Abandonment of the Lisbon force goals encouraged official pessimism on the possibility of ever matching Soviet conventional strength. The NATO force goals were reduced to 30 divisions, and hope was placed in the introduction of tactical nuclear weapons to compensate for numerical inferiority.

The resultant nuclear bias in NATO's force structure rendered the conventional option extremely radical; it would involve a major increase in manpower and a complete change of equipment and tactics for the ground forces. Few argued that NATO could abandon nuclear weapons, for, now that the Warsaw Pact was similarly armed, a deterrent was needed to nuclear aggression. Some were prepared to argue that if the Warsaw Pact attacked with conventional arms, NATO should be prepared to respond in kind, no matter how large the attack. Almost unique amongst Europeans in supporting this view (and even he soon backed away from it), Helmut Schmidt demonstrated the impressive intellectual arguments that could be summoned on its behalf.

Schmidt argued that a local defence known by the enemy to be capable of blocking an attack would be as good a deterrent as the threat of nuclear retaliation. In fact it would be better because the initial use of nuclear weapons would be such an irrational act that it could not be expected to influence another's actions.

In the interests of maintaining the substance of Europe and particularly of Germany, NATO must . . . have troops and weapons on a scale ample to make non-nuclear agression appear hopeless, and sufficient in an emergency to force one of two courses on the aggressor – to halt or extend the conflict.[5]

The practicality of this option depended, at least to some extent, on calculations on the character of the Warsaw Pact threat (including such factors as the reliability of the Pact's non-Soviet divisions and the speed of Soviet mobilization) and the forces necessary to provide an effective defence. On this latter point, Liddell Hart's formula of two defending divisions for every three attacking divisions was widely accepted. But even taking this ratio, common estimates of Warsaw Pact strength could suggest that an effective defence would require a doubling of NATO's front-line forces.[6]

The problem was not simply one of numbers. A further complication was that NATO had set itself a particularly difficult military problem. When Germany had agreed to re-arm, one condition was that no amount of her territory should be ceded in a war, even as part of an opening gambit designed to allow sufficient time for mobilization and counter-attack. The need therefore was for Forward Defence, interpreted by differing countries according to how far back they were from the front, but taken literally by Germany. Unfortunately the tactical concepts favoured by the US military were for mobile units, based some way back from the front ready to move to confront an invading force at the most opportune place and time. This did not involve a commitment to holding a particular 'line'.

One alternative was to prepare to move to the tactical offensive, but not only would this put extra demands on force levels, it was also somewhat unsuitable for forces based on Germany. Memories of past offensives launched from Germany were too strong. Tactical nuclear weapons, launched against an invading force massing across the border, might help; but only if used as a weapon of first resort. Delay in using nuclear weapons would only make matters worse, for once the targets were amongst the people who were supposed to be defended, their fate would be even more dire. The only alternative was to develop a firm defensive wall at the border that would make the first stage of an invasion difficult. This idea did not get very far. It was deemed politically unacceptable because a fortified border would in some way acknowledge the permanence of a divided Germany; the time for this symbolic step had not yet come. And it was dismissed on military grounds because of a similarity with the French Maginot Line, the failure of which in 1940 was taken as proof of the inadequacy of the concept, and because the proponents of such a line were suggesting a major rôle for local militias, of which professional soldiers did not think highly.

The proposal to make more effective use of militia had some respectable advocates, including Liddell Hart. He argued for militia forces in the front line, each 'organised to fight in its own locality, and maintain itself from local stores, distributed in numerous small underground shelters'. Such a force 'would provide a deep network of defence yet need much less transport than the present NATO type, be much less of a target, be less liable to interception, and become effective with far shorter training – so relieving the present burden of conscription'. By innovation in the design and deployment of conventional forces, Liddell Hart believed that, without greater expenditure, an alternative could be found to the prevailing view that a serious invasion could only be repelled with nuclear weapons. Plans based on this latter view amounted 'to nothing better than a despairing acceptance of suicide in the event of any major aggression'.[7]

Even if a full-scale conventional defence was feasible, doctrinal problems remained. It could be agreed that conventional warfare would be preferable and much more rational if deterrence failed. The problem was that the aggressor's preferences would probably be the same – leading to the 'war threshold' being lowered. Whereas the threat of nuclear war would make the risks of war too great, if the threat was only of conventional war the risks might be tolerable. Thus the problem with a nuclear strategy was that it was hard to demonstrate why the US, as the only power which could implement such a strategy, should be willing to risk nuclear war in the event of a conventional invasion of Europe; the problem with a conventional strategy was that it was hard to demonstrate why the Russians would be deterred. This latter problem grew if a full-scale conventional defence was not even practical.

If neither a strategy based wholly on nuclear weapons nor one based wholly on conventional weapons could be satisfactory, might there be a possible mixture of the two? The problem of extended deterrence was of the United States risking nuclear war to defend Europe. If the first US participation in a war was liable to be a decision on whether or not to 'go nuclear' there might be a great temptation in Washington to stay out of the conflict. One rôle therefore to be played by US forces based in Europe was to create an involvement in hostilities prior to a nuclear decision. The theory was that once young Americans had been killed by the invading forces the whole-hearted commitment of their country need no longer be in doubt. The important thing about US ground forces in Europe was thus their nationality and the consequent link they provided to the US nuclear deterrent. Tactical nuclear weapons, as US nuclear weapons directly committed to the defence of Europe, strengthened this link further. Seen in this way local defence served as a 'trip wire' or 'plate glass' designed to trigger the US nuclear deterrent.

Part of the criticism of massive retaliation was that limited engagements, even involving the death of American soldiers, ought not to trigger a nuclear war. A case could therefore be made for creating strong enough local defences capable of dealing with limited attacks, even if an all-out attack could not be blocked. In this way, particularly after the loss of confidence in strategies centred on tactical nuclear weapons, conventional weapons become associated with limited war while nuclear weapons were associated with total war.

Even with larger conventional forces, the 'trip-wire' concept could still operate. Though a nuclear response to invasion would now be less automatic, the aggressor would still have to accept a certain risk. Schelling made this point clear, dividing the threat to engage in a limited war into two parts:

One is the threat to inflict costs directly on the other side, in casualties, expenditures, loss of territory, loss of force, or anything else. The second is the threat to expose the other party, together with one's self, to a heightened risk of general war.[8]

Conventional forces could embody 'the threat that leaves something to chance'. Thus a deterrent could be forged relying on the strongest features of both conventional and nuclear forces. In hostilities beginning with conventional battles the US would not have too many qualms about intervening, yet the act of intervention would make future nuclear use more credible, so strengthening the deterrent. Once it was accepted that NATO could never fight a conventional total war then the strengthening of conventional forces at lower, feasible levels could only strengthen nuclear deterrence against total war. As Henry Kissinger explained:

The stronger the limited war forces of the free world, the larger will have to be the Communist effort designed to overcome them, the more the scale of conflict required for victory approaches that of all-out war, the greater will be the inhibitions against initiating hostilities. In this sense a capability of limited war is necessary in order to enhance the deterrent power of the retaliatory force.[9]

Furthermore, stronger local defences, even if they might eventually give way, would provide sufficient time to prepare the nuclear riposte and to allow for some diplomatic attempts to remind the adversary of the imminent consequences of a failure to withdraw.

What was not being proposed in the US up to 1961 was the capability of holding any Soviet invading force. Even one of the strongest proponents of redressing the balance in NATO's force structure in favour of conventional forces, General Maxwell Taylor, stopped short of this. What Taylor called 'counter-attrition forces' had important roles to play.

> In general war, they must cover the vital ground areas in which they are deployed and hold the enemy at arm's length while we punish him with our heavy weapons of great destruction. Thereafter they must have the residual strength to occupy his lands and claim whatever may be called victory. For limited war, they must be strong enough to turn back infiltrations, raids and border forays and gain the necessary time to make sure of an enemy's intentions.[10]

These were demanding requirements but it was still assumed that the only proper response to general war was the introduction of the nuclear arsenal.

It should not be thought that the Eisenhower Administration was unaware of the arguments in favour of strengthening local defences, particularly in view of the evident growth in Soviet nuclear forces. Even John Foster Dulles was willing to acknowledge that in the coming decade less reliance might be placed on the threat of nuclear retaliation.

> Thus, in contrast to the 1950 decade, it may be by the 1960 decade the nations which are around the Sino-Soviet perimeter can possess an effective defense against full-scale conventional attack and thus confront any aggressor with the choice between failing or himself initiating nuclear war against the defending country.[11]

The Supreme Allied Commander in Europe (SACEUR), General Lauris Norstad, did argue for improvements in conventional capabilities during the late 1950s as a means of holding up a Soviet invasion. The loss of momentum would allow for a 'pause' in which the Soviet leaders would have time to reconsider whether they were prepared for the full consequences of all-out war. Using NATO terminology, with the Shield of conventional forces and the Sword of nuclear retaliation, Norstad argued that if NATO's frontier could be held with reasonable force, then force would have to be used to breach it. 'The decision to apply that force would be terrible in its implications. It must consider not only the stout Shield in immediate defence, but the sharp Sword of our strategic retaliation.' Norstad then added a limited war function for the Shield – 'to save civilization from being whittled away by forays and incursions which otherwise could be halted only by invoking our full apparatus of destruction'.[12]

European Attitudes

Norstad had in mind a very limited capability, though even this proposal was enough to make America's allies nervous. After an anguished internal debate, the Christian Democrat Government in Germany had accepted the nuclear emphasis of the Eisenhower Administration's New Look and did not want to see it reversed. Also in 1957, the Conservative Government in Britain had expressed itself wholly converted to a version of massive retaliation and was preparing to cut drastically the numbers of conventional troops and arm those that remained with nuclear weapons.[13] Neither Government was keen to hear Americans expounding the arguments of their domestic oppositions.

The lukewarm European responses to even the modest proposals of Norstad were as nothing compared to the outrage that greeted the more ambitious proposals of the Kennedy Administration. Before commenting on the substance of their counter-arguments it is worth emphasizing the political context. The main Governments of Europe were right-of-centre and committed to strategies forged when the US Government had shared their nuclear bias. They did not take kindly to being asked to change their policies simply because the United States had a new Administration. Secondly, in any coalition such as NATO, change is always more difficult than reaffirmation of the *status quo*, because the prospect of change underlines differences in interests and outlook.[14]

It is always difficult to speak of 'European' views on any matter, though it may sometimes be convenient. Many Europeans and many Americans have accepted that life would be easier if Europe could act as one unit. But a collection of proud nations, with diverse cultures, who had worked out their identities in conflict and rivalry with each other, and who as democracies each contained many strands of opinion, does not reach a consensus easily. Part of the American frustration was with the uncertainty and confusion of European allies, as much as with the views that eventually emerged. The frustration can be found in some of William Kaufmann's description of his country's allies: 'they could not agree among themselves about objectives, they trusted one another less than they did the United States, and they had no particular inclination to incur the costs and risks of greater independence'.[15]

The fact remains, however, that European leaders of the time had an explicit nuclear bias which ought not to have taken anyone by surprise. For example, the then British Secretary of State for Defence, Duncan Sandys, provided a clear statement in 1958. First, he described the contentional capability of the Soviet Union. Then he wrote:

> The West, on the other hand, relies for its defence primarily upon the deterrent effect of its vast stockpile of nuclear weapons and its capacity to deliver them. The democratic Western nations will never start a war against Russia. But it must be well understood that, if Russia were to launch a major attack on them, even with conventional forces only, they would have to hit back with strategic nuclear weapons. In fact, the strategy of NATO is based on the frank recognition that a full-scale Soviet attack could not be repelled without resort to a massive nuclear bombardment of the sources of power in Russia. In that event, the rôle of the allied defence forces in Europe would be to hold the front for the time needed to allow the effects of the nuclear counter-offensive to make themselves felt.[16]

This position offered little advice on how to deal with low-level conflicts. The official view was that limited actions by the Soviet Union were unlikely, that it would be the Soviet Union's own fault if they were misinterpreted and escalated into General War, and that there was little point in spending vast sums of money to prepare for unlikely contingencies.

The Europeans found many US concepts of Limited War unpalatable. To them, any invasion of Europe, of virtually any size, should be taken as the start of a total war. They were concerned that to Americans, a war taking place across the ocean could still be seen as being limited, particularly so long as American cities were not being attacked.

It was at this point that the doctrine of flexible response began to make the Europeans nervous. Their fear, based on a recognition of how they would view their interests under comparable circumstances,[17] was that the primary American objective was to spare North America the ravages of nuclear war, and they would do this by attempting to hold back a Soviet invasion by conventional means, thus inflicting on Europe the ravages of conventional war. The Europeans were disturbed by the implication that a conventional war was, in some way, a limited event, a 'soft' option, equivalent almost to the 'phoney war' of 1939–40, the shadow-boxing before the really nasty business of nuclear exchanges began. The Europeans had an experience of two prolonged vicious and bloody twentieth-century wars, in which millions had been killed, vast areas of land devastated, powerful and unruly social and political forces unleashed, and economies ruined. Wars were harder to stop than to start; men came to be governed by deep passions and fury. It did not need nuclear weapons to make war a miserable and horrible affair.

Thus even when the distinction between limited and total war was meaningful to Europeans, as it was to some, it was not synonymous with the distinction between the use of conventional and nuclear explosives. This latter distinction was not as relevant to the European situation as a theatre of war as it was to the American situation – beyond the theatre but vulnerable to nuclear attack. For similar reasons, the distinction between deterrence and defence was far more pertinent for the Europeans than it was to the Americans. In strict terms, adequate military preparation to hold the line against attack, as the denial of gain, is as legitimate a part of deterrence as the subsequent imposition of cost. The Europeans were less impressed by notions of intra-war deterrence because of the catastrophic consequences for Europe of a series of land battles on the continent. *All* war had to be deterred. If the Soviet Union believed that a war would only be fought at a conventional level, not entailing a serious risk of nuclear war, then it might be tempted to try its luck. To talk of a 'threshold' below which nuclear weapons would not be used, or a 'pause' during which these weapons would not be used, eased the Soviet risk calculus too much.[18]

Finally, the absence of a clear link between America's nuclear arsenal and the defence of Europe would leave the Europeans vulnerable to intimidation by the Soviet Union without any confidence that the Americans would come to their rescue. The American proposals for a more impressive conventional option could be seen as being designed more to spare the US any sacrifice than to bolster the deterrent, while emphasizing Europe's vulnerability to a nuclear attack. When this was combined with a concerted American campaign against independent European nuclear forces, the suspicions grew.

In general the Europeans did not find the problems of deterrence to be as difficult as the US. It was not felt that the Soviet Union was gearing itself up for major aggression. So long as any aggression would entail a modicum of serious risk, it was felt that the Russians would remain content with peaceful coexistence. To those that, unlike the French, remained committed to NATO the need was to ensure that the Russians were reminded of the dangers connected with any adventures, and to keep the Alliance in working order so as to avoid being divided and ruled.

Towards a Conventional Balance

Though the Eisenhower Administration was backing away from the strictest massive retaliation concept, the main enthusiasm for strengthening local defences came from the Army and the Democrat opposition. Those responsible for forming the NATO policy of the Truman Administration remained true to their view that the optimum strategy involved strong local defences with nuclear weapons moving more into the background.[19] Aware of European attitudes, the new Kennedy Administration sought to reassure the Allies that the nuclear guarantee was not about to be withdrawn and that the conventional build-up need be no more than the fulfilment of existing commitments of men and equipment. The US, sensing the responsibilities of leadership, would set an example which, it was expected, the Europeans would follow. Not to do so would raise annoyance in Washington over the excessive burden that the US was felt to be bearing for the defence of Europe. Unlike the Europeans, who felt that Soviet adventures were unlikely, the Administration considered Europe to be 'alive with possibilities for small-scale action: in Berlin, on the flanks of NATO, and against the friendly neutrals. Consequently conventional rather than nuclear forces seemed to be the real need of the day.'[20]

The Berlin crisis of 1961 had an ambiguous conclusion. The building of the wall in August 1961 demonstrated the division of Europe in a crude and unpleasant manner, sealing the unfortunate citizens of East Germany off from their escape routes to the West. But the Russians held back from impeding Western access to West Berlin and West Berlin remained free. This could be taken as a successful invocation of the nuclear deterrent as Berlin itself was indefensible by conventional means. Nevertheless the crisis prompted some increase in European conventional forces, and the lesson drawn by McNamara was to continue this process. In 1962 he said to Congress:

> The events of last year have convinced us that the NATO forces in Europe must be greatly strengthened. While we will always be prepared to use our nuclear weapons when needed, we also want to have a choice other than doing nothing or deliberately initiating a general nuclear war; or as President Kennedy said, a choice between 'inglorious retreat or unlimited retaliation'. No one can put a precise figure on what the conventional strength ought to be, but we do know it must be more than what we had available last year.

To the chagrin of the Allies, McNamara then started to speculate on the feasibility of a full conventional defence. His case was simple. On close examination the Soviet threat receded to manageable proportions. The hopelessness engendered by contemplating the size of the Soviet Army was unnecessary. In a February 1962 speech he explained:

> A simple comparison of numbers of Allied and bloc divisions takes no account of the fact that many of the bloc divisions are a good deal smaller at full strength than our own, many are under strength, and some of them may be highly unreliable. The important point to bear in mind is that NATO has a strong defensive capability. Its further growth is limited by the degree to which its members are willing to devote resources to the task.[21]

Cutting the Russians down to size meant that the blame for the overdependence on nuclear weapons could be placed on the stinginess of the Allies.

A book written by two of McNamara's assistants gives an idea of the confident and rigorous analysis the Europeans had to face from McNamara's staff.

In *How Much is Enough?*, Enthoven and Smith noted how strategic nuclear weapons could only be reserved for the most 'desperate of circumstances'. They were 'an ineffective or at least unusable form of power in a local conflict, even in the critical area of Europe. Further, these weapons simply did not deter local wars'. Thus, the Europeans had to note, a local war in Europe was not a sufficiently desperate circumstance for the US to use strategic nuclear weapons.

Nor would they be happy with tactical nuclear weapons. These had a marginal rôle, helping to contribute to deterrence by confusing adversary calculations and ensuring that the enemy had no unilateral advantage in this area. But the strong impression was given that the most appealing reason for maintaining this option was that a lot of effort had been put into creating it. The stockpiles for use by the US and her Allies had been established. 'This was not a situation that defense officials could, or wanted to, change drastically at the time. To attempt to do so would have raised the specter of an imminent US withdrawal from Europe.' However, these weapons were not a substitute for conventional weapons. They could not guarantee stopping a Soviet invasion and their use carried enormous risks. 'They did not solve the suicide-or-surrender dilemma. They provided options, but only after forcing us to initiate a nuclear war.' Again to the discomfort of their European audience, the US reluctance to initiate nuclear war was acknowledged. The value of US nuclear forces as an inhibition on Soviet attacks was accepted, but it was made clear that Enthoven and Smith would not themselves be too impressed by nuclear threats if contemplating a solely conventional attack, noting that Soviet reliance on conventional strength did not seem to mean that the West took her less seriously. They quoted McNamara: 'One cannot fashion a credible deterrent out of an incredible action.'

It was accepted that nuclear weapons were in a category of their own and that use would not follow naturally from failure in conventional defences in a European war. Much was made of the concept of the *fire-break* between conventional and nuclear war.

> Because of differences in the effects of conventional and nuclear explosives, violations of the fire-break are readily detectable; thus there is no ambiguity of the kind of war being fought. This fire-break is the most obvious discontinuity in the spectrum of modern warfare.

Thus, while the 'rules of a limited nuclear war would be complex and unclear', those of conventional war would be 'simple and clear', with the 'upper limit on escalation' not 'shrouded in uncertainty'. The message was straightforward. The US would play to 'rules' in which a certain level of violence would be tolerated without the use of the US deterrent.

There was only one alternative:

The only satisfactory escape from the dilemma lay in NATO's having adequate conventional forces – which in the US view meant forces approximately equal in military power to those opposing them on M-day (the day after mobilization starts) and each day thereafter.

But here Enthoven and Smith detected a 'psychological complex' within NATO concerning the cost of conventional weapons and the invincibility of the Soviet Union in this area. This 'despair and hoplessness' was seen as a major contributory factor to keeping down NATO's forces. It had become a 'self-fulfilling prophecy'. NATO forces were only supplied with three days' supply of ammunition because they were not expected to survive for more than three days. In consequence little serious consideration was given to flexible response because it was assumed that it would cost too much. According to Enthoven and Smith, if a conventional capability had been viewed as viable (which meant financially feasible rather than prohibitively costly) most of the 'frustrating and divisive debate' would not have taken place.

Analysis led them to conclude that the conventional option was viable. Their main target was the assumption that each Soviet division was equivalent to each American division:

[B]y 1965, we knew that a Soviet division force cost only about a third that of a US division force, had only about a third as many men, and (we had strong reason to believe) was only about one-third as effective. . . . In short, eliminating paper divisions, using cost and firepower indexes, counts of combat personnel in available divisions, and numbers of artillery pieces, trucks, tanks and the like, we ended up with the same conclusion: NATO and the Warsaw Pact had approximate equality on the ground. Where four years earlier it had appeared that a conventional option was impossible, it now began to appear that perhaps NATO could have had one all along.[22]

The Administration's policy gained wide support from civilian strategists. The most notable dissenting voice came from Bernard Brodie, who broke ranks with his colleagues on this issue. He first did this in a 1963 article and then in 1966 in a short book.[23] One source of the differences between Brodie and his colleagues, with the exception of Kissinger, was the essentially political character of his thought. He was sensitive to the main currents in international affairs and particularly to the attitudes of the Europeans. He was not a formal strategist in that he lacked confidence in conclusions derived from 'war-gaming' or rigorous but abstracted analysis, isolated from the real world. Brodie felt it was possible to take a much more relaxed view of the dangers in the international environment. He saw little point in upsetting the Alliance in order to cope with remote contingencies. The Soviet leaders were well aware of the dangers of nuclear war and had shown no inclination to take on Western military might. 'It would probably take much persuasion on our part to shake the Soviet leaders from their apparent conviction that in the event of a substantial attack by them the nuclear weapons available to NATO forces in Europe would quickly be used. Why should we attempt to shake that conviction?'

The key decision, according to Brodie, was not whether or not to use nuclear weapons but whether to initiate war in the first place. By concentrating on the significance of 'going nuclear' the conventional weapon enthusiasts were devaluing the gravity of the decision to 'go to war'. Though he did not doubt the value of some conventional forces or of encouraging the Allies to meet agreed NATO commitments, he felt too much emphasis was being put on creating a certainty that nuclear weapons would not be used until a conflict reached a specified point. Despite his own lack of enthusiasm in the past for tactical nuclear weapons, the possibility of their use did complicate Soviet calculations. His concern was to emphasize, not reduce, 'the threat that leaves something to chance'.

In his book Brodie severely criticized the fire-break theory for this reason. The theory assumed that the distinction between nuclear and non-nuclear weapons was the only feasible demarcation line between local hostilities and General War. Both sides would not hesitate to outbid each other in violence up to this limit, yet would not consider further escalation, having reached it. It was then argued that: 'To attempt to place that kind of fire-break at a relatively low place in the scale of operations would subject it to an insupportable pressure such as would be missing – or which it could far better sustain at high levels.' Brodie argued this barrier to escalation was far too mechanical. He preferred to rely on 'the aims, intentions, or fears of the respective opponents'. Furthermore, for the fire-break notion to be feasible, especially at a high level of tactical operations, the opponent must accept the rules. 'Otherwise the whole environment for conventional fighting would simply be too precarious.' Yet the apparent rejection of the fire-break theory by the Soviet Union had thus far worked to NATO's advantage. The non-nuclear enthusiasts were assuming that it was only a matter of time before the Russians would sense the underlying incredibility of extended nuclear deterrence but were in fact accelerating this process. Brodie noted with approval Raymond Aron's view that it had been to the West's advantage that the Russians had been unready 'to accept these special strategic ideas that are so popular in the United States'.[24]

Conclusion

It was the pursuit of a strategic problem in isolation from its political context that caused the US Administration so much difficulty. The ideas for limited war had been developed during the 1950s in connection with regions other than Europe where conditions were unstable and when relations between East and West were confused and unsettled. Many European theorists of limited war had carefully distinguished the needs of Europe from those of other regions. Europe was a 'special case', inextricably linked to the United States, so that a blow from the Soviet Union against Europe would be felt unambiguously to be a blow against the vital interests of the United States and would trigger an uninhibited military reaction. What the Europeans feared, to quote Pierre Gallois, was losing their status as 'an integral part of the American security area'. Once the Americans became vulnerable to nuclear attack they had sought to reduce the dangers to themselves even at the expense of their European Allies. 'Now, because of "escalation" and its dangers, Western Europe is to be "de-nuclearized" – that is to say, reduced to the level of those countries which may become host to local conflicts on the pattern of Korea, Indochina, and Malaya.' Yet, asserted Gallois, 'most military authorities are convinced that a conventional defence of Europe is no longer feasible and that a nuclear withdrawal would seal Europe's fate'.[25]

This is where McNamara and his aides would differ from Gallois and those who thought like him. They had a far better case than the Europeans would accept; a conventional defence probably was feasible and in the event of a failure in deterrence would still be preferable for the inhabitants of European NATO. Part of the problem in the debate was that it did not really turn on strategic analysis but on the political realities of the 1960s. It was not about the best way to deter the Russians but about the best way to tie the United States to Europe. The European Governments had over-reacted to American insensitivity, especially when presenting proposed increases in US force levels in Europe as evidence of declining American commitment. By the end of the decade, with the liberal faction in America turning to the view that America's allies must do much more to help themselves, the Europeans came to fear a decrease in US conventional strength in Europe! Perhaps the best interpretation of the European view was that in conditions of relative peace and stability they saw no need to tamper with any aspect of the *status quo*.

20 The European Nuclear Option (i) Anglo-Saxon Views

As controversial as McNamara's desire to improve the Alliance's conventional option was his desire to dissuade the Europeans from developing their own nuclear options. The distaste for the independent nuclear deterrents was not solely a question of saving resources for conventional weapons. It was also related to concepts of controlled nuclear warfare, in which, even after the nuclear fire-break had been breached, an attempt would still be made to prevent matters getting out of hand. Reflecting the scientific bent of the time, and indicating the indeterminate possibilities for proliferation, the issue was then described as 'The Nth Country Problem', a term that has now happily passed out of fashion.[1] By giving anonymity to the offending country, the term suggested that the problems were similar whoever the Nth power might be. One of the frequent observations on this matter was that whereas the Nth power viewed his own acquisition of nuclear weapons as being fully justified, he would probably see any $N + 1$th power as a threat to world peace.

Herman Kahn spoke of this danger as much as anybody. He assumed that, in the absence of controls, large numbers of weapons would be distributed to advanced and even some less advanced countries by the early 1970s. This would put far greater dependence on responsible governments and sophisticated forms of crisis management. Many of the problems he envisaged were with small nuclear powers fighting amongst themselves.[2] He was less worried than others about the fear of 'catalytic' war, in which a small nuclear power triggers off the cataclysm of a super-power nuclear war.[3] Kahn shared the intuitive

303

concern that the probabilities of disaster were increased as more countries gained access to nuclear capabilities.

While noting the general concerns over the spread of nuclear weapons the main interest here lies with views on the impact of nuclear proliferation on NATO.

NATO and the Nth Problem

During the 1950s the Eisenhower Administration, while expressing concern over the possible spread of nuclear weapons, had sought to head off the problem by making the benefits of nuclear technology available to its allies. Under the 'Atoms for Peace' programme, assistance was given for the construction of energy-generating nuclear reactors. While there were no actual transfers of nuclear warheads to allies, a large number of tactical nuclear weapons were made available under the 'double-key' system of shared control by the US and the host country. Impediments to nuclear co-operation with the United Kingdom were removed by amending the McMahon Act and there were tentative discussions over facilitating the development of nuclear delivery systems in France. In the last days of the Eisenhower Administration an offer was made by the US to create a 'NATO Deterrent', a force of 300 *Polaris* missiles to be put under the control of the NATO council, with the aim of reinforcing the deterrent while averting pressure for independent nuclear forces. Thus, whatever the doubts about the general diffusion of nuclear weapons, it was accepted that major powers within the Alliance would want some access to nuclear capabilities, and that it was therefore best if this could be done in a spirit of sharing American capabilities rather than by a series of separate national initiatives.

There were doubts about the wisdom of this approach. They were expressed forcefully in one of Albert Wohlstetter's influential articles in *Foreign Affairs*. Wohlstetter discussed four alternatives for NATO: rejection of nuclear weapons; development of autonomous nuclear forces; a jointly controlled nuclear force; and reliance on the United States guarantees. This latter option he found the most compelling, feeling that, given the coincidence of American and European interests, an American response to an attack on Europe was not incredible. He noted that credibility required not a certainty of response but only a high probability. This probability was 'clearly large' and could be increased by improved conventional forces.

Having noted this preference, it is necessary to turn to Wohlstetter's criticisms of national strike forces.

These forces were extremely expensive for they required a large initial outlay for the basic technology without the economies of scale available to the super-powers. The military value of small forces tended to be exaggerated by noting the damage to be done if they could be delivered *in toto* to enemy territory without taking into account the problems of both surviving surprise attacks and of penetrating anti-ballistic missile defences. 'A small strike force ... could inflict, not proportionately small damage, but possibly no damage at all.' If the problems of developing a 'responsible deterrent', now seen to be many, could be overcome in the United States, this was because of 'incomparable advantages of distance, size and industrial strength'.

The danger was that the vulnerability of nuclear forces based in Europe would encourage a hair-trigger response system to reduce the dangers of forces being caught before launching. This was exactly what Wohlstetter and his colleagues were worried about with US forces. An ability to absorb a first strike was so important because it removed the need to rush to nuclear use out of a fear of surprise attack. In this way 'the problem of forestalling deliberate attack is inseparable from that of preventing war by miscalculation'. The danger was of a loss of control.

> With the multiplication of national strike forces, the control problem becomes especially acute. If many nations have the power of decision, and if, in addition, each nation decentralizes its control to a multiplicity of subordinates, or worse, to some electronic automata, it is evident that the situation could get out of hand very easily.[4]

It was, of course, this sense of control that was so important to the strategic ideas under development at the time and which were taken up by Robert McNamara. The notion was that nuclear decisions should not be forced on a President by a lack of alternatives or a fear of surprise attack or an involuntary process of escalation. If nuclear weapons were to be understood as instruments of coercive diplomacy then every move that involved them should be cool, deliberate, and to some purpose. The weapons would be used to signal something as well as to destroy targets, warning of the dangers of unrestrained attacks on cities rather than moving inexorably towards these attacks. All this raised important questions of command and control.

Schelling noted that these questions related 'less to *who* controls the nuclear weapons than to *how* they are controlled in their use'.[5] However, the line of Wohlstetter's argument was that by their very nature these weapons were incapable of controlled use.

The ideas of 'city-avoidance' that came to the fore in the first year of McNamara's tenancy at the Pentagon also clashed with the European view. Because of their size, small nuclear forces could only be suitable for all-out attacks against cities. There was no scope for holding the enemy's population as a hostage by directing a first volley against military targets while keeping a second in reserve. In this way Malcolm Hoag explained the difference between the US and the European nuclear powers:

> What our strategic plenty gives us is the ability to choose among alternative tactics, each of which poses so formidable a threat to Soviet interests that it is a compelling deterrent even where we impose severe restraints upon ourselves. Smaller and less sophisticated nuclear systems, in order to pose a serious deterrent, must promise to be used in as blunt and bloody a manner as possible.[6]

McNamara was very keen on the concept of control, hoping that at every level of violence matters could still be managed in such a way as to prevent further escalation. According to Kaufmann, because he felt that any strategic nuclear exchange would involve all the nuclear powers, 'he was appalled at the prospect that such an exchange might start in an uncoordinated way and involve the wrong mixture of targets'.[7] This would be a likely result of nuclear proliferation within the Alliance. Enthoven and Smith indicate another argument informing McNamara's critique of independent nuclear deterrents – 'it meant that fewer resources would go into British and French conventional forces'.[8]

In his June 1962 speech in Athens to NATO Ministers (the same that was repeated a month later to a rather different audience of graduating seniors at Ann Arbor, Michigan) McNamara made his concern known in a triumph of logic over tact.

> [R]elatively weak national nuclear forces with enemy cities as their targets are not likely to be sufficient to perform even the function of deterrence. If they are small, and perhaps vulnerable on the ground or in the air, or inaccurate, a major antagonist can take a variety of measures to counter them. Indeed, if a major antagonist

came to believe there was a substantial likelihood of it being used independently, this force would be inviting a pre-emptive first strike against it. In the event of war, the use of such a force against the cities of a major nuclear power would be tantamount to suicide, whereas its employment against significant military targets would have a negligible effect on the outcome of the conflict. Meanwhile, the creation of a single additional national nuclear force encourages the proliferation of nuclear power with all its attendant dangers.

In short, then, limited nuclear capabilities, operating independently, are dangerous, expensive, prone to obsolescence and lacking in credibility as a deterrent.[9]

This damning judgment was directed, above all others, at the French – the British nuclear force being too well established to dislodge.

The British Nuclear Force

Through the 1950s British strategists such as Liddell Hart, Blackett, and Buzzard played an important role in developing the critiques of massive retaliation, with their influence extended well beyond Britain. However, as nuclear strategy became subject to the application of sophisticated methodologies, this influence waned. Britain's intellectual community lacked both the technical competence and resources for engaging in the sort of studies for which RAND was becoming noted, finding it difficult enough keeping up with the burgeoning American literature.[10]

Moreover, there was little disposition to attempt to become *au fait* with these new methodologies. As already noted, the British scientists who had helped to develop operations research became concerned that far too much was being claimed by contemporary practitioners.[11] Sir Basil Liddell Hart, who had always prided himself on his 'scientific' approach to military problems, found himself out of sympathy with the new analysts. He wrote to an American inquiring of his interest in game theory: 'I find that the jargon used by its exponents is more puzzling than illuminating. It also leaves doubts in my mind about the value of deductions drawn from it.'[12]

John Garnett suggests that there may be a British tendency to avoid 'pure' as opposed to 'applied' strategic thought. He adds that it is a 'moot point' as to whether this is a strength or a weakness.[13] Certainly, the battle lines encouraged by Hedley Bull in his famous comparison between the 'classical' and 'scientific' approaches to international relations supported the view that the British were more comfortable with notions derived from history, philosophy, and law rather than seeking answers in a pure form of logic or in scientifically testable empirical propositions.[14] In one of the major American works exploring new forms of nuclear strategy the editors noted, somewhat defensively, that the work could be criticized as 'abstruse theorizing' and quoted a complaint from the magazine *Survey*, 'that in the thermonuclear age military strategy begins to look like a game of chess without a chess board, that its mental construction and strategic anticipations are made in a world in which Kafka meets Lewis Carroll'. The editors added: 'This viewpoint is especially prevalent in England.'[15]

Nevertheless, British writers on nuclear deterrence were well aware of American analyses. The stress on the importance of invulnerability for retaliatory forces was picked up and transposed to British circumstances.[16] British strategists still considered themselves to be conducting a trans-Atlantic dialogue. But Alastair Buchan, directing the new Institute for Strategic Studies, was as concerned to encourage a debate amongst proponents of existing strategic concepts as to develop new concepts.[17]

It is important to emphasize that the British conducted their debates with the Americans as if the relevant issues were matters of shared responsibility. Neither the need for some form of deterrence nor an alliance was questioned. Unlike in France, where intellectual stimulus was found by opposing the Americans, there was no comparable search in Britain for a European alternative to dependence on the United States.

As with the American community and its own nuclear forces, the existence of some British component to NATO's nuclear forces was taken for granted. The question was over the extent of the rôle of the British deterrent, not over whether it had any rôle at all. There was little serious challenge to the British deterrent from inside the community of specialists on military affairs. There were doubts within this community: nuclear weapons were proving to be more expensive and technically troublesome than had once been hoped, and it was difficult to see how the resultant force could make a significant contribution to the Alliance when American forces had grown so mighty. Doubts such as these were expressed within both major political parties. Many were aware of the problems of vulnerability under discussion in the United States, and felt that the British force of bombers would not score well on this criterion. However, the real pressure for abandoning the British deterrent came from outside the political establishment.

The intellectual case for nuclear disarmament has been discussed in an earlier chapter. In terms of the current discussion, it is worth noting only that the case was not presented in Alliance terms.[18] Though the argument could on occasions be heard that there was no need for the British to contaminate themselves with such immoral things as nuclear weapons so long as the United States was willing to carry the burden, the arguments of the unilateralists went well beyond this, criticizing any connection with weapons of mass destruction. For example, Stephen King-Hall wrote that:

It would be an essential feature of the UND (Unilateral Nuclear Disarmament) policy that we make it clear beyond all doubt to our American friends that *in no circumstances whatsoever did we wish to be 'protected' by, or in any way associated with, their nuclear capacity.*[19]

The unilateralists were thus not offering a better nuclear strategy for NATO as were the American critics of the European forces; they were shunning nuclear weapons altogether.

The supporters of the British nuclear force did not present their case as an exercise in strategic logic. The framework was that of the need for deterrence, but within that framework a variety of purposes were, at different times, discerned for the British force. It was, if anything, subject to a law of diminishing rationales. In terms of deterring the Soviet Union, it was felt in the late 1940s that a British force might be necessary to make up the numbers in a Western retaliatory force against the East. By the early 1950s, when it was recognized that the United States could provide an imposing threat without Britain's help, it was argued that there might be targets of particular interest to Britain that might be neglected if the responsibility for the retaliatory strike was solely in American hands. By the early 1960s, with America having sufficient warheads to cover the whole of the Warsaw Pact target structure, the British were reduced to making a marginal European contribution to the retaliatory forces.

In 1957 the Government had reaffirmed its commitment to a policy of massive retaliation in uncompromising terms at the same time that the US Administration was beginning to have doubts. The critique of massive retaliation, however, had been developed in Britain at the same time as in the United States and, led by Liddell Hart and Blackett, evolved during the 1950s towards the view that the balance in NATO's force structure ought to be redressed in favour of conventional defence. Labour Party defence specialists encouraged this trend. One chapter in a book written by John Strachey was entitled 'A reversal of NATO's strategy', and argued for more conventional forces.[20]

The debate over nuclear strategy was thus couched in NATO terms. As some sort of 'great power' status could still be taken for granted, there was no need (yet) for symbols that might proclaim the nation's significance to doubting foreigners. More important, the British had always viewed nuclear issues as an Anglo-American matter, seeking to gain access to US nuclear secrets as a matter of right, a proper return on Britain's own war-time investment in atom bomb research. Diplomatic effort had been devoted to encouraging interdependence with the Americans in nuclear matters rather than striving for independence. The 1958 amendments to the US McMahon Act made greater Anglo-American co-operation possible. This, plus the rhetoric of the 'special relationship', actively discouraged any interest in either an independent force or a strategic doctrine to support one.

The developing dependence of Britain on the US was most evident in the area of delivery vehicles. After plans for a British ballistic missile, *Blue Streak*, had been aborted, President Eisenhower agreed in 1960 to sell Britain the *Skybolt* air-launched missile, then under development. In return the British agreed to make available a base for US nuclear submarines at Holy Loch in Scotland. Unfortunately the *Skybolt* programme was beset with difficulties and these led to its cancellation in November 1962. The British affected surprise though they had been warned of the programme's problems.[21] The abrupt cancellation undermined Britain's nuclear programme and underlined the extent to which nuclear weapons were creating a form of dependence on the United States rather than becoming a source of influence. Britain's limited influence was clearly indicated by the minimal consultation Britain enjoyed during the Cuban Missile Crisis that had taken place two months before. To salvage Anglo-American relations, a hastily arranged summit conference was convened at Nassau between Prime Minister Macmillan and President Kennedy.

This resulted in a deal by which Britain was allowed to purchase *Polaris* submarine-launched missiles.

This put the British force on a much sounder basis, given the reduced vulnerability of a submarine-based force. The option had been available in 1960 and it had been foolishly rejected by the British in favour of *Skybolt*. The agreement at Nassau stipulated that the UK *Polaris* submarines would be used 'for the purpose of international defence of the Western Alliance in all circumstances.' In this way the proposals could be a compromise between Alliance integration and national independence. However the agreement was unclear as to whether the Alliance nuclear force to which Britain was contributing was to be constructed as a multilateral or multinational force. Moreover, the final decision on use was with the British, based on their own understanding of whether 'supreme national interests' were 'at stake'. It is, of course, only where supreme national interests are at stake that the question of whether or not to use nuclear weapons arises at all. Nevertheless, the underlying loyalty to the Alliance forced the British to pull their punches when explaining the need for their own forces.

The rationales used to justify this 'independent' force were as much political as strategic, stressing the opportunities for the exercise of benign influence when all nuclear issues, from disarmament to NATO planning, were discussed. The argument had never been far below the surface. Prime Minister Harold Macmillan spoke in 1958 of how:

> The independent contribution ... gives us a better position in the world, it gives us a better position with respect to the United States. It puts us where we ought to be, in the position of a Great Power. The fact that we have it makes the United States pay a greater regard to our point of view, and that is of great importance.[22]

After 1962 this argument was emphasized. Macmillan's successor, Alec Douglas-Home, spoke of the bomb as a 'ticket of admission', providing 'a place at the peace table as of right'.[23]

The second argument, which became more prominent in the 1960s and which came to constitute the strongest popular rationale for the force, was based on the unreliability of the Alliance. It was often presented as a simple assertion that in a cruel and uncertain world, where others may get nuclear weapons and the United States' own willingness to engage in nuclear war on Europe's behalf was open to doubt, an independent British force was a necessary form of insurance. Without actually going so far as to directly question the US guarantee, the 1964 Statement on Defence diplomatically raised this point: '[I]f there were no power in Europe capable of inflicting unacceptable damage on a potential enemy he might be tempted ... to attack in the mistaken belief that the United States would not act unless America herself were attacked.'[24] This theory of a 'second decision-centre', has been adhered to consistently because it provides little challenge to NATO orthodoxy.

There were problems in constructing plausible scenarios in which Britain 'stood alone' yet still had the US furnishing the necessary support to keep the *Polaris* fleet operational, or in which the USSR picked Britain out for special treatment in a crisis, or in which there was any particular point in Britain rattling its nuclear weapons while the Soviet Army made its way across Europe. However, the main difficulty in dwelling on the possibility of acting independently of an alliance was that NATO remained in existence and that its preservation, backed by a forceful US nuclear commitment, was a prime objective of British policy. Excessive speculation on how it might be possible to do without the US could provide Washington with the necessary excuse. Hence the need to argue that the danger was not of the US reneging on its nuclear guarantee but of a mistaken Soviet belief that this might happen, to be corrected by forcing it to worry about another centre of nuclear decision.

The British Government was pleased to stress Britain's force as a contribution to NATO. No attempt was made to keep up with American ideas on flexible options; the theory behind them was either ignored or dismissed as American faint-heartedness about the awfulness of the capability they had created. As the *Polaris* programme turned out to be remarkably inexpensive, only modest justification to the British public for it was deemed necessary.

In 1980, contemplating the obsolescence of *Polaris* in the 1990s, there seemed to be no better successor than the same type of submarine force, this time equipped with US *Trident* missiles.[25] It was justified within exactly the same strategic and political framework as before. The only doubt was whether the economically weak British could afford the new system without damaging the over-stretched conventional forces. As the American connection made the force possible, the British were happy to suppress doubts as to US intentions towards NATO in order to stay in the nuclear business. The intellectual satisfaction, but financial burdens, of devising arguments for completely self-sufficient forces was left to France.

21 The European Nuclear Option (ii) French and German Views

During the 1950s NATO strategy was dominated by nuclear weapons; the more the United States and Britain demonstrated their status and influence through a stockpile of nuclear weapons, the more France wanted to secure her place amongst the major powers by nuclear means. Following the humiliations of the German occupation and then the loss of Indo-China, nuclear weapons were seen as a possible aid to national recovery, boosting morale and ensuring that France returned to her proper rank amongst the nations. After de Gaulle became President in 1958, the nuclear programme became a key instrument in his endeavours to reassert France's distinctive identity and to enable Europe to become independent from the superpowers. 'A Great State', explained de Gaulle, which does not possess nuclear weapons while others have them 'does not command its own destiny.'[1]

Under de Gaulle, French nuclear strategy became linked to a challenge to the very concept of an Alliance. In this the French went further than the British, who considered an independent nuclear force to be an insurance against the withdrawal of America's nuclear protection but not a substitute for this protection. The French characterized the US nuclear guarantee as being a flimsy foundation for security, much inferior to a national effort. While the British spoke in a rather circumspect manner about America's future reliability, displaying embarrassment at questioning the scruples of a friend, the French enjoyed the frank disclosure of the unreliability of America's nuclear guarantees.

In mounting their challenge to NATO, the French articulated some distinctive strategic notions. They were distinctive, first because they opposed the dominant trends in US strategic thought and, second, because nothing quite so robust emerged from British strategists. The British Government did not encourage the souring of relations with the United States despite the policy differences which existed.

Gallois

French strategic thought became associated with two retired Generals, Pierre Gallois and André Beaufre. In an early article in an American journal Gallois spoke of the revolutionary consequences of the advent of nuclear weapons.[2] He introduced some themes which became prominent in his later writings, including the differences in attitudes caused by unequal access to nuclear weapons. Those who possessed nuclear weapons 'hold the trump cards for an active policy'. Their allies had to be more cautious, and those without weapons or the prospect of a useful alliance were neutralist. A nation with nuclear weapons, so long as they could deny the enemy the ability to destroy his retaliatory capacity, enjoyed 'self-protection', for no aggressor would launch an attack while there was a risk of serious retaliation. Gallois had confidence that ways could be found of assuring retaliation. Those who were denied this self-protection had to hope that they represented a sufficient stake for a super-power protector to risk nuclear war for their security. This represented a potential element of division within states – 'no one is sure of remaining on the right side of the atomic "bomb line"'. There was reason for doubt. 'As long as there remains an uncertainty about the air-nuclear power guaranteeing the sovereignty of Western Europe, the risk will remain complete for the attacker and for the defender.'

Gallois was sure in 1956 that a conventional defence of Western Europe was futile and he never wavered in this conviction. In the event of attack, resort to nuclear weapons would be unavoidable and he was nervous about the readiness of Western Governments to accept this requirement. He worried about the weaknesses of democracies in this regard. 'In the event of a crisis, the allied nations, if they want to survive, ought to rely on the resolution of the men charged with their defense.' Modern weapons allowed no time for hesitation. 'We are approaching the time when the menace will move faster than a mind can be made up.'

In 1960 Gallois published an influential book which took his thoughts further.[3] By now he was concerned about the credibility of NATO's deterrent. As the disincentives for US nuclear action grew, he sought for ways to enhance credibility. His analysis of the dynamics of nuclear war itself was not uniquely deep or original. He had little confidence in counter-force or in first strikes and believed that a nuclear war of any size soon escalated into a general war. Of greater interest were his observations on the problem of 'will':

> In principle, a determined policy of deterrence could solve all Western military problems. If the potential assailant believed that even on the occasion of a conflict of secondary importance to himself, the opposing side would not hesitate, rather than surrender, to use its nuclear arsenal, he would have to abandon force as a means of persuasion.[4]

The problem was that Western nations were not made of stern enough stuff. Gallois preferred retaliation so automatic that no unfriendly nation would dare be provocative, but even a small risk of retaliation might be sufficient. Unfortunately, the tendency to make reluctance to risk nuclear warfare so self-evident was reducing the deterrent effect of America's nuclear arsenal. The only way to regain this deterrent effect was to exploit the political sources of credibility.

Credibility, as noted earlier, was a difficult concept because it resided ultimately in the mind of the beholder rather than in the one who was trying to create the impression. In the pre-nuclear age, one's reputation could be related to past military performance, but in the nuclear age there were no such performances to refer to. Credibility had therefore to be based on speculations as to future reactions to specified circumstances, known as 'scenarios'. The problem was that in many cases it was hard to demonstrate how an opponent could be convinced that it would be rational to execute a retaliatory threat. One alternative was to demonstrate a certain recklessness, even irrationality. Gallois felt that an element of bluff in this area might work, but doubted whether it could be sustained by the West.[5] A better answer could be found in the interests at stake. Gallois did not succeed in demonstrating how a nuclear response would be rational even when supreme national interests were threatened, but intuitively he had a point in suggesting that retaliation was more likely following an attack on oneself than when the attack was directed at a friendly third party.

Though the nation-state, as a more solid unit than an alliance, might be more likely to respond, there was a problem over whether the available response would be unpleasant enough to deter the potential aggressor. Here Gallois developed one of his most influential concepts, that of 'proportional deterrence'. The theory was simple: 'The thermonuclear force can be proportional to the value of the stake it is defending.'[6] The pain that might be endured to eliminate America would not be endured if the prize was only France. A sort of cost/benefit calculus could be developed to identify the sort of punitive response necessary to hold back an aggressor from seizing any specified prize.

There were two criticisms of this view. First, a small country had to expend a disproportionate amount of resources as against a superpower to achieve a given amount of nuclear firepower. Second, the concept of sufficient cost to outweigh prospective gain was not so distant from those ideas of flexible or measured response that Gallois opposed. However, Gallois did not believe non-nuclear defence was feasible, nor did he believe in limited nuclear strikes. His interest was more in accumulating sufficient firepower to provide for national deterrence than in whether it was possible to get away with using only a small, measured proportion of this firepower.

Gallois' name also became associated with the idea of universal nuclear deterrence, in which all states, great and small, attain stability through a series of mutual nuclear threats. He also provided the intellectual source of de Gaulle's critique of NATO. However, though he did become a proponent of de Gaulle's ideas and though his ideas did tend towards universal deterrence, thus providing a rationale for any proliferation, his concepts were developed initially to support NATO. His view was that NATO should exploit the greater credibility of national nuclear deterents. He advocated a policy of nuclear decentralization within the Alliance. Generalizing 'the policy of national dissuasion' would 'force the aggressor to accept the responsibility and the risks inherent in any modification of the territorial *status quo* in Europe'. In facing a collection of nuclear forces, the Soviet Union would have to accept a greater risk of retaliation if it wished to invade.

Gallois believed in the obsolescence of conventional forces in the nuclear age. In an environment in which nuclear forces could be used it would not be possible to concentrate forces, organize lines of supply, and mobilize reserves as in the past. Preparations for nuclear war and those for conventional war could not coexist. 'Once committed to the atom, it is impossible to draw back.' His complaint against the US Administration was that it attempted to do just that. The result would be to leave the Europeans more vulnerable by denying them the best means of protection in the face of an enemy armed with both conventional and nuclear weapons. He also recognized that a conventional strategy, though militarily inadequate, reduced the risk for the United States. This divergence of strategic interests created a crisis in NATO. It could only be solved by the US fully sharing nuclear risks with its allies and by renewing the old promise 'of an unconditional guarantee of the security of Western Europe'. Otherwise, the Europeans would have to look to their own nuclear devices.[7]

The question raised by Gallois concerned the amount of automaticity there needed to be in the nuclear response before it acted as a deterrent. On the one hand it might be thought that the consequences of retaliation for the aggressor were so great that the slightest possibility of retaliation would suffice as a constraint. On the other hand, a bold enough aggressor could calculate that the consequences of nuclear war for the other side could well result in a lack of nuclear response. There was a tension in Gallois' thought between these two propositions, but he tended towards the latter, mainly because the responsibility for retaliation in a period of super-power nuclear monopoly rested with a country not directly threatened by an invasion of Western Europe. This tendency was encouraged by what he saw as an active US policy aimed at reducing the risks for any aggressor.

Nevertheless, even a national response would not be wholly automatic. A decision would still have to be made to retaliate. Alternatively, as the US critics of the European forces pointed out, there might be no decision to be made because an enemy surprise attack backed by air defences could render the deterrent useless. Gallois' case rested in the end not on automatic retaliation or on an unusually credible configuration of forces, but on the way that a nation-state could see itself as a unity in a way that an alliance of nation-states could not. It was therefore more likely to lash out when attacked.

But if the most plausible unit for a credible deterrent was a nation-state, then no coalition of states, even if they were all European, could rely on just one of their number holding nuclear weapons. The only exception to this rule might be where the nuclear state was the one that shared a border with the potential aggressor. In NATO's case this would be West Germany (Norway and Turkey could be discounted), a country for whom nuclear aspirations raised immense political problems. Gallois' strategic logic led to profound and difficult political conclusions, which became apparent when they were taken up by de Gaulle (without much prompting by Gallois).

Beaufre

The methodology of General André Beaufre was different from that of Gallois, relying more on abstract model-building, and he by no means shared Gallois' enthusiasm for the declining strategy of massive retaliation. He was not enamoured with ideas of 'proportional deterrence', nor was he dismissive of 'flexible response'. The essential feature of Beaufre's thought was his insistence on the new and distinctive requirements imposed by a strategy of deterrence and the rôle he saw for local nuclear forces within this strategy. Nuclear weapons involved a new level of conflict, a movement 'from a war strategy to a strategy of potential threat; in other words to a strategy of *deterrence*'. The object of this strategy was 'to *prevent* an enemy power *taking the decision* to use armed force'. The desired result was psychological, produced by 'the combined effect of a *calculation* of the risk incurred compared to the issue at stake and of the *fear* engendered by the risks and uncertainties of conflict'.[8]

The strategy depended on manipulating the enemy's sense of this risk, by 'the non-employment of nuclear weapons through judicious exploitation of the fact that they exist'. Because of this Beaufre felt that the technical qualities of weapons were far less important than their political and psychological impact.

The main political impact of nuclear weapons was the stability it introduced into relations between the super-powers. Whenever their major interests were at stake the situation congealed, both sides being aware of the dangers of any radical challenges. For the allies of a super-power the problem came if their interests were not coincident with those of the super-power. What risks would a super-power take in support on matters it considered marginal to its own survival? Unlike Gallois, Beaufre did not assume that alliances were virtually impossible in these conditions. Deterrence was a peacetime activity and alliances did not fall apart in peacetime. The need was to strengthen deterrence to compensate for weaknesses by increasing the risks for the potential enemy. Beaufre considered the best way to achieve this was a series of nuclear forces. By generalizing the danger this created a new form of solidarity; the Allies had to work together.

Because there would be multiple decision-centres, a new form of uncertainty was introduced for the enemy, inducing caution. This multilateral deterrence would be more stable than if only two opponents were involved.

In a 1965 article, Beaufre provided a succinct statement of his views. The problem was to restore 'the credibility of a threat which everyone knows to have become unreal'. To achieve this 'everything possible should be done to ensure that the threat should retain that minimum of spontaneous risk which leads to that prudence indispensable to the maintenance of peace'. To do this:

Different methods must simultaneously be used to keep the enemy's mind in that *state of uncertainty* which alone can render deterrence effective; thus, to enable several methods of deterrence to be used simultaneously, *there must be several centres of decision.* The basic conclusion is contrary to American policies; in fact these have for too long focused upon the stabilisation of the nuclear threshold although it is today so stable that it needs to be, so to speak, 'destabilised' to restore its deterrent effect.[9]

Beaufre's response to the growing incredibility of threats of nuclear retaliation was not to assert the greater plausibility of a purely national response or that conditions could be created in which any single decision on activating the deterrence threat could be made rational. He could not even demonstrate how a multiplicity of decisions made nuclear use more likely, only that it added complexity to the enemy's calculations. The impact was felt through the psychology of uncertainty rather than the logic of certainty. It was a threat that left a lot to chance, based on the danger of a situation getting out of control. In this it was completely at variance with McNamara's attempts to establish a capacity for measured escalation with every step under centralized control.

Beaufre was motivated by a desire to increase the solidarity of the Alliance and not to compensate for its fragmentation. However, the mechanisms by which Alliance solidarity would come into play in the nuclear sense remained unclear. For example much of the discussion of the French nuclear forces in the 1960s spoke of its rôle as a detonator of the American nuclear arsenal. According to Raymond Aron: 'The threat, though no explicit, of using the French atomic force as a detonator is its sole conceivable deterrence function within the framework of the present Atlantic organization.'[10] Many in the

US Administration certainly felt this to be a key part of the opposition case with which they had to contend. Perhaps it indicated a more precise causal relationship than the vaguer notions of multilateral deterrence. To the extent that they understood the notion they found it unimpressive.[11]

The most sophisticated discussion of the concept was by an American, Glenn Snyder, who himself did not favour it. He noted two types of triggering. The first was 'emotional'. If the Russians were provoked into a counter-force nuclear attack on a European country to disarm her of a nuclear capacity, then the shock to the US could be strong enough to stimulate a nuclear response. The second type was 'attritional' in which the expenditure of nuclear weapons in a disarming first strike would leave the Soviet Union vulnerable to a US attack. In both these cases Snyder saw the feasibility of the strategy to be dependent on the balance of forces at the time. In particular he felt it related to 'the first-strike counter-force capability of the United States', in that without a significant capability of this sort the United States could not afford to let her nuclear arsenal be triggered by someone else.[12]

The difficulty in believing in the 'detonator' concept was the difficulty in believing that even in the most favourable of strategic conditions the Americans would allow such a fundamental act as the use of nuclear weapons to be shaped simply by the force of events and not by deliberate decision. Nevertheless, there was an argument that the existence of independent nuclear forces simply raised the stakes of a conflict to the extent that general war became harder to avoid. It was no worse an argument, though somewhat more irresponsible, than that which stated that a substantial conventional force, even if capable of holding a determined assault, would force the enemy to throw more resources into the battle, so making it a less limited affair and more likely to degenerate into general war. In any attempt to demonstrate the plausibility of nuclear use it was extremely difficult to demonstrate why a rational actor should behave in such a way: the most convincing cases were those where the environment in which the decision on use had to be made was not conducive to rationality.

De Gaulle

Though not responsible for the conception of the French *force de frappe* President Charles de Gaulle turned it into a central instrument of his own diplomacy. He does not appear to have been influenced by his country's strategic theorists, though he did adopt the idea of 'proportional deterrence'. De Gaulle is reported to have replied to one strategist who had sent him a copy of his latest book that the analysis was all very interesting, but there was but one issue: 'Est-ce que la France restera la France?'[13]

The main rôle he saw for France's nuclear force was determined by his view that nuclear weapons were the major source of contemporary international power and influence. Towards the end of the 1950s he attempted to use the French force to justify participation in a proposed Alliance Directorate (with America and Britain). Later he saw nuclear weapons as a way of providing France with a distinctive identity and a power base from which to criticize the hegemonic aspirations of the United States. Any original contribution to nuclear strategy comes from this intensely political approach. Nuclear weapons provided the starting point for a radical critique of the Alliance system within Europe.

The argument was simple and had an old-fashioned appeal. Dependence on the United States for nuclear protection created a political dependence. The United States, via the flexible response strategy, was attempting to maintain this dependency relationship by assigning to Europe only a non-nuclear function in the Alliance. Europe was thus left vulnerable, in any crisis, to the whims of Washington. In the long run the situation was even more dangerous, for Europe's political position would be determined by the character of the political relations between the super-powers. A war between them, even if its origins had nothing to do with Europe, could be the ruination of the continent; in a condominium Europe could get sold out and her interests forgotten in a super-power agreement. De Gaulle noted in 1959, not long after becoming President of the Fifth Republic: 'Probably the sort of equilibrium that is establishing itself between the atomic power of the two camps is, for the moment, a factor in world peace, but who can say what will happen tomorrow.'[14]

By the mid-1960s his views had matured. The Soviet threat had diminished while the Americans were becoming more threatening, by getting themselves into dangerous adventures in Vietnam. In 1966, though not leaving the Atlantic Alliance, de Gaulle withdrew French forces from NATO's Integrated Military Command. Participation in a joint military effort in the future would be conditional. It would not be enough to know that her Allies were under attack; France would want to know who started the conflict.

The full strategic rationale for this policy was presented by General d'Armée, Charles Ailleret. Ailleret's argument was that it was no longer possible to plan for war against 'a single, well-defined, possible enemy' because the future was so uncertain:

> The world situation offers us ... a spectacle of such disorder, such agitation, such development, that while it is hardly possible to identify anywhere precisely the potential threats to our own country, it is also impossible to rely on the present balances of power in order to forecast the future.

Meanwhile, NATO was too constricting. It atrophied the nation's 'independent means of defence'. The determination of the Americans to keep the Alliance under their control made it unresponsive to European interests. The propensity of the Americans to get themselves into fights elsewhere in the world could result in Europeans being dragged into an unnecessary war. 'NATO thus presented a great danger for us'. Ailleret saw the need for flexibility, not in the way the Americans used this term in referring to military options, but as a capacity to respond to threats anywhere on the globe.

To provide this flexibility all that was needed was a significant number of 'megaton ballistic missiles of a world-wide range'. Ailleret had a simple faith in the efficiency of nuclear weapons, particularly for deterrent purposes, no matter who needed deterring and for what reasons. Those missiles would not be orientated in only one direction but 'be capable of intervening everywhere, or as we say in our military jargon, at every point of the compass (*tous azimuts*).' Such a system for France:

> [W]ould wield the maximum power afforded by its national resources and ... handled with as much sang-froid as determination, should enable it, by dissuasion, to avoid certain major wars and, if it cannot, then to take part in them under the best conditions; in short, a system which, during future crises that may rock the world, would place France in a position where she could freely determine her own destiny.[15]

There were three main flaws in this bold conception. First, Gaullist strategy was not merely anticipating a new international strategy but helping to create it. By helping to destroy NATO the arrival of the anticipated new world order could be accelerated. Yet though de Gaulle shook the Alliance, it did not fall apart. The division of Europe into two armed camps persisted, only now France occupied an anomalous position within this system. De Gaulle failed to develop any alternative. Though he spoke of a united Europe 'from the Atlantic to the Urals' this conception was riddled with contradictions. The British were to be excluded as being an extension of the American super-power. At least part of the other super-power was apparently to be included, but how?; and what about her attempts at hegemony, particularly over Eastern Europe? At the centre of it all, France was to be the focal point for the new Europe, but the problem of inconsistencies between the national interests of France and the more general interests of her neighbours was not followed up. The consequences of de Gaulle's policy were the opposite to those intended. Germany became the *de facto* leader of Europe within NATO while the French efforts only divided Western Europe, rendering super-power hegemony easier.

The second flaw in the Gaullist strategy was that the French lacked the resources to carry it out. They failed to develop a global nuclear capability; only one with a regional range. Nor were they ever able to explain how they could present a credible nuclear deterrent *tous azimuts*, especially given problems of warning time and vulnerability.

The consequence of these two flaws was to leave France as an essentially European power, operating within an environment in which the core political arrangements, in contrast to those in other regions, appeared quite stable. The continuity in political relationships ensured that NATO's traditional strategic problem – that of a major Soviet invasion of Europe – remained the most serious and the one French planners had to address. Here they came up against the third flaw in the Gaullist strategy – the tension between the suggestion that through the *Force de Frappe*, France could become a sanctuary, aloof from a war in which she may not wish to take sides, and the admission that in certain cases she might wish to take sides. The more planners concentrated on scenarios which would touch upon France's NATO obligations, the more Gaullist notions of a dignified independence would have to be qualified by the logic of alliance.

In the standard NATO scenario of a Soviet attack on Germany, France might feel sufficiently threatened to join her Allies in battle but not inclined to start a nuclear war. As with any other responsible Government, it would want to leave some opportunity for diplomatic activity. As with NATO generally in the 1950s, tactical nuclear weapons were seized upon as a means of demonstrating a seriousness of purpose, perhaps to useful military effect, but without triggering the holocaust. To fulfil this purpose a short-range missile, *Pluton*, was produced. Unfortunately when deployed on French soil they could only bombard German soil, recognition of which caused consternation in both Bonn and Paris.

When the Gaullist hold of French Government was eased in 1974 with the election of President Giscard d'Estaing, these problems were addressed and there were tentative indications of a move towards something akin to 'flexible response'. In March 1976, General Guy Mery introduced the concept of *extended sanctuarization*, to 'allow us to intervene with the whole or part of our forces throughout the entire zone where the security of this country may be immediately threatened'. Such a concept recognized a possible need to 'participate in the forward battle area', from which it 'would be extremely dangerous' to remain aloof. A 'battle of the frontiers' would result only if the forward area crumbled too quickly, perhaps because the French were unable to make up their minds on intervention or were impeded in doing so by the enemy.[16]

None of this went down very well with orthodox Gaullists. A year later, when Prime Minister Raymond Barre was describing Government thinking, he drew more on Gaullist rhetoric, but he could not hide the drift back to a more Alliance-oriented approach. However he was able to make it clear that France, like Britain, would have little to do with any selective, counter-force targeting. The 'anti-cities strategy' was the only one that could be 'truly deterrent'.[17]

German Strategy

Unlike the French, the Germans were not responsible for any innovation in strategic thought. They provided some of the most fervent critics of flexible response, but only within a framework derived from the theories of the Eisenhower Administration with which they had become accustomed as they re-armed themselves under NATO auspices in the 1950s. Catherine Kelleher notes that even though by 1966 Germany was once again Western Europe's largest conventional power there was little capacity within the Bonn Government to sustain a dialogue on strategy with Washington, let alone the independent analyses of the type performed at RAND. The major German contribution to the dialogue came from the colourful language of the formidable Defence Minister from 1956 to 1962, Franz Josef Strauss, who once described some of the sophisticated concepts used by the Americans to be 'conceptual aids for the precalculation of the inconceivable and incalculable nature of the specific'.[18]

Whatever their formal contribution to theory, their sensitive geographical and political position had given the Germans a determining influence on the character of NATO. To a West Germany contemplating the follies of the 1930s and 1940s and the consequent division of the country there was a strong impulse to integrate itself fully within the community of Western nations. A national identity could only be regained in an international context, by solidarity with others, either through the European Community or NATO. Germany sought to answer its own problems within a multilateral framework and thus provided a strong force for cohesion within the Alliance. Solidarity with the West was reinforced by fear and loathing of the East, particularly in view of the continued occupation of a portion of the country. Through the 1950s and much of the 1960s Germany brooked no thought of sanctifying the division of Germany, insisting that reunification remained an objective of Western policy. Though most Western Governments had no intention of doing anything about this policy, the German position on this matter imposed limits on Western diplomacy. Forms of East–West detente and disengagement were held up until the late 1960s when the Bonn Government finally accepted the *status quo* and then became a major force behind the detente process.

In military terms West Germany also had a constraining influence. It was on German soil that NATO and the Warsaw Pact faced each other, and if the Soviet Union decided on expansion it was expected that West Germany would be the first to face the invasion. Because Germany was the wrong shape for defence (having little East–West depth) it was in the country's interest to insist on holding the line as close as possible to the border. The need was for 'forward defence'. It was difficult to see how this could be guaranteed absolutely with conventional weapons. A barrier defence at the border was unacceptable because it gave the border a political status. The mobile forces favoured by NATO's armies could not avoid ceding some territory. Given Germany's history an offensive or pre-emptive strategy was politically unthinkable. This meant that battles would be fought on German soil and the consequences would be devastating, particularly if the Alliance had to resort to tactical nuclear weapons.

As it was difficult to imagine any war which Germany could survive, the emphasis had to be on deterrence. Furthermore, the more automatic the deterrent threat the better. There was a fear in concepts of a 'pause' or a limited conventional engagement. By the time the nuclear threat became explicit, a portion of Germany would have been occupied. A Soviet agreement to go no further, accepted with relief by the Allies, would leave Germany dismembered. To quote Strauss:

> Does anyone believe that if a dividing line between atomic and conventional weapons is allowed, the democracies will then say 'If you don't go back and surrender [your] booty, then tomorrow at six o'clock, total atomic war begins with which we will drive you back.'[19]

As Germany was being rehabilitated during the 1950s, views such as these constituted the official and American-inspired wisdom within NATO. The fledgling German forces were planned along these lines. As in many other areas, the German response to attempts to revise NATO canons was rigid support of the *status quo*. There was only one area where the Germans argued for a change, and that was the area of the control of nuclear weapons.

In order to make German rearmament more palatable, the Bonn Government had agreed in 1954 'not to manufacture in its territory any atomic weapons'. There is no evidence that there has ever been any interest in, let alone plans for, reneging on this pledge. However, German leaders did become adept at playing on fears of a Germany armed with nuclear weapons. Many in the West as well as the East feared the consequences of a resurgent nationalism in a nuclear Germany. The fears were given credence by those who saw nuclear proliferation as a sort of epidemic rather than a consequence of a series of individual national decisions. The Germans were interested in control over nuclear decisions that affected them. They argued for some responsibility for the decisions and control of the relevant weapons.

Because nuclear weapons were presented during the 1950s as the most modern and only really decisive armament, to be without them meant relegation to a second class. Such a position would be contrary to Germany's desire to demonstrate her return as a responsible country. In addition, if everyone else had tactical nuclear weapons there was little point in Germany being left out. NATO's deterrent would be weakened if the country most in danger of invasion lacked the best means of countering that invasion. Germany's position gave her a better argument than any other European country that access to nuclear weapons could strengthen deterrence by making their use more plausible.

The Multilateral Force (MLF)

It was not an independent German arsenal that was proposed, nor special rights of access to US nuclear weapons. The proposal was for a shared NATO nuclear force, distinct from the independent forces. The advantage of such a force would be the participation of all the Allies in these life-and-death decisions. It would be a force that embodied and expressed NATO solidarity and, because this force would be based in and around Europe, it would provide a specific counter to the large medium-range forces accumulated by the East and targeted upon Europe. In different ways both the Eisenhower and Kennedy Administrations felt a need to respond to this idea. It seemed to offer a compromise between the independent forces and an American monopoly. Rather than resist the tide of proliferation it could be harnessed.[20]

A great variety of schemes for a multilateral force were devised and one was almost implemented. The thought of devolving nuclear capabilities occurred to a number of strategists in the 1950s, including Kissinger and Paul Nitze. General Norstad proposed a medium-range ballistic missile force to replace NATO strike aircraft as they became obsolescent. The missiles would be under SACEUR's control, but manned by international crews and operating on 'guidelines' laid down by the NATO Council. After an initial loss of enthusiasm, the Kennedy Administration proposed a comparable system that came to be known as the Multilateral Force (MLF), involving an internationally manned fleet of surface or submarine missile ships under the command of Supreme Commander Atlantic (as SACEUR, an American) or under a new NATO command, also operating according to NATO Council 'guidance'. Finally in 1965 the British Government proposed yet another scheme; the Atlantic Nuclear Force (ANF). This was to be a multinational force, composed of an equal number of British and American *Polaris* submarines, with a mixed-manned *Polaris* surface fleet on the MLF pattern (which would not have included Britain). All this would be placed at NATO's disposal. As intended, the effect of the British proposal for the ANF was to deprive the MLF of any momentum it might have had left.

Throughout the whole episode it was only the Germans who displayed any real interest in the proposals. Alastair Buchan wrote in 1964: 'In the depths of German thought the MLF had been, and still is, conceived as the German equivalent of the British and French independent deterrents.'[21] On the whole, while most other Governments could think of no strong objections to the proposals, few could think of any strong grounds for approbation.

The difficulty with all these schemes was straightforward. McNamara argued cogently for a centralized decision-making process in which every move up or down the escalatory ladder could be carefully controlled. A degree of consultation in forward planning or in the management of small local crises was tolerable but no more. Others, such as Beaufre, argued for multiple decision-centres so as to sow the seeds of uncertainty in the enemy by demonstrating a lack of single control. To both these schools nuclear sharing was a futile compromise. It would lead to clumsy control mechanisms and, because of the nature of pluralistic decision-taking, would encourage inaction in a crisis rather than action.

Though the MLF became US policy, the impetus came from the State Department rather than the Pentagon. An indication of the views of those surrounding McNamara is found in a critique by Albert Wohlstetter. Wohlstetter suggested that one motive for nuclear sharing was the desire to have a veto over US 'trigger-happiness'. However, 'if those who jointly control the NATO force are principally interested in the power to say "No", then the response of the joint force is less credible than the US guarantee'. The Americans would have a vote and so could still exercise a veto if a strike was not considered to be in the US interest. The nature of coalition decision-making made it likely that one country could exercise a veto. On the other hand, because the bulk of US forces would remain outside the sharing scheme, no serious control could be exercised over the US.[22]

Pierre Gallois also noted the problem of the veto-power of individual allies as a source of paralysis in a multilateral force. He saw the US proposals as an attempt to circumscribe the NATO nuclear forces by placing them under American control, again helping to guarantee against the risk of escalation in Western Europe. He also noted that the MLF under offer was a numerically small anti-city force, exactly the sort that McNamara had considered dangerous when discussing national nuclear forces.[23] Beaufre felt that any new force to be effective had to represent an autonomous centre of decision, and such a centre could not be international.[24]

Perhaps the most effective critic of MLF was Alastair Buchan. In 1963, Buchan argued that control, and not the manning of a weapon system, was the issue. Control would involve either a single military officer or the NATO council or some appendage: 'Fifteen fingers on the safety catch – or one on the trigger. Neither formula seems a recipe for stability, or for Soviet confidence in the responsibility as well as the determination, of the NATO Alliance.'[25] In 1964 Buchan published a detailed analysis of the origins of the proposal and the course of the Alliance debate. By exposing the diplomatic mess into which the Alliance had managed to get itself, Buchan helped to create a climate of opinion conducive to the demise of the concept.[26] The alternative, though less ambitious, was to encourage a greater consultation amongst the Allies on nuclear policies. This approach was adopted with the formation of the Nuclear Planning Group.

Conclusion

While a large number of European countries have been capable of becoming weapons states, only two of them have thus far done so. Until the late 1970s, when the question of long-range nuclear forces based in Europe re-emerged as an issue,[27] the question of European nuclear options remained dormant, with the United States recognizing that undue pressure on its Allies on this matter could well be counterproductive, and most Allies preferring to live with the known uncertainties of the US nuclear guarantee than with the political and strategic uncertainties of nuclear independence. The French and British have both found the diplomatic benefits stemming from their nuclear possessions to be elusive, while the military benefits inevitably remained matters for conjecture. The French found themselves staying closer to NATO than originally envisaged, but with Gaullist vigilance preventing any formal return to the integrated military organization. Familiarity with the British and French forces bred not so much contempt within NATO, but appreciation that their nuisance value to the Russians was somewhat greater than that to the Alliance. In the declaration issued at Ottawa on NATO's silver jubilee, recognition was accorded, in tones of mild approbation, to the British and French nuclear forces, which were 'capable of playing a deterrent role'.[28]

Section 8

Retreat from Assured Destruction

22 Military–Industrial Complexities

The strategic debates of the 1970s within the United States were as passionate as any that had gone before. After some delay, a challenge was mounted to the concepts developed during the McNamara period, in particular the notion of mutual assured destruction. Although an impressive critique was developed, attempts to create a compelling alternative were less successful. As confidence that a nuclear war could and would be fought in a specific way waned, the argument came to be heard that it was necessary to prepare to fight in almost any way. As uncertainty grew as to what dimension of military power created the desired deterrent effect on the Soviet Union, it was argued that imposing strength must be demonstrated on every dimension.

The debate was reminiscent of the critique of massive retaliation developed during the 1950s and applied in the first years of the Kennedy Administration. There were the same complaints over a rigid reliance on an incredible retaliatory threat in the face of a possible diversity of challenges from the Soviet Union. There was the same desire to create a large menu of options from which the President could pick and choose according to the circumstances of a particular crisis. When Secretary of Defense James Schlesinger announced in early 1974 that the Nixon Administration had decided to change US targeting doctrine to allow for more variety in nuclear exchanges, including small strikes and attacks on military targets, the importance of control, selectivity, and flexible response were emphasized as they had been in 1961 and 1962.

In fact, a number of the people around Schlesinger had played a part in the formation of McNamara's 'no-cities' policy, many of them, like Schlesinger himself, having had a long spell at RAND. Andrew Marshall, who had performed some of the earliest RAND studies on counter-force options in the mid-1950s, was put in charge of Net Assessments first in the NSC and then in the Pentagon and William Kaufmann was on call, once again, to draft the annual posture statements. There was a continuity in the thoughts of these men, from the 1950s to the 1970s, involving a distaste for basing national security on threats of genocide and terror, and a belief in the possibilities of using nuclear weapons as an extension of conventional military forces.

Despite the constancy in principles, the strategic environment of the 1970s was different. The Soviet Union had caught up, in raw military power, with the United States and went ahead in quantity if not quality. Another new and related development was continuing and serious negotiation over arms control between the United States and the Soviet Union. The Strategic Arms Limitation Talks (SALT) began in November 1969 and were still under way at the end of the 1970s, providing the most significant focal point for strategic debate throughout the decade.

The talks were supposed to mark the demise of the cold war, an era of negotiation to replace the passing of an era of confrontation. The message, and a proper sense of progress, was contained in the titles of President Nixon's annual foreign policy reports to Congress: 1970 – *A New Strategy for Peace*; 1971 – *Building the Peace*; 1972 – *The Emerging Structure of Peace*; 1973 – *Shaping a Durable Peace*.

Detente did not turn out quite as expected. It held at a minimum level with a mutual desire to avoid nuclear war, but there was a lack of accommodation in those areas of the Third World where the two sides' interests continued to clash. In SALT itself the strain of trying to achieve some symmetry in force structures turned the negotiations into a source of dispute in East–West relations rather than comity. As agreement was found at force levels high enough not to disturb or inconvenience the military planning of either side, the liberal supporters of SALT discovered to their dismay that arms control and arms competition need not be exclusive activities.

There was a perceptible shift during the decade in the consensus amongst the informed public and this was reflected in the Congress. The view at the start of the decade was that nuclear weapons were far more of a problem than the Soviet Union, and that the co-operation of the Soviet Union should be sought to deal with the problem. The old rhetoric of the cold war appeared overdrawn; the Soviet Union was seen as an unattractive but cautious power, bound to the *status quo* and, on the evidence of the past decade, less ready than the United States to resort to arms in a crisis. As important as not being alarmed by the Russians was not alarming them. Emphasis was placed on the importance of restraint to create the necessary stability.

By the end of the decade the Soviet Union again appeared to menace the West, allowing conservatives to claim that the Kremlin, still wedded to expansionist goals, was incapable of reciprocating American restraint. A surge in Soviet military construction coincided with the recovery of conservatism in the United States. After years of being on the defensive over the past neglect of America's social problems and the folly of American global interventionism, the conservatives rediscovered their voice. Following the ignominious American withdrawal from Indo-China, concern grew over inaction in Third World conflicts. Warnings came to be heard from the right against conceding any nuclear advantages to the Soviet Union.

The McNamara Legacy

The dominant views at the start of the 1970s were derived from the framework established by McNamara, and were concerned with stabilizing the condition of Mutual Assured Destruction. As the Democrats moved into opposition after the 1968 election, their approach took on a more critical edge; a number of propositions tentatively offered while in office were now put forward as basic axioms. McNamara's speech of September 1967, in which he had explained the dynamics of the arms race and argued for restraint, was particularly influential.

With the authority of a Secretary of Defense, McNamara had argued that the only nuclear capability that really mattered was to assure destruction in a second strike and that all procurement decisions should be taken with a view to preserving this capability. Furthermore, he admitted, the presumption of the worst in estimating future Soviet capabilities, an unavoidable necessity in force planning, resulted in a built-in tendency to procure more military power than required. Meanwhile the Soviet Union over-reacted in turn to the premature and exaggerated response of the United States, so stimulating yet another American reaction. This action–reaction phenomenon appeared as the key to the dynamics of the arms race. The restraint needed to escape from this action–reaction phenomenon was made more difficult by the many domestic pressures, once new systems had been shown to work well, to procure and deploy them 'out of all proportion to the prudent level required'.[1]

The desire to avoid a rush into ABMs had encouraged analysis of the dynamics of the arms race in these terms. McNamara's strongest support in this endeavour had come from those nuclear scientists who had long been at the fore of all attempts to control and reverse the arms race. To these scientists the most disappointing feature of the September 1967 speech was the appended announcement that an ABM system, known as *Sentinel*, would be constructed to protect US cities against an attack from China in the early 1970s, indicating that McNamara had succumbed to the very domestic pressures from the military, industry, and his President's political opponents to which he had alluded. Weakened by his failure in managing both the arms race and the Vietnam War, he was obviously on the way out.[2] In these circumstances the powerful 'liberal wing' of the scientific community began to demonstrate their disaffection with the establishment on nuclear weapons policy. Using the journal *Scientific American* as their main vehicle, articles began to appear which mingled formidable scientific expertise and distinctive strategic views with a detail and authority unusual for unclassified publications.

The first was by Richard Garwin and Hans Bethe in March 1968, questioning the wisdom of the *Sentinel* system. Their criticisms, which moved beyond their strictly scientific competence, were concerned not only with the physical capacity of the proposed system in the face of postulated attack, but also with arguments over what deterred China and the Soviet Union and the character of the weapons-procurement process in the United States. Thus, the most pertinent argument against the system, they felt, was 'that it will nourish the illusion that an effective defense against ballistic missiles is possible and will lead almost inevitably to demands that the light . . . be expanded into a heavy system'.[3]

When the new Nixon Administration announced in March 1969 that the ABM system was to be reoriented to protect US ICBM silos against Soviet attack, it seemed to these scientists that their fears were being realized, though by strict assured destruction criteria the new version was unobjectionable as it protected the US deterrent without threatening the Soviet deterrent. Nevertheless, the *Safeguard* concept was flawed, having been designed in too much of a hurry, and the scientific community set out to expose these flaws. Nuclear scientists descended upon Washington to testify before Congress against

Safeguard. Again the case involved a combination of technical judgments ('We conclude that the system is unlikely to perform to specifications in the event of a nuclear attack, . . . is highly susceptible to penetration, . . . is not well adapted to perform the missions assigned to it by either the previous Administration or the present one'), and a view of the arms race ('We conclude that deployment of *Sentinel/Safeguard* now would probably start a new round in the arms race, and would seriously impede the conclusion of an arms control agreement'.)[4]

The circumstances of 1969 were not favourable to the American military. The failures of Vietnam policy, the evidence of low morale and indiscipline in the services, and concern over the level of military spending and its effect on the economy all meant that its advice was treated warily. Former advisers to Democratic Administrations with long experience of bureaucratic fights with the military over force plans encouraged this scepticism. Meanwhile Congress was being fortified by expert advice, much of it from people with recent access to classified material. In an unprecedented vote, the Senate divided evenly on the *Safeguard* system, which meant approval, but it meant also that the authorization of new weapons, which had been virtually automatic in the past, could no longer be taken for granted.

This debate had important consequences for the liberal position on strategy and arms control. It confirmed the tendency to concentrate attention on the means by which new weapons are conceived, developed, and produced. Strategic debate was to revolve around procurement decisions.

There were practical reasons for this. The political, economic, and military consequences of new weapons were tangible compared with the abstractions of strategic debate. The sums of money involved were often huge and this alone ensured that minds were concentrated and political lobbies mobilized. The process of procuring new weapons inside the executive branch and the legislature provided an occasion for debate. However, more than this was a particular view of the procurement process, current in the 1969–72 period, which encouraged an extra effort to influence decision-makers, even at the late Congressional stage.

The Military–Industrial Complex

It was assumed that the US was the major source of innovation in military technology and thus was responsible for triggering each new round of the arms race.[5] If the United States demonstrated restraint then there would be no cause for a Soviet reaction and the arms race could be concluded. This unilateral restraint would be necessary even if formal negotiations were under way towards a super-power treaty on arms limitation. Examining the prospects for such negotiations in early 1969, George Rathjens observed that there would be a basis for hope if both powers 'recognized that breaking the action–reaction cycle should be given first priority in any negotiations, and also in unilateral decisions'.[6]

The onus was on the United States to provide the restraint as the dangerous tendency to react to 'worst-case' projections of the other's forces was accentuated in the American case by its superior technology. The result was both ironic and tragic: Jerome Wiesner observed that 'we are running an arms race with ourselves'.[7] In another of the brightly illustrated articles in *Scientific American*, Herbert York attempted to counter the 'deep seated belief that the only appropriate response to any new technical development on the other side is further complexity of our own'.[8]

One example of the influence of ideas such as these was a 1975 sequel to the celebrated 1960 *Daedalus* issue on arms control. Reviewing the changes in attitudes over the past fifteen years, F. A. Long noted the greater realization that 'arms control begins at home' as well as the 'costly and often destabilizing impacts of new military technologies'. One contributor wrote of how a 'less frenetic research effort in military technology would reduce the pressures for deployment of the resulting, often unnecessary, weapons systems'. Another analysis went so far as to argue that 'the central problems of defense policy now include not only the international balance of strategic forces, but the internal dynamics of defense institutions'.[9]

Strategy and arms control were thus branches of bureaucratic as much as international politics. Indeed one contributor to the *Daedalus* volume argued that bureaucratic politics were all-important; rather than interacting through the action–reaction phenomenon, the force structures of the two super-powers developed quite separately; the result, predominantly, of factors internal to each nation.[10]

A multiplicity of internal pressures did not inevitably result in any particular outcome. However there was a powerful coalition between the scientists and engineers who developed the new weapons, the industrial contractors who would produce them, the Congressmen in whose districts this production would take place, and the military who would use the final product. All had an interest in higher expenditure on military hardware, and this biased the force planning process against restraint. Against this 'military–industrial complex' the voices of moderation within the Pentagon were faint. Therefore controlling the arms race meant controlling the 'military–industrial complex'. In the absence of a strong manager comparable to McNamara, Congress would have to do the best it could.

A hint of this view can be found in the Chayes and Wiesner anti-ABM book[11] in an essay by Adam Yarmolinsky, another former McNamara aide, on 'The problem of momentum' which noted the vested interests in ABM procurement. The ABM opponents' conviction and influence on both the technical and doctrinal aspects of the debate, compared with the occasionally desperate arguments but imposing political pressures mounted by the pro-ABM side, encouraged the view that it was a virtual conspiracy that was preventing the proper exercise of US restraint. A rich literature flourished briefly, a mélange of radical sociology and investigative journalism, which exposed the 'military–industrial complex', and warned of the general 'militarization' of US society. The variety of forms this criticism took, from the Marxist to the mildly reformist, need not be discussed here. It is only necessary to note the belief that it was a systematic bias in favour of weapons procurement within the US than ensured the persistence of the arms race.[12]

In time, extreme versions of the military–industrial complex theories were undermined by scholarly analysis.[13] Nevertheless, there was a residual fascination with the mechanisms of weapons procurement as the key to a general understanding of the arms race. Biographies of weapons, from conception to birth (but rarely to old age), became standard subjects for graduate theses, often conducted in the belief that such studies would illuminate the areas where responsible control might be exercised.[14] McNamara's observations on the pressures to produce and deploy new systems threatened to be turned into an Iron Law of Weapons Innovation.[15]

The politicization of the arms debate in this manner, and the growing suspicion that key weapons decisions were taken more to satisfy the needs of the engineers, contractors, and military managers involved in their production than the needs of national security, encouraged dogmatism. Doubts were cast on the validity of the case for any new weapons system emerging from this biased procurement process. Any strategic perspectives other than those derived from McNamara's 1967 speech were liable to be seen as deviations and as *post-hoc* rationalizations for new weapons. The view was captured by a Senator's description of the ABM as a 'missile in search of a mission'. Rather than identify a strategic problem and then search for a technology to solve it, the sequence appeared to be reversed, with invention becoming the mother of necessity. It was thus wariness over the motives of the proponents of the ABM, combined with respect for the scientific credentials of the opponents, that helped to endow the principles of Mutual Assured Destruction and the associated views on the dynamics of the arms race with their canonical status. The legitimization of a balance of terror, once a matter of much liberal and radical distaste, had become a liberal cause. The vice of the perpetual nuclear threat was displaced by the virtue of stability.

Jerome Kahan, in a thorough presentation of the liberal position, discussed policy issues under the general heading of 'The search for stability'. The three principles of 'stable deterrence' he advocated were: maintaining 'a confident retaliatory deterrent posture'; reducing the 'relative reliance on nuclear power in US defense policy'; and 'avoiding weapons and doctrines that pose a threat to the USSR's deterrent and seeking security through negotiated arms limitations'.[16]

Force Planning Under Nixon

While all these critiques were being developed, the Nixon Administration remained remarkably quiet. This was despite the presence of one of the leading academic strategists, Dr Henry Kissinger, as Nixon's Assistant for National Security Affairs. We have already observed Kissinger the strategist in action. His skill had been in clarifying and then popularizing some of the key theories and concepts that had been under development since the mid-1950s. He had also acted as a weather-vane for changes in the intellectual climate, reflecting the dominant ideas of any period yet able to anticipate movements in fashion. His description of his views on joining Nixon's staff demonstrate this. He shared with his former academic colleagues a fear that 'Strategic forces, at once highly vulnerable and extremely powerful, could in a crisis tempt one side to strike first, especially if it feared that it might lose its means of retaliation to a first blow'. He thus favoured 'a conscious policy of stabilizing the arms race'. He parted company with the academic community on the sources of Soviet conduct. 'I did not accept the proposition that unilateral restraint in weapons precurement on our part would evoke a comparable response from the Kremlin'.[17]

In the early years of the Nixon Administration the political issue was whether new military programmes could be initiated against the pressure, particularly strong in Congress, for unilateral restraint. Kissinger records an argument before the inauguration with John Erlichman, in charge of Nixon's domestic programmes, in which Erlichman had asserted that 'everyone' knew that Defense had been getting too much. Thus though Kissinger was interested in revising strategic doctrine this did not seem a propitious moment for anything too strong.

While there was no shortage of weapons programmes to incite the liberals they were therefore not supported by any new strategic rationales. Although Nixon had campaigned on a 'security gap' platform, calling for clear US superiority, and had gathered around him a number of 'hawks' the initial pronouncements of the new Administration were moderate. The first studies in the National Security Council, now under the direction of Henry Kissinger, demonstrated that the sort of superiority the US had enjoyed in the past was now unobtainable. Kissinger encouraged Nixon to settle for something more modest, to be described as 'sufficiency', a term able neither to inspire nor to inform.

When Deputy Secretary of Defense David Packard was asked what was meant by 'sufficiency' he replied: 'It means that it's a good word to use in a speech. Beyond that it doesn't mean a God-damned thing'.[18] Other officials admitted that the concept was unclear and elastic. President Nixon did not attempt to explain the term until February 1971, when he noted two meanings:

> In its narrow military sense, it means enough force to inflict a level of damage on a potential aggressor sufficient to deter him from attacking. . . . In its broader political sense, sufficiency means the maintenance of forces adequate to prevent us and our allies from being coerced. Thus the relationship between our strategic forces and those of the Soviet Union must be such that our ability and resolve to protect our vital security interests will not be underestimated.[19]

The second, political, meaning of sufficiency eventually turned out to be the most important, yet in the early 1970s the debate was conducted in terms of the first military meaning. One reason for this was that Nixon and Kissinger did not devote a great deal of time to developing the idea. Another was that the first two years of the Administration were dominated by issues related to the military version of sufficiency.

The Administration had to face a sustained challenge within Congress from those urging restraint in order to keep the military budget down and to induce comparable restraint from the Soviet Union. The Nixon Administration did not seek initially to change the terms of the debate. The *Safeguard* ABM system was justified in 'assured destruction' terms as a means of protecting second-strike forces and avoiding first-strike provocations. The concept of military 'sufficiency' was presented as something new but it was hard to discover whether or not this meant any new operational criteria in force planning. For those reared in the McNamara tradition, a lack of specificity here was unforgivable. Criteria for strategic sufficiency, when provided, appeared as vague desiderata, described by the Secretary of Defense as 'not rigid and unchanging', but 'developed as broad guidance for planning'.[20]

The fact was that Melvin Laird was of a quite different mould to McNamara. He was a hard-liner, who had once written a book advocating a first-strike capability.[21] As a Congressman he had learnt the importance of 'threatmanship' in selling weapons projects and therefore based his own rationales for new systems on postulated increases in Soviet military capabilities. If there was any doctrine with which he might be associated it was the doctrine of the *triad*. This required that each leg of the triad of ICBMs, SLBMs and bombers approximated towards an independent second-strike capability. This created a 'mutually supporting deterrent capability'. The word 'synergism' was discovered, stripped of theological connotations, and taken to refer to the combined triad creating a deterrent effect greater than the sum of the individual parts.

The case for the triad is not without merit. There is an obvious danger in putting all 'eggs in one basket'. If the deterrent depended solely on one type of delivery vehicle, then the adversary's defensive problem would be simplified. To mount an attack simultaneously on three completely different types of system would be an awesome task; one system might be manageable. Furthermore while bombers, ICBMs, and SLBMs might all be able to mount a formidable second strike against cities, each had some unique feature which could allow for extra options – the ICBM for example had greater accuracy, allowing for attacks on discrete targets, while the human control over the bomber made possible second thoughts after launching. However, although these arguments justified a variety in offensive systems, they did not necessarily mean that all types must be maintained in large numbers or at an equivalent level of modernity.

The force of the concept of the triad in this analysis derived less from intellectual compulsion than political convenience. The 'participatory management' approach of Melvin Laird returned to the Services much of the autonomy lost under McNamara. In return for this they agreed to respect budget ceilings. By splitting up the budget into three equal parts competition between the Services was limited. While making political sense, this inhibited the development of a coherent strategic perspective at the centre. It reflected the acceptance by the civilian leadership of the pre-existent division of responsibilities between the Services and showed the civilians unwilling to challenge military judgment on the structures and systems deemed necessary to fulfil military responsibilities. The political relationships encouraged conservatism in force planning and stability was achieved by replacing obsolete systems with follow-on systems. Otherwise Laird contented himself with justifying new weapons as an insurance policy, a prudent investment in case something terrible happened in the future.

His successor, James Schlesinger, observed to a Congressional Committee: 'To some extent I think the rationale of the Triad was a rationalization'.[22] As such, despite its political value in helping to maintain the bureaucratic calm inside the Pentagon, the triad concept, like that of sufficiency, was an inadequate basis with which to confront a Congress supported by assorted lobbyists that was becoming increasingly well-informed and sophisticated on strategic arms issues.

23 The Consensus Undermined

The strategic debates of the 1970s in the United States could not be restricted to a qualified few, versed in the mysteries of the atom and informed through the most secret sources. The debate was noisy, even cacophonous, and frequently linked to wider issues, such as Presidential elections and the struggle to establish the demarcation line between executive and legislative spheres of competence, and embracing all parts of the political system.

As the nuclear age progressed there was a natural accumulation of scientists, officials, diplomats, and servicemen who had enjoyed access at some point in their careers to classified information and who had participated in the relevant debates on new weapons, strategies, and arms control initiatives. SALT rapidly increased their number. Continuing negotiations with the Russians, involving as they did questions on future force planning, relations with adversaries and allies, and verification, all of which demanded a series of decisions at the highest level, imposed intensive demands on the military and civilian bureaucracies for over a decade. The result was a substantial increase in the numbers of Americans who felt qualified to speak on nuclear weapons subjects.

Meanwhile, emboldened by the 1969 ABM debate, Congressmen began to expect a rôle in reaching major decisions, and acquired large staffs to advise them. Independent institutes, offering expertise and prescription in a variety of mixes, were established to disseminate relevant information and analyses to Congressmen and the attentive public. This was in addition to the many organizations with some

344

sort of consultancy arrangement with branches of the bureaucracy who were pushing out a stream of commissioned studies on issues ranging from the trivial to the fundamental. Finally, the circulation of individuals in and out and around the Government machine ensured the flow of information and concepts.

Technical details on warheads, delivery systems, and basing modes, once subjects for the highest classification, were widely distributed. The provisions of SALT agreements in force and those still the subject of negotiation were widely available, often while still matters of sensitive discussion. Similarly, intelligence information on virtually every detail of the Soviet force structure became common fare. What some senior officials felt ought to remain secret, others felt was just the thing for a leak to the *New York Times* or the *Washington Post*. The Freedom of Information Act and the general distrust of Government furtiveness following the Pentagon Papers and the Watergate revelations encouraged this process.

Widespread intimacy with nuclear weapons and every detail of the strategic balance, encouraged a many-sided debate. A diversity of views emanated from the Executive branch, Congress, the military and civilian specialists. The result was to undermine the established liberal consensus, but not to present a new consensus to take its place.

The Soviet Build-Up

In the early 1960s, the Soviet Union had appeared content with a modest force, well below the American level but sufficient to guarantee a powerful second strike. In 1965–1966 there were signs of substantial construction at missile sites; soon new missiles were sprouting throughout the Soviet Union. McNamara viewed this development with a remarkable lack of alarm. Numbers in themselves made little difference. All that mattered was whether or not destruction was assured. The Soviet build-up was scrutinized for signs of a developing first-strike capability. Evidence of an anti-ballistic missile system resulted in a compensatory improvement of US offensive capabilities, of which multiple independently-targeted re-entry vehicles (MIRVs) were the most important step. But so long as the new Soviet ICBMs were of medium size and inaccurate they caused little concern. The larger type of ICBM – designated the SS-9 – was watched with more care because, if MIRVed, the individual re-entry vehicles might each operate as a 'silo-buster'. But as deployment of these types remained limited the problem was not felt to be great.

By the start of the 1970s the Soviet Union had caught up in numbers of ICBMs, and was building up fast in numbers of SLBMs. Throughout the 1970s there was Soviet superiority in both. The United States maintained a much larger bomber force and kept ahead in the quality of its missiles. As the US completed the MIRVing of its ICBMs and SLBMs in the mid-1970s, the Soviet Union was only beginning to introduce MIRVed ICBMs and it took until the end of the decade for Soviet MIRVed SLBMs to appear.[1] Despite the fact that the United States was as active as the Soviet Union in the modernization of its force structure and kept ahead in technical sophistication, the impression grew that the Soviet Union was seizing the strategic initiative.

The persistence of the build-up, beyond levels where a crude but visible parity with the United States had been attained, raised doubts. It seemed a disturbingly open-ended process, without an obvious full-stop. The effect was accentuated by not phasing out older ICBMs, as was the practice in the United States. The most remarkable feature of the Soviet force structure was that investment was concentrated in ICBMs, more numerous and, on average, individually larger than anything in the American arsenal. This extra size meant that, when the Soviet Union did decide to modernize their force with high-accuracy multiple warheads, it would be more imposing than the equivalent United States force. There were no breakthroughs in technology originating in the Soviet Union sufficient to tilt the strategic balance, and the military problems created were limited.

With each aspect of the build-up it was difficult to explain how the Soviet strategic or political position had really benefited. The sort of scepticism that had developed in liberal circles over whether the US had gained much advantage when it enjoyed a margin of superiority was applied to the USSR. Could it not be that programmes enforced upon the Kremlin by its own military-industrial complex were as wasteful and extravagant as comparable US programmes? In addition, the traditional insecurity of the Russians, their dependence on raw military power as the only instrument of global diplomacy (given their economic weakness), the example of the US build-up in the 1960s, could all be cited as explanations for the momentum that had developed behind Soviet weapons production. While all these points were necessary to ensure that Soviet military developments were kept in perspective, they could not dispel the nagging doubt that the

USSR was arming itself because it felt this to be advantageous, and that it had yet to acquire the Western scepticism over the limited utility of military forces in the modern world. It might be mistaken, but if it acted upon such beliefs, however wrong, the consequences for everyone could be extremely dangerous.

The Action–Inaction Phenomenon

New uncertainties were introduced by active Soviet procurement of strategic arms. The arms race itself could no longer be presented as the simple, almost mechanical, affair suggested by such terms as the 'action–reaction phenomenon'.[2] In an influential series of articles, Albert Wohlstetter attacked what he considered to be some of the legends of the arms race. He demonstrated that the costs and destructiveness of US strategic forces had been on the decline rather than accelerating, that technology could be benign as well as malign, and that there was no evidence of 'invariable' overestimation of Soviet strategic forces in US intelligence estimates. If anything, there had been 'underestimation, especially with projections of Soviet offensive forces'.[3]

There were criticisms of Wohlstetter's methodology, but his polemic was effective. He punctured much of the rhetoric about the arms race and forced the liberals to return to the evidence to sort out what was and had been going on. As Wohlstetter observed, a better model of the interaction between the two sides would have to take into account institutional factors, operational doctrines, and resource constraints. Nor could the two sides' arms decisions be taken simply as 'unfortunate cases of reciprocal failure . . . to see that all their important interests were in common. They are not.'[4] The model of the arms race driven by technology, intelligence overestimates, and flawed force planning was replaced by a complex interaction, competitive rather than racing, between two powers with 'partially, but sometimes intensely opposed aims'. 'Strategic forces', Wohlstetter reminded his readers, 'are the ultimate back-up for alliance commitments.'[5]

This was taken up by Colin Gray, one of the few prominent British contributors to the debate in the 1970s, though he often took on the appearance of a partisan American. Gray also stressed the origins of the arms race (a term he had fewer qualms in using than Wohlstetter) in genuine conflicts of interests. 'Arms race behaviour', he concluded, following an investigation of alternative theories, 'is really only normal Great Power behaviour somewhat accentuated.'[6]

The Shame of Assured Destruction

One underlying theme in Wohlstetter's exposé of the legends of the arms race was a deep distaste for the prescriptions of assured destruction. He noted the development of the view that the best way to avoid an arms race was to aim strategic weapons exclusively at populations. He concluded his series by questioning the morality of this, of measuring 'the adequacy of our weapons in terms of the number of civilians they can kill' and proposing that 'we face up to evasions making "murder respectable" in such chaste phrases as "counter-value attacks" and in all the unreflective vocabulary of the arms race'.[7]

This unhappiness over the moral basis of US policy was neither new nor confined to any particular part of the political spectrum. At times of peace few can contemplate mass destruction of human life with relish, or can advocate it as an end in itself.[8] The theorists of mutual assured destruction believed themselves to be coming to terms with a fact of life so as to control it. They argued that the danger of mutual destruction grew if one pretended to be able to fight a nuclear war in such a way as to avoid this outcome. The prescription was not to prepare for genocide as the foundation of defence policy, but to reduce dependence on genocidal weapons in America's military posture, keeping them in the background as weapons of last resort.[9] Unfortunately for this approach the failure to build up conventional forces along the lines implied by NATO's flexible response strategy meant that there was still a great dependence on nuclear forces, and the threat they posed to the Soviet Union was still essentially against its population.

Unease over the state of affairs was widely expressed. During the course of the 1969 ABM debate, Donald Brennan made the case for population defence. Brennan noted that mutual assured destruction meant mutual assured vulnerability. Instead of reducing the Soviet threat to them, Americans increased their threat to the USSR. This he thought bizarre: 'We should rather prefer live Americans to dead Russians, and we should not choose deliberately to live forever under a nuclear sword of Damocles.' He argued that so long as it could be assured that the Russians would have inflicted upon them the same amount of damage that they inflicted on the US in a nuclear attack, then deterrence would be sustained even in the presence of significant damage-limiting capacities on both sides. The trend in procurement in favour of offensive systems and against defensive systems should be reversed.[10]

Brennan's case depended on an optimistic view on the effectiveness of ballistic missile defences and the costs to the offence of degrading extra defensive capability. The idea was considered important enough to be investigated by the incoming Nixon Administration in 1969, but the technical and financial foundations were discovered not to be sufficiently sound and there were major strategic problems involved in the transition. The Administration carried on in SALT in the spirit of McNamara, negotiating away the defensive option and confirming the ascendancy of the offence. However Brennan did signal an unease with reliance on assured destruction, claiming that this was shared by a majority of the 'defense community'.[11]

The most influential critique came from Fred Iklé in an article in *Foreign Affairs*.[12] Iklé's eloquence demanded attention:

> The jargon of American strategic analysis works like a narcotic. It dulls our sense of moral outrage about the tragic confrontation of nuclear arsenals, primed and constantly perfected to unleash widespread genocide. It fosters the current smug complacency regarding the soundness and stability of mutual deterrence. It blinds us to the fact that our method for preventing nuclear war rests on a form of warfare universally condemned since the Dark Ages – the mass killing of hostages (p. 14).

He challenged the presumption that mutual assured destruction represented a stable state. He believed that a threat which, if carried out, would lead to mutual destruction was not inherently credible. It involved on the American side a threat to respond to one particular type of Soviet attack – the massive surprise attack – and might be less relevant to other types. It neglected the problem of lunacy and recklessness at the top,[13] of men of power 'willing to see their nation destroyed in pursuit of causes which only they and their henchmen espouse'. And it neglected the persistent danger of the 'fatal accident or unauthorized act'. Furthermore, stabilizing deterrence by keeping arsenals for instant and unrestrained slaughter would impose a 'wrenching philosophy' on the officialdom of both nations. There could never be an end to hostility. 'Toward each other as a people, Americans and Russians harbour practically no feelings of hostility, but by our theories they must indefinitely face each other as the most fearful threat to their future existence'.

Iklé's capacity to bring into the open a nagging unease over reliance on a balance of terror, kept below the surface by the success in preventing war for almost three decades, was not matched by his capacity to offer ways out of this situation. One reason for this was that he had the mistaken idea that speed was an essential feature of the retaliatory response advocated in the dogmas he was opposing. His ideas for making the US deterrent forces invulnerable and capable of a slow considered response were thus unexceptionable and upset nobody. He believed that modern technology would help by making it possible to 'escape the evil dilemma that the strategic forces must either be designed to kill people or else jeopardize the opponent's confidence in his deterrent'. New technologies would permit precise and discriminatory attacks on the military, industrial and transportation assets – 'the sinews and muscles of the regime initiating war'.[14]

Iklé's unease struck a responsive chord. Herbert York, for example, an eminent defence scientist and leading arms-control advocate, added his voice to those who felt that to accept a substantial chance that the world will 'go up in a nuclear smoke' was 'too frightful and too dangerous a way to live indefinitely; we *must* find some better form of international relationship than the current dependency on a strategy of mutual assured destruction'. Yet York did not agree with Iklé on the means of escape. A policy of targeting only military installations would be no more than an 'administrative arrangement', and could not prevent sizeable loss of life in the vicinity of the targets. It could be used to justify increases in force levels and then be abandoned. York preferred to reduce surplus capacity, popularly known as 'overkill', advocating deep cuts in force levels. But, as he admitted, even reductions far beyond anything realistically possible would not end the state of mutual assured destruction, but only assure destruction of a more limited number – the populations of large cities. The prospects for those in rural areas, small towns and third countries might be improved. This combined modest ends with ambitious means and did not indicate an alternative form of strategic relationship.[15]

In an article written as a reply to Iklé, another defence scientist, Wolfgang Panofsky, accepted the moral discomfort of the current situation while doubting whether 'we can do better'. He criticized, in similar terms to York, views of limited nuclear war and counter-force strategies as potentially making the situation worse, by providing justification for more forces and by weakening the barriers against the employment of nuclear weapons. Central to Panofsky's position was the view that the state of mutual assured destruction was beyond a policy decision but a 'tension of modern life' that will have to be endured, but responsible, as well, for the prevention of war. The 'mutual-hostage relationship' was a matter of 'physical fact' and 'grossly insensitive to any change in strategic policy'. The best he could offer was a reduction of the rôle of nuclear weapons in international political and military affairs, through a relaxation of tensions, arms reductions, and doctrines preserving the nuclear 'fire-break' in the use of weapons in war.[16]

Through these arguments the moral and empirical foundations of established strategy and arms control theory, and the consensus which they supported, were being undermined. Yet no alternative doctrine which commanded broad support had emerged to take its place.

New Technologies

It had been presumed that it would be technology, rather than either the Soviet Union or moral qualms, that would present the greatest source of instability. This was another of the dogmas attacked by Wohlstetter. The problem he noted was one of political choice. Innovation increased the range of choice, allowing for new capabilities and a redeployment of resources. Not all innovations increased the danger and destructiveness of nuclear war. Those which improved reconnaissance, the political control over strategic weapons, and their invulnerability were on the whole benign.[17]

The impact of technology during the 1970s turned out to be similar to the other changes in the strategic environment discussed above; it did not fundamentally alter anything very much, but it introduced new uncertainties and complexities that blurred old distinctions and qualified old verities.

In a number of ways nuclear weapons developed along the lines anticipated in the 1960s. The manned bomber showed few signs of revival and ballistic missiles reigned supreme, with the submarine-based force ensuring that the deterrent remained invulnerable. The development of anti-ballistic missile systems continued, but with little sign that they were going to provide a challenge to the dominance of the offence. The most influential changes, the full implications of which were not foreseen by McNamara, came in the quality of offensive systems.

Of these changes the most significant was the relentless improvement in guidance systems. During the 1970s accuracies improved from CEPs (circular error probable) of half of a mile to under a sixth of a mile.[18] This development had been anticipated. What was less expected was the capacity to combine high accuracy with two other features – multiple warheads and mobility.[19] The sea-based deterrent had demonstrated the virtues of mobility since the start of the 1960s and by the middle of the decade the *Polaris* A-3 warhead, which split up in a shotgun effect into three re-entry vehicles, had been deployed but each separate warhead was unguided. However, it was accepted that mobility and multiple warheads came at the expense of accuracy. The sea-based deterrent was considered to be a model second-strike force – invulnerable to a first strike, while so incapable of attacking anything other than cities that it could not threaten a first strike itself. In terms of stability this was exemplary. When it came to surprise attacks, submarines neither threatened first strikes nor were they threatened by one.

A 'bus' system was devised to carry a number of individual re-entry vehicles on one launch vehicle and then distribute them with some precision. This was the multiple independently-targetable re-entry vehicle system (MIRV). Although ensuring that a greater diversity of targets would be available for attack, it was not expected originally that MIRVs would render hardened targets, particularly the protected missile silos of the Soviet Union, vulnerable. They were approved as a means of degrading ABM systems and removing the necessity for further increases in launch vehicles. MIRVing meant that each re-entry vehicle had a smaller yield than a single warhead missile. So it was not enough to avoid a loss of accuracy in MIRVing. If it was desired that MIRVed missiles showed as high a kill probability against hardened targets as could be obtained with single warhead missiles, accuracy would have to be improved.

No attempt was made to achieve such high kill probabilities in the MIRVed SLBM, *Poseidon*, developed in the late 1960s. The warhead was split up into ten or more small units each yielding some 60 kilotons. The Air Force was initially suspicious of MIRVs because it felt that it would lose the counter-force capabilities it had.[20] The MIRVed *Minuteman III* ICBM had three warheads each of some 170 kilotons yield. To give it a significant hard-target capability the accuracy was brought to a quarter of a mile – not enough to be able to be sure of destroying the best-protected missile, but indicating a direction for future technology which, if followed, would make any fixed target vulnerable to accurate warheads with quite small yields. There was little doubt that, if it was so desired, this capability could be achieved. This meant that whereas before, given problems of reliability, at the very least two ICBMs would be needed to destroy one enemy ICBM – a basically unfavourable exchange rate – one MIRVed ICBM could take out one or more enemy ICBMs, so reversing this exchange rate.

After some delays, programmes were eventually authorized to exploit precision guidance to the full.[21] These, with improvements in command and control capabilities, meant that individual warheads could be prepared in a matter of minutes and in any circumstances to attack and destroy virtually all types of fixed targets with some certainty. This widened the range of options available to a President, but they remained limited in one key respect. Moving targets, such as submarines, put far greater demands on the attacking force and remained beyond the scope of these evolving counter-force capabilities. Any first strike, however completely it eliminated the ICBM portion of the triad, would leave another portion, SLBMs, virtually intact, or at least that portion which were on station and not in port.

The problem of the growing vulnerability of US ICBMs was related to the fact that only they could respond in kind to an attack upon them. Only ICBMs offered an option for attacking hard targets and so a counter-force option. Their loss would not, however, remove all semblance of flexibility and confine retaliation purely to cities. Many other types of targets relevant to military operations and the functioning of the economy could still be attacked (for example, fuel depots).

Furthermore, eventually SLBMs could have some hard-target capability. This would admittedly be expensive, and there would be problems of command and control. It was also feared that the submarine's position would be disclosed if only one SLBM was launched thus giving the enemy a chance to attack it. Cruise missiles, on the other hand, would allow for single shots of high accuracy at reasonable cost, but the disadvantage here was the slow speed. Nevertheless, it should not be thought that ICBMs were the only weapon with any flexibility.

It was the provision of the hard-target option that was the key feature of ICBMs. Consequently, they took on the attributes of first-strike weapons for which bombers had been criticized in the late

1950s. They remained vulnerable so long as they rested in their silos and a threat to the equivalent force of the enemy once launched. With anti-submarine warfare (ASW) techniques still unable to challenge the pre-eminence of the submarine, SLBMs remained the only pure second-strike weapon, invulnerable to an enemy first strike while incapable of mounting one of their own. (Two qualifications are needed: the most vulnerable component of either sides' retaliatory force would always be submarines in port; Soviet submarines are much more vulnerable to ASW than those of the United States.) But even here, the relentless improvement in guidance technology offered the eventual prospect of a loss of doctrinal purity, with sea-based systems capable of attacking all fixed land-based assets.

This capacity to knock out practically all of the adversary's ICBMs, SLBMs in port and bombers at bases, while still holding a portion of one's own in reserve was widely seen as the crucial shift in the strategic environment, though it remained beyond both sides' capabilities throughout the 1970s. The validity of the claim that it would represent a significant advantage will be examined in Chapter 25.

A combination of mobility and accuracy (using either ICBMs or SLBMs or cruise missiles) offered an escape from the problems of vulnerability without a loss in offensive capability. But this only started to be seriously considered in the second half of the 1970s. Cruise missiles, pilotless aircraft with continuous propulsion, were descended from the German V-1 of World War II, as ballistic missiles were descended from the V-2. After experiments in the 1950s, they had been neglected because of their slow speed, high fuel consumption and consequently small warhead (though the *Snark* was available as a strategic weapon until 1961). Improvements in munitions design and jet engines, and a guidance system which allowed the attainment of impressive accuracy by the missile recognizing and adjusting to the terrain on the approach to the target, helped to create a weapon with a promise of great versatility, able in theory to operate at a variety of ranges, with either conventional or nuclear warheads and from a variety of launch platforms, though still at a relatively slow speed.

Arms Control

All these factors – the perplexing growth in Soviet missile forces, the critique of arms race theories relying on over-exuberant weapons designers and intelligence estimators, the uncertainties over Soviet intentions, the moral qualms, and the confusion of technological progress – all impacted on the process that was supposed to consolidate stability in strategic relations between the super-powers and advance political relations. In consequence, the experience of arms control was extremely unsatisfactory.

There were many different sets of arms control negotiations, including those covering the non-proliferation of nuclear weapons, force reductions in Europe and comprehensive test bans. Concern here is with strategic theory rather than with arms control *per se*, so the only negotiations of central relevance are the Strategic Arms Limitation Talks (SALT). These were first proposed in 1967 and began in November 1969. SALT dominated public debate in the US on nuclear matters throughout the 1970s, with important consequences for the character of strategic thought.

McNamara's motives in encouraging President Johnson to offer talks to the Soviet Union had been linked to a distinct theory of the arms race, with the main objective of keeping deployment of ABMs down to a minimum so as to prevent the evolution of first-strike capabilities. This objective was achieved in May 1972 when the first SALT Treaty was signed in Moscow, limiting the number of ABM launchers to 200 for each side. This number was halved in 1974 and the US eventually mothballed its system. The Soviet Union maintained its small system around Moscow, probably with China in mind.

SALT also embraced offensive arms and here the negotiations were much more difficult. ABMs were a distinct type of weapon only just starting to be deployed. The vast research and development effort in ABMs had palpably failed to produce convincing and cost-effective solutions to the many problems of effective ballistic missile defence, for the tolerance of failure was very low. Because both the US and Soviet ABM programmes had lost momentum, they were easy to stop altogether with arms control measures and there were good doctrinal reasons, at least for the Americans, as to why this should be done.

The same conditions did not apply to offensive weapons. Both sides had many weapons which, though nationally comparable, displayed important variations. Technology was still adding new types of weapons to the inventories of both super-powers. The start of SALT was coterminous with the introduction of MIRVed missiles, cruise missiles were first mooted in the mid-1970s and the accuracy of all strategic missiles was improving all the time.[22] Furthermore, there was a lack of clarity in the setting of goals for offensive arms limitation. The concept of mutual assured destruction did not indicate any value in reductions of offensive weapons. If anything, excessive reductions could be destabilizing if they went past the point where destruction could no longer be assured.

The most compelling argument was that, as existing force levels guaranteed assured destruction for both sides, extra weapons provided no benefit and an agreement not to build them could save resources which could then be put to better use.[23] In addition, both sides had to accept explicitly the futility of continuing the arms race and to agree on restraint which could create the atmosphere in which they might settle political differences. In this way, SALT became the centrepiece of the detente process. By declaring an honourable draw in the military sphere it would be possible to come to terms in the political sphere.

The character of arms control agreements is influenced by the mechanisms of international politics that are required to reach them. Because negotiations proceeded on the basis of a *quid pro quo*, a definition of parity that demanded asymmetrical adjustments in force structures was unacceptable. Tolerable definitions required the simplification of strategic relationships, the exclusion of many military relevant factors and concentration on a few prestige weapons. The consequent agreements were partial rather than comprehensive and barely radical in their strategic effects.

Much of the argument over SALT, between and within the super-powers, was over the proper definitions of parity. One consequence of this was to exaggerate the importance of parity as a feature in the military balance, encouraging the tabulation of strategic credits and debits and the codification of differences between super-powers. Furthermore, the consequence of high-level negotiations on matters that touch on each side's most vital security interests is to ensure that the subject-matter increases, not decreases, in salience.

The arguments did not centre on the concept of parity or its value in principle but on its practical content. There were distinct asymmetries between the two force structures and it was difficult to decide what weight to attach to them. The Americans had more bombers and a more advanced technology; their forces were MIRVed earlier. On the other hand the ICBMs which dominated the Soviet force structure were more numerous, much larger than the American equivalents and eventually, when all MIRVed, could carry more warheads of larger individual yield. A larger Soviet SLBM force was being constructed but this seemed to be of inferior quality and efficiency to that of the US. In addition to weapons of intercontinental range the Soviet Union had a large force directed solely against European targets. On the Western side medium-range forces were much smaller, but the relevant weapons could reach the Soviet Union and they included British and French missiles and bombers as well as those of the United States. The Soviet Union had to consider the growing Chinese nuclear force to the East. There was thus no simple formula to describe parity.

In 1972 an interim five-year agreement was reached on the limitation of offensive arms. This put a freeze on numbers of missile launchers, with an allowance for the momentum in the Soviet construction programme. The US was allowed 1054 ICBMs and 656 SLBMs, the Soviet Union 1409 ICBMs, and 950 SLBMs,[24] with a sub-limit of 308 'heavy' ICBMs. Implicit in the agreement was a trade of Soviet numerical superiority in missiles for US superiority in technology and bombers. This was not altogether appreciated in the Senate, where Senator Jackson secured an amendment requesting the President to 'seek a future treaty that, *inter alia*, would not limit the United States to levels of intercontinental strategic forces inferior to the limits provided for the Soviet Union'.[25]

Under these terms negotiations for a more permanent Treaty proceeded. Apparent success came in Vladivostock in November 1974, when President Ford and Secretary Brezhnev agreed on a framework for a new Treaty which would allow ceilings of 2400 strategic nuclear delivery vehicles (SNDVs), that is bombers and missiles, and dealt with MIRVs by counting not warheads but MIRVed missiles, for which a sub-ceiling of 1320 was set.

Unfortunately, it was not found possible to transform this simple if undemanding framework into a Treaty. New complicating issues emerged connected with a Soviet missile (SS-19) that disrupted the distinction between 'heavy' and 'light' ICBMs, and, most important, the cruise missile which was both a unilateral American advantage and new and versatile.[26] It took until late 1977 (by which time the Democrats had returned to office under the leadership of President Carter) to construct a new framework to sort out these and other problems. It took almost another two years to turn this into a Treaty and even then the result was hardly definitive. This second Treaty was to last until only 1985 and would limit SNDVs to 2250, with sub-limits on MIRVed missiles and bombers carrying air-launched cruise missiles (1320), on MIRVed missiles (1200), on MIRVed

ICBMs (820) and 'heavy' MIRVed ICBMs (308). It was still necessary to put a number of particularly intractable problems, including ground- and sea-launched cruise missiles, and mobile missiles, into a three-year protocol to allow time for further negotiation and to relegate the controversial Soviet TU-22M *Backfire* bomber to a Letter of Understanding appended to the Treaty.

By this time the broad consensus supporting SALT had been badly shaken. The process was criticized for not doing enough to reduce numbers, for stimulating the arms race because of the need to gain military endorsement by promises of new weapons, for exacerbating rather than calming East–West tensions, and for failing to solve the pressing strategic problems of the day. In January 1980, after it had already become evident that it would be difficult to muster the necessary two-thirds majority in the Senate for Treaty ratification, the Soviet invasion of Afghanistan made further progress impossible and President Carter asked for the vote to be deferred. SALT had become an unhappy affair, projecting and reflecting the doubts and uncertainties of the 1970s.

24 Parity

In 1975 Secretary of Defense James Schlesinger noted the inability of either side in the foreseeable future to acquire the means for either a disarming first strike or effective damage limitation, because of the demise of ABM systems confirmed by the 1972 SALT Treaty. 'In these circumstances', he continued, 'one may ask, has nuclear strategy not reached a dead end?' He answered that this might well be the case 'as far as the massive attacks that preoccupied us in the 1960s', but went on to claim that 'unfortunately', there remained 'a number of more limited contingencies that could arise and that we should be prepared to deter'.[1]

Schlesinger identified four requirements for a credible nuclear deterrence. One referred, though not by name, to an assured destruction capability, a survivable force able to retaliate against the economic base of the enemy. The novelty came with the other three requirements. First was *essential equivalence*, a basic symmetry in all 'factors which contribute to the effectiveness of strategic weapons and to the perception of non-super-power nations'. The second was for a 'force that, in response to Soviet actions, could implement a variety of limited pre-planned options and react rapidly to retargeting orders so as to deter any range of further attacks that a potential enemy might contemplate'. The third requirement brought the first two together. It was for 'a range and magnitude of capabilities such that everyone – friend, foe, and domestic audiences alike – will perceive that we are the equal of our strongest competitors'.[2]

These two themes – of unambiguous parity and wide flexibility –

were the basis of the attempt to construct a distinctive doctrine to replace that of mutual assured destruction. This and the next chapter will examine the origins of these themes, and the extent to which they became part of a new consensus and were able to prevent strategy reaching a 'dead end'.

Calm over Parity

As the Soviet Union built up its strategic forces during the late 1960s and early 1970s, the initial response from American analysts was quite sanguine. Ever since the first Soviet atomic test in 1949 there had been an anticipation of effective parity – a balance of terror – and by the mid-1950s there was already a sense of a neck-and-neck race between the super-powers. The first half of the 1960s had been one of numerical US superiority but the Administration of the time, while happy to point to this superiority when reassuring Congressmen, did not discuss this in such a way as to suggest that it made life easier for the US in its global diplomacy. McNamara evaluated military capability by reference to assured destruction criteria: once a blatant first strike was evidently unobtainable there could be no superiority that could be exploitable militarily. It was doubted that serious political benefits could flow from an unusable military capability. This line of argument was presented more strongly as the Soviet build-up began, and with it pressure for a US response. Enthoven and Smith provided a clear statement:

> [S]uch 'nuclear superiority' as the United States maintains is of little significance, since we do not know how to use it to achieve our national security objectives. In other words, since the Soviet Union has an assured-destruction capability against the United States, 'superior' US nuclear forces are extremely difficult to convert into real political power. The blunt, unavoidable fact is that the Soviet Union could effectively destroy the United States even after absorbing the full weight of a US first strike, and vice versa.[3]

This approach survived McNamara. Laurence Martin observed in 1973: 'An increasingly dominant view holds that the strategic nuclear forces of the super-powers do nothing but deter the use of each other by making it suicidal.'[4] The main reason for this view was the horrendous consequences of the use of nuclear weapons for all concerned. Joseph Coffey, for example, argued cautiously that US strategic nuclear forces did not have to be 'larger and more powerful than those of an opponent in order to deter him from starting a war or risking a confrontation'. The main reason was that only a few nuclear weapons were needed to kill millions of people. Additional nuclear weapons were surplus to requirements. Variations in comparative levels of damage might be achieved, but this would be of interest 'only to defence analysts'. A national leader might 'deem 10 million casualties as unacceptable as an incomprehensible 100 million dead'.[5]

In an influential article, the former Special Assistant to the President for National Security Affairs, McGeorge Bundy, made the same point forcefully:

> There is an enormous gulf between what political leaders really think about nuclear weapons and what is assumed in complex calculations of relative 'advantage' is simulated strategic warfare. Think Tank analysts can set levels of 'acceptable' damage well up in the tens of millions of lives. They can assume that the loss of dozens of great cities is somehow a real choice for sane men. They are in an unreal world. In the real world of real political leaders – whether here or in the Soviet Union – a decision that would bring even one hydrogen bomb on one city of one's own country would be recognized in advance as a catastrophic blunder; ten bombs on ten cities would be a disaster beyond history; and a hundred bombs on a hundred cities are unthinkable. Yet this unthinkable level of human incineration is the least that could be expected by either side in response to any first strike in the next ten years, *no matter what happens* to weapons systems in the meantime.[6]

The limited political utility of weapons, so horrific in their consequences that they could be brought to bear only in the most extreme circumstances, was reinforced by past experience. It was hard to identify any 'golden age of deterrence' when the Soviet Union had been kept absolutely passive by an imposing US arsenal.

The Cuban missile crisis of 1962 was often cited as an example of the practical benefits of a military superiority. However, examination of the evidence suggested that the sources of American strength lay in a preponderance of conventional strength in the Caribbean, enabling them to adopt the tactic of quarantine which pushed the onus of escalation onto the Russians, so providing a clear demonstration that the prevention of the establishment of missiles in Cuba was a vital US interest.[7]

This stress on the importance of interests in determining respective stakes in a confrontation was a feature of the empirical research on super-power crises that was starting to become available.[8] Critics of post-war American foreign policy, fortified by the sorry experience of the Vietnam War, stressed over-commitment to areas of peripheral interest, over-concentration on a global struggle to the neglect of regional complexities and subtleties. They also criticized over-reliance on deterrent threats in preference to other, more positive, instruments of foreign policy and over-drawn images of opponents which were insensitive to their motivations and calculations. A more realistic policy, it was argued, would note the difficulties of actually applying military force successfully, would therefore be more circumspect about issuing threats of military action (especially in an effort to retrieve a deteriorating situation) and, most important, would clarify national interests with greater care.

In circumstances where there were severe limits on the application of military power, the credibility of military threats would depend on factors such as 'will' or 'resolve'. But in earlier deterrence literature these factors had appeared as almost independent variables, barely influenced by what was actually at stake in each successive crisis. Schelling and others had emphasized the interdependence of commitments; how a retreat when one commitment was challenged would undermine the credibility of all others. Such fears over the consequence of appearing irresolute in any particular crisis for a general strategic position had become an important feature in the rhetoric of American foreign policy. However as soon as the costs of standing firm had to be weighed against the costs of retreat, as they had been in Vietnam, the 'intrinsic interests' at stake in a particular conflict came to the fore. George and Smoke wrote:

> Theorists would do better to caution that sophisticated opponents will judge credibility on the basis of a more fundamental analysis of the defender's interests. For this purpose, the opponent is likely to pay more attention to strategic, political, economic, ideological factors determining the nature and magnitude of these interests than to rhetorical and other signalling devices the defending power may employ to enhance credibility.[9]

Those arguing, in the face of the Soviet build-up, that any strategic superiority short of a first-strike capability was of only marginal value drew on the centrality of interests to the credibility of a deterrent posture. Concluding, for the IISS, the first serious discussion of the implications of visible parity, Walter Slocombe wrote:

> The pattern of effects of parity in Europe – probably the political theatre most sensitive to changes in the American–Soviet relationship – can be expected to be essentially congruent to that elsewhere: negligible technically, and politically significant only when parity acts in parallel with other, stronger forces.[10]

The belief that increments of nuclear power made little difference politically was accepted by the Nixon Administration. President Nixon specifically ruled out an increase in the numbers of US ICBMs as a response to the Soviet build-up. The American approach remained one of ensuring high unit-quality in designing the force structure, discounting numbers *per se*. While the Soviet Union rarely removed old missiles to make way for the new, the United States withdrew from service almost 1000 ICBMs and over 300 B-52 bombers between the early 1960s and the mid-1970s. If they had remained operational, a quite different image to the one that actually prevailed could have been presented. Yet, as Edward Luttwak has noted, even after the start of SALT, in which aggregate numbers were obviously going to be relevant, this policy of removal continued.[11] One of Henry Kissinger's most memorable public statements concurred in the general disposition to doubt the political value of extra nuclear weapons. It came as he was having a difficult time with domestic opponents in his efforts to negotiate a second SALT Treaty:

> And one of the questions which we have to ask ourselves as a country is what in the name of God is strategic superiority? What is the significance of it, politically, militarily, operationally, at these levels of numbers? What do you do with it?[12]

Finally it appeared, with the conclusion of SALT I, that the Soviet Union had come to similar conclusions. After the first ABM Treaty of May 1972, for example, Herbert York wrote a paper on the 'common understandings about basic issues' that were 'clearly implicit' in the Agreement. Among the most important of these was an understanding that 'the deployment of defensive weapons can accelerate the arms race just as much as the deployment of offensive weapons; 'defence of the nation against a massive nuclear attack is impossible'; and 'a strategic situation of approximate parity and mutual deterrence is the best that is now within reach'.[13] This is what the liberal arms controllers had been saying all along! Henry Kissinger presented the Agreement in similar terms. In a briefing to Congress he spoke of how, despite deep and bitter rivalries, the vast power at each side's disposal created 'a certain commonality of outlook, a sort of interdependence for survival between the two of us . . . now that both we and the Soviet Union have begun to find that each increment of power does not necessarily represent an increment of usable political strength'.[14]

Concern over Superiority

The calm over parity was undermined by growing doubts over whether the Kremlin was operating on a similar premise. These doubts grew after SALT as the Soviet Union continued to modernize its strategic forces in an energetic fashion to the accompaniment of an active diplomacy. Wohlstetter's influential articles in *Foreign Policy*[15] had identified the persistent underestimation of the Soviet build-up by the US intelligence community during the 1960s. There had been an assumption that the build-up would stop at the magic figure of 1000 ICBMs, which would mean equality with the US. But the build-up continued to over 1500 ICBMs. It was increasingly suggested that this could only be explained in terms of a drive for superiority; moreover a superiority of the sort that would allow the USSR to fight and 'win' a nuclear war.[16]

A suspicion was introduced into the debate that, in marked contrast to what had previously been believed, the Soviet Union enjoyed a greater insight into the military and political utility of nuclear power than the United States. Colin Gray, who was particularly emphatic on this matter, discerned an evangelical streak in American arms controllers. So confident had they been of the righteousness of their cause that signs of divergent Soviet attitudes and behaviour were taken to be a consequence of strategic illiteracy to be corrected by dialogue with the Americans. 'The most persistent source of error among Western arms race and arms control analysts has been of an ethnocentric character . . . we should discard the last vestiges of the notion that there is a general theoretical enlightenment towards which all arms race actors must necessarily strain.'[17]

The observation was not wholly unfair and was reminiscent of some liberal critiques of arms race behaviour in the United States which noted the tendency to justify the US exploiting some new technology by presuming a similar Soviet interest. Arguments for unilateral restraint were based largely on an apprehension that moves considered defensive by the US would appear fearsome and offensive from a Soviet perspective. For example, Jeremy Stone, one of the leading members of the arms control community, wrote a thoughtful, if somewhat discursive, book in 1967 on methods of improving the strategic dialogue between the two super-powers to improve mutual understanding. Stone analysed the many sources of interference in communications on strategic matters that could impede the develop- ment of the necessary understanding. He observed the danger of ignoring the other's point of view, of forgetting 'that ours is not the universal language and that an apparent stupidity can mask a fully developed opinion of an altogether different kind. The presumption of adversary error is a serious obstacle to effective persuasion.' One of his conclusions was relevant to the debate of a decade later. He stressed the primary importance of determining the goals of US policy. 'So long as we remain unsure of the strategic relations which we and the Soviets ought to seek, we shall be unable to speak and act with complete assurance about them.' Stone cited 'our ambivalence over strategic superiority' as a clear example of how different answers to the desirability of superiority would result in quite different policies.[18]

Gray took matters further, suggesting that if doctrine was to con- verge it would be along the lines preferred by the Soviet Union, that 'strategic numerical appearances were the stuff of which international respect and influence were made', and that 'the best way to prevent war is to be able to fight it effectively'.[19] The superior Soviet under- standing he detected came particularly in the political sphere. Mili- tary power gave strength to the international political offensive of the USSR.[20]

The accuracy of this view of the Soviet approach to nuclear super- iority became a matter of some dispute in the West in the 1970s, even among Sovietologists. By compiling statements from the Soviet mili- tary, a picture soon emerged of a constant yearning for superiority in all departments, a belief that the outcome of any war would be favourable to the cause of socialism if the proper preparations had been taken with men and equipment.[21]

It would have been difficult, both professionally and ideologically, for the Soviet military to take a different line. However, by compiling statements from Soviet political and military leaders on the desirabi- lity of nuclear war, an equally impressive picture soon emerged of an utter catastrophe which must be avoided. Even the notion of 'mutual suicide', somewhat loaded in an ideology which stressed the inevitable historical ascent of socialism, now and again appeared. A statement such as that by Major-General Rair Simonyon was similar to many heard in the United States:

> Given the priority of strategic forces, when both sides possess weapons capable of destroying many times over all life on earth, neither the addition of new armaments nor an increase in their destructive power can bring any substantial military – and still less political – advantage.[22]

In November 1978 a number of US Senators met President Brezhnev, who reminded them of the lasting effects of the 'losses of the Soviet people' during the war. He added 'We do not want to unleash a nuclear war because we are not crazy', and then went on to remind the Senators of the retaliatory capability of the USSR: 'We will never be the first to let such weapons fly. I will still have time to respond. There will be no more United States. But we will still get it in the neck.'[23]

What this mainly indicated was that Brezhnev could not think of occasions when resort to war would be politically expedient. However, this did not preclude the view that evident Soviet military power has fortunate and beneficial effects on the general state of international affairs. Unlike the United States, which never experienced effective military inferiority, the USSR had undergone this experience and disliked it. The climb-down over Cuba and, probably more important, the irritation at the ease with which American forces moved into Vietnam in 1965, convinced the Soviet leaders that they did need a form of parity to 'sober the imperialists'. The growth of Soviet military might could be understood in terms of the *correlation of forces*, the sum of the economic, political, moral, and military forces behind the contending parties in the international arena. Soviet writings have assured readers that this correlation was moving in favour of socialism, a proposition that would be difficult to support empirically unless major weight was attached to the military factor.[24]

The main benefit of the improving condition was considered to be the realism induced in the imperialist camp as its room for manoeuvre became constrained. Thus parity in strategic forces was 'a special factor behind the realization by Western ruling circles of the new realities of our day and the corresponding correction of their political line'.[25] Such a view of the political utility of nuclear power was more modest and defensive than others attributed to the Soviet Union, but it did indicate a belief that there was some positive relationship between military and political power.

Perceptions

During the 1970s the view gained ground, first in Europe and then in the United States, that the real Soviet threat was political rather than military. The German Defence White Paper of 1970 declared: 'The narrowing, through pressure or threats, of their freedom of political decision is the real danger which the Federal Republic and her Allies might have to face. By comparison, the danger of military aggression is not very great at present.'[26] The term *Finlandization* came into vogue to describe the situation in which a country, despite notional independence, continually accommodated itself to the interests of another power which it dared not offend. A variant, *Self-Finlandization*, described such accommodation taking place without the other power actually exerting pressure. These terms, while pointing to a genuine process, illustrate the crudity of the political concepts commonly employed in strategic studies. Apart from the fact that it appeared to write off a country still enjoying substantial autonomy, it neglected unique factors, including the small size and isolation of Finland and its past conflict with the USSR. It was these factors which produced the current relationship between Finland and the Soviet Union, and offered this worst case (short of actual satellite status) as almost exhausting the arrangements, alternative to an alliance-assisted independence, that could develop.

A measure of accommodation to Soviet interests had been a necessary feature of East–West relations since the 1940s. It resulted first from a recognition of Soviet conventional strength and its hold on Eastern Europe, and then because of substantial changes in absolute Soviet power brought about by its acquisition of a large nuclear stockpile. The question was whether further, and politically more radical, accommodation, might result from changes in *relative* strategic power, particularly when it was admitted that there were severe inhibitions on the successful military exploitation of this power. The issue returned to the source of political will and the rôle played by perceptions of military balance.

The same empirical research that stressed the importance of the interests as the key determinant of crisis behaviour also provided arguments which could be used to suggest that more emphasis should be given to perceptions of the balance. Analysts had become impressed by the difficulty in ensuring that the message one believed to be communicated by declarations or shows of force was properly understood by the recipient. Distortions could be introduced by a combination of psychological, cultural, and bureaucratic factors.

Loyalty to an organization, the stress of crisis, the pressures of 'group think', the need to make sense of confusing and perplexing situations, world-views that fix and limit understanding of the world, the human frailties which lead to excessive confidence in hunches or refusal to acknowledge evidence which undermines favoured theories and so on, all made it difficult to assert that reality would be perceived 'correctly' or in such a way as to be manipulable from the outside.[27]

If military power was in the eyes of the beholder, then there could be no guarantee that it would be beheld in any particular way. However true it may be that additional missiles made little difference, one could not guarantee that this would be universally realized. As Luttwak noted:

> The political utility and military effectiveness of a given structure of armed forces exist in different worlds: one, the world of appearances, impressions, and the culturally determined value judgements of international politics; the other, the world of physical reality in actual warfare.[28]

This line of argument pushed strategic theory into quite the opposite direction from the 1960s, away from the emphasis on rationality and the construction of unambiguous deterrent threats to concern with the imperfection of cognitive and decision processes and the consequent inadequacy of perceptions of military strength, no matter how well they had been constructed. John Steinbruner illustrated the shift by suggesting that the problem in the game of 'Chicken', beloved by the 1950s/1960s strategists, was that a typical decision-maker when playing the game 'would not observe his opponent's behavior at all as the cars approached each other. Rather, he would execute a preestablished program for driving down the center of the road and would notice only whether the line still ran between his wheels.'[29]

This theme found its way into US doctrine, encouraged by the SALT negotiations, which as has been noted,[30] tended to focus on questions of parity. The term adopted to describe US objectives in this area was 'essential equivalence', defined as conferring 'no unilateral advantage to either side'. According to Schlesinger, this was important 'for symbolic purposes, in large part because the strategic offensive forces have come to be seen by many – however regrettably – as important to the status and stature of a major power'. Lack of equality, he explained, could

> become a source of serious diplomatic and military miscalculation. Opponents may feel that they can exploit a favourable imbalance by means of political pressure, as Hitler did so skilfully in the 1930s, particularly with Neville Chamberlain at Berchtesgaden. Friends may believe that a lack of willingness on our part to accept less than equality indicates a lack of resolve to uphold our end of the competition and a certain deficiency in staying power. Our own citizens may doubt our capacity to guard the nation's interests.[31]

His successor in the Carter Administration, Harold Brown, also accepted that 'essential equivalence' was important; it 'guards against any danger that the Soviets might be seen as superior – even if the perception is not technically justified'.[32]

Once subjective factors were accorded critical importance in the formation of a deterrent posture then all aspects of military power became of potential importance and nothing could be discounted.

Measuring the Balance

The first problem, if the quantity and quality of strategic forces was to be taken as an index of political will, as was soon discovered in SALT, was that there was no self-evident index of military power. The impression of the balance created could vary according to which measure was chosen, for example delivery vehicles or warheads. The more an index was sought which conveyed military effectiveness the more difficult the calculations became. Two popular measures became *equivalent megatonnage*, which acknowledged that destructive power does not grow proportionately with yield and indicated counter-city potential, and *lethality*, which indicated counter-force potential.[33] Schlesinger argued that it would be a mistake to allow any major asymmetry to develop between the United States and the Soviet Union in the 'basic technological and other factors that shape force effectiveness'.[34]

The greater the concern with factors that shape force effectiveness (target structure; defences; reliability; tactics; as well as accuracy, yield, and numbers of warheads) the more complicated the analysis became, and the more unknowables and unquantifiables were involved.

The anxiety was supposedly over the perceptions of simple-minded politicians and other amateurs in military matters; it would have been surprising if their views of the military balance were influenced by arcane and complex calculations which could only be performed with the aid of a computer. If visible disparities did matter, it was in the crude and quantifiable measures, such as delivery vehicles. The desire to construct measures that conveyed real force effectiveness betrayed an American inclination to place confidence, in the final analysis, in the real quality of the hardware rather than in subjective perceptions.[35]

The second problem was the lack of evidence (market research) used to justify the stress on 'perception'. The only serious empirical work on the topic found that, in a variety of relevant publics (in Europe, Japan, and in the Middle East), there was a lack of agreement on which super-power was ahead, and that a large number of respondents believed that the question had little point because the two super-powers could so easily destroy each other. The study demonstrated that the issues were treated with great common sense and perspective and that there was little disposition to take radical political steps on the basis of marginal shifts in super-power capabilities.[36] Similarly, opinion poll data in the late 1950s had shown US Allies believing the USSR to be forging ahead in military power, without this making the slightest difference to their allegiance to the Western side (which if anything strengthened with perception of gains in Soviet military strength).[37]

It was arguable that the problem, if there was one, had much to do with the collapse of self-confidence in the United States following the debacle in Vietnam and the Watergate scandals, particularly when contrasted with what seemed to be the clear and positive view on the political value of military power held in the Kremlin. America appeared hesitant and fumbling, overwhelmed by the limits of power, whereas the Soviet Union, in propaganda for both internal and external purposes, took care to project a confident image, with a world correlation of forces moving inexorably in its favour. The perpetual lobbying in the United States encouraged a harping on American weaknesses and Soviet strengths.

Bemoaning American decline became a regular theme among conservative pundits. The weakness the critics deplored was a growing reluctance to solve foreign-policy problems by military means, even in areas where the Soviet Union was relying on a militaristic approach. The issue came to a head at the start of 1980 following the Soviet invasion of Afghanistan. While this was a clear sign that the Soviet Union was prepared to exert its military power in a ruthless manner if necessary, the fact that it was considered necessary reflected a failure in the political attempts to establish a Marxist regime in Afghanistan. The consequent Soviet experience against determined, but poorly armed, Afghan tribesmen served to remind the Kremlin of the difficulties of this sort of exercise. Earlier interventions, using Cuban troops, such as those in Angola and Ethiopia, had not been walkovers.

The very fact that the Soviet Union was throwing its weight around the third world was sufficient to generate alarm in the West, particularly as the exercise of Soviet power was coming to be too close for comfort to regions vital to the economies of the West, such as the oil wells of Arabia and the mines of Africa. The trend of the West during the 1970s – to avoid further military entanglements in the third world – was reversed, with plans for a Rapid Deployment Force to confront any Soviet excursions into the Gulf area. Because of Soviet proximity to the area there was even less hope that the United States could hold a Soviet advance in this region than in Europe. The concept was very much a 'trip-wire' one, borrowed from the European theatre, by which it was hoped that the fear of a super-power confrontation, rather than the likely outcome of a confrontation, would serve to deter Soviet adventures. This move indicated a preference for useable military power to signal and protect interests and suggested the limited impact of the overall strategic balance on local conflicts.

Stressing the perceptions of others reflected an uncertainty over the quality of American perceptions: giving way to subjectivity reflected the lack of any clear empirical basis for nuclear strategy. The concept of essential equivalence contributed only a crude political insight, pointing to something so transitory and elusive that it could form no consistent guide to force planning and was of only slight relevance to international crises.

25 Selective Options

If Deterrence Should 'Fail'

The preoccupation with 'essential equivalence' in the US was a consequence of anxiety, in the face of a sustained Soviet build-up, over the real state of the strategic balance, compounded by continual negotiations in SALT to find a formula to express that balance in a mutually satisfactory manner. It was a concept which Congressmen and diplomats could readily understand, though they may have found the details unduly complicated. It was not, however, a concept which naturally appealed to the community of professional strategists.

Members of this community had become extremely competent in the technical analysis of military capabilities and tactics. Their focus of attention was what could be done, and how, to and by whom, in an actual combat. This might be called the 'RAND tradition', and it had certain results. One was the dismissal of tendencies towards mechanical force matching, as this provided imprecise and unsatisfactory guidance for military planners. Another, which has already been discussed at some length here, was a growing irritation that the concept of mutual assured destruction discouraged the development of any operational nuclear options other than an all-out attack.

The natural instinct of those working within this tradition was to solve the 'credibility' problem of the US deterrent by making it possible to fight a nuclear war in a non-suicidal manner, rather than by manipulating perceptions. The stress on the appearance of weapons, individually and in aggregate, contrasted with the professional's interest in real capabilities.

This approach can be illustrated by reference to an influential article by William Van Cleave and Roger Barnett. They found it unsatisfactory that deterrence should be based upon 'unusable weapons'. Deterrence they saw as a product of capability and credibility. The greater the capability 'to use nuclear forces in a rational and non-apocalyptic fashion', the greater the credibility and thus the strength of deterrence. Apart from anything else 'deterrence may fail . . . and the weapons may have to be used'. While they did not reject the concept of 'essential equivalence' nor were they overly impressed by it: 'To be realistic . . . it must be acknowledged that essential equivalence may go the way of other labelled policies and become little more than flummery. While it is an admirable goal, it is not an exact one and may become more elastic over time'. One reason for that was that the definition necessary to achieve a SALT agreement might 'render the concept sterile'.[1]

The strength of this approach lay in the conviction that the question of what to do if war broke out (normally posed as 'what happens if deterrence fails?') deserved a serious and constructive answer, rather than a pained assertion that there could be no sensible or useful policy for nuclear war. Albert Wohlstetter argued:

We cannot assure that a nuclear war will never occur simply by repeating that it would be an unlimited catastrophe. And we cannot eliminate the possibility of nuclear war simply by *assuring* that if it occurs it *will* be an unlimited catastrophe.[2]

In planning for nuclear war it appeared implausible that the sort of nuclear strike most discussed in the US debate, an all-out attack on Soviet population and industry, would be the most appropriate. The sort of priorities which governed the stress on counter-city threats during peace-time, to remind the other side of the risks of combat while reassuring him that no surprise first strike was being planned, would be reversed in war: attacks on Soviet civilians would provide no relief to American civilians while, possibly, attacks on Soviet military capabilities might; all-out attacks would be acts of despair while limited attacks offered some hope of war termination at a level of destruction that was something less than total and on terms of some political value. Michael May argued:

The main usefulness of weapons, if we are attacked, will be to make sure that the attacker is prevented from following up his attack with steps that would lead to further destruction or domination of this country and its allies. We will want to do this more urgently than we will want to carry out any previously set level of destruction against the attacker.[3]

To those who argued along these lines it was axiomatic that a statesman who knew that he could fight a nuclear war with some chance of his society surviving could take a far more credible and robust stand in a crisis than one knowing that a failure in crisis management could lead to nothing but utter disaster. In this way any serious war-fighting capabilities would enhance deterrence.

The proposition that more impressive war-fighting capabilities would produce an increment of 'resolve' was unassailable. Critics of this approach feared that the increment might be so large as to lead to recklessness. More likely, however, the increment would be so small as to make little difference. Implicit, and often explicit, in many descriptions of the consequences of a 'failure' in deterrence was a loss of resolve in a crisis of the Cuban Missile sort, in which the stark alternatives appeared as either peace or total war.

Appeal to the October 1962 crisis was not the best guide for future crises. Leaving aside the purely military factors, Cuban missiles were a prominent issue in US domestic politics and could be portrayed as a direct threat to American cities. America's NATO allies did not have a direct stake in the matter and so neither required intensive consultation nor were expected to implement any decisions. The resolution of the crisis had little to do with the internal politics of Cuba. It was a two-party confrontation over a straightforward movement of military equipment. For all these reasons it fitted, unusually well, into the 'eyeball-to-eyeball' dramas that many felt to be the essence of super-power crises. Less well remembered was the Berlin crisis of 1961: this involved many more actors and a much more complicated diplomacy, and was a matter of less obvious intrinsic interest to the US. The important shifts in the international political structure since the early 1960s made it even less likely that a crisis outside the NATO area would be politically simply enough to appear as a question of resolve between Washington and Moscow.

The fact that, despite occasional alarms during the Vietnam War and one moment of great tension towards the end of the October 1973 Arab–Israeli war, there had been no super-power crisis that even hinted at a decisive showdown, made all scenarios other than major political and military upheavals in the centre of Europe seem quite manageable. Elsewhere the West had sufficient conventional forces available for most contingencies. These were not always deployed during the 1970s, but less because of a decline in options at the higher range of the escalation ladder, and more because of doubts over the value of military intervention into difficult situations in Third World countries.

To talk simply of deterrence 'failing' without further elaboration of the probable circumstances surrounding the failure provided little guidance for strategic planning. Implicit in much of the discussion of options was the scenario of a deliberate Soviet attack on NATO, but the history of East–West crisis was replete with conflicts of more equivocal origins, often the result of intransigence or unruliness among client states, and best treated with cautious circumspection (as was invariably the case) rather than bluster and sabre-rattling, and managed with care.[4]

The importance of the strategic balance as a factor in crises would thus vary according to the nature of the conflict and, until matters reached a harrowing level, and unless one side enjoyed unambiguous superiority, it was unlikely to be overriding. In these cases where comparative strategic advantage might be determinant, impressive war-fighting capabilities could, in principle, prove to be significant. The question was whether any feasible moves in this direction could make a fundamental difference to the appreciation of the risks in the respective capitals.

The Search for Options

The Nixon Administration was inclined to answer this question positively, because of its fascination (which at times seemed obsessive) with the sources of 'resolve' and 'will' in international affairs. In addition Henry Kissinger had long been interested in the possibility of limited nuclear war and a range of options to fortify deterrence.

Kissinger has written of his own distaste for the strategy of assured destruction. It implied the most inhuman strategy for conducting a war. The threat to mutual suicide was not credible, because to make such a thing credible required a diplomacy that suggested irrationality, yet the American political system required an image of 'calculability and moderation':

And if deterrence failed and the President was finally faced with the decision to retaliate, who would take the moral responsibility for recommending a strategy based on the mass extermination of civilians? How could the United States hold its allies together as the credibility of its strategy eroded? How would we deal with Soviet conventional forces once the Soviets believed that we meant what we said about basing strategy on the extermination of civilians?[5]

In June 1969 he described to the President the dilemma he might face in the event of a limited Soviet nuclear attack. The dilemma was raised in a rhetorical manner, in Nixon's *Foreign Policy* report to Congress in February 1970:

> Should a President, in the event of a nuclear attack, be left with the single option of ordering the mass destruction of enemy civilians, in the face of the certainty that it would be followed by the mass slaughter of Americans.[6]

The question was repeated in slightly expanded form in the Reports of the next two years, affirming the need 'for forces and procedures that provide us with alternatives appropriate to the nature and level of the provocation'.[7]

The President already had a number of options, but they were apparently still too large and unsubtle for his taste and that of his advisors. In the first couple of years of the Nixon Administration the desire for new options remained wishful thinking. There were no major studies on the problems of limited nuclear strikes in the earlier years. Orders to devise strategies to meet contingencies other than all-out nuclear challenge were issued to the Pentagon where little was done. The military saw this as another attempt by civilians to meddle in force planning, while the civilians in the Pentagon worried about new demands on a defence budget that was already under pressure.[8]

In the course of studies conducted by the NSC on the 'survivability' of US retaliatory forces in early 1971, this often expressed but still rather vague aspiration for options caused some problems, for it left uncertainty as to US second-strike requirements. As a consequence, in April 1971 a 'Strategic Objectives' study was initiated in the NSC. Just over a year later it moved from a staff study to the highest level, when Kissinger was put in charge of an interdepartmental group to consider a variety of limited-war options involving small-scale nuclear exchanges, demonstration 'shots across the bow' as well as the problems liable to be caused by a removal of the US counter-force option by a Soviet attack on the *Minuteman* ICBMs.[9] The implementation of a new targeting policy was not a high priority in 1972. Far more important, at least to Kissinger, was SALT. He considered his efforts to shore up deterrence through detente more important than arguments over what to do if events moved in exactly the opposite direction to the one in which he was trying to push them. Furthermore, the hardware requirements of the new policy could cause political problems. These requirements were qualitative rather than quantitative. Highly sophisticated command and control capabilities would be needed to extend the range of effective choice. Also, and more awkward, was the need for highly accurate warheads, capable of destroying hard targets.

By 1972 there had been considerable technological progress in this area but a decision to exploit it was restrained by the widespread feeling amongst Senators that accurate warheads were likely to accelerate the arms race, by raising fears of a first strike. Moreover, 1972 was an election year and candidate George McGovern was one of these suspicious Senators. When the story leaked that these new strategic options had been under study in the NSC and that hard-target warheads were now considered desirable by the Administration, opposition was immediately generated in the Senate. Because of the sensitivity of explaining a move which many considered to be destabilizing, in the midst of a Presidential campaign that posed the achievement of SALT I as a major triumph, the Administration did not push the matter until after November 1972. In the first half of 1973 President Nixon authorized implementation of the doctrine. About this time James Schlesinger became Secretary of Defense. It was he who announced the new strategy in a January 1974 press conference and then became an energetic lecturer on the subject to Congress and the public. While he was not responsible for its formulation, his name became associated with the new strategy and he did give it a gloss of his own.

'The Schlesinger Doctrine'

Schlesinger, who had spent much of the 1960s at RAND, was the first professional civilian strategist to become Secretary of Defense. As an economist by training he had become disturbed by some of the exaggerated claims being made for methodologies such as systems analysis, and this had brought him into dispute with some of his colleagues.[10] Nevertheless, on strategic issues he shared the growing scepticism on the value of the emphasis being accorded assured destruction criteria in US policy.

In one paper, written while at RAND, he expressed concern that one consequence of the arguments over ABM deployment had been 'to turn our thoughts away from city avoidance and minimizing collateral damage to the civil fabric of our opponent's society and toward employment of military capabilities in their most destructive mode'.[11] Elsewhere, he argued that a more rational posture ('under almost any imaginable circumstances') than city-busting would be to 'reserve one's own forces – and thereby to create every incentive for the enemy to refrain from striking at one's own cities'. This would be more credible and held out some hope of reducing damage to the societies of the belligerents. It would, however, require a 'sophisticated' capability, the key to which would be 'the ability to implement a number of options':

> It requires at the outset a very large force, so that numerous vehicles and weapons can be allocated to strikes at the extended forces of the foe. It requires a hyper-protected force for intra-war deterrence, with long endurance and excellent communications and control. It requires, in the counterforce stage, the ability to assess damage – and to reassign vehicles – thereby compounding the requirements for the command, control and communications system. It requires knowledge of the deployment of the opponent's forces.[12]

When Schlesinger became Secretary of Defense in 1973, the main shift towards this sort of strategy had been undertaken and the requisite capabilities were being developed. There was therefore a unique opportunity to turn theory into practice. As soon as he was appointed, Schlesinger made clear the sort of strategic options he wanted. On 10 January 1974 he was able to tell a meeting of the Overseas Writers Association that his wish was fulfilled, with a change 'in the strategies of the United States with regard to the hypothetical employment of central strategic forces'. As he explained the change[13] it became apparent that the objective was to have as wide a range of nuclear options, from the very small to the very large, and that the bias was on the development of the smaller strikes which were to be counter-force rather than counter-city in character.

The objective would be to limit the chances of uncontrolled escalation and 'hit meaningful targets with a sufficient accuracy–yield combination to destroy only the intended target and to avoid widespread collateral damage'. Planning had to assume that deterrence might fail but it was not possible 'to forecast the situations that would cause it to fail'. Contingencies mentioned included accidental acts, the escalation of conventional conflicts, a challenge to 'a nuclear test of wills' by 'ill-informed or cornered and desperate leaders' involving the nuclear equivalent of 'shots across the bow'. Nor could 'a massive surprise attack on our forces' be precluded, although Schlesinger considered its probability 'close to zero under existing conditions'.[14]

This approach did not generate the enormous debate that the Administration appeared to have anticipated. A trickle of articles appeared attacking the new strategy, but the attack was muted.[15] There were three central points to this attack: the unreality of the belief that nuclear war could be controlled; if it were believed that nuclear war could be controlled at tolerable levels of damage this could increase the risk of premature resort to nuclear weapons; and the renewed stress on counter-force options could raise fear of first-strike ambitions, introducing the danger of an arms race and jeopardizing SALT. The danger was in forgetting that 'the primary objective of nuclear strategy is to avoid wars, not to fight them',[16] and the problem was that the two objectives were in tension.

The critique lacked force in part because it was difficult to argue against flexibility and options *per se*. Only Bernard Brodie, increasingly disenchanted with the preoccupation with what he described as 'strategic fiction' (borrowing the term from Raymond Aron), questioned whether 'expanding the President's military options is always a good thing', because of the burden it put on his 'wisdom' (and, one might add, his capacity to make a decision in a crisis by complicating enormously the process of choosing). Brodie noted that Congress had recently been taking steps to decrease the President's capacity for independent action, after the experience of the exercise of free and wide choice over Vietnam. Nor did he think most of the options would be considered practical. The rigidity which appeared to limit options in the past, he argued, lay not in the thinking of past Secretaries of Defense, but in the situations they were contemplating.[17]

Most of Schlesinger's critics, however, conceded the need for flexibility as soon as they protested that there had always been a measure of flexibility, even in the later McNamara period. Thus Barry Carter observed that there was 'general agreement among strategic analysts that the US should have a variety of response options other than massive retaliation against cities'. The argument, he later indicated, was over 'where the line should be drawn' in development of these options.[18] What concerned him and other critics were the counterforce options.

But here the question was whether or not the balance of terror was 'delicate', in that new weapons innovations could lead to serious instability. Schlesinger's predecessor, Melvin Laird, had once insisted that an effective first-strike capability was both possible and the major Soviet objective. But the claim could not be sustained, mainly because of the invulnerability of SLBMs. Schlesinger dismissed first-strike fears. He was concerned with restricted attacks. Furthermore he could point to the development of Soviet counter-force capabilities to which some response was in order, claiming that nothing would be gained by unilateral restraints. The critics could not have it both ways, arguing simultaneously that the strategic balance was so stable that counter-force options would provide no advantages while insisting that their introduction would be destabilizing.[19] By the same token, of course, these conditions did not promise major increments of credibility. Put in perspective, the prospectus was for a wider, but still extremely constrained and unpleasant range of choice.

There were obvious parallels with McNamara's fated attempt to introduce similar options and 'no-cities' policy in 1961–2. However, there were three important differences. First, the technologies of precision and control were now at hand. It is arguable that the requisite capabilities were emerging through the impact of the microelectronics revolution, almost independently of political choice. Second, both sides possessed secure second-strike forces. Third, the Russians were on the way to achieving a comparable, controlled counter-force capability.

If a new mode of nuclear war was to be formulated out of this set of circumstances then some Soviet connivance was necessary. It takes two to keep a nuclear war limited. Here the proponents of selective options were in difficulty for the USSR still lacked a doctrine of this sort. Soviet pronouncements on the Schlesinger doctrine were unremittingly hostile, recalling similar distaste in the early 1960s over rules for nuclear war. Benjamin Lambeth, sympathetic to the new doctrine, noted with regret: 'Of all the conceptual and weaponry asymmetries that currently obtain in the US–Soviet strategic confrontation, the one which rests on the assumption of targeting limitation and intra-war "crisis management" seems to be the most dominant and irreconcilable'.[20]

In the late 1960s Soviet doctrine began to concede the possibility of forms of limitation particularly with regard to the threshold of nuclear use, and possibly then with regard to containing any nuclear use to a theatre of battle so long as there were no direct attacks on the Soviet Union. However, the stress on the need for victory meant that avoidance of collateral damage around important military targets, let alone preserving the enemy populations from the consequences of their government's folly, did not rank high as a priority. Nor was the idea of withholding forces in order to allow time for negotiations attractive. Military force was applied as a consequence of the breakdown of diplomacy. Here there was an important difference with the American tendency to see early military exchanges as a continuation of pre-war diplomacy and a last attempt to restore some form of deterrence, rather than as the start of an attempt to resolve matters by military means. This would be no time for gestures, experiments, and half-measures. The most explicit Soviet treatment of nuclear employment in the European theatre, Colonel A. A. Sidorenko's *The Offensive* (1970), suggested that the first employment of nuclear weapons, whatever the state of fighting with conventional armaments, would mark a dramatic shift in the character of the war. 'In the case of their employment, nuclear weapons will become the main means for destroying the enemy in battle.'[21]

If the US policy was designed only as a reaction to plausible opening nuclear shots from the USSR, then a Soviet proclivity for large strikes rendered it futile; if it was designed for opening shots for the US then it could be folly, for it would invite a massive Soviet response without gaining any of the advantages of a first blow. To sustain the Schlesinger initiative it was therefore necessary to find grounds for believing that the Soviet military could, conceivably, move in this direction. The only available grounds were the range of capabilities actually developed, the interest in control mechanisms shown in the Soviet literature, and inferences from observation of Soviet military exercises. But no documentary evidence could be found to support the proposition that, privately, Soviet thoughts might be moving in these directions. It is somewhat ironic to find an article by William Van Cleave which opened by deriding past US hopes of doctrinal convergence on the basis of mutual assured destruction, and closed straining to find evidence of a serious Soviet interest in the sort of selective targeting envisaged by Schlesinger. ('Soviet thought on nuclear warfare may be undergoing some refinement'.)[22]

While the Soviet leaders could, in time, overcome their scepticism over selective targeting, despite these sort of stylized and subtle exchanges being at variance with predispositions towards uninhibited expression of raw power, their initial negative reaction cast doubt upon what might be achieved by limited strikes.

Possible objectives could be divided into those which sought to remind the enemy of the dangers of continuing with his aggression by capitalizing on fears of the destructive potential of the bomb, and those which sought to exploit the innate qualities of nuclear weapons by attacking targets of high military value. With the first set of objectives all that might be necessary was to explode one nuclear warhead on some enemy target. The problems here would be connected with ensuring that the enemy understood the message one was trying to convey. The willingness to use nuclear weapons would be apparent, but the enemy might conclude that the feebleness of the attack demonstrated cowardice in pushing the matter too far rather than the exercise of controlled restraint. Nor could one guarantee that the attack would be experienced as restraint. This might be because of confusion in the enemy's HQ over what had actually happened in some distant region (from which, in the aftermath of a nuclear explosion, communications would be far from perfect) or greater damage being actually caused than expected (because, for example, of fallout). Even if properly understood, the enemy might not be able to respond in kind because of the quality of weapons or the target structure. These difficulties would also apply in the case of a limited first attack by the USSR. What constituted a response in kind? a similar number of casualties, an explosion of similar yield, a delivery vehicle of similar type, or a target of equivalent significance and value (a regional capital or a naval base)? There were certain attacks for which there could be no responses in kind. For example, it is arguable that the most likely Soviet 'limited' strike would be against targets in Western Europe to disrupt the cohesion of NATO; attacks on the non-USSR Warsaw Pact could not have a similar effect.

A greater source of difficulty in keeping exchanges limited would be the temptation to gain military advantage in the attack. In the elaboration of the Schlesinger doctrine it became apparent that three military objectives would be germane: (a) aid to conventional forces engaged in major fighting, probably in Europe; (b) destruction of remaining enemy strategic forces to limit further damage; and (c) attainment of effective military superiority at a particular point in the escalation ladder (escalation dominance). To attain each of these objectives would require sizeable strikes.

Options for a European War

The first of these contingencies, a conventional war at a worrisome stage, represented the basic NATO problem and much of the Schlesinger doctrine could be seen as yet another attempt to solve it. The RAND tradition pointed in this direction rather than towards limited strikes, which Wohlstetter described as 'devoid of political context' and as ignoring the likelihood 'that each side would have powerful incentives to select targets for their military significance in relation to a continuing conventional war. These targets would not be abstract counters to be exchanged in a game of nuclear checkers where each player demonstrates his "resolve"'.[23]

When pressed for scenarios, Schlesinger frequently mentioned an attack on Western Europe. In an interview with Laurence Martin, he stressed the importance of 'coupling' US nuclear forces to the defence of Europe and identified it as a major reason behind the change in doctrine.[24] Schlesinger made it clear that he would consider first use of nuclear weapons to fulfil Alliance obligations, which he distinguished from initiating a war in a surprise first strike. The sort of targets often specified – airfields, submarine bases, oil fields and railway marshalling yards – were of obvious military relevance. The whole emphasis on nuclear weapons as precise instruments of low collateral damage, rather than being blunt and crude, weapons of mass destruction, encouraged this sort of target structure. Such strikes would need to be related to the situation on the ground. While nuclear use might be the easiest of all at sea, with no collateral damage to worry about, this would be of little help to a hard-pressed army commander being pushed back to the Channel.

The question of whether new technologies could be used to improve NATO's over-all defensive position was first considered in the 1970s in the context of innovations in conventional weapons. Developments in the ability to find, track, identify, target, and destroy enemy units, from any distance and with great precision, at all times of day and in all weather, raised hope that forces configured essentially for defensive purposes would benefit from these new technologies and so be able to hold back a much larger invading force. Some engagements during the later stages of the Vietnam War and, more impressively, during the Yom Kippur War of October 1973, convinced many that aircraft and tanks were being made virtually obsolete by precision weapons. This enthusiasm dampened somewhat with the growing awareness of opportunities for counter-measures, the possibilities for the exploitation of the new technologies in offensive tactics, and problems in the actual organization of forces to operate with and against these weapons.

The hope, shared by Schlesinger, was that these new conventional weapons would raise the nuclear threshold. Often using similar arguments to McNamara, he spoke of 'the gradual evolution towards increasing stress on the conventional components, a dimunition of the threat of recourse to nuclear weapons'.[25]

To the surprise of some, this hope did not cause the same ructions within the Alliance as had McNamara's push for the conventional option. This was because of a conscious desire to avoid the arguments of the 1960s, the more qualified claims made by the Americans, and the fact that the Europeans managed to convince themselves that this sort of option was both effective (as shown in October 1973) and relatively inexpensive. However the Europeans showed no inclination to over-exert themselves in mapping out a new NATO strategy and, as it became apparent that the new technologies were of benefit without making a radical difference (except at a high cost), the enthusiasm waned and they contented themselves with extremely incremental force improvements.

The question of the impact of both new conventional and nuclear technologies for the defence of Europe came together with renewed consideration of tactical nuclear weapons. Here again Schlesinger encouraged modernization of an arsenal that was large but obsolete,[26] again with the aim of controlling the level of violence in any conflict. As a topic for concerted intellectual effort, nuclear weapons based in the European theatre had been lying fallow for many years. The position reached in the 1960s was that the Europeans welcomed the presence of these shorter-range systems at the front line as a direct link between the defence of the continent and American nuclear forces, but there was very little idea as to how they could be put to good use in an actual conflict. The political pressure would be to delay use; and the weapons were of disproportionate yield for the tasks they might be expected to perform and so would cause immense collateral damage in the territory being defended.

In keeping with the general mood reflected by Schlesinger, there were a number of schemes put forward for the modernization of this arsenal, all with the aim of making its employment more precise and less damaging to those being defended, and thus more credible for deterrence. More than other sets of programmes relevant to the new doctrine, this occasioned a political row within NATO, which posed (with a number of more diversionary questions) the difficult question of how much one did wish to make nuclear use easier, weighing increments of credibility against the danger of premature moves towards the holocaust. The answer to this question was beyond the competence of a technical strategist – it was a political question over what was feared most – nuclear war or the Soviet Union.

The debate was triggered somewhat accidentally. One of the new 'tailored' nuclear munitions (the 'neutron bomb') enhanced radiation effects and reduced the others. It was designed to disable tank crews, and it became the subject of controversy in 1976 and 1977 after it had been misleadingly characterized as a weapon that killed people and left property intact. As one that stressed rather than minimized the singularly nuclear effect of radiation it was an unfortunate advertisement for a strategy that aimed to use nuclear weapons interchangeably with their conventional counterparts. The public unease in Europe with this weapon demonstrated that the special fears aroused by any nuclear weapon, and the consequent impediments to their use in a crisis, could not be resolved simply by greater tailoring. The debate, in which both sides exaggerated the extent to which this innovation would make nuclear weapons 'easier' to use (their use in quantity would still be exceptionally unpleasant for the local population and could well trigger an unlimited Soviet response), left the whole matter as unresolved as ever.[27]

A related problem was another collection of systems, hitherto ignored because they were of little relevance to either close combat or intercontinental exchanges. These were longer-range systems for 'rear-echelon' attacks (which might include reserve forces or communication systems) but which could also be directed against the cities of the Warsaw Pact or, from the other side, against the European segment of NATO. Furthermore, the Soviet modernization priorities appeared to be focused on weapons of this range, of which the USSR in any case enjoyed a preponderance, rather than on its short-range systems, which remained large in yield and 'dirty' in effects, mocking any Western ideas of keeping a two-sided nuclear war in Europe 'clean' and confined to military targets.

The conceptual framework available to NATO for dealing with the questions of employment of nuclear weapons in the European theatre was inadequate and far less elaborate than that for dealing with central systems. The connection between mutual capabilities for intercontinental attacks on the cities of the super-powers (strategic) and intermediate-to-short-range attacks on military targets within

Europe (theatre or tactical) broke down both with explicit moves, supported by Schlesinger, to use 'strategic' weapons to attack military targets related to a European battle, and the growing awareness of the vulnerability of European cities to weapons based in the continent, hitherto ignored or classified as 'tactical'. (To a German, practically any nuclear weapon is potentially 'strategic' in its consequences.)

The link between the US nuclear forces and the defence of Europe, which dominated European perceptions of the issue, might well be strengthened by extending the direct value of US strategic forces to fighting on NATO's central front. On the other hand, a renewed stress on systems based in Europe as strategic threats to the USSR, with even talk of a 'Euro-strategic' balance separate from the central strategic balance, might weaken the link. It would seem that an important feature of Schlesinger's approach was to take the first of these routes, so enhancing the credibility of the US nuclear guarantee. Yet the impact of this move was undermined by the growing willingness of the Europeans themselves, particularly the Germans, to move in exactly the opposite direction. This went against precedent and against notions of the 'indivisibility of deterrence'. It was assumed that threats uniquely directed against Western Europe deserved, in part, a uniquely European response. The reasons for this were complex; the consolidation of strategic parity in SALT had focused attention on asymmetries lower down the line which were compounded by the growing obsolescence of NATO's long-range theatre forces when compared with the modernization of Soviet forces. The consequence was that Western Europeans were not convinced that new targeting options for US ICBMs (or even for the 32 Poseidon SLBMs assigned to SACEUR) were sufficiently credible to fully deter a set of limited contingencies specifically related to the European theatre.

In December 1979 NATO eventually decided to deploy 572 American medium-range ballistic and cruise missiles on European soil. The feature of the decision that aroused the most satisfaction was that it had been made at all, given the domestic political difficulties it caused in a number of member states (still by no means wholly resolved). The substance of the decision was to establish a distinctive regional response to the modernization of Soviet missiles designed solely for European use, without denying the essential link between the defence of Europe and America strategic forces. Thus, though American-owned and manned, the forces were to be ground-based so as to make their activation in the face of a Soviet advance credible. There were to be sufficient missiles to make a difference, but not so many as to suggest that they could fully satisfy NATO's nuclear needs without involving the rest of the American nuclear arsenal.[28]

ICBM Vulnerability

Schlesinger did not succeed in steering the US strategic debate away from consideration of large-scale nuclear exchanges between the super-powers and towards analysis of their direct relevance to any land battle in Europe. This was not surprising. Super-power strategic relations had become a highly charged political issue because of SALT. The concepts of first and second strikes had taken root and provided the frame of reference for the public debate on strategic forces since the late 1950s. The fact that the US had accepted an obligation to possibly employ its nuclear arsenal on behalf of its allies if they were suffering a conventional invasion was less well under-stood, and often only alluded to somewhat cryptically by senior US officials (except at NATO gatherings). Even when this issue was understood, it was normally felt that the state of the strategic balance would determine the US response to a crisis in Europe.

Finally, as Schlesinger sought to justify the creation of new Ameri-can options by pointing to their acquisition in the Soviet Union, it was the growth in counter-force capabilities embodied in their large force of large ICBMs, to which he directed attention. It was to the deteriorating balance in counter-force capabilities upon which Henry Kissinger (when out of office) in a celebrated speech to an orthodox, and consequently somewhat distressed, NATO audience, based his assertion that it was no longer possible to offer the assurances which he, with his predecessors and successors, had regularly provided, of an 'undiminished American military commitment'.[29]

The main scenario which came to dominate the debate was an attack by USSR ICBMs against US missile silos, effectively elimin-ating the ICBM force, when by contrast a similar US attack on Soviet silos would be far less complete. Colin Gray claimed that the question of what to do about this growing vulnerability of fixed-site, land-based missile forces would, in the 1980s, be 'the question of the decade'. The loss of one leg of the strategic triad would be 'an event so momentous that its anticipation should be the occasion for a fundamental review of strategic doctrine'.[30] Of course, a change in strategic doctrine was needed to make the event 'momentous', for under established concepts the hypothetical 'loss' of this leg in a surprise attack was more than compensated for by the other two legs (bombers and SLBMs) which, even somewhat depleted themselves, would still be capable of delivering a powerful retaliatory blow. When, in the mid-1960s, Pentagon planners had first begun to consider the possible vulnerability of the *Minuteman* ICBM force, the most natural reaction seemed to be to strengthen the 'survivable' submarine-based missile force. In 1969 the Nixon Administration first identified the ICBM vulnerability issue as a central problem, for which it was offering the *Safeguard* ABM system as a solution. Melvin Laird then conceded that it only really mattered because the rest of the triad might also become vulnerable.[31]

This argument proved difficult to sustain, as did Laird's central contention that the *Minuteman* force might be vulnerable by the mid-1970s. Nevertheless, the simple arithmetic of MIRVing, combined with the large size of Soviet warheads, meant that there was a good chance that this threat would develop one day. Meanwhile the attack by liberal arms controllers on the advanced US MIRVing programme as destabilizing because of its counter-force (taken to be synonymous with first strike) implications helped to create a climate in which MIRVed ICBMs held in quantity by either side were seen as profoundly disturbing. The eventual Soviet development of MIRVs in 1974, after a number of false alarms, meant that, for the rest of the decade, the evolving vulnerability of *Minuteman* could be charted and its nadir projected, usually at some point in the first half of the 1980s, in a manner similar to intelligence calculations of the first years of the cold war on the imminent 'year of maximum danger'.[32]

Senator Jackson, as he berated the SALT I Treaty in mid-1972 for doing nothing to prevent this threat, explained why it was in fact threatening. He acknowledged the capacity to retaliate as required by assured destruction concepts after a Soviet attack against US ICBM and bomber bases but he felt that Soviet forces left in reserve would then present an even more fearful threat. The US President would have only one option: to annihilate Russian cities, 'knowing full well, however, that the Russians could strike back at our populated centers far more effectively, killing more people, virtually wiping out our population'. This possibility might undermine deterrence because the Russians 'might conclude that no American President would order such a move'.[33]

Jackson put the problem as one of a balance of forces after the Soviet surprise attack, in which there was a Soviet advantage in counter-city capabilities. In the same hearings, William Van Cleave began the shift in the terms of reference of the debate away from that of assured destruction towards theories of *escalation dominance*, in which the key question was the burden of responsibility for escalating to higher levels of violence:

> [I]nstead of the simple model of aggressive Soviet first strike and US retaliation, we may face a situation where the Soviets could strike first and still retain their own assured destruction retaliatory force, leaving the United States in a position of being the initiator of nuclear war against civilian populace and the Soviet Union being in the position of retaliator.[34]

By the end of the decade, this scenario had become established as real and serious, with the associated concept of escalation dominance. Colin Gray used this term in a 1978 explication of the danger, perhaps reflecting the influence of Herman Kahn who had developed the concept in the early 1960s and in whose Hudson Institute Gray was now residing:

> On current trends in the strategic balance, an American President should, prudently, be deterred from initiating strategic nuclear employment; should he proceed nonetheless, the war would very likely terminate after an almost wholly counter-military exchange (which the Soviet Union should win unequivocally) because the United States could not possibly secure an improved war outcome by initiating attacks against Soviet industry and (through relocation) population.[35]

As only ICBMs were really suitable for counter-force attacks on enemy ICBMs, the fear was that, using only about one-third of its force to destroy US ICBMs, the USSR would deprive the President of the option of responding in kind. All that he could do would be to attack softer targets, destructive of life and property, but of less military significance, thus inviting retaliation against American cities. Moreover, after the attack envisaged in this scenario, the Soviet Union would be left with a far greater capacity for engaging in counter-value strikes, so making it an even more unattractive option.[36]

How realistic was this scenario? Even if it is assumed that a force with the requisite number of warheads of the requisite accuracy and yield was available at combat readiness in the USSR, and the Soviet leadership had been convinced that it was of sufficient reliability to perform efficiently in all departments, a perplexing risk calculus would then have to be faced. The first question would be of the undoubted American capacity to launch its ICBMs on warning of an attack. There have been strong indications, as we have noted, that this is what Soviet planners believe that they would do, faced with a similar attack. It became conventional wisdom in the US to caution against relying on warning systems and making retaliatory decisions in twenty minutes, preferring to 'ride out' attacks so that their extent and significance could be properly evaluated. However, the option was never explicitly ruled out and, as anxiety over ICBM vulnerability increased, so did the Administration's ambiguity on this matter.[37]

Even if it were felt that a full-blooded US retaliation would not be automatic, the Russians could not at all be sure that their attack would be experienced as a solely counter-force effort, thus putting pressure on the US President, when considering his retaliatory options, to search for something as patently restrained. If the Soviet first strike was of a size large enough to significantly reduce US retaliatory options, then it would result in massive casualties on the North American continent. The extent of the casualties would depend on a number of factors, such as prevailing weather conditions or warheads going astray quite uncontrollably. American estimates suggested that they could easily be of the order of 10 million dead, perhaps as high as 20 million. More important, in estimating prompt casualties, insufficient attention was being paid to the longer-term disruption of societies with impaired fuel supply, communications and agriculture, and, presumably, somewhat traumatized by their 'limited' experience of nuclear war. A Soviet attack on the US in mid-summer might cause less casualties than one in winter, because the winds would be calmer and so the distribution of fallout would be moderate; however, if the US response, at comparable numbers of megatons, made it impossible to gather the harvest in the USSR the consequences for Soviet society could be devastating.[38]

The idea that attacks of this sort could be considered a limited 'surgical' attack had no reference to anything within human experience, only to a knowledge that it could be worse. Up to 1975, all the wars of America's two centuries had resulted in deaths of less than 1,200,000. An attack on US ICBMs would be an immoderate act, that could not deserve a moderate reaction. The President, in response, might be paralysed with fear and horror, or stirred into a ferocious retaliation. That fallible and unpredictable human beings might be faced with such a choice has always been the fundamental uncertainty upon which nuclear deterrence has depended.

The same loss of perspective on the human meaning of nuclear attacks appeared with the concern over a comparative Soviet advantage in counter-value capabilities after this first Soviet volley, when *absolute* US capabilities could still destroy the USSR as a viable society.[39]

In explaining why the growing Soviet counter-force capability was a matter of real concern, Schlesinger accepted that it would not produce 'anything approximate to a disarming first strike against the United States':

> But such a development could bring into question our ability to respond to attacks in a controlled, selective, and deliberate fashion. It could also give the Soviets a capability that we ourselves would lack, and it could bring into question the sense of equality that the principles of Vladivostok so explicitly endorse. Worst of all, it could arouse precisely the fears and suspicions that our arms control efforts are designed to dispel.[40]

The loss of command and control facilities would be the only sort of truly limited attack relevant to the first of these concerns. If only a portion of *Minuteman* ICBMs were destroyed then sufficient would remain for a suitably selected response; if all *Minuteman* ICBMs were destroyed then this would not necessarily create conditions conducive to a controlled and selected response. These conditions in fact could be varied by moving relevant bases closer to or further from centres of population. The question was whether one wanted to discourage this sort of escalation dominance by deliberately blurring (even more) the distinctions between different stages in the process of escalation, or whether one wanted to increase the enemy's pure counter-force options on the grounds that if there were to be a nuclear war it would be preferable if it could be fought in this sort of manner!

Equally, the proper response was considered not just to reduce vulnerability (for example by a move out to sea) but to increase counter-force capabilities to match those of the adversary. If the aim was to increase the possibilities for both sides to engage in pure counter-force attacks, then over-eagerness to protect forces could be as destabilizing! It would not be possible for both sides to have nothing *but* an invulnerable counter-force capability. A counter-force race could tend to this, although both would probably end up with a 'modern' missile force on each side, mobile, MIRVed with excellent accuracy against hard targets, and a vulnerable fixed-site ICBM force. But counter-force attacks which could *not* eliminate the most modern segment of the enemy's force would presumably be only of marginal value, and so the scenarios of controlled and selective strikes become even more dubious!

However, the main sources of anxiety exhibited by the Schlesinger quotation above appeared to be derived more from notions of essential equivalence than escalation dominance. If major asymmetry was perceived in counter-force capabilities of a sort that could be used to the Soviet advantage, then, however implausible the actual scenario when examined closely, it might influence attitudes. Repetition of concern that such perceptions might develop could become self-fulfilling. These perceptions did not develop independently but were shaped largely by the pronouncements of authoritative Americans. Most Europeans, for example, relied on US sources for their information and ideas on the state of the strategic balance.

As the 1970s progressed, the conventional wisdom became one of alarm over the increasing vulnerability of ICBMs. This was considered a matter of enormous significance, such that the Americans would only feel comfortable in offering, and Western Europe (and Japan) in accepting, a nuclear guarantee if the situation were remedied at once. By the end of the decade large amounts of money were being allocated to the best available remedy, the *MX* ICBM, which would, at the same time, enhance both counter-force options and survive the worst the Russians could offer – once the most appropriate form of mobility had been chosen from a number of singularly unpromising schemes.

The attention devoted to this matter could be taken as a reflection more of the crisis in American self-confidence and confusion over what made deterrence 'work' than any serious movement in the military balance. In 1980, the fact that ICBM vulnerability provided the greatest cause for concern, could be taken as a symptom of the underlying stability of the strategic balance.

The Political Science of Nuclear Strategy

Yet the question of how nuclear weapons could be used in war remained and continued to nag at responsible officials as well as academic strategists. Once one openly admitted that the nuclear arsenal was unlikely ever to be activated then the deterrent lost all credibility. If weapons had to be designed for operational use then some sort of guidance was necessary, which required stating a preference for one form of nuclear employment against another.

The difficulty in avoiding targeting issues can be illustrated by the Carter Administration. At the start of his Administration, President Carter displayed a marked aversion to nuclear weapons, toyed with ideas of minimum deterrence, and dismissed notions of limited nuclear war. In 1979 his Secretary of Defense, Harold Brown, provided a sceptical assessment of the possibility of controlled counterforce exchanges:

> [C]ounterforce and damage-limiting campaigns have been put forward as the nuclear equivalents of traditional warfare. But their proponents find it difficult to tell us what objectives an enemy would seek in launching such campaigns, how these campaigns would end, or how any resulting symmetries could be made meaningful.[41]

Despite these doubts there was a continual search during the Carter Administration for a set of satisfactory targeting options. The military had been converted to the idea under Schlesinger, much of the relevant technology was in hand and there was nothing in the development of the Soviet force structure to suggest that they completely ruled out limited nuclear war. It was decided to maintain and then refine the targeting guidelines developed under Schlesinger.

The key innovation was to begin to think in terms of limited strikes against political and economic targets rather than solely against military targets. A major (but largely futile) effort was put into assessing economic recovery so as to maximize the long-term impact of attacks on economic targets.[42] This approach was open to the objection that a military victory would provide access to what was left of the world economy. There was also an interest in destroying targets of particular political importance to the Soviet leaders and those relevant to the control over their country.

In July 1980 President Carter approved Presidential Directive 59 which aimed to improve deterrence by improving the capacity for a prolonged but limited nuclear war. The prime targets would be those 'the Soviet leadership values most – its military forces and its own ability to maintain control after a war starts'. Part of the plan would be to find Soviet leaders in their bunkers. The ability to fight a prolonged war would be maintained by a 'secure strategic reserve', that is invulnerable missiles that would not be employed in the early stages. The plan would be flexible enough to allow for retargeting based on information from such sources as surveillance satellites on the course of the war.[43]

Thus more and more flexibility was built into the system. The concentration was on the first faltering steps into a nuclear war rather than on the conclusion. The political objective remained unclear: if the aim was to affect the course of a conventional military conflict already under way, why prolong matters and keep strikes limited? If the aim was to demonstrate resolve while still holding out the possibility of a negotiated settlement, would it be wise to target the Soviet leadership for if it were destroyed who could issue the orders to stop firing and with whom would one negotiate? What happened if Soviet strategy followed its traditional approach of doggedly attacking the West's war-making capacities while protecting its own, accepting the unavoidability of a terrible war of attrition, without wasting time on tentative gestures or subtle manoeuvres?

Some outside Government, not content solely with devising a remotely plausible operational plan, suggested that an attack specifically directed against the Soviet political culture could actually bring victory. Thus Colin Gray and Keith Payne wrote:

> The USSR with its gross overcentralization of authority . . . should be highly vulnerable to such an attack. The Soviet Union might cease to function if its security agency, the KGB were severely crippled. If the Moscow bureaucracy could be eliminated, damaged, or isolated, the USSR might disintegrate into anarchy. . . .[44]

Somehow it was assumed that the Soviet command structure was so fragile that once the leaders were removed the Strategic Rocket Forces would immediately cease to function, or that the Soviet leaders did not already feel that a nuclear war threatened their political position, or that an American President who announced such a strategy would be seen to have a more credible deterrent available than one who merely reminded the Soviet Union of the incalculable consequences of any super-power confrontation.

The debate had thus come full circle, back to the crude political science of early airpower theorists, such as Douhet and Fuller, who believed that strategic bombardment could detach the elite from the mass and thus cause swift social breakdown, and by implication the cessation of military operations. When we even try to imagine how soldiers and statesmen will cope with the stress of the opening shots of a nuclear war, and start to choose from the vast array of options offered to them, we can see how difficult it is to imagine the political and psychological state of the societies they represent, or the futility of banking on an ability to find some flaw in the adversary's political structure before he has time to do his worst.

This legion of uncertainties ought to have created a common humility – to be so much in the dark with so much at stake. Unfortunately the frustration with this predicament led many strategists to show astonishing confidence in their own nostrums, combined with vindictiveness against those who differed.

The question of what happens if deterrence fails is vital for the intellectual cohesion and credibility of nuclear strategy. A proper answer requires more than the design of means to wage nuclear war in a wide variety of ways, but something sufficiently plausible to appear as a tolerably rational course of action which has a realistic chance of leading to a satisfactory outcome. No operational nuclear strategy had yet been devised that did not carry an enormous risk of degenerating into a bloody contest of resolve or a furious exchange of devastating and crippling blows against the political and economic centres of the industrialized world. In 1981 the Reagan Administration made a final attempt to square the circle.

26 The Reagan Administration and the Great Nuclear Debate

From the Second Cold War to the Second Detente

At the start of the 1980s, the international system was passing through a stormy period. A run of mini-crises exhausted the scenarios dreamed up by strategists to give verisimilitude to war-games and exercises in crisis management – the death of Tito in Yugoslavia, the collapse of a major American ally in the Gulf and subsequent retribution against the United States by a new militant leadership, a vicious war between two oil-producing states, a Soviet move into a hitherto non-aligned country, a major challenge to communist rule in Eastern Europe, the collapse of arms control negotiations, the election of a hard-line President in the United States.

The ascendant view in Washington was that after years of accumulating military strength the Soviet behemoth was at last on the move. The invasion of Afghanistan, following closely on the less direct interventions in Angola and Ethiopia, was taken as confirmation of a dangerous new stage in East–West relations. The Carter Administration had spent its last, troubled year identifying new areas of vital American interest, boycotting the Olympic games, encouraging rearmament and devising a new nuclear doctrine. Nevertheless, Carter still nurtured a lingering hope that, having demonstrated resolve, constructive relations could be re-established with the Soviet Union. In 1981 he was succeeded by a leader taken from the right of the American political spectrum, who was apparently convinced of the need to prepare for a decisive showdown with the

396

Soviet Union. It appeared as if the world was moving into a 'second cold war'.

During the years of the Reagan Presidency, there was plenty of super-power acrimony – especially over the shooting down of a stray Korean airliner by Soviet air defences in September 1983. At various times, the Reagan Administration sought to tighten up the embargo on the export of strategic goods to communist countries, impose sanctions in response to martial rule in Poland, and gain release from arms control obligations. The President spoke of consigning the Soviet Union to the ash-can of history, just as two decades earlier Nikita Khrushchev had promised to 'bury the West'. (In both cases it was claimed that the confidence in the adversary's eventual historical collapse was a reflection of its likely ideological rather than military failings; in both cases the adversary interpreted the remarks in a less generous light.)

The ideological competition became intense during the 1980s. Perhaps the internal pressures for reform of the Soviet system constituted a *de facto* concession of defeat. Certainly the Reagan Administration's combative instincts were tempered by the lack of enthusiasm in Moscow for a fight. With the leadership sobered by frustrating experiences in Africa and Afghanistan there were no Soviet adventures in the 1980s comparable to those of the previous decade. Moscow appeared content for the United States to draw political fire for its interventions in Central America and the Middle East, while keeping a determinedly low profile for itself. The Soviet leadership saw benefit in appearing as the voice of openness and sweet reason.

So despite an unpromising start, the 1980s were survived without evident difficulty and indeed without great finesse. Despite some tense moments and harsh language, fingers never moved close to the nuclear button. Fortunately exceptional diplomatic skill and cool judgment turned out to be less critical than might have been feared.

By the last years of the decade the most intriguing questions concerned the nature and extent of the political transformation of the Soviet Union. After Mikhail Gorbachev took over in early 1985 he embarked upon a courageous programme of reconstruction (*Perestroika*) and openness (*Glasnost*).[1] Western leaders watched sympathetically, wondering if the 'Gorbachev effect' would turn out to be anything more than surface-deep, and then possibly be reversed as the old guard fought back, or whether they really wanted the Soviet Union to be turned into a dynamic, modern economy. There

was some, but not conclusive, evidence of a relaxation in the
fundamentals of Soviet power in the post-war world – the pervasive
influence of the Communist Party, the close control of Eastern
Europe and predominant military power around the periphery of the
USSR. The evidence was sufficient for President Reagan himself,
despite all that he had said and done in the early days of his
Administration, to start to establish a working relationship with
Gorbachev. This resulted in a flurry of four summits and one major
arms control treaty. The political context in which the theories of
nuclear strategy had been developed and nurtured was showing signs
of change.

There has been a persistent tension in Western debate over the
post-war period as to whether it was more important to worry about
the 'Soviet threat' than the 'nuclear threat'. At the start of the decade
this tension was unusually sharp, with protest movements in all
Western countries challenging the Reagan Administration's conviction that most of the world's security problems could be traced to
Moscow. The resultant debate forced into the open many of the
particular dilemmas of nuclear strategy and gave strength to those
who argued that this dilemma could only be resolved by measures of
radical disarmament – multilateral if possible but unilateral if necessary. As East–West relations relaxed it was a natural assumption that
the time had come to do something about the nuclear threat.

Nuclear disarmament had provided a stock of diplomatic pieties
for forty years. It remains unusual for political leaders to take
seriously the possibility of escape from something taken for granted
by most of their profession. What was striking about the new Reagan–
Gorbachev relationship was an apparent shared interest in taking
these pieties seriously. Many who had been known to utter these
pieties themselves, especially in the governments of Western Europe,
soon demonstrated that they remained more comfortable with the
orthodoxies of NATO strategy. Their satisfaction with the *status quo*
turned into a reluctance to tamper with one of its main pillars –
nuclear deterrence. They considered it paradoxical and unwelcome
that one of the consequences of improved East–West relations should
be a readiness to eliminate the very condition that made it possible.
The Administration's interest in radical disarmament was not made
any more tolerable by the fact that it appeared as an over-correction
to the equally exaggerated doctrines that governed the rearmament
of the Administration's first years.

It had begun with a determined effort to refine the instruments of nuclear deterrence to render them more credible. By its close it appeared prepared to abandon the whole exercise. This chapter will attempt to explain the character of this shift in nuclear policies. If we can understand how this has come about we may be better placed to judge whether this was just another paradox in a generally paradoxical Administration or a significant trend that can be expected to be sustained in subsequent years. There is a constant in the Reagan Administration: the desire to escape the nuclear dilemma – the situation of dependence upon nuclear threats to achieve security when the implementation of these threats could well lead to mutual annihilation. There are many means by which this escape might be achieved even though few are very promising. The Administration explored a number in a reasonably logical sequence.

The Rise of Anti-Nuclear Protest

Up to the late 1970s most sections of the public seemed to have grown accustomed to living with the 'bomb'. Public indifference combined with the experts' celebration over the taming of both the arms race and the great powers' worst tendencies towards conflict. Public and experts alike now paused to consider whether this achievement could endure. A generation that had never really had to face up to the meaning of nuclear war suddenly discovered the potential for mass destruction, carefully nurtured for so long.

Certainly, to suggest in the early 1980s that the international system had adjusted to the nuclear age led to accusations of complacency. During this time, the fear of nuclear war exercised a powerful hold on the Western imagination. The first stirrings of a revival in anti-nuclear protest had come during the arguments over the 'neutron bomb' (enhanced radiation weapons) in 1977–78. Calmed by President Carter's decision against deployment of these weapons, the protest movements began to grow rapidly in strength in the early 1980s. This followed NATO's more decisive approval in December 1979 of proposals to introduce 572 *Tomahawk* cruise and *Pershing 2* ballistic missiles into five European countries. During the early 1980s the membership of the anti-nuclear movements grew, massive demonstrations were mounted in most European capitals, although with protest more evident in the north than the south of the continent.[2] An intellectual climate developed in which the risk of nuclear war and its awful consequences should it occur was pushed to the fore. All this led to a vast literature and some notable movies. Political parties, especially those on the centre and left, began to find the nuclear issue extraordinarily troublesome and divisive, with the unilateralist inclinations of activists not so widely shared by electorates.

The domestic political impact of the anti-nuclear movements was considerable. Although individual elements of the anti-nuclear movement's platform had widespread appeal the package as a whole did not.[3] Left-of-centre parties found themselves torn between those supporting the old NATO orthodoxies and the new radicalism. As a result, rather than sweeping to power on the basis of anti-nuclear sentiment the splits in these parties kept them out of government, which meant that policy in practice was framed by European governments who had little wish to tamper with NATO orthodoxy.

Nonetheless they could not ignore the anxieties being recorded in opinion polls and reflected in public debate, and this required that they took questions of arms control more seriously than they might have otherwise been inclined to do, and also that they encouraged the Reagan Administration to offer a more moderate image than it seemed inclined to do. Furthermore, NATO orthodoxy had been allowed to develop without serious critical attention for so long that merely subjecting it to public scrutiny could not help but raise awkward questions as to its internal consistency and strategic value.

Although the anti-nuclear movement naturally stressed a moral abhorrence of weapons of mass destruction, and based its appeal on a fear of nuclear war, its leaders sought to broaden their support by building up a strategic case for rapid, and if necessary unilateral, disarmament. In constructing this case they drew attention to the concepts of limited nuclear options that had been influencing US policy-makers throughout the 1970s, with special prominence being given to the more extreme versions of these concepts associated with figures such as Colin Gray and Edward Luttwak. The American debate on the future of nuclear strategy which had been developing among specialists in the 1970s spilled over into partisan European politics. Some views reflected in that debate and given full expression in the Reagan Administration appeared at best frivolous and at worst downright dangerous. Articles suggesting that 'victory' was possible in a nuclear war were considered particularly sinister.[4] Statements by President Reagan helped to fuel the fears.[5]

This was then combined with a sense that under Reagan's leadership, and with East–West relations deteriorating, the United States was simply becoming too dangerous an ally. The December 1979 decision was interpreted as a move in the 'second cold war'.[6] It may have been the sensation of a return to the bad old days of sharp East–West tension that provided the most powerful stimulant to the new protest movements.

The political thrust of the critique was that the United States was setting up Europe to suffer the consequences of its global anti-communist crusade, and that the cruise and *Pershing* missiles were the chosen instrument of this policy. This critique can be illustrated by a representative quote from E. P. Thompson, who had been influential in the first wave of nuclear protest in the late 1950s, and now became one of the leading voices of the new European Nuclear Disarmament (END) campaign.

European war is to be one 'choice' or 'option' for the United States strategists, although what might appear to be 'limited' on that side of the Atlantic might appear to be spasmodic and apocalyptical on this. The cruise missiles which are being set up in Western Europe are the hardware designed for exactly such a 'limited' war, and the nations which harbour them are viewed, in this strategy, as launching platforms which are expendable in the interests of 'Western' defence.[7]

As an interpretation of the motives behind the cruise missile pro-gramme this left something to be desired. Apart from anything else, these were unlikely instruments of limited nuclear war in that their range threatened Soviet territory, and there was no reason to believe that any war in which Soviet targets were being attacked could long stay limited.[8] New peace research institutes, often with close links with the anti-nuclear movement, sponsored quite detailed studies of developments in military technology or the nuances of the military balance, and also came up with proposals for alternative strategies for defence based on conventional forces.[9]

In addition to demonstrating that it took defence seriously, the anti-nuclear movement took care to avoid accusations of being pro-Soviet, although that did not prevent the allegation that at the very least they served the Kremlin's interest.[10] In many ways their specific demands required more of the Soviet Union than the United States, for in seeking the dissolution of the two alliances they challenged the Soviet position in Eastern Europe. Moscow did not therefore endorse the protest movements with the sort of enthusiasm that might have been expected, even though inevitably it was far better placed to resist their demands than Western governments. Although the direct influence on Western policy remained limited, and the movements themselves began to decline after 1983, the indirect influences were significant, both in terms of encouraging moves to ease the East–West confrontation through arms control, and in illuminating many of the problems associated with the logic of nuclear deterrence.

The Changing American Climate

The anti-nuclear movement in the United States gained momentum slightly later than its European counterpart, again in part a reaction to similar tendencies. The reaction took the form of the 'freeze' movement. The spark was a 'Call to Halt the Nuclear Arms Race' drafted by Randall Forsberg in April 1980. The attraction of the idea of the freeze was said to lie in its simplicity, requiring the super-powers to stop the production and testing of nuclear weapons without getting too bogged down in the complexities of arms control negotiations (although of course as it became necessary to turn the call for a freeze into practical policy the complexities reasserted themselves).[11]

The American anti-nuclear movement operated within more con-strained political limits than did that in Europe. A degree of political moderation was also wise in that, unlike in Europe where changes in government were required before fundamental policy changes could take place, there was always Congressional sentiment to play for, and 'freeze' resolutions came close to success.

Despite this pragmatic tendency, from the United States also came one of the most powerful anti-nuclear tracts of the period – Jonathan Schell's *The Fate of the Earth*. But in a sense this was the exception which proved the rule, for the policy conclusions were absolutist – world government – and within a couple of years had been abandoned by the author in return for an equally grand and equally impractical scheme but which this time was based upon, instead of transcending, the sovereignty of states.[12]

The power of Schell's writing was based on his vivid and disturbing descriptions of the physical, human and social consequences of nuclear war. In 1983 some scientific backing was given to apocalyptical concerns as to the consequences of nuclear war by the publication of an article by Carl Sagan, describing the conclusions of work by himself and colleagues on the 'Global atmospheric consequences of nuclear war'. Sagan wrote of 'climactic catastrophe and cascading biological devastation'.[13] Further analysis suggested that while important problems had been raised, the 'nuclear winter' hypothesis was based on taking the extreme worst view on a number of areas of great uncertainty.[14] It also became evident that few policy conclusions could be drawn from the hypothesis.[15] Nor was it necessarily the case that the likelihood of 'nuclear winter' and the obliteration of the human species was required to make the prospect of nuclear war horrific. Even the most limited of nuclear exchanges would involve widespread death and destruction. Public opinion was probably more impressed by the smaller-scale but insidious consequences of the accident at the Chernobyl nuclear reactor in the Soviet Union in April 1985, which demonstrated the difficulties of confining the effects of nuclear detonations to one particular locality.

The sensitivity to the evils of nuclear war created a political climate of unease with dependence on nuclear weapons. This helped give an edge to the more narrowly focused policy debates. The most important focal point for those grappling with the moral dimension was the drafting of a pastoral letter on the subject by the American National Conference of Catholic Bishops. What was significant about the letter itself was that in seeking to reconcile nuclear deterrence with their ethical principles the bishops eventually concluded that it was permissible to own nuclear weapons for purposes of deterrence but improper to use them.[16] The significance of the bishops' pastoral letter was not in the quality of its reasoning or its conclusions but in throwing the fundamental dilemma of nuclear policy into such stark relief.[17]

In the ensuing debate, the critics of the bishops charged either that they had missed the higher moral necessity of opposing communism, or that they had missed the opportunity to endorse nuclear systems that were more in tune with the injunction of the just war theory to distinguish between combatants and non-combatants.[18] Others were less worried as to whether nuclear deterrence could be made to conform to timeless ethical principles and more concerned with whether a prudent policy was being followed.[19]

To Prevail or Countervail

The alternative methods of escape from the nuclear dilemma are either to transform nuclear threats so that they do not imply mutual annihilation or to stop making them altogether and obtain security through non-nuclear means. For those advocating either alternative, threatening mass destruction is intolerable. This is deemed immoral and repugnant, with little strategic logic and inspired only by a spirit of vengeance. Dissatisfaction with mutual assured destruction was thus shared by both the anti-nuclear movement and conservatives.

By and large the ascendant strategic view during the 1970s had been conservative. With the election of Reagan in the November 1980 election the conservatives now had their opportunity to shape nuclear strategy in accordance with the ideas developed during the previous decade. Many of the veterans of the Committee on the Present Danger moved into positions of power and influence.[20] It was now assumed that the policies devised during their period of opposition could now be put into practice.

The new strategists derived their inspiration from the Soviet Union which provided both the threat against which it was necessary to prepare and a model of what could be achieved with a proper grasp of strategy. Liberal confidence that in future crises the Soviet Union could be relied upon to be cautious was rebuffed. Soviet military writings did not follow Western pessimism as to the inevitability of mutual assured destruction. While the Soviet military recognized the risks of any war, they saw it as their duty to plan to fight to victory and had devised plans accordingly.[21] Soviet strategic realism was contrasted unfavourably with the pusillanimity of the liberal old guard, provided the excuse for some fiery polemics and helped create the intellectual climate for the policy shifts proposed by the Administration.

At the core of the new approach was the rediscovery of the 'operational art' – which, up to this point, had been lost somewhere between strategy and tactics. This was most obviously relevant to conventional warfare, during which the application of this art could produce the decisive campaign, a series of imaginative operations, skilfully executed, that could by itself determine the outcome of war. From this perspective the military establishment of the United States appeared not only uninspired but quite hopeless. From an operational perspective US performance during the various limited post-1945 conflicts was not impressive. The military was handicapped by inter-service rivalries, failures of command and a decline in the military art. The system was severely criticized for becoming geared to the procurement of highly complex, advanced weaponry and the management of a substantial budget. Old-fashioned generalship had been forgotten.[22] The critics went on to warn that the Soviet Union had never allowed itself to forget the 'operational art' (the term itself was taken from the Soviet literature). Following further what was believed to be the Soviet example, it was argued that a revival of the operational art would require a move away from a simple reliance on attrition through concentrated firepower and towards greater awareness of the potential of manoeuvre.[23] The 'new strategists' toyed with the possible application of the operational art to the nuclear area, based on advances in the technologies of precision-guidance and small-yield warheads, and especially those of command and control. Thus they argued not only for a return to classical strategic thinking in the conventional sphere, but also claimed that this should be achieved in the nuclear sphere.

This approach was close to what was described in the previous chapter as the 'RAND tradition'. The influence of these ideas was evident in the Reagan Administration. They were carried into the Administration by such senior figures as Fred Iklé in the Pentagon and Paul Nitze as chief arms negotiator – though the latter acquired first by comparison and then by deed a more moderate image.[24] Albert Wohlstetter remained true to the basic approach he had adopted while at RAND in the late 1950s.[25] As co-chairmen of a high-level Presidential Commission on Integrated Long-Term Strategy, he produced with Iklé a document towards the end of the Administration with a provocative message dimmed by the sense that the intellectual ground had now shifted once again.[26] Herman Kahn, responsible for many of the key concepts and ideas favoured by the conservative strategists, reinterpreted his views for contemporary circumstances before he died in 1983.[27]

As we have seen, conservative critics had argued during the 1970s that a strategy based on a nuclear bluff would soon be revealed as such and with disastrous results. The integrity of Western security required a convincing answer to the question, 'What do we do if deterrence fails?' The continued inability to provide such an answer increased the chances that deterrence would indeed fail. If all that the United States could do was implement massive nuclear strikes against the Soviet Union then the strategy could have little credibility and virtually no morality.

There had been a move away from the doctrine of mutual assured destruction in terms of declared changes in targeting policy during the 1970s: NSDM 242 as announced by Secretary of Defense James Schlesinger in early 1974, and PD59, announced by Secretary of

Defense Harold Brown in June 1980. However, to use Brown's term, the change was justified as a *countervailing* strategy – in terms of the need to deny the Soviet Union a range of limited nuclear options rather than to develop these options for the United States.[28] The Reagan Administration sought to take this further. In a strategic modernization programme announced in October 1981 the whole range of American nuclear capabilities was to be improved.

The programmes of the Carter Administration were sustained. One hundred of the *M-X* ICBM (improbably and ineffectually renamed the *Peacekeeper*), were to be procured for interim basing in superhardened silos. The *Trident D-5* SLBM and air-launched cruise missile programmes were to be accelerated and sea-launched cruise missiles to be developed for use on submarines and ships. The *B-1B* bomber was reinstated, with 100 to be procured. The whole range of command, control, communications and intelligence capabilities was to be revamped in order to make it possible to manage nuclear operations at a far greater level of sophistication than had hitherto been possible.[29]

Some idea of the form that these operations might take was indicated in the defence guidance (leaked to the *New York Times* and *Washington Post*) which stated that:

> Should deterrence fail and strategic nuclear war with the USSR occur, the United States must prevail and be able to force the Soviet Union to seek earliest termination of hostilities on terms favorable to the United States.
>
> The United States must have plans that assure US strategic nuclear forces can render ineffective the total Soviet military and political power structure . . . and forces that will maintain, throughout a protracted conflict period and afterward, the capability to inflict very high levels of damage against the industrial/economic base of the Soviet Union . . . so that they have a strong incentive to seek conflict termination short of an all-out attack on our cities and economic assets.[30]

In public statements Administration officials insisted on the need to prepare military forces to cope with a wide range of contingencies including nuclear war. The emphasis shifted from countervailing to prevailing. 'You show me a Secretary of Defense who's planning not to prevail,' intoned Caspar Weinberger, 'and I'll show you a Secretary of Defense who ought to be impeached.'[31] The idea that a nuclear war would follow the conventions of former wars and conclude with obvious winners and losers appeared to influence Administration thinking.

There was no enthusiasm for war but it was argued that the United States could put its relations on a far more satisfactory footing if the military balance had been attended to. The source of international instability was seen as the 'remorseless' build-up of Soviet military power, often presented in Administration briefings as an unbroken line on a graph pointing ever upwards.[32]

The Counter-Attack

While the strategic modernization programme went ahead and new targeting plans and doctrines were developed, major problems soon became apparent. The Administration did not seem too concerned about accusations that it had misrepresented the character of the Soviet build-up and its rationale, nor the argument that few international problems could be traced simply to Soviet mischief. A cottage industry producing alternative military balances, normally based on a thorough trawl of all information officially and unofficially released from the executive branch, came to challenge the Administration's position on the extent to which the United States had slipped behind the Soviet Union.[33] Sovietologists deplored the caricatures of the Soviet Union and its policies and pleaded for a more sensitive appreciation of its character and behaviour.[34] None of this cut much ice, at least not until late in the Administration when the contrary indicators were proving strong and it suited the Administration to refine its view.

More troublesome were studies demonstrating the problems likely to be faced when turning theory into practice. From the Schlesinger doctrine of 1974 onwards improvements in command, control, communications and surveillance systems had been central to claims that it was becoming possible to design and execute subtle nuclear tactics during a prolonged conflict.

A number of studies questioned whether it would be at all feasible to undertake sophisticated and protracted nuclear operations, given the havoc wreaked upon communications in a nuclear environment.[35] Paul Bracken in an original contribution to the debate warned that the interactions of the alert and command systems in a high-level nuclear crisis were imperfectly understood and could well be disastrous.[36] This renewed interest in the nuances of nuclear operations was coupled with analyses based on studies of the origins of non-nuclear conflicts which stressed the impact of misperceptions, communication failures and the implementation of plans devised in peace-time, especially those based on speedy mobilization.[37] Indeed to read some of the literature it was possible to doubt whether any diplomatic communications – let alone deterrent threats – were understood by those receiving them as they had been sent.[38] Inevitably the most favoured case study was the outbreak of World War I.[39]

The literature offered a catalogue of all the many things that can possibly go wrong during attempts to manage crises, with the clear warning that they probably would go wrong in any conflict involving the nuclear powers. In terms of policy this suggested reducing the extent to which nuclear weapons could at all get caught up in a crisis or even a conventional war.

A second source of counter-attack, not surprising given the vigour of the challenge to the old orthodoxies of mutual assured destruction, came from the liberal old guard.[40] They were concerned with the apparent reckless disregard of what they had previously taken to be self-evident. Robert McNamara, on retirement from the World Bank, took the arguments he had been developing as Secretary of Defense a stage further in making the case for a minimum deterrent. Another important contribution came from one of his key aides of that period, Morton Halperin. Both argued that the impossibility of devising means of using nuclear weapons in a way that made any military sense undermined their overall value in security policies. As total abolition would not be possible the best course was to constrain their numbers, location and command procedures to reduce as much as possible the risk of accidental detonation. In this they were influenced by the studies referred to above on the problems of command and control in a nuclear environment.[41]

A focus on removing all possible causes of nuclear war raised the question of whether success in this objective could only come at the expense of undermining whatever benefits the condition of mutual assured destruction provided in terms of deterrence and international stability. In the 1960s, after all, the response to the evident problems with attempts to develop operational nuclear strategies had been to stress uncertainty and the prospect of nuclear war arising out of a loss of control in conventional war as sustaining deterrence. This had been one of the main themes in the work of Thomas Schelling, who with Halperin had written the seminal work on arms control in the early 1960s. Schelling had become preoccupied with more civilian concerns in the intervening years, although he did provide one clear restatement of his basic views. In this he stressed again his preference for deterrence as against defence, arguing that it need not depend on fear:

> People regularly stand at the curb watching trucks, buses and cars hurtle past at speeds which guarantee injury and threaten death if they so much as attempt to cross against the traffic. They are absolutely deterred. But there is no fear. They just know better.[42]

His influence was still felt in many of the critiques of the Reagan Administration, perhaps most notably in Robert Jervis's thorough dissection of the Reagan strategy, which he dedicated to 'James King, Thomas Schelling, Glenn Snyder, and the memory of Bernard Brodie, who developed so many of the ideas I have used'. His analysis draws upon the notion of 'the threat that leaves something to chance' which he contrasts favourably with strategies based on Herman Kahn's idea of 'escalation dominance'.[43]

As in the 1960s, the liberal critique started from the premise that the nuclear stalemate was a fact of life from which some benefit might be derived as a result of its sobering influence. The nagging question was always whether it would be possible to benefit from nuclear threats that one dare not implement. But with the passage of time mutual deterrence appeared less delicate than ever. There was no reason to believe that the threats would ever need to be implemented. All this suggested that deterrence was much easier than many assumed. Those who felt confident in this felt obliged to make the case against the anti-nuclear movement as well as the Reagan Administration.[44]

McGeorge Bundy who had advised Presidents Kennedy and Johnson on national security affairs, suggested that the deterrent effect of nuclear weapons resided in their mere existence as opposed to the nuances of targeting doctrine.

> As long as each side has thermonuclear weapons that *could* be used against the opponent, even after the strongest possible preemptive attack, existential deterrence is strong and it rests on uncertainty about what could happen.[45]

Here the deterrent effect is almost wholly impervious to the location and capabilities of nuclear weapons, and the doctrines that would notionally govern their use. All that is required is the availability of some nuclear weapons that *could* be used in anger. In this way the most perplexing problems of nuclear policy are rendered virtually irrelevant. Forces were to be judged by essentially negative criteria: they should not be vulnerable, provocative, disruptive of arms control or prone to accidental detonation. So long as these criteria were met it did not matter what was procured, where and in what numbers it was deployed, and against what it was targeted.[46] Thus the answer to the question, 'What do we do if deterrence fails?' was that the question could be ignored, because even without a satisfactory answer there was no reason to believe that deterrence would fail.

From Prevailing to Defending

The Administration faced political problems in selling its programme from early on. There were difficulties from the start in persuading Congress and the American people that the approach to nuclear strategy being adopted was realistic and responsible. An unfortunate interview granted by a junior official concerned with civil defence and a journalist for the *Los Angeles Times* conveyed the impression that the Administration was unusually relaxed in its contemplation of nuclear war.[47] More senior figures such as Richard Perle in the Pentagon managed to acquire a reputation for zealous anti-communism unconstrained by any sense of risk.

The Administration sought to moderate a politically unattractive image based on militant anti-communism and the robust espousal of a radical nuclear doctrine. But in distancing itself from extreme formulations it also lost intellectual coherence. Thus it was deeply distrustful of Soviet intentions, considered past arms control agreements to be 'fatally flawed' and *still* violated by the Soviet Union, and yet it continued to negotiate with Moscow. It made preparations to fight a protracted and tactically complex nuclear war yet the President was obliged to insist that he was personally convinced that there could be no winners in a nuclear war. Most seriously, while the Administration found few problems in justifying their policies as an effort to deny a range of aggressive nuclear options to the Soviet Union they equivocated in terms of how much they would like comparable options for themselves.

The dilemma was all the more stark because it was one the Reagan

Administration had promised – and then failed – to resolve. The fundamental critique of mutual assured destruction was that it provided no guidance as to what to do if deterrence failed. The new Reagan strategy had to provide convincing *nuclear* answers to this question or it had failed according to its own standards. While it could multiply the different means by which it might initiate a nuclear war it seemed to fare little better than earlier Administrations when it came to demonstrating how such a war could be brought to a tolerable conclusion.

The most serious political trouble came with the *M-X*. This missile was required to meet two criteria which were not necessarily complementary: it was to have an ability to attack vital, protected Soviet military targets but also able to survive a comparable attack from Soviet ICBMs. The Carter Administration had sought to solve this problem by means of a 'racetrack' that would allow each missile 23 possible hiding places, each of which the Soviet Union would need to target. It had been argued by hawkish critics that the problem had been exacerbated by the insertion of a third criterion – the need to ensure that the missile could still be subject to the verification provisions of an arms control agreement. However, it soon turned out that the main problem was the sheer scale of the project and the environmental impact on the states of Utah and Nevada.

At a time when the Administration was encouraging Europeans to accept intermediate nuclear forces in their midst, it turned out to be less successful in persuading its own supporters to accept ICBMs. The racetrack was abandoned and it was decided to put the new missiles in old ICBM silos as an interim measure. In November 1982 the Administration came forward with its own solution to the basing problem, known as 'densepack'. This depended on the 'fratricide effect', whereby if the missile silos were close enough together, the nuclear effects resulting from the explosions of the first attacking warheads would disable those coming in behind. Whatever the scientific merits of this notion, it proved to be almost impossible to convince an increasingly sceptical Congress that it would achieve the necessary results.

With the *M-X* in trouble and the Administration accused of failing to take arms control seriously, it sought to create a bipartisan consensus to save the new ICBM programme. This was achieved through a bipartisan commission, chaired by President Ford's former national security advisor, General Brent Scowcroft, and which included President Carter's Secretary of Defense, Harold Brown. The

Scowcroft Commission did succeed in saving the *M-X* by coming up with a lukewarm rationale to support a modest programme. But in the process it removed the cutting edge from the debate on nuclear strategy by stressing its limits. In particular it dispatched the great bogy which had dogged strategic debate since the early 1970s – the fear that the Soviet Union might obtain a decisive advantage through a capacity to mount a counterforce attack to remove the bulk of US ICBMs.

We saw in the previous chapter how this issue had come to dominate the American strategic debate. It had even been suggested by no less a figure than Henry Kissinger during the hearings on the SALT II Treaty that a developing Soviet advantage in comparative counterforce capabilities (made possible by the sheer size of their ICBMs and the large number of warheads that could be placed atop each launcher) could result in a historic shift in the balance of power.[48] Unless something were done the Soviet Union would be granted in the first half of the 1980s a 'window of opportunity' to capitalize on this fundamental strategic weakness.

The problems with the *M-X* programme and the loss, with the deferred SALT II Treaty, of the opportunity to reduce Soviet counterforce capabilities ensured that in the first years of the Reagan Administration nothing practical had been done to close this particular window. But neither Moscow nor Washington acted as if the Soviet Union was *really* enjoying the sort of commanding strategic position that the hawks' rhetoric proclaimed it did enjoy. In practice the whole scenario had always been overdrawn. As the Scowcroft Commission pointed out:

> The existence of several components of our strategic forces permits each to function as a hedge against possible Soviet successes in endangering any of the others . . . . Although the survivability of our ICBMs is today a matter of concern (especially when that problem is viewed in isolation) it would be far more serious if we did not have a force of ballistic missiles, submarines at sea and a bomber force.[49]

However, to some extent the Scowcroft Commission went along with the '*Minuteman* vulnerability' scenario in identifying the process of MIRVing as the most unsettling feature of the strategic balance. It sought remedy in a move away from large launchers with many warheads to many small launchers with single warheads (soon dubbed

Midgetman) and in a new approach to strategic arms control, known as 'build-down', which allowed the modernization of strategic forces only so long as more old warheads were removed than entered service. Congress found this idea attractive and for a while an extraordinarily complex version of build-down was incorporated into the American negotiating position at the Geneva arms control talks.[50] Increasingly the *M-X* was itself presented as a bargaining chip, a means of obtaining concessions from the Soviet Union. It had become dependent upon the arms control process and was no longer an alternative.

The readiness of President Reagan to accept the recommendations of the Scowcroft Commission meant acknowledging implicitly that the attempt to escape from mutual assured destruction through the proliferation of nuclear options was effectively over. In practical terms options would accumulate as new weapons systems became available and command and control systems were refined, but the political argument was lost. If the Administration was still serious about ending the condition of mutual assured destruction then it now had to find another way of achieving this.

This 'other way' was revealed in a Presidential broadcast on 23 March 1983, a month before the release of the Scowcroft Commission's report. The launch of what was almost immediately described as 'star wars' by the media and later officially known as the Strategic Defense Initiative was widely perceived at the time to be a response to the growing disquiet over trends in American nuclear policy. No other words of President Reagan have been quite so widely quoted as those in which he asked rhetorically, 'Wouldn't it be better to save lives than to avenge them?'; and 'What if free people could live secure in the knowledge that their security did not rest upon the threat of instant US retaliation to deter a Soviet attack, that we could intercept and destroy strategic ballistic missiles before they reached our own soil or that of our allies?'; and where he called upon the scientific community to provide the means to render nuclear weapons 'impotent and obsolete'.[51]

There is even some evidence that in a very real personal sense, the President had been repelled by the full implications of the policies his own Administration had been pursuing and so sought to push policy in a quite different direction. One of the greatest burdens passed on from one President to another on inauguration day is the responsibility for America's nuclear arsenal. Having a 'finger on the button' is the definitive feature of supreme executive authority. Those who have carried this responsibility have often found it troubling and are relieved when it is passed on to a successor.

Presidents do not become fully familiar with the implications of their responsibility until they pass through the initiation ceremony known as 'the briefing on the SIOP'. The SIOP – or Single Integrated Operations Plan – is developed at Omaha. It describes to the President the range of targeting options he would have available should the moment of truth arrive.[52] It is framed in terms of launch procedures and the target sets against which weapons will be launched. It gives a terrible, practical reality to the familiar clichés of nuclear war.

It is reported that President Reagan was reluctant to be confronted with the SIOP and resisted it until well into his Administration. It is further reported that having been through the ceremony he was sufficiently impressed to launch his Strategic Defense Initiative which, if successful, would relieve his successors of the need to confront the awful choices on which he had been briefed.[53]

If this is the case then it underscores both the sincerity of his commitment, its logical extension into radical nuclear disarmament and the irrelevance of the attempts of his subordinates actually running SDI to recast the presidential vision into a feasible project. SDI sought a Great Escape from the nuclear dilemma. There was to be a switch from mutual assured destruction to mutual assured survival, its mutuality made possible by an out-of-character promise to share the critical secrets of the Great Escape with the Soviet Union.

There was always a disjunction between this idealistic rhetoric and the Initiative's practical expression and political complexities.[54] The attempt by SDI's friends to rescue it from the laws of physics, the obligations of treaties, the scepticism of Congress and the anxieties of allies by turning it into something more mundane could not but trivialize the President's message.[55] He was not attempting a new move in the prolonged game of nuclear deterrence but seeking to terminate the game. The objective was not to protect vital military assets but society itself.

Even in its more mundane form SDI faced serious problems. It was a project for several Presidents and Congresses and was never likely to sustain its appeal for sufficient time. The critics found the President's extreme formulation almost irresistible and they set about demolishing it with enthusiasm.[56] The scientific community argued against SDI in similar terms to those used in the late 1960s and early 1970s against the *Sentinel* and *Safeguard* anti-ballistic missiles. The terms of the debate were set by some of the first books.[57] Meanwhile, allies and other supporters of traditional nuclear deterrence were appalled at the implications of the nuclear-free rhetoric surrounding SDI.[58]

The proponents hoped that scientific breakthroughs would provide the necessary momentum but the problem to be cracked was strategic rather than technical. It was not the same as landing men on the moon because the moon was not attempting to repel boarders and counter-attack.[59] From early on, analyses of SDI's prospects suggested that it could never come to fruition without the active connivance of the Soviet Union. If Moscow sought to defeat the Initiative it could – simply through the proliferation of missile warheads or a move towards alternative forms of delivery to ballistic missiles. Unless it were possible to ensure that the cost of future offences would be greater than the defences designed to stop them, SDI would be little more than a recipe for a sustained arms race.[60] While Soviet hostility to the project gave its proponents hope that there must be some merit in something which so alarmed the adversary, it also meant that there was little chance of a co-operative transition to a defence-dominated world.

President Reagan could take the initiative, but the time-scale for implementation had to be measured in decades rather than years. In the face of technical doubts and worries over cost, the programme could only be sustained with serious Presidential commitment. A move towards early deployment of an 'intermediate' system, capable of dealing with limited threats and demonstrating some of the new technologies was canvassed before the end of the Reagan Administration, but by 1988 the impact of budget cuts meant that the Initiative was rapidly losing both its lustre and its credibility. Thus the Reagan legacy in the area of strategic defence would be the output of a substantial research effort but not a developing programme with a momentum of its own.

From the start the future of SDI was bound up with the future of arms control. So long as the ABM Treaty was honoured then SDI could not get very far. Initially the logical course appeared to be for the Administration to ditch the ABM Treaty altogether, using as a pretext an unusually clear case of a Soviet violation with the building of a phased-array radar at Krasnayorsk, a location prohibited under the terms of the Treaty.[61] However, the Administration sought to promote SDI without abandoning the Treaty by means of an attempt to reinterpret the 1972 ABM Treaty. Up to 1985 the only, and thereafter known as 'narrow', interpretation of the Treaty was that anything other than research on ballistic missile defences (except for fixed land-based systems) was prohibited. The interpretation favoured by the Administration would allow development and testing to proceed on strategic defences based on 'new physical principles'.[62] This failed to impress Congress and again left the future of SDI uncertain.

The Soviet leadership was hostile even to SDI research and linked various arms control proposals to the abortion of the Initiative. This effort backfired in that it gave more credibility to SDI than was deserved – something which alarmed Moscow so much could not be *so* foolish – and also put the Soviet Union in the position of having gradually to soften its position on this matter in order to get progress elsewhere. By 1987 the Soviet assessment of SDI appeared to be much more relaxed so long as the basic framework of the ABM Treaty remained intact. Mr Gorbachev had been obliged to recognize that President Reagan would not be denied his 'vision' of freedom from nuclear threats, but could be confident that this particular vision would not become reality, at least not by means of SDI.

From Defence to Arms Control

The last option for an escape from mutual assured destruction was arms control. As the excitement surrounding SDI subsided it became apparent that radical arms control offered a more plausible means of meeting many of the same objectives. As the elusiveness of a technical fix to the nuclear dilemma was rediscovered a political fix started to look much more likely.

The last years of the Reagan Administration were dominated by an attempt to put in place a comprehensive nuclear arms control regime. In December 1987 a treaty eliminating intermediate nuclear forces was signed and was even ratified by the US Senate. Substantial progress was made towards a strategic arms reductions treaty that would lead to reductions of some 25 to 30 per cent (50 per cent on the Administration's count) in offensive warheads. All this was done within a framework which accepted the long-term goal of the complete elimination of nuclear weapons. This conclusion to the Reagan Administration was all the more surprising given that it had appeared initially hostile to arms control, arguing that the exercise had lost credibility because of the unacceptable nature of the Soviet Union as a partner in negotiations.

From the start the Administration was arguing for a much more radical approach to arms control. The radicalism took two forms. First, because it was convinced that the Soviet Union had a high propensity to cheat (and a number of allegations were made to this effect[63]) it wanted intrusive verification procedures. The only sanction that was ever taken against the alleged cheating was to cease to recognize the SALT II limits in the summer of 1986. However, the fact that the Administration had observed for as long as it did the terms of a Treaty that candidate Reagan had described in 1980 as being 'fatally flawed' was in itself remarkable.

The second element of radicalism was to argue for reduction rather than limitation. Along with many liberals, the conservatives claimed that a collection of permissive ceilings which confirmed the *status quo* was wholly unsatisfactory. To their critique was added the thought that when the *status quo* favoured the Soviet Union it was not at all surprising that it was so interested in consolidating its advantages. What is important here is that from the start of the Administration there was a rhetorical willingness to contemplate substantial nuclear disarmament. It is always difficult to assess how seriously all this should have been taken. It was part of the tendency towards absolute standards, against which arms control and strategic doctrine were both judged. If arms control could not produce deep cuts then it was of little value, while if doctrinal innovation could not produce a formula for victory it too was deficient. As the Administration progressed the initial optimism with regard to meeting the absolute standards set for nuclear doctrine was shown to be unwarranted, while the pessimism on arms control subsided.

The Administration claimed that progress on arms control was a result of sticking to firm principles and holding out until they were met. A readiness to improve America's military strength created a proper bargaining position where there had been none before. This argument has to be examined with care. The sort of radical arms control deals considered in the strategic arms area only became possible because one jewel in the Administration's crown, namely *M-X*, was in serious trouble and so no longer needed to be protected, and then was held up because the other jewel, SDI, had to be protected. The most dramatic breakthroughs were made in the area of intermediate nuclear forces, where the initial programme had been approved under the Carter Administration.

The INF programme had initially been developed as a means of meeting the nuclear dilemma by providing a degree of reassurance to Western Europe as to the quality of the American nuclear commitment. Many in the Reagan Administration were critical of the programme because of the vulnerability of land-based systems and because they did not accept that it was necessary to reassure Europeans by local basing. If some tangible American nuclear superiority could be created then that would be superiority enough.

In this sense it is not wholly correct to describe the 'zero option' of November 1981 as a cynical political move designed to wrong-foot both the Soviet Union and the disarmament movement. To be sure these were seen as advantages but there was also a very real sense in which these 'Euro-missiles' were deemed unnecessary. Nonetheless, few had any expectations at the time that anything could come of it, because it required the Soviet Union to give up a substantial force already deployed in return for one that was still on paper and might yet be stopped by domestic political action.[64]

Politically it was undoubtedly effective, for there was an obvious symmetry in the proposal. Soviet attempts to construct a balance that they could argue was being disrupted by the new American missiles could appear by contrast to be cynical and self-serving. Gradually, in an effort to demonstrate reasonableness the Reagan Administration allowed itself to be eased away from the zero solution in early 1983, in the process pushing to one side what orthodox NATO circles considered to be a doctrinal heresy. The Soviet Union further obliged by walking out of the Geneva talks in late 1983 as the first *Pershing* and cruise missiles arrived. Perhaps the objective was to create a NATO crisis over arms control, but NATO was perfectly happy that the Soviet Union had cast itself in the role of spoiler. The only crisis was in Soviet diplomacy.

Once it became clear that the walk-out was a failure and that Reagan was to be re-elected the Soviet return to arms control began (each of these factors was far more important than SDI). What was critical was that the return was effectively with a new leader – Mikhail Gorbachev. He immediately began to seize the initiative with a succession of proposals that began to wrong-foot the West. The fact that the Soviet Union had a relatively young and dynamic leader in itself appeared to require a Western response. A succession of ailing leaders had up to this point provided Reagan with no real contest. Gorbachev was also more relaxed about intrusive verification. He was not so worried about this being used as a cover for espionage. This in itself eased the negotiating path considerably. Gorbachev had a clearer view of Soviet interests. His own framework was less dominated by security concerns than was that of the Second World War leadership, while he had the flexibility of mind to examine ideas on their merits rather than in terms of past positions. He saw that the opposition to the zero option which made sense when it could not be sure that the NATO deployments would go ahead made less sense once they had gone ahead. The option now offered the Soviet Union an opportunity to trade missiles which could only hit the allies of the United States for weapons that could actually hit the Soviet Union.

Gorbachev offered a schedule for complete nuclear disarmament in a speech on 15 January 1986, which in terms of vision provided his equivalent to Reagan's 'star wars' speech of March 1983. As with SDI, it was hard to take seriously the ultimate goal. However, in this case the first steps were practical. Towards the end of the year, in a remarkable and hastily arranged summit in Reykjavik in Iceland, the two leaders appeared ready not only to take the first steps along the road to Gorbachev's vision but to travel the distance. In a set of extraordinary discussions the two began to outbid each other in their utopianism. Their bureaucracies were spared the traumas of having to implement this by Reagan's refusal to swop his vision of strategic defences in exchange for Gorbachev's vision of complete disarmament. He saw them as compatible.[65]

Among the NATO establishment in Europe there was a stunned astonishment that Reagan had been prepared to compromise nuclear deterrence in so cavalier a fashion. Ideas raised by the American team, such as the abolition of all ballistic missiles with a return to manned bombers as the main means of nuclear delivery, appeared to have been barely thought through. European leaders, such as Margaret Thatcher of Britain, urged a more cautious approach.

Gradually the Reykjavik package began to be reassembled, starting with the agreement on the elimination of all intermediate nuclear forces. In different circumstances NATO might have found this cause for mild celebration. After all Gorbachev had conceded the Western position and the unilateralist disarmament campaigns had been proved wrong. The NATO establishment was now uncertain where this might lead. When they began to suggest conditions in the form of restrictions on shorter-range missiles (500–1000 km) Gorbachev unbalanced them further by offering to eliminate these as well. European leaders balked at this apparent generosity until they received evidence that their electorates viewed it favourably. The

INF Treaty was prepared for signing at the Washington summit of December 1987.

Soviet Doctrine

Influencing the changing American attitude towards arms control was a widespread perception that there had been a fundamental change in the Soviet approach. It might be too much actually to trust the Soviet Union to comply with the provisions of treaties, but it did now appear willing to allow intrusive verification. This changing attitude towards the Soviet Union was one of the most important developments of the 1980s, for the debate at the start of the decade was over what might be read into the offensive character of Soviet military doctrine.[66] Part of the change in the 1980s can be attributed to the policies of Gorbachev. However, even before Gorbachev there were indications of a shift in Soviet military doctrine.

The impression that had been gained in the West at the start of the decade suggested that Soviet strategy in a major European war would involve three stages: (a) the conventional stage, during which one of the priority tasks for conventional forces would be to attack and destroy as much of NATO's nuclear assets as possible;[67] (b) nuclear strikes designed to remove surviving nuclear assets and then destroy major sources of conventional strength; and (c) a mopping-up stage when conventional forces would remove remaining sources of resistance and then occupy enemy territory. This envisaged that Warsaw Pact forces would take the nuclear offensive not in the sense often considered in NATO as a desperate act of last resort but as a deliberate step towards victory.[68] For this strategy to succeed the Soviet Union had to be able to maintain the initiative by being able not only to pre-empt a NATO nuclear strike at the first sign of its preparation, but also to do so without NATO even contemplating such a step until virtually the last moment, when it would have lost most of its nuclear assets. The second critical assumption was that Soviet territory would be respected as a sanctuary. This in turn depended on NATO (especially the United States) respecting this sanctuary status, presumably in return for its own territory being respected as a sanctuary.

In the event of nuclear war there was little reason to doubt that the Soviet Union would share the American interest in keeping the exchanges as limited as possible. However this did not mean that the two countries shared the same concept of limitations. A substantial counterforce exchange between the super-powers directed against missile silos, command and control centres and submarine pens, might be characterized by the United States as being limited in the sense of focusing on one set of targets to the exclusion of others, yet to the Soviet Union this would appear as the most logical form of attack – the essence of strategic warfare.[69] Given the proximity of key military targets to civilian areas the presumption would have to be that such attacks would be experienced as total. Soviet planners appear to have found it very difficult to envisage nuclear exchanges at the super-power level being at all limited in any useful sense of the word.

Soviet statements emphasized that any nuclear attacks on Soviet territory would not be deemed limited even if they were launched from European bases, were on a relatively small scale and related to the course of a land war in Europe. The late Defence Minister, Marshal Ustinov, was quite blunt in 1982: 'There can be no kind of limited nuclear war at all.'[70] Nevertheless there was still a Soviet concept of limitations. As we have noted, attacks on the territory of the super-powers were considered to be of a quite different order to attacks on allies. Soviet leaders recognize a concept of *homeland sanctuaries* in which the major nuclear powers inflict damage on each other's allies but not each other. In this sense the transformation from limited to total war takes place when the first weapons explode on Soviet territory. This concept informed much of the opposition to US cruise and *Pershing* missiles as theatre weapons intended to extend the war to Soviet territory, thus undermining any distinction between the theatre of operations and the homeland.[71]

Secondly, it was possible to put targets in order of priority without a specific policy of limitation. Priorities are needed because potential target lists outrun available weapons. Soviet theorists also are aware of powerful reasons for not attacking targets of a largely civilian nature as a matter of course. This would involve deliberately *not* attacking certain targets in certain circumstances. One Soviet planner spoke of the need to identify targets that might disorganize the enemy economy but stressed that:

> The objective is not to turn large economic and industrial regions into a heap of ruins (although great destruction is apparently unavoidable) but to deliver nuclear strikes which will destroy strategic combat means, paralyze enemy military production,

making it incapable of satisfying the priority needs of the front and rear, and sharply reducing the enemy capability to conduct strikes.

Another described tactical nuclear engagements in terms of limited political objectives: '. . . they should not encompass objectives that would put into question the very existence of the opponent's social system'.[72]

The problem for the Soviet leaders – as with the American – was whether their concept of limitations had any practical applications. Their notion of a decisive nuclear strike within Europe must always have seemed a bit hopeful even if they allowed their planners to make the best of a bad job by way of developing a credible strategy.[73] Two factors completely undermined this approach. First the general Reagan modernization programme and the attitude it was believed to betray. According to John Erickson:

> In the US and the 'imperialist camp' at large, the USSR faces a formidable adversary, whose real purposes are not disclosed by declaratory doctrinal positions – the reality in Soviet eyes lies in the US pursuit of war-waging counterforce capabilities with offensive strategic forces eminently capable of 'first-strike': the 'punishment' concept has given way to coercion and constraint, with counterforce capability growing constantly.[74]

Second, with the arrival of cruise and *Pershing* missiles the likelihood of Soviet territory being granted sanctuary status declined, and the chances of being able to fight a nuclear war that left Soviet territory virtually unscathed was reduced.[75]

These problems raised a question mark against the wisdom of using the initial conventional phase to prepare the ground for the nuclear phase, as a result of which some favourable opportunities in the conventional area might be lost. As a result, Soviet planners began to attach more importance to the conventional stage and would hope to achieve their basic objectives without resort to nuclear strikes and with NATO strikes also remaining deterred. Soviet planners became less sanguine about the possibility of controlling a nuclear war and more confident in the conventional strengths of the Soviet Union. In this sense the shift in the Soviet position towards a no-first-use policy, however unreliable a guide it might be to Soviet behaviour in the actual event of war, does seem to have a significance beyond its immediate propaganda value to the Soviet leadership.[76] Now the main task of Soviet military thinking is to develop and enhance the conventional option.[77]

There is of course here a certain convergence with trends in NATO thinking towards a more substantial conventional phase in future warfare, although NATO has not renounced the option of using nuclear weapons first. There are reasonable grounds for confidence that neither side would expect to open a future war with nuclear volleys or to move in this direction early on. To put it no higher, there no longer appears to be a presumption of inevitable nuclear escalation.

These practical grounds for a renewed emphasis on conventional strategy became coupled with a political interest in playing down the conflict. We noted above Gorbachev's proposals for general and complete nuclear disarmament. The most cynical Western interpretation was that this was an attempt to create the conditions in which a conventional strategy could work. However, others saw signs of a growing Soviet conviction that there was nothing to be gained militarily in a nuclear exchange and that it was hopeless to pretend any more that socialism could triumph in these conditions.[78]

In addition, and in the spirit of *Glasnost*, civilian strategists began to argue that Soviet doctrine had been unnecessarily provocative. In an intriguing analysis, Alexi Arbatov wrote of the discrepancy between the 'socio-political' aspects of Soviet doctrine which have been consistently and clearly defensive, and its 'military-technical aspects' which could convey a completely different impression. The old view was that

... if a war were unleashed against the USSR and its allies, their armed forces should have the capability necessary for crushing the enemy, primarily including the waging of resolute offensive operations at all levels of the conflict. The greater the capacity for such operations the stronger the defense, the more reliable the deterrence of hostile actions of the other side, and the better the conditions for the maintenance of peace.

Arbatov identified two problems with this view. First, that it erroneously supposed the possibility of a victor in a major East–West confrontation. Second, if both sides decided to work on the basis of a quick move into offensive operations then there would be a risk of damaging instability at a time of crisis. Arbatov describes this as the problem of feed-back.

If the military potential exceeds limits of reasonable sufficiency for defense, it will inevitably be perceived by other countries as a sign of aggressive intentions, outweighing any political obligations and statements. Such a situation causes distrust and suspicion, and generates political tension in relations between states, which, in some unforeseen crisis, could turn into an uncontrollable military conflict.[79]

If war cannot be won then it must be prevented, and if it is to be prevented the greater priority must now be given to eliminating the risk of aggravating a crisis than to preparing to deliver 'a crushing blow to an aggressor'. Arbatov applied this to both conventional and nuclear doctrine. This suggested that at last Soviet doctrine was coming into line with the concern for crisis stability that has provided the basis for Western thinking on nuclear arms control for much of the past three decades.

Extended Deterrence

Throughout this book considerable emphasis has been placed on the importance of extended deterrence in driving American nuclear strategy. If the problem had simply been one of deterring a nuclear attack against the American homeland then it would have been declared 'solved' some time ago. The difficulties come with the promise made by the United States to use all the means at its disposal, not excluding nuclear weapons, to prevent its allies being overrun by conventional forces. The American nuclear guarantee to Europe was a commitment upon which Western Europe depended, which the Soviet Union appeared to take seriously, yet for which it had proved to be almost impossible to plan sensibly.[80]

The Reagan Administration had begun by taking this requirement seriously, acknowledging that the United States must be prepared in extreme circumstances to initiate nuclear war but in the belief that appropriate options could be devised to make such a step strategically rational and credible both to allies and adversaries. If it had discovered some way of making nuclear threats imply something other than *mutual* destruction then their strategic credibility might have been bolstered. As it was, the consequence of the Administration's failure to meet the standards it had set for itself was to make the challenge to first-use strategies even more intense.

In this chapter we have noted the various political, intellectual and practical challenges to orthodox nuclear deterrence. While there was no evidence that the United States under Reagan or any likely successor would cease to deter nuclear threats against allies, there was reason to believe that the commitment to deter conventional aggression through nuclear threats was on the decline.

In 1982, four former senior policy-makers (who became known as the 'gang of four') advocated a policy of 'no-first-use-of-nuclear-weapons'.[81] The next year one of this gang – Robert McNamara – published an article suggesting that in practice, during his tenure in office, the United States had been following a *de facto* no-first-use policy:

> In long private conversations with successive Presidents – Kennedy and Johnson – I recommended, without qualification, that they never initiate, under any circumstances, the use of nuclear weapons.[82]

The more an earlier generation of policy-makers who had sustained the first-use commitment in the past described their own doubts as to its validity, the harder it was to accept the assurances of the current generation of policy-makers that the commitment was intact. Apart from the fact that a senior member of the Administration had written an impressive article sympathetic to 'no first use' just prior to the start of taking office,[83] and that the Administration's own statements in support of first use were couched in circumspect language, its failure to generate a compelling nuclear strategy reinforced rather than assuaged the doubts. The President's support for utopian schemes of strategic defence and then of nuclear disarmament, which reached its peak at the 1986 Reykjavik summit, created a deep gloom amongst those committed to an orthodox NATO strategy. The 1987 INF Treaty reinforced this gloom and even led to exaggerated talk of Europe becoming denuclearised.

The talk was exaggerated because many American (as well as British and French) nuclear systems would remain after the missiles covered by the Treaty departed. The real change was in political attitudes towards nuclear deterrence. The critics could be found on both sides of the Atlantic and on both sides of the Iron Curtain. So could supporters, but they made their case with less conviction and more qualification than before. For example, although there was a vigorous German response to the original 'gang of four', they accepted that any nuclear use should be late rather than early.[84] Moreover, as the decade progressed the German political consensus demonstrated considerable unease with the requirements of deterrence. A compelling case could still be made for flexible response,[85] and its very 'flexibility' allowed for adjustments to new circumstances without great upheavals. Nonetheless the events of the decade created a sense of crisis in deterrence. The traditional argument was that there would be little need for nuclear deterrence if only Europe would make the effort to match Warsaw Pact conventional forces. Apart from the fact that there was still a residual problem in terms of the United States deterring *nuclear* attacks on its non-nuclear allies, there was no evidence that the decline in nuclear deterrence would be matched by a surge in conventional capabilities.

In terms of the old orthodoxies this meant that Europe was becoming 'safe for conventional war', although this hackneyed warning reflected no tangible political developments on the continent. It was challenged by a series of analyses claiming that the conventional imbalance had been exaggerated.[86] Even more significant was the fact that the crisis in deterrence made little impression on the actual course of East–West relations – which were mainly influenced by the travails of the socialist system. Crude containment backed by crude nuclear threats was having to give way to a more complex set of relationships with the East, with stability resulting from active diplomacy, the institutional inertia of decades and the shared fear of any sort of armed confrontation. The Reagan Administration had tried and failed to provide a form of nuclear deterrence that would meet its own exacting standards of credibility. Fortunately international order had never been as dependent on this effort succeeding as those involved had believed.

27 Conclusion

In the first major contribution by a civilian to nuclear strategy, Bernard Brodie observed that 'everything about the atomic bomb is overshadowed by the twin facts that it exists and its destructive power is fantastically great'.[1] Since then the major additional fact is that the bomb is no longer monopolized by the United States. Otherwise most developments have served to increase this destructive power and the ease with which it can be delivered. Strategic thinking over the past four decades has been conditioned by these facts. Simplifying somewhat, three basic responses can be identified.

The first, taking the line of least resistance, has been to exploit this destructive power to make total war appear a greater folly than ever before.

The second has been to search for a way to deny an enemy the benefits of its destructive power by devising either an effective defence or a form of first strike that could eliminate the enemy's capacity to retaliate. This was the obvious line for the military to follow. It has turned out to be futile, although it enjoyed a brief revival during the Reagan Administration.

The third response takes the form of attempts to deny the essence of nuclear weapons and to contrive to develop types of weapons and tactics for their use which minimize their destructive power. These attempts usually involve small-yield weapons, capable of guidance with the utmost precision to wholly military targets, these targets to be destroyed with minimum damage to the surrounding civil society. The strength of this approach is that few can relish the prospect of a war fought by two sides attempting to maximize the impact of the destructive power of nuclear weapons. The difficulties reside not in capabilities but in establishing rules for meticulous control and self-restraint, capable of comprehension and obedience in the most exceptional and fraught of circumstances. Fortunately, there has yet to be an opportunity to see if these difficulties would prove insuperable in practice. Meanwhile, it is doubtful that there has been any significant success in breaking the popular association between any nuclear use and utter catastrophe.

As Soviet nuclear capabilities undermined American commitments made to allies at a time of effective superiority, the logical response was to reduce dependence on nuclear weapons, relying more on conventional forces. But this was deemed too expensive and risky and so the quest continued in the West for a plausible nuclear strategy. Moving to large thermonuclear weapons and small 'tactical' weapons, contemplating disarming first strikes, seeking to demonstrate resolve and commitment as well as sensitivity to the horrors of all-out war, there has been a search for some formula that would work to the West's advantage. The advantage has been sought in the superiority of weapons themselves, in the support they could give to defences against invasion, and in the artfulness of American strategists. At the same time there have been regular expressions of anxiety over how the real advantages would accrue to the USSR – supposedly more aggressive in intent, indifferent to human suffering, and able to plan and execute surprise attacks. In practice, neither side emerges with a decisive advantage: each remains capable of confounding the most ruthless and devious plans of the other, by ensuring an unavoidable risk of unendurable destruction.

The essence of the problem is the difficulty of attaching any rationality whatsoever to the initiation of a chain of events that could well end in the utter devastation of one's own society (even assuming indifference to the fate of the enemy society). No means of controlling events to be sure of avoiding the worst outcome have been developed. In consequence any strategy that requires the threat of first use of nuclear weapons suffers from incredibility. Even threats confined to retaliation, which may achieve little except another volley from the enemy, suffer from this incredibility. The resulting sense of an enormous, and somewhat transparent, bluff is, however, more likely to worry those relying on these threats (who tend to believe themselves to be rational and prudent) than those against whom they are directed (who can never be 100 per cent sure of the mental equilibrium of their adversaries). It would be foolish to rely on a national leader taking any particular course when the likely consequences of any action (including doing nothing) in a confused and highly charged atmosphere are incalculable. By their nature these are threats which impress those who receive them more than those who make them. This explains why so much of nuclear policy within NATO is more concerned with mutual reassurance than warning the Soviet Union.

The second major set of problems, in constructing nuclear strategies, revolves around the enormity of the uncertainties. Despite the technical bias of contemporary strategic studies, its most important problems can only be approached through speculation and conjecture, for in essence much of it is about influencing the thought processes of political leaders, current and still to come, in circumstances so horrific and facing pressures so extreme that we can barely comprehend them. We do not know how political leaders will react to the news of even only a few nuclear weapons exploding on their territory. The response could be a reckless fury, lethargic submission, craven cowardice, or a firm and resolute action. We do not know how an American President will react to the news that Soviet forces are advancing through Western Europe. He may be struck most by the danger to his country's population if any steps are taken towards nuclear war, or else by a sense of obligation in honouring alliance commitments. Not only do we not know how our leaders will respond; still less do we know the expectations of Soviet leaders as to Western responses or how they themselves would cope with their own moments of truth: and even less do we know how things will have changed in a decade or so when the weapons now being conceived will become operational. All we can draw on is our knowledge of human nature and specific personalities, and on our experience of diplomacy and non-nuclear war.

Uncertainties abound even with the objective of deterrence, requiring as a continuous peacetime activity speculation on the course of a nuclear war. The actual workings of the strategic relationship between East and West are more enigmatic than often admitted: whether the Soviet Union actually has serious designs on Western Europe; whether, if they exist, they are the sort that can readily be deterred by means available to NATO; whether, if they are capable of deterrence, NATO has been employing the right means in the past and whether these will suffice in the future; and how great is the margin of error – is NATO on the edge of tolerable risk or enjoying a far more comfortable relationship than it in fact realizes?

What we do know is that since 1945 Europe has been at peace. This underlines the point that nuclear deterrence may be a viable policy even if it is not credible; the legion of uncertainties means that no one could contemplate aggression with a confident forecast of the full consequences. Despite preparations for nuclear war as if it could be tamed and controlled, it is probably the fear of the whole process getting out of control that is the strongest source of caution in the modern world. The Emperor Deterrence may have no clothes, but he is still Emperor. This may also mean that the regular proposals for re-designing force structure and war plans, introducing new weapons and explaining them through new doctrines, may have less to do with keeping the peace in Europe than is often supposed (except in the sense mentioned earlier of serving the function of mutual reassurance within NATO).

These paragraphs may seem unduly optimistic or even complacent. In the short term, in all conceivable scenarios, only the most appalling set of accidents and miscalculations would cause a full-scale nuclear war. It is therefore not surprising that so much effort goes into shoring up the *status quo*, in keeping the alliances in good repair and ensuring that military relations between them are managed, rather than transformed, through the mechanisms of arms control. The international system has proved to be less sensitive than anticipated to shifts in the superpower nuclear relationship. This was less true during the first years of the nuclear age as the system sorted itself out following the upheaval of the Second World War. Over this period nuclear developments and deployments, doctrinal pronouncements and commitments to allies had an urgency and intensity to them that has now been dimmed with the passage of time. In a sense this was the most substantial period of nuclear strategy – not because of the ingenuity of the prescriptions dreamed up by academics but because there was a close relationship between nuclear means and political ends. Nuclear policies were critical when it came to defining the terms of the cold war or facilitating alliance formation. By the time that contemporary strategic studies began to 'take off' in the mid 1950s many of the great strategic issues of the post-war era had already been settled.

The study of strategy was nevertheless influenced by the continuing uncertainty over the future of East–West relations. It was particularly stimulated by the need to clarify the emerging military relationship between the superpowers and to explore the implications of this relationship for the political commitments made to allies and its possible impact on future crises. The strategic studies community never stopped addressing these issues even as they were gradually becoming less urgent. There was reluctance to accept that the relationship between nuclear strategy and international stability might be less close than previously imagined. Indeed from the mid 1970s on, the contrary view was asserted with great vigour. From the right there were warnings that an inadequate strategic posture creates opportunities for aggressive states; the left's anxieties focused on the consequences of reckless strategic postures and an arms race.

Nevertheless the experience of the past decades suggests that while the basic structure of the contemporary international system was shaped by the arrival of nuclear weapons it is now only marginally affected by variations in nuclear policies. This is why governments have been reluctant to accept high political and economic costs of resolving the evident contradictions in deterrence strategies. Deterrence has become not so much a function of the policies adopted by individual states and alliances, but the condition created by the stocks of weapons, their widespread deployment, the character of the command and control arrangements, the links with conventional forces, and underlying conflicts of interest. It works less through conditional threats but through a sense of a wholly unacceptable risk. The major powers are in shared awe at the speed with which civilized societies could be comprehensively demolished. Deterrence also works because it is barely put to the test. The fear of nuclear war adds stability to a political system that is already reasonably stable for other reasons.

There are three obvious qualifications to this judgment. First, even while this may hold with regard to the relationship among the major powers it tells us little with regard to the possible implications of nuclear proliferation in the world's more unsettled regions. The fact that nuclear proliferation has been much slower than forecast does not alter the point that should it occur in the future it cannot be assumed that it will always reinforce the *status quo* and dampen drives towards war. This leads to the second qualification which concerns the possibility that, for reasons which have more to do with the unavoidable processes of political change than shifts in nuclear policies and practices, the strategic environment could become unsettled. There must then be a risk of nuclear restraint being overwhelmed by political turbulence. In this sense we ought to be disturbed by the apparently permanent position of nuclear weapons in the international system, even acknowledging that there is now little that can be done about it. This will be the most terrible legacy with which each generation will endow the next. To believe that this can go on indefinitely without major disaster requires an optimism unjustified by any historical or political perspective.

The standard question, 'What do we do if deterrence fails?' is largely beside the point not because failure is inconceivable, but because it is extremely unlikely under current political circumstances. If it does fail this will be in completely different political circumstances that will in themselves shape the strategic options available. It is more likely that the international system, and perhaps eventually the nuclear balance, will become unstuck because of fundamental political changes than by purely military factors. In this sense the challenge for strategic studies is to consider the strategic implications of political change and the sort of military responses that might result. The most optimistic prospect is not that international leaders will band together to agree some grand scheme for general and complete disarmament but that if political relations become even more stable, nuclear weapons will be seen to be playing a marginal role in international affairs and less care and attention will be lavished upon them.

Because of the remarkable constancy in the fundamental relations between the major powers throughout the nuclear age, the political framework has been taken too much for granted and strategic studies have become infatuated with the microscopic analysis of military technology and the acquisition of equipment by the forces of both sides. This has been the one major area of change with the additional advantage of generating the most concrete and profuse data. The literature abounds with calculations and graphs and matrices – computing the kill probabilities of missiles of given range and accuracy against point targets with a certain hardness, considering the prospect for successful defence against cruise missiles, discussing the relative merits of Equivalent Megatonnage and Counter Military Potential as measures of military power, comparing the surviving missile throw-weight and bomber payload after the initial nuclear exchange, identifying the level at which destruction is both assured and unacceptable, and so on, as if this is the real stuff of strategy.

At the end of over 40 years of attempts at constructing nuclear strategies one is forced to the conclusion that there has been a move to the analysis of second- and third-order issues. If strategic thought in the future is to consist of no more than permutations of old concepts in response to new military capabilities, or the exigencies of arms control negotiations in a desperate attempt to preserve the *status quo*, then it may have reached a dead end. For the position we have reached is one where stability depends on something that is more the antithesis of strategy than its apotheosis – on threats that things will get out of hand, that we might act irrationally, that possibly through inadvertence we could set in motion a process that in its development and conclusion would be beyond human control and comprehension.

This threat is credible because it is clear that if there were a major breakdown in East–West relations in Europe, and fighting began, there would be great confusion with plans drawn up before a war soon overtaken by events, and nobody able to promise victory. Those who have responsibility for unleashing nuclear arsenals live by the motto that if they ever had to do so they would have failed. Remarkably, up to now they have succeeded. C'est magnifique, mais ce n'est pas la stratégie.

Notes

INTRODUCTION

1. George Quester, *Nuclear Diplomacy: The First Twenty-Five Years* (New York: Dunellen, 1970); Jerome Kahan, *Security in the Nuclear Age: Developing US Strategic Arms Policy* (Washington DC, Brookings Institute, 1975); Michael Howard, 'The Classic Strategists', in Alastair Buchan (ed.), *Problems of Modern Strategy* (London, Chatto & Windus, 1970). The late James King was engaged in an important study of the major works of nuclear strategy (under the title *The New Strategy*); this was never published.
2. Gregg Herken, *The Winning Weapon: The Atomic Bomb in the Cold War* (New York: Alfred A. Knopf, 1980).
3. John Gaddis, *The Long Peace: Inquiries into the History of the Cold War* (New York: Oxford University Press, 1987).
4. David Rosenberg, 'American atomic strategy and the hydrogen bomb decision', *Journal of American History*, LXVI (Summer 1985).
5. David Rosenberg, 'The origins of overkill: nuclear weapons and American strategy, 1945–1960', *International Security*, 7:4 (Spring 1983). See also the documents edited by Rosenberg in 'A smoking, radiating ruin at the end of two hours': documents on American plans for nuclear war with the Soviet Union, 1954–1955', *International Security* (Winter 1981/82).
6. See the transcripts produced, with an accompanying article by Marc Trachtenberg, 'The influence of nuclear weapons in the Cuban missile crisis', *International Security*, vol. 10 (Summer 1985).
7. Michael Charlton, *From Deterrence to Defense: The Inside Story of Strategic Policy* (Harvard University Press, 1987).
8. Steven Rearden, *The Evolution of American Strategic Doctrine: Paul H.*

434

Nitze and the Soviet Challenge, SAIS papers in International Affairs, (Boulder, Col.: Westview, 1984).

9. Glenn Seaborg, *Kennedy, Khruschev and the Test Ban* (Berkeley: University of California Press, 1981); Herbert York, *Making Weapons, Talking Peace: A Physicist's Odyssey from Hiroshima to Geneva* (New York: Basic Books, 1987).

10. See Ian Clark and Nicholas Wheeler, *British Origins of Nuclear Strategy, 1945–55* (Oxford University Press, forthcoming).

11. David Yost, *France's Deterrent Posture and Security in Europe: Part I, Capabilities and Doctrine, Part II, Strategic and Arms-Control Implications*, Adelphi Papers 194 and 195, (Winter 1984/85).

12. David Holloway, *The Soviet Union and the Arms Race* (Yale University Press, 1983).

13. David Skaggs, 'Michael Howard and strategic policy', *Armed Forces and Society* (Summer 1985); Barry Steiner, 'Using the absolute weapon: early ideas of Bernard Brodie on atomic strategy', *The Journal of Strategic Studies* (December 1984).

14. I have examined the development of the concept of escalation in Lawrence Freedman, 'On the tiger's back: the development of the concept of escalation' in Roman Kolkowicz (ed.), *The Logic of Nuclear Terror* (Boston: Allen & Unwin, 1987).

15. Gregg Herken, *Counsels of War* (New York: Alfred A. Knopf, 1985); Fred Kaplan, *The Wizards of Armageddon* (New York: Simon & Schuster, 1983).

16. B. H. Liddell Hart, *Strategy: The Indirect Approach* (London: Faber & Faber, 1968), p. 334.

17. Michael Howard, 'The Transformation of Strategy', in Major-General J. L. Moulton (ed.), *Brassey's 1972* (London: William Clowes, 1972), p. 1.

CHAPTER 1

1. The most notable exceptions to this statement are guerrilla leaders, for a war of attrition has appeal only to those who begin hostilities at a disadvantage but have grounds to believe that, given time and a chance to mobilize to their full potential, the balance of advantage will eventually work out in their favour.

2. *Hansard*, 10 November 1932, cols. 613–18.

3. Quoted in George Quester, *Deterrence Before Hiroshima: The Influence of Airpower on Modern Strategy* (New York: John Wiley, 1966), p. 52.

4. Giulio Douhet, *The Command of the Air*, as translated by Dino Ferrari (New York: Coward-McCann Inc., 1942), pp. 220, 202.

5. *Ibid.*, p. 128.

6. *Ibid.*, p. 58.

7. Quoted in Quester, *Deterrence before Hiroshima*, p. 56.

8. The efforts to secure formal international agreement on restraint are described by Donald Cameron Watt in 'Restraints on war in the air

before 1945', in Michael Howard (ed.), *Restraints on War: Studies in the limitation of Armed Conflict* (London: Oxford University Press, 1979).

9. B. H. Liddell Hart, *The Revolution in Warfare* (London, Faber & Faber; 1946), p. 31.
10. David Irving, *The Mare's Nest* (London: William Kimber, 1964), pp. 181, 210, 291, 294.
11. Richard G. Hewlett and Oscar Anderson, *The New World 1939/46*: vol. I of a history of the ASAEC (Pennsylvania: Pennsylvania University Press, 1962); Margaret Gowing, *Britain and Atomic Energy*, 1939–1945 (London Macmillan, 1964).
12. Henry L. Stimson and McGeorge Bundy, *On Active Service in Peace and War* (London: Hutchinson, 1948), p. 361.
13. Herbert Feis, *The Atomic Bomb and the End of World War II*, (Princeton: Princeton University Press, 1966), p. 87; Margaret Gowing, *op. cit.*, p. 106.
14. Feis, *op. cit.*, p. 38.
15. This is discussed in detail in Lawrence Freedman, 'The Strategy of Hiroshima', *The Journal of Strategic Studies*, I, 1 (May 1978).
16. Quoted by L. Giovannitti and F. Freed, *The Decision to Drop the Bomb* (London: Methuen & Co., 1967), p. 35.
17. Leslie R. Groves, *Now It Can Be Told: The Story of the Manhattan Project* (New York: Harper, 1962) p. 267.
18. Basil Liddell Hart, *The Revolution in Warfare*, p. 25.
19. Stimson and Bundy, *op. cit.*, pp. 36, 369–70, 373.
20. Giovannitti and Freed, *op. cit.*, p. 36.
21. Robert J. C. Butow, *Japan's Decision to Surrender* (Stanford: Stanford University Press, 1954), p. 180.
22. Liddell Hart, *The Revolution in Warfare*, pp. 30–2, 83.

CHAPTER 2

1. Perry McCoy Smith, *The Air Force Plans for Peace 1939–1945*. (Baltimore: John Hopkins Press, 1970), p. 46, 17.
2. Quoted in David MacIsaacs, *Strategic Bombing in World War Two: The Story of the United States Strategic Bombing Survey* (New York: Garland, 1976), p. 165. The survey was a thorough investigation, directed by civilians, into the effects of the bombing campaigns on the economies and civilian morale of Germany and Japan. MacIsaacs has edited the reports in ten volumes, also published by Garland in 1976.
3. General H. H. Arnold, 'Air Force in the Atomic Age', in Dexter Masters and Katherine Way (eds.), *One World or None* (New York: McGraw Hill, 1946), pp. 26–9. Arnold admitted that his calculations were 'rough'. The USSBS estimate for the number of B-29s needed to commit an Hiroshima was 210, and 120 for Nagasaki. Their conclusion was that: 'The atomic bomb in its present state of development raises the destructive power of a single bomber by a factor of between 50 and 250 times, depending upon the nature and size of the target.' Summary Report,

Pacific War, *United States Strategic Bombing Survey, III*, p. 29. This conclusion was not altogether popular with those airmen, such as General Curtis Le May, who looked forward to ever-expanding fleets of long-range bombers.

4. See Edmund Beard, *Developing the ICBM: A Study in Bureaucratic Politics* (New York: Columbia University Press, 1976).
5. *New York Times*, 13 August 1945.
6. Major-General J. F. S. Fuller, 'The atomic bomb and warfare of the future', *Army Ordnance* (January–February 1946), p. 34.
7. Report of the President's Advisory Commission on Universal Military Training, *A Programme for National Security*, known as *The Compton Report* (Washington DC; USGPO, 1947), p. 12.
8. Bernard Brodie and Eilene Galloway, *The Atomic Bomb and the Armed Services* Public Affairs Bulletin No. 55 (Washington DC: Library of Congress Legislative Reference Service, May 1947), pp. 30–1.
9. Arnold, in Masters and Way, *op. cit.*, p. 30.
10. Vannevar Bush, *Modern Arms and Free Men* (London, Heinemann, 1950), pp. 90, 96–7.
11. Brodie and Galloway, *op. cit.*, p. 32; Bush, *op. cit.*, p. 117; P. M. S. Blackett, *The Military and Political Consequences of Atomic Energy* (London, Turnstile Press, 1948), p. 68.
12. Reprinted in Morton Grodzins and Eugene Rabinowitch (eds.) *The Atomic Age: Scientists in National and World Affairs* (New York: Basic Books, 1963), p. 13.
13. Edward Condon, 'The new techniques of private war', in Masters and Way, *op. cit.*, p. 41 ('We must no longer expect the special agent to be special'). On this concern see Roberta Wohlstetter, 'Terror on a grand scale', *Survival*, xviii:3 (May/June 1976), pp. 98–9.
14. In *The Atomic Bomb and American Security* (Yale University, Memorandum No. 18, 1945), p. 5, he wrote of how a war of the future 'might take the form of a revelation by one nation to another that the latter's major cities had atomic bombs planted in them and that only immediate and absolute submission to dictates would prevent them from going off'.
15. Bernard Brodie, *The Absolute Weapon* (New York: Harcourt Brace, 1946), p. 49.
16. Blackett, *op. cit.*, p. 50.
17. Bernard Brodie, *Absolute Weapon*, p. 41; idem., 'Compiler's critique on U.S. navy views', in Brodie and Galloway, *op. cit.*, pp. 46–7.
18. Brodie and Galloway, *op. cit.*, p. 68; *The Compton Report*, p. 12; *New York Times*, 3 October 1949.
19. William Fox, *Atomic Energy and International Relations* (Mimeo: Yale Institute of International Affairs, June 1948), p. 4.
20. Vannevar Bush, *op. cit.*, pp. 104, 139.
21. Jacob Viner, 'The implications of the atomic bomb for international relations', *Proceedings of the American Philosophical Society*, xc:1 (January 1946), p. 55. Fox (*Atomic Energy*, pp. 11–12) doubted that small countries would find bombs much use for 'blackmail' purposes, though he thought 'they might strengthen respect for neutrality'. Others were less certain of the advantages: 'Even small countries can make these bombs in

numbers if they are such utter fools as to engage in this lethal business. They will not because they know they would be completely destroyed if bombs were used', Harold Urey, 'How does it all add up?', in Masters and Way, *op. cit.*, p. 55.

22. There was some wishful thinking on this score. In October 1949 Commander Eugene Tatom of the US Navy still felt confident enough to assert that it would be possible to stand on the runway at Washington National Airport 'with no more than the clothes you now have on, and have an atom bomb explode at the other end of the runway without serious injury to you' Quoted by Albert Wohlstetter in unpublished letter to Michael Howard, 6 November 1968, p. 26. Professor Wohlstetter has kindly permitted quotation from this letter.

23. See Brodie, *Absolute Weapon*, pp. 28, 31.

24. Summary (Pacific War), *United States Strategic Bombing Survey, IV*, p. 29.

25. Brodie and Galloway, *op. cit.*, p. 32.

26. Bush, *op. cit.*, p. 59.

27. 'Very greatly increased bomber speeds will immensely increase the difficulties of providing adequate warning and effective interception, and indeed the fighter's superiority of speed over the bomber . . . may well dwindle to almost nothing'. Lord Tedder, *Air Power in the War* (London: Hodder & Stoughton, 1947), p. 44.

28. Bush, *op. cit.*, pp. 116–17.

29. Blackett, *op. cit.*, p. 54.

30. Bush, *op. cit.*, p. 100.

31. Louis Ridenour, 'There is no defense', in Masters and Way, *op. cit.*, p. 37; *idem.*, 'A US physicist's reply to Professor Blackett', *Scientific American* (March 1949), reprinted in York (ed.), *Arms Control.* (San Francisco: W. H. Freeman & Co., 1973).

CHAPTER 3

1. Quoted in Wohlstetter letter to Howard, p. 5.

2. 'In no other type of warfare does the advantage lie so heavily with the aggressor', the Franck Report, reprinted in Grodzins and Rabinowitch, *op. cit.*, p. 21.

3. H. D. Smyth, *A General Account of the Development of Methods of Using Atomic Energy for Military Purposes under the Auspices of the United States Government 1940–1945* (Washington DC, USGPO, August 1945), p. 134.

4. Caryl Haskins, 'Atomic energy and American foreign policy', *Foreign Affairs*, XXIV:4 (July 1946); The Eliot quote comes from *The Atomic Age Opens*, prepared by the editors of Pocket Books (New York, August 1945) – this is a useful compilation of immediate reactions to the bomb; Robert Oppenheimer, 'Atomic weapons', *Proceedings of the American Philosophical Society*, XC:1 (January 1946), p. 9; D. Lilienthal, *The Journals of David E. Lilienthal*, vol. II, *The Atomic Energy Years 1945–50* (New York, Harper & Row, 1964).

5. Edward Mead Earle, 'The influence of air power upon history', *The Yale*

Review, xxxv:4 (June 1946), pp. 577–93; 'The effects of the atomic bomb on national security (an expression of War Department thinking)', in Brodie and Galloway, *op. cit.*, p. 70. See also Bernard Brodie, *Atomic Bomb and American Security*, p. 9.

6. Ian Brownlie, *International Law and the Use of Force by States* (Oxford: Clarendon Press, 1963), pp. 351–6.
7. Cited in Robert W. Tucker, *The Just War: A Study in Contemporary American Doctrine* (Baltimore: Johns Hopkins Press, 1960), p. 12.
8. A report to the President by the Special Counsel to the President, *American Relations with the Soviet Union* (24 September 1946). Reprinted in Thomas H. Etzold and John Lewis Gaddis, *Containment: Documents on American Policy and Strategy 1945–50* (New York: Columbia University Press, 1978), p. 66.
9. Quoted in *ibid.*, p. 21, fn. 14.
10. Title of book edited by Masters and Way.
11. One book examined how a war would be fought after the adoption of an international control agreement. The conclusion seemed to be that prior to a war both sides would build up their forces and develop their facilities as much as possible without actually contravening the treaty, available facilities would be seized on the outbreak of war, and, until they became operational, the main military activity would consist of trying to destroy the facilities and delivery vehicles of the other side. Ansley J. Coale, *The Problem of Reducing Vulnerability to Atomic Bombs* (Princeton: Princeton University Press, 1947).
12. Cited in Blackett, *op. cit.*, p. 177.
13. 'The prevention of war', in Grodzins and Rabinowitch, *op. cit.*
14. Cited in Margaret Gowing, *Independence and Deterrence: Britain and Atomic Energy 1945-1952*, vol. 1, *Policy Making* (London: Macmillan, 1974), p. 79.
15. Quoted in Wohlstetter letter to Howard, 6 November 1968. Wohlstetter emphasizes the importance of this 'sooner or later' syndrome.
16. Arnold, in Masters and Way, *op. cit.*, p. 31.
17. Gowing reports the comments of UK scientists in June 1945 that 'the only answer to the bomb was to use it in retaliation', and by October of that year the chiefs of staff were emphatic that the best means of defence would be 'the possession of the means of retaliation' (*op. cit.*, p. 164).
18. NSC 20/2, *Factors Affecting the Nature of the US Defense Arrangements in the Light of Soviet Policies* (25 August 1948). Reprinted in Etzold and Gaddis, *op. cit.*, p. 298.
19. B. M. Liddell Hart, *The Revolution in Warfare*, pp. 85–6.
20. Viner, *op. cit.*, p. 54. This was a lecture given in November 1945.
21. Brodie, *Absolute Weapon*, pp. 74, 85; Frederic S. Dunn: 'The bomb is well adapted to the technique of retaliation' (p. 16); Arnold Wolfers: 'The threat of retaliation in kind is probably the strongest single means of deterrent' (p. 134).
22. William L. Borden, *There Will Be No Time* (New York: Macmillan, 1946), p. 83.
23. Brodie, *The Absolute Weapon*, pp. 76, 88–91. The 1947 War Department paper suggested that: 'The initial strategy of the armed forces, . . . , is that

of absorbing or diverting initial attacks, delivering immediate counter-attacks with long-range bombers or missiles, accomplishing initial essential deployment, and effecting without delay the necessary mobilization of national resources' (Brodie and Galloway, *op. cit.*, p. 78). This suggests a greater optimism than Brodie as to the capacity for mobilization in war.

24. General Arnold raised this possibility in 1946: 'In a world in which atomic weapons are available, the most threatening program that a nation could undertake would be one of *general* dispersal and fortification', *One World or None*, p. 31. Brodie, in a discussion of the need to deter through the threat of atomic retaliation, noted the difficulty of stopping the 'irresponsibility of madmen', *Absolute Weapon*, p. 15.

CHAPTER 4

1. Walter Lippmann, 'Why are we disarming ourselves?', *Redbrook Magazine* (September 1946), p. 106.
2. Bernard Brodie, 'The atom bomb as policy-maker', *Foreign Affairs*, XXVII:1 (October 1948), p. 21.
3. William Fox, *The Superpowers: The United States, Britain and the Soviet Union and Their Responsibility for Peace* (New York: Harcourt & Brace, 1944), p. 102.
4. Perry Smith, *The Air Force Plans for Peace*, pp. 52–3.
5. William Fox, *Atomic Energy and International Relations*, p. 14.
6. 'Spaatz Report', *The Implications of the Atom Bomb for the Size, Composition, Organization and Role of the Future Air Force* (23 October 1945); Joint Staff Strategic Survey, *Statement of the Effect of Atomic Weapons on National Security and Military Organization* (12 January 1946). See Frank Klotz, *The US President and the Control of Strategic Nuclear Weapons*, unpublished D.Phil. Thesis (Oxford, 1980).
7. 'X', 'The sources of Soviet conduct', *Foreign Affairs*, XXV (July 1947); George F. Kennan, *Memoirs, 1925–1950* (Boston, Little Brown: 1967), p. 358.
8. Lilienthal, *The Atomic Energy Years*, p. 391.
9. Walter Millis (ed.), *The Forrestal Diaries* (London: Cassell & Co. 1952), p. 45.
10. NSC-30, *United States Policy on Atomic Weapons* (10 September 1948). Reprinted in Etzold and Gaddis, *op. cit.*, p. 341. It was suggested that a decision against employment 'might gain the praise of the world's radical fringe'.
11. Millis, *op. cit.*, pp. 433–4, 457.
12. Blackett had raised a similar problem in a November 1945 memorandum and then later in his book. He argued that it would be in the interest of any nation faced with an atomic threat to neutralize enemy bases close at hand. Threatened with atomic bombs she would 'expand her effective frontiers to include all possible potential bases from where such attacks

might be launched'. Once ensconced in Western Europe they could not be removed as this would involve attacking friendly populations. (Reprinted in Gowing, *Independence and Deterrence*, p. 203.)

13. Brodie argued that any attacks on the Soviet homeland, even if not directly related to the progress of an invasion of Western Europe, were likely to impede the invasion. He argued that 'the destruction of Soviet cities and industries would make a great deal of difference in the ability of the Soviet armies to overrun Western Europe, or to maintain themselves in that area if they got there', 'Atom Bomb as Policy-Maker', *op. cit.*, p. 30.

14. Air Staff, *Strategic Implications of the Atomic Bomb on Warfare* (3 February 1947). See Klotz, *op. cit.*

15. Joint Chiefs of Staff, *Evaluation of Current Strategic Air Offensive Plans*, (21 December 1948), in Etzold and Gaddis, *op. cit.*, pp. 357–60.

16. The Harmon Report, *Evaluation of Effect on Soviet War Effort Resulting from the Strategic Air Offensive* (11 May 1949). Reprinted in Etzold and Gaddis, *op. cit.*, pp. 360–4.

17. H. S. Dinerstein, *War and the Soviet Union* (New York: Praeger, 1959), p. 32.

18. In 1949, cited in Raymond L. Garthoff, *Soviet Military Doctrine* (Illinois: The Free Press, 1953), p. 174.

19. Colonel-General of Aviation Nikitin, cited in Raymond L. Garthoff, *Soviet Strategy in the Nuclear Age* (New York: Praeger, 1958), pp. 173–4.

20. *Ibid.*, p. 67.

21. Marshal of Aviation Vershinin in 1949, cited by Garthoff, *Soviet Military Doctrine*, p. 175. 'Marshallized Countries' were these that had accepted US economic aid under the Marshall Plan.

22. On the Soviet atom bomb project see Arnold Kramish, *Atomic Energy in the Soviet Union* (Stanford, Calif.: Stanford University Press, 1960).

23. The similarities of views on this particular matter between such figures as Blackett and the Soviet Union were widely noted. As many felt that the only reason that Kremlin disparaged the bomb was that they wished to undermine Western confidence in its major strategic asset, those in the West who assisted in this effort were open to the charge of being virtual fifth-columnists. For example Louis Ridenour on Blackett's book, *The Military and Political Consequences of Atomic Energy*,

His ideas coincide remarkably with the standard Russian views. He belittles the atomic bomb – which Russia had not got, but wants. He depreciates strategic air power – which is the only arm we have that can strike a blow at Russia. . . . Blackett's argument carries its own antidote. The excesses and absurdities of the political views he urges are so clearly the result of bias, and so clearly dominated by pro-Soviet prejudice, that the whole work is suspect, and will appear so to the least discerning. 'A US physicist's reply to Professor Blackett', *Scientific American* (March 1949).

In the April 1949 issue of the *Bulletin of Atomic Scientists*, Edward Shils described the book as a 'gift to Soviet propaganda'. The British delegation to the UN Atomic Energy Commission felt obliged to issue a refutation.

CHAPTER 5

1. This could be the only explanation for the mid-1953 report of an advisory committee (written before the introduction of the TU-16) of a plausible current threat of 100 atomic bombs being accurately delivered on the US, sufficient to destroy up to one-third of America's industrial potential, with up to 13 million casualties. Charles Murphy, 'The US as a bombing target', *Fortune* (November 1953), p. 119.
2. *GAC Report of October 30 1949*, reprinted in Herbert York, *The Advisors: Oppenheimer, Teller and the Superbomb* (San Francisco: W. H. Freeman, 1976). See also Warner R. Schilling 'The H-Bomb decision: how to decide without actually choosing', *Political Science Quarterly* LXXVI (March 1961).
3. Lilienthal, *The Atomic Energy Years*, pp. 628–9.
4. Samuel F. Wells Jr, 'Sounding the Tocsin: NSC-68 and the Soviet Threat', *International Security*, IV:2 (Fall 1979), pp. 120–1.
5. York, *The Advisors*, p. 59.
6. Dean Acheson, *Present at the Creation* (London: Hamish Hamilton, 1969), p. 349.
7. Viner, 'The implications of the atomic bomb', *op. cit.*, p. 53.
8. Omar Bradley, 'This Way Lies Peace', *Saturday Evening Post* (15 October 1949).
9. *Scientific American*, November 1951.
10. *A Report to the National Security Council by the Executive Secretary on United States Objectives and Programs for National Security*, NSC-68 (14 April 1950). It is reprinted in Etzold and Gaddis, *op. cit.* See Paul Hammond 'NSC-68: Prologue to Rearmament', in Warner Schilling, Paul Hammond and Glenn Snyder, *Strategy, Politics and Defense Budgets* (New York: Columbia University Press, 1962).
11. See Bernard Brodie, *Strategy in the Missile Age* (Princeton: Princeton University Press, 1959), pp. 319–20.
12. Robert Osgood, *NATO: The Entangling Alliance* (Chicago: The University of Chicago Press, 1962).
13. Testimony of Secretary of State Acheson, Hearings of the Senate Foreign Relations and Armed Services Committees, *Assignment of Ground Forces of the United States in the European Area*, (February 1951).

CHAPTER 6

1. Bernard Brodie, 'Nuclear weapons: strategic or tactical'?, *Foreign Affairs*, XXXII:2 (January 1954), p. 222.
2. Gowing, *Independence and Deterrence*, p. 184.
3. Gowing, *op. cit.*, p. 441; Glenn Snyder, 'The new look of 1953', in Schilling, Hammond and Snyder, *Strategy, Politics, and Defense Budgets*; Charles Murphy, 'Defense and strategy', *Fortune* (January 1953).
4. Sir John Slessor, 'The place of the bomber in British strategy', *International Affaires*, XXIX:3 (July 1953), pp. 302–3; *idem.*, 'Air power and world strategy', *Foreign Affairs*, XXXI:1 (October 1954), pp. 48, 51; *idem.*, *Strategy for the West* (London: Cassell 1954).

5. NSC-162/2 is reprinted in full in The Gravel Edition, *Pentagon Papers*, vol. I (Boston: Beacon Press, 1971), pp. 412–29.

6. Field Marshal Bernard Law Montgomery, 'A look through a window at World War III', *The Journal of the Royal United Services Institute*, XCIX:596 (November 1954), p. 508.

7. See John Foster Dulles, 'A policy of boldness', *Life* (19 May 1952), p. 151; Snyder, 'The new look', in Schilling, Hammond and Snyder, *op. cit.*, p. 390. See also Martin C. Fergus, 'The massive retaliation doctrine: a study in United States military policy formation', *Public Policy*, XVII (1968).

8. Sherman Adams, *Firsthand Report* (New York: Harper, 1961), pp. 102, 48–9; David Rees, *Korea: The Limited War* (London: Macmillan 1964), pp. 417–20; Robert J. Donovan, *Eisenhower: The Inside Story* (New York: Harper, 1956), pp. 116–19.

9. Speech is reprinted as 'The evolution of foreign policy', *Department of State Bulletin*, XXX (25 January 1954), pp. 107–10.

10. John Foster Dulles, 'Policy for security and peace', *Foreign Affairs*, XXXII:3 (April 1954).

11. *Pentagon Papers*, p. 92.

CHAPTER 7

1. The growing concern on these matters is described in Robert A. Divine, *Blowing on the Wind: The Nuclear Test Ban Debate 1954–60* (New York: Oxford University Press, 1978).

2. P. M. S. Blackett, *Atomic Weapons and East–West Relations* (Cambridge: Cambridge University Press, 1956), p. 3.

3. Robert Oppenheimer, 'Atomic weapons and American policy', *Foreign Affairs*, XXXI:4 (July 1953), p. 529.

4. Paul Kecskemeti, *Strategic Surrender; The Politics of Victory and Defense* (Stanford, Calif.: Stanford University Press, 1958).

5. See James King, 'Strategic Surrender: The Senate Debate and the Book', *World Politics*, XI (April 1959).

6. These attempts are discussed in M. Howard (ed.), *Restraints on War*.

7. Liddell Hart, *Strategy: The Indirect Approach*, p. 25. On Liddell Hart's theories see Brian Bond, *Liddell Hart: A Study of his Military Thought* (London: Cassell, 1977).

8. Liddell Hart, *The Revolution in Warfare*, pp. 99–102.

9. Edward Mead Earle, 'The Influence of Air Power upon History', *op. cit.*

10. Taken from a piece written in April 1954 that was later reprinted in B. H. Liddell Hart, *Deterrent or Defence* (London: Stevens & Sons, 1960), p. 23.

11. Letter of 26 April 1957: 'you led all the rest of us in advocating the principle of limited war'. Quoted in Bond, *op. cit.*, p. 196.

12. Bernard Brodie, 'Unlimited Weapons and Limited War', *The Reporter* (1 November 1954).

13. William Kaufmann (ed.), *Military Policy and National Security* (Princeton: Princeton University Press, 1956), pp. 21, 24–5.

14. Robert Endicott Osgood, *Limited War: The Challenge to American Strategy* (The University of Chicago Press, 1957), pp. 26, 242.

15. Henry Kissinger, *Nuclear Weapons and Foreign Policy* (New York: Harper, 1957).
16. Brodie, 'Unlimited Weapons and Limited War', *op. cit.*
17. Osgood, *op. cit.*, p. 18.
18. W. Kaufmann, *Military Policy*, p. 117.
19. James King, 'Limited War', *Army* (August 1957).

CHAPTER 8

1. Bernard Brodie, 'Strategy hits a dead end', *Harpers* (October 1955); Osgood, *Limited War*, p. 230. Osgood was not totally convinced of the value of tactical nuclear weapons. His discussion of the costs and benefits attached to their use is careful and balanced. For a discussion of the debate about how best to fight a limited war see Morton Halperin, *Limited War in the Nuclear Age*, (New York: John Wiley, 1963). This book contains an excellent bibliography.
2. Denis Healey 'The bomb that didn't go off', *Encounter* (July 1955); Blackett, *Atomic Weapons and East-West Relations*, p. 8.
3. Kissinger, *Nuclear Weapons and Foreign Policy*, pp. 174–83.
4. James E. King, 'Nuclear weapons and foreign policy. II – Limited annihilation', *The New Republic* (15 July 1957), p. 18.
5. William Kaufmann, 'The crisis in military affairs', *World Politics*, x:4 (July 1958), p. 594.
6. For a devastating critique of the Army's attempts to do so, see T. N. Dupuy, 'Can America fight a limited nuclear war?', *Orbis*, v:1 (Spring 1961): '[T]here is every reason to believe that our ground troops – the basic components of a limited war force – are not capable of existing, let alone operating in the very nuclear environment to which our strategy has consigned them' (p. 32).
7. All quotations are from Chapter 7 of Garthoff, *Soviet Strategy in the Nuclear Age*.
8. Originally in *Deterrence by Denial and Punishment*, Research Monograph No. 1, Center of International Studies, Princeton University, 2 January 1959, and then to a wider audience in *Deterrence and Defense* (Princeton: Princeton University Press, 1961).
9. In a letter to the London *Times* of 29 August 1955 in which he spoke of the principle of 'applying the minimum force necessary to repel any particular aggression and deter its extension'.
10. Rear-Admiral Sir Anthony Buzzard, 'Massive retaliation and graduated deterrence', *World Politics*, viii:2 (January 1956); *On Limiting Atomic War* (London: Royal Institute of International Affairs, 1956), written by Richard Goold-Adams on the basis of discussions with Buzzard, Blackett and Denis Healey M.P.
11. Richard Goold-Adams, *On Living Atomic War*, p. 20.
12. 'Graduated deterrence', *Economist* (5 November 1955), p. 458.
13. Colonel Richard S. Leghorn, 'No need to bomb cities to win war', *US News & World Report* (28 January 1955), p. 84.
14. Buzzard, *op. cit.*, p. 229. These ideas are early versions of the concept of escalation dominance, see pp. 218 and 389.

15. Bernard Brodie, 'Strategy hits a dead end', *op. cit.*; *idem.*, *Strategy in the Missile Age*, pp. 321–5.
16. Bernard Brodie, 'More about limited war', *World Politics*, x:1 (October 1957), p. 117.
17. James King, 'Limited war', *op. cit.* William Kaufmann had never been convinced that preparations for limited war would not require large conventional forces or that tactical nuclear weapons offered decisive advantages to the West. See his essay on 'Limited war' in his book *Military Policy and National Security*.
18. Liddell Hart, *Deterrence or Defence*, p. 81; P. M. S. Blackett, 'Nuclear weapons and defence', *International Affairs*, xxxiv:4 (October 1958).
19. Henry A. Kissinger, 'Limited war: conventional or nuclear? A reappraisal', *Daedalus*, vol. 89, No. 4 (1960). This was published in book form a year later by George Braziller in New York, edited by Donald Brennan as *Arms Control, Disarmament and National Security*, p. 145.

CHAPTER 9

1. Paul Nitze, 'Atoms, strategy and policy', *Foreign Affairs*, xxxiv:2 (January 1956), pp. 190–1. See also Glenn Snyder, *Deterrence and Defense*, p. 68: 'The concepts of "winning" and "losing" have to do with the military or *power* outcome of the war.... They have nothing to do with the *intrinsic* costs of damage suffered in the war.'
2. For example John Foster Dulles: 'Khruschev does not need to be convinced of our good intentions. He knows we are not aggressors and do not threaten the security of the Soviet Union', quoted in Robert Jervis, *Perception and Misperception in International Politics* (Princeton: Princeton University Press, 1976), p. 68. The most careful critique of preventive war as a policy can be found in Brodie, *Strategy in the Missile Age*, pp. 228–91.
3. W. D. Puleston, *The Influence of Force in Foreign Relations* (New York: Van Nostrand, 1955), From extract in *US News & World Report* (4 February 1955), p. 133.
4. Col. Jack Nicholas, 'The element of surprise in modern warfare', *Air University Quarterly Review* (Summer 1956), pp. 3–4.
5. T. F. Walkowicz, 'Counter-Force strategy: how we can exploit America's atomic advantage', *Air Force Magazine* (February 1955), p. 51.
6. Charles Murphy, *Fortune* (July 1953). Though accepting the need for a limited air defence effort, Murphy insists that protection against nuclear attack is 'unattainable and in any case completely impractical, economically and technically'.
7. Quoted in George E. Lowe, *The Age of Deterrence* (Boston: Little, Brown & Co., 1964), pp. 100–1.
8. Colonel Robert Richardson, 'Do we need unlimited forces for limited war', *Air Force* (March 1959).
9. For example, Lord Tedder in 1947: 'The most effective defence against air attack is to stop it at source, and in the future it may become the only way; it is certainly the only method of dealing with the rocket. The only

decisive air superiority is that established over the enemy country'. *Air Power in the War*, pp. 44–5.

10. Quoted in Daniel Yergin, *Shattered Peace: The Origins of the Cold War and the National Security State* (London: André Deutsch, 1976), p. 478.

11. In Borden, *There will Be No Time*. See p. 43.

12. Richard Leghorn, commenting on a 1954 news report that the military were studying earth satellites, noted that: 'The present state of the aeronautical art makes the satellites feasible in the not-too-distant future. A few simple calculations, assuming lenses no larger than those now used in aerial photography, show that these might see, and return to earth by electronic means, gross details of larger military installations.' 'No need to bomb cities to win war: a new counter-force strategy for air warfare', *US News & World Report* (28 January 1955), p. 87.

13. Bernard Brodie, *The Reporter* (11 October 1954).

14. Brodie, *Strategy in the Missile Age*, pp. 270, 278, 311, 397. See James King's excellent review, 'Airpower in the missile gap', *World Politics*, XII:4 (July 1960), pp. 628–39.

15. H. Kahn, *On Thermonuclear War*. (Princeton: Princeton University Press, 1960), pp. 559–60.

16. *Ibid.*, p. 32 (emphasis in original).

17. One who took the problem seriously was Thomas Finletter, Secretary of the Air Force in the Truman Administration. In 1954 he wrote a book which suggested that: 'the Russians will not use their air-atomic power to destroy our cities and industry unless they can simultaneously knock out enough of the US Atomic-Air to stop it from making an overwhelming counter-attack on Russia ... and ... they are very busy working on a plan to do just that'. *Power and Policy* (New York: Harcourt & Brace, 1954), p. 26.

18. The story of the strategic bases study is told in Bruce L. R. Smith, *The RAND Corporation: Case Study of a Non-profit Advisory Corporation* (Harvard: Harvard University Press, 1966). The Report was published as A. J. Wohlstetter, F. S. Hoffman, R. J. Lutz and H. S. Rowen, *Selection and Use of Strategic Air Bases*, RAND R-266, 1 April 1954 (declassified 1962).

19. Albert Wohlstetter, 'The delicate balance of terror', *Foreign Affairs*, XXXVII:2 (January 1959).

20. Bernard Brodie, *Strategy in the Missile Age*, p. 282.

21. For example, Kissinger in his 1961 book, *Necessity for Choice* (New York: Harper & Row): 'A precondition of deterrence is an invulnerable retaliatory force' (p. 22).

22. George F. Kennan, *Russia, the Atom and The West* (New York: Harper & Brothers, 1958), pp. 52–4.

CHAPTER 10

1. On the response to *Sputnik*, see J. R. Killian, *Sputniks, Scientists and Eisenhower* (Cambridge, Mass.: MIT Press, 1977) and Herbert York, *Race to Oblivion: A Participant's View of the Arms Race* (New York: Simon & Schuster, 1971). Killian reports how the Soviet satellite

did violence to a belief so fundamental that it was almost heresy to question it. A belief I shared that the United States was so far advanced in its technological capacity that it had in fact no serious rival. That others possessed their share of technology I was aware, but somehow I pictured them all laboring far behind this country, looking towards the United States for guidance, envying our skills, our trained capacity, and above all our enormous industrial substructure that could be put to the task of converting advanced technological notions into performing hardware (p. 3).

2. The evidence upon which these projections were based is discussed in Lawrence Freedman, *US Intelligence and the Soviet Strategic Threat* (London: Macmillan, 1977). Though the Air Force was the most extreme in its projections, many of the fears were shared by other intelligence analysts, including those in the CIA.

3. So starting an intelligence debate that has persisted to this day.

4. General Thomas S. Power, *Design for Survival* (New York: Coward-McCann, 1964), p. 111.

5. Wohlstetter, 'The Delicate Balance of Terror' *op. cit.*, p. 222.

6. Herman Kahn, in his *On Thermonuclear War*, continually uses the 20 million figure as a benchmark for judging the losses likely to be acceptable or bearable for the Soviet Union. So 5 to 10 million casualties is presented as 'only a fraction as many people as they lost in World War II' (p. 132), the implication being that this would be insufficient hurt to ensure deterrence.

7. P. M. S. Blackett, *Studies of War – Nuclear and Conventional* (London: Oliver & Boyd, 1962), p. 139.

8. Power, *op. cit.*, pp. 112–13.

9. Colonel G. C. Reinhardt, 'Atomic weapons and warfare' in B. H. Liddell Hart (ed.), *The Soviet Army* (London: Wiedenfeld & Nicolson 1956), p. 429.

10. Herbert S. Dinerstein, 'The Revolution in Soviet Strategic Thinking', *Foreign Affairs*, xxxvi:2 (January 1958), p. 252.

11. H. S. Dinerstein, *War and the Soviet Union*, pp. 37–45.

12. *Ibid.*, p. 186.

13. See Frederic S. Burin, 'The communist doctrine of the inevitability of war', *American Political Science Review*, lvii:2 (June 1963), pp. 334–54.

14. For example Major-General Talensky: 'at any moment . . . mankind might be faced with the accomplished fact of the beginning of a destructive nuclear war'. Dinerstein, *War and the Soviet Union*, p. 141.

15. *Ibid.*, p. 142.

16. In a November 1957 interview with an American reporter Khruschev explained the virtues of Russia's size. In a nuclear war, 'we too, of course, will suffer great losses. But look at the vast spaces on our map and look at Germany, France and Britain'. He agreed that the US also had vast spaces but then pointed out the American industry was much more concentrated.

17. Dinerstein, *War and the Soviet Union*, pp. 186, 187.

18. It also referred to intelligence capabilities out of a recognition that a timely warning of attack would be essential to a pre-emptive strike: 'It is absolutely clear and beyond argument that Marxist–Leninist science is fully capable of foreseeing such a significant phenomenon in the life of society as the transition from a condition of peace to a condition of war'.

19. Dinerstein, *War and the Soviet Union*, pp. 216–20.

20. Garthoff, *Soviet Strategy in the Nuclear Age*, pp. 222–3.

21. *Ibid.*, pp. 230, 231.

22. By September 1957 General Pokrovsky was cautioning that some defence against ICBMs could and would be developed in the future, noting that radar detection might be sufficient to allow for the launch of a defensive rocket.

23. See Arnold Horelick and Myron Rush, *Strategic Power and Soviet Foreign Policy* (Chicago: University of Chicago Press, 1966).

24. See p. 111.

CHAPTER 11

1. Denis Healey, 'The Sputnik and western defence', *International Affairs*, XXXIV:2 (April 1954), p. 147.

2. 'The meaning of Stalemate', *Army* (August 1958).

3. John Foster Dulles, 'Challenge and response in US policy', *Foreign Affairs*, XXXVI:1 (October 1957).

4. Cited in Samuel P. Huntington, *The Common Defense: Strategic Programs in National Politics* (New York: Columbia University Press, 1961), p. 101.

5. Herbert York wrote in 1970: 'Surprising as it may seem, the wild outbursts of ideas inspired by Sputnik and the missile-gap psychology has produced nothing of direct value to our current strategic posture more than twelve years later'. *Race to Oblivion*, p. 144.

6. As an example he adds: 'I have not seen any figures, but I surmise that relatively thin margins of cost prevent us from doing such extraordinary projects as melting ice caps and diverting ocean currents' (this is for 1965!). *On Thermonuclear War*, p. 484.

7. Emphasis in the original. Quotations from report are taken from section reproduced in James R. Killian Jr., *Sputniks, Scientists and Eisenhower*, pp. 71–9.

8. In both Killian and Gaither Reports 'decisive' was defined as: (1) ability to strike back is essentially eliminated; or (2) civil, political or cultural life are reduced to a condition of chaos; or both (1) and (2).

9. Security Resources Panel of the Scientific Advisory Committee, *Deterrence and Survival in the Nuclear Age*, Washington DC: November 1957 (declassified January 1973). Though the President was not happy with the report, in a speech he made a week after its presentation to the National Security Council he showed signs of having been influenced by this forecast of the shape of things to come:

I assure you . . . that for the conditions existing today they [the US military forces] are both efficient and adequate. But if they are to remain so for the future, their design and power must keep pace with the increasing capabilities that science gives both to the aggressor and the defender.

Quoted in Morton Halperin, 'The Gaither Committee and the Policy Process', *World Politics*, XIII:3 (April 1961), p. 370.

10. Henry Kissinger, 'Arms control, inspection and surprise attack', *Foreign Affairs*, XXXVIII:3 (April 1960), p. 557.
11. Kennan, *Russia, the Atom and the West*, p. 54.
12. See J. David Singer, *Deterrence, Arms Control and Disarmament: Towards a Synthesis in National Security Policy* (Ohio State University Press; 1962).
13. Brodie, *The Reporter* (18 November 1954); Kahn, *On Thermonuclear War*, p. 192. Senator John Kennedy wrote (in the middle of his Presidential Campaign), reviewing Basil Liddell Hart's book, *Deterrence or Defence?* for the *Saturday Review* on 3 September 1960: 'We have no right to tempt Soviet planners and political leaders with the possibility of catching our aircraft and unprotected missiles on the ground, in a gigantic Pearl Harbor'.
14. Thomas Schelling, *The Strategy of Conflict* (New York: Oxford University Press, 1960).
15. Snyder, *Deterrence and Defense*, p. 108. Snyder also noted that if the enemy was only allowed the second strike, and if his strategic forces were not eliminated, his attack was much more likely to be counter-city than it would have been as a first strike, so, perhaps, increasing the severity of the damage.
16. Kahn, *On Thermonuclear War*, p. 495. (He considered this a possibility for 1969).
17. Bernard Brodie, 'The Development of Nuclear Strategy', *International Security*, II:4 (Spring 1978), p. 68. Brodie, though sympathetic to Wohlstetter's motives, adds that he 'could never accept . . . that the balance of terror . . . ever has been or ever could be delicate'.
18. The quotations are from an unclassified summary of *National Policy Implications of Atomic Parity* (Naval Warfare Group Study, Number 5, 1958) and a speech by Admiral Burke to the Press Club on 17 January 1958. They are taken from George Lowe, *The Age of Deterrence*, a rendition of the arguments against the Air Force view from the viewpoint of a Navy partisan. For similar arguments see George Fielding Eliot, *Victory without War: 1958–61* (Annapolis, Maryland: US Naval Institute, 1958).
19. Snyder, *Deterrence and Defense*, p. 88 (pp. 85–95 provides a thorough discussion of the issues discussed in this section). See also George Rathjens Jr, 'NATO strategy: total war', in Klaus Knorr (ed.), *NATO and American Security* (Princeton: Princeton University Press, 1959).
20. Kahn, *op. cit.*, p. 13.
21. J. King, 'Air Power in the Missile Gap', *op. cit.*, p. 635.
22. Oskar Morgenstern, *The Question of National Defense* (New York: Random House, 1959), p. 74.

23. Snyder, *op. cit.*, pp. 110, 94–5. He also made the valid point that a mixed force complicates the enemy's counter-force attacks and his air defence problem. There would be a diversity of targets and a diversity of sources of retaliatory attacks.

CHAPTER 12

1. Charles Hitch and Roland N. McKean, *The Economics of Defense in the Nuclear Age* (Cambridge: Harvard University Press, 1960).
2. P. M. S. Blackett, *Studies of War–Nuclear and Conventional*, p. 201. For a brief history see Chapter 3 of Andrew Wilson, *War Gaming* (London: Pelican, 1970).
3. Sir Solly Zuckerman, 'Judgement and control in modern warfare', *Foreign Affairs*, xxxx:2 (January 1962), p. 208.
4. Dr Samuel Glasstone, *The Effects of Nuclear Weapons* (US Atomic Energy Commission, 1957) is the most authoritative compilation.
5. Letter to Michael Howard, 6 November 1968, p. 49. He names J. F. Digby, E. J. Barlow, E. S. Quade, P. M. Dadant, E. Reich, F. Hoffman and H. Rowen.
6. Albert Wohlstetter, 'Strategy and the Natural Scientists', in Robert Gilpin and Christopher Wright (ed), *Scientists and National Policy Making* (New York: Columbia University Press, 1964), pp. 189, 193, 195.
7. P. M. S. Blackett, 'Critique of some contemporary defense thinking', in *Studies of War*.
8. Sir Solly Zuckerman, *Scientists and War, The Impact of Science on Military and Civil Affairs* (London: Hamish Hamilton, 1956), p. 63.
9. John von Neumann and Oskar Morgenstern, *Theory of Games and Economic Behavior* (Princeton: Princeton University Press, 1944).
10. Schelling's *The Strategy of Conflict* is a collection of some of his seminal essays. A less technical presentation of his ideas is to be found in a later work, *Arms and Influence* (New Haven: Yale University Press, 1966). A game theory type of analysis by Morton Kaplan is found in his 'The calculus of nuclear deterrence', *World Politics*, xi:1 (October 1958). The influence of Game Theory is evident in Oskar Morgenstern's *The Question of National Defense*. Game Theory, he claims, 'has clarified the conceptual problem of decision-making', established the necessary theorems and shown the methods for selecting and computing the optimal strategies' (p. 164). Anatol Rapaport provides useful guides to the subject in *Fights, Games and Debates* (Ann Arbor: Michigan University Press, 1960) and *Strategy and Conscience* (New York: Harper & Row, 1964). The latter provides his most fervent attack on the abuses of Game Theory.
11. Schelling, *The Strategy of Conflict*, p. 3. Bernard Brodie, while considering the 'refinements' of Game Theory to be 'generally of little importance to the strategic analysts', applauded its spirit: 'the constant awareness that we will be dealing with an opponent who will counteract our moves and to whom we must in turn react'. 'The Scientific Strategists', Gilpin and Wright (eds.), *Scientists and National Policy-Makers*, p. 252. Wohlstetter also saw this as its main value, while adding that taking every

reaction into account 'need not be done in the framework of a formal game'. In general he took a 'temperate view' of the uses of Game Theory, considering it 'still a long way from direct application to any complex problem of policy'. 'Analysis and design of conflict systems', in E. S. Quade, *Analysis for Military Decisions* (Chicago: RAND McNally, 1964), pp. 130–1.

12. The most thorough critique of the methods adopted by the new strategists is to be found in Philip Green, *Deadly Logic: The Theory of Nuclear Deterrence* (Columbus, Ohio: Ohio State University Press, 1966). See also Rapaport's *Strategy and Conscience*. For critiques of the critics see D. G. Brennan's review of Rapaport's book, *Bulletin of the Atomic Scientists*, xxi:12 (December 1965), and Hedley Bull, 'Strategic Studies and its Critics', *World Politics* (July 1968).

13. Green, *op. cit.*, p. 98.

14. Schelling, *The Strategy of Conflict*, p. 4.

15. Hedley Bull, *The Control of the Arms Race* (London: Weidenfeld & Nicolson, 1961), p. 48.

16. See Glenn Snyder, '"Prisoner's Dilemma" and "Chicken" models in international politics', *International Studies Quarterly*, xv:1 (March 1971).

17. *Ibid.*, p. 98.

CHAPTER 13

1. Schelling, *The Strategy of Conflict*, p. 15.

2. Morgenstern, *The Question of National Defense*, pp. 9–10.

3. C. W. Sherwin, 'Securing peace through military technology', *Bulletin of the Atomic Scientists* (May 1956). A short piece by Amster entitled 'Design for deterrence', was appended. The original Amster study appeared as *A Theory for the Design of a Deterrent Air Weapon System* (San Diego, Calif.: Convair Corporation, 1955). For evidence of the influence of Amster/Sherwin see Schelling, *Strategy of Conflict*, p. 7 and Arthur Lee Burns, 'Disarmament or the balance of terror', *World Politics*, xii:1 (October 1959), p. 134.

4. Amster, 'Design for Deterrence', *op. cit.*, p. 165.

5. Sherwin, *op. cit.*, p. 162.

6. *Ibid.*, p. 161.

7. Schelling, *Arms and Influence*, pp. 12, 35.

8. Schelling, *The Strategy of Conflict*, pp. 239–40.

9. Schelling, *The Strategy of Conflict*, p. 233. This essay on 'Surprise attack and disarmament' first appeared in Klaus Knorr (ed.), *NATO and American Security*.

10. *Ibid.*, p. 288.

11. Schelling, *Strategy and Conflict*, p. 236. See also Arthur Lee Burns, *op. cit.*

12. Thomas Schelling and Morton Halperin, *Strategy and Arms Control* (New York: Twentieth Century Fund, 1961), pp. 1–2.

13. Kahn, *On Thermonuclear War*, p. 232.

14. Schelling and Halperin, *op. cit.*, p. 5.

15. Bernard Bechhoefer, *Postwar Negotiations for Arms Control* (Washington DC: Brookings Institution 1961).

16. There is some link with the earlier usage in Hedley Bull's definition of arms control as 'restraint internationally exercised upon armaments policy'. Hedley Bull, *The Control of the Arms Race*, p. 1.

17. Schelling and Halperin, *op. cit.*, p. 2.

18. Alva Myrdal, *The Game of Disarmament: How the United States and Russia Run the Arms Race* (Manchester: Manchester University Press, 1977), p. xiv.

19. Robert Osgood, 'Stabilizing the military environment', *American Political Science Review*, LV:1 (March 1961).

20. Malcolm Hoag, 'On Stability in Deterrent Races', *World Politics*, XIII:4 (July 1961), p. 522.

21. The term is taken from Thomas Murray, *Nuclear Policy for War and Peace*, (Ohio: World Publishing Co., 1960), p. 28. Murray, a catholic member of the Atomic Energy Commission, attempted more than most others connected with the nuclear programme to inject a moral element into the debate. A discussion of a variety of ethical problems is found in Green, *Deadly Logic*, chap. 6. Green also provides a useful bibliography. Green's ideas are discussed, unsympathetically, in Morton A. Kaplan (ed.), *Strategic Thinking and Its Moral Implications* (Chicago: University of Chicago Press, 1973). See also Sydney Bailey, *Prohibitions and Restraints in Warfare* (London, Oxford University Press, 1972).

22. Lieutenant-General Sir John Cowley, 'Future trends in warfare', *Journal of the Royal United Services Institute* (February 1960), p. 13.

23. The 1961 review in *Scientific American* is collected with other small pieces by Newman in *The Rule of Folly* (London, George Allen & Unwin, 1962). Kahn became a particular *bete noire* of the nuclear pacifists. Philip Green's *Deadly Logic* is largely an attack on Kahn. Anatol Rapaport was inspired to write his critique of the abuses of Game Theory after listening with mounting anger to a lecture by Kahn. Bertrand Russell's book was entitled *Commonsense and Nuclear Warfare* (London, Allen & Unwin, 1959).

24. *Accidental War: Some Dangers in the 1960s*, Mershon National Security Program Research Paper (June 1960).

25. Eugene Burdick and Harvey Wheeler, *Fail-Safe* (London: Hutchinson, 1963); Sidney Hook, *The Fail-Safe Fallacy*, (New York, Stein & Day, 1963).

26. Kenneth E. Boulding, *Conflict and Defense: A General Theory* (New York: Harper & Row, 1963).

27. Aaron Wildavsky, 'Practical consequences of the theoretical study of defence policy', *Public Administration Review*, XXV (March 1965). Reprinted in *The Revolt Against the Masses* (New York, Basic Books, 1971).

28. Robert Jervis, 'Hypotheses on misperception', *World Politics*, XX (April 1968), p. 455.

29. On the British campaign see Christopher Driver, *The Disarmers* (London: Hodder & Stoughton, 1964).

30. Philip Noel-Baker, *The Arms Race* (London: John Calder, 1958).

31. Leo Szilard, 'Disarmament and the Problem of Peace', *Bulletin of the Atomic Scientists*, XI:8 (October 1955), p. 298.

32. One notable attempt to integrate the insights of the formal strategists

with those of the nuclear pacifists was J. David Singer, *Deterrence, Arms Control and Disarmament, op. cit.*

33. Leo Szilard, 'How to Live with the Bomb and Survive', *Bulletin of the Atomic Scientists*, XVI:2 (February 1960), p. 59.
34. Green, *op. cit.*, p. xii.

CHAPTER 14

1. Thorton Read, in Knorr and Read (eds.), *Limited Strategic War*, (New York: Praeger, 1962), p. 93.
2. Herman Kahn, *On Escalation: Metaphors and Scenarios* (New York: Praeger, 1965), p. 138.
3. In Kaufmann (ed.), *Military Policy and National Security*, p. 122. The basic ideas can be found in Clausewitz.
4. There is no reference to escalation in the index of *Strategy of Conflict*; only two in *Arms and Influence*.
5. Kahn, *On Escalation*; Bernard Brodie, *Escalation and the Nuclear Option* (Princeton: Princeton University Press, 1966).
6. Morton Halperin, *Limited War in the Nuclear Age*, p. 3.
7. Richard Smoke, *War: Controlling Escalation* (Cambridge, Mass.; Harvard University Press, 1977), pp. 19, 32, 34.
8. Kaplan, in Knorr and Read, *op. cit.*, p. 146.
9. Schellings *Strategy of Conflict*, pp. 57, 77. Whether or not game theory, with its formalised conflicts, could cope with the introduction of such unfathomable phenomena as the cultural landmarks on mental maps is beyond the scope of this study.
10. Schelling, *Arms and Influence*, p. 137.
11. See p. 192.
12. Leo Szilard, 'Disarmament and the problem of peace', p. 299.
13. Morton Kaplan, 'The calculus of nuclear deterrence', pp. 40–3.
14. Morton Kaplan, *The Strategy of Limited Retaliation*, Policy Memorandum No. 19, Center of International Studies, Princeton University, 9 April 1959.
15. Knorr, in Knorr and Read, *op. cit.*, p. 3.
16. Kaplan, in *Ibid.*, pp. 145–6. See also Read's essay.
17. Read, in *ibid.*, p. 89.
18. Khan in *ibid.*, pp. 44–5.
19. Schelling, in *ibid.*, p. 254.
20. Kahn had first raised the concept in *On Thermonuclear War*, and then discussed it further in *Thinking About the Unthinkable* New York: Horizon Press, 1962) where he introduced an escalation ladder of 16 rungs.
21. Kahn, *On Escalation*, pp. 186, 190, 221. He noted that Canadians and Europeans had yet to reach this higher level of consciousness; mainly, he suspected because of an absence of serious discussion.
22. *Ibid.*, pp. 217–20. He admits that 'in most of this book, I have committed the besetting sin of most US analysts and have attributed to the Soviets a kind of behaviour that may in fact be appropriate to US analysts – and not at all relevant to Soviet conditions and attitudes.'
23. *Ibid.*, p. 137.

24. *Ibid.*, p. 290.
25. *Ibid.*, p. 290.
26. *Strategy of Conflict*, p. 188 (emphasis in the original).
27. See Glenn Snyder, *Deterrence and Defence*: 'it cannot be too often repeated that the Soviets can never be sure of the degree of rationality in their victim' (p. 164). For a discussion of this point see Patrick Morgan, *Deterrence: A Conceptual Analysis*, (London: Sage Publications, 1977), Chap. Five.
28. *Arms and Influence*, p. 93.
29. *Strategy of Conflict*, p. 193.
30. *Ibid.*, pp. 200, 193.
31. *Arms and Influence*, p. 182.
32. *Strategy of Conflict*, p. 194.
33. *Ibid.*, pp. 193, 196.
34. *Arms and Influence*, p. 194.
35. One is reminded of Assistant Secretary of Defense John McNaughton's 1965 memorandum to Robert McNamara on US aims in Vietnam:
    70 per cent – To avoid a humiliating US defeat (to our reputation as a guarantor).
    20 per cent – To keep SVN (and the adjacent) territory from Chinese hands.
    10 per cent – To permit the people of SVN to enjoy a better, freer way of life.
    Cited in *Pentagon Papers* (New York, Bantam Books, 1971), p. 432.

CHAPTER 15

1. Henry Kissinger could still write in 1960, in a book published in 1961, that 'there is no dispute about the missile gap as such. It is generally admitted that from 1961 until at least the end of 1964 the Soviet Union will possess more missiles than the United States.' *Necessity for Choice*, p. 15.
2. Roswell L. Gilpatric, 'Address before the Business Council, Hot Springs, Virginia, 10 October 1961'. Reprinted in *Documents on Disarmament 1961* (Washington DC: US Arms Control and Disarmament Agency, 1962), pp. 542–50.
3. William M. Kaufmann, *The McNamara Strategy* (New York: Harper & Row, 1964), p. 49.
4. John F. Kennedy, *The Strategy of Peace* (New York: Harper & Row 1960), pp. 37–8.
5. The best account of the development of strategic doctrine under the Kennedy Administration is contained in Desmond Ball, *Policies and Force Levels: The Strategic Missile Program of the Kennedy Administration* (Berkeley: University of California Press, 1980). An enthusiastic account of the first few years is found in Kaufmann's *The McNamara Strategy*. This probably contains a few recycled words, as Kaufmann quotes liberally from McNamara's speeches and statements, a number of which were drafted by Kaufmann. Two of McNamara's former aides, Alain C. Enthoven and K. Wayne Smith, have provided in *How Much is*

Enough? Shaping the Defense Program 1961–1969 (New York: Harper & Row, 1971) a thorough description of the McNamara approach in action, with some lucid explanations of most of the important themes of the period. The views of McNamara in the later 1960s are found in a collection of his speeches: Robert S. McNamara, *The Essence of Security: Reflections in Office* (London: Hodder & Stoughton Ltd, 1968).

6. To House Armed Services Committee in February 1961. Quoted in Kaufmann, *op. cit.*, p. 53.

7. Kaufmann, *op. cit.*, p. 88.

8. See Ball, *Policies and Force Levels*.

9. Robert S. McNamara, 'Defense Arrangements of the North Atlantic Community'. *Department of State Bulletin*, **47** (9 July 1962), pp. 67–8.

10. Kaufmann, *op. cit.*, p. 75.

11. Kahn, *On Thermonuclear War*, pp. 174–5.

12. Schelling, *Arms and Influence*, p. 25. See also Thomas Schelling, *Controlled Response and Strategic Warfare* (London: IISS, June 1965).

13. Morton Halperin, 'The "No Cities Doctrine"', *New Republic* (8 October 1962). This was one of four articles in *New Republic* which discussed the new strategy. The others were an editorial on 'McNamara's strategy' (2 July 1962); Michael Browner, 'Controlled thermonuclear war' (30 July 1962); and Robert Osgood, 'Nuclear arms: uses and limits', (10 September 1962).

14. *The Times* (London), 4 July 1962. The comparable figures for Western Europe were 115 million with Soviet counter-city targeting and 15 million with counter-force targeting.

15. See Halperin, 'The "no cities" doctrine', p. 19.

16. Secretary of Defense, Robert S. McNamara, Statement on the Defense Budget for Fiscal Years 1964–1968, *Defense Program and 1964 Defense Budget* (27 January 1963), p. 41.

17. Marshal V. D. Sokolovsky, *Soviet Military Strategy* (2nd edn), p. 88.

18. Cited in Browner, *op. cit.*, p. 12.

19. Testimony of Secretary McNamara, House Armed Services Committee, *Hearings on Military Posture* (1963), p. 332.

20. US Air Force, *This is Counterforce*, dated 7 February 1963 (from IISS files). By the time this document was prepared the doctrine was at its most refined.

21. Ball, *op. cit.*, p. 290.

22. Claude Witze, 'Farewell to Counterforce', *Air Force Magazine* (February 1963). Compare this to the approving tones of John Loosbrock in 'Counterforce and Mr. McNamara' in the same magazine in September 1962.

23. See George Quester, *Nuclear Diplomacy*, p. 246.

24. Arthur Schlesinger, Jr, *A Thousand Days: John F. Kennedy in the White House* (Boston: Houghton Mifflin, 1965), p. 769.

CHAPTER 16

1. Enthoven and Smith, *How Much is Enough?* p. 174.

2. *Ibid.*, pp. 177–8. See also Freedman, *US Intelligence and the Soviet Strategic Threat*, pp. 84–6.

3. Fred Iklé reports that in order to calculate the number of the enemy population that would be killed, a method known by the distasteful term 'cookie cutter' was used, in which nuclear weapons are assumed to 'take out' people in a neat circle, like a piece of dough, so that all are killed or injured within this circumference and none outside. Fred Iklé, *Can Nuclear Deterrence Last Out the Century?* (Santa Monica, Calif.: Arms Control and Foreign Policy Seminar, January 1973) pp. 13, 34.

4. Enthoven and Smith, *op. cit.*, pp. 207–8.

5. Donald Brennan was most responsible for drawing attention to the acronym. Donald Brennan, 'Symposium on the SALT agreements', *Survival*, September/October 1972.

6. Warner Schilling has demonstrated how one can play with acronyms to make any point you care to make, e.g.: Capability of Firing First If Necessary = COFFIN. Warner Schilling *et al.*, *American Arms and a Changing Europe* (New York: Columbia University Press, 1973), p. 44.

7. Schlesinger, *A Thousand Days*, p. 301.

8. James Trainor, 'DOD says AICBM is Feasible' *Missiles and Rockets*, 24 December 1962.

9. Address at University of Michigan, Ann Arbor, 19 December 1962. This speech is quoted at length in Kaufmann, *The McNamara Strategy*, pp. 138–47.

10. Stewart Alsop, 'Our new strategy: the alternatives to total war', *The Saturday Evening Post* 1 December 1962.

11. John Kennedy, as a Senator, contributed to the belief in the strategic value of space by writing: 'Control of space will be decided in the next decade. If the Soviets control space, they can control earth.' This was cited by General Power to justify a call to 'surpass them [the Soviets] in every phase of the space effort so as to prevent them from gaining control of space, denying us the space medium, and using space for aggressive purposes'. Power, *Design for Survival*, p. 239. One example of the 'space war' literature of the time is M. N. Golovine, *Conflict in Space: A Pattern of War in a New Dimension.* (New York: St Martin's Press, 1962). He argued that earth might be spared if the super-powers could be persuaded to decide their conflicts in space.

12. Kaufmann, *The McNamara Strategy*, pp. 57–8.

13. Henry Rowen, 'Formulating strategic doctrine', *Appendices to the Report of the Commission on the Organization of Government for the Conduct of Foreign Policy*, Vol. IV, Appendix K (Washington DC: GPO, 1975), p. 227.

14. See Robert Gilpin, *American Scientists and Nuclear Weapons Policy* (Princeton, Princeton University Press, 1962).

15. Herbert York and Jerome Wiesner, 'National security and the nuclear test ban', *Scientific American* (October 1964). This article became caught up in a general debate over whether military technology had now reached a plateau or whether there were to be more quantum jumps, and from that whether or not enough money was being spent in the Department of Defense on new projects. For a denunciation of the York/Wiesner thesis as it affected the welfare of the defence industry see Hanson Baldwin, 'Slow-down in the Pentagon', *Foreign Affairs* (January 1965).

16. See Edward Randolph Jayne, *The ABM Debate; Strategic Defense and National Security* (MIT Center for International Studies, June 1969), Morton Halperin, 'The decision to deploy the ABM', *World Politics*, xxv (October 1972) and Freedman, *US Intelligence and the Soviet Strategic Threat*, Chapter Seven.
17. Secretary of State, Robert S. McNamara, 'The dynamics of nuclear strategy', *Department of State Bulletin*, LVII (9 October 1967). Morton Halperin was the actual author of the speech.

CHAPTER 17 •

1. Roman Kolkowicz *et al., The Soviet Union and Arms Control: A Superpower Dilemma* (Baltimore, Md.: Johns Hopkins University Press, 1970), pp. 34–7.
2. Interview with Robert McNamara, 15 February 1966, in *Documents on Disarmament 1967* (Washington, DC: US Arms Control and Disarmament Agency, 1967).
3. Richard Pipes, 'Why the Soviet Union thinks it could fight and win a nuclear war', *Commentary*, **64** (1) (July 1977).
4. This indictment is forcefully set out in Chapter Three of Colin Gray, *The Soviet-American Arms Race* (Farnborough, Hants: Saxon House, 1976). Its significance for the strategic debate of the 1970s is discussed below, pp. 364–7.
5. Benjamin S. Lambeth, *Selective Nuclear Options in American and Soviet Strategic Policy* (Santa Monica, Calif.: RAND Corporation, 1976), p. 14.
6. R. S. McNamara, *The Essence of Security*, pp. 159–60.
7. Nikita Khruschev, *Khruschev Remembers*, vol. 2, *The Last Testament* (London: André Deutsch, 1974), pp. 48–50. Khrushchev also describes how, drawing on the physics he had learnt as a youth, he explained to M. K. Yangel, the head of the Soviet rocketry programme, the rockets might be kept at constant readiness. He illustrated his point using two glasses on the coffee table in front of him.
8. Edward L. Warner, *The Military in Contemporary Soviet Politics* (New York: Praeger, 1977), pp. 99–100.
9. Thomas Wolfe, *Soviet Power and Europe 1945-70* (Baltimore: Johns Hopkins University Press, 1970), p. 134.
10. Warner, *op. cit.*, pp. 139–40.
11. A. W. Tupolev, the leading designer of Soviet aircraft, presented the case for the manned bomber in terms that would have been appreciated by SAC:

> A rocket-carrying aircraft can be considered the first stage of a multistage system which has important advantages over multistage missiles. It does not require permanent launch sites or complex and expensive launch equipment. The first stage, the piloted aircraft, is used repeatedly. When necessary, the aircraft can be redirected after a command decision. If the target is relocated, the aircraft crew can make a decision in order to successfully execute the combat mission. Only rocket-carrying aircraft possess these qualities.

A. W. Tupolev, 'Missile-carrying aircraft', *Aviation and Cosmonautics* (June 1962). Quoted in Warner, *op. cit.*, p. 146.
12. The book went through three editions – 1962, 1963, and 1968. A translation of the first edition was published with an introduction by Herbert Dinerstein, Leon Gouré, and Thomas Wolfe of RAND as *Soviet Military Strategy* (Englewood Cliffs, N.J.: Prentice-Hall, 1963). The third edition, with full details of all amendments from previous editions was published under the same title with an introduction by the editor, Harriet Fast Scott (London: Macdonald & Jane's, 1975).
13. Horelick and Rush, *Strategic Power and Soviet Foreign Policy*, p. 88.
14. This idea was given credence following an interview given by Khruschev to C. L. Sulzberger of the *New York Times* in September 1961. Sulzberger reported:

> Khruschev believes absolutely that when it comes to a showdown, Britain, France and Italy would refuse to join the United States in a war over Berlin for fear of their absolute destruction. Quite blandly he asserts that these countries are, figuratively speaking, hostages to the USSR and a guarantee against war.

Quoted in Horelick and Rush, *op. cit.*, p. 94.
15. In October 1961 Marshall Malinovsky chided the Americans for underestimating the damage the USSR could inflict upon them, asserting that calculations had been made with 'only' a 5 megaton warhead. He continued: 'we have nuclear charges equivalent to several tens of thousands and up to 100 million tons of TNT, and our ballistic rockets have proved to be so splendid no one can doubt their ability to lift and deliver such charges to any point on earth' (quoted in *ibid.*, p. 98). In the event the largest yield ever employed on a Soviet ICBM warhead was 25 megatons.
16. *Military Strategy* (first edition), pp. 91, 308, 314, 399–400.
17. Quoted in Raymond L. Garthoff, 'Mutual deterrence and strategic arms limitation in Soviet policy', *International Security*, III:1 (Summer 1978), pp. 129–30. Garthoff provides a number of similar quotes.
18. Warner, *op. cit.*, p. 81. One can note here the similarity with American views of the Soviet Union which divide the ruling group into 'modernist' or 'orthodox' factions, the former being the most realistic and moderate. See for example Lawrence Caldwell, *Soviet Attitudes to SALT* (London: IISS, 1972). Of course, at moments when defence issues have become highly politicized, in either country, it may well be legitimate to describe debate in such polarized terms (as with 'hawks' and 'doves' in the US over the Vietnam War). At times when the argument is less heated, a less rigid, pluralistic system can be assumed to operate.
19. Warner, *op. cit.*, pp. 77–9, 181–2.
20. *Ibid.*, pp. 88–9; Garthoff, *op. cit.*, pp. 115–22.
21. Leon Gouré, Foy Kohler, and Mose Harvey, *The Role of Nuclear Forces in Current Soviet Strategy* (Miami, Florida: Center for Advanced Studies, University of Miami, 1974). Fritz Ermarth has referred to two very unpleasant features in Soviet military doctrine: 'a strong tendency to pre-empt and a determination to suppress the enemy's command and control

systems at all costs'. 'Contrasts in American and Soviet strategic thought', *International Security*, III:2 (Autumn 1978), p. 152.

22. Dennis Ross, 'Rethinking Soviet strategic policy: inputs and implications', *The Journal of Strategic Studies*, 1:2 (May 1975), pp. 3–30, argues that the Soviet Union has opted for deterrence through denial (convincing an enemy that an attack will be unsuccessful) rather than punishment.
23. Gouré *et al.*, *op. cit.*, pp. 35–6.
24. Garthoff, *op. cit.*, p. 126.
25. Quoted by Gouré *et al.*, *op. cit.*, pp. 119–20.
26. Leon Gouré, *War Survival in Soviet Strategy* (University of Miami Press, 1976) takes this more seriously. For a critique, Fred M. Kaplan, 'Soviet civil defense: some myths in the Western debate', *Survival*, XXX:3 (May/June 1978). Also see introductory note by Malcolm Mackintosh.
27. Warner, *op. cit.*, p. 152.
28. Garthoff, *op. cit.*, p. 137.

CHAPTER 18

1. Sensitive observers had become aware of the strains much earlier. For example, Donald Zagoria, *The Sino-Soviet Conflict 1956–1961* (Princeton: Princeton University Press, 1962).
2. Quoted in Alice Langley Hsieh, *Communist China's Strategy in the Nuclear Age* (Englewood Cliffs, N.J.: Prentice-Hall, Inc., 1962), p. 132.
3. Ralph Powell, 'Maoist military doctrine', *Asian Survey* (April 1968).
4. Lin Piao, 'Long live the People's War', quoted in Raymond Garthoff 'Politico-Military Issues in the Sino-Soviet Debate, 1963–65', in Raymond Garthoff (ed.), *Sino-Soviet Military Relations* (New York: Praeger, 1966), p. 178.
5. Ralph Powell, 'Great powers and atomic bombs are "paper tigers"', *China Quarterly*, No. 23 (July/September 1965).
6. Quotes from Allen S. Whiting, *China Crosses the Yalu: The Decision to Enter the Korean War* (New York: Macmillan, 1960), pp. 142, 198. A 'resist America' drive began in late October 1950, which attempted to reassure the audience both about the improbability of employment of atomic bombs and their effects should they be used.
7. Quoted in Alice Langley Hsieh, 'The Sino-Soviet nuclear dialogue 1963', in Garthoff (ed.), *op. cit.*, pp. 156–7.
8. John Thomas, 'The limits of alliance: the Quemoy crisis of 1958', in Garthoff (ed.), *op. cit.*, pp. 114–49.
9. The parallels between Chinese and French rationale have been pointed out by B. W. Augenstein, 'The Chinese and French programs for the development of national nuclear force', *Orbis* (Autumn 1967).
10. Hsieh, 'The Sino-Soviet nuclear dialogue', in Garthoff (ed.), *op. cit.*, pp. 160, 161.
11. I. Yermashev, 'The Peking version of "total strategy"', reprinted in *ibid.*, pp. 239–52.

12. *Khruschev Remembers*, vol. 1 (London: André Deutsch, 1971), pp. 467–70. In 1962, by which time relations had become even less cordial, Khruschev discovered to his fury that the military had been reprinting Mao's works on warfare. This he considered 'absurd': 'The Soviet Army crushed the crack forces of the German army, while Mao Tse-tung's men have spent between twenty and twenty-five years poking each other in the backsides with knives and bayonets' (p. 471). One of the few significant changes between the first (1962) and second (1963) edition of Marshall Sokolovsky's major work on *Military Strategy* was that all positive references to the Chinese were expunged.

13. An editorial in an army paper of February 1966 explained:

> We acknowledge the tremendous role played by modern weapons and equipment, yet ultimately they cannot solve problems. In solving problems ultimately, we must still rely on man, on rifles, on hand grenades, on bayonets, on close range fighting, on night-fighting, and on close quarter fighting. ... Modern, long-range weapons, the atom bomb included, are useless for close-range fighting or night-fighting.

Quoted in Jonathan D. Pollack 'Chinese attitudes towards nuclear weapons, 1964–9', *China Quarterly*, No. 50 (1972), p. 269; Jonathan D. Pollack, 'The logic of Chinese military strategy', *Bulletin of the Atomic Scientists* (January 1979).

CHAPTER 19

1. Communiqué, *Ministerial Meeting of North Atlantic Council*, 14 December 1967.
2. Quoted in Wilfred Kohl, *French Nuclear Diplomacy* (Princeton: Princeton University Press, 1971), p. 227.
3. Henry Kissinger, *Necessity for Choice*.
4. For a discussion of the debate see Halperin, *Limited War in the Nuclear Age*.
5. Helmut Schmidt, *Defence or Retaliation* (New York: Praeger, 1972), p. 211.
6. A pessimism on Soviet offensive strength led Alastair Buchan and Philip Windsor to rule out a full conventional defence in *Arms and Stability in Europe* (London: Chatto & Windus, 1963).
7. *Deterrent or Defense*, pp. 89–96, 165–73. Discussion of these ideas can also be found in F. O. Miksche, *The Failure of Atomic Strategy* (New York: Praeger, 1958) and in Malcolm Hoag, 'Rationalizing NATO strategy', *World Politics*, XVII:1 (October 1964).
8. Schelling, *Strategy of Conflict*, p. 190. Characteristically, Schelling saw limited war in terms of the imposition of hurt rather than the denial of gain.
9. Henry Kissinger, *Necessity for Choice*, p. 62.
10. Maxwell D. Taylor, *The Uncertain Trumpet* (New York: Harper & Row, 1960), p. 153.
11. John Foster Dulles, 'Challenge and response in US policy', *op. cit.*
12. *NATO Letter*, V:12 (December 1957).

13. *Defence; Outline of Future Policy*, Cmnd 124 (London, HMSO, April 1957).
14. Alastair Buchan suggested: 'In practical terms, the British reaction to new American policy may be somewhat negative. But in France and Germany, it is almost hostile.' *NATO in the 1960s* (London: Chatto & Windus, 1963). This is an excellent guide through the issues of the period.
15. Kaufmann, *The McNamara Strategy*, p. 104. It should be remembered that coincident with this debate was the first French veto on Britain's application to join the Common Market.
16. *Report on Defence, Britain's Contribution to Peace and Security*. Cmnd 363 (London: HMSO, 1958), para 12.
17. In late 1945, when considering a proposal prepared by some officials for nations owning atomic bombs to all agree to use them against any country which initiated use, the British Prime Minister Clement Attlee commented: 'What British Government in view of the vulnerability of London would dare accept the obligation of entering on atomic warfare against an aggressor who might be able, before going down, to destroy London?' Quoted in Gowing, *Independence and Deterrence*, vol. 1, p. 71.
18. See James L. Richardson, *Germany and the Atlantic Alliance* (Cambridge, Mass.: Harvard University Press, 1966), Chapter 4.
19. See, for example, *Power and Diplomacy* by Dean Acheson, Truman's Secretary of State (Cambridge, Mass.: Harvard University Press, 1958). Acheson became one of the most determined advocates of greater conventional forces during the Kennedy Administration, seeing in these forces the key to greater diplomatic strength in confrontations with the Soviet Union.
20. Kaufmann, *The McNamara Strategy*, p. 106.
21. Citations are from *ibid.*, pp. 112, 113.
22. All quotations are taken from Chapter 4 of Enthoven and Smith, *How Much is Enough?*
23. Bernard Brodie, 'What price conventional capabilities in Europe', *The Reporter* (23 May 1963) and *Escalation and the Nuclear Option*. A sharp review by Brodie of Kaufmann's book appeared as 'The McNamara phenomenon', *World Politics*, xvii:4 (July 1965).
24. The quotations are all taken from Brodie, *Escalation and the Nuclear Option*, Chapter X. Aron's views are found in his *The Great Debate* (New York, Doubleday 1965), pp. 152–4.
25. Pierre M. Gallois, 'US strategy and the defense of Europe', *Orbis*, vii:2 (Summer 1963).

CHAPTER 20

1. See, for example, National Planning Association, *The 'Nth Country' Problem and Arms Control* (New York: NPA, 1959). A corrective to some of the pessimism on the subject is found in Fred Iklé, 'Nth countries and disarmament', *Bulletin of the Atomic Scientists*, XVI:10 (December 1960). A useful compilation of articles is R. N. Rosencrance (ed) *The Dispersion of Nuclear Weapons* (New York, Columbia University Press, 1964).

2. 'In a nuclear world, the "small" nuclear powers, vis-à-vis one another, would have: greater opportunities for blackmail and mischief-making; greater likelihood of an accidental triggering of weapons; an increased possibility of a "local" Munich, a Pearl Harbor, and blitzkriegs; pressures to pre-emption because of the preceding three items; a tendency to neglect conventional capabilities because of an over-reliance on nuclear capabilities; internal (civil war, a *coup d'état*, irresponsibility, etc.) and external (the arms race, fear of fear, etc.) political problems.' Herman Kahn, 'The arms race and some of its hazards', in Brennan (ed.), *Arms Control, Disarmament and National Security*, p. 119.

3. The most extreme version of this notion was developed by Arthur Lee Burns, in which a minor nuclear power would devise a means to make one super-power believe it had been attacked by the other, so causing a nuclear war. *The Rationale of Catalytic War* (Princeton University Center of International Studies, April 1959).

4. Albert Wohlstetter, 'Nuclear sharing: NATO and the N + 1 country', *Foreign Affairs*, XXXIX:3 (April 1961).

5. Thomas Schelling, 'Nuclears, NATO and the "New Strategy"', in Henry Kissinger (ed.), *Problems of National Strategy* (New York: Praeger, 1965), p. 179. Schelling regretted (with hindsight) that McNamara's new strategy was used as an 'argument against independent nuclear deterrents. The new strategy was new enough, at least in public discussion, to need a sympathetic audience.'

6. Malcolm Hoag, 'Nuclear strategic options and European force participation' in R. N. Rosencrance (ed.), *op. cit.*, p. 227.

7. Kaufmann, *The McNamara Strategy*, p. 116.

8. Enthoven and Smith, *How Much is Enough?*, p. 131.

9. Cited in Kaufmann, *The McNamara Strategy*, pp. 116–17.

10. One could also add the unwillingness of the British Government to release information on strategic matters, and the more rigid demarcation line between Government and Academia. It is less easy to move in and out of Government in Britain than in America.

11. See p. 177.

12. D. G. Brennan, 'Review of "Strategy and Conscience"', *op. cit.*, p. 28.

13. John Garnett, 'British strategic thought', in John Baylis (ed.), *British Defence Policy in a Changing World* (London: Croom Helm, 1977), p. 163.

14. Hedley Bull, 'International theory: the case for a classical approach', *World Politics* (April 1966). The key articles in the resultant debate are collected in Klaus Knorr and James Rosenau (eds.), *Contending Approaches to International Relations* (Princeton: Princeton University Press, 1969).

15. Klaus Knorr and Thornton Read (eds.), *Limited Strategic War*, pp. v–vi. The quote was taken from 'On thermonuclear coexistence', *Survey*, No. 39 (December 1961).

16. Laurence Martin saw 'the heavy reliance of British politicians upon American authors for their arguments' as a symptom of the lack of interest in national security policy amongst academics. He wondered whether Labour Party leaders, such as Denis Healey, had not overdone this reliance 'and acquired opinions – favourable observers would say

sophistication – which partly accounts for their losing touch with the sentiments of many of their followers'. 'The market for strategic ideas in Britain', *American Political Science Review*, LVI:1 (March 1962), pp. 40–1.

17. John Groom's *British Thinking About Nuclear Weapons* (London: Frances Pinter, 1974) has virtually nothing on the period after the early 1960s.

18. One attempt to do so is a sharp little book by Emanuel J. de Kadt, *British Defence Policy and Nuclear War* (London: Frank Cass, 1964). He spoke of Britain's '[non-independent] contribution to the total Western nuclear force', as being 'insubstantial and, moreover, unwanted', p. 130.

19. Stephen King-Hall, *Power Politics in the Nuclear Age: A Policy for Britain* (London: Gollancz Ltd, 1962), p. 171 (emphasis in original).

20. John Strachey, *On the Prevention of War* (London: Macmillan, 1962).

21. The problems of miscommunication in this affair are examined in Richard Neustadt, *Alliance Politics* (New York: Columbia University Press, 1970).

22. Television interview of February 1958. Andrew Pierre, *Nuclear Politics: The British Experience with an Independent Strategic Force, 1939–1970*, (London: Oxford University Press, 1972), p. 178.

23. *Ibid.*

24. *Statement on Defence 1964*, Cmnd 2270 (London: HMSO, 1964), p. 6.

25. Lawrence Freedman, *Britain and Nuclear Weapons* (London: Macmillan, 1980).

CHAPTER 21

1. Speech of November 1961 quoted in Wilfred Kohl, *French Nuclear Diplomacy*, p. 129.

2. Pierre Gallois, 'The policy and strategy of air-nuclear weapons', *Bulletin of the Atomic Scientists*, XII:6 (June 1956).

3. *Stratégie de l'age Nucléaire* (Paris: Calmann-Levy, 1960). The English edition appeared as *The Balance of Terror: Strategy for the Nuclear Age*, translated by Richard Howard (Boston; Houghton Mifflin, 1961).

4. *Ibid.*, (English edn.), p. 93.

5. He was correct in his suspicions. Schelling commented on some of Gallois's views on the efficacy of 'irrational outbursts' in shoring up deterrence: '[T]he American Government ought to be mature enough and rich enough to arrange a persuasive sequence of threatened responses that are not wholly a matter of guessing a President's temper.' 'Nuclears, NATO and the new strategy', in Kissinger (ed.), *op. cit.*, p. 185.

6. Gallois, *Balance of Terror*, p. 22.

7. Gallois, US strategy and the defence of Europe', *Orbis*, VII:2 (Summer 1963).

8. Quotations are from André Beaufre, *Deterrence and Strategy* (London: Faber & Faber, 1965). This was originally published as *Dissuasion et Stratégie* (Paris: Armand Colin, 1964). (Emphasis in original.)

9. André Beaufre, 'The sharing of nuclear responsibilities: a problem in need of solution', *International Affairs*, XXXI:3 (July 1965), p. 416. (Emphasis in original.)

10. Aron, *The Great Debate*, p. 142.

11. For example, Enthoven and Smith thought it involved:

> a curious piece of logic: the Americans can't be trusted to retaliate against the Soviets for attacking France (or Great Britain); therefore, we will have our own independent nuclear force to cause the Americans to retaliate against the Soviet Union for a French (or British) attack on the Soviet Union. *How Much is Enough?*, p. 131.

12. Snyder, *Deterrence and Defense*, pp. 162-4.
13. Cited in Kohl, *French Nuclear Diplomacy*, p. 150.
14. Quoted in *ibid.*, p. 129 (Press Conference, 10 November 1959).
15. General D'Armée Ailleret, 'Directed defence', *Survival* (February 1968), pp. 38-43. Translated from 'Défense 'dirigée' ou défense 'tous azimuts'', *Revue de Défense Nationale* (December 1967).
16. General Guy Mery, 'French defence policy', *Survival* (September/October 1976). President Giscard d'Estaing gave explicit support to these ideas.
17. Prime Minister Raymond Barre, 'Speech on defence policy', *Survival* (September/October 1977).
18. Catherine McArdle Kelleher, *Germany and the Politics of Nuclear Weapons* (New York: Columbia University Press, 1975), pp. 165, 282.
19. Quoted in *ibid.*, p. 160.
20. For arguments in favour of the MLF, see Robert Bowie, 'Strategy and the Atlantic alliance' *International Organization*, XVII:3 (Summer 1963).
21. Alastair Buchan, *The Multilateral Force: A Historical Perspective* (London: IISS, 1964).
22. A. Wohlstetter, 'Nuclear sharing: NATO and the N + 1 country'.
23. Gallois, 'US strategy and the defense of Europe', *Orbis*, VII:2 (Summer 1963).
24. Beaufre, 'The Sharing of Nuclear Responsibilities', *op. cit.*
25. *NATO in the 1960s* (2nd edn.), p. 92.
26. Buchan, *The Multilateral Force*.
27. See p. 386.
28. North Atlantic Council, *Declaration on Alliance Relations* (Ottawa: 19 June 1974).

CHAPTER 22

1. McNamara, *The Dynamics of Nuclear Strategy*. See pp. 254-6.
2. He retired as Secretary of Defense in February 1968, to be replaced by Clark Clifford.
3. Richard L. Garwin and Hans Bethe, 'Anti-ballistic missile systems', *Scientific American* (March 1968). Reprinted in York (ed.), *Arms control*, p. 164.
4. Abram Chayes, Jerome Wiesner, George Rathjens, and Steven Weinberg, 'An Overview', in Abram Chayes and Jerome Wiesner (ed.), *ABM: An Evaluation of the Decision to Deploy an Anti-Ballistic Missile System* (New York: Harper & Row, 1969), pp. 58-9. This was the key anti-ABM document.
5. 'It is my contention that with minor exceptions, the United States has led in the development of military technology and weapons production

throughout the Cold War. .... This ... has placed the United States in a position of being fundamentally responsible for every major escalation of the arms race'. Edgar Bottome, *The Balance of Terror: A Guide to the Arms Race* (Boston: Beacon Press, 1971), pp. xv–xvi.

6. George Rathjens, 'The dynamics of the arms race', *Scientific American* (April 1969). Reprinted in York (ed.), *Arms Control*, p. 187.

7. Quoted in Nancy Lipton and Leonard Rodberg, 'The missile race: the contest with ourselves', in Leonard Rodberg and Derek Shearer, *The Pentagon Watchers* (New York: Doubleday & Co., 1970), p. 303.

8. Herbert York, 'Military technology and national security', in *Scientific American* (August 1969) reprinted in York (ed.), *Arms Control*, p. 198. York developed his views in *Race to Oblivion*.

9. F. A. Long, 'Arms control from the perspective of the nineteen-seventies'; Harvey Brooks, 'The military innovation system and the qualitative arms race'; John Steinbruner and Barry Carter, 'Organizational and political dimensions of the strategic posture: the problems of reform', in *Daedalus*, CIV:3 (Summer 1975).

10. Graham T. Allison and Frederic A. Morris, 'Exploring the determinants of military weapons', in *ibid*. The force of this point was diminished by the acknowledgment of boundaries, within which the level of forces, defence budgets, and specific weapons must fall, determined by some 'minimum set of widely shared values (eg a secure second-strike capability)'. The quality of the analysis suffered by failing to ask where these 'values' came from, but the interest lay in the fact that the essence of an assured destruction capability could be taken so easily for granted, beyond internal debate, a part of the general consensus.

11. See note 4.

12. Some of the better works of this genre are: Ralph Lapp, *The Weapons Culture* (New York: W. W. Norton, 1968); Adam Yarmolinsky, *The Military Establishment* (New York: Harper & Row, 1971); and Richard Kaufman, *The War Profiteers* (New York: Doubleday, 1972). To gain the flavour of the 1969 fervour on this matter and the general strategic views of the critics, see the report of a conference organised by *The Progressive* magazine involving Congressmen and a sundry collection of critics. Published as Erwin Knoll and Judith Nies McFadden (eds.), *American Militarism 1970* (New York: The Viking Press, 1969).

13. For example, Sam Sarkesian (ed.), *The Military–Industrial Complex: A Reassessment* (Beverly Hills, Sage Publications: 1972).

14. The best of the studies is Ted Greenwood, *Making the MIRV: A Study in Defense Decision-Making* (Cambridge, Mass: Ballinger, 1975).

15. The inevitable tendency to concentrate research on weapons proposals that did actually come to fruition, rather than those that fell by the wayside, helped to confirm this Law.

16. Jerome H. Kahan, *Security in the Nuclear Age*, p. 330.

17. Henry Kissinger, *The White House Years* (London: Weidenfeld & Nicolson, 1979), pp. 202–3.

18. Quoted in Desmond Ball, *Déjà Vu: The Return to Counterforce in the Nixon Administration* (California: Seminar on Arms Control and Foreign Policy, 1974), p. 8.

19. Richard M. Nixon, *United States Foreign Policy for the 1970s: Building the Peace* (25 February 1971), pp. 53-4.
20. Quoted in Ball, *Déjà Vu*, p. 8. The criteria involved a second-strike capability; denying the Soviet Union any incentives to attempt a first strike; a capacity 'to cause considerably greater destruction than the United States could inflict in any type of nuclear exchange'; and a measure of damage limitation against small attacks or accidental launches.
21. Melvin Laird, *A House Divided: America's Security Gap* (New York: Henry Regnery, 1962). When questioned about this book when he was appointed Secretary of Defense he said it had been written at a time of confrontation that had now passed.
22. Hearing before the Subcommittee on Arms Control, International Law and Organization of Senate Foreign Relations Committee, *US-USSR Strategic Policies* (Washington DC, USGPO, March 1974), p. 25. He also suggested that in his position statement there had been a switch away 'from what I will call the canonical logic of the triad'. There is little substantive evidence of this switch.

CHAPTER 23

1. An important source on the programmes of both sides is John M. Collins, *American and Soviet Military Trends since the Cuban Missile Crisis* (Washington, DC: The Center for Strategic and International Studies, Georgetown University, 1978).
2. Proponents of explanations of the arms race in this way often acknowledged, to quote George Rathjens, that it would be 'an obvious oversimplification' to use the action–reaction hypothesis to 'explain all the major decisions of the super-powers'. Unfortunately in the polemics of defence debate the qualifications tend to get lost, rendering the argument unduly dogmatic. 'The dynamics of the arms race', *Scientific American* (April 1969).
3. Albert Wohlstetter, 'Is there a strategic arms race?'; 'Rivals but no "race"'; 'Optimal ways to confuse ourselves', *Foreign Policy*, xv (Summer 1974); xvi (Autumn 1974); xx (Autumn 1975).
4. *Foreign Policy*, xv (Summer 1974), p. 8.
5. *Foreign Policy*, xvi (Autumn 1974), p. 79.
6. Colin S. Gray, *The Soviet-American Arms Race*, p. 182.
7. *Foreign Policy*, xx:198.
8. There were exceptions. Norman Moss recounts the story of a SAC General being given a briefing on counter-force strategies in the 1950s. The briefing drew on Game Theory and had matrices indicating the alternative payoffs. The General needed to look at only one square to know he was against the strategy, the square that showed the number of Soviet casualties. He commented: 'Counter-force means less Russians dead. So I'm against it'. Norman Moss, *Men Who Play God: The Story of the Hydrogen Bomb* (London: Penguin, 1970), p. 260.

9. Kahan, *A Strategic Policy for the 1970s*, pp. 336–7.
10. Donald Brennan, 'The case for population defense', in Johan Holst and William Schneider (eds.), *Why ABM?* (New York: Pergamon Press, 1969).
11. *Ibid.*, p. 109. Brennan himself was a recent convert to this view.
12. 'Can nuclear deterrence last out the century', *Foreign Affairs*, LI:2 (January 1973). This was also published under the same title at the same time in an extended version, including an interesting collection of footnotes, by the Californian Arms Control and Foreign Policy Seminar. It is from this latter version that the quotations are taken.
13. On this see Yehezkel Dror, *Crazy States: A Counter-conventional Strategic Problem* (Lexington, Mass.: D. C. Heath, 1971).
14. Iklé, *op. cit.*, p. 15. It is not clear whether Iklé believed this could be done wholly with 'smart' conventional weapons. A similar approach can be found in Arthur Lee Burns, *Ethics and Deterrence: A Nuclear Balance Without Hostage Cities?* (London: IISS, 1970). See Chapter 5.
15. Herbert York, 'Reducing the overkill', *Survival*, XVI:2 (March/April 1974).
16. Wolfgang Panofsky, 'The Mutual-Hostage Relationship Between America and Russia', *Foreign Affairs*, LII:1 (October 1973).
17. *Foreign Policy*, XVI:71–9.
18. CEP is defined as the radius of a circle centred on the target within which 50 per cent of the re-entry vehicles would impact if the tests were repeated many times.
19. See D. G. Hoag, 'Ballistic-missile guidance', in B. T. Feld *et al.* (eds.), *Impact of New Technologies on the Arms Race* (Cambridge, Mass., MIT Press, 1971): Hoag estimated that 'an overall ICBM CEP of 30 meters may be expected with reasonable and practical application of science and technology to the task', and that 'there was no theoretical justification to feel that individual MIRV warheads will not have a CEP essentially the same as that of a single-warhead missile using the same technology' (pp. 81, 90). In a paper written in 1967 on 'Strength, interest and new Technologies', Albert Wohlstetter singled out as particularly significant 'the multiplication of armed offensive re-entry vehicles carried in a single launch vehicle (MIRVs) and the great improvements in offence accuracy and reliability'. In IISS *The Implications of Military Technology in the 1970s* (London: IISS, 1968).
20. See Ted Greenwood, *Making the MIRV*.
21. See p. 377.
22. The main consequences of mobility were felt in arms control. One of the valuable features of strategic weapons had been that they could be placed in clear categories and readily counted. Reconnaissance satellites meant that military bases could be located with precision, so aiding counter-force targeting, and their contents identified, so aiding the verification of arms control agreements.
23. Bernard Brodie, 'On the objectives of arms control', *International Security*, I:1 (Summer 1976), pp. 17–36.
24. To make way for the extra SLBMs, the Soviet Union had to dismantle 209 old ICBMs. On SALT I see John Newhouse, *Cold Dawn: The Story of SALT* (New York, Holt, Rinehart & Winston, 1973); Mason Willrich

and John B. Rhinelander, *SALT: The Moscow Agreements and Beyond* (New York: The Free Press, 1974).
25. *US Public Law*, 92-448.
26. On the developing problems of SALT, see Christoph Bertram (ed.), *Beyond SALT II* (London: IISS, 1978).

CHAPTER 24

1. Secretary of Defense James Schlesinger, *Annual Defense Report FY 1976* (5 February 1975), pp. II-3-II-4.
2. *Ibid.*, pp. I-13, I-14.
3. Enthoven and Smith, *How Much is Enough?*, p. 184. This did not stop McNamara shifting the indicator for measuring military strength from numbers of delivery vehicles, where the Soviet Union was catching up, to numbers of warheads, where the US was about to move ahead.
4. Laurence Martin, 'The utility of military force', in Francois Duchêne (ed.), *Force in Modern Societies: Its Place in International Politics* (London: IISS, 1973), p. 16. For an early discussion of the issue, see Klaus Knorr, *On the Uses of Military Power in the Nuclear Age* (Princeton: Princeton University Press, 1966).
5. J. I. Coffey, *Strategic Power and National Security* (Pittsburgh: University of Pittsburgh Press, 1971).
6. McGeorge Bundy, 'To cap the volcano', *Foreign Affairs*, XLVIII:1 (October 1969), pp. 9-10. (Emphasis in original.)
7. See Walter Slocombe, *The Political Implications of Strategic Parity* (London: IISS, 1971), Appendix II; Benjamin Lambeth, 'Deterrence in the MIRV era', *World Politics* (January 1972), pp. 230-3.
8. The most important book, blending theory with research, was Alexander George and Richard Smoke, *Deterrence in American Foreign Policy: Theory and Practice* (New York: Columbia University Press, 1974).
9. George and Smoke, *op. cit.*, pp. 560-1. For similar observations see Patrick Morgan, *Deterrence: A Conceptual Analysis*, Chapter Six; Stephen Maxwell, *Rationality in Deterrence* (London: IISS, 1968), p. 19. The 'third wave' of deterrence theory is discussed by Robert Jervis in 'Deterrence theory revisited', *World Politics*, XXXI:2 (January 1979), pp. 289-324.
10. Slocombe, *op. cit.*, p. 25. Lambeth argued, after a review of various crises, that: 'The lesson of the examples thus seems to be that the overall nature of the objective rather than strategic "superiority" ultimately determines which protagonist will prevail in a crisis', *op. cit.*, p. 233.
11. Edward N. Luttwak, 'The missing dimension of US defense policy: force, perceptions and power', in Donald C. Daniel (ed.), *International Perceptions of the Superpower Military Balance* (New York: Praeger, 1978), pp. 21-3.
12. Henry Kissinger, Press Conference of 3 July 1974, reprinted in *Survival*, XVI:5 (September/October 1974).
13. Reprinted in York, *Arms Control*, p. 276.

14. In Senate Foreign Relations Committee, *Strategic Arms Limitation Talks* (Washington DC, USGPO, 1972), pp. 394–5.
15. See p. 347.
16. The dominant view in the intelligence community in 1969 had been that: 'We believe that the Soviets recognize the enormous difficulties of any attempt to achieve strategic superiority of such order as to significantly alter the strategic balance.' Seven years later, after an exercise in which a team of notable outside hawks had been allowed to challenge the 'home' team of intelligence estimaters from within in the drawing-up of National Intelligence Estimates, this question was left much more open. See Freedman, *US Intelligence and the Soviet Strategic Threat*, pp. 133, 194–8. The next year the NIE reverted to the earlier view.
17. Gray, *The Soviet–American Arms Race*, p. 181. For a similar point of view from a conservative source see Leon Gouré, Foy Kohler, and Mose L. Harvey, *The Role of Nuclear Forces in Current Soviet Strategy*. Foy Kohler in the Foreword noted a tendency

    to perceive the Soviet leaders as thinking and seeing things as we do, and, in effect, to project into Soviet affairs a mirror-image of ourselves and our own concepts. The consequence of such an approach . . . is that it has led to serious misjudgments in understanding and forecasting Soviet behaviour (p. x).

18. Jeremy Stone, *Strategic Persuasion: Arms Limitations Through Dialogue* (New York: Columbia University Press, 1967), pp. 8–9, 169.
19. Gray, *op. cit.*, p. 79.
20. For support for this view of Soviet perception of military power see Lawrence L. Whetten (ed.), *The Future of Soviet Military Power* (New York: Crane Russak, 1976). Whetten noted in the Introduction: 'The Soviets expect to use this new strategic posture as a back-drop for the conduct of a more flexible foreign policy that may, when appropriate, include an increase in their willingness to accept risk in the face of challenge or to be more assertive under favourable circumstances' (p. 14). In the same volume William Van Cleave wrote of 'the Soviet concept that military force confers meaningful political power, and thus that inferiority is a political liability and superiority an important political asset'. 'Soviet doctrine and strategy', p. 48.
21. Joseph Douglass and Amoretta Hoeber, *Soviet Strategy for Nuclear War* (Stanford, Calif.: Hoover Institution Press, 1979).
22. *Pravda*, 14 June 1977. Quoted by Garthoff, 'Mutual deterrence and strategic arms limitation in Soviet policy', *International Security*, III:1 (Summer 1978), p. 142.
23. David Shipler, 'Soviet tested a neutron weapon, Brezhnev tells group of senators', *New York Times*, 18 November 1978. This quote, plus a reference to the fact that 'Carter and I know we both have a couple of dozen minutes when satellites will tell us missiles are coming', provides added confirmation of a Soviet dependence on a launch-on-warning strategy (see pp. 267–8).
24. Michael Deane, 'Soviet perceptions of the military factor in the correlation of world forces', in Daniel (ed.), *op. cit.*, pp. 72–94.

25. D. Tomashevsky, November 1976, quoted in *ibid.*, p. 77.
26. Quoted in John Vincent, *Military Power and Political Influence: The Soviet Union and Western Europe* (London: IISS, 1975), p. 15.
27. See Jervis, *Perception and Misperception in International Politics* (Princeton: Princeton University Press, 1976); also Irving Janis, *Victims of Group-Think* (Boston: Houghton Mifflin, 1972).
28. Luttwak, *op. cit.*, p. 28. He notes that: 'If "true" combat capabilities were always perceived correctly, then all distinctions between power and force, or between political utility and military effectiveness, would not matter at all from the viewpoint of defense planning'.
29. John Steinbruner, 'Beyond rational deterrence: The Struggle for New Conceptions', *World Politics*, XXVIII:2 (January 1976), p. 237.
30. See p. 356.
31. Schlesinger, *Annual Defense Report FY 1976*, p. II-7.
32. Secretary of Defense Harold Brown, *Department of Defense Annual Report Fiscal Year 1979* (Washington, DC: 2 February 1978), p. 5.
33. One of the better examples of this sort of analysis is Fred A. Payne, 'The strategic nuclear balance: a new measure', *Survival*, XX:3 (May/June 1977).
34. Schlesinger, *Annual Defense Report FY 1976*, p. II-8.
35. See Lawrence Freedman, 'Balancing acts', *Millennium*, VII:2 (Autumn 1978).
36. Daniel (ed.), *op. cit.*, pp. 185–90. One interesting finding was a trend among American Allies to prefer parity to US superiority because of the perceived gain in international stability.
37. Gabriel A. Almond, 'Public opinion and the development of space technology: 1957–60'. In Joseph M. Goldsen (ed.), *Outer Space in World Politics* (London: Pall Mall Press, 1963), pp. 71–96.

CHAPTER 25

1. William R. Van Cleave and Roger W. Barnett, 'Strategic adaptability', *Orbis*, XVIII:3 (Autumn 1974), pp. 655–76.
2. Albert Wohlstetter, 'Threats and promises of peace: Europe and America in the new era', *Orbis*, XVII:4 (Winter 1974), p. 1126. This point had been made forcefully in the 1950s by Kahn, see earlier, pp. 133–4.
3. Michael May, 'Some advantages of a counterforce deterrent', *Orbis*, XIV (Summer 1970), p. 274.
4. Phil Williams, *Crisis Management: Confrontation and Diplomacy in the Nuclear Age* (London: Martin Robertson, 1976).
5. Kissinger, *The White House Years*, p. 216.
6. Richard M. Nixon, *United States Foreign Policy for the 1970s* (18 February 1970), pp. 54–5.
7. *Ibid.* (25 February 1971), pp. 54–5.
8. Kissinger, *The White House Years*, p. 217.
9. The main sources on the development of these options are found in Lynn Etheridge Davis, *Limited Nuclear Options: Deterrence and the New Amer-*

ican Doctrine (London: IISS, 1976) and Desmond Ball, *Dèja Vu*. These accounts have been supplemented with some interviews of the author's.

10. J. R. Schlesinger, 'Quantitative analysis and national security', *World Politics*, xv (1963), pp. 295–315.

11. *Idem.*, *Arms Interaction and Arms Control* (Santa Monica, Calif.: RAND, September 1968), pp. 16–17.

12. *Idem.*, *European Security and the Nuclear Threat since 1945* (Santa Monica, Calif: RAND, April 1967), pp. 12–13. This passage came in the context of the feasibility of such forces for European states. The requirements were described as 'onerous'.

13. The main discussion of the policy was in a press conference of 24 January 1974 and the *Department of Defense Reports* for Fiscal Years 1975 and 1976 (4 March 1974 and 5 February 1975 respectively). Schlesinger was questioned in detail by members of the Senate Foreign Relations Committee in two sets of hearings: *US and Soviet Strategic Policies* (March 1974) and *Briefing on Counterforce Attacks* (September 1974).

14. Report of Secretary of Defense, James Schlesinger to the Congress on the *FY 1975 Defense Budget and FY 1975–79 Defense Program* (4 March 1974).

15. Such a debate as there was, which embraced the general questioning of assured destruction and the concern over perceptions is well covered in Ted Greenwood and Michael Nacht, 'The new nuclear debate: sense or nonsense', *Foreign Affairs*, LII:4 (July 1974). Among critiques of the Schlesinger doctrine see Herbert Scoville Jr., 'Flexible madness', *Foreign Policy*, No. 14 (Spring 1974) and Barry Carter, 'Nuclear strategy and nuclear weapons', *Scientific American*, 230:5 (May 1974). A useful compilation of relevant articles and documents is Robert J. Pranger and Roger P. Labrie (eds.), *Nuclear Strategy and National Security: Points of View* (Washington, DC: American Enterprise Institute, 1977).

16. Carter, *op. cit.*, p. 30 (Scoville used a similar phrase).

17. Bernard Brodie, 'The development of nuclear strategy', *International Security*, II:4 (Spring 1978), pp. 78–83.

18. Carter, *op. cit.*, pp. 24, 31.

19. 'If the nuclear balance is no longer delicate and if substantial force asymmetries are quite tolerable, then the kinds of changes I have been discussing here will neither perturb the balance nor stimulate an arms race. If, on the other hand, asymmetries do matter (despite the existence of some highly survivable forces), then the critics themselves should consider seriously what response we should make to the major programs that the Soviets currently have underway to exploit their advantages in numbers of missiles and payload.' *Report on FY 1975 Defense Budget*, p. 39.

20. Benjamin S. Lambeth, 'Selective nuclear options and Soviet strategy', in Johan Holst and Uwe Nerlich, *Beyond Nuclear Deterrence* (London: Macdonald & Janes, 1978).

21. Quoted in *ibid.*, p. 92.

22. William Van Cleave, 'Soviet doctrine and Strategy', *op. cit.* Lambeth also engaged in this search in his essay in a final section on 'possible private Soviet thinking and planning'. ('This silence as to the possible existence of a Soviet policy regarding controlled nuclear targeting should not auto-

matically be interpreted as a sign of Soviet uninterest'). However, he advised not to regard whatever changes there may be in Soviet policy 'as emulative reactions to the US retargeting policy or as mirror images of contemporary American strategic concepts but rather as uniquely "Soviet" responses to the potential of Soviet military power'. Lambeth, *op. cit.*, pp. 97, 100. Warner, too, deviated from his customary scrupulousness in citing Soviet sources when he claimed that 'Despite their frequent denials, the Soviets may in fact be prepared to launch deliberately controlled strategic attacks and thus engage in some form of limited warfare as long envisioned by Western military theorists and more recently endorsed as official US policy'. Warner, *The Military in Contemporary Soviet Politics*, p. 150.

23. Wohlstetter, *Threats and Promises of Peace*, p. 1136. For a sympathetic discussion of limited options in a European war see essays in Holst and Nerlich, *op. cit.*, particularly Peter Stratmann and René Hermann, 'Limited options, escalation and the central region'; and Laurence Martin, 'Flexibility in a tactical nuclear response'.
24. Quoted in Davies, *Limited Nuclear Options*, p. 6.
25. Quoted in Richard Burt, *New Weapons and Technologies: Debate and Directions* (London: IISS, 1976), p. 21. This is an excellent survey of these issues. See also Christoph Bertram (ed.), *New Conventional Weapons and East–West Security* (Two Parts) (London: IISS, 1978).
26. Michael J. Brenner, 'Tactical nuclear strategy and European defence: a critical reappraisal', *International Affairs*, LI:1 (January 1975).
27. S. T. Cohen, 'Enhanced radiation weapons: setting the record straight', *Strategic Review* (Winter 1978); Fred M. Kaplan. 'Enhanced radiation weapons', *Scientific American*, 238:5 (May 1978).
28. On this set of issues see Richard Burt, 'The SS-20 and the Euro-strategic balance', *World Today* (February 1977); Greg Treverton, 'Nuclear weapons and the gray area', *Foreign Affairs*, LVII (Summer 1979); Freedman, *Britain and Nuclear Weapons*; G. Philip Hughes, 'Cutting the Gordian knot: a theatre nuclear force for deterrence in Europe', *Orbis*, XXII (Summer 1978).
29. Henry Kissinger, 'NATO: the next thirty years', *Survival* (November/December 1979), p. 265.
30. Colin Gray, *The Future of Land-Based Missile Forces* (London: IISS, 1978), p. 1. This is a useful analysis of the problem and ways of 'solving it'.
31. The history of this issue is discussed in Freedman, *US Intelligence and the Soviet Strategic Threat*.
32. Lynn Etheridge Davis and Warner Schilling, 'All you ever wanted to know about MIRV and ICBM calculations but were not cleared to ask', *Journal of Conflict Resolution*, 17:2 (June 1973). John Steinbruner and Thomas Garwin, 'Strategic vulnerability: the balance between prudence and paranoia', *International Security*, L:1 (Summer 1976).
33. Senate Armed Services Committee, *Hearings on Military Implications of the Treaty on the Limitation of Anti-Ballistic Missile Systems and the Interim Agreement on Limitation of Strategic Offensive Arms* (Washington, DC: USGPO, 1972), p. 145.
34. *Ibid.*, p. 579.

35. Colin Gray, 'The strategic force triad: end of the road?', *Foreign Affairs*, LVI (July 1978), p. 775.
36. When large numbers of US submarines were lingering at port or bombers immobile at base were to be caught in the attack, and if (very) worst-case assessments of Soviet civil defences were included, the scenario approximated to a straightforward first strike. Paul Nitze did much to publicize these pessimistic versions of the scenario. See his articles: 'Deterring our deterrent', *Foreign Policy* No. 25 (Winter 1976–7); 'Assuring strategic stability in an era of detente', *Foreign Affairs*, LIV:2 (January 1976).
37. The term 'launch on assessment' was adopted, which sounded slightly less irresponsible. See Gray: 'As an operational firing tactic, it would be monumental folly, but as a veiled suggestion of the "we refuse to rule it out" variety, it should not be despised'. *The Future of Land-Based Missile Forces*, pp. 14–15.
38. United States Congress, Office of Technology Assessment, *The Effects of Nuclear War* (Washington, DC: USGPO, 1979); Kevin N. Lewis, 'The Prompt and Delayed Effects of Nuclear War', *Scientific American* (July 1979).
39. Jan Lodal, 'Assuring strategic stability: an alternative view', *Foreign Affairs*, LIV (April 1976). In a reply Paul Nitze argued that this would only be true if such retaliation as the US could muster was directed deliberately against counter-value rather than counter-force targets 'despite the desperate consequences to us and the world of doing so'. Paul Nitze, 'Strategic stability', *Foreign Affairs*, LIV (July 1976). Colin Gray suggested that, in the 1980s, the USSR 'might possibly be able to hold down its civilian casualties to a level below that suffered in the Great Patriotic War of 1941–5 – even if the United States should proceed all the way up the escalation ladder', as if the risk of losing 20 million people and probably more was in the realm of acceptibility. *Op. cit.*, p. 778. On an earlier version of this argument see p. 142. The sort of analysis of the military balance that presented a picture of comparative capabilities after the first volleys was known as a *dynamic* measure as opposed to a *static* measure. Such measures are somewhat misleading because they inevitably require a large set of arbitrary assumptions on areas of massive uncertainty.
40. *Defense Department Report of FY 1976*, p. I-16. Vladivostock was the scene of the November 1974 Brezhnev–Ford summit which set guidelines for SALT II.
41. Harold Brown, *Department of Defense Annual Report Fiscal Year 1980* (25 January 1979), p. 76.
42. Desmond Ball, *Developments in US Strategic Nuclear Policy under the Carter Administration* (California: Seminar on Arms Control and Foreign Policy, 1980).
43. Richard Burt, 'US stresses limited nuclear war in sharp shift on military strategy', *International Herald Tribune* (7 August 1980).
44. Colin S. Gray and Keith Payne, 'Victory is possible', *Foreign Policy*, No. 39 (Summer 1980), p. 21.

CHAPTER 26

1. Mikhail Gorbachev, *Perestroika* (London: Collins, 1987).
2. There has not yet been a full study of the anti-nuclear movements of the 1980s and their political significance. For some interesting essays see Peter Van Den Dungen (ed.), *West European Pacifism and the Strategy For Peace* (London: Macmillan, 1985). For a rich study with a slightly broader canvas (though confined only to Britain) see Philip Sabin, *The Third World War Scare in Britain* (London: Macmillan, 1986). On West Germany see David Yost and Thomas Glad, 'West German party politics and theater nuclear modernization since 1977', *Armed Forces and Society* (Summer 1982) and Jeffrey Boutwell, 'Politics and the peace movement in West Germany', *International Security* (Spring 1983). On France, where anti-nuclear protest is most remarkable for its absence, see Jolyon Howorth and Patricia Chilton (eds.), *Defence and Dissent in Contemporary France* (London: Croom Helm, 1984).
3. See David Capitanchik and Richard Eichenberg, *Defence and Public Opinion*, Chatham House Paper No. 20 (London: Routledge & Kegan Paul for RIIA, 1983).
4. The most quoted was probably that by Colin Gray and Keith Payne, 'Victory is possible', *Foreign Policy* No. 39 (Summer 1980), p. 21. At times it appeared that if Colin Gray did not exist, the anti-nuclear movement would have had to invent him as his writings seemed designed to confirm their worst fears.
5. In October 1981 the President noted that he 'could see where you could have the exchange of tactical weapons against troops in the field without it bringing either one of the major powers to pushing the button', *International Herald Tribune*, 21 October 1981.
6. Fred Halliday, *The Making of the Second Cold War* (London: Verso, 1983).
7. In E. P. Thompson and Dan Smith (eds.), *Protest and Survive* (London: Penguin, 1980). This book (the title of which is a pun on the British Government's civil defence leaflet *Protect and Survive*) provides the most accessible statement of the anti-nuclear movements' case. Thompson's most substantial critique of deterrence theory is found in 'Deterrence and addiction', included in a collection of essays, E. P. Thompson, *Zero Option* (London: Merlin Press, 1982).
8. I address these arguments in Lawrence Freedman, *The Price of Peace: Living with the Nuclear Dilemma* (London: Firethorne, 1986), ch. 4.
9. Such as Horst Afheldt of the Max-Planck-Institut. See, for example, his 'The necessity, preconditions and consequences of a no-first-use policy' in Frank Blackaby, Jozef Goldblat and Sverre Lodgaard (eds.), *No-First Use* (London: Taylor & Francis for SIPRI, 1984).
10. Vladimir Bukovsky, 'The peace movement and the Soviet Union', *Commentary* (May 1982).
11. See Randall Forsberg, 'A bilateral nuclear-weapon freeze', *Scientific American* 247:5 (November 1982). Senator Edward Kennedy and Senator Mark Hatfield, *Freeze: How You Can Prevent Nuclear War* (New York: Bantam Books, 1982). For analyses, see Adam Garfinkel, *The Politics*

of the Nuclear Freeze (Philadelphia: Foreign Policy Research Institute, 1984) and Paul Cole and William J. Taylor (eds.), *The Nuclear Freeze Debate* (Boulder, Col.: Westview, 1983).

12. Jonathan Schell, *The Fate of the Earth* (London: Cape, 1982); *The Abolition* (New York: Alfred A. Knopf, 1982).

13. Carl Sagan, 'Nuclear war and climatic catastrophe', *Foreign Affairs* (Winter 1983/84).

14. George Carrier, 'Nuclear winter: the state of the science', *Issues in Science and Technology* (Winter 1985). For a hostile critique, see Russell Seitz, 'In from the cold: "nuclear winter" melts down', *The National Interest* (Fall 1986).

15. Secretary of Defense Caspar Weinberger, *The Potential Effects of Nuclear War on the Climate* (A Report to the United States Congress, March 1985) uses the hypothesis to justify the Strategic Defense Initiative.

16. National Conference of Catholic Bishops, 'The challenge of peace: God's promise and our response', *Origins* (National Catholic Documentary Service), vol. 13 (19 May 1983).

17. The Church of England eventually opted for a no-first-use position, following a debate stimulated by the publication of a working party report which was much more unilateralist in tone, i.e. the report of a working party under the chairmanship of the Bishop of Salisbury, *The Church and the Bomb: Nuclear Weapons and the Christian Conscience* (London: Hodder & Stoughton, 1982). A leading British policy-maker who is a practising Catholic argued the moral case for nuclear deterrence in Michael Quinlan, 'Preventing war', *The Tablet* (July 1981). The Catholic bishops of France, not surprisingly, took a more relaxed view of the moral dilemma than did their American counterparts, and concluded that nuclear deterrence was justified as an 'ethic of distress'; see *Winning Peace* (December 1983).

18. Michael Novak, 'Moral clarity in the nuclear age', *National Review* (1 April 1983); Albert Wohlstetter, 'Bishops, statesmen, and other strategists on the bombing of civilians', *Commentary* (June 1983). For a response see Francis X. Winters, 'Bishops and scholars: the peace pastoral under siege', *The Review of Politics* (Winter 1986).

19. Robert Tucker, *The Nuclear Debate* (New York: Holmes & Meier, 1985). See also Joseph Nye, *Nuclear Ethics* (New York: The Free Press, 1986), Geoffrey Goodwin (ed.), *Ethics and Nuclear Deterrence* (London: Croom Helm, 1982).

20. For a list of 60 members of the Board of Directors of the Committee, starting with the President himself, who occupied a position with the Administration in either a government department or an advisory body, see Charles Tyroler II (ed.), *Alerting America: The Papers of the Committee on the Present Danger* (Washington, DC: Pergamon-Brassey, 1984), pp. ix–xi.

21. The distinctiveness of Soviet thinking and the danger of an American failure to appreciate its implications are constant themes in the writings of Colin Gray. For a recent version see Colin Gray, *Nuclear Strategy and National Style* (Lanham, Md.: Hamilton Books/Abt Associates, 1986).

22. See, for example, Edward Luttwak, *The Pentagon and the Art of War* (New York: Simon & Schuster, 1984).

23. The influence of this approach in the conventional sphere was reflected in the US Army Field Manual, FM 100/5 (Washington DC: Department of the Army, 1982).

24. Fred Iklé, 'The Reagan defense program: a focus on the strategic imperatives', *Strategic Review* (Spring 1982); Paul Nitze, 'Living with the Soviets', *Foreign Affairs* (Winter 1984/85).

25. Albert Wohlstetter, 'Between an unfree world and none: increasing our choices', *Foreign Affairs* (Summer 1985).

26. The Report of the Commission On Integrated Long-Term Strategy, *Discriminate Deterrence* (Washington DC: January 1988).

27. Herman Kahn, *Thinking About the Unthinkable in the 1980s* (New York: Simon & Schuster, 1984).

28. See Walter Slocombe, 'The countervailing strategy', *International Security* (Spring 1981).

29. On the continuities and contrasts between the Reagan and previous Administrations see Leon Sloss and Marc Dean Millot, 'US nuclear strategy in evolution', *Strategic Review* (Winter 1984) and Jeffrey Richelson, 'PD-59, NSDD-13 and the Reagan strategic modernization program', *The Journal of Strategic Studies* VI:3 (June 1983).

30. *Washington Post*, 10 November 1982. For early reports see *New York Times*, 30 May 1982; *Washington Post*, 4 June 1982.

31. Quoted in *New York Times*, 9 August 1982. There was an interesting exchange on this matter between Weinberger and the historian Theodore Draper. See Theodore Draper, *Present History: On Nuclear War, Détente, and Other Controversies* (New York: Random House, 1983).

32. In 1981 the Pentagon published the first in what became an annual presentation on *Soviet Military Power* (Washington DC: Department of Defense, 1981). In the introduction (p. 2) Secretary of Defense Caspar Weinberger wrote that 'For the past quarter century, we have witnessed the continuing growth of Soviet military power at a pace that shows no sign of slackening in the future.' The Soviet Union was provoked into publishing a counter-blast entitled *Whence the Threat to Peace* (Moscow: Military Publishing House, 1982).

33. Some of the most substantial work of this sort was undertaken under the auspices of the Natural Resources Defense Council who produced a series of Nuclear Weapons Databooks, opening with a volume which underlined the extent and the quality of the US nuclear arsenal: Thomas B. Cochran, William M. Arkin and Milton M. Hoenig, *US Nuclear Forces and Capabilities* (Cambridge, Mass.: Ballinger, 1984). Somewhat less careful is Tom Gervasi, *The Myth of Soviet Military Supremacy* (New York: Harper & Row, 1986) which exhibits many of the faults the author is criticizing.

34. See, for example, Seweryn Bialer and Joan Afferica, 'Reagan and Russia', *Foreign Affairs* (Winter 1982/83).

35. Bruce Blair, *Strategic Command and Control: Redefining the Nuclear Threat* (Washington, DC: The Brookings Institution, 1985); Desmond

Ball, *Can Nuclear War be Controlled?* Adelphi Papers 169 (London: IISS, 1981).

36. Paul Bracken, *The Command and Control of Nuclear Weapons* (New Haven: Yale University Press, 1983).
37. Richard Ned Lebow, *Nuclear Crisis Management: A Dangerous Illusion* (Ithaca: Cornell University Press, 1987).
38. Robert Jervis, Richard Ned Lebow and Janice Gross Stein, *Psychology and Deterrence* (Baltimore: John Hopkins University Press, 1985).
39. A debate on the relevance of August 1914 for the contemporary situation was carried out in the pages of *International Security*. See Stephen Van Evera, 'The cult of the offensive and the origins of the First World War' and Jack Snyder, 'Civil–military relations and the cult of the offensive' in *International Security* 9:1 (Summer 1984); Scott Sagan, '1914 revisited: allies, offense and instability', *International Security* 11:2 (Fall 1986) and correspondence between Snyder and Sagan, *International Security*, 11:3 (Winter 1986/87).
40. For an interesting compilation of the various positions in the nuclear debate which notes the continuities with previous decades see Robert Levine, *The Strategic Nuclear Debate* (Santa Monica, Calif.: The RAND Corporation, 1987).
41. Morton Halperin, *Nuclear Fallacy: Dispelling the Myth of Nuclear Strategy* (Cambridge, Mass.: Ballinger, 1987); Robert S. McNamara, *Blundering into Disaster: Surviving the First Century of the Nuclear Age* (New York: Pantheon Books, 1986). They are discussed in Lawrence Freedman 'I exist: therefore I deter?', *International Security* (Summer 1988).
42. Thomas Schelling, 'What went wrong with arms control?', *Foreign Affairs* (Winter 1985/86), p. 233.
43. Robert Jervis, *The Illogic of American Nuclear Strategy* (Ithaca: Cornell University Press, 1984).
44. Leon Wieseltier, *Nuclear War, Nuclear Peace* (New York: Holt, Rinehart & Winston, 1983).
45. McGeorge Bundy, 'The bishops and the Bomb', *The New York Review* (16 June 1983).
46. For a rare attempt to suggest targeting criteria from this perspective (which were essentially geared to terminating hostilities as soon as possible) see Leon Wieseltier, 'When deterrence fails', *Foreign Affairs* (Spring 1985).
47. The journalist was Robert Scheer and the offending official was T. K. Jones, Deputy Under Secretary of Defense for Strategic and Theater Nuclear Forces; the offending quote was:

> Dig a hole, cover it with a couple of doors and then throw three feet of dirt on top . . . It's the dirt that does it . . . if there are enough shovels to go around, everybody's going to make it.

This inspired the title of Robert Scheer's book, *With Enough Shovels: Reagan, Bush and Nuclear War* (New York: Random House, 1982).
48. There is now general agreement that their improvements in missile accuracy and warhead technology will put the Soviets in a position to

wipe out our land-based forces on Minuteman ICBMs by 1982.
Whether this capability is ever exercised or not – and I consider it
improbable – it reverses and hence revolutionizes the strategic equation
on which our security and that of our friends have depended through
most of the postwar period.

Henry Kissinger, Statement before the Senate Foreign Relations Committee on SALT II, 31 July 1979. Reprinted in Henry Kissinger, *For
the Record: Selected Statements, 1977–1980* (London: Weidenfeld &
Nicholson, 1981), p. 197.

49. *Report of the President's Commission on Strategic Forces* (Washington,
DC: April 1987). For an insider's assessment of the Commission's
analysis see James Woolsey, 'The politics of vulnerability: 1980–83',
Foreign Affairs (Spring 1984).

50. This is another example of how an apparently simple arms control idea
can soon become very complicated. See Glenn A. Kent, *A New Approach
to Arms Control*, R-3140-FF/RC (Santa Monica, Calif.: The RAND
Corporation, June 1984).

51. Address to the Nation by President Ronald Reagan, *Peace and National
Security* (23 March 1983).

52. The practicalities of nuclear war are discussed in full in Ashton Carter
et al. (eds.), *Managing Nuclear Operations* (Washington, DC: The
Brookings Institution, 1987).

53. Richard Ned Lebow, *Nuclear Crisis Management*, p. 121.

54. The issues are discussed in Franklin Long, Donald Hafner and Jeffrey
Boutwell (eds.), *Weapons in Space* (New York: W. W. Norton, 1986)
and William Durch (ed.), *National Interests and the Military Uses of
Space* (Cambridge, Mass.: Ballinger, 1984). Ashton Carter and David
Schwartz (eds.), *Ballistic Missile Defense* (Washington, DC: The Brook-
ings Institution, 1984). These also cover related issues of anti-satellite
weapons. For a thorough assessment from a critical perspective see
R. I. P. Bulkeley & Graham Spinardi, *Space Weapons: Deterrence or
Delusion* (Cambridge: Polity Press, 1986).

55. For one example, related to the previous concern over the developing
problems of ICBM vulnerability, see Zbigniew Brzezinski, Robert
Jastrow and Max Kampelman, 'Defense in space is not "Star Wars"',
New York Times Magazine (27 January 1985).

56. On the politics of SDI see Gerald Steinberg, *Lost in Space: The Domestic
Politics of the Strategic Defense Initiative* (Lexington, Mass.: Lexington
Books, 1988).

57. The first major critique was provided by the Union of Concerned
Scientists, *The Fallacy of Star Wars* (New York: Vintage Books, 1983).
For a rare scientific statement in favour of SDI see Robert Jastrow, *How
to Make Nuclear Weapons Obsolete* (London: Sidgwick & Jackson,
1985). For another early critique see Sidney Drell, Philip Farley and
David Holloway, *The Reagan Strategic Defense Initiative: A Technical,
Political and Arms Control Assessment* (A Special Report of the Center
for International Security and Arms Control: Stanford University, July
1984).

58. Ivo Daalder, *The SDI Challenge to Europe* (Cambridge, Mass.:

Ballinger, 1987). See also chs. 9 and 10 of Lawrence Freedman, *The Price of Peace*.

59. On which one of the most authoritative discussions is found in United States Congress, Office of Technology Assessment, *Ballistic Missile Defense Technologies*, OTA-ISC-254 (Washington, DC: USGPO, September 1985); Hans Bethe *et al.*, 'Space-based missile defense', *Scientific American* (October 1984).

60. One of the key criteria for the eventual deployment of SDI as set down by Paul Nitze was that 'they must be cheap enough to add additional defensive capability so that the other side has no incentive to add additional offensive capability to overcome the defense'. The other criterion was that the key components of the defence should be themselves 'survivable'. Paul Nitze, Speech before the World Affairs Council of Philadelphia, 20 February 1985.

61. George Schneiter, 'Implications of the strategic defense initiative for the ABM Treaty', *Survival* (Fall 1984); William Durch, *The Future of the ABM Treaty*, Adelphi Paper 223 (Summer 1987).

62. For a critical assessment of the new interpretation see Raymond Garthoff, *Policy Versus The Law: The Reinterpretation of the ABM Treaty* (Washington, DC: The Brookings Institution, 1987). The case in favour of the new interpretation is made by the State Department's legal counsel, Judge Sofaer, with a critique by Abram and Antonia Chayes in *Harvard Law Review* (June 1986). See also Alan Sherr, 'Sound legal reasoning or policy expedient: the new interpretation of the ABM Treaty', *International Security* (Winter 1986/7).

63. James Schear, 'Arms control treaty compliance: buildup to a breakdown', *International Security* (Fall 1985); Sanford Reback, 'Responding to Soviet non-compliance', *Arms Control* (December 1986); John Baker, 'Improving prospects for compliance with arms-control treaties', *Survival* (September/October 1987).

64. The definitive account of the development of nuclear arms control policies in the first term of the Reagan Administration is found in Strobe Talbott, *Deadly Gambits* (New York: Alfred A. Knopf, 1984).

65. See Michael Mandelbaum and Strobe Talbott, 'Reykjavik and beyond', *Foreign Affairs* (Winter 1986/87). For a discussion of some of the themes of the summit see articles in *International Security* (Summer 1987).

66. Two useful collections of essays indicating the range of debate on the nature of Soviet strategic thought are: John Baylis and Gerald Segal (eds.), *Soviet Strategy* (London: Croom Helm, 1981) and Derek Leebaert (ed.), *Soviet Military Thinking* (London: George Allen & Unwin, 1981). Also of great value is David Holloway, *The Soviet Union and the Arms Race* (London: Yale University Press, 1983).

67. The destruction of nuclear weapons and interference with command and control facilities will be a priority task of Warsaw Pact forces in a continental land battle. See C. N. Donnelly, 'The Soviet Operational Manoeuvre Group: a new challenge for NATO', *International Defense Review* xv:9 (1982).

68. For one analysis along these lines see Joseph D. Douglass Jr. and

Amoretta M. Hoeber, *Conventional War and Escalation: The Soviet View* (New York: Crane Russak, 1981).
69. Stephen M. Meyer, *Soviet Theatre Nuclear Forces, Part II*, p. 23. For elaboration of this point see Stephen M. Meyer, 'Soviet perspectives on the paths to nuclear war', in Graham T. Allison, Albert Carnesale, Joseph S. Nye (eds.), *Hawks, Doves and Owls: An Agenda for Avoiding Nuclear War* (New York: W. W. Norton, 1985), p. 169.
70. Quoted in William Garner, *Soviet Threat Perceptions of NATO's Eurostrategic Missiles*, Atlantic Papers No. 52–53 (Paris: The Atlantic Institute for International Affairs, 1983), p. 63. See also Garner's discussion on pp. 30–4 of Soviet perceptions of US strategy as an attempt to wage war against the Soviet Union and Warsaw Pact without being engaged itself.
71. In 1972 the Soviet Union even proposed to the United States a treaty in which the two sides would pledge not to use nuclear weapons against each others' homeland even if they were being used against the territory of their NATO and Warsaw Pact allies. See Henry Kissinger, *The White House Years* (Boston: Little Brown & Co., 1979), pp. 183–90, and Meyer in Allison *et al.*, *Hawks, Doves and Owls . . .*, pp. 181–2.
72. Cynthia A. Roberts, 'Soviet INF Policy and Euro-Strategic Options' in Gloria Duffy (ed.), *Intermediate Nuclear Forces in Europe* (Palo Alto: Stanford University, 1982), pp. 35–6; Stephen M. Meyer, *Soviet Theatre Nuclear Forces. Part I: Development of Doctrine and Objectives*, Adelphi Paper 187 (London: IISS, 1984), p. 32.
73. A useful corrective to the presumption of an adversary 'assured of its combat virtuosity and unencumbered by doubts over doctrine and capabilities' is found in Benjamin Lambeth, 'Uncertainties for the Soviet war planner', *International Security* (Winter 1982/83).
74. John Erickson, 'The Soviet view of deterrence: a general survey', *Survival* (November/December 1962), p. 249.
75. Stephen M. Meyer, *Soviet Theatre Nuclear Forces . . .*
76. President Brezhnev announced the new policy in a message to the UN General Assembly's Special Session on Disarmament in June 1982. Prior to this the option had been maintained to use nuclear weapons against other nuclear powers committing 'aggression' (which could take a variety of forms); now it was only to be maintained against 'nuclear aggression'. See James McConnell, *The Soviet Shift In Emphasis from Nuclear to Conventional*, 2 volumes (Virginia: Center for Naval Analyses, June 1984), vol. I, p. 19. See also Stephen Shenfield, 'The Soviet undertaking not to use nuclear weapons first and its significance', *Detente* (Oct. 1984).
77. See James McConnell, *The Soviet Shift . . .*; Michael MccGwire, *Military Objectives in Soviet Foreign Policy* (Washington, DC: The Brookings Institution, 1987). There is evidence of some dissatisfaction with this trend and of arguments for more emphasis on nuclear weapons. See, for example, Ilana Kass and Michael J. Deane, 'The role of nuclear weapons in the modern theater battlefield: the current Soviet view', *Comparative Strategy* IV:3 (1984).
78. Stephen Shenfield, *The Nuclear Predicament: Explorations in Soviet Ideology* (London: Routledge & Kegan Paul for RIIA, 1987).

79. A. Arbatov, 'Military doctrine' in *1988 Yearbook* (Moscow: IMEMO, 1988).
80. This point is made with great force in Philip Bobbitt, *Democracy and Deterrence: The History and Future of Nuclear Strategy* (London: Macmillan, 1988).
81. McGeorge Bundy, George F. Kennan, Robert S. McNamara and Gerard Smith, 'Nuclear weapons and the Atlantic Alliance', *Foreign Affairs* (Spring 1982).
82. Robert S. McNamara, 'The military role of nuclear weapons: perceptions and misperceptions', *Foreign Affairs* (Fall 1983), p. 79. He adds 'I believe they accepted my recommendations'.
83. Fred Iklé, 'NATO's "first nuclear use": a deepening trap?', *Strategic Review* (Winter 1980).
84. Karl Kaiser, Georg Leber, Alois Mertes and Franz-Joseph Schulze, 'Nuclear weapons and the preservation of peace: a German response to no first use', *Foreign Affairs* (Summer 1982).
85. J. M. Legge, *Theater Nuclear Weapons and the NATO Strategy of Flexible Response* (Santa Monica, Calif.: The RAND Corporation, 1983).
86. See, for example, John Mearsheimer, 'Why the Soviets can't win quickly in Central Europe', *International Security* (Summer 1982).

CONCLUSION

1. In Brodie (ed.), *The Absolute Weapon, op. cit.*, p. 52.
2. One of the few attempts to do so is found in David C. Gompert, Michael Mandelbaum, Richard L. Garwin and John H. Barton, *Nuclear Weapons and World Politics: Alternatives for the Future* (New York: McGraw Hill for the Council on Foreign Relations, 1977).

Bibliography

Primary Sources

1 United States

(a) STATEMENTS BY SECRETARIES OF DEFENSE

Statement of Secretary of Defense Robert S. McNamara before the House Armed Services Committee on The Fiscal Years 1964–68. *Defense Program and 1964 Defense Budget* (27 January 1963)

Report of Secretary of Defense James Schlesinger to the Congress on the *FY 1975 Defense Budget and FY 1975–79 Defense Program* (4 March 1974)

Report of Secretary of Defense James Schlesinger to the Congress on *FY 1976 and Transition Budgets, FY 1977 Authorization Request and FY 1978–1980 Defense Program* (5 February 1975)

Secretary of Defense Harold Brown, *Department of Defense Annual Report Fiscal Year 1979* (2 February 1978)

——, *Department of Defense Annual Report Fiscal Year 1980* (25 January 1979)

Report of Secretary of Defense Caspar Weinberger to the Congress on *The Potential Effects of Nuclear War on the Climate* (March 1985)

(b) REPORTS OF PRESIDENT NIXON

Nixon, Richard, President of the United States, *United States Foreign Policy for the 1970s: A New Strategy for Peace* (18 February 1970)

Nixon, Richard, President of the United States, *United States Foreign Policy for the 1970s: Building the Peace* (25 February 1971)

Nixon, Richard, President of the United States, *United States Foreign Policy for the 1970s: The Emerging Structure of Peace* (9 February 1972)

Nixon, Richard, President of the United States, *United States Foreign Policy for the 1970s: Shaping a Durable Peace* (3 May 1973)

(c) CONGRESSIONAL HEARINGS

Senate Foreign Relations and Armed Services Committee, *Assignment of Ground Forces of the United States in the European Area* (February 1951)

Senate Foreign Relations Committee, *Strategic Arms Limitation Talks* (1972)

Senate Foreign Relations Committee, *US and Soviet Strategic Policies* (March 1974)

Senate Foreign Relations Committee, *Briefing on Counterforce Attacks* (September 1974)

Senate Armed Services Committee, *Hearings on Military Implications of the Treaty on the Limitation of Anti-Ballistic Missile Systems and the Interim Agreement on Limitation of Strategic Offensive Arms* (1972)

(d) SPEECHES AND PRESS CONFERENCES

Dulles, John Foster, 'The evolution of foreign policy', *Department of State Bulletin*, xxx (25 January 1954)

Gilpatric, Roswell L., 'Address before the Business Council, Hot Springs, Virginia, 10 October 1961'. Reprinted in *Documents on Disarmament 1961* (Washington, DC: US Arms Control and Disarmament Agency, 1962)

McNamara, Robert S., 'Defense arrangements of the North Atlantic Community', *Department of State Bulletin*, XLVII (9 July 1962)

Interview with Robert McNamara, 15 February 1966, in *Documents on Disarmament 1967* (Washington, DC: US Arms Control and Disarmament Agency, 1967)

McNamara, Robert S., 'The dynamics of nuclear strategy', *Department of State Bulletin*, LVII (9 October 1967)

Kissinger, Henry, Press Conference of 3 July 1974, reprinted in *Survival*, xvi:5 (September/October 1974)

Address to the Nation by President Ronald Reagan, *Peace and National Security* (23 March 1983)

Nitze, Paul, Speech before the World Affairs Council of Philadelphia (20 February 1985)

(e) INTERNAL DOCUMENTS

Spaatz, General Carl, *The Implications of the Atom Bomb for the Size, Composition, Organization and Role of the Future Air Force* (The Spaatz Report) (23 October 1945)

Joint Staff Strategic Survey, *Statement of the Effect of Atomic Weapons on National Security and Military Organization* (12 January 1946)

Special Counsel to the President (Clark Clifford), *American Relations with the Soviet Union* (24 September 1946)

Air Staff, *Strategic Implications of the Atomic Bomb on Warfare* (3 February 1947)

NSC-30, *United States Policy on Atomic Weapons* (10 September 1948)

Joint Chiefs of Staff, *Evaluation of Current Strategic Air Offensive Plans* (21 December 1948)

NSC-20/2, *Factors Affecting the Nature of the US Defense Arrangements in the Light of Soviet Policies* (25 August 1948)

Harmon, General H. R. et al., *Evaluation of Effect on Soviet War Effort*

Resulting from the Strategic Air Offensive (The Harmon Report) (11 May 1949)

General Advisory Committee of the Atomic Energy Commission, *Report* (30 October 1949)

NSC-68, *A Report to the National Security Council by the Executive Secretary on United States Objectives and Programs for National Security* (14 April 1950)

NSC-162/2, *Basic National Security Plan* (30 October 1953)

Technological Capabilities Panel of the Scientific Advisory Committee of the Office of Defense Mobilization, *Meeting the Threat of Surprise Attack* (*The Killian Report*) (14 February 1955)

Security Resources Panel of the Scientific Advisory Committee of the Office of Defense Mobilization, *Deterrence and Survival in the Nuclear Age* (*The Gaither Report*) (November 1957)

US Air Force, *This is Counterforce* (7 February 1963) (from IISS files)

FM 100/5, *US Army Field Manual* (Washington, DC: Department of the Army, 1982)

(f) PUBLISHED DOCUMENTS

Smyth, H. D., *A General Account of the Development of Methods of Using Atomic Energy for Military Purposes under the Auspices of the US Government 1940–45* (Washington, DC: USGPO, August 1945)

US Strategic Bombing Survey, 10 vols. (New York: Garland, 1976)

Report of the President's Advisory Commission on Universal Military Training, *A Programme for National Security* (*The Compton Report*) (Washington, DC: USGPO, 1947)

Glasstone, Dr Samuel, *The Effects of Nuclear Weapons* (US Atomic Energy Commission, 1957)

United States Congress, Office of Technology Assessment, *The Effects of Nuclear War* (Washington, DC: USGPO, 1979)

Soviet Military Power (Washington, DC: Department of Defense, 1981)

United States Congress, Office of Technology Assessment, *Ballistic Missile Defense Technologies*, OTA-ISC-254 (Washington, DC: USGPO, September 1985)

Report of the President's Commission on Strategic Forces (Washington, DC: USGPO, April 1987)

Report of the Commission on Integrated Long-Term Strategy, Discriminate Deterrence (Washington, DC: USGPO, January 1988)

2   United Kingdom

Defence: Outline of Future Policy. Cmnd 124 (London: HMSO, April 1957)

Report on Defence, Britain's Contribution to Peace and Security. Cmnd 363 (London: HMSO, 1958)

Statement on Defence 1964. Cmnd 2270 (London: HMSO, 1964)

3 NATO

NATO Letter, v:12 (December 1957)
Communiqué, *Ministerial Meeting of North Atlantic Council* (14 December 1967)
North Atlantic Council, *Declaration on Alliance Relations* (Ottawa: 19 June 1974)

Unpublished

King, James, 'The New Strategy' (Unpublished Manuscript)
Klotz, Frank, *The US President and the Control of Strategic Nuclear Weapons* (D.Phil Thesis, Oxford: 1980)
Wohlstetter, Albert, Letter to Michael Howard, 6 November 1968

Secondary Sources

Books

Acheson, Dean, *Power and Diplomacy* (Cambridge, Mass.: Harvard University Press, 1958)
——, *Present at the Creation* (London: Hamish Hamilton, 1969)
Adams, Sherman, *Firsthand Report: The Story of the Eisenhower Administration* (New York: Harper & Row, 1961)
Afheldt, Horst, 'The necessity, preconditions and consequences of a no-first-use policy' in Blackaby, Frank; Goldblat, Jozef and Lodgaard, Sverre (eds.), *No-First Use* (London: Taylor & Francis for SIPRI, 1984)
Allison, Graham T.; Carnesale, Albert and Nye, Joseph S. (eds.), *Hawks, Doves and Owls: An Agenda for Avoiding Nuclear War* (New York: W. W. Norton, 1985)
Amster, Warren, *A Theory for the Design of a Deterrent Air Weapon System* (San Diego, Calif.: Convair Corporation, 1955)
Arbatov, A., 'Military Doctrine' in *1988 Yearbook* (Moscow: IMEMO, 1988)
Aron, Raymond, *The Great Debate* (New York: Doubleday, 1965)
Bailey, Sydney, *Prohibitions and Restraints in Warfare* (London: Oxford University Press, 1972)
Ball, Desmond, *Déjà Vu: The Return to Counterforce in the Nixon Administration* (California: Seminar on Arms Control and Foreign Policy. December 1974)
——, *Developments in US Nuclear Policy under the Carter Administration* (California: Seminar on Arms Control and Foreign Policy, 1980)
——, *Policies and Force Levels: The Strategic Missile Program of the Kennedy Administration* (Berkeley: University of California Press, 1980)
——, *Can Nuclear War be Controlled?* Adelphi Papers 169 (London: IISS, 1981)
Baylis, John (ed.), *British Defence Policy in a Changing World* (London: Croom Helm, 1977)

—— and Segal, Gerald (eds.), *Soviet Strategy* (London: Croom Helm, 1981)
Beard, Edmund, *Developing the ICBM: A Study in Bureaucratic Politics* (New York: Columbia University Press, 1976)
Beaufre, André, *Deterrence and Strategy* (London: Faber & Faber, 1965), originally published as *Dissuasion et Stratégie* (Paris: Armand Colin, 1964)
Bechhoefer, Bernard, *Postwar Negotiations for Arms Control* (Washington, DC: The Brookings Institution, 1961)
Bertram, Christoph (ed.), *Beyond SALT II* (London: IISS, 1978)
—— (ed.), *New Conventional Weapons and East–West Security* (London: IISS, 1978)
Blackaby, Frank; Goldblat, Jozef and Lodgaard, Sverre (eds.), *No-First Use* (London: Taylor & Francis for SIPRI, 1984)
Blackett, P. M. S., *Atomic Weapons and East–West Relations* (Cambridge: Cambridge University Press, 1956)
——, *The Military and Political Consequences of Atomic Energy* (London: Turnstile Press, 1948)
——, *Studies of War – Nuclear and Conventional* (London: Oliver & Boyd, 1962)
Blair, Bruce, *Strategic Command and Control: Redefining the Nuclear Threat* (Washington, DC: The Brookings Institution, 1985)
Bobbitt, Philip, *Democracy and Deterrence: The History and Future of Nuclear Strategy* (London: Macmillan, 1988)
Bond, Brian, *Liddell Hart: A Study of his Military Thought* (London: Cassell, 1977)
Borden, William L., *There Will Be No Time* (New York: Macmillan, 1946)
Bottome, Edgar, *The Balance of Terror: A Guide to the Arms Race* (Boston: Beacon Press, 1971)
Boulding, Kenneth E., *Conflict and Defense: A General Theory* (New York: Harper & Row, 1963)
Bracken, Paul, *The Command and Control of Nuclear Weapons* (New Haven: Yale University Press, 1983)
Brennan, Donald (ed.), *Arms Control, Disarmament and National Security* (New York: George Braziller, 1961)
Brodie, Bernard, *The Atomic Bomb and American Security* (Yale University, Memorandum No. 18, 1945)
——, *The Absolute Weapon* (New York: Harcourt Brace, 1946)
——, *Strategy in the Missile Age* (Princeton: Princeton University Press, 1959)
——, *Escalation and the Nuclear Option* (Princeton: Princeton University Press, 1966)
—— and Galloway, Eilene, *The Atomic Bomb and the Armed Services*, Public Affairs Bulletin No. 55 (Washington, DC: Library of Congress Legislative Reference Service, May 1947)
Brownlie, Ian, *International Law and the Use of Force by States* (Oxford: Clarendon Press, 1963)
Buchan, Alastair, *The Multilateral Force: A Historical Perspective*. Adelphi Papers No. 13 (London: IISS, 1964)
——, *NATO in the 1960s* (London: Chatto & Windus, 1963)
—— (ed.), *Problems of Modern Strategy* (London: Chatto & Windus, 1970)

—— and Windsor, Philip, *Arms and Stability in Europe* (London: Chatto & Windus, 1963)

Bulkeley, R. I. P. and Spinardi, Graham, *Space Weapons: Deterrence or Delusion* (Cambridge: Polity Press, 1986)

Bull, Hedley, *The Control of the Arms Race* (London: Weidenfeld & Nicolson, 1961)

Burdick, Eugene and Wheeler, Harvey, *Fail-Safe* (London: Hutchinson, 1963)

Burns, Arthur Lee, *The Rationale of Catalytic War* (Princeton University Center of International Studies, April 1959)

——, *Ethics and Deterrence: A Nuclear Balance Without Hostage Cities?* (London: IISS, 1970)

Burt, Richard, *New Weapons and Technologies: Debate and Directions* (London: IISS, 1976)

Bush, Vannevar, *Modern Arms and Free Men* (London: Heinemann, 1950)

Butow, Robert J. C., *Japan's Decision to Surrender* (Stanford: Stanford University Press, 1954)

Caldwell, Lawrence, *Soviet Attitudes to SALT* (London: IISS, 1972)

Capitanchik, David and Eichenberg, Richard, *Defence and Public Opinion*, Chatham House Paper No. 20 (London: Routledge & Kegan Paul for RIIA, 1983)

Carter, Ashton and Schwartz, David (eds.), *Ballistic Missile Defense* (Washington, DC: Brookings Institution, 1984)

—— *et al.* (eds.), *Managing Nuclear Operations* (Washington, DC: Brookings Institution, 1987)

Charlton, Michael, *From Deterrence to Defense: The Inside Story of Strategic Policy* (Harvard University Press, 1987)

Chayes, Abram and Wiesner, Jerome, (ed.). *ABM: An Evaluation of the Decision to Deploy an Anti-Ballistic Missile System* (New York: Harper & Row, 1969)

Clark, Ian and Wheeler, Nicholas, *British Origins of Nuclear Strategy, 1945– 55* (Oxford: Oxford University Press, forthcoming)

Coale, Ansley J., *The Problem of Reducing Vulnerability to Atomic Bombs* (Princeton: Princeton University Press, 1947)

Cochran, Thomas B.; Arkin, William M. and Hoenig, Milton M., *US Nuclear Forces and Capabilities* (New York: Ballinger, 1984)

Coffey, J. I., *Strategic Power and National Security* (Pittsburgh: University of Pittsburgh Press, 1971)

Cole, Paul and Taylor, William J. (eds.), *The Nuclear Freeze Debate* (Boulder, Col.: Westview, 1983)

Collins, John M., *American and Soviet Military Trends since the Cuban Missile Crisis* (Washington, DC: The Center for Strategic and International Studies, Georgetown University, 1978)

Daalder, Ivo, *The SDI Challenge to Europe* (Cambridge, Mass.: Ballinger, 1987)

Daniel, Donald (ed.), *International Perceptions of the Superpower Military Balance* (New York: Praeger, 1978)

Davis, Lynn Etheridge, *Limited Nuclear Options: Deterrence and the New American Doctrine*, Adelphi Paper 121 (London: IISS, 1976)

Dinerstein, H. S., *War and the Soviet Union* (New York: Praeger, 1959)

Divine, Robert A., *Blowing on the Wind: The Nuclear Test Ban Debate 1954–60* (New York: Oxford University Press, 1978)

Donovan, Robert J., *Eisenhower: The Inside Story* (New York: Harper, 1956)

Douglass, Joseph and Hoeber, Amoretta, *Soviet Strategy for Nuclear War* (Stanford, Calif.: Hoover Institution Press, 1979)

——, *Conventional War and Escalation: The Soviet View* (New York: Crane Russak, 1981)

Douhet, Giulio, *The Command of the Air*, as translated by Dino Ferrari (New York: Coward McCann Inc., 1942)

Draper, Theodore, *Present History: On Nuclear War, Détente, and Other Controversies* (New York: Random House, 1983)

Drell, Sidney; Farley, Philip and Holloway, David, *The Reagan Strategic Defense Initiative: A Technical, Political and Arms Control Assessment* (A Special Report of the Center for International Security and Arms Control, Stanford University, July 1984)

Driver, Christopher, *The Disarmers* (London: Hodder & Stoughton, 1964)

Dror, Yehezekel, *Crazy States: A Counter-conventional Strategic Problem* (Lexington, Mass.: D. C. Heath, 1971)

Durch, William (ed.), *National Interests and the Military Uses of Space* (Cambridge, Mass.: Ballinger, 1984)

——, *The Future of the ABM Treaty*, Adelphi Paper 223 (London: IISS, Summer 1987)

Editors of Pocket Books, *The Atomic Age Opens* (New York: Pocket Books, 1945)

Eliot, George Fielding, *Victory Without War: 1958–61* (Annapolis, Maryland: US Naval Institute, 1958)

Enthoven, Alain C. and Smith, K. Wayne, *How Much is Enough? Shaping the Defense Program 1961–1969* (New York: Harper & Row, 1971)

Etzold, Thomas H. and Gaddis, John Lewis, *Containment: Documents on American Policy and Strategy 1945–50* (New York: Columbia University Press, 1978)

Feis, Herbert, *The Atomic Bomb and the End of World War II* (Princeton: Princeton University Press, 1966)

Feld, B. T.; Greenwood, T.; Rathjens, G. N. and Weinberg, Stephen, *Impact of New Technologies on the Arms Race* (Cambridge, Mass.: MIT Press, 1971)

Finletter, Thomas, *Power and Policy* (New York: Harcourt & Brace, 1954)

Fox, William, *The Superpowers: The United States, Britain and the Soviet Union and Their Responsibility for Peace* (New York: Harcourt & Brace, 1954)

——, *Atomic Energy and International Relations* (Mimeo: Yale Institute of International Affairs, June 1948)

Freedman, Lawrence, *US Intelligence and the Soviet Strategic Threat* (London: Macmillan, 1977)

——, *Britain and Nuclear Weapons* (London: Macmillan, 1980)

——, *The Price of Peace: Living with the Nuclear Dilemma* (London: Firethorne, 1986)

——, 'On the tiger's back: the development of the concept of escalation' in

Kolkowicz, Roman (ed.), *The Logic of Nuclear Terror* (Boston: Allen & Unwin, 1987)

Gaddis, John, *The Long Peace: Inquiries into the History of the Cold War* (New York: Oxford University Press, 1987)

Gallois, Pierre, *Stratégie de l'âge nucléaire* (Paris: Calmann-Levy, 1960). English edition: *The Balance of Terror: Strategy for the Nuclear Age* translated by Howard, Richard (Boston: Houghton Mifflin, 1961)

Garfinkel, Adam, *The Politics of the Nuclear Freeze* (Philadelphia: Foreign Policy Research Institute, 1984)

Garner, William, *Soviet Threat Perceptions of NATO's Eurostrategic Missiles*, Atlantic Papers No. 52–53 (Paris: The Atlantic Institute for International Affairs, 1983)

Garthoff, Raymond L., *Soviet Military Doctrine* (Illinois: The Free Press, 1953)

——, *Soviet Strategy in the Nuclear Age* (New York: Praeger, 1958)

——, *Policy Versus The Law: The Reinterpretation of the ABM Treaty* (Washington, DC: Brookings Institution, 1987)

George, Alexander and Smoke, Richard, *Deterrence in American Foreign Policy: Theory and Practice* (New York: Columbia University Press, 1974)

Gervasi, Tom, *The Myth of Soviet Military Supremacy* (New York: Harper & Row, 1986)

Gilpin, Robert, *American Scientists and Nuclear Weapons Policy* (Princeton: Princeton University Press, 1962)

—— and Wright, Christopher (eds.), *Scientists and National Policy Making* (New York: Columbia University Press, 1964)

Giovannitti, L. and Freed, F., *The Decision to Drop the Bomb* (London: Methuen & Co., 1967)

Golovine, M. N., *Conflict in Space: A Pattern of War in a New Dimension* (New York: St Martin's Press, 1962)

Gompert, David C.; Mandelbaum, Michael; Garwin, Richard L. and Barton, John H., *Nuclear Weapons and World Politics: Alternatives for the Future* (New York: McGraw-Hill for the Council on Foreign Relations, 1977)

Goodwin, Geoffrey (ed.), *Ethics and Nuclear Deterrence* (London: Croom Helm, 1982)

Goold-Adams, Richard, *On Limiting Atomic Warfare* (London: Royal Institute of International Affairs, 1956)

Gorbachev, Mikhail, *Perestroika* (London: Collins, 1987)

Gouré, Leon, *War Survival in Soviet Strategy* (University of Miami Press, 1976)

——, Kohler, Foy, and Harvey, Mose, L., *The Role of Nuclear Forces in Current Soviet Strategy* (Miami, Florida: Center for Advanced Studies, University of Miami, 1974)

Gowing, Margaret, *Britain and Atomic Energy, 1939–1945* (London: Macmillan, 1964)

——, *Independence and Deterrence: Britain and Atomic Energy 1945–1952*, vol. 1, *Policy Making* (London: Macmillan, 1974)

Gray, Colin, *The Future of Land-Based Missile Forces* (London: IISS, 1978)

——, *The Soviet–American Arms Race* (Farnborough, Hants: Saxon House, 1976)

——, *Nuclear Strategy and National Style* (Lanham, Md: Hamilton Books/Abt Associates, 1986)

Gravel, Senator Michael (ed.), *Pentagon Papers* (vol. 1) (Boston: Beacon Press, 1971)

Green, Philip, *Deadly Logic: The Theory of Nuclear Deterrence* (Columbus, Ohio: Ohio State University Press, 1966)

Greenwood, Ted, *Making the MIRV: A Study in Defense Decision-Making* (Cambridge, Mass.: Ballinger, 1975)

Grodzins, Morton and Rabinowitch, Eugene (eds.), *The Atomic Age: Scientists in National and World Affairs* (New York: Basic Books, 1963)

Groom, John, *British Thinking About Nuclear Weapons* (London: Frances Pinter, 1974)

Groves, Leslie R., *Now It Can Be Told: The Story of the Manhattan Project* (New York: Harper, 1962)

Halliday, Fred, *The Making of the Second Cold War* (London: Verso, 1983)

Halperin, Morton, *Limited War in the Nuclear Age* (New York: John Wiley & Sons, 1963)

——, *Nuclear Fallacy: Dispelling the Myth of Nuclear Strategy* (Cambridge, Mass.: Ballinger, 1987)

Herken, Gregg, *The Winning Weapon: The Atomic Bomb in the Cold War* (New York: Alfred A. Knopf, 1980)

——, *Counsels of War* (New York: Alfred A. Knopf, 1985)

Hewlett, Richard G. and Anderson, Oscar, *The New World 1939/46:* Vol. 1 of a History of the ASAEC (Pennsylvania University Press, 1962)

Hitch, Charles and McKean, Roland N., *The Economics of Defense in the Nuclear Age* (Cambridge: Harvard University Press, 1960)

Holloway, David, *The Soviet Union and the Arms Race* (London: Yale University Press, 1983)

Hook, Sidney, *The Fail-Safe Fallacy* (New York: Stein & Day, 1963)

Horelick, Arnold and Rush, Myron, *Strategic Power and Soviet Foreign Policy* (Chicago: University of Chicago Press, 1966)

Howard, Michael (ed.), *Restraints in War: Studies in the Limitation of Armed Conflict* (London: Oxford University Press, 1979)

Howorth, Jolyon and Chilton, Patricia (eds.), *Defence and Dissent in Contemporary France* (London: Croom Helm, 1984)

Hsieh, Alice Langley, *Communist China's Strategy in the Nuclear Age* (Englewood Cliffs, N.J.: Prentice-Hall, Inc., 1962)

Huntington, Samuel P., *The Common Defense: Strategic Programs in National Politics* (New York: Columbia University Press, 1961)

Iklé, Fred, *Can Nuclear Deterrence Last Out the Century?* (Santa Monica, Calif.: Arms Control and Foreign Policy Seminar, January 1973)

International Institute for Strategic Studies (IISS), *The Implications of Military Technology in the 1970s* (London: IISS, 1968)

Irving, David, *The Mare's Nest* (London: William Kimber, 1964)

Janis, Irving, *Victims of Group-think* (Boston: Houghton Mifflin, 1972)

Jastrow, Robert, *How to Make Nuclear Weapons Obsolete* (London: Sidgwick & Jackson, 1985)

Jayne, Edward Randolph, *The ABM Debate: Strategic Defense and National Security* (MIT Center for Strategic Studies, June 1969)

Jervis, Robert, *Perception and Misperception in International Politics* (Princeton: Princeton University Press, 1976)
——, *The Illogic of American Nuclear Strategy* (Ithaca: Cornell University Press, 1984)
——, Lebow, Richard Ned and Stein, Janice Gross, *Psychology and Deterrence* (Baltimore: Johns Hopkins University Press, 1985)
Kadt, Emanuel J. de, *British Defence Policy and Nuclear War* (London: Frank Cass, 1964)
Kahan, Jerome, *Security in the Nuclear Age: Developing US Strategic Arms Policy* (Washington, DC: Brookings Institution, 1975)
Kahn, Herman, *On Thermonuclear War* (Princeton: Princeton University Press, 1960)
——, *Thinking About the Unthinkable* (New York: Horizon Press, 1962)
——, *On Escalation: Metaphors and Scenarios* (New York: Praeger, 1965)
——, *Thinking About the Unthinkable in the 1980s* (New York: Simon & Schuster, 1984)
Kaplan, Fred, *The Wizards of Armageddon* (New York: Simon & Schuster, 1983)
Kaplan, Morton, *The Strategy of Limited Retaliation*, Policy Memorandum No. 19 (Center of International Studies, Princeton University, 9 April 1959)
—— (ed.), *Strategic Thinking and its Moral Implications* (Chicago: University of Chicago Press, 1973)
Kaufman, Richard, *The War Profiteers* (New York: Doubleday, 1972)
Kaufmann, William (ed.), *Military Policy and National Security* (Princeton: Princeton University Press, 1956)
——, *The McNamara Strategy* (New York: Harper & Row, 1964)
Kecskemeti, Paul, *Strategic Surrender: The Politics of Victory and Defense* (Stanford, Calif.: Stanford University Press, 1958)
Kelleher, Catherine McArdle, *Germany and the Politics of Nuclear Weapons* (New York: Columbia University Press, 1975)
Kennan, George F., *Russia, The Atom and the West* (New York: Harper & Brothers, 1958)
——, *Memoirs, 1925–1950* (Boston: Little, Brown & Co., 1967)
Kennedy, Edward and Hatfield, Mark, *Freeze: How You Can Prevent Nuclear War* (New York: Bantam Books, 1982)
Kennedy, John F., *The Strategy of Peace* (New York: Harper & Row, 1960)
Kent, Glenn A., *A New Approach to Arms Control*, R-3140-FF/RC (Santa Monica, Calif.: The RAND Corporation, June 1984)
Khruschev, Nikita, *Khruschev Remembers*, 2 volumes (London: André Deutsch, 1971 and 1974)
Killian, James R., *Sputniks, Scientists and Eisenhower* (Cambridge, Mass.: MIT Press, 1977)
King-Hall, Stephen, *Power Politics in the Nuclear Age: A Policy for Britain* (London: Gollancz, 1962)
Kissinger, Henry, *Nuclear Weapons and Foreign Policy* (New York: Harper, 1957)
——, *Necessity for Choice* (New York: Harper & Row, 1961)
—— (ed.), *Problems of National Strategy* (New York: Praeger, 1962)

——, *The White House Years* (London: Weidenfeld & Nicolson, 1979)

——, *For the Record: Selected Statements, 1977–1980* (London: Weidenfeld & Nicolson, 1981)

Knoll, Erwin and McFadden, Judith Nies (eds.), *American Militarism 1970* (New York: The Viking Press, 1969)

Knorr, Klaus, *On the Uses of Military Power in the Nuclear Age* (Princeton: Princeton University Press, 1966)

—— (ed.), *NATO and American Security* (Princeton: Princeton University Press, 1959)

—— and Read, Thornton (eds.), *Limited Strategic War* (New York: Praeger, 1962)

—— and Rosenau, James (eds.), *Contending Approaches to International Relations* (Princeton: Princeton University Press, 1969)

Kohl, Wilfred, *French Nuclear Diplomacy* (Princeton: Princeton University Press, 1971)

Kolkowicz, Roman, *et al.*, *The Soviet Union and Arms Control: A Superpower Dilemma* (Baltimore, Md.: Johns Hopkins University Press, 1970)

Kramish, Arnold, *Atomic Energy in the Soviet Union* (Stanford, Calif.: Stanford University Press, 1960)

Laird, Melvin, *A House Divided: America's Security Gap* (New York: Henry Regnery, 1962)

Lambeth, Benjamin S., *Selective Nuclear Options in American and Soviet Strategic Policy* (Santa Monica, Calif.: RAND Corporation, 1976)

Lapp, Ralph, *The Weapons Culture* (New York: W. W. Norton, 1968)

Lebow, Richard Ned, *Nuclear Crisis Management: A Dangerous Illusion* (Ithaca: Cornell University Press, 1987)

Leebaert, Derek (ed.), *Soviet Military Thinking* (London: George Allen & Unwin, 1981)

Legge, J. M., *Theater Nuclear Weapons and the NATO Strategy of Flexible Response* (Santa Monica, Calif.: RAND Corporation, 1983)

Liddell Hart, B. H., *The Revolution in Warfare* (London: Faber & Faber, 1946)

—— (ed.), *The Soviet Army* (London: Weidenfeld & Nicolson, 1956)

——, *Deterrent or Defense* (London: Stevens & Sons, 1960)

——, *Strategy: The Indirect Approach* (London: Faber & Faber, 1968)

Lilienthal, David, *The Journals of David E. Lilienthal*, vol. II, *The Atomic Energy Years 1945–50* (New York: Harper & Row, 1964)

Long, Franklin; Hafner, Donald and Boutwell, Jeffrey (eds.), *Weapons in Space* (New York: W. W. Norton, 1986)

Lowe, George E., *The Age of Deterrence* (Boston: Little, Brown & Co., 1964)

Luttwak, Edward, *The Pentagon and the Art of War* (New York: Simon & Schuster, 1984)

McConnell, James, *The Soviet Shift in Emphasis from Nuclear to Conventional*, 2 vols (Virginia: Center for Naval Analyses, June 1984), vol. I

MccGwire, Michael, *Military Objectives in Soviet Foreign Policy* (Washington, DC: Brookings Institution, 1987)

MacIsaacs, David, *Strategic Bombing in World War Two: The Story of the United States Strategic Bombing Survey* (New York: Garland, 1976)

McNamara, Robert S., *The Essence of Security: Reflections in Office* (London: Hodder & Stoughton, 1968)
——, *Blundering into Disaster: Surviving the First Century of the Nuclear Age* (New York: Pantheon Books, 1986)
Masters, Dexter and Way, Katherine (eds.), *One World or None* (New York: McGraw-Hill, 1941)
Maxwell, Stephen, *Rationality in Deterrence* (London: IISS, 1968)
Mershon National Security Program, *Accidental War: Some Dangers of the 1960s* (Research Paper, June 1960)
Meyer, Stephen M., *Soviet Theatre Nuclear Forces. Part I: Development of Doctrine and Objectives*, Adelphi Paper 187 (London: IISS, 1984)
Miksche, F. O., *The Failure of Atomic Strategy* (New York: Praeger, 1958)
Millis, Walter (ed.), *The Forrestal Diaries* (London: Cassell & Co., 1952)
Morgan, Patrick, *Deterrence: A Conceptual Analysis* (London: Sage Publications, 1977)
Morgenstern, Oskar, *The Question of National Defense* (New York: Random House, 1959)
Moss, Norman, *Men Who Play God; The Story of the Hydrogen Bomb* (London: Penguin, 1970)
Murray, Thomas, *Nuclear Policy for War and Peace* (Ohio: World Publishing Co., 1960)
Myrdal, Alva, *The Game of Disarmament: How the United States and Russia Run the Arms Race* (Manchester: Manchester University Press, 1977)
National Conference of Catholic Bishops, 'The challenge of peace: God's promise and our response', *Origins* (National Catholic Documentary Service), vol. 13 (19 May 1983)
National Planning Association, *The 'Nth Country' Problem and Arms Control* (New York: NPA, 1959)
Neustadt, Richard, *Alliance Politics* (New York: Columbia University Press, 1970)
New York Times, *Pentagon Papers* (New York: Bantam Books, 1971)
Newhouse, John, *Cold Dawn: The Story of SALT* (New York: Holt, Rinehart & Winston, 1973)
Newman, James, *The Rule of Folly* (London: George Allen & Unwin, 1962)
Noel-Baker, Philip, *The Arms Race* (London: John Calder, 1958)
Nye, Joseph, *Nuclear Ethics* (New York: The Free Press, 1986)
Osgood, Robert Endicott, *Limited War: The Challenge to American Strategy* (Chicago: University of Chicago Press, 1957)
——, *NATO: The Entangling Alliance* (Chicago: The University of Chicago Press, 1962)
Pierre, Andrew, *Nuclear Politics: The British Experience with an Independent Strategic Force, 1939–1970* (London: Oxford University Press, 1972)
Power, General Thomas S., *Design for Survival* (New York: Coward-McCann, 1964)
Pranger, Robert J. and Labrie, Roger P. (eds.), *Nuclear Strategy and National Security: Points of View* (Washington, DC: American Enterprise Institute, 1977)
Puleston, W. D., *The Influence of Force in Foreign Relations* (New York: Van Nostrand, 1955)

Quester, George, *Deterrence Before Hiroshima: The Influence of Airpower on Modern Strategy* (New York: John Wiley, 1966)

——, *Nuclear Diplomacy: The First Twenty-Five Years* (New York: Dunellen, 1970)

Rapaport, Anatol, *Fights, Games and Debates* (Ann Arbor: Michigan University Press, 1960)

——, *Strategy and Conscience* (New York: Harper & Row, 1964)

Rearden, Steven, *The Evolution of American Strategic Doctrine: Paul H. Nitze and the Soviet Challenge*, SAIS Papers in International Affairs (Boulder, Col.: Westview, 1984)

Rees, David, *Korea: The Limited War* (London: Macmillan, 1964)

Richardson, James L., *Germany and the Atlantic Alliance* (Cambridge, Mass.: Harvard University Press, 1966)

Roberts, Cynthia A., 'Soviet INF policy and Euro-strategic options' in Duffy, Gloria (ed.) *Intermediate Nuclear Forces in Europe* (Palo Alto: Stanford University, 1982)

Rosencrance, R. N., *The Dispersion of Nuclear Weapons* (New York: Columbia University Press, 1964)

Russell, Bertrand, *Commonsense and Nuclear Warfare* (London: Allen & Unwin, 1959)

Sabin, Philip, *The Third World War Scare in Britain* (London: Macmillan, 1986)

Salisbury, the Bishop of, The Report of a Working Party under the chairmanship of the Bishop of Salisbury, *The Church and the Bomb: Nuclear Weapons and the Christian Conscience* (London: Hodder & Stoughton, 1982)

Sarkesian, Sam (ed.), *The Military-Industrial Complex: A Reassessment* (Beverly Hills: Sage Publications, 1972)

Scheer, Robert, *With Enough Shovels: Reagan, Bush and Nuclear War* (New York: Random House, 1982)

Schell, Jonathan, *The Fate of the Earth* (London: Cape, 1982)

——, *The Abolition* (New York: Alfred A. Knopf, 1982)

Schelling, Thomas, *The Strategy of Conflict* (New York: Oxford University Press, 1960)

——, *Controlled Response and Strategic Warfare* (London: IISS, June 1965)

——, *Arms and Influence* (New Haven: Yale University Press, 1966)

—— and Halperin, Morton, *Strategy and Arms Control* (New York: Twentieth Century Fund, 1961)

Schilling, Warner; Hammond, Paul and Snyder, Glenn, *Strategy, Politics, and Defense Budgets* (New York: Columbia University Press, 1962)

——, *et al.*, *American Arms and a Changing Europe* (New York: Columbia University Press, 1973)

Schlesinger, Arthur, *A Thousand Days: John F. Kennedy in the White House* (Boston: Houghton Mifflin, 1965)

Schlesinger, J. R., *Arms Interaction and Arms Control* (Santa Monica, Calif.: The RAND Corporation, September 1968)

——, *European Security and the Nuclear Threat since 1945* (Santa Monica, Calif.: The RAND Corporation, April 1967)

Schmidt, Helmut, *Defence or Retaliation* (New York: Praeger, 1972)

Seaborg, Glenn, *Kennedy, Khruschev and the Test Ban* (Berkeley: University of California Press, 1981)

Shenfield, Stephen, *The Nuclear Predicament: Explorations in Soviet Ideology* (London: Routledge & Kegan Paul for RIIA, 1987)

Singer, J. David, *Deterrence, Arms Control and Disarmament: Towards a Synthesis in National Security Policy* (Ohio State University Press, 1962)

Slessor, Sir John, *Strategy for the West* (London: Cassell, 1954)

Slocombe, Walter, *The Political Implications of Strategic Parity*, Adelphi Paper 77 (London: IISS, 1971)

Smith, Bruce I. R., *The RAND Corporation: Case Study of a Non-profit Advisory Corporation* (Harvard: Harvard University Press, 1966)

Smith, Perry McCoy, *The Air Force Plans for Peace 1939–1945* (Baltimore: Johns Hopkins University Press, 1970)

Smoke, Richard, *War: Controlling Escalation* (Cambridge, Mass.: Harvard University Press, 1977)

Snyder, Glenn, *Deterrence and Defense* (Princeton: Princeton University Press, 1961)

Sokolovsky, Marshal V. D., *Soviet Military Strategy*, 1st edn., edited by Dinerstein, Herbert; Gouré, Leon and Wolfe, Thomas (Englewood Cliffs, N.J.: Prentice-Hall, 1963). 3rd edn., by Fast Scott, Harriet (London: Macdonald and Jane's, 1975)

Steinberg, Gerald, *Lost in Space: The Domestic Politics of the Strategic Defense Initiative* (Lexington, Mass.: Lexington Books, 1988)

Stimson, Henry L. and Bundy, McGeorge, *On Active Service in Peace and War* (London: Hutchinson, 1948)

Stone, Jeremy, *Strategic Persuasion: Arms Limitation Through Dialogue* (New York: Columbia University Press, 1967)

Strachey, John, *On the Prevention of War* (London: Macmillan, 1962)

Talbott, Strobe, *Deadly Gambits* (New York: Alfred A. Knopf, 1984)

Taylor, Maxwell D., *The Uncertain Trumpet* (New York: Harper & Row, 1960)

Tedder, Arthur William, Lord, *Air Power in the War* (London: Hodder & Stoughton, 1947)

Thompson, E. P., *Zero Option* (London: Merlin Press, 1982)

—— and Smith, Dan (eds.), *Protest and Survive* (London: Penguin, 1980)

Tucker, Robert W., *The Just War: A Study in Contemporary American Doctrine* (Baltimore: Johns Hopkins University Press, 1960)

Tucker, Robert, *The Nuclear Debate* (New York: Holmes & Meier, 1985)

Tyroler, Charles, II (ed.), *Alerting America: The Papers of the Committee on the Present Danger* (Washington, DC: Pergamon-Brassey, 1984)

Union of Concerned Scientists, The, *The Fallacy of Star Wars* (New York: Vintage Books, 1983)

Van Den Dungen, Peter (ed.), *West European Pacifism and the Strategy For Peace* (London: Macmillan, 1985)

Vincent, John, *Military Power and Political Influence: The Soviet Union and Western Europe*, Adelphi Paper 119 (London: IISS, 1975)

Von Neumann, John and Morgenstern, Oskar, *Theory of Games and Economic Behavior* (Princeton: Princeton University Press, 1944)

Warner, Edward L., *The Military in Contemporary Soviet Politics* (New York: Praeger, 1977)

Whetten, Lawrence L. (ed.), *The Future of Soviet Military Power* (New York: Crane Russak, 1976)

Whiting, Allen S., *China Crosses the Yalu: The Decision to Enter the Korean War* (New York: Macmillan, 1960)

Wieseltier, Leon, *Nuclear War, Nuclear Peace* (New York: Holt, Rinehart & Winston, 1983)

Williams, Phil, *Crisis Management: Confrontation and Diplomacy in the Nuclear Age* (London: Martin Robertson, 1976)

Willrich, Mason, and Rhinelander, John B., *SALT, The Moscow Agreements and Beyond* (New York: The Free Press, 1974)

Wilson, Andrew, *War Gaming* (London: Pelican, 1970)

Wohlstetter, A. J.; Hoffman, F. S.; Lutz, R. J. and Rowen, H. S., *Selection and Use of Strategic Air Bases*, RAND R-266, 1 April 1954 (declassified 1962)

Wolfe, Thomas, *Soviet Power and Europe 1945–70* (Baltimore: Johns Hopkins University Press, 1970)

Yarmolinsky, Adam, *The Military Establishment* (New York: Harper & Row, 1971)

Yergin, Daniel, *Shattered Peace: The Origins of the Cold War and the National Security State* (London: André Deutsch, 1976)

York, Herbert, *Race to Oblivion: A Participant's View of the Arms Race* (New York: Simon & Schuster, 1971)

—— (ed.), *Arms Control* (San Francisco: W. M. Freeman, 1973)

——, *The Advisers: Oppenheimer, Teller and the Superbomb* (San Francisco: W. M. Freeman, 1976)

——, *Making Weapons, Talking Peace: A Physicist's Odyssey from Hiroshima to Geneva* (New York: Basic Books, 1987)

Yost, David, *France's Deterrent Posture and Security in Europe: Part I, Capabilities and Doctrine, Part II, Strategic and Arms-Control Implications*, Adelphi Papers 194 and 195 (London: IISS, 1984/85)

Zagoria, Donald, *The Sino-Soviet Conflict 1956–1961* (Princeton: Princeton University Press, 1962)

Zuckerman, Sir Solly, *Scientists and War, The Impact of Science on Military and Civil Affairs* (London: Hamish Hamilton, 1956)

Articles

Ailleret, Général D'Armée, 'Directed defence', *Survival* (February 1968). Translated from 'Défense "dirigée" or défense "tous azimuts"', *Revue de Défense Nationale* (December 1967)

Allison, Graham T. and Morris, Frederic A., 'Exploring the determinants of military weapons', *Daedalus*, CIV:3 (Summer 1975)

Almond, Gabriel A., 'Public opinion and the development of space technology: 1957–60', in Goldsen, Joseph M. (ed.), *Outer Space in World Politics* (London: Pall Mall Press, 1963)

Alsop, Stewart, 'Our new strategy: the alternatives to total war', *The Saturday Evening Post* (1 December 1962)

Amster, Warren, 'Design for deterrence', *Bulletin of the Atomic Scientists*, XII (May 1956)

Arnold, General H. H., 'Air force in the atomic age' in Masters, Dexter and Way, Katherine (eds.), *One World or None* (New York: McGraw-Hill, 1946)

Augenstein, B. W., 'The Chinese and French programs for the development of national nuclear force', *Orbis*, IX:3 (Autumn 1967)

Baker, John, 'Improving prospects for compliance with arms-control treaties', *Survival* (September/October 1987)

Baldwin, Hanson, 'Slow-down in the Pentagon', *Foreign Affairs*, XLIII:2 (January 1965)

Barre, Prime Minister Raymond, 'Speech on defence policy', *Survival*, XIX:5 (September/October 1977)

Beaufre, André, 'The sharing of nuclear responsibilities: a problem in need of solution', *International Affairs*, XXXI:3 (July 1965)

Bethe, Hans *et al.*, 'Space-based missile defense', *Scientific American* (October 1984)

Bialer, Seweryn and Afferica, Joan, 'Reagan and Russia', *Foreign Affairs* (Winter 1982/83)

Blackett, P. M. S., 'Nuclear weapons and defence', *International Affairs*, XXXIV:4 (October 1958)

Boutwell, Jeffrey, 'Politics and the peace movement in West Germany', *International Security* (Spring 1983)

Bowie, 'Strategy and the Atlantic alliance', *International Organization*, XVII:3 (Summer 1963)

Bradley, Omar, 'This Way Lies Peace', *Saturday Evening Post* (15 October 1949)

Brennan, Donald, 'The case for population defense', in Holst, Johan and Schneider, William (eds.), *Why ABM?* (New York: Pergamon Press, 1969)

——, 'Symposium on the SALT agreements', *Survival* (September/October 1972)

——, 'Review of "Strategy and Conscience"', *Bulletin of the Atomic Scientists*, XXI:12 (December 1965)

Brenner, Michael J., 'Tactical nuclear strategy and European defence: a critical reappraisal, *International Affairs*, LI:1 (January 1975)

Brodie, Bernard, 'The Atom Bomb as Policy-Maker', *Foreign Affairs*, XXVII:1 (October 1948)

——, 'Nuclear weapons: strategic or tactical?' *Foreign Affairs*, XXXII:2 (January 1954)

——, 'Unlimited weapons and limited war', *The Reporter* (11 November 1954)

——, 'Strategy hits a dead end', *Harpers* (October 1955)

——, 'More about limited war', *World Politics*, X:1 (October 1957)

——, 'What price conventional capabilities in Europe', *The Reporter* (23 May 1963)

——, 'The scientific strategists', in Gilpin and Wright (eds.), *Scientists and National Policy-Makers* (New York: Columbia University Press, 1964)

——, 'The McNamara phenomenon', *World Politics*, xvii:4 (July 1965)

——, 'On the objectives of arms control', *International Security*, i:1 (Summer 1976)

——, 'The development of nuclear strategy', *International Security*, ii:4 (Spring 1978)

Brooks, Harvey, 'The military innovation system and the qualitative arms race', *Daedalus*, civ:3 (Summer 1975)

Browner, Michael, 'Controlled thermonuclear war', *New Republic* (30 July 1962)

Brzezinski, Zbigniew; Jastrow, Robert and Kampelman, Max, 'Defense in space is not "Star Wars"', *New York Times Magazine* (27 January 1985)

Bukovsky, Vladimir, 'The peace movement and the Soviet Union', *Commentary* (May 1982)

Bull, Hedley, 'International theory: the case for a classical approach', *World Politics*, xviii:3 (April 1966)

——, 'Strategic studies and its critics', *World Politics*, xx:4 (July 1968)

Bundy, McGeorge, 'To cap the volcano', *Foreign Affairs*, xlviii:1 (October 1969)

——, 'The bishops and the Bomb', *The New York Review* (16 June 1983)

——; Kennan, George F.; McNamara, Robert S. and Smith, Gerard, 'Nuclear weapons and the Atlantic Alliance', *Foreign Affairs* (Spring 1982)

Burin, Frederic S., 'The communist doctrine of the inevitability of war', *American Political Science Review* (June 1963)

Burns, Arthur Lee, 'Disarmament or the balance of terror', *World Politics*, xii:1 (October 1959)

Burt, Richard, 'The SS-20 and the Eurostrategic balance', *World Today* (February 1977)

——, 'US stresses limited nuclear war in sharp shift on strategy', *International Herald Tribune* (7 August 1980)

Buzzard, Rear-Admiral Sir Anthony, 'Massive retaliation and graduated deterrence', *World Politics*, viii:2 (January 1956)

Carrier, George, 'Nuclear winter: the state of the science', *Issues in Science and Technology* (Winter 1985)

Carter, Barry, 'Nuclear strategy and nuclear weapons', *Scientific American* 230:5 (May 1974)

Catholic Bishops of France, 'Winning the Peace' in Scholl, James (ed.), *Out of Justice, Peace: Winning the Peace* (San Francisco: Ignatius Press, 1984)

Chayes, Abram and Handler Chayes, Antonia, 'Testing and development of "esoteric" systems under the ABM Treaty: the great reinterpretation caper', *Harvard Law Review*, vol. 99 (June 1986)

——; Wiesner, Jerome; Rathjens, George, and Weinberg, Steven, 'An overview' in Chayes, Abram and Wiesner, Jerome (eds.), *ABM: An Evaluation of the Decision to Deploy an Anti-Ballistic Missile System* (New York: Harper & Row, 1969)

Cohen, S. T., 'Enhanced radiation weapons: setting the record straight', *Strategic Review* (Winter 1978)

Condon, Edward, 'The new techniques of private war', in Masters, Dexter and Way, Katharine (eds.), *One World or None* (New York: McGraw-Hill, 1946)

Cowley, Lieutenant-General Sir John, 'Future trends in warfare', *Journal of the Royal United Services Institute* (February 1960)

Davis, Lynn Etheridge, and Schilling, Warner, 'All you ever wanted to know about MIRV and ICBM calculations, but were not cleared to ask', *Journal of Conflict Resolution*, 17:2 (June 1973)

Deane, Michael, 'Soviet perceptions of the military factor in the correlation of world forces', in Daniel (ed.), *International Perceptions of the Superpower Military Balance* (New York: Praeger, 1978)

Dinerstein, Herbert S., 'The revolution in Soviet strategic thinking', *Foreign Affairs*, xxxvi:2 (January 1958)

Donnelly, C. N., 'The Soviet Operational Manoeuvre Group: a new challenge for NATO', *International Defense Review* xv:9 (1982)

Dulles, John Foster, 'Challenge and response in US policy', *Foreign Affairs*, xxxvi:1 (October 1957)

——, 'A policy of boldness', *Life* (19 May 1952)

——, 'Policy for security and peace', *Foreign Affairs*, xxxii:3 (April 1954)

Dupuy, T. N., 'Can America fight a limited nuclear war?', *Orbis*, v:1 (Spring 1961)

Earle, Edward Mead, 'The influence of air power upon history', *The Yale Review*, xxxv:4 (June 1946)

Erickson, John, 'The Soviet view of deterrence: a general survey', *Survival* (November/December 1962)

Ermarth, Fritz, 'Contrasts in American and Soviet strategic thought', *International Security*, iii:2 (Autumn 1978)

Fergus, Martin C., 'The massive retaliation doctrine: A study in United States military policy formation', *Public Policy*, xvii (1968)

Forsberg, Randall, 'A bilateral nuclear-weapon freeze', *Scientific American* 247:5 (November 1982)

Freedman, Lawrence, 'The strategy of Hiroshima', *The Journal of Strategic Studies*, i:1 (May 1978)

——, 'Balancing acts', *Millennium*, vii:2 (Autumn 1978)

——, 'I exist: therefore I deter?', *International Security* (Summer 1988)

Fuller, Major-General, J. F. S., 'The atomic bomb and warfare of the future', *Army Ordnance* (January–February 1946)

Gallois, Pierre, 'The policy and strategy of air-nuclear weapons', *Bulletin of the Atomic Scientists*, xii:6 (June 1956)

——, 'US strategy and the defense of Europe', *Orbis*, vii:2 (Summer 1963)

Garnett, John, 'British strategic thought', in Baylis, John (ed.), *British Defence Policy in a Changing World* (London: Croom Helm, 1977)

Garthoff, Raymond L., 'Politico-military issues in the Sino-Soviet debate, 1963–65', in Garthoff, Raymond L. (ed.), *Sino-Soviet Military Relations* (New York: Praeger, 1966)

——, 'Mutual deterrence and strategic arms limitation in Soviet policy', *International Security*, iii:1 (Summer 1978)

Garwin, Richard L. and Bethe, Hans, 'Anti-ballistic missile systems', *Scientific American* (March 1968)

'Graduated deterrence', *Economist* (5 November 1955)

Gray, Colin, 'The strategic force triad: end of the road', *Foreign Affairs*, lvi (July 1978)

—— and Payne, Keith, 'Victory is possible', *Foreign Policy*, No. 39 (Summer 1980)

Greenwood, Ted and Nacht, Michael, 'The new nuclear debate: sense or nonsense', *Foreign Affairs*, LII:4 (July 1974)

Halperin, Morton, 'The Gaither Committee and the policy process', *World Politics*, XIII: 3 (April 1961)

——, 'The "no cities doctrine"', *New Republic* (8 October 1962)

——, 'The decision to deploy the ABM', *World Politics*, XXV (October 1972)

Haskins, Caryl, 'Atomic energy and American foreign policy', *Foreign Affairs*, XXIV:4 (July 1946)

Healey, Dennis, 'The Sputnik and western defence', *International Affairs*, XXXIV:2 (April 1954)

——, 'The bomb that didn't go off', *Encounter* (July 1955)

Hoag, D. G., 'Ballistic-missile guidance', in Feld, B. T.; Greenwood, T.; Rathjens, G. W. and Weinberg, S. (eds.), *Impact of New Technologies on the Arms Race* (Cambridge, Mass.: MIT Press, 1971)

Hoag, Malcolm, 'On stability in deterrent races', *World Politics*, XIII:4 (July 1961)

——, 'Rationalising NATO strategy', *World Politics*, XVII:1 (October 1964)

——, 'Nuclear strategic options and European force participation', in Rosencrance, R. N. (ed.), *The Dispersion of Nuclear Weapons* (New York: Columbia University Press, 1964)

Howard, Michael, 'The classic strategists' in Buchan, Alastair (ed.), *Problems of Modern Strategy* (London: Chatto & Windus, 1970)

——, 'The transformation of strategy', in Moulton, Major-General J. L. (ed.), *Brassey's Annual 1972* (London: William Clowes, 1972)

Hsieh, Alice Langley, 'The Sino-Soviet nuclear dialogue 1963', in Garthoff, R. (ed.), *Sino-Soviet Military Relations* (New York: Praeger, 1966)

Hughes, G. Philip, 'Cutting the Gordian knot: a theatre nuclear force for deterrence in Europe', *Orbis*, XXII (Summer 1978)

Iklé, Fred, 'Nth countries and disarmament', *Bulletin of the Atomic Scientists*, XVI:10 (December 1960)

——, 'Can nuclear deterrence last out the century?', *Foreign Affairs*, LI:2 (January 1973)

——, 'NATO's "first nuclear use": a deepening trap?' *Strategic Review* (Winter 1980)

——, 'The Reagan defense program: a focus on the strategic imperatives', *Strategic Review* (Spring 1982)

Jervis, Robert, 'Hypotheses on misperception', *World Politics*, XX (April 1968)

——, 'Deterrence theory revisited', *World Politics*, XXXI:2 (January 1979)

Kahn, Herman, 'The arms race and some of its hazards', in Brennan, D. (ed.), *Arms Control, Disarmament and National Security* (New York: George Braziller, 1961)

——, 'Some comments on controlled war', in Knorr, Klaus and Read, Thornton (eds.), *Limited Strategic War* (New York: Praeger, 1962)

Kaiser, Karl; Leber, Georg; Mertes, Alois and Schulze, Franz-Joseph,

'Nuclear weapons and the preservation of peace: a German response to no first use', *Foreign Affairs* (Summer 1982)

Kaplan, Fred M., 'Enhanced radiation weapons', *Scientific American*, 238:5 (May 1978)

——, 'Soviet civil defense: some myths in the Western debate', *Survival*, xxx:3 (May/June 1978)

Kaplan, Morton A., 'The calculus of nuclear deterrence', *World Politics*, xi:1 (October 1958)

——, 'Limited retaliation as a bargaining process', in Knorr, Klaus and Read, Thornton (eds.), *Limited Strategic War* (New York: Praeger, 1963)

Kass, Ilana and Deane, Michael J., 'The role of nuclear weapons in the modern theater battlefield: the current Soviet view, *Comparative Strategy* iv:3 (1984)

Kaufmann, William, 'The crisis in military affairs', *World Politics*, x:4 (July 1958)

Kennan, George ('X'), 'The sources of Soviet conduct', *Foreign Affairs*, xxv:4 (July 1947)

Kennedy, Senator John, 'Book review of *Deterrence or Defense*', *Saturday Review* (3 September 1960)

King, James E., 'Limited war', *Army* (August 1957)

——, 'Nuclear weapons and foreign policy. II – Limited annihilation', *The New Republic* (15 July 1957)

——, 'Strategic surrender: the Senate debate and the book', *World Politics*, xi: (April 1959)

——, 'Airpower in the missile gap', *World Politics*, xii:4 (July 1960)

Kissinger, Henry, 'Arms control, inspection and surprise attack', *Foreign Affairs*, xxxviii:3 (April 1960)

——, 'Limited war: conventional or nuclear? A reappraisal', in Brennan, D. (ed.), *Arms Control, Disarmament and National Security* (New York: George Braziller, 1961)

——, 'NATO: the next thirty years', *Survival* (November/December 1979)

Knorr, Klaus, 'Limited strategic war' in Knorr, Klaus and Read, Thornton (eds.), *Limited Strategic War* (New York: Praeger, 1962)

Lambeth, Benjamin S., 'Deterrence in the MIRV era', *World Politics* (January 1972)

——, 'Selective nuclear options and Soviet strategy', in Holst, Johan and Nerlich, Uwe (eds.), *Beyond Nuclear Deterrence* (London: MacDonald and Jane's 1977)

——, 'Uncertainties for the Soviet war planner', *International Security* (Winter 1982/83)

Leghorn, Colonel Richard S., 'No need to bomb cities to win war: a new counter-force strategy for air warfare', *US News & World Report* (28 January 1955)

Lewis, Kevin N., 'The prompt and delayed effects of nuclear war', *Scientific American* (July 1979)

Lippmann, Walter, 'Why are we disarming ourselves?', *Redbrook Magazine* (September 1946)

Lipton, Nancy and Rodberg, Leonard, 'The missile race: the contest with ourselves', in Rodberg, Leonard and Shearer, Derek, *The Pentagon Watchers* (New York: Doubleday & Co., 1970)

Lodal, Jan, 'Assuring strategic stability: an alternative view', *Foreign Affairs*, LIV (April 1976)

Long, F. A., 'Arms control from the perspective of the nineteen-seventies', *Daedalus*, CIV:3 (Summer 1975)

Loosbrock, John, 'Counterforce and Mr McNamara', *Air Force Magazine* (September 1962)

Luttwak, Edward N., 'The missing dimension of US defense policy: force, perception and power', in Daniel, Donald C. (ed.), *International Perceptions of the Superpower Military Balance* (New York: Praeger, 1978)

'McNamara's strategy', *New Republic* (2 July 1962) (editorial)

McNamara, Robert S., 'The military role of nuclear weapons: perceptions and misperceptions', *Foreign Affairs* (Fall 1983)

Mandelbaum, Michael and Talbott, Strobe, 'Reykjavik and beyond', *Foreign Affairs* (Winter 1986–87)

Martin, Laurence, 'The market for strategic ideas in Britain', *American Political Science Review*, LVI:1 (March 1962)

——, 'The utility of military force', in Duchêne, François (ed.), *Force in Modern Societies: Its Place in International Politics* (London: IISS, 1973)

——, 'Flexibility in a tactical nuclear response', in Holst, Johan and Nerlich, Uwe (eds.), *Beyond Nuclear Deterrence: New Aims, New Arms* (London: Macdonald and Jane's, 1977)

May, Michael, 'Some advantages of a counterforce deterrent', *Orbis*, XIV (Summer 1970)

——, 'The meaning of stalemate', *Army* (August 1958)

Mearsheimer, John, 'Why the Soviets can't win quickly in Central Europe', *International Security* (Summer 1982)

Mery, General Guy, 'French defence policy', *Survival*, XVIII:5 (September/October 1976)

Montgomery, Field Marshal Bernard Law, 'A look through a window at World War III', *The Journal of the Royal United Services Institute*, XCIX:596 (November 1954)

Murphy, Charles, 'Defense and strategy', *Fortune* (January 1953; July 1953)

——, 'The US as a bombing target', *Fortune* (November 1953)

Nicholas, Colonel Jack, 'The element of surprise in modern warfare', *Air University Quarterly Review* (Summer 1956)

Nitze, Paul, 'Atoms, strategy and policy', *Foreign Affairs*, XXXIV:2 (January 1956)

——, 'Assuring strategic stability in an era of detente', *Foreign Affairs*, LIV:2 (January 1976)

——, 'Strategic stability', *Foreign Affairs*, LIV:3 (July 1976)

——, 'Deterring our deterrent', *Foreign Policy*, No. 25 (Winter 1976–7)

——, 'Living with the Soviets', *Foreign Affairs* (Winter 1984/85)

Novak, Michael, 'Moral clarity in the nuclear age', *National Review* (1 April 1983)

On thermonuclear coexistence', *Survey*, no. 39 (December 1961; editorial)

Oppenheimer, Robert, 'Atomic weapons', *Proceedings of the American Philosophical Society*, XC:1 (January 1946)

——, 'Atomic weapons and American policy', *Foreign Affairs*, XXXI:4 (July 1953)

Osgood, Robert, 'Stabilizing the military environment', *American Political Science Review*', LV:1 (March 1961)

——, 'Nuclear arms: uses and limits', *New Republic* (10 September 1962)

Panofsky, Wolfgang, 'The mutual hostage relationship between America and Russia', *Foreign Affairs*, LII:1 (October 1973)

Payne, Fred A., 'The strategic nuclear balance: a new measure', *Survival*, XX:3 (May/June 1977)

Pipes, Richard, 'Why the Soviet Union thinks it could fight and win a nuclear war', *Commentary*, 64 (1) (July 1977)

Pollack, Jonathan D., 'Chinese attitudes towards nuclear weapons 1964–9', *China Quarterly*, No. 50 (1972)

——, 'The logic of Chinese military strategy', *Bulletin of the Atomic Scientists* (January 1979)

Powell, Ralph, 'Great powers and atomic bombs are "paper tigers"', *China Quarterly*, No. 23 (July/September 1965)

——, 'Maoist military doctrine', *Asian Survey* (April 1968)

Quinlan, Michael, 'Preventing war', *The Tablet* (July 1981)

Rathjens, George, 'NATO strategy: total war', in Knorr, Klaus (ed.), *NATO and American Security* (Princeton: Princeton University Press, 1959)

——, 'The dynamics of the arms race', *Scientific American* (April 1969)

Read, Thornton, 'Limited strategic war and tactical nuclear war', in Knorr, Klaus and Read, Thornton (eds.), *Limited Strategic War* (New York: Praeger, 1962)

Reback, Sanford, 'Responding to Soviet non-compliance', *Arms Control* (December 1986)

Reinhardt, Colonel G. C., 'Atomic weapons and war', in Liddell Hart, B. H. (ed.), *The Soviet Army* (London: Weidenfeld & Nicolson, 1956)

Richardson, Colonel Robert, 'Do we need unlimited forces for limited war?', *Air Force* (March 1959)

Richelson, Jeffrey, 'PD-59, NSDD-13 and the Reagan strategic modernization program', *The Journal of Strategic Studies* VI:3 (June 1983)

Ridenour, Louis, 'A US physicist's reply to Professor Blackett', *Scientific American* (March 1949)

——, 'There is no defense', in Masters, Dexter and Way, Katherine (eds.), *One World or None* (New York: McGraw-Hill, 1946)

Rosenberg, David, '"A smoking, radiating ruin at the end of two hours": documents on American plans for nuclear war with the Soviet Union, 1954–1955', *International Security* (Winter 1981/82)

——, 'The origins of overkill: nuclear weapons and American strategy, 1945–1960', *International Security*, 7:4 (Spring 1983)

——, 'American atomic strategy and the hydrogen bomb decision', *Journal of American History*, LXVI (Summer 1985)

Ross, Dennis, 'Rethinking Soviet strategic policy: inputs and implications', *The Journal of Strategic Studies*, I:2 (May 1975)

Rowen, Henry, 'Formulating Strategic Doctrine', *Appendices to the Report of the Commission on the Organization of Government for the Conduct of Foreign Policy*, Vol. IV, Appendix K (Washington, DC: USGPO, 1975)

Russell, Bertrand, 'The prevention of war', in Grodzins, Morton and Rabinowitch, Eugene (eds.), *The Atomic Age: Scientists in National and World Affairs* (New York: Basic Books, 1963)

Sagan, Carl, 'Nuclear war and climatic catastrophe', *Foreign Affairs* (Winter 1983/84)

Sagan, Scott, '1914 revisited: allies, offense and instability', *International Security* 11:2 (Fall 1986)

Schear, James, 'Arms control treaty compliance: buildup to a breakdown', *International Security* (Fall 1985)

Schelling, T. C., 'Comment', in Knorr, Klaus and Read, Thornton (eds.), *Limited Strategic War* (New York: Praeger, 1962)

——, 'Nuclears, NATO and the new strategy', in Kissinger, Henry (ed.), *Problems of National Strategy* (New York: Praeger, 1965)

——, 'What went wrong with arms control?', *Foreign Affairs* (Winter 1985/86)

Schlesinger, J. R., 'Quantitative analysis and national security', *World Politics*, xv (1963)

Schneiter, George, 'Implications of the Strategic Defense Initiative for the ABM Treaty', *Survival* (Fall 1984)

Scoville, Herbert Jr, 'Flexible madness', *Foreign Policy*, No. 14 (Spring 1974)

Seitz, Russell, 'In from the cold: "nuclear winter" melts down', *The National Interest* (Fall 1986)

Shenfield, Stephen, 'The Soviet undertaking not to use nuclear weapons first and its significance', *Detente* (October 1984)

Sherr, Alan, 'Sound legal reasoning or policy expedient; the new interpretation of the ABM Treaty', *International Security* (Winter 1986/87)

Sherwin, C. W., 'Securing peace through military technology', *Bulletin of the Atomic Scientists*, xii (May 1956)

Shilling, Warner, 'The H-Bomb decision: how to decide without actually choosing', *Political Science Quarterly*, lxxvi (March 1961)

Shipler, David, 'Soviets tested a neutron weapon, Brezhnev tells group of senators', *New York Times*, 18 November 1978

Skaggs, David, 'Michael Howard and strategic policy', *Armed Forces and Society* (Summer 1985)

Slessor, Sir John, 'The place of the bomber in British strategy', *International Affairs*, xxix:3 (July 1953)

——, 'Air power and world strategy', *Foreign Affairs*, xxx:1 (October 1954)

Slocombe, Walter, 'The countervailing strategy', *International Security* (Spring 1981)

Sloss, Leon and Millot, Marc Dean, 'US nuclear strategy in evolution', *Strategic Review* (Winter 1984)

Snyder, Glenn, '"Prisoner's dilemma" and "chicken" models in international politics', *International Studies Quarterly*, xv:1 (March 1971)

Snyder, Jack, 'Civil–military relations and the cult of the offensive', *International Security* 9:1 (Summer 1984)

Snyder and Sagan, Correspondence, *International Security*, 11:3 (Winter 1986/87)

Sofaer, Judge Abraham D., 'The ABM Treaty and the Strategic Defense Initiative', *Harvard Law Review*, vol. 99 (June 1986)

Steinbruner, John, 'Beyond rational deterrence: the struggle for new conceptions', *World Politics*, xxviii:2 (January 1976)

—— and Carter, Barry, 'Organizational and political dimensions of the strategic posture: the problems of reform', *Daedalus*, civ:3 (Summer 1975)

—— and Garwin, Thomas, 'Strategic vulnerability: the balance between prudence and paranoia', *International Security*, i:1 (Summer 1976)

Steiner, Barry, 'Using the absolute weapon: early ideas of Bernard Brodie on atomic strategy', *The Journal of Strategic Studies*, vii:4 (December 1984)

Strattman, Peter and Hermann, René, 'Limited options, escalation and the central region', in Holst, Johan and Nerlich, Uwe (eds.), *Beyond Nuclear Deterrence: New Aims: New Arms* (London: Macdonald & Jane's, 1977)

Szilard, Leo, 'Disarmament and the problem of peace', *Bulletin of the Atomic Scientists*, xi:8 (October 1955)

——, 'How to live with the bomb and survive', *Bulletin of the Atomic Scientists*, xvi:2 (February 1960)

Thomas, John, 'The limits of alliance: the Quemoy crisis of 1958', in Garthoff, Raymond (ed.), *Sino-Soviet Military Relations* (New York: Praeger, 1966)

Trachtenberg, Marc, 'The influence of nuclear weapons in the Cuban missile crisis', *International Security*, 10:1 (Summer 1985)

Trainor, James, 'DOD says AICBM is feasible', *Missiles and Rockets* (29 December 1962)

Treverton, Greg, 'Nuclear weapons and the gray area', *Foreign Affairs*, lvii:3 (Summer 1979)

Urey, Harold, 'How does it all add up?', in Masters, Dexter and Way, Katherine (eds.), *One World or None* (New York: McGraw-Hill, 1946)

Van Cleave, William R., 'Soviet doctrine and strategy', in Whetton, Lawrence, *The Future of Soviet Military Power* (New York: Crane Russack, 1976)

—— and Barnett, Roger W., 'Strategic adaptability', *Orbis*, xviii:3 (Autumn 1974)

Van Evera, Stephen, 'The cult of the offensive and the origins of the First World War', *International Security* 9:1 (Summer 1984)

Viner, Jacob, 'The implications of the atomic bomb for international relations', *Proceedings of the American Philosophical Society*, xc:1 (January 1946)

Walkowicz, T. F., 'Counter-force strategy: how can we exploit America's atomic advantage', *Air Force Magazine* (February 1955)

Watt, Donald Cameron, 'Restraints on war in the air before 1945', in Howard, Michael (ed.), *Restraints in War: Studies in the Limitation of Arms Conflict* (London: Oxford University Press, 1979)

Wells, Samuel F., 'Sounding the tocsin: NSC-68 and the Soviet threat', *International Security*, iv:2 (Autumn 1979)

Wieseltier, Leon, 'When deterrence fails', *Foreign Affairs* (Spring 1985)

Wildavsky, Aaron, 'Practical consequences of the theoretical study of defence policy', *Public Administration Review*, xxv (March 1965)

Winters, Francis X., 'Bishops and scholars: the peace pastoral under siege', *The Review of Politics* (Winter 1986)

Witze, Claude, 'Farewell to counterforce', *Air Force Magazine* (February 1963)

Wohlstetter, Albert, 'The delicate balance of terror', *Foreign Affairs*, xxxvii:2 (January 1959)

——, 'Nuclear sharing: NATO and the N + 1 country', *Foreign Affairs*, xxxix:3 (April 1961)

——, 'Analysis and design of conflict systems', in Quade, E. S., *Analysis for Military Decisions* (Chicago: RAND McNally, 1964)

——, 'Strategy and the natural scientists', in Gilpin, Robert and Wright, Christopher (eds.), *Scientists and National Policy Making* (New York: Columbia University Press, 1964)

——, 'Strength, interest and new technologies, in IISS', *The Implications of Military Technology in the 1970s* (London: IISS, 1968)

——, 'Threats and promises of peace: Europe and America in the new era', *Orbis*, xvii:4 (Winter 1974)

——, 'Is there a strategic arms race?', *Foreign Policy*, xv (Summer 1974)

——, 'Rivals but no "race"', *Foreign Policy*, xvi (Autumn 1974)

——, 'Optimal ways to confuse ourselves', *Foreign Policy*, xx (Autumn 1975)

Wohlstetter, Albert, 'Bishops, statesmen, and other strategists on the bombing of civilians', *Commentary* (June 1983)

——, 'Between an unfree world and none: increasing our choices', *Foreign Affairs* (Summer 1985)

Wohlstetter, Roberta, 'Terror on a grand scale', *Survival*, xviii:3 (May/June 1976)

Woolsey, James, 'The politics of vulnerability: 1980–83', *Foreign Affairs* (Spring 1984)

Yermashev, I., 'The Peking version of "total strategy"', in Garthoff, Raymond (ed.), *Sino-Soviet Military Relations* (New York: Praeger, 1966)

York, Herbert, 'Military technology and national security', *Scientific American* (August 1969)

——, 'Reducing the overkill', *Survival*, xvi:2 (March/April 1974)

—— and Wiesner, Jerome, 'National security and the nuclear test ban', *Scientific American* (October 1964)

Yost, David and Glad, Thomas, 'West German party politics and theater nuclear modernization since 1977', *Armed Forces and Society* (Summer 1982)

Zuckerman, Sir Solly, 'Judgement and control in modern warfare', *Foreign Affairs*, xxxx:2 (January 1962)

Subject Index

507

Name Index

515